Geoffrey Khan, Masoud Mohammadirad
Language Contact in Sanandaj

Language Contact
and Bilingualism

Editor
Yaron Matras

Volume 32

Geoffrey Khan, Masoud Mohammadirad

Language Contact in Sanandaj

A Study of the Impact of Iranian on Neo-Aramaic

DE GRUYTER
MOUTON

Funded by the European Union (ERC, ALHOME, 101021183). Views and opinions expressed are however those of the author(s) only and do not necessarily reflect those of the European Union or the European Research Council Executive Agency. Neither the European Union nor the granting authority can be held responsible for them.

ISBN 978-3-11-221528-9
e-ISBN (PDF) 978-3-11-120918-0
e-ISBN (EPUB) 978-3-11-121007-0
ISSN 2190-698X
DOI https://doi.org/10.1515/9783111209180

This work is licensed under the Creative Commons Attribution-NonCommercial-NoDerivatives 4.0 International License. For details go to https://creativecommons.org/licenses/by-nc-nd/4.0/.

Creative Commons license terms for re-use do not apply to any content (such as graphs, figures, photos, excerpts, etc.) not original to the Open Access publication and further permission may be required from the rights holder. The obligation to research and clear permission lies solely with the party re-using the material.

Library of Congress Control Number: 2023942757

Bibliographic information published by the Deutsche Nationalbibliothek
The Deutsche Nationalbibliothek lists this publication in the Deutsche Nationalbibliografie; detailed bibliographic data are available on the internet at http://dnb.dnb.de.

© 2025 the author(s), published by Walter de Gruyter GmbH, Berlin/Boston
This volume is text- and page-identical with the hardback published in 2024.
This book is published open access at www.degruyter.com.

Cover image: Anette Linnea Rasmus/Fotolia
Typesetting: Integra Software Services Pvt. Ltd.
Printing and binding: CPI books GmbH, Leck

www.degruyter.com

Preface

Sanandaj, a town in western Iran, was home to a Jewish Aramaic-speaking community since its foundation early in the 17th Century. This book is a study of the impact of Iranian languages, most notably Gorani and Kurdish, but also to a lesser extent Persian, on the Jewish Neo-Aramaic dialect of the town.

The book is a follow up to Geoffrey Khan's *The Jewish Neo-Aramaic Dialect of Sanandaj* (2009). It draws on first-hand material gathered from the field as the basis for studying contact between Neo-Aramaic and Iranian.

We began working together on the project early in 2020 in the middle of the Covid pandemic while Masoud was a PhD student in Paris. As we discussed the convergences between Neo-Aramaic and Iranian during our weekly zoom meetings, we became more and more excited by this fascinating topic. We identified convergences in all levels of the languages. It was clear to us that a study of language contact in the region had to include all linguistic levels. As a result, our book presents a comprehensive comparison of the phonology, morphology and syntax of Neo-Aramaic with Iranian.

The book would not have been possible without the kind collaboration of many native speakers of Jewish Neo-Aramaic, Gorani, and Kurdish from Sanandaj, to all of whom we owe a deep debt of gratitude.

For Jewish Neo-Aramaic these include in particular Danny (Daryuš) Avrahami, who enthusiastically helped Geoffrey Khan at all stages of the original documentation project pubished in 2009 and also during the preparation of the current book. Other Neo-Aramaic speakers who supplied important data for the original documentation project were Sarah Avrahami, Dr. Bahruz Qamran, Ḥabib Nurani, Victoria Amini, Eli Avrahami, David Avrahami, Dr. Yeskel Paz and his wife Negar Paz.

For the Iranian material, we would like to thank in particular Dr. Mahdi Sadjadi for answering our many questions about his native dialect, Gorani (Hawrami) Takht. In addition, we are grateful to Mazhar Ebrahimi and Masoumeh (Hana) Mohammadirad for providing us with recorded material from the Kurdish dialect of Sanandaj and its environs.

We are very grateful to several academic colleagues who generously devoted time to reading drafts of the book and gave us many insightful comments. These included Geoffrey Haig, who was a visitor in Cambridge in 2022, Paul Noorlander and Dorota Molin.

The research on the book from September 2021 onwards was made possible by funding from the European Research Council, which we acknowledge with gratitude.

January 2023
Geoffrey Khan and Masoud Mohammadirad

Contents

Preface —— V

List of tables —— XIX

List of figures —— XXIII

Abbreviations and symbols —— XXV

1	Introduction —— 1	
1.1	Sanandaj and its Languages —— 1	
1.2	The Neo-Aramaic Dialects of the Sanandaj Region —— 2	
1.3	The Iranian languages of the Sanandaj Region —— 6	
1.4	Bilingualism and language shifts in Sanandaj —— 10	
1.4.1	The NENA-speaking Jews of Sanandaj —— 10	
1.4.2	The Iranian-speaking Muslims of Sanandaj —— 11	
1.5	The aims and methodology of the book —— 14	
2	Phonology —— 18	
2.1	Introductory overview —— 18	
2.2	Consonant phonemes —— 19	
2.2.1	Phoneme inventory —— 19	
2.2.2	Notes on the phonetic realisation of the Consonants —— 21	
2.2.2.1	/p/, /t/, /k/ —— 21	
2.2.2.2	/ṭ/, /ṣ/ —— 22	
2.2.2.3	/ḷ/ —— 26	
2.2.2.4	Rhotic consonants —— 28	
2.2.2.5	Pharyngeal consonants —— 30	
2.2.2.6	Inserted word-initial /h/ —— 36	
2.2.2.7	Zagros /d/ —— 39	
2.2.2.8	/w/ —— 41	
2.2.2.9	/č/ —— 42	
2.2.2.10	/q/ —— 43	
2.2.2.11	Phonetic processes relating to voicing —— 44	
2.2.2.12	Consonant gemination —— 45	
2.3	VOWELS —— 47	
2.3.1	Vowel quality —— 47	
2.3.1.1	JSNENA vowel system —— 47	
2.3.1.2	Kurdish vowel system —— 48	

2.3.1.3	Gorani vowel system —— **49**	
2.3.1.4	Comparison of vowel systems —— **49**	
2.3.2	Vowel length —— **49**	
2.4	Stress position —— **51**	
2.4.1	Nominals —— **52**	
2.4.2	Adverbials —— **54**	
2.4.3	Verbs —— **56**	
2.4.4	Copula —— **60**	
2.4.5	Clitic additive particle —— **61**	
2.5	Summary —— **62**	
3	**The morphology of pronouns —— 64**	
3.1	Introductory overview —— **64**	
3.2	Independent pronouns —— **64**	
3.3	Demonstrative pronouns —— **70**	
3.3.1	Independent proximate deixis pronouns —— **70**	
3.3.2	Independent remote pronouns —— **73**	
3.4	Attributive demonstrative pronouns —— **76**	
3.5	Pronominal suffixes on nouns and prepositions —— **79**	
3.6	Independent oblique pronouns —— **84**	
3.7	Summary —— **89**	
4	**The morphology of nouns and particles —— 91**	
4.1	Introductory overview —— **91**	
4.2	Gender —— **92**	
4.2.1	Gender of loanwords —— **97**	
4.2.1.1	Masculine consonant-final loanwords —— **97**	
4.2.1.2	Masculine nouns ending in a stressed vowel —— **98**	
4.2.2	Marking female gender —— **100**	
4.3	Derivational affixes on nouns —— **100**	
4.4	Plural endings —— **101**	
4.5	The definite article —— **104**	
4.6	The indefinite suffix —— **106**	
4.7	Nouns in the absolutive state —— **107**	
4.8	Genitive annexation constructions —— **107**	
4.9	Ezafe on prepositions —— **110**	
4.10	Adjectives —— **112**	
4.10.1	Inflection —— **112**	
4.10.2	Unadapted adjective loans —— **114**	
4.10.3	Compound adjectives —— **115**	

4.11	Numerals —— **116**	
4.11.1	Ordinals —— **118**	
4.11.2	Fractions —— **121**	
4.12	Days of the week —— **121**	
4.13	Seasons —— **123**	
4.14	Adverbs —— **123**	
4.15	Prepositions —— **124**	
4.15.1	ba-, b- —— **124**	
4.15.2	bāqa 'to, for' —— **125**	
4.15.3	bayn 'between' —— **126**	
4.15.4	bē 'without' —— **126**	
4.15.5	dawr, ba-dawr 'around' —— **126**	
4.15.6	ġēr 'az 'apart from' —— **127**	
4.15.7	lāga 'at the home of, by the side of, with' —— **127**	
4.15.8	mangol, mangal 'like' —— **127**	
4.15.9	mənták=ē 'with' —— **128**	
4.16	Miscellaneous uninflected particles —— **129**	
4.17	Summary —— **130**	
5	**The morphology of verbs —— 133**	
5.1	Introductory overview —— **133**	
5.2	Verb stems —— **134**	
5.2.1	Imperatives —— **143**	
5.3	Verbal inflectional suffixes —— **144**	
5.4	Inflection of the resultative participles —— **153**	
5.5	Indicative particle —— **155**	
5.6	Subjunctive —— **165**	
5.7	Deontic particles —— **166**	
5.7.1	bā —— **166**	
5.7.2	magar —— **167**	
5.7.3	dā —— **168**	
5.8	The copula —— **168**	
5.8.1	Present copula —— **168**	
5.8.2	Further types of copulas —— **172**	
5.9	Existential copula —— **180**	
5.10	Pronominal direct objects on present, imperative and past stem verbs —— **184**	
5.10.1	Pronominal direct objects on present stem verbs —— **184**	
5.10.2	Imperative —— **190**	
5.10.3	Pronominal direct objects on past stem verbs —— **190**	

5.11	Compound verbal forms containing the verb 'to be' —— **194**	
5.11.1	Realis perfect —— **194**	
5.11.2	Irrealis perfect —— **198**	
5.11.3	Indirective function of the perfect —— **205**	
5.11.4	The perfect of the copula —— **205**	
5.11.5	Indirective past perfect —— **207**	
5.11.6	Summary of direct past, direct perfect and indirective verbal functions —— **208**	
5.12	Light verb constructions —— **209**	
5.12.1	Pronominal direct objects on light verb constructions —— **211**	
5.13	Pronominal indirect object —— **213**	
5.14	Negation of verbs and copulas —— **217**	
5.15	Summary —— **222**	
6	**The syntax of nominals and particles —— 225**	
6.1	Introductory overview —— **225**	
6.2	The Expression of indefiniteness —— **226**	
6.2.1	Indefinite specific referent with discourse salience —— **227**	
6.2.2	Temporal adverbial referring to specific time —— **228**	
6.2.3	Indefinite specific referent without discourse salience —— **229**	
6.2.4	Non-specific indefinite —— **230**	
6.2.5	Heavy coding for discourse structuring —— **233**	
6.2.6	Cardinal numeral —— **234**	
6.2.7	Kurdish yak as indefinite marker —— **236**	
6.2.8	Summary —— **236**	
6.2.9	Pronominal use of xa —— **236**	
6.2.10	JSNENA xa dana —— **237**	
6.2.11	Borrowing by JSNENA of Kurdish indefinite suffix -ēk —— **240**	
6.3	The definite article –akē —— **241**	
6.3.1	Anaphora —— **241**	
6.3.2	Associative anaphora —— **242**	
6.3.3	Marking a discourse boundary —— **244**	
6.4	Demonstrative pronouns —— **245**	
6.4.1	Deictic function —— **245**	
6.4.2	Anaphoric function —— **247**	
6.4.3	Demonstratives with cardinal numeral 'one' —— **256**	
6.4.4	Discourse presentative function of demonstratives —— **257**	
6.5	Presentative particles —— **259**	
6.5.1	JSNENA wā —— **259**	

6.5.1.1	Referent —— **259**	
6.5.1.2	Situation —— **259**	
6.5.2	Iranian wā —— **260**	
6.5.3	JSNENA ʾayānē —— **261**	
6.5.4	JSNENA hā —— **261**	
6.6	Pronominal suffixes on adverbials —— **263**	
6.7	Attributes —— **264**	
6.7.1	Adjectives —— **264**	
6.7.2	Adverbial modifiers —— **266**	
6.7.3	Modifiers of active participles —— **266**	
6.7.4	Non-attributive modifiers —— **266**	
6.7.4.1	kulē —— **266**	
6.7.4.2	tamām 'all' —— **267**	
6.7.4.3	xēt 'other' —— **268**	
6.7.4.4	har, har čī 'each, every' —— **269**	
6.7.4.5	čəkma 'how much/many?' 'several' —— **270**	
6.7.4.6	xančī 'some, a little' —— **271**	
6.7.4.7	hīč —— **272**	
6.8	Comparative constructions —— **273**	
6.8.1	bīš —— **273**	
6.8.2	bīš-zoa, bī-zoa —— **274**	
6.9	Conjoining of phrases —— **275**	
6.10	Numerals —— **277**	
6.11	Adverbial expressions —— **278**	
6.11.1	Temporal adverbials —— **278**	
6.11.2	Spatial adverbials —— **279**	
6.11.3	Destinations —— **279**	
6.11.4	Manner adverbials —— **280**	
6.12	Summary —— **280**	
7	**The syntax of verbs —— 283**	
7.1	Introductory overview —— **283**	
7.2	The function of verb forms derived from the present stem —— **284**	
7.2.1	Function of irrealis forms —— **284**	
7.2.1.1	Speaker-oriented modality in main clauses —— **284**	
7.2.1.2	Epistemic modality in main clauses —— **287**	
7.2.1.3	Generic relative clauses —— **288**	
7.2.1.4	Subordinate complements —— **289**	
7.2.1.5	Conditional constructions —— **295**	

7.2.2	Realis form of the present-stem verbs —— **295**	
7.2.2.1	Progressive —— **296**	
7.2.2.2	Habitual —— **297**	
7.2.2.3	Narrative present —— **299**	
7.2.2.4	Performative —— **300**	
7.2.2.5	Future —— **301**	
7.2.3	Present-stem verbs with past converter suffix —— **302**	
7.2.3.1	Realis —— **302**	
7.2.3.2	Irrealis —— **304**	
7.3	The function of verb forms derived from past stems —— **306**	
7.3.1	Past-stem forms without the past converter affix —— **306**	
7.3.1.2	Past perfective —— **306**	
7.3.2	Past-stem forms with the past converter affix —— **309**	
7.3.2.1	Past perfect —— **309**	
7.3.2.2	Indirective —— **312**	
7.4	The imperative —— **313**	
7.5	The copula —— **315**	
7.5.1	The present copula —— **315**	
7.5.2	Past copula —— **317**	
7.6	The existential particle —— **318**	
7.7	The JSNENA verb h-w-y —— **320**	
7.7.1	k-wē —— **320**	
7.7.2	hawē —— **320**	
7.7.2.1	Speaker-oriented modality in main clauses —— **320**	
7.7.2.2	Conditional constructions —— **321**	
7.7.2.3	Generic relative clauses —— **321**	
7.7.2.4	Subordinate complements —— **321**	
7.8	Iranian *w-/ b-* copula —— **321**	
7.8.1	Realis functions of the *w-/ b-* copula —— **322**	
7.8.2	Irrealis functions of the *w-/ b-* copula —— **323**	
7.8.2.1	Speaker-oriented modality in main clauses —— **323**	
7.8.2.2	Conditional constructions —— **324**	
7.8.2.3	Generic relative clauses —— **324**	
7.8.2.4	Subordinate complements —— **325**	
7.9	JSNENA resultative participle + copula —— **325**	
7.9.1	Present perfect —— **325**	
7.9.2	Indirective —— **326**	
7.9.2.1	Reports of past events —— **327**	
7.9.2.2	Folktales and legends —— **327**	
7.9.2.3	Remote past —— **328**	

7.10	Iranian resultative participle + copula —— **329**	
7.10.1	Present perfect —— **329**	
7.10.2	Indirective —— **329**	
7.10.2.1	Reports of past events —— **329**	
7.10.2.2	Folktales and legends —— **330**	
7.10.2.3	Remote past —— **331**	
7.11	Morphological coding of transitivity —— **332**	
7.12	Expression of the passive —— **339**	
7.12.1	Passive past stem —— **339**	
7.12.2	Passive resultative participle —— **341**	
7.12.3	Passive formed with an ingressive auxiliary —— **342**	
7.12.4	Impersonal 3pl. subject —— **343**	
7.13	Labile verbs with transitive—unaccusative alternation —— **344**	
7.14	The post-verbal particle -o —— **347**	
7.14.1	'again, back' —— **348**	
7.14.2	Telicity —— **348**	
7.14.3	'opening' —— **350**	
7.14.4	Combination with other verbal affixes —— **351**	
7.14.5	On adverbials —— **351**	
7.15	Direct object —— **352**	
7.15.1	Present stem verbs and imperatives —— **352**	
7.15.1.1	No grammatical marking of object —— **352**	
7.15.1.2	Grammatical marking of object —— **354**	
7.15.2	Past stem verbs —— **357**	
7.15.2.2	Compound verbal forms —— **362**	
7.16	The infinitive —— **364**	
7.16.1	Nominal function —— **364**	
7.16.1.1	Complement of a preposition —— **364**	
7.16.1.2	Complement of a nominal —— **366**	
7.16.1.3	Nominal arguments in copula or existential clauses —— **367**	
7.16.2	Verbal functions —— **368**	
7.16.2.1	Placement before finite verb —— **368**	
7.16.2.2	Placement after finite verb —— **369**	
7.17	Summary —— **370**	
8	**The Clause —— 374**	
8.1	Introductory overview —— **374**	
8.2	The copula clause —— **375**	
8.2.1	Preliminary remarks —— **375**	
8.2.2	Subject constituents —— **377**	

8.2.3	Postposing of subject constituent —— **378**	
8.2.4	Postposing of predicate —— **380**	
8.2.5	Omission of copula —— **381**	
8.2.6	Interrogative predicates —— **381**	
8.2.7	Predicative complements of the JSNENA Verb x-Ø-r —— **382**	
8.3	Clauses with existential particles —— **384**	
8.3.1	Existential clauses —— **384**	
8.3.2	Possessive constructions —— **386**	
8.4	Verbal clauses —— **387**	
8.4.1	Direct object constituent —— **387**	
8.4.1.1	Object—verb —— **387**	
8.4.1.2	Verb—object —— **389**	
8.4.1.3	Predicative complements and expressions of content —— **393**	
8.4.2	Subject constituent —— **394**	
8.4.2.1	Subject—(Object)—verb —— **394**	
8.4.2.2	Object—subject—verb —— **396**	
8.4.2.3	Verb—subject —— **397**	
8.4.2.4	Subject Verb Agreement —— **400**	
8.4.2.5	Independent subject pronouns —— **401**	
8.4.3	Prepositional phrases —— **406**	
8.4.3.1	Verb—prepositional phrase —— **406**	
8.4.3.2	Prepositional phrase—verb —— **407**	
8.4.3.3	Nominal complements expressing goals after verbs of movement —— **409**	
8.4.3.4	Nominal complements of verbs of naming —— **411**	
8.4.3.5	Interrogative clauses —— **412**	
8.5	Negated clauses —— **413**	
8.5.1	Negator before verb —— **413**	
8.5.1.1	Unstressed negator —— **414**	
8.5.1.2	Negator with non-nuclear stress —— **414**	
8.5.1.3	Negator with nuclear stress —— **414**	
8.5.1.4	Negated verb with nouns negated by hīč —— **415**	
8.5.2	Negated clauses in Iranian —— **415**	
8.5.2.1	Unstressed —— **416**	
8.5.2.2	Stressed with non-nuclear stress —— **416**	
8.5.2.3	Stressed with nuclear stress —— **416**	
8.5.2.4	Negated verb with nouns negated by hič —— **417**	
8.5.2.5	Negator before other elements in the clause —— **417**	
8.5.3	Idiomatic usage —— **418**	
8.6	Extrapositional constructions —— **419**	

8.7	Placement of adverbials —— 424	
8.7.1	In clause initial position —— 424	
8.7.2	At the end or in the middle of a clause —— 425	
8.8	Summary —— 427	
9	**Clause sequences** —— 429	
9.1	Introductory overview —— 429	
9.2	Expression of co-ordinative clausal connection —— 429	
9.2.1	Asyndetic connection —— 429	
9.2.1.1	Sequential actions —— 429	
9.2.1.2	Temporally overlapping actions or situations —— 431	
9.2.2	The co-ordinating particle *ū* —— 432	
9.2.2.1	Sequential actions —— 433	
9.2.2.2	Temporally overlapping actions or situations —— 435	
9.2.3	The co-ordinating particle *wa* —— 437	
9.3	=əč —— 438	
9.3.1	Scope over a constituent —— 438	
9.3.1.1	Inclusive focus ('too') —— 438	
9.3.1.2	Scalar additive focus ('even') —— 439	
9.3.1.3	Establishing a new topic —— 440	
9.3.2	Scope over the proposition —— 441	
9.3.2.1	Thetic clauses —— 441	
9.3.2.2	Concessive clauses ('even if') —— 443	
9.4	Intonation group boundaries —— 444	
9.5	Incremental repetition —— 448	
9.6	Summary —— 449	
10	**Syntactic subordination of clauses** —— 451	
10.1	Introductory overview —— 451	
10.2	Relative clauses —— 451	
10.2.1	Syndetic relative clauses —— 451	
10.2.1.1	kē —— 454	
10.2.1.2	=ē —— 455	
10.2.2	Asyndetic relative clauses —— 456	
10.2.2.1	har-čī, har-kas —— 458	
10.3	Cleft constructions —— 460	
10.4	Modifier clauses —— 461	
10.5	Indirect questions —— 462	
10.6	Subordinate content clauses —— 465	
10.6.1	kē —— 465	

10.6.1.1	Factive complement content clauses — **465**
10.6.1.2	Non-factive complement — **468**
10.6.1.3	Purpose — **469**
10.6.2	tā- — **470**
10.6.2.1	'when' — **470**
10.6.2.2	'until' — **470**
10.6.2.3	Purpose — **472**
10.6.2.4	Result — **472**
10.7	Temporal clauses — **473**
10.7.1	waxt=ē — **473**
10.7.2	ba-mudat=ē kē — **475**
10.7.3	zamān=ē ke — **476**
10.7.4	čun — **476**
10.7.5	Asyndetic temporal constructions — **477**
10.8	Conditional constructions — **478**
10.8.1	Constructions with the particle ʾagar — **478**
10.8.2	Clauses introduced by ʾagar čanānčē — **478**
10.8.3	Asyndetic conditional constructions — **479**
10.9	Concessive constructions — **480**
10.10	Summary — **481**

11	**Lexicon — 483**
11.1	Loanwords from Gorani and Sanandaj Kurdish — **483**
11.1.1	Introductory remarks — **483**
11.1.2	Kinship terms — **484**
11.1.3	Body parts — **486**
11.1.4	Cultural objects — **490**
11.1.5	Names of locations — **491**
11.1.6	Spatial and temporal terms — **491**
11.1.7	Food and fruit — **492**
11.1.8	Animals and insects — **493**
11.1.9	Abstract, Intangible and mass nouns — **493**
11.1.10	Plants — **494**
11.1.11	Natural world — **494**
11.1.12	Professions — **495**
11.1.13	Fabrics — **495**
11.1.14	Clothing — **495**
11.1.15	Adjectives and adverbs — **495**
11.1.16	Verbs — **496**
11.1.17	Prepositions — **498**

11.1.18	Indefinites and interrogatives —— **499**	
11.1.19	Conjunctions —— **500**	
11.2	Loanwords from Persian —— **501**	
11.2.1	Nouns —— **501**	
11.2.2	Adjectives and adverbs —— **504**	
11.2.3	Verbs —— **504**	
11.2.4	Particles —— **505**	
11.3	Loanwords from the Kurdish of the Sulemaniyya region —— **505**	
11.4	Loanwords from Bahdini Kurdish —— **505**	
11.5	NENA loanwords in Kurdish and Gorani —— **506**	
11.6	Summary —— **508**	
12	**Conclusion —— 510**	
12.1	Preliminary remarks —— **510**	
12.2	Layers of contact —— **510**	
12.2.1	Gorani —— **511**	
12.2.2	Kurdish —— **513**	
12.2.3	Persian —— **514**	
12.2.4	Sulemaniyya Kurdish —— **515**	
12.2.5	Kurmanji Kurdish —— **515**	
12.3	Processes —— **515**	
12.3.1	Matter borrowing —— **515**	
12.3.1.1	Loanwords —— **516**	
12.3.1.2	Borrowed bound morphemes —— **517**	
12.3.1.3	Loanblends —— **518**	
12.3.1.4	Hybrid loanwords —— **519**	
12.3.1.5	Phonetic matching —— **520**	
12.3.1.6	Borrowed phonemes —— **520**	
12.3.2	Pattern replication —— **521**	
12.3.2.1	Phonology —— **521**	
12.3.2.2	Morphosyntax —— **521**	
12.3.2.3	Impact of internal exponence of JSNENA —— **522**	
12.3.2.4	Impact of Preference for Matching a Discrete Word —— **523**	
12.3.2.5	Impact of imperfect matching —— **524**	
12.3.2.6	Impact of a later overlay of Kurdish —— **524**	
12.3.2.7	Impact of grammatical category —— **525**	
12.3.2.8	Calques —— **526**	
12.3.2.9	Replication of syntactic and discourse patterns —— **526**	
12.4	Metatypy and communal identity —— **527**	
12.5	Theoretical models of language contact —— **528**	

Appendix —— 541

References —— 575

Index —— 587

List of tables

Table	Description	Page
Table 1	Phoneme inventory of JSNENA, Kurdish, and Gorani	19
Table 2	Phonological loans from Iranian in JSNENA	62
Table 3	Phonological loans in Gorani and Kurdish through contact with Semitic	62
Table 4	Phonological changes in JSNENA triggered through contact with Gorani, Kurdish or Persian	62
Table 5	Features exhibiting different convergence patterns with contact languages	63
Table 6	Independent direct pronouns in JSNENA	64
Table 7	Gender distinction in 2sg pronouns across NENA	65
Table 8	Gender distinction in 3sg pronouns across NENA	65
Table 9	Third person pronouns in JSNENA	66
Table 10	1st and 2nd independent pronouns in JSNENA	66
Table 11	Independent pronouns in NENA	67
Table 12	Independent direct and oblique pronouns in JSNENA	67
Table 13	Independent direct and oblique pronouns in Ch. Sulemaniyya	67
Table 14	Independent pronouns in Kurdish and Gorani	68
Table 15	Independent pronouns in JSNENA and J. Kerend, compared	69
Table 16	Independent proximate deixis pronouns in JSNENA	70
Table 17	Independent proximate deixis pronouns in Gorani	71
Table 18	Proximate anaphoric pronouns in Gorani	71
Table 19	The structural correspondence of proximate anaphoric pronouns in JSNENA and Gorani	72
Table 20	Independent proximate deictic pronoun in Kurdish	73
Table 21	Independent proximate deixis pronoun in JSNENA and Kurdish compared	73
Table 22	Independent remote pronouns in JSNENA	73
Table 23	Independent remote deixis pronouns in Gorani	74
Table 24	Additional deictic pronouns in Gorani	75
Table 25	The structural correspondence of remote anaphoric pronouns in JSNENA and Gorani	75
Table 26	Independent remote deixis pronouns in Kurdish	76
Table 27	The structural correspondence of remote anaphoric pronouns in JSNENA and Kurdish	76
Table 28	Attributive proximate demonstrative pronouns in JSNENA	76
Table 29	Attributive remote demonstrative pronouns in JSNENA	77
Table 30	Attributive proximate demonstrative pronouns in Gorani	77
Table 31	Attributive remote demonstrative pronouns in Gorani	78
Table 32	Attributive proximate demonstrative pronouns in Kurdish	79
Table 33	Attributive remote demonstrative pronouns in Kurdish	79
Table 34	JSNENA pronominal suffixes on nouns and prepositions	80
Table 35	L-suffixes in JSNENA	81
Table 36	Pronominal person clitics in Kurdish and Gorani	81
Table 37	Pattern replication of morphological features of pronouns in JSNENA	89
Table 38	Pattern matching of morphological features of pronouns in NENA with contact languages	89
Table 39	Morphological features of pronouns in JSNENA lost due to contact	90

Open Access. © 2024 the author(s), published by De Gruyter. This work is licensed under the Creative Commons Attribution-NonCommercial-NoDerivatives 4.0 International License.
https://doi.org/10.1515/9783111209180-204

Table 40	Nominal gender marking in Gorani —— 93	
Table 41	Definiteness paradigm of Gorani —— 104	
Table 42	Token frequency of different definite forms in Gorani —— 106	
Table 43	Direct borrowing of nominal morphological features into NENA —— 131	
Table 44	Pattern replication of nominal morphological features in NENA —— 131	
Table 45	Nominal morphological features in JSNENA reinforced due to contact with Iranian —— 132	
Table 46	Nominal morphological features in JSNENA lost due to contact —— 132	
Table 47	Direct inflectional suffixes in JSNENA, Gorani, and Kurdish —— 144	
Table 48	Oblique Clitics in Iranian and L-suffixes in JSNENA —— 147	
Table 49	Person suffixes and person clitics in the Bajalani variety of Gorani —— 151	
Table 50	Person suffixes and person clitics in Kurdish of Kirkuk —— 152	
Table 51	Copula paradigms in JSNENA —— 169	
Table 52	Copula paradigms in Ch. Barwar (Khan 2008b, 180–81) —— 169	
Table 53	Copula paradigm in Gorani in comparison with inflectional person suffixes —— 170	
Table 54	Copula paradigm in Kurdish in comparison with inflectional person suffixes —— 170	
Table 55	Copula paradigm in Gorani Bajalani in comparison with inflectional person suffixes —— 171	
Table 56	The copula paradigm in proto-Iranian and Old Iranian —— 171	
Table 57	Past copula paradigm in JSNENA —— 172	
Table 58	Past copula paradigm in J. Arbel —— 173	
Table 59	Past copula paradigm in Ch. Barwar (Khan 2008b, 183–84) —— 173	
Table 60	Past copula paradigm in Gorani Bajalani (Iraq) (MacKenzie 1956, 424) —— 174	
Table 61	Past copula paradigms in Gorani —— 176	
Table 62	Past copula paradigm in Kurdish —— 177	
Table 63	Functions of copula forms in JSNENA, Gorani, and Kurdish —— 179	
Table 64	The paradigm of negated copulas in JSNENA —— 219	
Table 65	The paradigm of negated copulas in Gorani —— 219	
Table 66	The paradigm of negated copulas in Kurdish —— 220	
Table 67	Direct borrowing of verbal morphological features into NENA —— 222	
Table 68	Pattern replication of verbal morphological features into JSNENA —— 222	
Table 69	Pattern matching of verbal morphological features in NENA with contact languages —— 223	
Table 70	Verbal morphological features of JSNENA reinforced due to contact —— 223	
Table 71	Verbal morphological features of JSNENA lost due to contact —— 224	
Table 72	Nominal syntax of JSNENA and the type of convergence it shares with contact languages —— 281	
Table 73	The syntax of attributive modifiers in JSNENA and its convergence with similar phenomenon in contact languages —— 281	
Table 74	Transitive vs. intransitive coding of sound emission verbs across NENA —— 335	
Table 75	Encoding transitivity in JSNENA, Gorani, and Kurdish, compared —— 338	
Table 76	Convergence of JSNENA with Iranian in the function of present-stem verbal forms —— 371	
Table 77	The function of past-converter suffixes in JSNENA and Gorani —— 371	
Table 78	Convergence of JSNENA with Iranian in the function of past-stem verbal forms —— 372	
Table 79	Convergence of JSNENA with Iranian in the function of constructions with resultative participles —— 372	

Table 80	Convergence of JSNENA with Iranian in other features of verbal syntax —— 373	
Table 81	Percentage of post-predicate objects across JSNENA, Kurdish, and Gorani —— 390	
Table 82	Rate of post-predicate realisation of nominal indirect objects in JSNENA and Kurdish —— 406	
Table 83	Negator formatives in Gorani and Kurdish —— 415	
Table 84	Features in JSNENA showing total convergence with Kurdish and Gorani contact languages —— 427	
Table 85	Features showing different convergence patterns with Contact languages —— 428	
Table 86	Subordinating and other particles in JSNENA and their origin —— 481	

List of figures

Figure 1 Jewish NENA dialects (simplified) —— 4
Figure 2 Christian NENA dialects (simplified) —— 6
Figure 3 Iranian languages of the region —— 9
Figure 4 Phonetic realisation of vowels in JSNENA —— 48
Figure 5 Phonetic realisation of vowels in Kurdish —— 48
Figure 6 Phonetic realisation of vowels in Gorani —— 49
Figure 7 Phonetic realisation of vowels in JSNENA, Gorani, and Kurdish compared —— 50

Abbreviations and symbols

ADD	additive
AUX	auxiliary
CAUS	causative
CLF	classifier
CMPR	comparative
COMPL	complementiser
COP	copula
DEF	definite
DEIC	deictic
DEM	demonstrative
DIM	diminutive
DIR	direct
DIST	distal
DRCT	directional
EMPH	emphatic
EP	epenthetic
EXIST	existential
EXCM	exclamative
EZ	ezafe
F	feminine
FUT	future
HORT	hortative
IMP	imperative
IND	indicative (realis)
INDF	indefinite
IPFV	imperfective
INF	infinitive
INTJ	interjection
LVC	light verb complement
M	masculine
NA	not analysed
NEG	negative
OBL	oblique
PERF	perfect
PFV	perfective
PL	plural
PN	proper noun
POST	postposition
PRS	present
PRSNT	presentative
PROG	progressive
PRON	pronominal
PROX	proximate
PRSNT	presentative

Open Access. © 2024 the author(s), published by De Gruyter. This work is licensed under the Creative Commons Attribution-NonCommercial-NoDerivatives 4.0 International License.
https://doi.org/10.1515/9783111209180-206

PST	past
PSTC	past converter affix
PTCL	particle
PTCP	participle
PVB	preverbal derivational particle
Q	question
RDP	reduplicant
REFL	reflexive
REL	relativiser
RESTR	restrictive
SG	singular
SBJV	subjunctive
SBRD	subordinator
SIM	similative
TAM	tense-aspect-mood
TELIC	telicity marker
Ch.	Christian NENA dialect
CK.	Central Kurdish
G.	Gorani
JSNENA	Jewish Neo-Aramaic dialect of Sanandaj
K.	Kurdish Sanandaj
NK.	Northern Kurdish
P.	Persian
|	intonation group boundary
=	clitic boundary
-	separates segmentable morphemes
Ø	'non-overt, but reconstructable morpheme'

1 Introduction

1.1 Sanandaj and its Languages

Sanandaj (Kurdish *Sine* [səna]) is the administrative capital of Kordestan province in western Iran, situated close to the border with the neighbouring Kurdish regions in Iraq. There was a small village on the site until the 17th century, when the governor of the region, Suleyman Khan Ardalan, built a castle known as Səna-dij ('Səna fortress'), which became the basis of the town. Sanandaj gained historical importance especially in the 17th and 18th century, during the rule of the Ardalan principality. The region remained a semi-autonomous frontier province ruled by the Ardalan dynasty down to the middle of the 19th century.

In the first half of the 20th century, Sanandaj was home to Muslims, Jews and Christians. The dominant spoken language of the Muslims at that period was Kurdish. The Jews and Christians were minority groups who spoke Neo-Aramaic as an ancestral communal language and also spoke the Kurdish dialect of the Muslim majority. Standard Persian was becoming more widely used in the region as a language of education and administration and was spoken by many people in all religious communities. Neo-Aramaic belongs to the Semitic family of languages whereas Kurdish and Persian belong to the Iranian family.

As a result of this multilingual situation in Sanandaj there was contact between the various languages, which laid the ground for contact-induced change. This book focuses on the changes that took place in one of the Semitic Neo-Aramaic dialects of Sanandaj due to contact with Iranian languages. The book, therefore, is a case study of contact-induced change in one of the languages of the multilingual situation of Sanandaj rather than a systematic study of contact-induced change in all languages of the town. The Neo-Aramaic dialect that is made the focus is that of the Jews of Sanandaj. The main justification for this is that we have a detailed description of this dialect in the grammar published by Khan (2009). The Christian Neo-Aramaic dialect and the Iranian vernacular dialects of Sanandaj and the surrounding region have not been described in any detail. The grammar of Khan, therefore, forms the basis for the study. In addition to being a study of language contact, the book is a systematic description of Gorani (the vernacular of Hawraman Takht) and Sanandaj Kurdish on the model of Khan's (2009) grammar of JSNENA. We have described constructions and features in Gorani and Sanandaj Kurdish in all areas of grammar, including phonology, morphology, syntax, clausal coordination, clausal subordination, and lexicon. We have done so systematically regardless of whether linguistic features of JSNENA match those of the Iranian languages or not. This approach is justified also by our aim in the book to investigate systematically contact-induced change in all levels of the language and all grammatical constructions (see below §1.5 for more details about our methodology). This approach is greatly facilitated by making an existing detailed description its foundation. Throughout the book, however, numerous comments are made about cases of contact-induced change also in the other languages of Sanandaj, especially the Iranian languages. The change in the Jewish Neo-Aramaic dialect of Sanandaj developed through contact with the Iranian languages of the area. There is no evidence that the Christian Neo-Aramaic dialect of Sanandaj had any impact on the Jewish Neo-Aramaic dialect. Indeed, the Christian dialect was so different from the Jewish dialect that the Jews spoke to the Christians in Kurdish rather than in Neo-Aramaic. The book, therefore, is a study of linguistic change arising from contact between the Semitic Neo-Aramaic dialect of the Jews with Iranian.

1.2 The Neo-Aramaic Dialects of the Sanandaj Region

The Neo-Aramaic dialects spoken in the region of Sanandaj belong to the North-Eastern Neo-Aramaic subgroup of Neo-Aramaic. North-Eastern Neo-Aramaic (NENA)[1] is a highly diverse subgroup of over 150 dialects spoken by Christians and Jews originating from towns and villages east of the Tigris river in northern Iraq, south-eastern Turkey and western Iran. Within NENA itself one may identify a number of subgroups on the basis of linguistic structure and lexicon.

There is a fundamental split between the dialects spoken by the Christians and those spoken by the Jews. This applies even to cases where Jewish and Christian communities lived in the same town, such as Koy Sanjak, Sulemaniyya (both in northern Iraq), Urmi (north-western Iran) and Sanandaj (western Iran). In these towns the dialect of the Christians differed radically from the dialect of the Jews in all levels of grammar (phonology, morphology, syntax) and lexicon.[2]

Within Jewish NENA dialects two main subgroups are clearly identifiable:

One of these was spoken in north-western Iraq, mainly in Dohuk province in locations to the west of the Great Zab river, such as Zakho (Avinery 1988; Sabar 2002; Cohen 2012), Dohuk, Amedia (Greenblatt 2011), Betanure (Mutzafi 2008a), also across the Zab in Iraq near the Turkish border in villages such as Nerwa and in small communities in what is now south-eastern Turkey in, for example, Challa (Fassberg 2010) in Hakkâri province, and Cizre (Nakano 1969; 1973) in Şırnak province. This subgroup is generally referred as *līšāna dēnī* ('our language'), the native

---

[1] The term was coined by Hobermann (1988, 557).
[2] In this article Christian dialects are distinguished from Jewish dialects by the abbreviation Ch. and J. respectively before the name of the location of the dialect.

term used by speakers of the dialects, which contains the form of the 1pl. genitive pronoun that is distinctive of the group.

The dialects of the other Jewish subgroup were spoken in locations east of the Great Zab river in Iraq, north-western Iran and western Iran. This subgroup is generally referred to as trans-Zab (following Mutzafi 2008b). In Iraq this included the dialects of locations in the Arbel (Erbil) and Sulemaniyya provinces, e.g. Rustaqa (Khan 2002b), Ruwanduz, Koy Sanjak (Mutzafi 2004a), villages of the plain of Arbel (Khan 1999),[3] the village of Dobe which is on the western bank of the Great Zab, Ḥalabja and Sulemaniyya to the east (Khan 2004), and as far south as Khanaqin on the Iranian border. In north-western Iran it includes the Jewish dialects of the towns of Urmi, Šəno (official name Ushnuye), Solduz (official name Naqadeh) and Sablagh (now Mahabad) (Garbell 1965; Khan 2008a), the district of Salamas north of the Urmi plain (Duval 1883; Mutzafi 2015) and in adjacent towns that are now situated in the east of Turkey, such as Başkale and Gawar (official name Yüksekova). In western Iran the trans-Zab subgroup includes a cluster of dialects spoken by Jewish communities in various localities in the Kordestan and Kermanshah provinces in an area that includes Sainqala, Bokan, Saqqəz on its northern border, Sanandaj in the centre, Bijar on the eastern border, and in the south Kerend and Qasr-e Širin (Hopkins 1999; Khan 2009; Yisraeli 1998). Various native names of the language are used by the trans-Zab Jewish communities, e.g. *līšānət nošan* (north-eastern Iraq), *līšāna nošan* (western Iran), *līšāna dīdan* (north-western Iran), all of which mean 'our language', also *hūlāūla* (western Iran), which is an abstract noun meaning 'Jewishness/Judaism' (< *hūḏāyūṯā*).

The divisions among the Christian NENA dialects on structural and lexical grounds are not so clear-cut. One may, nevertheless, identify clusters of dialects with distinctive features.[4]

The NENA dialects of northern Iraq, south-eastern Turkey and north-western Iran exhibit considerable diversity. The NENA dialects of the Kordestan and Kermanshah provinces of western Iran, by contrast, exhibit very little diversity. The main split within the dialects of western Iran is between Jewish and Christian varieties of NENA. The Jewish variety consists of a cluster of dialects spoken by Jewish communities in various localities in an area that includes Sainqala, Bokan, Saqqəz on its northern border, Sanandaj in the centre, Bijar on the eastern border, and in the south Kerend and Qasr-e Širin. The Christians variety consists of a single dialect spoken by Christians in the town of Sanandaj.

The Jewish cluster of dialects in western Iran is remarkably uniform and only minor differences are found among the dialects of the aforementioned places where

---

[3] The Jews in the town of Arbel itself spoke Arabic (Jastrow 1990).
[4] For more details, see Khan (2018c; 2018e; 2018d).

the dialects were spoken. As remarked, the comparative analysis that is presented in this book takes the Jewish dialect of Sanandaj as its central case study. This is the dialect of the region that has been described in the greatest detail. An extensive documentation of the dialect (grammar, lexicon and text corpus) was published in Khan (2009). Studies on other Jewish NENA dialects include Yisraeli (1998) on the dialect of Saqqəz and Hopkins (2002) on Kerend. The Jewish dialects of the region belong to the so-called trans-Zab subgroup of Jewish NENA. Within trans-Zab they are most closely related to the Jewish dialect of Sulemaniyya in north-eastern Iraq (Khan 2004). Their relationship to the Jewish trans-Zab cluster of dialects of the West Azerbaijan province of Iran in the Urmi region is more distant to the extent that speakers of dialects from the western Iran cluster had difficulties communicating with Jews from Urmi (See Figure 1 for a map of Jewish NENA dialects).

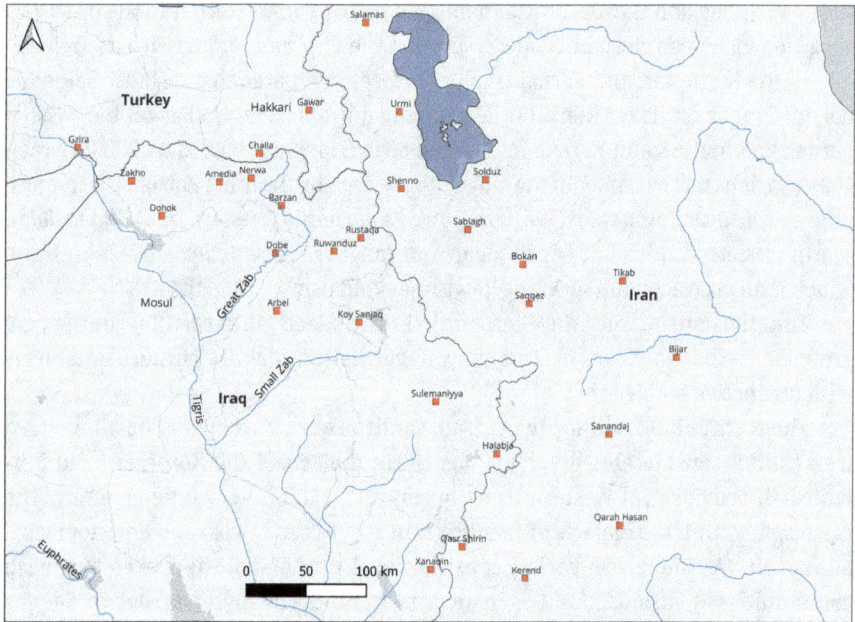

Figure 1: Jewish NENA dialects (simplified).

The Christian NENA dialect of Sanandaj (henceforth referred to Ch. Sanandaj) is, likewise, very similar to the Christian dialect of Sulemaniyya but substantially different from the Christian dialects spoken in the Urmi region of Iran. Grammatical and lexical studies on the Ch. Sanandaj include Panoussi (1990; 1991), Heinrichs (2002) and Kalin (2014). Short extracts of texts in the dialect can be found in Panoussi (1990, 120–28) and Macuch & Panoussi (1974, 39).[5] These authors refer to the dialect as the Senaya dialect, from the Kurdish name of the town 'Sena'. Brief overviews of the NENA dialect situation in Iran in general can be found in Hopkins (1999) and Khan (2020b).

Very little is documented concerning the history of the NENA-speaking communities of western Iran before the twentieth century. The lack of diversity in the Jewish cluster of dialects suggests that the communities who spoke them migrated in a single wave into the region in relatively recent centuries. The ancient heartland of NENA must have been in what is now northern Iraq and south-eastern Turkey, where there is great dialectal diversity. The close relationship of the Jewish dialects of western Iran with the J. Sulemaniyya dialect points to north-eastern Iraq as the origin of the migration. Our study in this book has found linguistic evidence of this migration route.

The isolated Christian dialect spoken in Sanandaj must, likewise, have been the result of migration. It is closely related to the Christian dialect of Sulemaniyya and there were family relationships between these two communities in the living memory of speakers. It is likely, therefore, that the Christians of Sanandaj were originally migrants from the region of Sulemaniyya in Iraq. As remarked, the Christian dialect of Sanandaj is radically different in its structure from the Jewish dialect of Sanandaj (See Figure 2 for a map of Christian NENA dialects).

We know that some of the Jewish communities who settled in the towns of western Iran originally lived in surrounding villages. The Jews of Sanandaj, for example, moved into the town after its foundation in the 17th century from a village known as Qal'at Ḥasan-ʾābād (Khan 2009, 1).

The Christians of Sanandaj belong to the Chaldean Church. In the 19th century several Christian families moved to Qazvīn, where their speech developed the distinctive trait of the realisation of /w/ as /v/ under the influence of Persian (Heinrichs 2002, 238). In the middle of the twentieth century, the Chaldean diocese of Sanandaj moved to Tehran and the Christian Neo-Aramaic speakers moved with it.

In 1952 many NENA-speaking Jews from the region emigrated to the newly founded State of Israel. Over the subsequent two decades there was a gradual emigration of the Jews either to Tehran or abroad, mostly to Israel. After the Iranian Revolution in 1979, most of the remaining Jews left the region, the majority settling in Los Angeles in the USA and the remainder in Israel or Europe. Today only a few elderly Jews are reported to be still living in the town.

After the Christian NENA-speaking community moved *en masse* from Sanandaj to Tehran, they gradually left Iran and settled abroad. The majority of the migrants

---

[5] Data on Ch. Sanandaj cited in this chapter are mainly taken from the publications of Panoussi or from personal communications from him and other informants, which I acknowledge with gratitude. I also thank Matthew Nazari for assistance with the gathering of data.

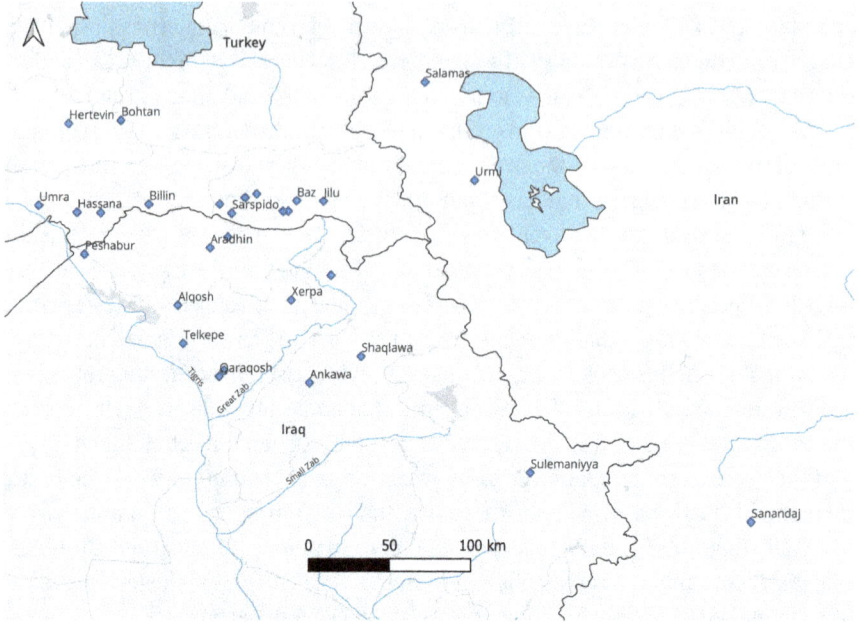

Figure 2: Christian NENA dialects (simplified).

have settled in the Los Angeles area of the USA. As a result of these migrations and the disintegration of the NENA speech communities, the NENA dialects that were spoken in western Iran are now highly endangered.

1.3 The Iranian languages of the Sanandaj Region

Three Iranian languages are spoken in the Sanandaj area: Kurdish, Hawrami (Gorani), and Persian. Traditionally, Iranian languages are divided into eastern and western groups. The western group is classified into southern and northern subgroups. Kurdish and Hawrami belong to the north-western Iranian languages. Persian, on the other hand, is considered a member of the south-western subgroup.[6] The genetic affiliation of Kurdish and Gorani is different within the family tree of Iranian languages. Gorani shares features with Zazaki and other north-western Iranian languages (e.g. Taleshi), while Kurdish shares features with languages of the south-western subgroup (Paul 1998), which makes it a 'transition' variety (Windfuhr 2009, 19).

---

6 The traditional dichotomy of Iranian languages has been refuted in the light of recent scholarship (cf. Korn 2016; 2019). This has, nonetheless, no bearing on the claims of this book.

1.3 The Iranian languages of the Sanandaj Region

Since the 20th century, the indigenous population of Sanandaj has been Kurdish-speaking. Kurdish is an Iranian language spoken in neighbouring regions of eastern Turkey, northern Iraq, western Iran, and north-eastern Syria. It is classified into three general varieties: Northern Kurdish (Kurmanji); Central Kurdish (Sorani), and Southern Kurdish (which also is known by other terms, such as Kalhuri, Kirmashani, Feyli, etc.). The Kurdish dialect spoken in Sanandaj belongs to the southernmost dialects of the Central Kurdish (CK) speech zone and is in close contact with the neighbouring Southern Kurdish and Hawrami dialects.[7] The Kurdish vernacular of Sanandaj has not been subject to a proper linguistic description. Publications in European languages are restricted to small grammatical notes in De Morgan (1904). Other publications include a succinct grammatical overview in Persian (Ebrahimpour *undated*), a Kurdish-Persian dictionary (Razi 2009) and a few journal articles in Persian (see Paul 2022 for an analytical bibliography). As remarked in §1.1, the current book offers a systematic description of Sanandaj Kurdish on the model of Khan's (2009) grammar of NENA.

The data for the description of the Kurdish dialect of Sanandaj come from a corpus of eleven transcribed spoken narratives recorded in Sanandaj and its surrounding villages (Mohammadirad 2022b).[8] Moreover, some examples of Sanandaj Kurdish in our book are excerpts from additional recordings from Sanandaj that have not been fully processed. Throughout the book, We have specified whether a linguistic example comes from Sanandaj itself, in which case we have put 'Kurdish' next to the example number, or whether the example comes from the region around Sanandaj, in which case we have put 'Kurdish of Sanandaj region' next to the example number. In a few cases, reference has been made to other varieties of Kurdish from which the examples come from.

Persian is another Iranian language spoken in Sanandaj. It was the main language of administration, official correspondence, and perhaps for *medrese* education during the ruling of the Ardalan principality in the region (cf. Leezenberg 2020, 57). Persian was fully introduced into the region in the early 20th century, following its designation as the sole means of nationwide compulsory schooling.

---

7 Kurdish is often used as a cover term in a wider ethnic and socio-cultural sense to encompass the closely related but genetically different languages of Gorani (with Hawrami as its best known and the most archaic dialect), which is spoken in small pockets in western Iran and north-eastern Iraq, and Zazaki, which is spoken in south-eastern Turkey in the region north of Diyarbakir (cf. Leezenberg 1992; Öpengin 2021).
8 For metadata on the location of the texts, the speakers, their sex, etc. see the heading "Kurdish (Central, Sanandaj)" in "The Word Order in Western Asia Corpus": https://multicast.aspra.uni-bamberg.de/resources/wowa/

Hawrami is the third major Iranian language spoken in the Sanandaj region. Following Mahmoudevysi et al. (2012), we use 'Gorani' as a cover term for a group of West Iranian languages spoken in the area of Hawraman on the Iranian and Iraqi sides of the border, and also in various small pockets in northern Iraq, extending as far west as the Mosul plain. These pockets of Gorani in Iraq are the vernacular language of communities such as the Kaka'ī, Šabak, Sarlī, or Bājałānī (cf. Bailey 2018 for a classification of Gorani dialects). Among Gorani dialects, Hawrami is the most complex morphologically, and the best known. The Hawrami spoken along the Iranian side of the border can be roughly classified into three dialect areas: Takht, Luhon, and Zhawaro. So far, the only available grammar of a Hawrami variety is MacKenzie's (1966) description of the Luhon dialect.

The data for the Gorani material in this book comes primarily from the vernacular of Hawraman Takht in western Iran, which is classified as the Takht dialect. The linguistic material comes from recordings that Mohammadirad collected in his various trips to Hawraman during the last few years. Some of these narratives form the basis of a Hawrami corpus currently under construction (Mohammadirad *in prep*). In addition to spoken narratives, we have also made use of elicitation tasks as a means of data gathering. Hawrami Takht is one of the most conservative Gorani dialects. It is nearest in terms of morphosyntactic features to the Luhon dialect studied by MacKenzie (1966), though geographically Hawrami Takht is closer to Sanandaj. Publications on Hawrami Takht are mostly in Persian, e.g. Sadjadi (2015) on the category of gender. Hawrami Takht is different from the more Kurdicised Gorani dialects of Gawraju and Zarda described in Mahmoudveysi et al. (2012), and Mahmoudveysi and Bailey (2013), respectively. Throughout the book, we have put 'Gorani' next to the example number whenever the data come from Hawrami Takht. If examples are from other varieties of Gorani, these are identified with specific labels. We have used the general term 'Gorani' in place of Hawrami throughout the book.

Gorani is assumed to have been the dominant language in earlier times in the areas where Central and Southern Kurdish are now spoken (cf. Minorsky 1943; MacKenzie 1961b).[9] It flourished as the literary language at the court of the Ardalan principality.[10] Gorani also serves as the language of the religious texts of the heterodox Yarsan community in western Iran.

---

[9] Note that the term Guran (Goran) has been used in different senses, e.g. to name a dynasty, a tribal confederation, a social class, etc. (Leezenberg 1992). It is thus possible that the place name Gûran that Minorsky (1943, 77 fn. 2) lists for some areas in Urmi in western Iran and Bohtan in south-eastern Turkey could have any of the senses above. Likewise, Jaba's (1860) mentioning of families of Guran in Bayzid (south-eastern Turkey) and its neighbourhoods, probably denote a social class.
[10] Gorani was also the court language of the neighbouring Baban principality, based in Sulemaniyya, up until early in the 18th century, when it was later replaced by Sorani (cf. Leezenberg 1992).

The existing accounts of the history of Kurdish assume Kurdish to be a late arrival to the region and advocate the existence of an older layer of Gorani, especially to the east of the Great Zab river (cf. MacKenzie 1961b; 2002; Leezenberg 1992; Matras 2019; Öpengin 2021). These accounts assume that there was a language shift from Gorani to Kurdish.[11] Leezenberg (1992) reports that a shift from Gorani to Central Kurdish is probably a recent phenomenon, during the last two centuries.

MacKenzie (1961b) has argued that Kurdish was originally a dialect continuum and that the differences between Northern Kurdish and Central Kurdish result from the merging of the latter with Gorani, while Northern Kurdish remained more archaic. An alternative view, proposed by Jügel (2014), Haig and Öpengin (2014), and Matras (2019), is that Kurdish was from the beginning composed of two distinct groups, which spoke closely related varieties. The differences between Northern and Central Kurdish are then partly attributed to distinct source languages, and partly due to contact with other languages, e.g. Armenian, Gorani, Neo-Aramaic.

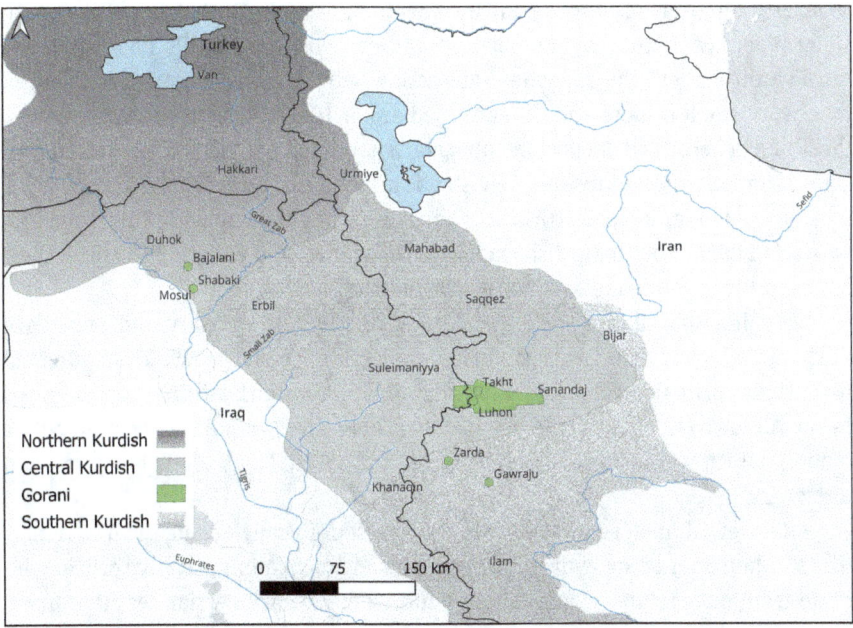

Figure 3: Iranian languages of the region.

---

11 Note, however, that much is unknown about the linguistic history of Kurdish (cf. Öpengin 2021 for an overview).

1.4 Bilingualism and language shifts in Sanandaj

1.4.1 The NENA-speaking Jews of Sanandaj

The Jews from Sanandaj who were the informants for Khan's grammar of the Jewish NENA dialect of Sanandaj (henceforth JSNENA) grew up in the town in the middle of the twentieth century. They report that in the 1950s there were approximately 200 Jewish families in Sanandaj, amounting to around 4,700 people, which constituted about 10% of the total population of the town.[12] The relationship between the Jews and the majority population of Sunni Muslim Kurds was amicable. All the Jews of the NENA-speaking Sanandaj community spoke also the local Kurdish dialect. A large proportion of the community also had a knowledge of Standard Persian.

Jews spoke JSNENA at home, so NENA can be said to be their native language. Most Jewish families, however, had Kurdish-speaking servants who lived with them in their houses, so children from an early age became bilingual NENA–Kurdish speakers. Children also spoke Kurdish with Muslim Kurdish friends and with shopkeepers when they went on errands. Adult Jewish men would typically speak Kurdish throughout the day when interacting with Muslims at work. Most Jewish men were small traders and itinerant pedlars or had service professions such as those of teachers, medical doctors, pharmacists, dentists, all of which required constant interaction with Muslims. Jewish adult women, who typically did not work outside the home, spoke Kurdish sporadically during the day with Kurdish neighbours and friends, with Kurdish traders in the market and with their Kurdish servants. Most Jews tended to live in a special quarter.

Most Jewish children spoke Persian at school, both primary and secondary school, in which teaching was conducted in Persian. The Jewish children attended two private primary schools, one for boys and one for girls, which were founded by the Alliance Israélite Universelle in 1904. Thereafter the children went to public schools, which were attended also by Muslim children. Many of the Jews attended university.

Adult Jewish men generally spoke Persian sporadically during the day, in particular when interacting with employees in government administrative offices who came from outside the region. Jewish adult women spoke Persian less than men, but usually had a knowledge of the language from their schooling. When Jews communicated with NENA-speaking Christians in Sanandaj, they spoke in Kurdish, since the two NENA dialects were not mutually comprehensible.

---

[12] Similar statistics are reported by Magnarella (1969).

It is reported that a few families of NENA-speaking Jews came to settle in Sanandaj from various towns in the region, including Merivan, Saqqəz, Sainqala, Baneh and Dehgulan. Khan's informants do not recall that any Jews from Sulemaniyya migrated to Sanandaj. Our study has shown that the JSNENA dialect contains some lexical elements from Sulemaniyya Kurdish. These must, therefore, have entered the dialect at a more remote historical period.

Some Jews who migrated from mountain villages to Sanandaj in the twentieth century spoke only Kurdish. There were only a few Jewish families in these villages among a majority Muslim population. When they settled in Sanandaj, they learnt to speak NENA from the Sanandaj Jewish community. Such migrants are reported to have spoken NENA with an 'accent', suggesting that they had learnt NENA imperfectly.

As will be discussed in the next section, there was a language shift in the Iranian-speaking Muslim population of Sanandaj at some point in the recent past from Gorani to Kurdish. The NENA-Iranian bilingual Jews, therefore, underwent the same language shift. We shall show in detail throughout this book that Gorani had a deep influence on the structure and lexicon of JSNENA, more so than Kurdish. The Gorani influence extended to core areas of the morpho-syntax and vocabulary of JSNENA. This Gorani influence had become entrenched in JSNENA as it was spoken in the twentieth century, although by that period Jewish NENA-Iranian bilinguals spoke Kurdish rather than Gorani.

1.4.2 The Iranian-speaking Muslims of Sanandaj

The Muslims of Sanandaj today speak Kurdish as their vernacular language. A large proportion of the population also speak Persian, which they have learnt mainly by attending Persian-speaking schools. There are still, however, some people of the older generation (over 60) who are monolingual in Kurdish. The same language situation among the Muslims existed in the second half of the twentieth century, when Khan's JSNENA informants were growing up in Sanandaj, except that knowledge of Persian is likely to have been slightly less. The Muslims would have used Persian outside of school in similar contexts as the Jews used Persian, i.e. when interacting with government administration and with Persian-speaking people who had migrated to Sanandaj from elsewhere in Iran. The Muslims of Sanandaj did not learn to speak JSNENA with the Jews. Jews and Muslims communicated in Kurdish.

There is evidence that the Kurdish dialect spoken today in Sanandaj had a Gorani (specifically Hawrami) substrate. This is reflected, for example, by morpho-syntactic features that set it apart from the rest of Central Kurdish. One such feature is the ordering of core arguments on past tense verbs. In Sanandaj Central Kurdish

(1a) and Hawrami (1b) the object index comes first and the subject index second. This ordering is the reverse in upper Central Kurdish dialects, e.g. Mukri Central Kurdish (1c) (cf. Öpengin & Mohammadirad (2022); Mohammadirad *(in review)*.

(1) a. *bərd=mān=yān*
        take.PST=1PL=3PL
    b. *bard-īmē=šā*
        take.PST-1PL=3PL
    c. *bərd=yān-īn*
        take.PST=3PL-1PL
        'They took us (away).'

Another piece of evidence for a Gorani substrate in Sanandaj Kurdish is that the additive particle has the form *=īč* as in Gorani, whereas it has the form *=īš* in the rest of Central Kurdish.[13]

There are some accounts of the linguistic history of Sanandaj that indicate that Gorani was once widely spoken in the town. In an introduction to the book *Les dialectes d'Awroman et de Pawa*, Benedictsen gives a report concerning the linguistic situation in Sanandaj in 1900. He writes that 'learned people' in the city knew and spoke *Maço* (an epithet of Gorani/Hawrami, meaning 'S/he says'). He adds:

> À Sänä où le kurde est maintenant la langue commune hors des communautés persane, juive et syrienne, on prétendait que l'awromānī y avait été communément entendu autrefois ('In Sänä [Sanandaj, Kurdish Sine], where Kurdish is now the common language outside of the Persian, Jewish and Syriac communities, it was claimed that Awromānī had been commonly heard there in the past] (Christensen and Benedictsen 1921, 5)

This quotation shows that Gorani (Awromānī) was once widely spoken in Sanandaj. A more concrete account of the language shift in Sanandaj from Gorani to Kurdish is found in a translation of the Bible into Hawrami Gorani by Kurdistānī (1930). The author was a famous physician from Sanandaj named Dr. Sa'eed Khan Kordestani (1863–1943). The author reports with sadness that when he returned to his hometown Sanandaj after an absence of fifty years, "Hawrami, the original 'sweet' dialect of the city, is now completely extinct and can be seen spoken only by a handful of old women in the corners and alleyways of Sanandaj."

The aforementioned accounts of the linguistic history of the region roughly match the historians' accounts of the recent history of the region, even though these accounts remain speculative. Following Izadi (1992), Ardalan (2004, 24–25) suggests

---

13 After a series of migrations of Kurds from surrounding localities to Sanandaj, especially in the past four decades, the additive particle is now shifting to the common Kurdish *=īš*.

that the Sanandaj region westward to Shahrezur (in the Sulemaniyya region) was once populated by Gorani-speaking people who were followers of the Yarsan (Ahlehagh) religion. It appears that Islam only had a superficial influence on the region until the beginning of the 17th century, i.e. the beginning of the Ardalan dynasty. The continuing intermittent war between the Persians and the Ottomans over territorial issues from the 16th century to the 17th century had a devastating socio-economic impact on the Gorani people in this conflict zone. This paved the way for the expansion of the nomadic Kurds, who came from the north and imposed their religion, Sunnite Islam, and their language, Kurdish, on the Gorani people (Izady 1992).

The aforementioned account of the recent history of the region remains speculative in the absence of historical records. It connects linguistic shift from Gorani to Kurdish to religious shift from Yarsan to Islam. What follows from this account is that some Gorani people have kept their language and religion up until today (e.g. Gorani-speaking localities in Gawrajo, Zarda, Kandula). The majority of Goran people who converted to Islam, however, shifted to Kurdish (barring the Hawraman region where language shift to Kurdish has not occurred).

A language shift from Gorani to Kurdish took place also outside the Sanandaj region. This was the case in northern Iraq over the last 150 years (Leezenberg 1992). Now Gorani only survives in small pockets in Iraq. It is significant that some of the surviving Gorani-speaking communities in the region still have not adopted an orthodox form of Islam, but follow ancestral religions.

Similarly, Mahmoudveysi (2016, 3) reports that when Mann and Hadank (1930) conducted fieldwork among speakers in the localities of Bēwänījī, Rijābī and Gähwārāī around Kerend (western Iran), they were speaking Gorani, but they have now shifted to vernaculars of Southern Kurdish.

There is clear evidence, therefore, of a language shift from Gorani to Kurdish in the Sanandaj region and more broadly in the southern region of the Central Kurdish speech zone. If there was a Gorani substrate in Sanandaj and its environs, some assumptions can be made regarding bilingualism in the region. In earlier times, Gorani was the dominant language in the region. With the influx of Kurdish into the area, Gorani-Kurdish bilingualism would have become the norm. Later Gorani was overwhelmed by Kurdish and a language shift occurred from Gorani to Kurdish. As remarked above, this would have brought about a shift in the profile of the bilingualism of the NENA-speaking communities in Sanandaj. The development would have been NENA-Gorani bilingualism > NENA-Gorani-Kurdish multilingualism > NENA-Kurdish bilingualism. In addition, as we have seen, there has been an increasing knowledge of Persian in the population of the Sanandaj region in the last century due to the introduction of school education. Gorani has survived in various pockets around Sanandaj, mainly in the mountainous Hawraman region. Speakers of Gorani in Hawraman today also speak Kurdish and Persian.

1.5 The aims and methodology of the book

As remarked, this book investigates language contact in Sanandaj from the perspective of the Jewish NENA dialect of the town. The description of the various features of the JSNENA dialect in Khan (2009) is made the starting for each of the sections of the book. The description of each JSNENA feature is followed by a comparison with the Iranian languages of the region. The Iranian languages that are compared are, in the vast majority of cases, Sanandaj Kurdish and Gorani of the Takht region of Hawraman, which is one of the closest locations to Sanandaj where Gorani is still spoken today. Occasional reference is made to other Iranian languages, in particular those of western Iran and in the adjacent regions of eastern Iraq.

The relationship between the JSNENA feature and the corresponding feature in the Iranian languages is discussed. Parallels and differences in structure and function are identified. Assessments are made as to whether the parallels are contact-induced innovations in JSNENA and, if so, whether the model of the innovation is Gorani or Kurdish. In some cases there are exact parallels, but on many occasions contact-induced change in JSNENA has resulted in only partial matches in structure or function. Some JSNENA features, moreover, have no direct parallel in Iranian. Possible reasons for these varying degrees of matching and change are discussed, taking into account typological tendencies in language contact.

The book presents a systematic comparison of the grammar and lexicon of JSNENA with Iranian. It is divided into a series of chapters, which correspond to the chapters in Khan's (2009) grammar of JSNENA, covering phonology, morphology, syntax, discourse structure and the lexicon. Where JSNENA examples are citations from the text corpus of Khan's grammar, these are given references to the place they occur in the text corpus. A concluding chapter categorises the various types of contact-induced change that have been identified in JSNENA and the processes that have given rise to them. The conclusion ends with a discussion of various possible theoretical models of the language situation in which such change has taken place, taking into account the fact that this situation has changed diachronically. Short glossed texts of JSNENA, Sanandaj Kurdish and Gorani of Takht are presented at the end of the book.

There have been a number of previous studies of the contact of NENA with Iranian. These are typically article-length studies that focus on a selection of features, sometimes taken from various dialects of NENA. Articles of this nature include Chyet (1995), Matras (2002), Khan (2007a; 2018b; 2020c; 2022a; 2022b), Borghero (2015), Haig (2015), Noorlander and Stilo (2015), Stilo and Noorlander (2015). Most of these are concerned specifically with the contact of NENA with Kurdish, though the papers co-authored by Stilo and Noorlander examine features of NENA in the context of what they call the Araxes-Iran Linguistic Area. Matras

(2002) is a study of the structure of complement clauses in Kurmanji Kurdish in the context of languages spoken in the Middle East. The volume *The Languages and Linguistics of Western Asia* (ed. Haig and Khan 2018) includes overview sections of language contact across various languages of western Asia, including NENA and Iranian languages. These, likewise, focus on selected features only. None of the studies just listed addresses the impact of Gorani on NENA. The current book is the first comprehensive study of contact-induced change across all levels of a NENA dialect and the first study that takes account of the important role Gorani played in such contact-induced change.

In recent years there has been an increasing number of studies on language contact outside of Semitic languages. Some of these are detailed studies of specific language contact situations around the world or specific language areas. Some publications are concerned with selected features of contact taken from a wide range of typologically diverse languages with a view to establishing cross-linguistic principles of contact-induced change.[14] The latter type of studies tend to be more widely read and more influential. It is our view that a comprehensive investigation of contact-induced change in all levels of a language leads to a better understanding of the phenomenon. Having now completed the task, we see that the phenomenon is far more complex than we had anticipated. Factors that contribute to this complexity include the scalar nature of some kinds of convergence, the relationship between internal and external forces of change, the historical layers of contact-induced change in JSNENA and the multiple synchronic and diachronic sociolinguistic dimensions of the language situations that formed JSNENA.

Our target audience is primarily that of specialists in Semitic and Iranian. It is hoped, however, that this case study will be of interest to the wider community of linguists working in the field of language contact studies.

A few remarks are in order on the terminology we use in book in connection with contact-induced change. In the main body of the book we use the term 'borrowing' for 'matter borrowing' (Matras and Sakel 2007; Matras 2009), which involves the transfer of lexical, morphological, or phonetic material from the Iranian source languages to JSNENA. Where JSNENA develops innovations in structural patterns under the influence of Iranian, we use terms such as 'replication', 'imitation' and 'convergence'.

'Replication' (the term originates in Weinreich 1953, 30–31) and 'imitation' denote transfers that do not involve phonetic substance. These could involve the transfer of semantic patterns or the transfer of the syntactic ordering of elements.

---

14 See Hickey (2010b) and Grant (2020) for overviews of the burgeoning literature in the field.

They typically involve the extension of existing patterns to new contexts and, in some case, grammaticalisation (Heine and Kuteva 2010).

The term 'convergence' is a scalar term and is used to refer to various degrees of approximation of patterns and systems of JSNENA with those of Iranian. It is typically used where the convergence of the internal JSNENA feature with the external feature of Iranian is not complete but only partial. This may result in the replica feature being less grammaticalised than the corresponding feature in the model language (Heine and Kuteva 2010, 94). Convergence often occurs when there is an internal 'tension' in the JSNENA language system that is developed under the influence of the external Iranian language.[15] Our use of the term 'convergence' is in most cases unidirectional, i.e. we discuss the convergence of JSNENA with Iranian. We occasionally use the term to refer to the mutual approximation of the structures of two languages in contact.[16]

In various places, features of JSNENA are said to 'match' features in Iranian. This reflects a process that lays the ground for convergence and replication, whereby a particular feature in Iranian is perceived to correspond to a particular feature in JSNENA. This process is equivalent to what Matras and Sakel (2007) call 'pivot matching' in the replication of syntax or morpho-syntax (cf. also Matras 2009, 240–43; 2010, 71–72). The process of pivot matching involves identifying a structure in the model language as the equivalent of a structure in the replica language and reorganising the inherited structure in the replica language in terms of grammatical and semantic meaning, and also distribution, to replicate those of the structure in the model language. In intense contact situations, the mechanism of pattern replication is characterised by adapting meanings and functions of inherited structures and enhancing them to carry out organisational procedures that are replicated from the model language (Matras 2009, 238), a process that leads to syncretising the "mental planning operations" while interacting in each language. The pivot in the model language can be replicated in the target language through different means: semantic extension (e.g. JSNENA extends the original meaning of š-q-l 'to take' to include also 'to buy' in an attempt to replicate the Gorani model sānāy 'to take, to buy' see §11.1.16); morpho-phonological similarity (e.g. JSNENA

---

[15] Cf. the remarks of Hickey (2010b, 15) regarding convergence processes in the contact between Irish and English. Such an interaction between internal and external linguistic systems is widely discussed in the language contact literature. See, for example, the papers in Aikhenvald and Dixon (2001). Many linguists (e.g. Dorian 1993; S. Thomason 2010) argue that there is no clear-cut dichotomy between internally and externally motivated change. Within Semitic, Butts (2016, 148) engages with this issue in his study of the contact of Syriac and Greek.

[16] In some of the literature on language contact the term is used specifically with this latter meaning, e.g. Hickey (2010a, 154, 162).

demonstrative pronouns structurally correspond to equivalent forms in Gorani see §3.3); discourse management (e.g. the JSNENA indefinite form *xa* 'one' matches the functional distribution of the pivot of the Iranian indefinite suffixes see § 6.2). On the level of syntax, the model pivot structure results in the reorganisation of word-order structures, clause complementation, etc., in the replica language. For instance, JSNENA has replaced the historical VO constituent order by OV following the model of Iranian (§8.4.1). Likewise, JSNENA has lost the historical genitive particle in nominal-genitive constructions, by matching the Kurdish model, which features simple juxtaposition in such constructions (§4.8).

Hickey (2010b, 12) refers to such a process as the search for categorial equivalence. In the contact of phonological systems it corresponds to the process of matching of particular phonetic tokens of one language with particular phonological prototypes in a contact language, as described by Blevins (2017). Compare also the models of contact-induced change in bilinguals of Bolonyai (1998) and Myers-Scotton (2006, 271) as a combination, i.e. matching, of surface-level forms from one language with an underlying abstract structure from another language.

In the section on theoretical models of contact in the final concluding chapter, we use the term 'borrowing' to refer specifically to the incorporation of material by a linguistically dominant recipient language (RL), in our case JSNENA, from a less dominant source language (SL), in our case Iranian. We use the term 'imposition' to refer to a process whereby grammatical structures and phonological systems of the Iranian source language are replicated in the JSNENA recipient language when the Iranian source language is linguistically dominant.[17] One of our various hypotheses is that the ancestor of JSNENA was originally linguistically dominant among the Jewish speakers, i.e. it was the language they were most fluent and proficient in. This, therefore, resulted in borrowing of lexical material. At a later historical period, Iranian became linguistically dominant for NENA-Iranian bilinguals, and this led to the imposition of Iranian grammatical structure and phonology being imposed on JSNENA.

---

[17] For the distinction between 'borrowing' and 'imposition' see in particular van Coetsem (1995; 2000) and Winford (2005).

2 Phonology

2.1 Introductory overview

The original inventory of NENA consonantal phonemes has undergone change in JSNENA due to convergence with the phonological systems of the Iranian languages of the region. This includes the loss of the original interdental consonants *θ and *ð, which have mostly been replaced by the lateral /l/. The interdentals originally shifted to the stop /d/, and this underwent lenition to /l/ due to the areal phenomenon known as the 'Zagros /d/', which resulted in the lenition of /d/ with various outcomes in the non-Semitic languages of the area. Some sounds of the original NENA consonantal inventory have undergone phonological change, although they still exist in some contexts on the phonetic level. This includes the dephonemicisation of the pharyngealised consonants *ṣ and *ṭ. Another case of this is the occurrence of the voiced pharyngeal /ʿ/ [ʕ] by a process of segmentalisation of flat resonance (i.e. pharyngealisation) rather than by the historical preservation of etymological *ʿ. This has resulted in the loss of etymological *ʿ in many words and the occurrence of non-etymological /ʿ/ in some words that were pronounced with flat resonance. In a few words an unvoiced pharyngeal /ḥ/ has developed by pharyngealisation of an *h. In all attested cases the *h has itself developed by debuccalisation of an original unvoiced interdental *θ. In some cases an etymological voiced pharyngeal *ʿ [ʕ] in JSNENA undergoes devoicing to the pharyngeal /ḥ/ [ħ], which matches a process that occurs in Gorani and Kurdish. The pharyngealised sonorant sounds [rˤ] and [lˤ], by contrast, have undergone phonemicisation (/ṛ/, /ḷ/) by a process of matching corresponding pharyngealised phonemes /ṛ/ and /ḷ/ in the Iranian languages of the region. Word-initial /ʿ/ in JSNENA shifts to /ḥ/ in some words in imitation of a parallel process in Gorani and Kurdish of the region.

Several consonants have been borrowed by JSNENA from the Iranian languages, mostly in loanwords. These include /č/ [tʃʰ], /f/ [f], /j/ [dʒ], /ř/ (trilled rhotic), /ž/ [ʒ], and /ġ/ [ʁ]. These are only marginal phonemes in JSNENA.

Stress patterns of JSNENA correspond to patterns of stress in the Iranian languages of the region.

Some phonological features of JSNENA exhibit different degrees of convergence with Gorani or Kurdish respectively. The quality of JSNENA vowels correspond slightly more closely to those of Gorani of the region than those of Sanandaj Kurdish. The labio-dental [v] realisation of JSNENA /w/ corresponds to Gornani but not Kurdish. Patterns of stress, on the other hand, correspond slightly closer to those of Kurdish.

2.2 Consonant phonemes

2.2.1 Phoneme inventory

Table 1: Phoneme inventory of JSNENA, Kurdish, and Gorani.

	Labial	Alveolar	Post-alveolar	Palatal	Velar	Uvular	Pharyngeal	Laryngeal
Stops								
Unvoiced	p	t			k	q		ʾ
Voiced	b	d			g			
Emphatic		ṭ						
Affricates								
Unvoiced			č					
Voiced			j					
Fricatives								
Unvoiced	f	s	š		x		ḥ	h
Voiced	w	z	ž	y	(ġ)		ʿ	
Emphatic		ṣ						
Nasal	m	n						
Lateral								
Plain		l						
Emphatic		ḷ						
Rhotic								
Tap/trill		r						
Trill		ř						
Emphatic		ṛ						

JSNENA, Gorani and Kurdish share the same inventory of consonant phonemes, which is represented in the Table 1.

Some of these consonants in JSNENA occur predominantly in loanwords or loan verbal roots from Iranian languages. These include the following:

/č/ [tʃʰ]
(2) JSNENA   Gorani/ Kurdish
    čīn   'lock (of hair)'   G. čīn
    čamčá   'spoon'   G. čamča, čəmča
    čəngā́ḷ   'fork'   G./K. čəngāḷ
    čāḷ   'hole (in the ground)' K. čāḷ; G. čāḷī
    pīčyā́w   'twisted'   K. pīčyāw
    pārčá   'material, fabric'   G./K. pārča; P. pārče

/f/ [f]

(3) JSNENA | | Gorani/ Kurdish
- *flānakás* 'so-and-so' K. *flānakas*
- *frīštá* 'angel' G./K. *frīšta*
- *təf* 'spittle' G./K. *təf*
- *ləfká* 'loofah' G. *ləfka*
- *laʿēfá* 'quilt' G. *lēfa*; K. *lāf*
- *haftá* 'week' G./ K. *hafta*

/j/ [ʤ]

(4) JSNENA | | Gorani/ Kurdish
- *jogá* 'stream' G. *jūa*; K. *jo*
- *jəlé* 'clothes' G./K. *jəl*
- *payjá* 'ladder' G./K. *payja*
- *jolāná* 'nest, hammock' G. *jolānē*
- *kománj* 'roof chamber' G. *komānja*
- *gurj, gwərj* 'fast' G./K. *gurj*

/ř/ [r]

(5) JSNENA | | Gorani/ Kurdish
- *řag* 'vein' G./K. *řag*
- *pařá* 'feather' G. *pařa*; K. *pař*
- *řēwí* 'fox' K. *řēwī*; G. *řūāsa*

/ž/ [ʒ]

(6) JSNENA | | Gorani/ Kurdish
- *māmožná* 'paternal uncle's wife' G. *māmožanī*; K. *mamožən*
- *žān* 'pain' G./K. *žān*

The sound /ġ/ is found only marginally in a few loanwords from Persian. In such cases it is realised as a voiced uvular fricative [ʁ]. It is a reflex of a voiced uvular stop [ɢ] in Persian:

(7) Persian | JSNENA | Kurdish
- [šoɢl] (< Arab.) 'profession' *šoġlé* (pl.) [ʃɔʁlˁeː] *šuġḷ* [šuʁḷ]
- [ɒˈɢɒ] (< Turk.) 'master' *ʾaġá* [ʔaːˈʁa] *āġa* [aːˈʁa]

In most loanwords from Persian in Kurdish the reflex of Persian [ɢ] is /x/ or /q/. In word-final position the normal reflex is /x/, e.g.

(8) Kurdish   Persian
    bāx   'garden' [bɒɢ]
    dāx   'hot'   [dɒɢ]
    čāx   'fat'   [ʧɒɢ]
    wəjāx 'stove'   [oʤɒɢ]

Some of these Persian loans in Kurdish have come into JSNENA. e.g. JSNENA *dāx* 'hot'.

Examples of /x/ in Kurdish that are reflexes of Persian [ɢ] in word-medial position include:

(9) Kurdish   Persian
    naxt   'cash'   [naɢd]
    naxša 'map'   [naɢše]

In a few cases in word-medial position the reflex of Persian [ɢ] in Persian loanwords in Kurdish is /q/. This applies to words that are ulimately of Arabic origin and have [q] in their original Arabic form, e.g.

(10) Kurdish   Persian
     sāqī   'butler'   [sɒɢi:] < Arabic *sāqī*
     māqūl 'sensible' [ma:ɢu:l] < Arabic *maʿqūl*

Note the following Persian loanword in JSNENA in which the reflex of Persian [ɢ] is /q/:

(11) JSNENA   Persian
     ʾotā́q   room   [o:tʰɑ:ɢ]

2.2.2 Notes on the phonetic realisation of the consonants

2.2.2.1 /p/, /t/, /k/
These unvoiced stops are generally pronounced with some aspiration before vowels in JSNENA, Kurdish and Gorani, e.g.

/p/
(12) JSNENA *pēx-ó* [pʰe:ˈxo:] 'It cools'
     K.   *pāk* [pʰa:k]   'clean'
     G.   *pal* [pʰal]   'feather'

/t/
(13) JSNENA *tará* [tʰaˈra]   'door'
     K.   *tař* [tʰær]   'wet'
     G.   *tātá* [tʰaːˈtʰæ]   'father'

/k/
(14) JSNENA *kol* [kʰoːl]   'he does'
     K.   *kar* [kʰær]   'donkey'
     G.   *karga* [kʰargæ]   'hen'

There is no aspiration when these unvoiced stops follow an unvoiced fricative in a cluster, e.g.

/p/
(15) JSNENA *maspé* [masˈpeː]   'he delivers'
     K.   *aspāw* [æspˈaːw]   'utensil'
     G.   *spārāy* [spaːraːj] 'entrust'

/t/
(16) JSNENA *baxtá* [baxˈta]   'woman'
     K.   *xəstən* [xəsˈtən]   'to throw'
     G.   *āstay* [aːstˈay]   'to let'

/k/
(17) JSNENA *skītá* [skiːˈta]   'knife'
     K.   *pəská* [pəsˈkæ]   'whisper'
     G.   *āska* [ˈaːskæ]   'gazelle'

In word-final position unvoiced stops tend to remain unreleased without aspiration, e.g.

(18) JSNENA *ʾāt* [ʔaːt]   'you'
     K.   *kāḷak* [kʰaːḷæk]   'melon'
     G.   *qap* [qap]   'bite'

2.2.2.2 /ṭ/, /ṣ/

The JSNENA consonants /ṭ/ and /ṣ/ are historically 'emphatic' in Aramaic and were originally pronounced with pharyngealisation. This involved the retraction of the back of the tongue into the upper pharynx and increased muscular tension, resulting in the /ṭ/ being realised as an unaspirated stop [tˤ]. In the current state of the JSNENA dialect, however, the consonants /ṭ/ and /ṣ/, which derived historically from emphatic consonants, are in most cases realised without any clear pharyngealisation. This can be demonstrated by instrumental acoustic analysis. Pharyngealisation of a consonant segment is reflected in spectographs by the lowering ('flatting') of high frequency energy, specifically by the lowering of the second formant (Ladefoged and Maddieson 1996, 360–63), in the transition to the adjacent vowels and also, if the consonant is voiced, in the consonantal segment. In most environments there is no significant difference in the second formant (F2) frequency between sequences of /ṭ/ or /ṣ/ and adjacent vowels and equivalent sequences containing the corresponding non-emphatic consonants /t/ and /s/. In what follows the mean F2 frequency is given for the transition points between these sets of unvoiced consonants and the following vowels:

(19)　JSNENA
　　a.　ṣīwá [siˈwa]　　　　　'wood'　　　　　　　/ṣī/ F2=2245
　　　　ʾəsīrī-ó [ˈəsiˑriːˈjoː]　'they were tied'　　/sī/ F2=2255
　　b.　xāṣḗ [xaːˈseː]　　　　'backs'　　　　　　/ṣē/ F2=1898
　　　　sērakḗ [seːraˈkʰeː]　　'the moon'　　　　/sē/ F2=1941
　　c.　máṭē [ˈmɪtʰeˑ]　　　　'he arrived'　　　　/ṭē/ F2=2072
　　　　tēmá [tʰeːˈma]　　　　'it (f.) finishes'　　/tē/ F2=2037
　　d.　plíṭa [ˈpliːtʰa]　　　　'it (f.) came out'　　/ṭa/ F2=1618
　　　　tlītá [tliːˈtʰa]　　　　　'hung (f.)'　　　　/ta/ F2=1603
　　e.　ṭūrá [tʰuːˈra]　　　　　'mountain'　　　　/ṭū/ F2=1523
　　　　xaétun [xaˈeːtʰʊn]　　'you (pl.) see'　　　/tu/ F2=1557

The stop /ṭ/ is pronounced with aspiration before vowels in the same environments as /t/ is aspirated, e.g. ṭūrá [tʰuːˈra] 'mountain'.

Occasionally, however, historical /ṭ/ or /ṣ/ retain their pharyngealisation, which is reflected by a significant lowering of F2 frequency of the syllable compared to corresponding syllables with /t/ and /s/. This is encountered mainly in the environment of /l/ or /m/. The F1 in pharyngealised environments is higher than in the equivalent plain syllables, indicating that the vowel is lower, e.g.

(20)　JSNENA
　　a.　ṭalabḗ [tˤalaˈbeː]　　　'criticism'　　　　/ṭal/ F1=623, F2=1265
　　　　talgá [tʰalˈga]　　　　　'snow'　　　　　　/tal/ F1 721, F2=1818
　　b.　zmáṭēla [ˈzmaːtˤeːla]　'it (f.) is full'　　　/āṭ/ F1=612, F2=1095
　　　　bātḗ [baːˈtʰeː]　　　　　'houses'　　　　　/āt/ F1=577, F2=1625

  c. *qaṭə́l* [qɑˈtˤəlˤ] 'he kills' /ṭ/ F1=628, F2=1357
    təlyén [tʰɪlˈjeˑn] 'they are hung' /təl/ F1=330, F2=2114
  d. *ṣalmáx* [sˤalˤˈmax] 'your (sg.f) face' /ṣa/ F1=637, F2=1309
    saroqḗ [saroːˈqeː] 'to comb' /sa/ F1=595, F2=1523

This indicates that the historical pharyngealisation of the consonants /ṭ/ and /ṣ/ remains as a potential feature that may be conditioned by certain phonetic environments but generally remains unrealised. This variable and unstable realisation of the pharyngealisation of /ṭ/ and /ṣ/ in JSNENA contrasts with more stable pharyngealisation of these consonants in NENA dialects in the western and northwestern sectors of NENA that are in contact with Arabic (Khan 2013). This is doubtless due the conservative influence of Arabic, in which these pharyngeal consonants are stable.

  The variable pharyngealisation of /ṭ/ and /ṣ/ in JSNENA matches closely what is found in Kurdish and Gorani of the Sanandaj region. In the latter languages, pharyngealised /ṭ/ and /ṣ/ occur in some lexical items, but they are not stable and they are realised as plain consonants by some speakers.

  In these Iranian languages /s/ becomes pharyngealised before or after the vowel /a/ in some words. This is shown in the following pairs by the lower F2 in /ṣa/ than in /sa/. Note that there is generally a higher F1 in the pharyngealised sequence, which indicates a greater lowering of the vowel than in the plain syllable.

(21) Kurdish
  a. *ṣa* [sˤɑ] 'hundred' /ṣa/ F1=483, F2=949
    sam [sæm] 'poison' /sa/ F1=579 F2=1456
  b. *ṣag* [sˤɑg] 'dog' /ṣa/ F1=572 F2=918
    sar [sæɾ] 'head' /sa/ F1=566 F2=1459

(22) Gorani
  a. *šaṣ* [ʃɑsˤ] 'sixty' /aṣ/ F1=623 F2=982
    mas [mæs] 'drunk' /as/ F1=589 F2=1464
  b. *ṣa* [sˤɑ] 'hundred' /ṣa/ F1=604 F2=942
    īsá [ʔiːˈsæ] 'now' /sa/ F1=438 F2=1708

The pharyngealisation in some tokens of the words is unrealised, indicating that it is unstable and variable, as in JSNENA. This is seen in the following Gorani pairs.

(23) Gorani
    a. *šaṣ* [ʃɑṣ]   'sixty'   /aṣ/ F1=623 F2=982
       šas [ʃæs]   'sixty'   /as/ F1=547 F2=1427
    b. *ṣa* [ṣɑ]   'hundred' /ṣa/ F1=604 F2=942
       sa [sæ]   'hundred' /sa/ F1=536 F2=1329

A pharyngealised stop [tˤ] is marginally attested in the Iranian languages of Sanandaj. It has been identified in the pronunciation by one Kurdish speaker of the following word. The same word is also pronounced plain:

(24) Kurdish
    ṭāḷ [tˤɑːlˤ] 'bitter'   /ṭā/ F1=727 F2=1058
    tāl [tʰɑːl] 'bitter'   /tā/ F1=660 F2=1345

The pharyngealisation of /t/ and /s/ in the Iranian languages of Sanandaj was a feature that was acquired from Semitic, either Arabic or NENA, or both. Pharyngealised consonants are found also in Kurmanji (Kahn 1976, 49–52; Öpengin 2020).

The process of acquisition of pharyngealised consonants in the Iranian languages may have involved a perception of an equivalence between the Iranian sounds /t/ and /s/ and the Semitic pharyngealised /ṭ/ and /ṣ/ in 'flat' contexts, i.e. contexts in which the F2 tends to be lowered. These are typically syllables containing labial consonants and low vowels (Barry 2019). The Iranian sounds would have then converged with the Semitic sounds and acquired their phonetic feature of pharyngealisation by a 'perceptual magnet effect', as Blevins (2017) puts it. It would appear that pharyngealisation only became an allophonic phonetic property of the Iranian /t/ and /s/ and there was no clear phonemic split into /t/ : /ṭ/ and /s/ : /ṣ/. For this reason the pharyngealisation is unstable. In the trancriptions above, therefore, the symbols ṭ and ṣ do not strictly speaking represent phonemes but rather represent phonetic features of /s/ in particular contexts.

Although the pharyngealisation of the Iranian sounds appears to have had its origin in Semitic emphatic phonemes, JSNENA merged with the sound system of the Iranian languages in contact with it. This involved the perceptual matching of the NENA emphatic phonemes /ṭ/ and /ṣ/ with the Iranian sounds /t/ and /s/, which were pronounced pharyngealised in some contexts. Since the pharyngealisation of these sounds in the Iranian languages, however, was not a stable phonological feature, the perceptual matching resulted in the dephonemicisation of pharyngealisation in JSNENA. The process would have involved convergence from both directions. The Iranian languages partially converged with Semitic by acquiring the phonetic property of pharyngealisation in /t/ and /s/ and JSNENA would have converged with the Iranian languages by dephonemicisation of the pharyngealisation and shifting it to a phonetic property.

In most words in the Iranian languages of Sanandaj, /t̟/ is regularly pronounced as an aspirated stop without pharyngealisation. The lack of pharyngealisation is reflected by the relatively high F2 in the following pairs.

(25) Kurdish
    a. *tāj* [tʰaːʤ]   'crown'   /tā/ F1=520 F2=1481
       tāq [tʰaːq]   'recess'   /tā/ F1=689 F2=1205
    b. *tamáʿ* [tʰæˈmaːʕ] 'greed'   /ta/ F1=477 F2=1436
       taqá [tʰæˈqæ]   'knocking' /ta/ F1=632 F2=1274

(26) Gorani
    tāja [tʰaːˈʤæ]   'crown'   /tā/ F1=546 F2=1330
    tāta [tʰaːˈtʰæ] 'father' /tā/ F1=624 F2=1292

2.2.2.3 /ḷ/

Unlike the historical emphatics /t̟/ and /s̟/, which have largely lost their emphatic quality, JSNENA has an emphatic /ḷ/ that is regularly realised with pharyngealisation. This emphatic is phonemically distinct from plain /l/, as is demonstrated by several minimal pairs, e.g.

(27) JSNENA
    lālá   'maternal uncle'   : *ḷāḷá*   'lung'
    mālá   'village'   : *māḷá*   'spatula'
    mīlá   'dead'   : *mīḷá*   'circumcision'
    naqolé 'to extract unclean offal' : *naqoḷé* 'to dance'
    pēlá   'radish'   : *pēḷá*   'eyelash'

The pharyngealisation of /ḷ/ is demonstrated instrumentally by the fact that it consistently has a significantly lower second formant than /l/. This lowering of F2 is discernible also in the surrounding vowels, especially /a/ and back vowels. Adjacent high front vowels generally do not exhibit a significant difference in the mean frequency of F2, although it tends to be lower in the onset phase. The F1 in pharyngealised /ḷ/ and its environment is higher than in words with plain /l/, indicating a lower articulation. This is shown in the following F1 and F2 readings for one of the minimal pairs:

(28) JSNENA
  naqolé 'to extract offal' /o/ F1=444, F2=1001
                                /l/ F1=298, F2=1704
                                /ē/ F1=390, F2=1696
  naqol̤é 'to dance'   /o/ F1=528, F2=871
                                /l̤/ F1=417, F2=1097
                                /ē/ F1=458, F2=1494

An emphatic /l̤/ phoneme is an innovative development in JSNENA. In NENA dialects in the western sector of the NENA area a pharyngealised [lˤ] occurs only on the phonetic level by spread of pharyngealisation from an adjacent /ṭ/ or /ṣ/ phoneme, e.g. Ch. Qaraqosh *xálṣa* [ˈxɑlˤsˤɑ] 'she finishes'.

The phonemic distinction between plain /l/ and emphatic /l̤/ has a counterpart in the Iranian languages of the Sanandaj region. The pharyngealisation of /l̤/ [lˤ] in the pairs below is reflected by a lower F2 of the segment and its surrounding vowels than is the case with plain /l/. Note also that the F1 in the environment of the pharyngealised /l̤/ is regularly higher than the F1 in the environment of plain /l/, which indicates that the tongue is close to the bottom of the oral cavity.

(29) Gorani
  a. *tal* [tʰæl]   'wire'   /a/ F1=633, F2=1505
                                          /l/ F1=292, F2=1517
     tal̤ [tʰɑlˤ]   'unique'   /a/ F1=671, F2=1143
                                          /l̤/ F1=719, F2=977
  b. *kal* [kʰæl]   'mountain pass' /a/ F1=607, F2=1539
                                          /l/ F1=329, F2=1618
     kal̤ [kʰɑl̤]   'mountain goat' /a/ F1=681, F2=1106
                                          /l̤/ F1=627, F2=982
  c. *pīyála* [piːˈjaːlæ] 'man'   /ā/ F1=576, F2=1480
                                          /l/ F1=292, F2=1557
                                          /a/ F1=492, F2=1502
     pīyál̤a [piːjaːˈlˤɑ] 'cup'   /ā/ F1=748, F2=1135
                                          /l̤/ F1=473, F2=923
                                          /a/ F1=746, F2=1030

(30) Kurdish
  kal [kʰæl] 'mountain pass' /a/ F1=443, F2=1636
                                 /l/ F1=267, F2=1834
  kal̤ [kʰɑlˤ] 'mountain goat' /a/ F1=690, F2=1030
                                 /l̤/ F1=594, F2=1068

As is the case with emphatic /ṣ/ and /ṭ/, the pharyngealisation of the lateral [lˁ] in Kurdish and Gorani is likely to have entered these languages originally from Semitic (Arabic and/or Aramaic). The fact that in the western sector of NENA it does not have phonemic status, suggests that its phonemicisation in JSNENA of Sanandaj was induced by contact with the Iranian languages. The phonemicisation of phonetic [lˁ] would have first developed in Iranian and subsequently emphatic [lˁ] in JSNENA was matched with the Iranian phoneme /ḷ/.

In NENA dialects spoken in the North of Iraq that are in contact with Kurmanji Kurdish sporadic cases of phonemic oppositions between emphatic /ḷ/ and plain /l/, e.g.

(31) J. Amedia (Greenblatt 2011, 36)
   mḷēlē 'he filled' : mlēlē 'it sufficed'

This is, likewise, motivated by the sporadic occurrences of emphatic [lˁ] in Bahdini Kurmanji, in words like māḷ 'house'; sāḷ 'year'; guḷk 'calf'. The emphatic [lˁ] is not phonemically contrastive in Bahdini Kurmanji.

2.2.2.4 Rhotic consonants

JSNENA has three rhotic consonants: /r/, /ṛ/ and /ř/.

The /r/ phoneme is generally realised as a voiced alveolar trill [r]. There is a certain degree of variation in the number of periods of vibration of the tongue tip. In word-internal position, however, it is sometimes realised as a single tap [ɾ] with no vibration or even an alveolar approximant [ɹ], e.g.

(32) JSNENA
   ʾəsīrī-ó [ˈəsiˑɾiːˈoː] 'they closed'
   baṣīrtá [basiˑɹtʰa] 'grape'

The consonant /ṛ/ is an emphatic rhotic. This has only been identified in the word zoṛa 'water jar', which has an Aramaic etymology. It has apparently developed in this word to distinguish it from the adjective zora 'small'. The emphatic quality of /ṛ/ in zoṛa involves increased muscular tension, which results it being realised as a trill rather than a tap, and pharyngealisation, which gives rise to flat resonance. The flat resonance causes a significantly lower F2 in the consonantal segment and in the adjacent vowel transitions. In the following the F2 reading of the transition from /o/ to /ṛ/ and from /ṛ/ to /a/ is given together with the F2 at the equivalent points in the word zoṛa:

(33) JSNENA
zoṛá [zoˈrˤa] 'water jar' /o/ F2 1131
/a/ F2 1206
zorá [zoˈra] 'small' /o/ F2 1526
/a/ F2 1770

The rhotic consonant /ř/ is a trill that has a greater number of periods of vibration than is typical for /r/. It occurs only in loanwords from Kurdish, e.g.

(34) JSNENA
řangú [rːaŋˈguː] 'their colour'
řag [rːag] 'vein'

Its phonemic status in JSNENA is marginal, since it does not contrast with other rhotics.

The phonemic contrast between plain /r/ and emphatic /ṛ/ is a feature of many of the NENA dialects of Iraq (Khan 2018e, 317; 2008b, 59) and north-eastern Turkey (Khan 2018d, 201). In some dialects there is a three-way phonemic contrast of /r/, /ṛ/ and retroflex /ɻ/ (Mutzafi 2014; Mole 2015).

The phonemic contrast of /r/ and /ṛ/ is not a feature of the Arabic dialects adjacent to the western periphery region (Procházka 2018, 247–48) nor is it a feature of the Bahdini Kurdish dialects of Iraq (Shokri 2002). It appears, therefore, to be an internal development of NENA. Its existence in JSNENA, therefore, is likely to be an inherited feature. Its preservation as a stable phonemic contrast has been supported by the existence of a corresponding phonemic contrast in the Iranian languages of the region.

In Kurdish and Gorani of the Sanandaj region there is a three-way contrast of the rhotics /r/ [ɾ], /ř/ [r] and /ṛ/ [rˤ]. As shown in the following examples, the flat resonance of the pharyngealisation of /ṛ/ is reflected by the fact that the F2 of /ṛ/ is lower than that of /r/ and /ř/. This applies also to the adjacent vowels. The F1 of /ṛ/ and its environment is higher, reflecting vowel lowering. Furthermore, the trilled /ř/ in *bař* 'fruity' has a slightly lower F2 than that of /r/ in *mara* 'grassland' and *hara* 'donkey', reflecting a flatter resonance.

(35) Gorani
 a. *mara* [ˈmæræ] 'grassland' /a/ F1=523, F2=1526
/r/ F1=427, F2=1542
/a/ F1=490, F2=1562

	mara ['mɑrˤæ]	'cave'	/a/ F1=725, F2=1119
			/r̝/ F1=637, F2=1036
			/a/ F1=643, F2=1131
b.	*bař* [bær]	'product'	/a/ F1=528, F2=1403
			/r̝/ F1=447, F2=1469
	bar̝ [bɑrˤ]	'dried'	/a/ F1=653, F2=1112
			/r̝/ F1=705, F2=1143
c.	*hara* [hæ'ræ]	'donkey'	/a/ F1=559, F2=1526
			/r/ F1=486, F2=1525
			/a/ F1=515, F2=1561
	har̝a [hɑ'rˤæ]	'mud'	/a/ F1=668, F2=1145
			/r̝/ F1=634, F2=1049
			/a/ F1=637, F2=1164

(36) Kurdish
    a. *kar* [kʰær]   'donkey'   /a/ F1=500, F2=1706
                                                       /r/ F1=413, F2=1545
        kar̝ [kʰɑrˤ]   'deaf'   /a/ F1=902, F2=1405
                                                       /r̝/ F1=399, F2=997
    b. *fəra* [fəræ]   'a lot'   /r/ F1=331, F2=2129
                                                        /a/ F1=548, F2=1517
        fər̝a [fərˤɑ]   'throwing' /r̝/ F1=473, F2=1112
                                                               /a/ F1=519, F2=1066

The fact that /r̝/ is not contrastive in JSNENA suggests that it has not been integrated into the phonemic system of the language but exists only as a fossilised feature of loanwords. The distributional patterns of internal items of the sound system of JSNENA are matched with those of the contact Iranian languages, but there is not complete borrowing and systemic integration of external phonemic sounds.

2.2.2.5 Pharyngeal consonants

Aramaic originally contained the pharyngeal consonants **ḥ* [ħ] and **ʿ* [ʕ]. In JSNENA, as in NENA dialects in general, these have been lost in most words of Aramaic stock. In most cases the unvoiced pharyngeal **ḥ* has shifted to the velar fricative /x/, e.g.

(37) JSNENA
     xmará   'ass'   < **ḥmārā*
     qamxá   'flour'   < **qamḥā*
     xamšá   'five'   < **ḥamšā*

In word initial position the reflex of an historical voiced pharyngeal *ʿ is normally the laryngeal stop /ʾ/, e.g.

(38) JSNENA
　　ʾaprá　'soil'　　< *ʿap̄rā
　　ʾēlá　'festival'　< *ʿēḏā

In word-internal or word-final position the voiced pharyngeal *ʿ has been weakened to zero in most cases, e.g.

(39) JSNENA
　　bētá　'egg'　　< *bēʿtā
　　tará　'door'　　< *tarʿā
　　zará　'wheat'　< *zarʿā
　　šamḗ　'he hears'　< *šāmaʿ
　　bḗē　'eggs'　　< *bēʿē
　　šoá　'seven'　< *šoʿa < *šaḇʿā

The original pharyngeals have been preserved in some words and verbal roots of Aramaic stock that contain, or contained at some point of their development, a pharyngealised consonant. The pharyngealised consonants include historical *ṭ, *ṣ, *q or a consonant that acquired pharyngealisation, especially the labial consonants /m̰/, /ḇ/ and the sonorant consonants /ḻ/ and /ṛ/, e.g.

(40) JSNENA
　　ḥ-n-q　　'to be throttled, to drown'　< *ḥ-n-q
　　d-b-ḥ　　'to slaughter'　　< *d-ḇ-ḥ < *d-b-ḥ
　　t-s-ḥ　　'to stuff, pack'　< *ṭ-ḥ-s < *d-ḥ-s (?)
　　ʿaqəwrá　'scorpion'　　< *ʿaqəbrā
　　taʿná　'load'　　< *ṭaʿnā
　　tamʿá　'she tastes'　< *ṭāmʿā
　　dəmʿḗ　'tears'　　< *dəmʿē < *dəmʿē
　　guḻʿá　'kernel of fruit'　< *guḻʿa < *gulʿā
　　maʿḻēlá　'eve of festival'　< m̰aʿḻēla < *maʿlē ʿēḏā
　　pərtaʿná　'flea'　　< *pərtaʿna < *purtaʿnā
　　zaʿṛá　'barley'　　< *zaʿṛa < *sʿārā
　　b-ʿ-y　　'to bleat'　　< *ḇ-ʿ-y
　　z-ʿ-r　　'to plant'　　< *z-ṛ-ʿ < *z-r-ʿ
　　b-l-ʿ　　'to swallow'　< *ḇ-ḻ-ʿ < *b-l-ʿ
　　ʾəčʿá　'nine'　　< *ʾəčʿa < *tšʿā

In a few words an unvoiced pharyngeal /ḥ/ has developed by pharyngealisation of an *h. In all attested cases the *h has itself developed by debuccalisation of an original unvoiced interdental *ϑ, e.g.

(41) JSNENA
    ʼaḥrá   'town'   < *ʼahra < *ʼaϑrā
    təlḥá   'three'   <*tḷāhā < *tlāϑā
    láḥmal   'day before yesterday'   < *lahəṃmaḷ < *lāṯəmmal
    naḥālḗ   'ears'   < *nahāḷḗ < *nāϑāϑā

The source of the pharyngealisation is likely to be the sonorant /l/ and labial /m/. In the J. Urmi dialect, spoken in north-western Iran, cognates of some of these words have suprasegmental pharyngealisation (indicated below by a superscribed ⁺) and contain the laryngeal /h/. This can be regarded as the historical forerunner of the corresponding forms with /ḥ/ in JSNENA. The Trans-Zab Jewish NENA dialects in Iraq have mainly /ḥ/ in these words as in JSNENA, with a few vestiges of /h/ and an adjacent pharyngealised /ḷ/ in the J. Arbel, J. Koy Sanjak and J. Ruwanduz:

(42) | JSNENA | J. Urmi | J. Sulemaniyya | J. Arbel | J. Ruwanduz | J. Koy Sanjak |
|---|---|---|---|---|---|
| ʼaḥrá | ⁺ahrá | ʼaḥrá | — | — | — |
| təlḥá | ⁺tahá | tlaḥá ~ təlḥá | tḷahá | tḷahá | tḷahá |
| láḥmal | lalúmmal | láḥmal | laləṃmal | laləṃmal | laləṃmal |
| naḥālḗ | ⁺nahālḗ | naḥālḗ | naḥālḗ | naḥālḗ | nḥālḗ |

J. Rustaqa
—
tḷahá ~ təlḥá
lalúmmal
naḥālḗ

In some words in JSNENA, a non-etymological voiced pharyngeal /ʿ/ has developed within a pharyngealised long /a/ vowel. This is found in the following words, in which the pharygnealisation of the /a/ originated in the adjacent labial /m/:

(43) JSNENA
    tmaʿnisár   'eighteen'   < *tṃānīsar
    tmaʿní   'eighty'   < *tṃānī
    tmaʿnisár   'eighteen'   < *tṃānīsar

Similar examples of non-etymological /ʿ/ are found in the neighbouring Jewish dialect of Sulemaniyya:

(44) J. Sulemaniyya
 maʿē 'water' < **mā̤ʾē* < **māyē*
 maʿdanūsī́ 'parsley' < *m̤adanusī*
 (Khan 2004, 35)

In sum, in words of Aramaic stock in JSNENA the historical pharyngeal consonants **ḥ* and **ʿ* are preserved in pharyngealised environments and non-etymological /ḥ/ and /ʿ/ have developed in pharyngealised environments. As can be seen in the examples adduced above, when the pharyngeal segments /ḥ/ and /ʿ/ have arisen in this way, the historical pharyngealisation of the adjacent environment in the word has been lost. The adjacent consonants and vowels are now plain. The retraction of the tongue root, which is associated with suprasegmental pharyngealised coarticulation, has become 'segmentalised' in the form of a pharyngeal segment, either through the preservation of a historical pharyngeal or the development of a non-etymological pharyngeal.

This process of segmentalisation of pharyngealisation does not, however, affect the consonant /q/. Whereas the historical emphatics **ṭ* and **ṣ* and pharyngealised labials and sonorants are converted to plain consonants, a /q/ remains in the word, e.g.

(45) JSNENA
 ḥ-n-q 'to be throttled, to drown'
 ʿaqəwrá 'scorpion'

The consonant /q/ is considered to be an emphatic consoant in Semitic. It shares with the other emphatic consonants the articulatory property of a greater muscular tension than the corresponding plain consonants (*ṭ—t, ṣ—s, q—k*). The explanation as to why it does not shift to the corresponding plain consonant /k/ may be that, unlike the other emphatics, it typically does not have the acoustic property of inducing flat resonance, i.e. reduced F2, in NENA (Khan 2016, vol. 1, 116). The process of segmentalisation consists of the conversion of flat resonance into a pharyngeal segment, which results in the conversion of emphatic consonants that produce flat resonance into plain consonants. Since /q/ does not produce flat resonance, it is not affected by the process.

The pharyngeals /ḥ/ and /ʿ/ are also found in Arabic loanwords in JSNENA, the majority of which have entered the language through Kurdish, e.g.

(46) JSNENA
 ḥamä́m 'bath'
 ḥaná 'henna'
 ḥ-q-y 'to speak' < Arab. *ḥky*
 ma'lə́m 'teacher'
 'ayzá 'good' < Arab. *'azīz*

Pharyngeal consonants exist in Kurdish both in loanwords from Arabic and in words of Iranian stock (Barry 2019; Öpengin 2020). This is due to contact with Arabic and, possibly also with Aramaic at an earlier period. According to Barry (2019), the pharyngeal segments in words of Iranian stock have developed mainly in environments that have acoustic properties of pharyngealisation, i.e. 'flat' environments with lowered F2. These include, in particular, pharyngealised consonants, labial consonants and rounded vowels. This phenomenon is found in both Northern Kurdish and Central Kurdish. It is found in both Kurdish and Gorani of the Sanandaj region, e.g.

(47) Kurdish
 ḥaft [hæft] 'seven' cf. P. *haft*
 ḥava [hæˈvæ], *ḥavva* 'seventeen' cf. P. *hevdah*

(48) Gorani
 ḥawt [hæwt], 'seven' cf. P. *haft*
 ḥaft, ḥot
 'əna [ʕəˈnæ] 'buttock' cf. K. *qəŋ* (Sanandaj), *qūn* (elsewhere in Central and Northern Kurdish), P. *kun*

In these examples a pharyngeal /ḥ/ or /ʕ/ has arisen in a word of Iranian etymology in a syllable that contains a labial consonant or, historically, a labial vowel *u*.

Pharyngeal segments also occur in Arabic loanwords in Sanandaj Kurdish and Gorani, e.g.

(49) Kurdish
 səḥb [səħb], *saḥb* 'morning' < Arab. *ṣabāḥ*
 tamā' [tʰæˈmaːʕ] 'greed' < Arab. *ṭama'*
 ḥaz [hæz] 'liking' < Arab. *ḥaẓẓ*

(50) Gorani
  sáb [sæʕb]   'morning'   < Arab. ṣabāḥ
  ḥagáḷ [hæˈgɑːlˤ]   'scarf'   < Arab. ʼiqāl
  ḥīz [ḥiːz]   'lecherous'   < Arab. ḥazz
  wáza [ˈwæʕzæ]   'situation'   < Arab. waẓʻ < waḍʻ

These loanwords exhibit the segmentalisation process that has been described in JSNENA above. The emphatic consonants /ṭ/, /ṣ/ and /ẓ/ of the Arabic source word have lost their flat resonance and become plain. The same applies to the native Gorani word ʼəna 'buttock', which has lost the round labial vowel *u, which existed historically in this word. The only exception is Gorani ḥagáḷ 'scarf', which has an emphatic final /ḷ/. The explanation appears to be that plain /l/ does not occur after /a/ in word-final position but only emphatic /ḷ/, e.g. sāḷ 'year', tāḷ 'bitter', pāḷ 'leaning'. In an optimality framework, one may say that this rule outranks the rule of segmentalisation.

In JSNENA and the Iranian languages of Sanandaj, the segmentalisation of flat resonance is a fixed process. In some Kurdish dialects in other regions there is some degree of free variation between flat resonance and a pharyngeal segment. This has been documented by Margaret Kahn (1976, 49–52) in Northern Kurdish dialects of the Urmi region, e.g. ṭæza ~ tæʻza 'fresh'.

We see, therefore, that although pharyngeal segments are inherited from earlier Aramaic in JSNENA, their distribution and development have come to match those of the pharyngeals in the Iranian languages in contact.

In Kurdish and Gorani of the Sanandaj region, the pharyngeal segments /ḥ/ and /ʻ/ are not phonemically contrastive. The same applies to these segments in JSNENA. In fact in JSNENA the voiced pharyngeal /ʻ/ is in some cases realised with less muscular tension as a laryngeal [ʼ]:

(51) JSNENA
  ṭamʻá [tʰamˈʕa ~ tʰamˈʔa]   'she tastes'
  ʼəčʻá [ʔɪtʃʕa ~ ˈɪtʃʕa]   'nine'

JSNENA exhibits some further developments of pharyngeal consonants that also match the behaviour of pharyngeals in the Iranian languages of the region.

JSNENA exhibits a change in the original voicing of the pharyngeal in the following verb, in which the voiced *ʻ is devoiced to /ḥ/:

(52) JSNENA
  t-ḥ-y 'to find' < *ṭʻy

Such changes in voicing are also found in the Iranian languages. These include devoicing of *ʿ and voicing of *ḥ, e.g.

(53) Kurdish
   tamāḥ (variant of *tamāʾ*) 'greed'   < Arab. *ṭamaʿ*

(54) Gorani
   ḥagāḷ [hæˈgɑːlˤ]   'scarf'   < Arab. *ʿiqāl*
   saʾb [sæʕb]   'morning'   < Arab. *ṣabāḥ*
   dáḥfa [ˈdæħfæ]   'exclusion'   < Arab. *dafʿa*

A further feature of pharyngeals in JSNENA is that word-final pharyngeals are sometimes metathesised with the preceding consonant, e.g.

(55) JSNENA
   z-ʿ-r 'to plant'   < *z-r-ʿ*

This feature of metathesis of a word-final pharyngeal is found in Kurdish and Gorani of the region, e.g.

(56) Kurdish
   səḥb [səhb], *saḥb* 'morning'   < Arab. *ṣabāḥ*

(57) Gorani
   saʾb [sæʕb]   'morning'   < Arab. *ṣabāḥ*
   wáʿza [ˈwæʕzæ]   'situation'   < Arab. *waẓʿ* < *waḍʿ*
   joʿma [dʒoʕˈmæ],   'Friday'   < Arab. *jumʿa*
   joḥma [dʒoħˈmæ]
   dáḥfa [ˈdæħfæ]   'exclusion'   < Arab. *dafʿa*

2.2.2.6 Inserted word-initial /h/

In JSNENA words do not begin with a vowel. Initial vowels are preceded by a laryngeal stop /ʾ/. The initial stop has shifted in some words to the laryngeal fricative /h/. This is attested mainly in verbs and particles, e.g.

(58) JSNENA
   hamə́r 'he says'   < *ʾamər*
   hamḗ   'he brings' < *ʾamē*
   hēzə́l 'he goes'   < *ʾēzəl*

hē	'he comes'	< ʾe < *ʾāṯē
hol	'he does'	< ʾol > ʿābeḏ
hīt	'there is'	< ʾīt
həl	'to'	< ʾəl
hḗka	'where?'	< ʾēka
hḗma	'which?'	< ʾēma
hamə́r	'he says'	< ʾamər

This shift is not completely regular. In some verbs an original initial /ʾ/ is retained, e.g.

(59) JSNENA
ʾaxə́l 'he eats'
ʾalḗ 'he knows'

Sporadically, the shift of /ʾ/ > /h/ is attested in word-internal position, e.g.

(60) JSNENA
šahə́l 'he coughs' < šaʾə́l

The shift is attested also in the neighbouring Jewish NENA dialect of Sulemaniyya, where it occurs both word-initially and word-internally. In many cases the /h/ alternates freely with the original /ʾ/ in such cases in this dialect, e.g.

(61) J. Sulemaniyya
bēhḗ ~ bēʾḗ 'eggs'
hulāhá ~ hulāʾá 'Jew'
yahḗn ~ yaʾḗn 'they are coming'
(Khan 2004, 37)

It occurs also in loanwords in J. Sulemaniyya, e.g.

(62) J. Suleimaniyya
hodá ~ ʾoda 'room'
hatarí ~ ʾatarí 'general store'
hestár ~ ʾestár 'mule'
jamahtá 'community' < jamaʾta

The shift of word-initial /ʾ/ to /h/ matches a similar development in Kurdish and Gorani of the region. In these Iranian languages, vowels do not occur word-initially but, as in JSNENA, an initial vowel is generally preceded by laryngeal stop /ʾ/, e.g.

(63) Kurdish
  ʼāw   'water'
  ʼēwa 'you (pl)'

In some words, however, the laryngeal fricative /h/ is added to vowel-initial words. This is found predominantly before the vowel /a/ [æ], e.g.

(64) Kurdish
  hangūr [hænˈguːr]   'grape'   cf. P. angūr
  halūja [hæluːˈdʒæ] 'sour plum'   cf. P. ālūče
  hanjīr [hænˈdʒiːr] 'fig'   cf. P. anjir
  hasaḷ [hæˈsɑḷ]   'honey'   < ʼasal < Arab. ʼasal)

(65) Gorani
  hanār [hæˈnaːɾ]   'pomegranate'   cf. P. anār
  hangwīn [hæŋgˈwiːn]   'honey'   cf. P. angbīn >angubīn
  hawr [hæwɾ]   'cloud'   cf. P. abr

Less frequently, word-initial /h/ is inserted before close-mid front and back vowels /e/ and /o/.

(66) Kurdish
  hēsər [heːˈsəɾ]   'mule'   < estər
  homēwār [homeːˈwaːɾ]   'sanguine'   cf. P. omidvār
  hoḷāxdārī [holˤaːxdaːˈriː] 'donkey husbandry'   cf. P. olāɣ

(67) Gorani
  hēma [heːˈmæ]   'we'   < ēma
  hēḷakī [heːḷæˈkiː]   'fine sieve'   < T. elek

This phenomenon is, indeed, an areal feature of languages of western Iran. In the Turkic varieties of western Iran a non-etymological laryngeal *h* has developed at the beginning of many words that historically began with a vowel or in loanwords that would have begun with a vowel without the added *h*, e.g.

(68) Turkic varieties of western Iran
  helämɪjälär   'they do not do'   < elämiyirlär
  helbet   'naturally'   < Arab. albatte
  häqīq   'agate-stone'   < P. < Arab. ʽaqīq
  (Bulut 2018b, 413)

In Bakhtiari an intervocalic laryngeal stop develops into /h/ in some dialects, e.g.

(69) Bakhtiari
sāhat 'hour' < Ar. sāʿa
(Anonby and Taheri-Ardali 2018, 450)

2.2.2.7 Zagros /d/

In several languages of the region a /d/ in post-vocalic position undergoes a process of lenition. This phenomenon has come to be known as 'Zagros /d/'. It has a variety of outcomes across the languages.

In JSNENA this is manifested in several ways. The most prominent of these is the development of a postvocalic *d into a lateral /l/. The lateral appears both where there is historically a voiced interdental *ð and also where there is an unvoiced interdental *ϑ, e.g.

(70) JSNENA
ʾilá 'hand' < *ʾīðā
ʾēlá 'festival' < *ʾēðā
hol 'he does' < *ʿāwəð
mālá 'village' < *māϑā
belá 'house' < *bayϑā
mīlá 'dead' < *mīϑa

An intermediate stage of development appears to have been *θ > d, *ð > d, whereby both interdentals became a voiced stop d. This intermediate stage is attested in some NENA dialects of north-western Iran, e.g.

(71) J. Urmi
īdá 'hand' < *ʾīðā
adé 'he comes' < *ʾāϑē
(Khan 2008a, 30)

The lateral /l/ would have, therefore, been the outcome of a lenition of the stop *d. This lenition of *d to /l/ is a feature of all Jewish Trans-Zab dialects. In Iranian and Turkic languages across the region of western Iran and north-eastern Iraq the outcome of the lenition of a post-vocalic /d/ is generally an approximant or a sonorant (/r/ or /l/) (Khan 2018f, 386; Mahmoudveysi and Bailey 2018, 540–41; Anonby and Taheri-Ardali 2018, 449; Haig 2018, 271; Bulut 2018, 413–14). Such lenition of *d to /l/ in Jewish Trans-Zab NENA, therefore, is likely to be due to the 'perceptual magnet effect' (Blevins 2017) of the weakened Zagros *d*, whereby Neo-Aramaic speakers match this perceptually with the sonorant /l/ in their existing sound inventory.

In the JSNENA dialect, the Zagros /d/ areal feature has induced other types of lenition of historical **d* that are not attested in the majority of Trans-Zab NENA dialects that are more distant from the Zagros region.

In some words the reflex of a historical **d* in post-vocalic position is the voiced sibilant /z/, e.g.

(72)	JSNENA		J. Koy Sanjak, J. Arbel
	kozá	'liver'	*kodá*
	gūzá	'wall'	*gūdá*
	dəzwá	'fly'	*dədwá*

The articulation of the consonant has been further weakened in a few cases to zero after a vowel or sonorant consonant, e.g.

(73)	JSNENA		J. Koy Sanjak	J. Arbel
	xar	'he becomes'	*ġadər*	*ġadər*
	šar	'he sends'	*žadər*	*šadər*
	bī-zóa	'more'	*bíz-zoda*	*bīz-zóda*
	qómē	'tomorrow'	*qádomē*	*qádomē*

This weakening is attested also after a sonorant consonant, e.g.

(74) JSNENA
Kursán 'Kurdistan' < **Kurdəstān*

The lenition of /d/ is a feature of both Gorani and Kurdish of the Sanandaj region. This occurs after a vowel or a sonorant consonant. The lenition of /d/ generally results in the alveolar approximant [ɹ] in Gorani, represented in the transcription by the symbol *ḋ*.[1] In Sanandaj Kurdish, the lenition of the /d/ results in the sonorant [w], zero, a palatalised [gʲ], or assimilation to the preceding lateral or fricative. Examples:

---

[1] For other outcomes of the lenition in the varieties of Hawrami outside of Hawraman, see Mahmoudveysi and Bailey (2018, 540–41).

(75) Gorani
 xuđā́ [xuˈɹaː]   'God'   cf. P. *xodā*
 'ā́đa [ˈʔaːɹæ]   'she (3sg.f direct)'
 'ā́đ [ˈʔaːɹ]   'he (3sg.m direct)'
 karđəš [ˈkʰæɾɹəʃ]   'he/she did'.

(76) Kurdish
 pāwšā, [paːwˈʃaː], *pāšā*   'king'   cf. P. *pādšā*
 nagʸār [nægʲaːr]   'poor'   cf. P. *nadār*
 bāḷḷār, bāḷār [baːlˤˈlaːɾ]   'bird'   < *bāḷdār*
 ḥavva, ḥava [ḥæˈvæ]   'seventeen'   cf. P. *hevdah*

It is significant that these outcomes of the lenition of the /d/ in the Iranian languages of the Sanandaj region do not correspond to those of JSNENA. Evidently JSNENA matches the generic feature of lenition and manifests this by outcomes that are available in its internal sound inventory (/l/, /z/) or by zero.

2.2.2.8 /w/

In JSNENA, the phoneme that is transcribed /w/ is realised as a labio-dental [v] in most cases, e.g.

(77) JSNENA
 ṣīwá [siːˈva]   'wood'
 hawḗ [haˈveː]   'may he be'
 hēwālḗ [heˑvaːˈleː]   '(that) he could'

The friction is sometimes reduced and it is pronounced as a labio-dental approximant [ʋ]. This is heard mainly after back consonants, e.g.

(78) JSNENA
 dóqwa [ˈdoˑqʋa]   'he used to hold'
 gwərté=ya [gʋərˈteːja]   'he has married her'

It tends to be realised as a bilabial continuant [w] when in contact with a sibilant, when it is between two instances of the low vowel /a/, or when it is adjacent to back rounded vowels, e.g.

(79) JSNENA
    ruwá [ruˈwa]   'big'
    yatûwa [yaˈtʰuːwa]   'he used to sit'
    šwāwá [ʃwɔːˈwʌ]   'neighbour'

In Kurdish of the Sanandaj region /w/ is realised as a labio-velar semivowel [w]. There is, however, a match for the labio-dental realisation [v] of JSNENA in the Takht and Nodsha dialects of Gorani (Hawrami). In these dialects of Gorani /w/ is sometimes realised as a labio-dental [v] in word-initial position followed by front open unrounded vowels, e.g.

(80) Gorani
    waná [væˈnæ]   'at'
    wắt=əm [vˈaːt-əm]   'I said'
    warbán [værˈbæn]   'apron'
    wīarū́ [viːjæˈɾuː]   'I cross'

The sound sometimes undergoes lenition and is realised as a labio-dental approximant [ʋ], e.g.

(81) Gorani
    məró kánēwa [məɾo kˈæneːʋæ]   'pear-picking'
    sənoqaká=š kárd̠-wa [kˈæɾ.ɪʋæ]   'he opened the box'

It is realised as [w] in environments that are similar to those that condition the [w] realisation of the sound in JSNENA, viz. between two instances of the low vowel /a/, or when it is adjacent to back rounded vowels, e.g.

(82) Gorani
    ja awaz-na [dʒæ ˈʔæwæznæ]   'in return'
    lūwā́-ymē [luːˈwaːjmeː]   'we went'
    na-tắwā=m [næˈtaːwaːm]   'I could not'.

We see, therefore, that the realisation of /w/ in JSNENA matches that of the sound in Takht and Nodsha Gorani very closely.

2.2.2.9 /č/

The affricate /č/ occurs in a few words of Aramaic etymology, although the consonant did not exist in the consonant inventory of earlier Aramaic. These include ʿ-y-č 'to knead', in which the /č/ has developed from an original emphatic /ṣ/ (< *ʿ-ṣ-ṣ). It can be assumed that at some stage the affricate was emphatic *ʿy-č̣. The increased muscular tension of the emphatic articulation no doubt was a factor in inducing the development of the affricate, which has a stronger onset than a fricative. The existence of the affricate /č/ in the Iranian languages of the region, however, is likely to have facilitated this, by the perceptual magnet affect. The emphatic fricative *ṣ with its muscular tension would have been matched perceptually with the Iranian /č/ with its strong onset.[2]

Some cases of the affricate /č/ have developed from a fusion of *t and *š. This is the case in numeral 'əč'a 'nine' < *'ətš'a < *taš'a. The preservation of the historical pharyngeal /ʿ/ must have been conditioned by suprasegmental emphasis at some stage of the word's development. Indeed, in some NENA dialects the affricate in this word is pronounced emphatic, e.g. Ch. Barwar 'əččạ (Khan 2008b, 60). Again, this internal development was no doubt facilitated by a perceptual matching of the sequence *tš with the Iranian affricate /č/.

The verb č-y-r 'to go around' appears to have developed by affrication of *k > č from *k-y-r (derived ultimately from *k-r-r, cf. Heb. kirker 'to go around, to whirl'). Such affrication of *k is not found elsewhere in JSNENA, although it is attested in numerous other NENA dialects. If the verb č-y-r indeed has an Aramaic etymology, it is possible that the affrication has arisen by assimilation to the phonetic form of the semantically related Kurdish verb čarxīn, čarxāndən 'to go around, to turn'.

2.2.2.10 /q/

In JSNENA the phoneme /q/ is normally realised as an unvoiced uvular stop, e.g. bāqá [bɑːˈqa] 'to'.

This is the normal realisation of /q/ in NENA dialects in Iraq and south-eastern Turkey. After a vowel or /w/, the phoneme occasionally undergoes lenition and is realised as an unvoiced uvular fricative, e.g.

(83) JSNENA
    qoqḗ [qoːˈχeː]   'pots'
    šəwqá=y [ʃɪfχaj]   'he has left'

This suggests that it has lost the muscular tension that is characteristic of emphatic consonants. Although historically /q/ would have been an emphatic phoneme corresponding to plain /k/, its emphatic status appears to have been lost. This has come about by speakers of JSNENA perceptually matching it with the /q/ of the Iranian

---

2 For the development of affricate /č/ other NENA dialects see Khan (2008b, 61–62; 2016, vol. 1, 175).

languages of the region, which undergoes lenition and is sometimes realised as a fricative after vowels. In the Kurdish of Sanandaj, this is an unvoiced velar fricative [x], an unvoiced uvular fricative [χ] or a voiced uvular fricative [ʁ], e.g.

(84) Kurdish
wəjā́q [wəˈʤaːx] 'hearth' cf. T. ojāq
āqá [aːˈʁa] 'Mr' cf. P. āqā
suqā́n [suˈχaːn] 'bone' cf. P. ostoxān

2.2.2.11 Phonetic processes relating to voicing

In JSNENA a voiced consonant tends to be devoiced when it is in contact with a following unvoiced consonant, e.g.

(85) JSNENA
  a. rabtá [rapˈta] 'big (sg.f)'
    cf. rā́ba [ˈrɑːba] 'much (sg.m)'
  b. nawagtá [nawakˈta] 'granddaughter'
    cf. nawāgá [nawaːˈga] 'grandson'
  c. ʿayztá [ʕajsˈta] 'good (sg.f)'
    cf. ʿayzá [ʕajˈza] 'good (sg.m)'

Voiced consonants tend to be devoiced at the end of words, e.g.

(86) JSNENA
šoḷtā́lī do-làgˈ [doˑlak] (A:24) 'I threw it on that side'

This is regularly the case with the 3sg.m. and 3sg.f. suffixes -ēf and –af (< *-ēw, *-aw) and the devoicing is represented in the transcription.

The devoicing of word-final consonants is not a regular feature of the Iranian languages of Sanandaj, although it is occasionally found in loanwords in Sanandaj Kurdish, e.g.

(87) Kurdish
sahā́t [sæˈhaːt] personal name (f). < Arab. saʿāda
                                     'happiness'

Word-final devoicing is more common in the Kurdish dialect of Sulemaniyya, e.g.

(88) CK Sulemaniyya
      Sulemaniyya   Sanandaj
      kətēb [kʰəˈtʰeːp]   'book'   *kətēb* [kʰəˈtʰeːb]
      ṣag [ṣɑk]   'dog'   *ṣag* [ṣɑg]
      'āzād [ʔaːˈzaːt]   'free'   *'āzād* [ʔaːˈzaːd]
      bərənj [bəˈrəntʃ] 'rice'   *bərənj* [bəˈrəndʒ]
      (Hamid 2014, Ahmed 2019)

2.2.2.12 Consonant gemination

In JSNENA consonant gemination has been completely lost. All NENA dialects have lost historical consonantal gemination in some contexts, but in JSNENA this loss is systematic and occurs in contexts where other NENA dialects preserve it.

As in other NENA dialects, gemination is lost after /a/ and /u/ vowels occurring within words of Aramaic stock. The forms in the closely related dialects of J. Sulemaniyya and J. Saqəz are give for comparison:

(89) JSNENA   J. Sulemaniyya/J. Saqəz
      kāká   *kāká*   'tooth'   < *kakkā
      rắba   *rắba*   'much'   < *rabbaṯ
      gūzá   *gudá ~ guzá*   'wall'   < *guddā

We may say that the gemination in these contexts was weakened in Proto-NENA. Unlike other documented NENA dialects, however, in JSNENA consonant gemination is lost within a word also after /ə/. The gemination may be considered to have been preserved in this context in Proto-NENA and its loss to have been subsequent to this stage of development. The /ə/ vowel remains short, e.g.

(90) JSNENA   J. Sulemaniyya/J. Sǟqəz
      šəné   *šənné*   'years'
      šərá   *šərrá*   'navel'
      dəmá   *dəmmá*   'blood'
      ləbá   *ləbbá*   'heart'
      təná   *tənná*   'smoke'
      xəmá   *xəmmá*   'father-in-law; heat'

The /ə/ vowel may be stressed, as is the case in the following adverbial form:

(91) JSNENA   J. Sulemaniyya/J. Sǟqəz
      tə́mal   *tə́mmal*   'yesterday'

Short /a/ and /u/ vowels before a consonant that was geminated in proto-NENA likewise remain short when the gemination of the consonant is weakened, e.g.

(92) JSNENA   J. Sulemaniyya/J. Săqəz
 laxá   laxxá   'here'
 xalú   xallú   'I (f.) wash them'
 kúlē   kúllē   'all'

This general loss of gemination in JSNENA can be correlated with the same phenomenon in the Kurdish of Sanandaj. Gemination has been documented in the neighbouring Kurdish dialect of Sulemaniyya in laterals and nasals (Ahmed 2019, 51). In the corresponding forms in the Kurdish of Sanandaj the consonants have no gemination, e.g.

(93)   Kurdish Sanandaj   Kurdish Sulemaniyya
 gula [gʊˈlæ]   gulla   'bullet'
 kuna [kʊˈnæ]   kunna   'water sack'
 šama [ʃæˈmæ]   šamma   'Saturday'

This would match the differences in gemination between the J. NENA dialects of Sanandaj and Sulemaniyya described above.

In the Kurdish of Sanandaj, gemination of consonants is likewise lost in Arabic loanwords, e.g.

(94) Kurdish
 banā [bæˈnaː]   'builder' < Arab. *bannā'*
 mərabā [məɾæˈbaː]   'jam'   < Arab. *murabbā*

Gemination, however, does occur in the Kurdish of Sanandaj, and in Gorani, as a result of the assimilation of a weakened Zagros /d/ to a preceding consonant in the following words. These are all compound constructions with the original /d/ at the onset of a separate morpheme:

(95) Kurdish
 ḥavvá [ħævˈvæ]   'seventeen'   < ḥav-dah
 bāḷḷár [baːlˤˈlɑːɾ]   'bird'   < bāḷ-dār
 mənāḷḷár [mənaːlˤˈlɑːɾ]   'having children' < mənāḷ-dār

(96) Gorani
čənna 'how much' cf. P. *čand*
ənna 'that much' cf. CK. *awanda*

This can be compared to the occurrence of gemination in JSNENA across a word boundary in stress groups such as the following:

(97) JSNENA
har-rḗṭ 'he just trembles'

2.3 VOWELS

The vowel inventory of JSNENA and the Iranian languages of Sanandaj are very similar. An exception is the close-mid front rounded vowel [Ø]—represented as /ö/— in the vowel inventory of Sanandaj Kurdish, e.g. *kör* 'blind'; *göčka* 'ear', which does not occur in either JSNENA or Gorani. This shows that the vowel inventory of JSNENA corresponds more closely to that of Gorani than to that of Kurdish.

2.3.1 Vowel quality

In JSNENA phonological distinctions between vowels are mainly made through quality distinctions. The only phonological distinction in length is between short and long *a*, which contrast in a few cases in identical syllabic contexts. The mean quality plots of the various vowel phonemes are represented on Figure 4 below.

2.3.1.1 JSNENA vowel system

The JSNENA vowels in Figure 4 were plotted based on their acoustic properties averaged out for at least ten words and in different syllabic environments. Details of the words in question can be found in Khan (2009, 34-43).

This matches closely the vowel system of Kurdish and Gorani, in which phonemic oppositions are mainly made through quality distinctions, with the exception of a length distinction between long and short *a*. The systems of Kurdish and Gorani are represented by mean quality plots in Figures 5 and 6.

48 — 2 Phonology

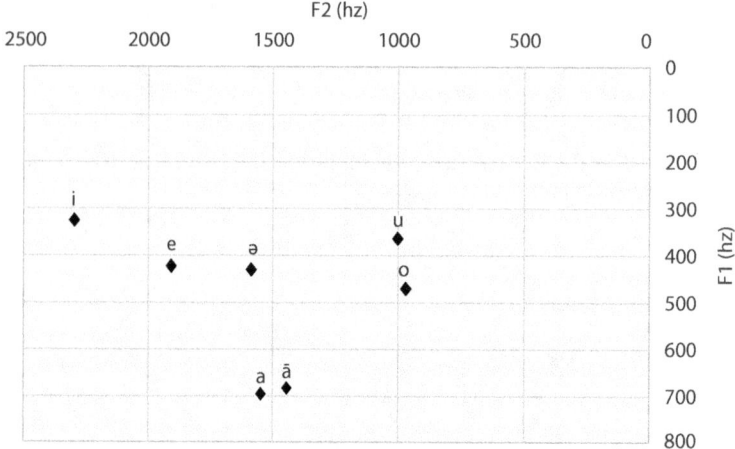

Figure 4: Phonetic realisation of vowels in JSNENA.

2.3.1.2 Kurdish vowel system

The Kurdish vowels in Figure 5 were plotted based on their acoustic properties averaged out for at least ten words and in different syllabic environments. The words were mainly produced by a 40-year old male speaker of CK Sanandaj. A few words were produced by a 50-year-old female speaker from Sanandaj.

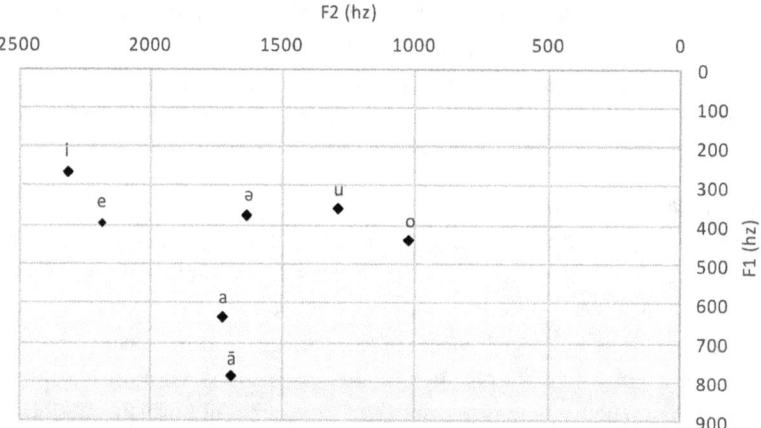

Figure 5: Phonetic realisation of vowels in Kurdish.

2.3.1.3 Gorani vowel system

The Gorani vowels in Figure 6 were plotted on the basis of their acoustic properties. At least ten words were analysed for plotting each individual vowel. The words were produced by a 50-year-old male speaker of Hawrami Takht.

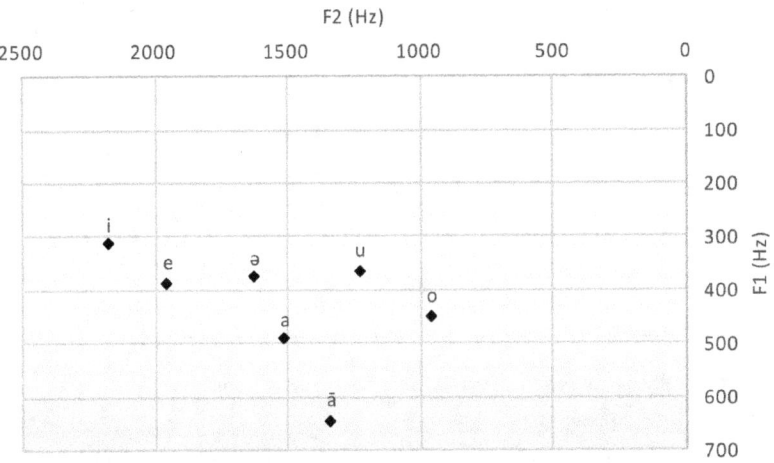

Figure 6: Phonetic realisation of vowels in Gorani.

2.3.1.4 Comparison of vowel systems

The following chart (Figure 7) compares the vowel systems of JSNENA (red), Kurdish (blue) and Gorani (green). The chart also shows the relationship of the vowels of the various languages with the cardinal vowels, which are marked in square brackets in black.

The chart shows that most of the JSNENA vowels are closer in quality to the corresponding Gorani vowels than to the Kurdish vowels.

2.3.2 Vowel length

The transcription that is used in this volume for JSNENA aims to correspond as far as possible to Iranist conventions of transcription that are used for Gorani and Kurdish. This is to make comparison between JSNENA and Iranian clearer. Most distinctions in vowel length in JSNENA, other than those of /a/ and /ā/, are either predictable from the syllabic structure and the position of the stress or are results of communicative strategies expressed in the division of speech into intonation groups (see Khan 2009, 47-52 for details). In such circumstances the length of a

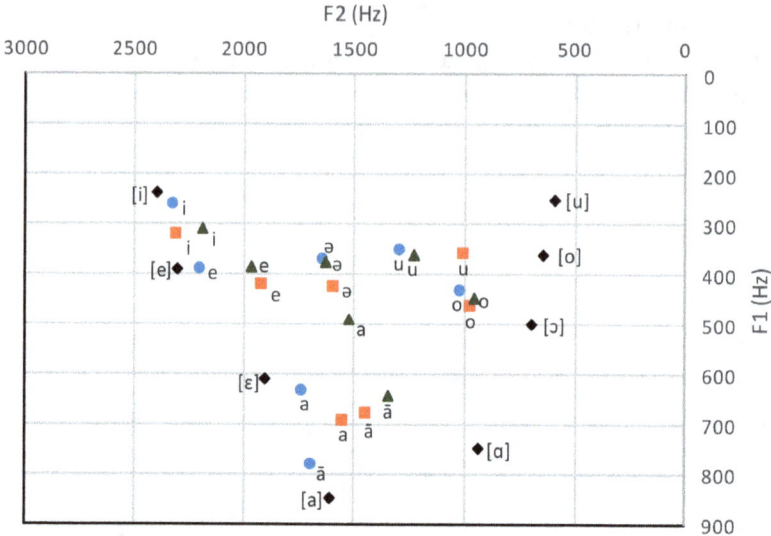

Figure 7: Phonetic realisation of vowels in JSNENA, Gorani, and Kurdish compared.

vowel does not have phonemic status since it is not crucial for expressing semantic distinctions between words. In the transcription, however, not only is long *ā* marked with a macron but also long *ē*, *ū* and *ī* in accordance with Iranian conventions. Also the marking of vowel length has been normalised to some extent and does not reflect allophonic variations due to speed of delivery and position in the intonation group.

Verbal forms with short vowels in an open penultimate syllable such as *šatéx* 'we drink' can form minimal pairs with homophonous noun forms that differ only in the length of the vowel. In the phonological system of JSNENA, therefore, there is phonemic opposition between short /a/ and long /ā/, e.g.

(98) JSNENA
  kasé 'he covers' : *kāsé* 'stomachs'
  garé 'he shaves' : *gāré* 'roof'

Similar oppositions between /a/ and /ā/ are found in loanwords, e.g.

(99) JSNENA
  paró 'rag' : *pāró* 'snow shovel'

A vowel that is regularly long in a word-final open syllable is marked with a macron sign, e.g.

(100) JSNENA
  lā́ ['læː] 'by the side of'

In most words a word-final -*a* varies in length according to its position within the intonation group. In such words no diacritic is marked on the vowel.

As remarked above, a phonemic length distinction between long and short *a* is found also in Gorani and Kurdish of the region, which would match the vowel system of JSNENA. This is shown by the following pairs (the last pair is specific to Kurdish):[3]

(101) Gorani and Kurdish
  das [dæs] 'hand' : *dās* [daːs] 'sickle'
  mas [mæs] 'drunk' : *mās* [maːs] 'yoghurt'
  kar [kʰær] 'donkey' : *kār* [kʰaːr] 'job'

2.4 Stress position

The transcription marks the boundaries of intonation groups by a short vertical sign |. Intonation contours are not represented, but a distinction is made between the nuclear stress of the intonation group and non-nuclear stress. The nuclear stress, which is the most prominent stress of the intonation group, is marked by a grave accent (v̀) and the non-nuclear stress is marked by an acute accent (v́). It is our convention in this volume to mark only the nuclear stress where the contents of the whole intonation group is cited. The non-nuclear stress mark (v́) is used only where isolated words and phrases are cited to indicate stress position.

In JSNENA there is some degree of variability in the position of stress in words. It is determined to a large extent by the relations between words on the level of syntax and discourse. The same applies to the choice of where the speaker places the nuclear stress and the intonation group boundaries. In what follows the predominant position of the stress in the various categories of word is described.

---

3 While these pairs clearly suggest that vowel length is phonemically distinctive between long and short /a/, there is some debate as to whether vowel length distinctions are phonemic in Kurdish. MacKenzie (1961a); Ahmad (1986); McCarus (1997); and Hamid (2015) hold that there is a phonemic distinction between long and short /a/. On the other hand, Öpengin (2016); and Ahmed (2019) claim that length is not contrastive in Central Kurdish.

2.4.1 Nominals

In JSNENA, most nouns and pronouns have word-final stress in most words in all contexts, and this may be regarded as the basic stress position. It is the usual position in nominals that occur in pause before an intonation group boundary and also in the citation form of nominals:

(102) JSNENA
    bēlà[|]   'house'
    tātà[|]   'father'
    yālè̯[|]   'children'
    'ānà[|]   'I'

Possessive suffixes are treated by stress placement as components of the word and the stress falls on the suffix in word-final position, e.g.

(103) JSNENA
    bēlèf[|]   'his house'
    bēlaxùn[|]   'your (pl) hours'
    bēlàn[|]   'our house'
    bēlanī̀[|]   'our house' (variant 1pl suffix)

An exception to this is the reflexive form *noš-* 'self', which is regularly stressed on the penultimate syllable when it has a pronominal suffix, e.g.

(104) JSNENA
    nòšī[|]   'myself'
    nòšan[|]   'ourselves'
    nòšaxun[|]   'yourselves'

When a noun is used in the vocative, the stress is realised on the penultimate syllable.

(105) JSNENA
    tàta![|]   'Father!'
    bàxta![|]   'Wife!'
    gyànī![|]   'My soul!'

In Iranian, the default stress pattern is for words to receive stress on the final syllable. There is some variation in the stress patterns associated with nouns in Gorani.

In masculine nouns, the stress consistently falls on the final syllable. In feminine nouns, the stress is usually placed on the penultimate syllable, except in nouns ending in -ē, and a few nouns in -ā:

(106) Gorani
    làma˩   'stomach' (f.)
    sàwī˩   'apple' (f.)
    yāgè˩   'place' (f.)
    čamčà˩   'spoon' (m.)
    hēḷà˩   'egg' (m.)

On the other hand, in Kurdish nouns the stress falls consistently on the final syllable.

(107) Kurdish
    haḷūjà˩   'plum'
    xasù˩   'mother-in-law'
    kunà˩   'hole'

JSNENA patterns with Kurdish rather than Gorani on assigning stress to the citation form of nominals. In JSNENA and Kurdish the final syllable in the citation form of the nominals receives stress. In Gorani, by contrast, the penultimate syllable is stressed in some feminine nouns.

In both Kurdish and Gorani, nominal formatives such as the infinitive formative, and the definite suffix receive the word stress. The indefinite formatives in the singular in Kurdish and in the singular and plural in Gorani are not stress-bearing. They should, therefore, be identified as clitics.

(108) Kurdish   Gorani
    xwand-ə́n   'reading'   mařī-áy   'break'
    kotər-aká   'the pigeon'   pīā-ká   'the man'
    mənāḷ-gál   'children'   kárd-ē   'knives'
    kārakár=ēk   'a worker'   kətéb=ēw   'a book'

Possessive pronominal formatives are clitics in Gorani and Kurdish and do not take the stress.

(109) Kurdish and Gorani
G. *kitèb=tā*ˈ 'your book'
K. *dāyagawrà=yān* 'Their grandmother'
G. *bāxčakà=mā*ˈ 'our garden'
K. *kanîškakà=yān* 'their daughter'
G. *wḗ=mā* 'ourselves'
K. *xó=yān* 'themselves'

Vocative nouns

Kurdish and Gorani nouns in the vocative have penultimate stress:

(110) Kurdish and Gorani
G./K. *ròḷa!*ˈ 'Child!'
G. *àḍā!*ˈ 'Mother!'
K. *bàba!*ˈ 'Father!'

The occurrence of penultimate stress in the JSNENA reflexive forms *nóši*, *nóšan*, *nóšaxun* etc. can be explained as the result of these forms being matched with the corresponding Iranian phrases, which have unstressed clitic pronouns:

(111) JSNENA Kurdish Gorani
    nóši   *xó=m*   *wḗ=m*
    nóšan   *xó=mān*   *wḗ=mā*
    nóšaxun   *xó=tān*   *wḗ=tā*

Speakers of JSNENA evidently do not parse the reflexive phrases compositionally as consisting of a nominal stem *noš-* and a possessive suffix. Rather they have lost their compositionality and are perceived as unitary phrases. This would have been facilitated by the fact that the stem *noš-* is not used in a nominal phrase without a suffix, i.e. there is no form **noša* in the synchronic state of the dialect. The reflexive forms for each person have been matched with the corresponding lexical item in the Iranian languages and have undergone convergence with the Iranian forms by a replication of prosody.

2.4.2 Adverbials

In JSNENA some adverbials exhibit the same stress patterns as nominals, in that the basic stress position is on the word-final syllable, e.g.

(112) JSNENA
    *laxà*ˈ   'here'
    *dokà*ˈ   'there'
    *waryà*ˈ   'outside'
    *loʾà*ˈ   'inside'

In several adverbials, however, the stress regularly falls on the penultimate syllable, e.g.

(113) JSNENA
    *ràba*ˈ   'much, many'
    *làʿēl*ˈ   'above'
    *qàmē*ˈ   'forwards'
    *xàrē*ˈ   'backwards'
    *bəqàta*ˈ   'in the morning'

The adverbials in Kurdish and Gorani usually have the same stress pattern as nouns, e.g.:

(114) Kurdish and Gorani
    G. *ēgà*ˈ   'here'
    G. *āgà*ˈ   'there'
    G./K. *īsà*ˈ 'now'
    K. *ērà*ˈ   'here'
    K. *önà*ˈ   'there'
    K. *fərà*ˈ   'much, many'

In some adverbials the stress shifts backward and falls on the penultimate syllable

(115) Kurdish and Gorani
    G. *dəmàwa*ˈ   'afterwards, from behind'
    G./K. *ə̀njā*ˈ   'then'
    G./K. *àwsā*ˈ   'then, long ago'
    K. *čừnka*ˈ   'because'

2.4.3 Verbs

(i) In JSNENA, the basic position of the stress in verb forms derived from the present stem (§4.3) is on the final syllable of the root or, if the vowel of this syllable is elided when an inflectional suffix is added, on the first syllable of the suffix:

(116) JSNENA
    *garə̀š-Ø*ˈ   'he pulls'
    pull.PRS-3SG.M
    *garə̀š-na*ˈ   'I pull'
    pull.PRS-1SG.M
    *garš-ī̀*ˈ   'they pull'
    pull.PRS-3PL
    *garš-ĕt*ˈ   'you pull'
    pull.PRS-2SG.M
    *garš-ĕtun*ˈ   'you (pl.) pull'
    pull.PRS-2PL

(ii) In verb forms derived from the past stem (§4.3), the placement of the basic stress follows the same principle:

(117) JSNENA
    *grə̀š-lē*ˈ   'he killed'
    pull.PST-3SG.M
    grə̀š-lox   'you killed'
    pull.PST-2SG.M
    grə̀š-laxun   'you (pl.) killed'
    pull.PST-2PL
    *smìx-ēt*ˈ   'you stood'
    stand.PST-2SG.M

The distinction between some past stem verbal forms and homophonous nominal forms depends uniquely on stress position, e.g.

(118) JSNENA
    *mìla*ˈ   'she died'
    *mīlà*ˈ   'dead (sg.m)'

(iii) The basic position of the stress in the imperative, on the other hand, is on the first syllable of the root:

(119) JSNENA
  *màxwē*ˈ   'show! (sg.)'
  *màxwē-mun*ˈ   'show! (pl.)'

This stress placement has phonemic significance in the singular imperative, since its non-final position contrasts with the final position of the stress in the otherwise homophonous 3sg.m. present form:

(120) JSNENA
  *maxwḕ*ˈ   'he shows'

(iv) When further pronominal suffixes are added to the verbal forms just described, the basic position of stress remains the same, e.g.

(121) JSNENA–Present stem
  *garə̀š-lū*ˈ   'he pulls them'
  pull.PRS-3PL
  *garə̀š-wā-lū*ˈ   'he used to pull them'
  pull.PRS-PSTC-3PL
  garə̀š-n-ēf   'I pull him'
  pull.PRS-1SG.M-3SG.M
  *garš-ī̀-lē*ˈ   'they pull him'
  pull.PRS-3PL-3SG.M
  *garš-ḕtu-lē*ˈ   'you (pl.) pull him'
  pull.PRS-2PL-3SG.M

(122) JSNENA–Past stem
  *grə̀š-wā-lē*ˈ   'he had killed'
  pull.PST-PSTC-3SG.M
  *smìx-ən-wa*ˈ   'I had stood'
  pull.PST-1SG.M-PSTC

(123) JSNENA– Imperative
 màxwē-lī| 'show me! (sg.)'
 show.IMP.S-1SG
 màxwēmū-lē| 'show (pl.) him!'
 show.IMP.PL-3SG.M

In the Iranian languages of the region, the verb forms based on the present stem have the same stress pattern as bare nouns. Thus, if syllabic, the inflectional suffixes take stress. If not, the last syllable of the root is stressed.

(124) Kurdish   Gorani
 a-nūs-ìn| 'We write' nəvīs-mḕ|
 a-xwà-m| 'I ate' war-ù|

In verb forms derived from the past stem, the stress consistently falls on the last syllable of the root. The inflectional suffixes (on intransitive verbs) and oblique suffixes (on transitive verbs) do not take stress. The reason why inflectional suffixes do not take stress, unlike their counterparts in the verb forms based on the present stem, is that the inflectional suffixes on past intransitive verbs were historically clitic copulas, which subsequently underwent univerbation. Past transitive verbs are inflected by historically oblique clitics, which are not stressed.

(125) Kurdish   Gorani
 hàt-īn| 'We came' āmà-ymē|
 nàrd=mān| 'We sent' kīyàst=mā
 kàft-ən| 'They fell' kòt-ē|
 bə̀rd=yān| 'They sent' kīyàst=šā

The imperative and preverbal prefixes, including the negator, are stressed, and thus are an exception to the final-syllable stress pattern.

(126) Kurdish and Gorani–Imperative
 K. bə̀-nūs-a!| 'Write!'
 G. bùs-a| 'Sleep!'

(127) Kurdish and Gorani– Subjunctive
 K. bə̀-xwa-m| 'That I eat!'
 G. bàr-ū| 'That I bring'

(128) Kurdish and Gorani– Prohibitive
  K. *mà-řo*| 'Don't go!'
  G. *mà-sān-a!*| 'Don't buy!'

(129) Kurdish and Gorani– Negative
  K. *nā́-xwa-m!*| 'I don't eat!'
  G. *nə̀-m-ār-ū*| 'I don't bring'

The addition of further suffixes on these verb forms does not cause a change in the stress pattern of preverbal inflectional prefixes.

(130) Kurdish and Gorani
  K. *nà=mān-xwa*| 'Don't eat us!'
  G. *nə̀-m-ār-ū=š*| 'I don't bring it'

In Gorani imperfect forms the stress retracts onto the past converter suffix. In the negation of the imperfect, the stress retracts further onto the negative prefix.

(131) Kurdish and Gorani
  G. *kar-ə̀n-ī*| 'You were doing'
  G. *nà-kar-ēn-ī*|| 'You were not doing'

The stress placement in JSNENA verbs exhibits a convergence with Iranian stress patterns.

The oblique L-suffixes in the inflection of JSNENA verbs remain unstressed as is the case with Iranian personal clitics:

(132) JSNENA   Kurdish
  grə́š-lē   *kešā́=y*
  grə́š-lan   *kešā́=mān*
  grə́š-laxun *kešā́=tān*

The Iranian verbal suffixes broadly correspond in function to the JSNENA direct suffixes (§4.3). The Iranian suffixes are stressed in present verbs but unstressed in past verbs, e.g.

(133) Kurdish   Gorani
  a-nēr-ə́m 'I send'   *kīyan-ū́*
  a-nēr-í 'you (s) send' *kīyān-í*

(134) Kurdish   Gorani
     hát-īn 'we came' āmá-ymē

The stress patterns of JSNENA direct suffixes replicate this. The direct suffixes are stressed when attached to the present stem and unstressed when attached to the past stem. The only exception is the 1sg.m present, in which the stress occurs on the verbal base rather than the suffix. This seems to be because the rule of stressing the suffixes is outranked by a rule that the stress should occur in a syllable containing a consonant of the verbal root. This explains also why the stress remains on the first syllable of the bisyllabic 2pl suffix -ētun:

(135) JSNENA–Present
      3sg.m garáš   'I pull'
      3pl   garš-í   'they pull'
      2sg.m garš-ét   'you (sg.m) pull'
      2pl   garš-étun   'you (pl) pull'
      1sg.m garáš-na   'I (m) pull'

(136) JSNENA–Past
      3sg.m smíx   'he stood'
      3pl   smíx-ī   'they stood'
      2sg.m smíx-ēt   'you (sg) stood'
      2pl   smíx-ētun   'you (pl) stood'
      1sg.m smíx-na   'I stood'

The JSNENA direct suffixes on the past stem were not historically enclitic copulas, unlike the Iranian suffixes on past verbs. The JSNENA direct suffixes however, are matched synchronically with the suffixes of the Iranian past verb, which are now identical with the suffixes of the Iranian present verb, and the Iranian stress patterns are replicated.

2.4.4 Copula

In JSNENA the present and past copulas (§4.8.1, §4.8.2) are clitics that are not stressed. They are attached at the end of a host word and the stress remains in the normal position of the host word, e.g.

(137) JSNENA
    naxóš 'ill'   *naxóš=yē*   'he is ill'
                    naxóš=yēna 'I (sg.m) am ill'
                    naxóš=yētun 'you (pl) are ill'
                    naxóš=yēlē 'he was ill'
                    naxóš=yēlī 'I was ill'
                    naxóš=yēlaxun 'you (pl) were ill'

This matches the stress pattern of present and past copulas in Iranian, which are not stress-bearing. Gorani adjectives inflect for gender and number, like nominals. Their stress pattern is not completely predictable (see above).

(138) Kurdish and Gorani
    G. *nawaš* (m.); K. *naxwaš* 'ill'
    nawáš=nā   'I am ill'   *naxwáš=əm*
    nawáša=nī   'You are ill' *naxwáš=ī*
    nawášē=nmē 'We are ill'   *naxwáš=ī*
    nawáš b-ḗn-ē 'I was ill'   *naxwáš=ū=m*
    nawáša b-ḗn-ī 'You were ill' *naxwáš=ū=y*
    nawášē b-ḗn-mē 'We were ill' *naxwáš=ū=yn*

2.4.5 Clitic additive particle

The additive particle *=ač* is a clitic in JSNENA. As with the copula, it is not stressed and when it is attached at the end of a host word, the stress remains in the normal position of the host word, e.g.

(139) JSNENA
    a. *'áy=ač*   'and he' (A:105)
        he=also
    b. *xét=ač*   'also other' (A:50)
        other=also

The inclusive particle in Kurdish and Gorani of the Sanandaj region likewise is not stress-bearing.

(140) Kurdish and Gorani
G. *ā́ đ=īč*   'and her'
G./K. *mə́n=īč*   'me too'
K. *bā́wk=īč=əm*   'my father too'

2.5 Summary

The sounds listed in Table 2 occur predominantly in Iranian loanwords in JSNENA. These sounds do not usually make their way into the JSNENA lexicon, which indicates that they are not productive.

Table 2: Phonological loans from Iranian in JSNENA.

feature attested in JSNENA	section
/č/ [tʃʰ]	§2.2.1
/f/ [f]	§2.2.1
/j/ [dʒ]	§2.2.1
/ř/ [r]	§2.2.1
/ž/ [ʒ]	§2.2.1
/ġ/ [ʁ]	§2.2.1

Table 3: Phonological loans in Gorani and Kurdish through contact with Semitic.

feature attested in Gorani and Kurdish	section
emphatic /ṣ/ and /ṭ/	§2.2.2.2
emphatic /ḷ/	§2.2.2.3
emphatic /ṛ/	§2.2.2.3
emphatic /ḥ/	§2.2.2.5

Table 4: Phonological changes in JSNENA triggered through contact with Gorani, Kurdish or Persian.

feature attested in JSNENA	section
dephonemicisation of pharyngealisation	§2.2.2.2
phonemicisation of phonetic [lˤ] /ḷ/	§2.2.2.3
phonemicisation of phonetic [rˤ] /ṛ/	§2.2.2.4
the segmentalisation of flat resonance	§2.2.2.5
change in the original voicing of the pharyngeal	§2.2.2.5
metathesis of word-final pharyngeals	§2.2.2.5

Table 4 (continued)

feature attested in JSNENA	section
The loss of consonant gemination	§2.2.2.12
Direct suffixes are not stressed in past-stem verbs	§2.4.3
Lenition of /q/ to a fricative [x], [ʁ], [χ]	§2.2.10
Three-way contrast of the rhotics	§2.2.2.4
The shift of word-initial /ʕ/ to /h/	§2.2.2.6

Table 5: Features exhibiting different convergence patterns with contact languages.

feature attested in JSNENA	type of convergence with contact languages		section
	Gorani	Kurdish	
vowel inventory	total	partial	§2.3
lenition of post-vocalic /d/	partial	partial	§2.2.2.7
Realisation of /w/ as a labio-dental [v]	total	not relevant	§2.2.2.8
The loss of consonant gemination	partial	total	§2.2.2.12
The quality of vowels	higher	lower	§2.3.1
final word-stress of nominals	partial	total	§2.4.1

3 The morphology of pronouns

3.1 Introductory overview

This chapter discusses independent personal pronouns, demonstrative pronouns and pronominal suffixes. JSNENA independent personal pronouns exhibit innovations in relation to earlier Aramaic in a number of features. Innovative oblique case inflection has developed in the 3rd person forms, which matches the oblique case inflection of 3rd person Gorani pronouns. JSNENA 3rd person pronouns have lost gender distinction. This matches the pronominal system of Kurdish. Gorani has retained gender distinction in the 3rd person pronouns.

The JSNENA demonstrative pronouns have undergone change by matching the morphological patterns of Gorani and Kurdish pronouns.

JSNENA and NENA dialects in general retain the inherited possessive pronominal suffixes on nouns and prepositions. NENA replicates the pattern of Iranian oblique clitic pronouns only in their function of verbal arguments. This reflects greater convergence of NENA with Iranian in verbal morphosyntax than in nominal morphosyntax. JSNENA independent oblique pronouns match the functions of Gorani 3rd person oblique pronouns, including possessor, complement of prepositions and direct object of present stem verbal forms. The last function (direct object) has not been documented elsewhere in NENA outside of JSNENA. A notable point of difference of JSNENA from Gorani is the expression of the agent of past transitive verbs. The use of the independent oblique third person pronoun to express the agent of past verbs in Gorani is not replicated in JSNENA, which only uses oblique verbal suffixes.

3.2 Independent pronouns

In JSNENA the independent pronouns are as follows, see Table 6. See §3.6 below for the so-called oblique forms of these pronouns.

Table 6: Independent direct pronouns in JSNENA.

3SG	'o
3PL	'oni
2SG	'āt
2PL	'axtū
1SG	'āna
1PL	'axnī

The third person pronouns are anaphoric pronouns that signal that the referent is identifiable in the discourse context or speech situation. The first and second person pronouns point to the participants in a speech situation (real or virtual).

There is no gender distinction in any of the pronouns. Lack of gender distinction is a regular feature of plural pronouns and the 1sg pronoun across NENA. Lack of gender distinction in the 2sg pronoun is also widespread across NENA. Dialects that distinguish between 2sg.m and 2sg.f independent pronouns are found mostly (though not exclusively) on the western periphery of the NENA area, represented in Table 7. The distinction appears to be a secondary innovation by analogy with 2sg.m and 2sg.f verbal suffixes, e.g.

Table 7: Gender distinction in 2sg pronouns across NENA.

	Ch. Qaraqosh	Ch. Baṭnaya		
2SG.M	ʼāhət	ʼāyət	< *ʼāt	cf. verbal direct suffix -ət
2SG.F	ʼāhat	ʼāyat	< *ʼāt	cf. verbal direct suffix -at

A distinctive feature of the Jewish trans-Zab dialects is their loss of gender differentiation in the 3sg pronoun, whereby the original 3sg.m pronoun ʼo (< *ʼahu) now has common gender (Mutzafi 2008b, 417–18). Most other NENA dialects distinguish between 3sg.m and 3sg.f, as shown in Table 8:

Table 8: Gender distinction in 3sg pronouns across NENA.

	Ch. Qaraqosh	Ch. Barwar	Ch. Shaqlawa	Trans-Zab
3SG.M	ʼāhu	ʼaw	ʼāwa	ʼo
3SG.F	ʼāhi	ʼay	ʼāya	ʼo

In some traditional literary texts in trans-Zab NENA dialects a separate 3sg.f pronoun is attested, e.g. ʼāhi and ʼāhən in J. Urmi, ʼāhi in J. Saqəz, ʼay in J. Koy Sanjak (Mutzafi 2008b, 418), ʼay in J. Ruwanduz (Rees 2008, 19). These texts are mainly written forms of oral traditions of Bible translations, which preserve an earlier form of the dialects. This indicates that the loss of the gender distinction of 3rd person singular pronouns is a relatively recent innovation.

The form of the 3pl pronoun in JSNENA ʼoni is common to trans-Zab. The initial syllable ʼo- appears to have developed by analogy with the singular form ʼo. The original form is likely to have been ʼāni, which is a form of the 3pl pronoun that is widespread in NENA.

In JSNENA the 3rd person pronoun has both a direct and an oblique form, the latter being used to express syntactic dependency, see Table 9:

Table 9: Third person pronouns in JSNENA.

	Direct	Oblique
3SG	ʾo	do
3PL	ʾoni	doni

The oblique form of the pronouns has been formed historically by bonding the subordinating particle *d* to the direct form of the pronoun.[1] This is widely attested in NENA in the central and eastern sectors of the dialect area. The oblique forms of the first and second person pronouns are supplied in JSNENA by another pronominal paradigm consisting of the stem *dīd-* and possessive suffixes, see Table 10:

Table 10: 1st and 2nd independent pronouns in JSNENA.

	Direct	Oblique
2SG.M	ʾāt	dīdox
2SG.F	ʾāt	dīdax
2PL	ʾaxtū	dīdaxun
1SG	ʾana	dīdī
1PL	ʾaxnī	dīdan, dīdanī

This pronominal oblique particle paradigm is found across the NENA region (with some phonetic variations, e.g. *dīð-*, *dīy-*) and is a feature inherited from earlier Aramaic. It is found in some dialects, such as those on the Mosul plain that do not have an oblique form of the independent third person pronoun (exemplified below by Ch. Qaraqosh), see Table 11. JSNENA and the NENA dialects of the immediately surrounding region differ from other NENA dialects in that they do not use the *dīd-* paradigm in the third person. Many of the dialects that have oblique forms of the third person pronouns consisting of *d* + direct pronoun also have a full paradigm of the pronominal oblique particle in all persons (exemplified below by Ch. Barwar):

In JSNENA the innovative oblique pronominal forms *do* and *donī* have suppressed the inherited third person oblique particle forms and have, in effect, become suppletive forms in the oblique particle paradigm, see Table 12. This suppletion is found in the Jewish trans-Zab dialects of the neighbouring area, e.g. J. Sulemaniyya (Khan 2004) and J. Saqez (Yisraeli 1998). It is also found in the Christian dialects of Sanandaj and Sulemaniyya, as shown in Table 13:

---

[1] See Khan (2016, vol. 1, 215–216) and Ariel (2018) for the historical process of its formation.

Table 11: Independent pronouns in NENA.

	Ch. Qaraqosh		Ch. Barwar		
	Direct	Oblique	Direct	Oblique	Oblique
3SG.M	'āhū	dīdəḥ	'aw	daw	dīyē
3SG.F	'āhī	dīdəḥ	'ay	day	dīya
3PL	'anhən	dədhən	'ani	dani	dīyē
2SG.M	'āhat	dīdux	'ātī	—	dīyux
2SG.F	'āhat	dīdax	'ātī	—	dīyəx
2PL	'axtun	dədxun	'axtū	—	dīyēxū
1SG	'āna	dīdī	'āna	—	dīyī
1PL	'axnī	dīdan	'axnī	—	dīyən

Table 12: Independent direct and oblique pronouns in JSNENA.

	Direct	Oblique
3SG	'o	do
3PL	'onī	donī
2SG.M	'āt	dīdox
2SG.F	'āt	dīdax
2PL	'axtū	dīdaxun
1SG	'āna	dīdī
1PL	'axnī	dīdan, dīdanī

Table 13: Independent direct and oblique pronouns in Ch. Sulemaniyya.

	Direct	Oblique
3SG.M	'āwa	dāwa
3SG.F	'oya	doya
3PL	'onī	donī
2SG.M	'āyət	dīyox
2SG.F	'āyat	dīyax
2PL	'axnoxən	dīyoxən
1SG	'āna	dīyī
1PL	'axnan	diyan

As shown in Table 14, in Gorani of the Sanandaj region the third person pronouns inflect for case, distinguishing between direct and oblique forms. The third person singular forms, moreover, inflect for gender, distinguishing masculine and feminine forms. The first and second person pronouns are unmarked morphologically for case and are used in both direct and oblique syntactic contexts. They are also unmarked for gender. In the Kurdish of Sanandaj, all the pronouns are unmarked morphologically for case and are used in both direct and oblique syntactic contexts. All the Kurdish pronouns, moreover are unmarked for gender.

Table 14: Independent pronouns in Kurdish and Gorani.

	Gorani		Kurdish
	Direct	Oblique	
3SG.M	āđ	āđī	aw
3SG.F	āđa	āđē	
3PL	āđē	āđīšā	awān
2SG		to	to
2PL	šəma, ašma		ēwa
1SG	mən		mən
1PL	ēma		ēma

The case inflection of JSNENA third person pronouns matches, therefore, the morphology of Gorani rather than that of Kurdish. The emergence of innovative oblique third person pronouns in NENA dialects further north in the region of Kurmanji Kurdish can be explained by the fact that Kurmanji has case distinctions in third person pronouns. Moreover, in upper Sorani Kurdish dialects, e.g. Mukri, Shaqlawa, Erbil, a 3sg oblique form *awī/ wī* occurs. It is unmarked for gender and corresponds to the 3sg oblique masculine form in Bahdini Kurmanji. In lower Sorani Kurdish (e.g. Sanandaj, Sulemaniyya), however, there is no case distinction, so the existence of the oblique forms in JSNENA must be due to contact with Gorani rather than Kurdish.

Moreover, the existence of gender distinction in third person singular pronouns in the Jewish trans-Zab NENA dialects at an earlier period would match the gender distinction in the morphology of Gorani. It is likely that the loss of gender distinction in third person pronouns in JSNENA and the rest of trans-Zab NENA was the result of the language shift from Gorani to Sorani Kurdish. The lack of gender morphological distinction in pronouns matches the morphology of Kurdish.

The generalisation of the original NENA 3sg.m pronoun *'o* (< **'aw* < **'āhū*) to a common gender, suppressing the 3sg.f pronoun *'ay* (< **'āhī*), may have been facilitated by the morphological shape of the Kurdish 3sg pronoun *aw*. It is relevant to point out that the corresponding pronoun in the Turkic languages of the region is common gender and has the form *o* (Bulut 2018), which is an even closer match to the NENA pronoun. Furthermore in documented forms of Gorani spoken in Iraq, the remote deixis pronoun has a *ū* vowel rather than an *ā* vowel, e.g. Bājalānī: *ūna* (independent), *ū . . . a* (attributive) (MacKenzie 1956, 421).

The development in JSNENA, and generally in Jewish trans-Zab dialects, of the 3pl pronoun *'*ānī* > '*onī*, in which the first syllable is levelled with that of the 3sg form '*o*, is likely to have been facilitated by the pattern of the paradigm of the third person pronouns in the Iranian languages, in which the singular and plural forms share the same initial syllable. This is, therefore, a case of paradigm pattern matching.

As remarked, in JSNENA and the immediately neighbouring NENA dialects the inherited *dīd-* oblique paradigm is supplanted by the innovative oblique independent third person pronouns. This can be regarded as a reflection of a greater degree of convergence with the Iranian contact languages than is the case with dialects such as Ch. Barwar in which the full *dīd-* paradigm is maintained alongside the innovative oblique independent third person pronouns. In JSNENA the *dīd-* oblique paradigm is retained in the first and second persons, although the first and second person pronouns in both Gorani and Kurdish of the region have no case distinction. The maintenance of a complete oblique paradigm was probably facilitated by the existence of oblique pronouns in the third person. It is significant that in the Jewish NENA dialect of Kerend, which was spoken further south, the *dīd-* paradigm has been lost and independent first and unmarked second person pronouns are used in both direct and oblique syntactic contexts, see Table 15. Moreover the oblique third person pronouns alternate with morphologically unmarked independent pronouns in oblique syntactic contexts.

Table 15: Independent pronouns in JSNENA and J. Kerend, compared.

	JSNENA		J. Kerend NENA	
	Direct	Oblique	Direct	Oblique
3SG	'*o*	*bēla do* 'his house (lit. house of him)'	'*o*	*bēla do* ~ *bēla* '*o*
3PL	'*onī*	*bēla donī* 'their house'	'*onī*	*bēla donī* ~ *bēla* '*onī*
2SG.M	'*āt*	*bēla dīdox* 'your (sg.m) house'	'*āt*	*bēla* '*āt*
2SG.F	'*ā*	*bēla dīdax* 'your (sg.f) house'	'*āt*	*bēla* '*āt*
2PL	'*axtū*	*bēla dīdaxun* 'your (pl) house'	'*axtu*	*bēla* '*axtū*
1SG	'*āna*	*bēla didi* 'my house'	'*ana*	*bēla* '*ana*
1PL	'*axnī*	*bēla didan* 'our house'	'*axni*	*bēla* '*axni*

This represents an even greater convergence to the Iranian paradigm than is the case with JSNENA. It has been facilitated by the fact that the oblique third person pronouns are in the process of decay, probably due to the fact that Gorani, which makes case distinctions, has had less impact on the J. Kerend dialect.

3.3 Demonstrative pronouns

3.3.1 Independent proximate deixis pronouns

In JSNENA there are three sets of independent proximate deixis demonstrative pronouns, see Table 16. All may function either as deictic pronouns or anaphoric pronouns. When used with a deictic function, they point to a visible referent in the speech situation near to the interlocutors. They are used anaphorically when the speaker assumes that the hearer is able to identify the referent in question near to the interlocutors in the speech situation. They are also used anaphorically to refer to a referent in the preceding discourse that is subjectively near due to its being a salient referent in the discourse (§6.4.2).

Sets 2 and 3 contain the augment elements -*a* and -*xa*, respectively. These suffixed augment elements are unstressed in all cases except the plural form of set 3. All of these demonstrative forms in JSNENA can form an oblique form by adding the prefix *d*:

Table 16: Independent proximate deixis pronouns in JSNENA.

	Set 1		Set 2		Set 3	
	Direct	Oblique	Direct	Oblique	Direct	Oblique
SG.M	ʾay, ʾē	day, dē	ʾéa	déa	ʾéxa	déxa
SG.F	ʾay, ʾē	day, dē	ʾéa	déa	ʾéxa	déxa
PL	ʾayní, ʾənyé	dayní, dənyé		ʾənyaxáē	dənyēxáē	

The singular forms in set 1 originate historically from two deictic elements **hā* + **ī*. It is possible that this goes back originally to **hā* + **ðī*. The element **ðī* is an inherited Aramaic sg.f deictic element that is preserved in archaising NENA dialects such as Ch. Qaraqosh *ʾāða* 'this (sg.m)', *ʾāðī* 'this (sg.f)'. These correspond to earlier Aramaic demonstrative forms *hāðā* (sg.m < *hā-dnā*) and *hāðī* (sg.f). The sg.f form would have become common gender; cf. Ch. Alqosh *ʾāðī* (cs), Ch. Ankawa *ʾāðī* (cs). In Ch. Alqosh, indeed, *ʾāðī* alternates with the form *ʾāy*, in which the /ð/ has been contracted.

The diphthong /ay/ of the singular JSNENA forms is contracted to /e/ by some speakers. The first syllable of the plural form *ʾaynī* is likely to have developed by analogy with the singular forms. The -*nī* reflects the original form of the demonstrative **ʾānī*, which is still used as a plural proximate deixis pronoun in the Christian dialects of Sanandaj and Sulemaniyya, and in other NENA dialects, especially in the western sector of NENA, e.g. J. Zakho, Ch. Baṭnaya, Ch. Karamlesh, Ch. Alqosh, Ch. Telkepe, Ch. Tisqopa, Ch. Ankawa, Ch. Bohtan. The alternative plural form 'ənyē has a nominal plural ending -ē. This is likely to have developed from the addition of -ē to the form *'ānī. J. Sulemaniyya has the form 'anyē. The original *a in the form 'ənyē has undergone centralisation.

The augment suffix in set 2 -a is a deictic particle with the original form *-hā. The form 'ēa, therefore, has developed from *hā-ī-hā. Some NENA dialects have proximate demonstratives that are formed from the combination *ī +*hā without the initial *hā, resulting in forms such as 'īya < (J. Barzan, J. Challa), 'iyya (J. Arbel, J. Koy Sanjak, J. Nerwa, Ch. Sanandaj), ya (J. Rustaqa, J. Ruwanduz, J. Urmi).

The augment -xa is the cardinal numeral 'one'. So, 'ēxa would mean 'this one'. The plural form 'ənyēxāē would be 'these ones' with the nominal plural ending.

As seen in Table 17, in Gorani of the Sanandaj region proximate demonstrative pronouns are inflected for gender and case and occur in three sets. As far as we can establish, these are used only as deictic pronouns:

Table 17: Independent proximate deixis pronouns in Gorani.

	Set 1		Set 2		Set 3	
	Direct	Oblique	Direct	Oblique	Direct	Oblique
SG.M	īna	īnay	ī dāna	ī dānay	a īna	a īnay
SG.F	īnē	īnē	ī dānē	ī dānē	a īnē	a īnē
PL	īnē	īnā, īnīšā	ī dānē	ī dānā	a īnē	a īnā

In addition to these proximate deictic independent pronouns, Gorani also has a set of proximate anaphoric pronouns, see Table 18.

Table 18: Proximate anaphoric pronouns in Gorani.

	Proximate Anaphoric	
	Direct	Oblique
SG.M	īd	īdī
SG.F	īda	īdē
PL	īdē	īdīšā

This anaphoric set is used to refer to a referent in the preceding discourse that is subjectively near due to its being a salient referent in the discourse (§6.4.2).

Set 1 and set 2 of the Gorani deictic forms match closely the morphological patterns of the JSNENA sets 2 (*'ēa*) and 3 (*'ēxa*). Set 1 in Gorani and and set 2 in JSNENA have an augment suffix with the form *a*. The classifier element *dāna* in Gorani set 2 matches the cardinal numeral *xa* in JSNENA set 3. Indeed in JSNENA this Iranian classifier element is often combined with the numeral 'one' in the phrase *xa dāna* 'one single' (Khan 2009, 232). According to some informants, moreover, in Gorani the classifier can be replaced by cardinal *yo* 'one', e.g. *ī yo* 'this one (m); *ī yoa* this one (f)'. The structural correspondences of the cs. (JSNENA) and sg.m (Gorani) singular forms can be summarised as follows, see Table 19 (a hyphen separates the stem of the demonstrative from the augment):

Table 19: The structural correspondence of proximate anaphoric pronouns in JSNENA and Gorani.

JSNENA	Gorani
'ay/'ē (cs.)	*īd* (sg.m)
'ē-a (cs.)	*īn-ā* (sg.m)
'ē-xa (cs.)	*ī-dāna/ī-yo* (sg.m)

The form *īna* in Gorani set 1 contains the vocalic elements /i/ and /a/, i.e. the vocalic melody *i–a*, which corresponds phonetically to the near form *'iyya* that is found in Ch. Sanandaj and several Jewish trans-Zab dialects in Iraq (e.g. J. Arbel, J. Koy Sanjak). The attributive adnominal form of the Gorani demonstrative is the discontinuous form *ī* NP *a* (§3.4). As remarked above, the components of the NENA form *'iyya* are in origin inherited Aramaic demonstrative elements. They have converged, however, in their phonetic form and ordering with the Gorani forms.

The case inflection of the JSNENA forms matches the Gorani distinction between direct and oblique forms.

The Gorani demonstratives distinguish between masculine and feminine gender, whereas this gender distinction is absent in JSNENA.

As represented in Table 20, in the Kurdish of Sanandaj, independent proximate pronouns occur in five sets. Sets 2–5 have augments to the basic form of set 1. The element *-ak* in set 3 (*am-ak-a*) is a shortened form of the cardinal numeral *yak* 'one'. Sets 1–3 can be used as deictic or anaphoric pronouns, though the basic form in set 1 is generally used as an anaphoric pronoun. The pattern of these three sets corresponds closely to the JSNENA sets 1–3 of proximate pronouns, in that in both languages set 2 has the augment suffix *-a* and set 3 has an augment of the cardinal numeral 'one'.

Sets 4 and 5 with the added attention drawing elements *ā* and *hā* respectively are used only as deictic pronouns:

Table 20: Independent proximate deictic pronoun in Kurdish.

	Set 1	Set 2	Set 3	Set 4	Set 5
SG	am	ama	amaka	ā ama	ama hā
PL	amān	amāna	amakān	ā amāna	amāna hā

There is no inflection for case or gender in the Kurdish demonstratives. The lack of gender distinction in JSNENA is likely to be due to convergence with the Kurdish demonstrative system. It is significant, however, that JSNENA has not lost the inflection for case, which it shares with Gorani. The structural parallels between the JSNENA and Kurdish sets of pronouns are summarised in Table 21:

Table 21: Independent proximate deixis pronoun in JSNENA and Kurdish compared.

JSNENA	Kurdish
'ay/'ē	am
'ē-a	am-a
'ē-xa	am-aka

3.3.2 Independent remote pronouns

JSNENA has three sets of remote pronouns (see Table 22), which correspond to the sets of near pronouns. Although three sets can be used with a deictic function, pointing to a visible referent far from the interlocutors, or with an anaphoric function (§6.4.1 & §6.4.2). Set 1 is the basic form and sets 2 and 3 have the augments -*a* and -*xa* (derived from the cardinal numeral 'one') respectively.

These three sets of pronouns inflect for case and include both direct and oblique forms.

Table 22: Independent remote pronouns in JSNENA.

	Set 1		Set 2		Set 3	
	Direct	Oblique	Direct	Oblique	Direct	Oblique
SG	'o	do	'óa	dóa	'óxa	dóxa
PL	'ónī	dónī	'onyḗ	donyḗ	'onyēxā́ē	donyēxā́ē

Set 1 are the basic forms of the pronoun, which were presented in §3.2 as the basic third person independent pronouns (corresponding to English 'he/him', 'she/her', 'they/them'). The morphologically augmented sets 2 and 3, however, can also be used anaphorically and in such cases correspond to English third person pronouns.

The form 'o is derived historically from the elements *hā-hū. The reflex of this historical form in some NENA dialects is 'āhu (e.g. Ch. Qaraqosh, Ch. Bāz Maha Xtaya, Ch. Dīz, Ch. Hertevin, J. Amedia). In some dialects this contracts to 'āwu (e.g. Ch. Arbuš, Ch. Sarspido, Ch. Telkepe, Ch. Txuma Gudəkθa, Ch. Txuma Mazṛa, Ch. Walto). A common further contraction is to 'āw or 'aw, which is found in numerous dialects. The form 'o, which is common to the Jewish NENA dialects, is a further contraction of 'āw/'aw.

In dialects that have the reflexes 'āhu, 'āwu, 'āw/'aw, these forms serve as anaphoric pronouns but not remote deictic pronouns. These dialects typically have, therefore, at least two deictic groups of demonstratives (proximate and remote) in addition to a group of anaphoric pronouns, all three sets being morphologically distinct. In the Jewish trans-Zab dialects and also the Christian dialects on the south-eastern periphery of NENA, such as Ch. Sanandaj and Ch. Sulemaniyya, all the remote pronouns can be used with an anaphoric or a deictic function.

The plural form in set 2 'onyē has been formed from the form 'oni by the addition of the nominal plural -e. It is possible that this was facilitated by the interpretation of the -a element in the singular form 'oa as the singular nominal inflection -a, e.g. goz-a (s) 'walnut', goz-ē (pl) 'walnuts'.

The demonstrative systems of Gorani and Kurdish include a remote group.

As shown in Table 23, in Gorani the remote pronoun set parallels the proximate deixis set in that it includes three sets, set 2 being augmented by the suffixed element dāna and set 3 by the prefixed element a. The pronouns are inflected for case and gender:

Table 23: Independent remote deixis pronouns in Gorani.

	Set 1		Set 2		Set 3	
	Direct	Oblique	Direct	Oblique	Direct	Oblique
SG.M	āna	ānay	ā dāna	ā dānay	a āna	a ānay
SG.F	ānē	ānē	ā dānē	ā dānē	a ānē	a ānē
PL	ānē	ānā, ānīšā	ā dānē	ā dānā	a ānē	a ānā

According to some informants, the classifier element can be replaced by the cardinal numeral yo 'one', e.g. ā yo 'that one (sg.m)'; ā yoa 'that one' (sg.f). These forms are now seemingly being replaced by the heavier form dāna.

In addition, as seen in Table 24, Gorani has a set of anaphoric pronouns which are differentiated from the third person independent pronouns presented in (§3.2):

Table 24: Additional deictic pronouns in Gorani.

	Direct	Oblique
SG.M	aw	awī
SG.F	awa	awē
PL	(awē), awēšā	awīšā

This set, with the basic form *aw* without a vocalic ending, could be seen as the equivalent to JSNENA *'o*, which is morphologically basic and generally functions as an anaphoric pronoun. Gorani sets 1 and 2, would correspond structurally to JSNENA *'oa* (set 2) and *'oxa* (set 3) respectively. The structural parallels between the JSNENA sg.c and Gorani sg.m forms are shown in Table 25 (a hyphen separates the stem of the demonstrative from the augment):

Table 25: The structural correspondence of remote anaphoric pronouns in JSNENA and Gorani.

JSNENA	Gorani
'o	aw
'o-a	ān-a
'o-xa	ā-dāna

The case inflection of the JSNENA remote pronouns match the case inflection of this group in Gorani. Although there are structural parallels with the various sets of pronouns between JSNENA and Gorani, there is no clear phonetic resemblance.

In the Kurdish of Sanandaj, there are five sets of remote independent pronouns (cf. Table 26), as in the near pronoun group. Sets 2–5 have augments to the basic form of set 1. The element *-ak* in set 3 (*awaka* < *aw-ak-a*) is a shortened form of the cardinal numeral *yak* 'one'. Sets 1–3 can be used as deictic or anaphoric pronouns, though the basic form in set 1 is normally used with anaphoric rather than deictic function. The pattern of these three sets corresponds closely to the JSNENA sets 1–3 of remote pronouns, in that in both languages set 2 has the augment suffix *-a* and set 3 has an augment of the cardinal numeral 'one'. Sets 4–6 with the added attention drawing elements *ā* and *hā* respectively are used only as deictic pronouns:

The pronouns are not inflected for case or gender:

The lack of gender distinction in JSNENA remote deixis pronouns matches the lack of gender distinction in Kurdish. The first three sets of Kurdish pronouns are structurally parallel to the JSNENA forms, as shown in Table 27.

Table 26: Independent remote deixis pronouns in Kurdish.

	Set 1	Set 2	Set 3	Set 4	Set 5	Set 6
SG	aw	awa	awaka	ā awa	awa hā	ā awa hā
PL	awān	awāna	awakān	ā awāna	awāna hā	ā awāna hā

Table 27: The structural correspondence of remote anaphoric pronouns in JSNENA and Kurdish.

JSNENA	Kurdish
'o	aw
'o-a	aw-a
'o-xa	aw-aka

3.4 Attributive demonstrative pronouns

In JSNENA the short form of the proximate pronoun *'ay* (contracted optionally to *'e*) is used when the pronoun is attributive, i.e. combined with a nominal, and this is generalised also to plural nouns. As demonstrated in Table 28, it occurs in a direct form and an oblique form with prefixed *d-*:

Table 28: Attributive proximate demonstrative pronouns in JSNENA.

	Direct	Oblique
SG.M	'ay, 'ē	day, dē
SG.F	'ay, 'ē	day, dē
PL	'ay, 'ē	day, dē

Examples:

(141) JSNENA
   'ay gora 'this man'
   'ay baxta 'this woman'
   'ay nāšē 'these people'
   'ay 'ənšē 'these women'
   bēla day gora 'the house of this man'
   bēla day baxta 'the house of this woman

When the remote pronoun is used attributively, it has the short form *'o* with both singular and plural nouns. It occurs in a direct form and an oblique form with prefixed *d-*, see Table 29:

Table 29: Attributive remote demonstrative pronouns in JSNENA.

	Direct	Oblique
SG.M	*'o*	*do*
SG.F	*'o*	*do*
PL	*'o*	*do*

Examples:

(142) JSNENA
  'o gora 'that man'
  'o baxta 'that woman'
  'o našē 'those people'
  'o ənšē 'those women'
  bēla do gora 'the house of that man'
  bēla do baxta 'the house of that woman'

These JSNENA near and remote pronouns can be used as deictics, pointing to a referent in the speech situation, or as anaphoric pronouns, signalling that the referent is identifiable in the context (§6.4.1 & §6.4.2).

In Gorani attributive demonstrative pronouns are discontinuous, as represented in Table 30 and Table 31. They consist of the vowels of the independent set 1 forms on both sides of the noun. The initial vowel of the independent form is placed before the noun and the final vowel, which expresses number, gender and case inflection, is placed after the noun. Only the plural form exhibits inflection for case. The augments of the longer form are not used:

Gorani

Table 30: Attributive proximate demonstrative pronouns in Gorani.

SG.M	*ī... a*
SG.F	*ī... ē*
PL	*ī... ē* (direct), *ī... ā* (oblique)

Table 31: Attributive remote demonstrative pronouns in Gorani.

SG.M	ā ... a/ aw ..... (a)
SG.F	ā ... ē/ aw ...... (ē)
PL	ā ... ē (direct), ā ... ā (oblique)/ aw .... (ē) (direct), aw ..... (ā)

Examples:

(143) Gorani–Proximate Deixis
    SG.M   ī har(a)-á   'this donkey'
    SG.F   ī māhar-ḗ   'this she-ass'
    PL. DIR   ī har-ḗ   'these donkeys'
    PL. OBL   hanā=w ī har-ā́   'the owner of these donkeys'

(144) Gorani–Remote Deixis
    SG.M   ā har-á   'that donkey'
    SG.F   ā māhar-ḗ   'that she-ass'
    PL. DIR   ā har-ḗ   'those donkeys'
    PL. OBL   hanā=w ā har-ā́   'the owner of those donkeys'

When separated from the noun, the postposed demonstrative particle changes to the generalised form -á:

(145) Gorani
    ā kənāčē=m-á   'that daughter of mine'
    DEM daughter=MY-DEM
    ā kətēb-ē=m-á   'those books of mine'
    DEM book-PL.DIR=my-DEM

In the Takht variety of Gorani, the demonstrative particle is deleted after a noun in the oblique case:

(146) Gorani
    ī har-ī   'this donkey'
    DEM donkey-OBL

The Gorani attributive demonstrative pronouns can be used with both a deictic function and an anaphoric function.

In the Kurdish of Sanandaj, the attributive demonstratives are also discontinuous, see Table 32 and Table 33. These are based either on the simplex set 1 forms, as is the case in Gorani, or on the more complex forms with postposed elements containing an augment. The full number of complex augments that appear in the independent pronouns, however, are not used in the attributive forms:

Table 32: Attributive proximate demonstrative pronouns in Kurdish.

	Simplex	Complex
SG	*am . . . a*	*am . . . ak-a*
PL	*am . . . gal-a*	—

Table 33: Attributive remote demonstrative pronouns in Kurdish.

	Simplex	Complex
SG	*aw . . . a*	*aw . . . ak-a*
PL	*aw . . . gal-a*	—

The remote attributive forms in Kurdish can also function as anaphoric pronouns.

The JSNENA paradigms of attributive demonstrative pronouns have been matched with the initial element of the Iranian attributive pronouns. This has resulted in the simplex singular form (*'ay*, *'o*) being generalised to the plural, since the number inflection in the Iranian pronouns is expressed by the postposed elements and, moreover, augments in Kurdish occur in the postposed elements. Evidently, matching with a single discrete morpheme was easier than matching with a complex discontinuous morpheme. This resulted in a partial convergence.

3.5 Pronominal suffixes on nouns and prepositions

NENA dialects have a paradigm of suffixes that are attached to nouns and prepositions, represented in Table 34. When attached to nouns, they function as possessive suffixes. When attached to prepositions, they express the pronominal complement of the preposition. The forms of these suffixes in JSNENA are as follows. In terms of stress placement they are treated as an integral part of the noun or preposition and stressed in accordance with the rule of word-final stress:

Table 34: JSNENA pronominal suffixes on nouns and prepositions.

3SG.M	-ēf
3SG.F	-af
3PL	-ū, -un
2SG.M	-ox
2SG.F	-ax
2PL	-axun
1SG	-ī
1PL	-an, -ani

These suffixes replace the final vowel of nouns and prepositions, as illustrated by the following, which presents the suffixed forms of the noun *bēla* 'house' and the preposition *bāqa* 'to, for':

(147) JSNENA

3SG.M	bēléf	'his house'	bāqéf	'to him'
3SG.F	bēláf	'her house'	bāqáf	'to her'
3PL	bēlú	'their house'	bāqú	'to them'
2SG.M	bēlóx	'your (sg.m) house'	bāqóx	'to you (sg.m)'
2SG.F	bēláx	'your (sg.f) house'	bāqáx	'to you (sg.f)'
2PL	bēlaxún	'your (pl) house'	bāqaxún	'to you (pl)'
1SG	bēlí	'my house'	bāqí	'to me'
1PL	bēlán	'our house'	bāqán	'to us'

For the sake of convenience these suffixes will be henceforth referred to as adnominal pronominal suffixes. Many prepositions, indeed, are in origin nouns.

As shown in Table 35, NENA dialects also have a paradigm of suffixes known as L-suffixes, which are historically prepositional phrases composed of the dative preposition *l-* and a prepositional suffix. These phrases have, however, now lost their compositionality. They are no longer interpreted as combinations of a preposition and the pronominal suffix paradigm, as in *bāq-ef* 'to-him' illustrated above. This is reflected by the fact that in many NENA dialects, including JSNENA, the third person singular forms of L-suffixes are more archaic than those of the adnominal paradigm of suffixes. The L-suffixes of JSNENA are as follows:

Table 35: L-suffixes in JSNENA.

3SG.M	-lē
3SG.F	-la
3PL	-lū, -lun
2SG.M	-lox
2SG.F	-lax
2PL	-laxun
1SG	-lī
1PL	-lan

The L-suffixes are added to verbal and existential forms to express a range of grammatical relations that include direct object (§4.10), recipient (§4.13), possessor (§4.9) and agent (§4.3). Unlike the adnominal suffixes, the L-suffixes are not stressed (§2.4.3).

In the Iranian languages of the region of Sanandaj, a single paradigm of pronominal elements covers the functional range of the JSNENA adnominal suffixes and the L-suffixes. These Iranian pronominal forms have the prosodic status of clitics and are not stressed. Historically, they are derived from the paradigms of oblique clitic pronouns in Old Iranian, which expressed the accusative, genitive, dative and agentive (Korn 2009). The paradigms of these clitics in the Kurdish and Gorani of Sanandaj are shown in Table 36:

Table 36: Pronominal person clitics in Kurdish and Gorani.

	Kurdish	Gorani
3SG	=ī	=š
3PL	=yān	=šā
2SG	=o, =t	=t, =ď
2PL	=tān	=tā
1SG	=m	=m
1PL	=mān	=mā

The Kurdish 2sg clitic has two alternative forms =o and =t, of which =o (=u in Sulemaniyya Kurdish) is the commoner. The form in =t, the most widespread in Central Kurdish, is derived from the Old Iranian genitive/dative -tai, while -o appears to be derived from an old Iranian accusative pronoun with the form *-θwā (Korn 2009, 163).

In the literature on the development of Iranian person clitics, it has been suggested that the use of oblique clitics as indexing objects and agents is an extension from the original general dative function of clitics, referred to as 'indirect participant' in Haig (2008, 112).

The NENA L-suffixes are replications of the Iranian oblique pronominal clitics. The fact that the L-suffixes were formed from the dative preposition *l-* indicates that NENA interpreted the basic function of the Iranian oblique clitics as dative.

The NENA L-suffixes have a clitic-like prosodic status, in that they are not stressed. They are, however, more prosodically bound to their verbal host than Iranian pronominal clitics, since, unlike the Iranian clitics, the NENA L-suffixes cannot be moved onto other clausal constituents. Moreover, in NENA dialects that have basic penultimate stress, i.e. Christian dialects and Jewish *līšāna dēnī* dialects, the attachment of L-suffixes affects the stress position, although they remain unstressed, e.g.

(148) Ch. Barwar
gárəš 'he pulls' *garə́š-lē* 'he pulls him'

This reflects a greater degree of integration into the word than would be expected of a clitic, which does not in principle affect the stress position in the host word. Since the basic position of stress in trans-Zab dialects such as JSNENA is word-final, this change of stress position does not occur:

(149) JSNENA
garə́š 'he pulls' *garə́š-lē* 'he pulls him'

Further details about the function and distribution of the NENA L-suffixes and Iranian pronominal clitics will be given in ensuing sections. On a more general level, however, the important observation is that NENA does not replicate the Iranian clitics in the full range of their functions. NENA retains the inherited adnominal possessive suffixes on nouns and prepositions. It replicates the Iranian clitics only in their function of verbal arguments. This reflects greater convergence of NENA with Iranian in verbal morphosyntax than in nominal morphosyntax.

The replication by NENA of the Iranian person clitics is linked to the convergence of the core inflectional patterns of the stems of NENA verbs with those of Iranian verbs (for more details see §4.3, §4.9, §4.11). This convergence through contact was no doubt facilitated by the greater number of inflectional variables across the stems of verbs than is the case in nouns. It was also motivated by the greater differences in core inflectional patterns in verbal stems (e.g. expression of Tense–Aspect–Mood) between earlier Aramaic and Iranian than was the case between the inflection patterns of nouns. Convergence brought closer the core inflectional patterns of the stems of verbs in Aramaic and Iranian and this brought with it by association a convergence in person markers on the periphery of verbal constructions. The key convergence was the use of participles for present and past stems in NENA that matched the present and past stems in Iranian. The past stem in Iranian was derived from the passive participle and the agent was an oblique pronoun or clitic in an ergative construction. This was matched by the passive particle and oblique L-suffix in NENA. The extension of the oblique L-suffix to the marking of objects of present stem verbs in NENA was a further convergence with Iranian that came by association with the convergence of the NENA present stem with the Iranian verbal system.

Nouns in Aramaic and Iranian have less inflectional variation than verbs and, probably due to this feature, they less readily underwent change and convergence, including in their systems of pronominal suffixes.

One possible case of convergence of NENA adnominal suffixes with Iranian clitics is the paradigm of reflexive pronouns. In JSNENA the paradigm is as follows:

(150) JSNENA
    3SG.M *nóšĕf* 'himself'
    3SG.F *nóšaf* 'herself'
    3PL *nóšū* 'themselves'
    2SG.M *nóšox* 'yourself (sg.m)'
    2SG.F *nóšax* 'yourself (sg.f)'
    2PL *nóšaxun* 'yourselves (pl)'
    1SG *nóšī* 'myself'
    1PL *nóšan* 'ourselves'

In this paradigm the suffixes are not stressed, unlike in other contexts. The items in the paradigm correspond prosodically, therefore, to the corresponding paradigm in the Iranian languages, which have unstressed clitics:

(151)   Gorani Kurdish
    3SG *wḗ=š* *xó=y* 'himself, herself'
    3PL *wḗ=šā* *xó=yān* 'themselves'
    2SG *wḗ=t* *xó=t* 'yourself (sg.m)'
    2PL *wḗ=tā* *xó=tān* 'yourselves (pl)'
    1SG *wḗ=m* *xó=m* 'myself'
    1PL *wḗ=mā* *xó=mān* 'ourselves'

Speakers of JSNENA evidently do not parse the reflexive phrases compositionally as consisting of a nominal stem *noš-* and a possessive suffix. Rather they have lost their compositionality and are perceived as unsegmentable items. This would have been facilitated by the fact that the stem *noš-* is not used in a nominal phrase without a suffix, i.e. there is no form **noša* in the synchronic state of the dialect. Likewise the

Iranian reflexive stems are not separable from the pronominal clitics. The JSNENA reflexive forms for each person have been matched with the corresponding lexical item in the Iranian languages and have undergone convergence with the Iranian forms by a replication of prosody.

3.6 Independent oblique pronouns

As indicated in §3.2, JSNENA has oblique inflections of third person independent anaphoric and deictic pronouns. These oblique independent pronouns serve the syntactic functions described below. The same functions are expressed by phrases consisting of the oblique particle *dīd-* + adnominal suffix in the first and second persons.

In Gorani of the Sanandaj region third person independent pronouns inflect for case and gender. The oblique third person pronouns appear in the functions listed below. Independent first and second person pronouns, which do not inflect for case, are used in the same position in these constructions.

In the Kurdish of Sanandaj none of the independent pronouns inflect for case.

(i) Possessor complement of a noun:

(152) JSNENA
    a. *bēla   do*
        house OBL.3SG
        'his house'
    b. *bēla   dīdī*
        house OBL.1SG
        'my house'
    c. *bēla   dīdox*
        house OBL.2SG.M
        'your (sg.m) house'

(153) Gorani
    a. *sawata=y   ādē*
        basket=EZ 3SG.f.obl
        'her basket'
    b. *'abd=ū   mən*
        servant=EZ 1SG
        'my servant'

3.6 Independent oblique pronouns

    c. *čī   dagā=w   ēma=nē*
       from.DEM.PROX village.OBL.SG=EZ 1PL= COP.3PL
       'They are from this villages of ours.'

(154) Kurdish
    a. *dāyk   aw*
       mother 3SG
       'his mother'
    b. *la   muḷk   mən*
       from property 1SG
       'from my property'
    c. *žən-aka=y   to*
       woman-DEF=EZ 2SG
       'your wife'

(ii) Complement of a preposition:

(155) JSNENA
    a. *bāqa do*
       to   OBL.3SG
       'to him'
    b. *bāqa dīdī*
       to   OBL.1SG
       'to me'
    c. *bāqa dīdox*
       to   OBL.2SG.M
       'to you (sg.m)'

(156) Gorani
    a. *p-āđī*
       to-3SG.OBL.M
       'to him.'
    b. *pay   mən*
       for   1SG
       'for me'
    c. *ba   to*
       to   2SG
       'to you.'

(157) Kurdish
    a. *ba*   *awàn=īč*   *ēž-əm*|
        to   3PL=ADD   IND.say.PRS-1SG
        'I say to them too'
    b. *kanīšk-aka=y*   *bo*   *mə̀n*   *māra*   *kərd*|
        girl-DEF=3SG   for   1SG   marriage   do.PST
        'He married his daughter to me.'
    c. *mən*   *čə̀t-ēg=əm*   *la*   *to*   *garak=a*|
        1SG   thing-INDF=1SG   from   2SG   necessary=COP.3SG
        'I want something from you.'

(iii) Direct object of a present stem verbal form

(158) JSNENA
    a. *do*   *garəš*
        OBL.3SG   pull.3SG.M
        'he pulls him'
    b. *dīdī*   *garəš*
        OBL.1SG   pull.3SG.M
        'he pulls me'
    c. *dīdox*   *garəš*
        OBL.2SG.M   pull.3SG.M
        'he pulls you (sg.m)'

(159) Gorani
    a. *mən*   *ādīšā*   *bar-ū*
        1SG   3PL.OBL   take.PRS-1SG
        'I (will) take them.'
    b. *mən*   *wīn-ī*
        1SG   see.PRS-2SG
        'You see me.'

(160) Kurdish
    a. *ēma*   *awān*   *nā-nās-īn*
        1PL   3PL   NEG-know.PRS-1PL
        'We don't know them'
    b. *ēwa*   *mən*   *nā-wa-n*
        2PL   1SG   NEG-take.PRS-2PL
        'You (pl) will not take me'

c. *ēma   to   a-wēn-īn*
   1PL   2SG   IND-see.PRS-1PL
   'We see you (sg)'

(iv) Agent of a past transitive construction

In Gorani the oblique independent third person pronoun is used to express the agent of past transitive verbs:

(161) Gorani
āđī=č   wāta-bē
3SG.OBL.M=ADD   say.PST.PTCP.M-COP.PST
'He had said.'

When the agent is a first or second person, this is expressed by an obligatory clitic and an independent pronoun is optional:

(162) Gorani
  a. *mən   na-zānā=m*
     1SG   neg-know.PST=1sg
     'I did not know.'
  b. *šəma   bard=tā*
     2PL   take.PST=2PL
     'You took'

In JSNENA oblique third person pronouns or phrases with the oblique particle *dīd-* are not used to express the agent. The agent is expressed by an oblique L-suffix and an independent pronoun is in the direct form:

(163) JSNENA
  a. *'o   grəš-lē*
     3SG.M   pull.PST-3SG.M.OBL
     'He pulled'
  b. *'āt   grəš-lox*
     2SG.M   pull.PST-2SG.M.OBL
     'You (sg.m) pulled'

In Kurdish the agent of past verbs is expressed by an oblique clitic. Independent pronouns are not inflected for case, so any independent pronoun occurring in the clause does not distinguish case:

(164) Kurdish
    a. *aw   hāwərd=ī*
       3SG   bring.PST=3SG
       'He brought (it)'
    b. *ēma   kaya=mān   a-kərd*
       1PL   play=1PL   IPFV-do.PST
       'We were playing'
    c. *to   na=w-wət*
       2SG NEG=2SG-say.PST
       'Didn't you say?'

In JSNENA the distribution of the oblique third person pronoun corresponds to that of the Gorani oblique third person pronoun in the functions of (i) possessor complement of a noun, (ii) complement of a preposition and (iii) direct object of a present stem verb. Functions (i) and (ii) of the NENA oblique third person pronoun are found across all the NENA dialects that have such oblique pronouns. The function of direct object (iii), however, has not been documented elsewhere in NENA outside of JSNENA. This represents, therefore, a greater convergence of the oblique pronoun with the morphosyntax of Iranian than has taken place in other NENA dialects. This convergence has taken place specifically with Gorani rather than Kurdish, since oblique independent pronouns do not occur in Sanandaj Kurdish. Most other NENA dialects with oblique pronouns can mark the pronoun as a direct object by a preceding preposition. This strategy, indeed, is available also in JSNENA, as an alternative to the use of the bare oblique pronoun:

(165) JSNENA
    həl-do   garəš   ~ do   garəš
    to-OBL.3SG.M pull.3SG.M   OBL.3SG.M pull.3SG.M
    'he pulls him'

The construction with the bare oblique pronoun has developed by eliding the preposition in the prepositional phrase *həl-do*. This has resulted in a closer replication of the Gorani construction with a bare oblique pronoun.

The inherited phrases containing the oblique particle *dīd-* are used in JSNENA to express the oblique first and second person, although there are no oblique equivalent first and second person forms in Gorani. The functions of the *dīd-* phrases include also the innovative function of direct object. This would have developed by analogy with the distribution of the oblique third person pronoun, which does have a direct match in Gorani.

The use of the independent oblique third person pronoun to express the agent of past verbs is not replicated in JSNENA. The reason is likely to be that agents of past verbs in JSNENA are obligatorily indexed by oblique L-suffixes on the verb. These L-suffixes are bonded to the verb and cannot be omitted or moved. When third person independent pronouns are used, these are in the direct case and they are cross-referenced by the oblique L-suffix, e.g.

(166) JSNENA
 'o graš-lē
 3SG.M pull.PST-OBL.3SG.M
 'He pulled'

This is, indeed, the pattern of constructions with independent pronouns that are not inflected for case in the Iranian languages, i.e. the first and second person pronouns in Gorani and all the pronouns in Kurdish. In Iranian the indexing of the agent by the oblique clitic in such cases is obligatory due to the lack of case inflection of the independent pronoun. In JSNENA there is a reverse causality, viz. the independent pronoun is in the direct case since the L-suffixes are obligatory.

3.7 Summary

Table 37: Pattern replication of morphological features of pronouns in JSNENA.

feature attested in JSNENA	Main Contact language	section
case inflection of third person pronouns	Gorani	§3.2
case inflection of deixis pronouns	Gorani	§3.3

Table 38: Pattern matching of morphological features of pronouns in NENA with contact languages.

feature attested in JSNENA	Main Contact language	section
3SG and 3PL pronouns share the same initial syllable	G. / K.	§3.2
The phonetic form of proximate deixis pronouns	Gorani	§3.3.1
The phonetic form of remote deixis pronouns	G./K.	§3.3.2
augment -a in deixis pronouns	G./K.	§3.3
Distribution of the oblique third person pronouns	Gorani	§3.6

Table 39: Morphological features of pronouns in JSNENA lost due to contact.

feature attested in JSNENA	contact language	section
loss of gender distinction of 3rd person singular pronoun	Kurdish	§3.2
loss of gender distinction in deixis pronouns	Kurdish	§3.3

4 The morphology of nouns and particles

4.1 Introductory overview

Nouns in JSNENA have either masculine or feminine gender. The same applies to Gorani. Gender distinctions, however, have been lost in the Kurdish of the region. In nouns of Aramaic etymology JSNENA retains to a large degree the gender inherited from earlier Aramaic and there does not appear to have been convergence with the gender of corresponding Gorani nouns. Gorani loanwords in JSNENA retain the gender they have in the Gorani source language. Loanwords in JSNENA from Kurdish and Persian, which do not have gender in the source language, are assigned gender according to semantic principles.

Some derivational affixes in JSNENA resemble Gorani and this may have reinforced of the choice in JSNENA of one particular derivational strategy in JSNENA rather than possible alternatives due to matching of one particular affix with an Iranian affix.

JSNENA nouns exhibit a variety of plural endings. The most frequent ending is *-ē*. This is inherited from earlier Aramaic but its frequent use may have been reinforced by the fact that it resembles phonetically the regular Gorani plural ending *-ē*. The use of *-ē* on loanwords in JSNENA from Gorani is, likewise, reinforced by the Gorani plural ending.

JSNENA has borrowed the Gorani definite article suffix *-akē*. In Gorani this suffix has various inflections. The form *-akē* is the most frequent form and it is this form that JSNENA has borrrowed. In Gorani and Kurdish the plural inflection is placed after the article. In JSNENA, on the other hand, the plural suffix is placed directly on the noun stem and the definite article suffix is attached at the end of the word. This reflects a lesser degree of morphological integration of the loaned article in the composition of the word than in Iranian.

The normal strategy for marking indefiniteness in JSNENA is by the inherited cardinal numeral 'one', viz. *xa*. JSNENA has, however, borrowed the Kurdish indefinite suffix *-ēk* in exclamatory expressions with subjective evaluative force.

Truncation of words in adverbial phrases in JSNENA replicates truncation in corresponding Kurdish and Gorani adverbial phrases.

The genitive particle *d-* occurs in the main body of NENA, but is rarely used in genitive constructions in JSNENA and closely related trans-Zab Jewish NENA dialects. This matches Sanandaj Kurdish rather than Gorani, which uses *ezafe* in genitive constructions. There is sporadic use in JSNENA of Persian *ezafe -ē*.

Persian *ezafe* occurs on a few prepositions in JSNENA.

In JSNENA there is a regular inflection of adjectives with distinct masculine and feminine endings in the singular and the invariable ending -ē in the plural. This matches the regular inflection of adjectives in Gorani, which have a phonetically identical plural ending -ē. The use of the invariable form *xēt* 'other' without gender or number distinction matches Kurdish rather than Gorani.

The loss of gender distinctions in cardinal numerals in JSNENA matches Iranian, especially Kurdish (Gorani has gender distinctions in the numerals 1 and 2). The pattern of numerals with pronominal suffixes ('one of us', 'two of us', etc.) matches Kurdish more closely than Gorani in some cases but Gorani in others. The constructions of ordinals in JSNENA borrow various morphological elements from the ordinal constructions of Iranian languages and also their syntactic patterns.

Names of days of the week in JSNENA exhibit the truncation of the final inflectional vowel -a. This is the case also in other Jewish dialects throughout the NENA area. It is a feature of Kurmanji rather than the Iranian languages of the Sanandaj region. This, therefore, appears to reflect the origin of JSNENA in Kurmanji-speaking areas of Iraq.

JSNENA has borrowed a number of prepositions from Iranian languages. In some cases these loans match the function and phonetic form of inherited NENA forms, which they have replaced. In some cases hybrid prepositions have developed, whereby Iranian elements are combined with inherited NENA prepositions. The purpose of this is to restrict the semantic range of the inherited preposition.

4.2 Gender

In JSNENA most nouns of Aramaic stock and loanwords that have been adapted to Aramaic morphology have in the singular one of the following endings: (i) -*a*, which is the reflex of the masculine singular determined state inflection of earlier Aramaic, (ii) -*ta* or its variants -*da* and -*la*, which are the reflexes of the feminine singular determined state inflection of earlier Aramaic, e.g.

(167) JSNENA
      lēš-a (m)   'dough'
      gup-ta (f)   'cheese'
      qar-da (f)   'cold'
      ksī-la (f)   'hat'

Nouns inflect for number with various plural endings, which are discussed below (§4.4).

In Gorani of the Sanandaj region nouns inflect for gender, number and case (direct vs oblique). In Gorani (Hawrami) Luhon nouns are classified into three declension classes (MacKenzie 1966, 14). This differs from Kurdish, in which nouns are invariable. Table (40) represent the inflection of two nouns from two different declension classes in Gorani Takht. Singular nouns in the direct case are generally unmarked, but display gender distinction in the oblique case: *-ī* (m), *-ē* (f). Plural nouns are marked in the direct case by *-ē*, and the oblique case by *-ā*, e.g.

Table 40: Nominal gender marking in Gorani.

	Masculine		Feminine	
Singular Direct	ásp	'horse'	báza	'goat'
Singular Oblique	asp-í		baz-é	
Plural Direct	ásp-ē		báz-ē	
Plural Oblique	asp-á		baz-á	

Gender assignment in Gorani depends on the phonological shape of the word. Several sub-classes of nouns that relate to gender assignment can be distinguished.

Masculine nouns end in a consonant, e.g. *varg* 'wolf', *goš* 'ear', *vārán* 'rain', *čam* 'eye'; in stressed *-á, -í, -ó, -ú*, e.g. *čəmčá* 'spoon', *məzgí* 'mosque', *māmó* 'paternal uncle', *haḷú* 'eagle'; and in *-ắ* (the majority of nouns), e.g. *zamắ* 'bridegroom'.

Feminine nouns end in unstressed *-ī*, unstressed *-a* and stressed *-ḗ*, e.g. *'ávī* 'water', *mắnga* 'moon', *kənắčḗ* 'girl'. Also a few nouns ending in *-ắ* and *-y* are feminine: *dagắ* 'village', *bay* 'quince'.

In JSNENA nouns of Aramaic stock that end in the feminine marker *-ta* or its phonetic variants are feminine and most words that end in *-a* are masculine. Several nouns ending in *-a*, however, are feminine in gender. Many of these can be classified into semantic categories such as names of parts of the body, insects and small animals, locations. Some of them are feminine in historical Aramaic, though the correspondence is not exact. Below we present a selection of these categories of nouns ending in *-a* that are feminine in JSNENA collated with their historical gender in earlier Aramaic[1] and the corresponding Gorani lexeme. In a few cases the historical Aramaic gender cannot be established due to the lack of a clear cognate in earlier forms of Aramaic.

---

[1] Based on the lexical data in the *Comprehensive Lexicon of Aramaic* (https://cal.huc.edu/).

Parts of the body

(168)

		JSNENA	Historical Aramaic gender	Gorani
	'hand'	ʾīla (f)	f	das (m)
	'leg, foot'	ʾaqla (f)	?	pā (m)
	'knee'	bərka (f)	f	čóka (f)
	'neck'	bqāra (f)	f	póšta (f)
	'stomach'	kāsa (f)	f	láma (f)
	'liver'	koza (f)	m	yahár (m)
	'kidney'	kulya (f)	f	wəḷk (m)
	'lung'	ḷāḷa (f)	f	šóšī (f)
	'palate'	šamāka (f)	?	āsmāná (m)
	'navel'	šəra (f)	m	nahá (m),
	'buttocks'	šərma (f)	?	qəp (m)
	'spleen'	taḥēla (f)	m	səpəḷ (m)
	'finger nail'	ṭəpra (f)	f	nāxūn (m)
	'beard'	təqna (f)	m	řīš (m)
	'vagina'	qūṭa (f)	?	kúsī (f)
	'handful'	xupna (f)	m	lámīšta (f)

Parts of the body with masculine gender

(169)

		JSNENA	Historical Aramaic gender	Gorani
	'bone'	garma (m)	m	pēšá (m)
	'tooth'	kāka (m)	m	dəðān (m)
	'shoulder'	kapāna (m)	f	šāná (m)
	'heart'	ləba (m)	m	dəḷ (m)
	'tongue'	ləšāna (m)	m	zuān (m)
	'brain'	moxa (m)	m	mažg (m)
	'mouth'	pəma (m)	m	dam (m)
	'nose'	poqa (m)	m	lúta (f)
	'head'	rēša (m)	m	sará (m)
	'face'	ṣalma (m)	m	řúa (f), dīdá (m)
	'back'	xāṣa (m)	m	māzī́ (m)
	'penis'	mara-mīla (m)	m	dəm (m)

Locations

(170)

		JSNENA	Historical Aramaic gender	Gorani
	'town'	ʼaḥra (f)	m	šār (m)
	'land'	ʼara (f)	f	zamīn (m)
	'road, way'	ʼurxa (f)	f	řā (f)
	'well'	bīra (f)	f	bı́rī (f)
	'place'	tʷka (f)	m	yāgḗ (f)
	'shop'	tʷkāna (f)	m (Arab.)	dūkān (m)
	'vineyard'	karma (f)	m	řaz (m)
	'kiln'	kūra (f)	m	koř̋ (f)
	'village'	māla (f)	f	dagā́ (f)
	'grave'	qora (f)	m	goř (m)
	'mountain'	ṭūra (f)	m	kaš (m)

Insects and small animals

(171)

		JSNENA	Historical Aramaic gender	Gorani
	'mouse'	ʼaqubra (f)	m	məlá (m)
	'sheep'	ʼərba (f)	m	máya (f)
	'flea'	pərtaʼna (f)	m	qolāčḗ (f)
	'cat'	qāṭu (f)	f	kətá (f)
	'fish'	nūnīla (f)	f	masáwī (f)
	'goat'	ʼəza (f)	f	bə́za (f)
	'horse'	sūsī (m)	m	asp (m)

Fruits and vegetables

(172)

		JSNENA	Historical Aramaic gender	Gorani
	'gallnut'	ʼapṣa (f)	m	bálčī (f)
	'walnut'	goza (f)	m	wázī (f)
	'gourd'	qara (f)	m	kulakḗ (f)
	'mulberry'	təla (f)	m	təfı́ (f)
	'almond'	šēza (f)	f	wámī (f)

Other nouns

(173)

		JSNENA	Historical Aramaic gender	Gorani
	'sieve'	ʾərbāla (f)	m	hēḷákī (f)
	'long needle'	ʾurədxa (f)	m	gočávanī (f)
	'kernel'	gulʿa (f)	m	mažgá (m)
	'ball of dough'	gūṣa (f)	m	gunká (m)
	'stone'	kēpa (f)	m/f	tawánī (f)
	'comb'	msərqa (f)	m	šāná (m)
	'meat'	pəsra (f)	m	gošt (m)
	'kernel'	qəna (f)	f	pēšá (m)
	'water pot'	qoqa (f)	m	pā́rča (f), sərahīlḗ (f)
	'wind'	roxa (f)	m/f	wā (m)
	'moon'	sēra (f)	m/f	mánga (f)
	'shirt'	ṣūra (f)	m	gəjī́ (m)
	'sun'	šəmša (f)	m/f	war (m)
	'snow'	talga (f)	m	wárwa (f)
	'oven'	tanūra (f)	m	tánūra (f)
	'load'	taʿna (f)	m	bār (m)
	'smoke'	təna (f)	m	dūkaḷ (m)
	'festival'	ʾēla (f)	m	jážna, yásna (f)
	'onion'	pəṣla (f)	m	pīyāz (m)
	'key'	qlīla (f)	m	krēḷ (m)
	'wedding'	xlūla (f)	m	zamávəna (f)
	'needle'	xmāta (f)	m/f	čánī (f)

The examples above show that a large proportion of the words in most of these categories do not exhibit a clear matching with the gender of the corresponding Gorani words. In many cases a feminine JSNENA word ending in -a is masculine in earlier Aramaic. In such cases, however, the corresponding Gorani word is often masculine. The gender change in JSNENA cannot, therefore be convincingly attributed to Gorani influence. It is more likely to be due to internal spreading of the feminine gender within JSNENA. This may be related to the tendency of JSNENA to assign feminine gender to genderless Kurdish and Persian loanwords referring to inanimate objects, body parts, small animals and flora (see below). The inherited Aramaic words ending in -a that have switched historically from masculine to feminine gender fall within these semantic categories.

4.2.1 Gender of loanwords

The lexicon of JSNENA includes many nouns that are loans from Iranian languages. A large proportion of these are loanwords from Gorani. This reflects the fact that Gorani was the main contact language with JSNENA at an earlier period. These loanwords in JSNENA retain the gender they have in Gorani.

4.2.1.1 Masculine consonant-final loanwords

(174)

	JSNENA	Gorani
'language'	zwān (m)	zwān (m)
'sugar'	šakar (m)	šakar (m)
'mattress'	došak (m)	dūšak (m)
'pepper'	'ālat (m)	hāḷat (m)
'harvest'	xarmān (m)	xarmān (m)
'thread (on carpet)'	frēt (m)	frēt (m)
'fog'	šawnam (m)	šawnəm (m)
'cracked wheat'	pařəšt (m)	pařəšt (m)
'beam on door'	klum (m)	kəḷom, kuḷom (m)
'coal'	zoxāḷ (m)	zoxāḷ (m)
'vein, artery'	řag (m)	řag (m)
'steam'	buq (m)	boq (m)
'chain'	zanjīr (m)	zanjīr (m)
'net'	toř (m)	toř (m)
'cover of a horse'	yaraq	yaraq (m)

Loanwords of ulimately Arabic origin usually end in a consonant and are assigned masculine gender in both JSNENA and Gorani, e.g.

(175)

	JSNENA	Gorani
'thought'	xīyāḷ (m)	xīyāḷ (m)
'condition'	ḥāl (m)	ḥāl (m)
'thought'	fəkr (m)	fəkr (m)
'mind, intelligence'	'aql (m)	'aql (m)
'mat'	ḥaṣīr (m)	ḥaṣīr (m)
'lock'	qfəl (m)	qəfl (m)
'line'	xat (m)	xat (m)
'bedding'	farš (m)	farš (m)

'material, stuff'	*jəns* (m)	*jəns* (m)
'ceiling'	*saqf* (m)	*saqf* (m)
'pillar'	*stun* (m)	*stun* (m)

4.2.1.2 Masculine nouns ending in a stressed vowel

(176)

	JSNENA	Gorani
'plate'	*dawrī́* (m)	*dawrī́* (m)
'fruit'	*mēwá* (m)	*mēwá* (m)
'quilt'	*laʿēfá* m.	*lēfá* (m)
'cloth'	*pārčá* (m)	*pārčá* (m)
'rag'	*paró* (m)	*pařó* (m)
'ground cloth'	*səfrá* (m)	*səfrá* (m)
'air, weather'	*hawá* (m)	*hawā́* (m)

Some Gorani loanwords in JSNENA have a slightly different phonological shape from what they have in the current Gorani of the region, but they have, nevertheless, preserved the Gorani gender.

(177)

	JSNENA	Gorani
'chair'	*sandalī́* (f)	*sandalī́a* (f)
'pillow, cushion'	*sarīná* (f)	*sarīn* (f)/*sərangá* (f)
'woman's head cover'	*čāčáw* (m)	*čāšéw* (m)
'chalk'	*gaj* (m)	*gač* (m)
'bunch, cluster'	*xošá* (m)	*hošá* (m)
'stream'	*jogá* (f)	*júa* (f)
'frog'	*qurbāqá* (f)	*qurwā́qī* (f)
'peach'	*štāḷwá* (f)	*haštālū́ī* (f)

In the following cases a loanword has been assigned the gender of a homophonous counterpart in Gorani that has a different meaning:

(178)

JSNENA		Gorani	
kūzī (f)	'pot for meat'	*kūzī* (f)	'stream of water'
darz (m)	'chink'	*darz* (m)	'lesson'

The lexicon of JSNENA also includes loanwords from Kurdish, some of which are of Persian origin. Kurdish and Persian have no grammatical gender distinctions and so these loanwords have been assigned gender in JSNENA according to semantic principles (Khan 2009, 180–84).

The majority of Kurdish and Persian loanwords referring to inanimate objects, body parts, small animals and flora are assigned to the feminine gender. These include words of ultimately Arabic origin that were originally masculine in Arabic:

(179)

		JSNENA	Kurdish	Gorani
	'churn'	*maška* (f)	*maška*	*halīza* (f)
	'handle'	*dasa* (f)	*dasa*	*dasá* (m)
	'mirror, glass'	*jām* (f)	*jām*	*jām* (m)
	'orange'	*burtaqāl* (f)	*pərtaqāḷ*	*pərtaqāl* (m)
	'black lentil'	*māša* (f)	*māš*	*māš* (m)
	'wooden bed'	*taxtaband* (f)	*taxteband* (Pers.)	*taxtaban* (m)
	'bee'	*hanga* (f)	*hang*	*hang* (m)
	'owl'	*bāyaquš* (f)	*bāyaquš*	*bāyaquš* (m)
	'frog'	*qurbāqa* (f)	*qurwāqa*, P. *qurbāqe*	*qurwāqī* (f)
	'melon'	*kāḷaka* (f)	*kāḷak*	*kāḷak* (m)
	'river'	*roxāna* (f)	*roxāna*	*roxāna* (m)
	'breast'	*mamona* (f)	*mamək, mamka*	*mamá* (m)

As can be seen, several of these loanwords are identical or similar in phonetic shape to the corresponding word in Gorani. The fact that JSNENA does not follow the gender assignment of Gorani indicates that they must have been loaned from Kurdish.

There is a residue of inanimate loans from Kurdish that are construed as masculine in gender. Most of the nouns in question either denote (i) a long, thin entity, (ii) fabrics, (iii) a collective or non-solid entity or (iv) a non-tangible, abstract entity:

(180)

		JSNENA	Kurdish	Gorani
	'tail'	*dūjka* (m)	*dūčka*	*qlīčka* (m)
	'match'	*gogərd* (m)	*gogərd*	*kəbrītī* (f)
	'feather'	*pařa* (m)	*pař* (Pers)	*pal* (m)
	'wire'	*sīm* (m)	*sīm, tal*	*tal* (m)
	'scissors'	*qayčī* (m)	*qayčī*	*dūwārdī* (f)
	'spindle'	*tašī* (m)	*tašī*	*latarē* (f)
	'baggy trousers'	*damaqopān* (m)	*damaqopān*	*pāntolē* (f)
	'dates'	*xorma* (m)	*xormā*	*xormāva* (f)
	'difficulty'	*saxtī* (m)	*saxtī* (Pers)	*saxtī* (m)

4.2.2 Marking female gender

In the case of animate referents, the addition of the feminine marker in JSNENA may designate the female counterpart of the masculine form, e.g.

(181) JSNENA
tora	'ox'	torta	'cow'
yāla	'young boy'	yalta	'young girl'
barūxa	'friend (m)'	baruxta	'friend (f)'
šwāwa	'neighbour (m)'	šwafta	'neighbour (f)'
ganāwa	'thief (m)'	ganafta	'thief (f)'

In Gorani, the feminine suffix *-a* may designate the female counterpart of a masculine noun, in particular those denoting professions (cf. Sadjadi 2019):

(182) Gorani
'cook'	čāčkar (m)	čāčkára (f)
'baker'	nānpač (m)	nānpáča (f)
'patient'	nawaš (m)	nawáša (f)
'physician'	doktor (m)	doktóra (f)

4.3 Derivational affixes on nouns

JSNENA makes use of various derivational affixes in the formation of nouns that are of Aramaic etymology. Some of the derivational affixes are phonetically similar to Iranian derivational affixes with a related function. It is possible, therefore, that the Iranian affixes have reinforced the use of the JSNENA affixes. The process would have involved the reinforcement of the choice of one particular derivational strategy in JSNENA rather than possible alternatives due to matching of one particular affix with an Iranian affix.

A possible case of this is the JSNENA derivational suffix *-āna*, which is used productively to form active participles from the present stem of verbs:

(183) JSNENA
ʾaxlāna	'(big) eater'	< ʾ-x-l 'to eat'
qaryāna	'reader'	< q-r-y 'to read'
yalpāna	'learner'	< y-l-p 'to learn'

This suffix *-āna* is phonetically similar to the Iranian suffix *-ana* that is used in Gorani and Kurdish of Sanandaj with the same function of forming active particles from the present stem of verbs. It is used in loans from Persian, which have the Persian suffix *-ande*, the /d/ being lost through the Zagros /d/ effect (§2.2.2.7), e.g.

(184) Kurdish and Gorani
 nəvīsana 'writer' Pers. *nevisande* < *nevis* 'to write'
 (G.)
 dawana 'runner' Pers. *davande* < *do* 'to run'
 (K.)
 gūyana 'speaker' Pers. *guyande* < *gū* 'to speak'
 (K.)

This differs from the normal means for forming active participles in Sanandaj Kurdish and Central Kurdish elsewhere, which is by the attachment of the suffix *-ar* to the present stem, e.g. *nūs-ar* 'writer'. In Bahdini active participles are formed by the suffixes *-ar*, *-kar* and *-kār*, e.g. *kūž-ar* 'killer', *dizī-kar* 'thief' (here the affix has been added to the past stem), *nivīs-kār* 'writer'.

There is a clear Aramaic etymology for the suffix *-āna* in JSNENA. It is not, however, the only possible strategy for deriving an active particle. Some NENA dialects, indeed, use a different pattern for the active particle, at least in Form 1 verbs, e.g. Ch. Qaraqosh *'axāla* 'eater' < *'-x-l* (Khan 2002a, 87). The existence of the Iranian parallel may have reinforced the choice of the suffix *-āna*.

4.4 Plural endings

JSNENA exhibits a variety of suffixes that are used to express the plural of nouns. There is no one-to-one correspondence between singular inflections and plural inflections and so the plural form of a singular noun is not predictable.

Examples of plural suffixes:

(185) JSNENA
 Singular Plural
 'īlān-a (m) 'īlān-ē 'tree'
 'aḥr-a (f) 'aḥr-ālē 'town'
 loʿ-a (m) loʿ-āē 'room'
 yom-a (m) yom-awāē 'day'
 'axon-a (m) 'axon-awālē 'brother'
 gūz-a (m) gūz-ānē 'wall'

’aqol-ta (f)	’aqol-yē	'ankle; elbow'
daš-ta (f)	daš-yālē	'field'
ḥaš-ta (f)	ḥaj-yānē	'work'

The most common plural ending is -ē. This is attached to a variety of singular forms ending in -a of both genders, e.g.

(186) JSNENA

Singular	Plural	
’īlāna (m)	’īlānē	'tree'
bēla (m)	bēlē	'house'
brona (m)	bronē	'son'
dəm‘a (m)	dəm‘ē	'tear'
goza (m)	gozē	'walnut'
gūza (m)	gūzē	'wall'
kalba (m)	kalbē	'dog'
mala (f)	mālē	'village'
’īla (f)	’īlē	'hand'

This plural ending is found throughout NENA and is clearly of Aramaic etymology. It is significant, however, that it is homophonous with the Gorani plural marker in the direct case, viz. -ē. The oblique form of the Gorani plural marker is -ā. This is the regular inflection of plural nouns in Gorani. It is possible, therefore, that the frequency of the NENA -ē plural ending may have been reinforced by matching it with the Gorani direct case plural marker.

Many of the nouns in JSNENA are loanwords from Iranian languages, a large proportion of which are from Gorani (§11.1). In numerous cases such loanwords are not adapted to Aramaic morphology in the singular by the addition of a singular inflectional ending. The plural of such loanwords is generally formed by adding the JSNENA plural ending –ē directly to the stem of the word. One factor conditioning this choice of plural ending may have been that the -ē ending is the most frequent and so 'unmarked' JSNENA plural ending. Another factor that is likely to have reinforced this phenomenon is the fact that in Gorani, the source of many of the loanwords, the words have the Gorani direct plural ending -ē, which is homophonous with the JSNENA unmarked ending:

(187)

		JSNENA		Gorani
		Singular	Plural	Plural (direct)
'lock of hair'		čīn	čīnē	čīnē/zólfē
'foreigner'		ġarīb	ġarībē	ġarībē

'kneading pot'	markan	markanē	makárē
'owl'	bāyaquš	bāyaqušē	bāīqúšē
'cock'	ḳalašēr	ḳalašērē	ḳaḷašīrē
'table'	mēz	mēzē	mézē
'line'	xat	xatē	xátē
'leaf'	gaḷa	gaḷaē	gáḷē (sg gaḷá)
'poor'	ga	gaē	gaḍē (sg gaḍā)
'snow shovel'	pāro	pāroē	pāřóē
'bud'	mlago	mlagoē	məlagóē
'cart'	gārī	gārīyē	gāríyē
'meat container'	kūzī	kūzīyē	kūzíyē
'small bird'	mrīčī	mrīčīyē	məríčḷē
'teapot'	qorī	qorīyē	qoríyē

In Sanandaj Kurdish the general plural marker is -gal, together with the variants -yal and -al used in dialects in the environs of Sanandaj. Another marker is the historically plural oblique -ān, which is normally used in combination with the definite marker -aka, yielding the form -akān, e.g. piyāwakān 'the men'. The ending -ān is also used independently of the definite article in some cases.

In JSNENA the normal plural ending of feminine nouns ending is -ta is -yē, which replaces the -ta, e.g.

(188) JSNENA
Singular	Plural	
baruxta	baruxyē	'friend (f.)'
bšəlmanta	bšəlmanyē	'Muslim woman'
dargušta	dargušyē	'cradle'

In a few cases the extended plural ending -yālē is used. This has an Aramaic origin, deriving from *-yāθā, which is found in some phonologically conservative NENA dialects, e.g. Ch. Barwar (Khan 2008b, 389–92). It is, however, only used marginally in JSNENA. It is possible that its use was reinforced by the Kurdish plural ending -yal, which is used in Kurdish dialects in the environs of Sanandaj. In the town of Sanandaj the plural ending has the form -gal. The probability of Kurdish influence is increased by the fact that it is found in loanwords whose source is Kurdish, e.g.

(189) JSNENA

Singular	Plural		Sanandaj Kurdish Plural	Kurdish of environs of Sanandaj Plural
dašta	dašyālē	'field'	daštgal	daštyal

In the loanword *dašta* in JSNENA the /t/ belongs historically to the stem of the word in the source language (Kurd. *dašt*) but has come to be interpreted as part of the feminine marker.

4.5 The definite article

In JSNENA, as is the case with other trans-Zab Jewish Neo-Aramaic dialects, the suffix *-akē*, which is of Iranian origin, is used as a definite article. The *-akē* suffix in NENA used considered a borrowing from Central Kurdish (see Khan 2007, 201; Coghill 2020, 510 among others). As will be shown later in this section, the more likely source for the borrowing of *-akē* is Gorani rather than Central Kurdish.

When this suffix is attached, the final inflectional vowel of the noun is removed. In cases where the singular and plural forms are distinguished only by the final vowels, this distinction is lost, e.g.

(190) JSNENA
 kalba 'dog' *kalbakē* 'the dog'
 kalbē 'dogs' *kalbakē* 'the dogs'

The plural suffix is placed before the article and is visible when it consists of more than one syllable, e.g.

(191) JSNENA
 'axon-awālē 'brothers' *'axon-awāl-akē* 'the brothers'

In Kurdish of Sanandaj the definite article is the suffix *-aka*, which, in combination with the plural ending *-ān*, yields the plural form *-akān*. In Gorani, the same definite article is used, but this inflects for gender and case. As shown in Table 41, it has the following forms:

Table 41: Definiteness paradigm of Gorani.

	Direct	Oblique
m	-aka	-akay
f	-akē	-akē
pl	-akē	-akā

As can be seen, in the Iranian languages the plural inflection is placed after the article. In JSNENA, on the other hand, the plural suffix is placed directly on the noun stem and the definite article suffix is attached at the end of the word. This reflects a lesser degree of morphological integration of the loaned article in the composition of the word than in Iranian. A further difference is that in JSNENA the article is not combined with possessive suffixes, whereas in the Iranian languages a possessive clitic may be placed after the article:

(192)
	JSNENA	Gorani	Kurdish
'the house'	bēl-akē	yāna-(a)ka	māḷ-aka
'my house'	bēl-ī	yāna-(a)ka=m	māḷ-aka=m

Another point of divergence is that in Gorani and Kurdish but not in JSNENA the definite suffix is used with kinship terms when they are used in the vocative. It is also used with body-part terms such as 'heart', 'eye' to express endearment:

(193) Kurdish and Gorani
pīyāw-aka (K.)/ *pīyāka* (G.)   'Husband!'
žən-aka (K.)/ *žan-akē* (G.)   'Wife!'
dəḷ-aka=m (K.)   'My love!' (lit. my heart)
čāw-aka=m (K.)   'Darling!' (lit. my eyes)

This seems to be a reflection of the origin of the *-aka* suffix as a diminutive marker.

The *-akē* does not occur in this context in JSNENA, which instead uses the diminutive suffix *-ona* of Aramaic origin in parallel constructions with kinship terms:

(194) JSNENA
brona 'son' (< *br* + diminutive *ona*),
'axona 'brother' (< *'ax* + diminutive *ona*)

It appears that JSNENA has not borrowed *-akē* in this diminutive sense, because it already possesses a corresponding language-internal resource, i.e. the diminutive suffix *-ona*. JSNENA only borrows *-akē* in its definite function because a definite marker is lacking in JSNENA.

The question arises as to whether the definite suffix *-akē* in JSNENA was loaned from Kurdish or Gorani. The definite suffix with the form *-akē* is found in most Jewish Trans-Zab NENA dialects, except in those spoken in the far north-west of Iran, such as J. Urmi and J. Salamas, in which it is absent. It is attested also in a few Christian dialects in the eastern periphery of NENA, such as Ch. Sulemaniyya and Ch. Sanandaj.

The Gorani *-akē* (f direct and oblique singular, and direct case pl) is the one closest in form to the article that is used in NENA. Our frequency count suggests that among the competing definite forms in Gorani, *-akē* has generally the highest token frequency in texts. The folktales 1 and 2 analysed are from MacKenzie (1966).

Table 42: Token frequency of different definite forms in Gorani.

Texts	Total no. of definite markers	-aka	-akay	-akā	-akē
Folktale 1	60	30%	22%	8%	39%
Folktale 2	25	48%	32%	4%	16%
Folktale 3	22	27%	27%	–	46%
Film narration 1	59	43%	12%	12%	32%
Film narration 2	33	21%	18%	15%	45%
Pear story	42	7%	12%	33%	50%
Personal or procedural arrative	17	23%	–	12%	65%
total	258	28%	18%	12%	42%

As the data show, in all but one text the token frequency of *-akē* is more than the phonetically similar masculine oblique form *-akay*. It can be concluded, therefore, that NENA has borrowed the most frequent form of the Gorani definite article. This would be compatible with the geographical distribution of *-akē* in NENA, which corresponds closely to the historical area of Gorani. It has been documented in the Jewish dialect of Shəno (Oshnavieh), which is situated south-west of lake Urmi and outside the historical Gorani area. It would appear that the feature entered this dialect through migrations from further south.

4.6 The indefinite suffix

JSNENA uses the cardinal numeral *xa* 'one' as an indefinite article, e.g. *xa gora* 'one man', 'a man' (§6.2). In a few isolated cases, the Kurdish suffix *-ēk* is used as an indefinite article, e.g.

(195) JSNENA
    a. ʾajáb   bron-èk=yē.ˈ
        wonder boy-INDEF=COP.3SG.M
        'He is a wonderful boy!' (A:17)
    b. bróna rắba ʾayz-èk=yēlē.ˈ
        boy   very good-INDEF=COP.PST.3SG.M
        'He was a very fine lad!' (A:14)

It is significant that both of these examples have a subjective evaluative force, which is likely to have motivated borrowing to give the statements added salience.

In Sanandaj Kurdish the indefinite suffix has the form *-ēk*, which is sometimes shortened to *-ē*. It is not stressed, e.g. *piyáw-ēk* 'a man', *róž-ē* 'one day'. In the exclamatory constructions (195a) and (195b) in JSNENA the full form of the article is used and it is stressed.

In Gorani the indefinite suffix is *-ēw* (m), *-ēwa* (f), *-ēwē* (pl.). The singular forms sometimes reduce to *-ē*, thus showing no gender distinction.

4.7 Nouns in the absolutive state

In JSNENA there are a few isolated cases of a noun being used without the nominal inflectional ending *-a*. We shall refer to these as nouns in the absolute state. They are mostly nouns that occur in adverbial phrases. The attested cases are the following:

(196) JSNENA
  'ay-šo 'this week' < *šoa* 'week'
  xa-šo 'a week' < *šoa* 'week'
  'əzyo 'today' < *yoma* 'day'

This truncation of words in adverbial phrases has replicated a model of truncation of nouns in adverbial phrases in Kurdish and Gorani, e.g.

(197) Kurdish: *īmro/amro* 'today' < *rož* 'day'
  Gorani: *ēsā́ḷ* 'this year' < *sā́ḷa* 'year'

4.8 Genitive annexation constructions

In JSNENA the most common way of annexing one nominal to another in a genitive relationship is simply to juxtapose the two. The Aramaic genitive/subordinating particle *d-*, which regularly occurs in such constructions in the main body of NENA dialects, is rarely used in the JSNENA dialect. Examples:

(198) JSNENA
  bēla barūxī 'the house of my friend'
  šəma 'axonaf 'the name of her brother'

brona Jahān	'the son of Jahān'
līšāna bšəlmānē	'the language of the Muslims'
pəsra rēša	'the meat of the head'

The equivalent to the Aramaic particle *d-* in Iranian languages is the so-called *ezafe* (< Arabic *'iḍāfa* 'joining, annexation'). This is a head-marking clitic particle that is used in the structure of the noun phrase in many West Iranian languages.

Two *ezafe* particles occur in Gorani of the Sanandaj region: Following MacKenzie's terminology (1961b, 82) *=ū/=w* occurs in 'genitival ezafe constructions' (199.a), and *=ī/=y* is used in 'epithetic ezafe constructions' (199.b).

(199) Gorani
 a. *zamāna=w šā-y*
   time=EZ Shah-OBL.M
   'in the Shah's time'
 b. *dua qarān-ēw=ī čarma*
   two kurus-INDF=EZ white
   'A white two-Kurus coin'

In the Kurdish of Sanandaj, however, the most common strategy in genitive constructions is the simple juxtaposition of two nouns without an *izafe* particle. JSNENA, therefore, has matched the model of Kurdish in this construction rather than Gorani:

(200) Kurdish
kanīšk pāwšā	'daughter of the king'
ark šāhī	'palace of the kingdom'
dašt xwā	'desert of God'
nəgabān dawr šār	'guardian of the suburbs of the city'
dār hamro	'tree of pear (i.e. pear tree)'

An *ezafe* particle with the form *ī/y* occurs in Kurdish when the head word ends in a vowel, e.g.

(201) Kurdish
 a. *qawr-aka=y bāwk=ī*
   grave-DEF=EZ father=OBL.3SG
   'the grave of his father'
 b. *pāwšā=y aw šār=a*
   king=EZ that city=DEM
   'the king of that city'

JSNENA on some occasions uses the Persian *ezafe* particle *=ē*. In the text corpus this is found most frequently when the head noun is an unadapted loanword that ends in a consonant rather than in a nominal inflectional vowel:

(202) JSNENA
 a. *ʾásər=ē šabàt*[|]
  eve=EZ sabbath
  'the eve of Sabbath' (A:51)
 b. *šamáš=ē knīštà*[|]
  beadle=EZ synagogue
  'the beadle of the synagogue' (A:43)
 c. *háft=ē xlūlà*[|]
  week=EZ wedding
  'the week of the wedding' (A:34)

The Persian *ezafe* particle is occasionally used also when the head noun has an Aramaic nominal inflectional vowel, e.g.

(203) JSNENA
 bēlá=ē barūx-í
 house=EZ friend-1SG
 'the house of my friend'

In JSNENA when the genitive complement of the head noun is an independent pronoun or attributive demonstrative, an oblique pronoun is used (§3.6), e.g.

(204) JSNENA
 bēla do 'the house of that one (= his house)'
 bēla day 'the house of this one'
 bēla dīdan 'the house of us (= our house)'
 bēla do gora 'the house of that man'

As discussed in §3.6, the oblique third person pronouns of JSNENA have developed on the model of the oblique third person pronouns of Gorani. The first and second person oblique pronominal phrases with the *dīd-* stem (e.g. *dīd-ī* 'of me', *dīd-ox* 'of you [SG.M]) have been preserved from historical NENA by analogy. In such constructions the Persian *ezafe* clitic *=ē* may optionally be added to the head noun. This is found particularly when the head noun is an unadapted loanword, but is also attested when it is a word of Aramaic etymology, e.g.

(205) JSNENA
    a. *fəšár=ē*   *do-mā̀ē*ˈ
        pressure=EZ   OBL.DEIC-water
        'the pressure of that water' (A:59)
    b. *bēlá=ē*   *do*
        house=EZ   OBL.3SG.M
        'his house' (lit. 'the house of that one')

In Gorani, the head of the oblique pronoun obligatorily has an *ezafe* clitic. This has not been matched regularly in the JSNENA construction. It appears that the occasional use of the Persian *ezafe* is due to influence from Persian, which requires *ezafe* in genitive annexation constructions, rather than Gorani. The model for the syntax of the JSNENA construction, therefore, is Kurdish (without *ezafe*) and Persian (with *ezafe =ē*), whereas the model for the morphology (the oblique form of the pronoun in the third person) is Gorani:

(206) Gorani
    a. *yāna=w*   *ānay*
        house=EZ   that.OBL
        'the house of that one (m)'
    b. *yāna=w*   *īnay*
        house=EZ   this.OBL
        'the house of this one (m)'
    c. *yāna=w*   *ādī*
        house=EZ   3SG.M.OBL
        'the house of him (= his house)'

4.9 Ezafe on prepositions

The Persian *ezafe* particle *=ē* occurs on the JSNENA preposition *məntak=ē* 'with', which is a hybrid of NENA and Iranian components (§4.15.9). This *ezafe* appears to be replicating the syntax of the Persian preposition *hamrāh* 'together with', which regularly appears with the *ezafe* particle, e.g. *hamrāh=e pedar=am* 'with my father'.

JSNENA has borrowed the preposition *lā* 'to the side of' from Iranian. This usually does not take an *ezafe* particle in JSNENA, e.g.

(207) JSNENA
    a. *zī́l-Ø*   *lá*   *táta*   *dāak-àf=ū*|
        go.PST-3SG.M   side   father   mother-3SG.F=and
        'He went to (the home of) her father and mother.' (D:19)
    b. *kúlē*   *hūlāḗ*   *lā-làxlē*   *yēlú*|
        all   Jews   side-each.other   COP.PST.3PL
        'All the Jews were close to one another.' (A:44)

Sporadically it is used with the Persian *ezafe =e*, e.g.

(208) JSNENA
     zī́-na   *lá=ē*   *pīrè*.|
     go.PST-1SG   side=EZ   old.PL
     'I went to the old folk.' (E:31)

This preposition is used in Gorani without an *ezafe* suffix. Examples are from MacKenzie (1966, 64–68):

(209) Gorani
    a. *nay-dē*   *lā*   *min*
        NEG.SBJV-come.PRS-2PL   side   1SG
        'Do not come to me.'
    b. *ā*   *tawana=w*   *lā*   *kursī=a*   *b-ār-a*
        DEM.DIST   stone=EZ   side   chair=DEM   SBJV-bring.PRS-2SG.IMP
        'Bring that stone by the chair.'
    c. *agar*   *bar-ī=m=o*   *pay*   *lā*   *tāta-y=m*
        if   take.PRS-2SG=1SG=TELIC   to   side   father-OBL.M=1SG
        'if you take me back to my father . . .'

In Sanandaj Kurdish, by contrast, *lā* takes the *ezafe* particle, following the regular practice of Sanandaj Kurdish of preserving *ezafe* after word-final vowels:

(210) Kurdish
    a. *ba*   *lā=y*   *min=īš=aw*   *nā-yž-ī*
        to   side=EZ   1SG=ADD=TELIC   NEG-say.PRS-2SG
        'Aren't you going to tell me either!?'
    b. *tēd=aw*   *lā=y*   *bāz*
        IND.come.PRS.3SG=TELIC   side=EZ   falcon
        'He comes back to the place of the falcon.'

It would appear, therefore, that JSNENA borrowed the preposition *lā* from Gorani rather than from Kurdish, since in both Gorani and, in most cases, in JSNENA *lā* appears without the *ezafe*. The sporadic use of Persian *ezafe* with the preposition in JSNENA can be regarded as a late convergence with Kurdish and/or Persian syntax.

4.10 Adjectives

4.10.1 Inflection

In JSNENA adjectives of Aramaic stock and loanwords that have been adapted to Aramaic morphology are inflected for gender and number both when used attributively and when used predicatively. In addition to the basic masculine singular form they are inflected for the feminine singular and the plural. Whereas the morphological form of a feminine noun and a plural noun are generally not predictable but rather are lexically specific, the gender and number inflection of adjectives is completely regular. The inflections are:

(211) JSNENA

	Inflection	Example	
SG.M	-a	kpīn-a	'hungry'
SG.F	-ta	kpīn-ta	
PL	-ē	kpīn-ē	

Due to the unpredictablility and lexical-specificness of gender and plural marking of nouns, the marking of gender and number are better characterised as a process of derivation rather than inflection. The regular marking of gender and number in adjectives, however, should be characterised as inflection.

The lack of gender distinction in the plural is a change from earlier Aramaic, in which adjectives of feminine plural nouns had feminine plural inflection, distinctive from masculine plural inflection, e.g. Syriac *neššē ṭāḇ-ātā* 'good women' vs. *gaḇrē ṭāḇ-ē* 'good men'.

When substantivised, Gorani adjectives inflect for gender, number, and case, with gender distinction in the singular but not in the plural. When used in a head-modifier relation, adjectives agree in gender and number with the head noun.
Example:

(212) Gorani

		M	F
pīr 'old (animate)'			
DIR.SG		pīr	pír-a

OBL.SG	pír-ī	pír-ē
DIR.PL	pír-ē	pír-ē
OBL.PL	pīr-ā́	pīr-ā́

This is the regular inflection in Gorani. The regular inflection of adjectives and the lack of gender distinction in the plural in JSNENA, as well as in NENA dialects in general, matches this regular pattern of inflection in Gorani adjectives. There is, indeed, phonetic similarity between the plural inflection *-ē* in JSNENA adjectives and the direct plural inflection of Gorani. In Gorani also nouns have the same regular plural inflection (direct *-ē*, oblique *-ā*), but JSNENA has not replicated this regular inflectional pattern. Convergence of JSNENA with Gorani, therefore, is greater in adjectives, which express properties, than in nouns, which express referential entities. Property expressions such as adjectives have a greater tendency to be contingent and not time-stable than nouns, which are typically time-stable.

In Kurdish, by contrast, adjectives are uninflected and appear in invariable form:

(213) Kurdish
    SG   *kuř-ēk bāḷābarz*   'a tall boy'
    PL   *kuř-gal-ē bāḷābarz*   'tall boys'

In JSNENA the non-attributive modifier 'other' is of invariable form, in that it has the same form irrespective of gender and number:

(214) JSNENA
    gora xēt (SG.M)   'another man'
    baxta xēt (SG.F)   'another woman'
    našē xēt (PL)   'other people'

The invariability of the non-attributive modifier 'other' is a feature of Jewish Trans-Zab dialects. In many other NENA dialects, however, it is inflected for gender and number like other adjectives, e.g. Ch. Barwar: *xēna* (SG.M), *xēta* (SG.F), *xēnē* (PL).

The invariability of JSNENA *xēt* corresponds to the corresponding invariable form *tər* 'other' in Kurdish, e.g.

(215) Kurdish
    pīyāw-ēk tər   'another man'
    žin-ēk tər   'another woman'
    xaḷk-ē tər   'other people'

The Gorani cognate form *tar* is inflected for gender and case:

(216) Gorani
sa'ātēw tar '(in) another hour'
kənāčēway tara 'another girl'
jəla konē xalqī tarī 'old clothes of other people'
kənāčē tarē 'other girls'

The invariability of JSNENA *xēt*, therefore, matches the distributional pattern of Kurdish rather than Gorani. The JSNENA non-attributive modifier, therefore, has converged with the pattern of the later contact language, Kurdish, whereas JSNENA attributive modifiers have not, but preserve the pattern of the older contact language Gorani. A relevant factor may be that *xēt* 'other' is more syntactic in nature than attributive adjectives.

4.10.2 Unadapted adjective loans

JSNENA has borrowed many adjectives from Iranian languages, including Gorani, Kurdish and Persian, without adapting them to Aramaic morphology and they are of an invariable form. Some examples of these are as follows:

(217)

		NENA	Kurdish	Gorani	Persian
	'blue'	*'ābī*	*kaw, āwī*	*kawa*	*ābi*
	'fast'	*gwərj*	*gurj*	*gurj*	*sariʿ*
	'blind'	*kwər*	*kwēr*	*kor*	*kur*
	'brown'	*qāway*	*qāwaī*	*qāwaī*	*qahvei*
	'deep'	*qūḷ*	*qūḷ*	*qūḷ, qūḷa*	*amiq*
	'heavy'	*qurs*	*qurs*	*qurs*	*sangin*
	'naked'	*řūt*	*řūt*	*řūt*	*loxt*
	'smooth'	*sāf*	*sāf*	*sāf*	*sāf*
	'hard'	*səft*	*səft*	*səft*	*seft*
	'mad'	*šēt*	*šēt*	*šēt*	*divāne*
	'happy'	*xošḥāḷ*	*šā, xošḥāḷ*	*kēfwaš, šā*	*xošḥāl*
	'excessive'	*zyādī*	*zīyā*	*zīyā*	*zyādi*

This category includes gentilic adjectives ending in *-ī* on the basis of an Iranian pattern, e.g.

(218) JSNENA
    sanandājī   'from Sanandaj'
    bījārī   'from Bijar'
    saqəzī   'from Saqqəz'

4.10.3 Compound adjectives

The most common types of compound adjectives in JSNENA are those that begin with the elements *mārē-* (literally: 'master of') or *bē-* 'without'. These are all invariable in form, even when the second element has an Aramaic nominal ending.

The form *mārē-* corresponds to *xāwan, xāwən* 'owner' in Kurdish:

(219)   JSNENA   Kurdish
    'strong'   *mārē-qəwta*   *xawān zor, zordār*
    'rich'   *mārē-dolta*   *xāwan dasaḷāt* ('authoritative')

The form *bē-* 'without' is a loan from either Gorani or Kurdish. Some of the compound adjectives of this type have also loaned Iranian complements, e.g.

(220)   JSNENA   Gorani/Kurdish
    'stupid'   *bē-ʿaql*   *bē-ʿaql*
    'with no solution, hopeless' *bē-čāra*   *bē-čāra*
    'shameless'   *bē-ḥaya*   *bē-hayā*
    'ownerless, abandoned'   *bē-māra*   *bē-xāwan, bē-xāwən*
    'tasteless'   *bē-təmʿa* *bē-tām*
    'weak'   *bē-qəwta* *bē-quwat*

Other attested compound adjectives in JSNENA have a preposition or numeral as their first component. These are calques of Iranian, e.g.

(221)   JSNENA   Gorani   Kurdish
    'tasty' (lit. 'with taste')   *ba-təmʿa* *ba-tām, tāmʿan* *ba-tām* (Kurdish of Sulemaniyya)
    'pregnant' (lit. 'two souls') *trē gyānē* *dəva gīyāna*   *du gīyan*

4.11 Numerals

In JSNENA the cardinal numerals are of invariable form and are not inflected for gender, see (222). This is a feature that is shared by all Jewish Trans-Zab dialects. In several NENA dialects, however, the numerals 1–10 have distinct forms according to whether the numeral is followed by a masculine noun or a feminine noun. Most of these dialects are in the western sector of NENA, e.g. Ch. Qaraqosh:

(222)

	JSNENA Invariable	Ch. Qaraqosh With masculine noun	With feminine noun
1	xa	xa	ġða
2	trē	trē	tə́tta
3	təlḥá	ṭláθa	ṭə́llaθ
4	ʾarbá	ʾárbʿa	ʾárbəʾ
5	xamšá	xámša	xámməš
6	ʾəštá	ʾə́šta	ʾə́ššət
7	šoá	šóʾa	šúwwəʾ
8	tmanyá	tmánya	tmä́nə
9	ʾəčʾá	tə́šʾa	tə́ššəʾ
10	ʾəsrá	ʾə́sra	ʾə́ssər

In Kurdish numerals are not inflected for gender. In Gorani, numeral 1 is inflected for gender. The numeral 2 distinguishes feminine gender in the compound adjective *dəva gīyāna* 'pregnant' (lit. two souls). The remainder of the numerals are invariable in Gorani:

(223)

	Gorani	Kurdish
1	yo (m); yoa (f)	yak
2	dūē (general); dəva (f)	dū
3	yarē	sē
4	čūār	čūār
5	panj	panj
6	šəš	šaš
7	hawt, hot	haft
8	hašt	hašt
9	no	no
10	da	da

The loss of gender inflection of numerals in NENA dialects in the eastern sector of the NENA area could have occurred through a process of internal simplification. It is possible, however, that a factor that catalysed this process was the lack of gender inflection in Iranian numerals, especially in Kurdish. The NENA dialects that have gender distinction have preserved a historical morphological distinction in Aramaic. This preservation is likely to have been reinforced by contact with Arabic dialects of the area, which have a gender distinction in their numeral systems, e.g. Mosul (Jastrow 1979, 48).

In JSNENA pronominal suffixes may be attached to the cardinals 2–10 to form partitive expressions. When the suffix is 1PL a /n/ element is added between the numeral and the pronominal suffix. The forms appear to be calques of the corresponding Kurdish construction, which is a phrase consisting of a numeral and a phrase with a pronominal clitic attached to the preposition *lē* 'from', i.e. 'one of us', 'two of us', etc. In Gorani the form consists of a preposition *ja* 'from' combined with the independent pronouns. The /n/ element in the JSNENA constructions, therefore, is most likely a phonetically reduced form of the NENA preposition *mən* 'from'.

(224)	JSNENA	Kurdish	Gorani
1PL Suffix			
'one of us'	xánan	yak-ēk lē-mān	yo ja ēma
'two of us'	tə́rnan, tə́nan	dū-wān lē-mān	dūē ja ēma
'three of us'	təlḥánan	sē-yān lē-mān	yarē ja ēma
'four of us'	ʾarbánan	čwār lē-mān	čūār ja ēma
'five of us'	xamšánan	panj lē-mān	panj ja ēma
'six of us'	ʾəštánan	šaš lē-mān	šəš ja ēma
'seven of us'	šoánan	ḥaft lē-mān	ḥot ja ēma
'eight of us'	tmanyánan	hašt lē-mān	hašt ja ēma
'nine of us'	ʾəčʿánan	no lē-mān	no ja ēma
'ten of us'	ʾəsránan	da lē-mān	da ja ēma

The original *mən* 'from' component in the JSNENA constructions is more transparent in some NENA dialects, e.g. cf. J. Urmi +tāhamnan 'three of us'.

In JSNENA when the suffix is 2PL or 3PL, it is attached directly to the numeral, as shown below. This corresponds to an alternative construction in Kurdish and Gorani in which the pronominal clitic is attached to the numeral. The correspondence with Gorani is closer, since in the case of numeral 1, the pronominal clitic attaches directly to the numeral, whereas in Kurdish the indefinite suffix comes between the numeral 1 and the pronominal clitic. In this case the numerals 2 and 3 have the plural ending:

(225) | | JSNENA | Kurdish | Gorani
2PL Suffix
'one of you' | xayaxun | yak-ēk-tān | yo-tā, yoa-tā
'two of you' | tə́rnaxun | dū-ān-tān | dūē-tā
'three of you' | təlḥaxun | sē-ān-tān | yarē-tā
'four of you' | 'arbaxun | čwār-tān | čūār-tā
'five of you' | xamšaxun | panj-tān | panj-tā
'six of you' | 'əštaxun | šaš-tān | šəš-tā
'seven of you' | šoaxun | ḥaft-tān | ḥot-tā
'eight of you' | tmanyaxun | hašt-tān | hašt-tā
'nine of you' | 'əč'axun | no-tān | no-tā
'ten of you' | 'əsraxun | da-tān | da-tā

(226) | | JSNENA | Kurdish | Gorani
3PL Suffix
'one of them' | xayū | yak-ēk-yān | yo-šā, yoa-šā
'two of them' | tənū, traū | dū-ān-yān | dūē-šā
'three of them' | təlḥaū | sē-ān-yān | yarē-šā
'four of them' | 'arbaū | čwār-yān | čūār-šā
'five of them' | xamšaū | panj-yān | panj-šā
'six of them' | 'əštaū | šaš-yān | šəš-šā
'seven of them' | šoaū | ḥaft-yān | ḥot-šā
'eight of them' | tmanyaū | hašt-yān | hašt-šā
'nine of them' | 'əč'aū | no-yān | no-šā
'ten of them' | 'əsraū | da-yān | da-šā

4.11.1 Ordinals

In JSNENA ordinals are formed by attaching the Iranian ending *–mīn* to the cardinal forms. These forms either remain invariable or are inflected for gender and number in agreement with the noun they qualify. The cardinal *xa* 'one' is an exceptional in that it does not usually form an ordinal in this way but rather is replaced by the invariable Iranian (< Arabic) loan form *'awaḷ*. The numeral *trē* 'two' is optionally replaced by the Iranian loan form *dū-*. The ordinal is placed either before or after the head noun. When following the noun, the noun is sometimes connected to it by the Persian *ezafe* clitic *=ē*:

(227) JSNENA
   a. 'The first man'
      'awaḷ gora   *gora 'awaḷ*   *gorá=ē 'awaḷ*
   b. 'The first woman'
      'awaḷ baxta   *baxta 'awaḷ*   *baxtá=ē 'awaḷ*
   c. 'The first people'
      'awaḷ nāšē   *nāšē 'awaḷ*   *nāšē=ē 'awaḷ*
   d. 'The second man'
      trēmīn gora   *gora trēmīn*   *gorá=ē trēmīn*
      dūmīn gora   *gora dūmīn*   *gorá=ē dūmīn*
   e. 'The second woman'
      trēmīn baxta   *baxta trēmīn*   *baxtá=ē trēmīn*
      trēmīnta baxta *baxta trēmīnta*   *baxtá=ē trēmīnta*
   f. 'The second people'
      trēmīn nāšē   *nāšē trēmīn*   *nāšē dūmīn*
      trēmīnē nāšē   *nāšē trēmīne*
   g. 'The third man'
      təlḥamīn gora   *gora təlḥamīn*   *gorá=ē təlḥamīn*
   h. 'The third woman'
      təlḥamīn baxta *baxta təlḥamīn*   *baxtá=ē təlḥamīn*
      təlḥamīnta baxta *baxta təlḥamīnta* *baxtá=ē təlḥamīnta*
   i. 'The third people'
      təlḥamīn nāšē   *nāšē təlḥamīn*
      təlḥamīne nāšē *nāšē təlḥamīnē*
   j. 'The fourth man'
      'arbamīn gora   *gora 'arbamīn*   *gorá=ē 'arbamīn*
   k. 'The fourth woman'
      'arbamīn baxta *baxta 'arbamīn*   *baxtá=ē 'arbamīn*
      'arbamīnta baxta *baxta 'arbamīnta* *baxtá=ē 'arbamīnta*
   l. 'The fourth people'
      'arbamīn nāšē   *nāšē 'arbamīn*
      'arbamīne nāšē *nāšē 'arbamīnē*

These various constructions of ordinals in JSNENA borrow various morphological elements from the ordinal constructions of Iranian languages and also their syntactic patterns. In Gorani and Kurdish of the region ordinals are formed by the addition of *-am*, *-amīn*. When occurring post-nominally, the definite *-a* appears on *-amīn* and in Kurdish the compound nominal marker *-a* (which is another form of *ezafe*) appears on the head noun. Persian ordinals are formed by the addition of *-omin* and *-om*. A post-nominal ordinal is connected to the noun by the *ezafe* clitic *=e*.

(228) a. Gorani　　　　　Kurdish　　　　　　　　Persian
　　　　'The first man'
　　　　yomīn pīyā　　　yakamīn/ awaḷ pīyāg　　avalīn mard
　　　　pīyā yoam　　　　pīyāg=a awaḷīn-a　　　　mard=e aval
　　b. 'The first woman'
　　　　yoamīn žanī　　　yakamīn/ awaḷ žən　　　avalīn zan
　　　　žanī yoam　　　　žən=a awalīn-a　　　　　zan=e aval
　　c. 'The first people'
　　　　yomīn xuḷk　　　yakamīn/ xaḷk　　　　　avalīn mardom
　　d. 'The second man'
　　　　duamīn pīyā　　　dūamīn pīyāg　　　　　dovomin mard
　　　　pīyā duwam-a　　pīyāg=a dūamīn-a　　　mard=e dovom
　　e. 'The second woman'
　　　　duamīn žanī　　　dūamīn žən　　　　　　dovomin zan
　　　　žanī duwam-a　　žən=a dūamīn-a　　　　zan=e dovom
　　　　žanī duwīšn-a
　　f. 'The second people'
　　　　duamīn xuḷk　　　dūamīn xaḷk　　　　　dovomin mardom(-ān)
　　　　xuḷk=ī duwam
　　g. 'The third man'
　　　　yaramīn pīyā　　　sēamīn pīyāg　　　　sevomin mard
　　　　pīyā yaram-a　　　pīyāg=a sēamīn-a　　mard=e sevom
　　h. 'The third woman'
　　　　yaramīn žanī　　　sēamīn žən　　　　　sevomin zan
　　　　žanī yaram-a　　　žən=a sēamīn-a　　　zan=e sevom
　　i. 'The third people'
　　　　yaramīn xuḷk　　　sēamīn xaḷk　　　　sevomin mardom(-ān)
　　　　xuḷk=ī yaram
　　j. 'The fourth man'
　　　　čūaramīn pīyā　　čūarəmīn pīyāg　　　čāromin mard
　　　　pīyā čūaram-a　　pīyāg=a čūarəmīn-a　mard=e čāromī
　　k. 'The fourth woman'
　　　　čūaramīn žanī　　čūarəmīn žən　　　　čāromin zan
　　　　žanī čūaram-a　　žən=a čūarəmīn-a　　zan=e čārom
　　l. 'The fourth people'
　　　　čūaramīn xuḷk　　čūarəmīn xaḷk　　　čāromin mardom(-ān)
　　　　xuḷk=ī čūaram

4.11.2 Fractions

In JSNENA special words for fractions exist only for 'half' and 'quarter':

(229) JSNENA
'half'   *pəlga*
'quarter'   *čārak*

The word for 'half' has an Aramaic etymology but the word for 'quarter' is loan from Kurdish (*čārak*).

4.12 Days of the week

The days of the week in JSNENA have the following forms:

(230) JSNENA
xšāba   'Sunday'
trúšab   'Monday'
təlḥúšab   'Tuesday'
'arbúšab   'Wednesday'
xamšúšab   'Thursday'
rotá   'Friday'
šabát   'Saturday'

The days Sunday—Thursday are derived historically from the phrases **xa b-šāba* 'the first in the week', **trē b-šāba* 'the second in the week', etc. The words for 'Monday'—'Thursday' are in the absolute state without the final nominal inflectional vowel *-a*. This feature of the absolute state in the words for 'Monday'—'Thursday' is common to Jewish dialects throughout NENA and contrasts with Christian dialects, which have forms with the nominal inflectional ending *-a*.

Examples of 'Tuesday' in NENA dialects

(231) Jewish dialects
J. Arbel   *trūšab*
J. Koy Sanjak   *trūšab*
J. Sulemaniyya   *trūšab*
J. Barzan   *trūšēb*
J. Challa   *trūšēb*
J. Nerwa   *trūšēb*

	J. Betanure	trošēb
	J. Dohok	trošēb

(232) Christian dialects

	Ch. Alqosh	trūšāba
	Ch. Ankawa	turšāba
	Ch. Karamlesh	turšāba
	Ch. Bne-Lagəppa	trešāba
	Ch. Bohtan	trūšoba
	Ch. Hasana	trüšāba
	Ch. Aradhin	trūšēba
	Ch. Barwar	trūšēba
	Ch. Umra	turšēba
	Ch. Urmi	trošība
	Ch. Jənnet	turšība
	Ch. Saṛa	trošība

The absoulte state of the forms 'Monday–Thursday' in the Jewish dialects may be related to the truncation of the -a in adverbials, e.g. JSNENA 'əzyo 'today' (< *'əd-yoma). This feature is found in adverbials in all NENA dialects, Jewish and Christian.

Another factor may have been convergence with the form of the days of the week in the Iranian languages of the region. these names are similar in structure to the NENA names. Most of them consist of a numeral and the word šam(a), which appears to be a loan from Aramaic šāba 'week'. In the Gorani and Kurdish of the Sanandaj region these names have a final -a. In the Kurmanji dialects, however, there is no final -a. The Jewish NENA dialects may have dropped the -a by convergence with the Kurmanji form. Since the -a is dropped also in the Jewish Trans-Zab dialects outside the Kurmanji area, it would follow that the Jewish Trans-Zab dialects were in contact with Kurmanji at some point in their history. Further evidence for this history of contact can be identified in the lexicon of JSNENA.

(233)

		Kurmanji	Sanandaj Kurdish	Gorani
	'Sunday'	yakšam	yakšama	yakšama
	'Monday'	dušam	dūšama	dəvašama
	'Tuesday'	sēšam	sēšama	yarašama
	'Wednesday'	čāršam	čwāršama	čwāršama
	'Thursday'	pēnjšam	panjšama	panjšama
	'Friday'	īnē	jəm'a	jum'a
	'Saturday'	šam, šamī	šama	šama

4.13 Seasons

The names of the seasons in JSNENA include inherited Aramaic words for 'Winter' and 'Summer', i.e. the two salient seasonal extremes, and Iranian loanwords for the intermediate seasons of 'Spring' and 'Autumn':

(234) JSNENA   Kurdish/Persian/Gorani
  sətwa   'Winter'
  bahār   'Spring'   cf. K./P. *bahār*; G. *wahār*
  qēṭa   'Summer'
  pāyīz   'Autumn'   cf. G./ K./ P. *pāyīz*

4.14 Adverbs

Numerous adverbial particles of JSNENA are either directly borrowed from Iranian or are parallel in structure to Iranian adverbial constructions. These include the following:

Loanwords

(235) JSNENA   Iranian
  'late'   *drắga*   cf. Gorani *drənga*; Kurdish *drang*
  'formerly'   *qablan*   < Persian *qablan*
  'never'   *hīč kā*   < Kurdish *hīč kā*
  'quickly'   *gurj*   < Gorani, Kurdish *gurj*
  'slowly'   *yawāš*   < Kurdish *yawāš, hēwāš*; Persian *yavāš*
  'well'   *ʿayza*   < Kurdish *ayz* <*azīz* 'well, dear'
  'badly'   *zāe*   < Kurdish *zāya* 'bad'
  'no, none'   *hīč*   < Gorani, Kurdish, Persian *hīč*

Parallel in structure

(236) JSNENA   Iranian
  'above'   *láʿēl*   cf. Kurdish *la bān* 'in above'
  'last night' *tə́mal lēlē*   cf. Gorani *hīzī šawē* 'yesterday night'
  'why?'   *bāqa ma*   cf. Kurdish *bo ča* 'for what'

Hybrid containing an Aramaic and an Iranian element

(237) JSNENA			Iranian
	how?'		ma-jor	cf. Persian če-jur
	'a little of'	xa-rīza	cf. Kurdish rēza-yk; Persian ye rize
	'a few'		xa-ʾəda	cf. Persian ye ede

4.15 Prepositions

Some prepositions in JSNENA are borrowed from Iranian. In some cases JSNENA treats the borrowed prepositions differently from the contact languages.

4.15.1 ba-, b-

The preposition *b-* has a clear Aramaic etymology and occurs in all NENA dialects. In most NENA dialects, however, it has the form *b-* without a lexical vowel. In the Iranian languages of the region there is a preposition with the form *ba-*, which has an Iranian etymology and is functionally similar to NENA *b-*. In JSNENA the NENA preposition *b-* has been matched with the Iranian *ba-* with the result that both *ba-* and *b-* are used in JSNENA as allomorphs of the same preposition.

In both Iranian and JSNENA this preposition may express an instrumental function, e.g.

(238) JSNENA	b-o skīta	'with that knife'
		b-šəmá		'by the name (of)'
	Kurdish	ba kārd		'with a knife'
		ba nāw		'by the name (of)'

In JSNENA, *ba-/b-* may express 'a point in time', which is also a function of *ba-* in Gorani and Kurdish.

(239) JSNENA	ba-do mudata	'at that period'
	Gorani	ba zāroḷayī	'in (my) childhood'
	Kurdish	ba šaw		'at night'

JSNENA *ba-, b-* can express spatial location, e.g.

(240) JSNENA *ba-tanūra*   'in the oven'
              b-ay-kujawā́ē   'in these streets'

The Iranian languages of the Sanandaj region usually employ other prepositions to mark spatial location. In Kurdish, however, *ba* combines with the postposition *ā* (a shortened form of *dā*) to express location:

(241) Gorani   *č-ī dənyā-na*   'in this world'
      Kurdish   *la māḷ-ā*   'at home'
      Kurdish   *ba dasī-ā*   'in his hand'

4.15.2 bāqa 'to, for'

In JSNENA the prepositon *bāqa* is used to encode both the recipient and the beneficiary of an action.

(242) *bāqa tātī*   'to, for my father'
      bāqa do gora   'to, for that man'

The phonetically-similar form *ba* in Gorani and Kurdish is used to express the recipient:

(243) Kurdish and Gorani
      ba mən   'to me'

A beneficiary is generally marked by *bo* in Kurdish (e.g. *bo mən* 'for me') and *pay* in Gorani (e.g. *pay āđī* 'for him').

The preposition *bāqa* is common to the Jewish Trans-Zab dialects. In some NENA dialects the corresponding preposition has the form *qa-/ḵa-*, without the initial *bā-*. This *qa-/ḵa-* appears to be derived historically from the Aramaic preposition *qam* < **qδām* 'before'; cf. Neo-Mandaic *qam* 'to, for' (Häberl 2009, 346). It is possible that *bāqa* is a hybrid preposition consisting of Iranian *ba-* and NENA *qa* (< **qam*). The formation of this hybrid may have been motivated by the need to distinguish the preposition with this meaning clearly from the cognate preposition *qam*, which is used in JSNENA with the orginal sense of 'before'. A similar case of hybridity motivated by the need to distinguish meaning is the preposition *məntak=ē* (§4.15.9).

4.15.3 bayn 'between'

The preposition *bayn* 'between' in JSNENA is a loan from Iranian languages and is ultimately derived from Arabic. Many NENA dialects use the inherited Aramaic form of the preposition, e.g. Ch. Barwar, Ch. Ankawa *bēn*. In many dialects the final /n/ shifts to /l/, e.g. Ch. Qočanəs *bēl*. The loaned form *bayn* is found mainly in Jewish NENA dialects, often with the prefix *ma-*, e.g. J. Betanure, J. Challa, J. Koy Sanjak, *ma bayn* 'what between'. This corresponds to the pattern of the phrase *čə bayn* what between' (= 'between'), which occurs in some dialects of Gorani. The Kurdish of the region uses the phrase *la bayn* 'in between'.

In JSNENA the preposition is regularly followed by the Persian *ezafe* particle =e:

(244) JSNENA
 bayn=ē tātī=ū dāakī 'between my father and my mother'

Likewise *bayn* in Gorani and Persian (but not in Sanandaj Kurdish) is connected with an *ezafe* particle. In Persian *bayn* is often preceded by *az* 'from'.

(245) Gorani
 bayn=ū wē=šān
 between=EZ REFL=3PL
 'between themselves'

(246) Persian
 az bayn=e pedar=o mādar=am
 from between=EZ father=and mother=1SG
 'between my father and my mother'

4.15.4 bē 'without'

The preposition *bē-* 'without' in JSNENA is a loan from Iranian:

(247) JSNENA *bē pūḷē* 'without money'
 Kurdish *bē poḷ* 'without money'

4.15.5 dawr, ba-dawr 'around'

This loaned preposition in JSNENA is regularly connected to the complement by the Persian *ezafe*. The preposition *dawr, ba-dawr* does not take the *ezafe* in Sanandaj Kurdish.

(248) JSNENA *dawr=ē mēz* 'around the table'
        ba-dawr=ē qat 'around the bed'
    Persian *dowr=e miz* 'around the table'
    Kurdish *ba-dawr šār* 'around the city'

4.15.6 ġēr ʾaz 'apart from'

This is a loan from Persian. No *ezafe* is used to link the particle to the complement.

(249) JSNENA *ġēr ʾaz tātī* 'apart from my father'
    Persian *qer az pedaram* 'apart from my father'

4.15.7 lāga 'at the home of, by the side of, with'

(250) JSNENA
    lāga tātī 'at my father's home'
    lāgēf 'at his home'

Before a noun, the preposition *lāga* is sometimes shortened to *lā*:

(251) JSNENA
    lā-ʾəlhá   *lol-ēna-wa-ò'*
    with-God   beseech.PRS-1SG.M-PSTC-TELIC
    'I was beseeching God' (literally: in the presence of God)

The form *lā* is borrowed from Kurdish. The form *lāga*, however, does not directly correspond to a cognate form in Iranian. It is relevant to note that a general feature of the Kurdish dialect of Sanandaj is that a velar stop /g/ is added to some vowel-final nouns and adjectives, e.g. *piyāg* 'man' (<Gorani *piyā*); *čarmig* 'white' (<Gorani *čarma*). The JSNENA form *lāga* could be considered to have its source in the over-generalisation of the phonological rule of adding -*g* to vowel-final words (here *lā*), to which the Aramaic ending -*a* is added, i.e. *lā-g-a*.

4.15.8 mangol, mangal 'like'

Most NENA dialects use inherited Aramaic forms for 'like', such as *ʾax* or *max*. JSNENA has the forms *mangol* and *mangal*, which appear to be from a different source. Some

Jewish Trans-Zab dialects have the form *magon* 'like', which may be derived from *ma-gon* 'what colour?' 'what kind?'. The component *gon* is a noun attested in Syriac, which is of Iranian origin (Ciancaglini 2008 vol. 2, 137). The JSNENA forms *mangol* and *mangal* may have developed by the shift of final *-n* to *-l*. The phonetic process that resulted in the insertion of the nasal /n/ before the /g/, however, is unclear. In literary Gorani the corresponding word for 'like' has the form *mangor*. It is easiest to identify the JSNENA form *mangol*, therefore, as a direct loan from Gorani. The JSNENA particle is sometimes connected to its complement with the Persian *ezafe* =*e*, as is the case with Persian *mānand*:

(252) JSNENA   *mangol tātī*   'like my father'
                    mangol=ē tātī
        Persian   *mānand=e pedaram*   'like my father'

4.15.9 məntákē 'with'

The JSNENA preposition *mən-tak=ē* is composed of the Aramaic particle *mən* 'from/with', the Iranian element *tak* and the Persian *ezafe* =*e*, e.g. *mən-tákē tātī* 'with my father'. The preposition is probably a calque of Kurdish *latak* 'with', which occurs also in the circumpositional form *la-tak . . . ā*. This is composed of *la* 'from, in' and *tak*. Unlike Kurdish *la-tak*, the JSNENA form *mən-tak=ē* has the *ezafe* particle. This appears to be replicating the syntax of the Persian preposition *hamrāh* 'together with', which is regularly used with the *ezafe* particle, e.g. *hamrāh=ē pedar-am* 'with my father'. The motivation for the formation of this hybrid preposition in JSNENA is that the NENA preposition *mən* in most NENA dialects is polysemous, meaning both 'from' and 'with'. The meaning of 'with' developed from reanalysis of a shortened form of the historical preposition **ʿam* meaning 'with'. Both *mən* 'from' and **ʿam* 'with' frequently shortened to *m-* before nouns. Due to this ambiguity *m-* meaning 'with' was reanalysed as a shortened form of *mən*. Many NENA dialects tolerate the polysemy of *mən* 'from/with'. JSNENA, however, has replicated the pattern and part of the material of a form in a contact language that unambiguously means 'with' to make a morphological distinction between the two meanings. The preposition *mən* 'from' has been matched with the *la* element in Kurdish *la-tak*. In Kurdish, as remarked, one of the basic meaning of *la* is 'from', which corresponds to JSNENA *mən* 'from'. Note that Kurdish *la-tak* is often accompanied by the postposition *-ā*, and has the circumposition form *la-tak . . .-ā*:

(253) JSNENA *mən-tak=ē tātī*   'with my father'
      Kurdish *la-tak bāwkəm-ā*
      Persian *hamrāh=e pedaram*

4.16 Miscellaneous uninflected particles

JSNENA makes use of numerous uninflected particles. These include those that operate within a clause, those that function as clausal conjunctions and those that function as discourse markers, to manage the discourse. The majority are loanwords from Gorani, Kurdish or Persian. Most of the words that are derived from Persian are likely to have been borrowed through Kurdish. Examples of loaned particles in JSNENA are the following:

(254)

		JSNENA	Iranian
	'if'	*'agar*	< G., K., P. *agar*
	'if not'	*'agar-nam*	cf. P. *age na*
	'indeed, in truth'	*'ensāfan*	< P. *ensāfan* < Arab.
	'too, also; as for'	*=əč, =č*	< G. *=īč, =č*
	'so much; so many'	*əqra*	cf. Bijar K. *awqara*
	'afterwards, then'	*baʿdan*	< P. *baʿdan* < Arab.
	'perhaps'	*baška, baškam*	< K. *baškam*, G. *bašqom*
	'still, again'	*bāz, bāz-ham*	< P. *bāz, bāz-ham*
	'if, whether'	*čanānče*	< P. *čenānče*
	'again'	*dūbára*	< G., K. *dūbāra*; P. *dobāre*
	'only'	*faqat*	< G., K., P. *faqat* < Arab.
	'apart from'	*ġēr ʾaz*	< P. *ġer az*
	'of course'	*halbata*	< G. *halbata*; P. *albate*
	'also'	*ham*	< G., K., P. *ham*
	'also the same'	*ham-čonīn*	< P. *hamčenin* 'too'
	'always'	*hamēša*	< P. *hamiše*; K. *hamīša*
	'everything that'	*har-čī*	< G., K., P., *har-čī*
	'because', 'when'	*čūn*	< K. *čūn* 'because, since'
	'even, even if'	*dāxom*	< K. *dāxom* 'I wish'
	'still, yet'	*hēštan*	cf. K. *hīštā*
	'now (connective)'	*jā*	< K. *jā*
	'on one side'	*jyā*	< G. *jīyā*; K. *ba jīyā*
	'perhaps'	*mágar*	< G., K., P. *magar*
	'for example'	*masalan*	< P. *masalan* < Arab.
	'especially'	*maxṣūṣan*	<. P. *maxsusan* < Arab.

'then, so'	*pas*	< K., P. *pas*
'concerning'	*rajə' ba-*	< P. *rāje' be*
'in truth, in fact'	*rāsī*	< K. *řāsī; rāstī*
'perhaps'	*šāyad*	cf. P. *šāyad*
'alone, only'	*tanhā*	< K., P. *tanhā*
'but'	*wálē*	< K. *walē*
'a little'	*xan*	cf. G., K. *xənj* 'small, tiny'
filler for word	*xéta*	cf. K. *čəta*
'or'	*yā*	< G. *yā, yām*; K. *yā, yān*; P. *yā*
relative particle	*yā*	< cf. Kurmanji *yā* (f. *ezafe*)
'that means, that is'	*yani*	< G., K., P. *yanī* < Arab.
'more'	*zoa*	cf. K. *zīyāw*

4.17 Summary

There are some linguistic constraints on borrowing morphology into a maintained language. Generally speaking, these can be divided into constraints based on (i) congruence of morphological structures, (ii) transparency, and (iii) functional considerations (cf. Winford 2003, 91–97 for overview).

As shown in Table 43, direct borrowings of morphological forms from Iranian into JSNENA are not numerous. Those 'matter' borrowings (Matras 2009) that have been identified in JSNENA reflect motivations for borrowing morphology into a maintained language. For instance, the definite article fills a gap in the morphemic inventory of JSNENA. It is also associated with discourse pragmatics and discourse management, which are dimensions of a language that are particularly prone to borrowing cross-linguistically (Matras 2009). On the other hand, the importation of the indefinite suffix *-ēk*, is not motivated by a gap in JSNENA, which has an indefinite marker, i.e. *xa* 'one'. Here the borrowing of *-ēk* is facilitated by congruence between morphological structures of the languages in the contact. As remarked in (§4.6) *-ēk* has a functional motivation, in that it is used in contexts which have a subjective evaluative force, e.g. 'he is a wonderful boy!' This is likely to have motivated borrowing to give the statements added salience. Another functional motivation for borrowing of morphology is the disambiguation or narrowing of meaning of inherited forms through hybrid constructions such as JSNENA *bā-qa* 'to', consisting of Iranian *ba-* 'to' and Aramaic *qa* 'to, before'.

Continuing with Winford's classification of morphological constraints on borrowing in a maintained language, transparency of morphological structures is another factor triggering contact. This applies to the borrowing by JSNENA of a number of Iranian morphological and morphosyntactic patterns. For instance, the

Table 43: Direct borrowing of nominal morphological features into NENA.

Feature attested in JSNENA	Main contact language	section
Definite article -akē	Gorani	§4.5
Indefinite suffix -ēk	Kurdish	§4.6
Particle -min used for forming ordinals	G./K./P.	§4.11.1
Ezafe on certain prepositions	Persian	§4.15

replication of the lack of *ezafe* in noun-genitive constructions is facilitated by the fact that the same noun-genitive ordering occurs in Kurdish, and the relative simplicity of the noun-genitive structure. Similarly, the use of certain nouns in the absolutive state in JSNENA is a replication of transparently corresponding nouns in Iranian. The same applies to the replication of compound adjectives, consisting of particles meaning 'owner' and 'without' combined with adjectives in JSNENA, and the replication of attaching pronominal suffixes to cardinal numbers, see Table 44 for pattern replication of nominal morphological features in JSNENA.

The gender assignment of loanwords in JSNENA and inflection of adjectives are facilitated by the close typological fit in gender systems between languages in contact, namely JSNENA and Gorani.

Table 44: Pattern replication of nominal morphological features in NENA.

Feature attested in JSNENA	Main contact language	section
Nouns in the absolutive state	Gorani/ Kurdish	§4.7
Simple juxtaposition in Noun-Genitive constructions	Kurdish	§4.8
2PL or 3PL pronominal suffix attaching directly to numerals	Gorani	§4.11
Gender assignment for loanwords	Gorani	§4.2.1
Inflection of adjectives	Gorani	§4.10.1
Compound adjectives	Kurdish, Gorani	§4.10.3

Language contact can act as a constraint on change if the contact language shares the feature with the recipient language. This is mostly the case with inflectional and derivational endings listed in Table 45, which happen to have similar forms in Iranian and have thus been preserved in JSNENA. The phenomenon attested here can be termed replica preservation (cf. Khan 2020).

Table 45: Nominal morphological features in JSNENA reinforced due to contact with Iranian.

feature attested in JSNENA	Main contact language	section
Plural ending -ē	Gorani	§4.4
Plural ending -yālē	Kurdish	§4.4
Plural of loanwords	Gorani	§4.4
Derivational suffix -āna	Gorani and Kurdish	§4.3

Similarly, contact can result in the loss of morphological distinctions in the recipient language. As represented in Table 46, JSNENA lost gender distinctions in numerals possibly under Kurdish influence. The original mismatch between languages in terms of the presence or lack of gender distinction was resolved by the loss of gender in JSNENA.

Table 46: Nominal morphological features in JSNENA lost due to contact.

Feature attested in JSNENA	Main contact language	section
Loss of gender distinction in numerals	Kurdish	§4.11

5 The morphology of verbs

5.1 Introductory overview

A distinctive feature of JSNENA verbal morphology is the use of different past stems and resultative participles for transitive agentive verbs, on the one hand, and intransitive unaccusative or passive verbs on the other. This is an innovation in NENA and appears to have come about through convergence with the morphological patterns of the verbal categories of Gorani. Another innovative feature of JSNENA, which is not found in the main body of NENA, is the extension of the causative inflection pattern of derived causative verbs to all agentive verbs. The catalyst for this appears to be the distribution of causative morphemes in Gorani and Kurdish.

The word-initial stress of imperatives of JSNENA matches the prosody of the Iranian languages.

JSNENA has direct and oblique verbal suffixes, the latter referred to as L-suffixes. In JSNENA and Gorani direct suffixes are used, among other functions, as inflections of the transitive past stem in order to express the undergoer of the action, while Sanandaj Kurdish uses oblique clitics for this purpose. In JSNENA and the Iranian languages the direct suffixes are attached to the past unaccusative/passive stem. The prosody of JSNENA in these paradigms has converged with that of the Iranian languages of the region.

In Gorani and Kurdish, oblique clitics are used to mark the agent of past stems in transitive constructions. JSNENA replicates this pattern by oblique L-suffixes to express the agent of agentive past stems. The loss of full clitic status of the NENA L-suffixes seems to have come about by analogy with the direct suffixes, which are fully bonded prosodically to the verbal stem.

In the main body of NENA dialects, whose heartland is Iraq, the oblique L-suffixes are used on both transitive and intransitive past stems. This is likely to be the historically earlier pattern in NENA. JSNENA attaches oblique L-suffixes only to agentive transitive past stems. This is an innovation that has come about through convergence with indexing patterns of the Iranian languages in western Iran.

An indicative particle *k-* is attached to a subset of present stem verbs in JSNENA. This lack of systematicity in the use of the particle matches Gorani, in which a corresponding indicative particle (*mə-*) appears with only certain lexical verbs. JSNENA uses the indicative particle on the infinitive in progressive constructions consisting of an infinitive and finite verb. This is a feature that is not found across other NENA dialects and has arisen by replication of a parallel construction in Gorani.

Although JSNENA has not replicated the Iranian subjunctive particle, it has borrowed several Iranian deontic particles.

The present copula of most NENA dialects has verbal inflection only in the 1ˢᵗ and 2ⁿᵈ persons. A distinctive feature of JSNENA is the complete levelling of the inflection of the present copula with verbal inflection. This matches more closely the profile of the copula in Kurdish than that of Gorani. The pattern of the past copula in JSNENA corresponds to Gorani.

In JSNENA the ingressive sense of 'becoming' is expressed by the lexical verb *x-Ø-r*. The Iranian languages, by contrast, use the same lexical verb to express 'to be' and 'to become'. The JSNENA ingressive verb exhibits parallels with Arabic rather than Iranian.

The pattern of direct object clitics on present stem verbs in Gorani is the closest match to that of JSNENA, in which the oblique L-suffixes expressing the object are placed after the person suffixes.

JSNENA matches the Gorani pattern of expression of pronominal objects ergatively by direct suffixes on past stem verbs, except for the fact that in JSNENA the object expressed by the direct suffixes is restricted to third person.

The JSNENA perfect constructions with the resultative participle and copula have developed on the model of Gorani rather than Kurdish.

The perfect in JSNENA can be used with an 'indirective' function, i.e. expressing events which the speaker has not witnessed or which occurred in the remote past. This matches the indirective use of the perfect also in Gorani and Kurdish of the Sanandaj region.

In JSNENA light verb constructions, consisting of a finite light verb and a non-finite element, are calqued on Kurdish and/or Gorani, which in turn often borrowed them from Persian. The JSNENA object constructions of light verb constructions are a replication of the Gorani constructions

5.2 Verb stems

In JSNENA verbs inflect for TAM by root and pattern morphology, which is a characteristic feature of Semitic languages. Discontinuous lexical roots consisting of three, or in some cases four, consonants are mapped onto discontinuous morphological patterns of vowels and consonants, e.g.

(255) JSNENA
root *g-r-š* 'to pull' + present pattern *CaCəC* > *garəš*
root *s-m-x* 'to stand' + past intransitive pattern *CCiC* > *smīx*

In addition to patterns of TAM inflection, the verbal system has derivational patterns, the main function of which is to increase the valency of the verb. In JSNENA two derivational patterns are used. The basic pattern will be referred to as Form I and two derivational patterns as Form II and Form III respectively. Form II is productive in earlier Aramaic and various other NENA dialects. In JSNENA, however, it is only marginal. Indeed in some trans-Zab NENA dialects it has been eliminated altogether (Mutzafi 2004b; Khan 2018e, 329). It is important to note that even Form III is not fully productive and is not available for all verbal roots. The derivational patterns are, as the term suggests, lexical items formed by derivation and not the result of regular inflection. Examples:

(256) JSNENA
 root *r-x-š* 'to walk'
 Form I present stem pattern *CaCəC* > *raxəš* 'he walks'
 Form III present stem pattern *maCCəC* > *marxəš* 'he causes to walk'

We present below for the three derivational forms the inflectional patterns of the various TAM stems. The discontinuous patterns are applied consistently across all lexical roots.

A distinction must be made between the stems of agentive verbs, on the one hand, and those of intransitive unaccusative and passivised transitive verbs, on the other, since intransitive unaccusative and passive verbs have forms of past stems and resultative participles that are different from those of agentive verbs. Unaccusative intransitive verbs express a change of state of the subject, including change of position (movement) and posture. With an unaccusative intransitive verb there is no necessarily implied external agent, whereas there is, in principle, the implication of an external agent or cause in passive constructions. An agentive verb is typically transitive with an object, but it may be intransitive. This applies particularly to verbs of omission of sound, e.g. *nwəxle* 'it barked'. Such intransitive agentive verbs will be referred to as unergative. There is a residue of a few verbs of perception that are treated grammatically as agentive in JSNENA although the subject cannot be felicitously classified as semantically agentive, e.g. *x-z-y* 'to see', *š-m-y* 'to hear'. They are, however, transitive in that they typically have a direct object, which is the prototypical construction of agentive verbs.

There are also differences between agentive and intransitive verbs in the imperative stems. In other stems (present and infinitive) intransitive verbs are identical in pattern to transitive verbs. There are no passive stems apart from those of the past stem and resultative participle.

Form I

(257) JSNENA
g-r-š 'to pull' (tr.), *s-m-x* 'to stand' (intr.)

	Agentive	Intransitive unaccasative	Passive
Present stem	garəš-	saməx-	—
Past stem	grəš-	smīx-	grīš-
Resultative participle	gərša	smīxa	grīša
Imperative	gruš ~ gárəš	smux ~ səmux	—
Infinitive	garošē	samoxē	—

Form II

(258) JSNENA
z-b-n 'to sell' (tr.)

	Agentive	Passive
Present stem	zabən-	—
Past stem	zbən-	zbīn-
Resultative participle	zəbna	zbīna
Imperative	zábən	—
Infinitive	zabonē	—

Form III

(259) JSNENA
m-r-š-x 'to cause to walk' (tr.), *m-s-k-r* 'to become lost' (intr.)

	Agentive	Intransitive unaccusative	Passive
Present stem	marxəš-	maskər-	—
Past stem	mərxəš-	məskīr-	mərxīš-
Resultative participle	mərxša	məskīra	mərxīša
Imperative	márxəš	máskur	—
Infinitive	marxošē	maskorē	—

The organisation of the verbal morphology into these categories, viz. present stem, past stem, resultative participle, imperative and infinitive, is a general feature of NENA dialects. The inflectional patterns of some of these categories in JSNENA, however, exhibit various innovations within the NENA dialect group. The most conspicuous one is the existence of two sets of past stem and resultative participle, one agentive and the other unaccusative/passive. The Form I agentive stem *grəš-* has developed by the imposition on it of the vocalic pattern of the Form III past agentive stem, viz. that of *mədməx*, the first vowel being deleted. Form III expresses the causative and most frequently expresses an increase in valency of an intransitive verb and its conversion from an unaccusative to an agentive, e.g. Form I *daməx* 'he sleeps', Form III *madməx* 'he causes to sleep'. The key factor is, in fact, agentivity rather than valency, since the Form III vocalic pattern is used with Form I intransitive agentive (unergative) verbs of sound emission. Such verbs have no passives, e.g.

(260) JSNENA
 n-w-x 'to bark'

	Agentive	Passive
Past stem	*nwəx-*	—
Resultative participle	*nəwxa*	—

The pattern of the Form I unaccusative/passive past stem *qṭīl-* is the original pattern of the past stem, which is ultimately derived historically from a stative/passive participle. This pattern has been extended to unaccusative/passive past stems of Form III, viz. *mədmīx*. Historically, the original past stem of Form III is *mədməx*. The same transfer of vocalic patterns between Form I and Form III has resulted in the morphological distinctions between agentive and unaccusative/passive in the resultative participles of stems I and III.

This splitting of the morphology of past stems and resultative participles is found in neighbouring Jewish NENA dialects in western Iran and Sulemaniyya. It appears to have come about through convergence with the morphological patterns of the verbal categories of Gorani.

The Iranian languages of the Sanandaj region exhibit a similar organisation of verbal morphological stems, including present, past, resultative participle, and infinitive. The imperative is based on the present stem:

(261) Gorani
 karḍay 'to do'
 Present stem *kar*
 Past stem *karḍ*
 Resultative participle *karḍa* (m); *karḍē* (f, pl)
 Imperative *kar*
 Infinitive *karḍay*

(262) Kurdish
 gərtən 'to take'
 Present stem *gər*
 Past stem *gərt*

Resultative participle *gərtəg, gərtē*
Imperative *gər*
Infinitive *gərtən*

This organisation is common to modern western Iranian languages. The present stem preserves the present stem of Old Iranian. The past stem derives historically from the passive participle. The NENA present stem *qaṭəl* is historically an active participle. The original Aramaic finite present form, the so-called prefix conjugation *yiqṭol*, however, had by late antiquity become restricted to modal functions and was supplanted by the active particle *qaṭal* in its present functions. It is for this reason that the Iranian present stem is matched by the NENA *qaṭəl* form. The NENA *qaṭəl* form, indeed, also came to replace the *yiqṭol* form in modal subjunctive functions. This is likely to be in imitation of the Iranian present stem, which is the stem of both the indicative present and the subjunctive. The historical origin of the past stem in NENA is the passive participle, in imitation of Iranian. The original finite past form, the so-called suffix conjugation *qṭal*, was replaced by the passive participle. The development in JSNENA of the split between agentive and unaccusative/passive past stems and participles is the result of a convergence with features of the Iranian languages of western Iran, in particular Gorani.

In the Iranian languages of Sanandaj, and in western Iranian in general, morphology is in principle agglutinative. In most cases the past form is formed by the addition of a phoneme to the present stem.

(263) Gorani
Present Past
kar   *karđ*   'do'
lēs   *lēsā*   'lick'

(264) Kurdish
Present Past
gər   *gərt*   'take'
zān   *zānī*   'know'

The passive is formed by adding a morpheme to the present stem of transitive verbs. These morphemes inflect for present and past:

(265)   Gorani   Kurdish
Present   *-īa*   *-(r)yē*
Past   *-īā*   *-(r)yā*

(266) Gorani
kūštāy 'to kill'

Present	Present passive	Past passive
kʷš	*kʷšīa*	*kʷšīā*

(267) Kurdish
xwārdin 'to eat'

Present	Present passive	Past passive
xo	*xoryē*	*xoryā*

The passive morpheme is a derivational morpheme that reduces the valency of a transitive verb, which is typically unmarked, without any derivational morpheme. In Gorani the passive morpheme is also used in the stem of some intransitive unaccusative verbs that are not derived from an unmarked transitive. Such unaccusative verbs typically express eventualities with internal causation rather than external causation, e.g.

(268) Gorani

Infinitive		Present	Past
ləkyāy	'to stick'	*ləkīa*	*ləkīā*
mānīāy	'to be tired'	*mānīa*	*mānīā*
māřīāy	'to break'	*māřīa*	*māřīā*
tāwīāy	'to melt'	*tāwīa*	*tāwīā*
gərīāy	'to boil'	*gərīa*	*gərīā*
wurīāy	'to itch'	*wurīa*	*wurīā*
gəžīāy	'to fight (intr.)'	*gəžīa*	*gəžīā*

The identical treatment of stem morphology for passives and (a subset of) intransitive unaccusative stems is seen in the table below, which presents the active and passive stems of the agentive verb *wātay* 'to say' and the stems of the intransitive unaccusative verb *māřīāy* 'to break':

(269) Gorani

	Active transitive	Passive	Intransitive
Present stem	*wāč*	*wāčīa*	*māřīa*
Past stem	*wāt*	*wāčīā*	*māřīā*
Participle	*wāta*		*māřīā(a)*
Infinitive	*wātay*		*māřīāy*

This morphological alignment of passive and intransitive unaccusative morphology corresponds to the alignment of past stems in JSNENA, whereby the same pattern is used for passive and intransitive unaccusative verbs, e.g.

(270) Gorani
      Form I   Passive   Intransitive unaccusative
      CCiC   grīš 'he was pulled' smīx 'he stood'

In JSNENA this parallel between passive and intransitive unaccusative stems is regular whereas in Gorani it applies only to a subset of intransitive stems. JSNENA appears to have converged with this pattern of morphological alignment in this subset of Gorani verbs. Since JSNENA distinguishes stems by regular vocalic patterns, i.e. the vocalic patterns in any particular verbal form (i.e. Form I, Form II or Form III) constitute inflection, this was generalised to all lexical verbs in a particular form. In Gorani, by contrast, the distinctions in stem morphology is by agglutinative derivation, which is specific to individual lexical verbs. JSNENA, therefore, has undergone a change in stem inflection by convergence with a subset of stem derivational patterns. Another factor was that all agentive active verbs in JSNENA acquired the vocalic pattern of causative Form III verbs. This would have facilitated the systematic division of the system into agentive/causative vs unaccusative/passive. This convergence between JSNENA and Gorani is, therefore, a case of the replication of a grammatical category but not its exponence, i.e. the manner of expressing it, which is a recognised phenomenon in language contact studies (Hickey 2010b, 11).

In Gorani the passive morpheme is used in both past and present stems of intransitive verbs. In JSNENA the alignment of passive and intransitive unaccusative morphology is found only in the past stem and resultative particle. This is because there is no passive inflection pattern for the present stem.

We shall now consider the possible Iranian background of the extension of the causative inflection pattern to agentive verbs in Form I in JSNENA. In Iranian, the valency of a verb is increased by adding a causative morpheme (Gorani: -n (present), -nā (past); Sanandaj Kurdish: -(ē)n (present), -n(d) (past)) to the present intransitive stems. In Gorani the causative suffix is infixed into the past intransitive stem:[1]

---

[1] By assuming that the causative affix attaches to the present stem of the verb, MacKenzie (1966, 49) takes the sequence -n-ā as a single affix, hence -nā, and labels it as a causative past suffix.

(271) Gorani[2]

Infinitive	Intransitive		Causative	
	present	past	present	past
wuřāy	wuř	wuřā	wuř-n	wuř-n-ā
	'to be destroyed'		'to destroy'	
ēšāy	ēš	ēšā	ēš-n	ēš-n-ā
	'to hurt (intr.)'		'to hurt (tr.)'	
gēḷāy	gēḷ	gēḷā	gēḷ-n	gēḷ-n-ā
	'to wander'		'to turn over'	
gərawāy	gəraw	gərawā	gəraw-n	gəraw-n-ā
	'to weep'		'to make weep'	
fīsāy	fīs	fīsā	fīs-n	fīs-n-ā
	'to overflow'		'to soak'	

(272) Kurdish

Infinitive	Intransitive		Causative	
	present	past	present	past
škān	škē	škā	škē-(ē)n	škā-n(d)
	'to break'		'to break'	
sotān	soz	sotā	sot-ēn	sotā-n(d)
	'to burn (intr.)'		'to burn(tr.)'	
ēšān	ēš	ēšā	ēš-ēn	ēšā-n(d)
	'to hurt (intr.)'		'to hurt (tr.)'	
fīsān	fīs	fīs(y)ā	fīs-ēn	fīsā-n(d)
	'to overflow'		'to soak'	

Gorani has also preserved the older pattern of Umlaut for the formation of causative stems, attested in Middle Persian (cf. Skjærvø 2009, 220), e.g. Middle Persian *ahram* 'go up' vs. *ahrām* 'lead up' (tr.).

---

[2] In one case the causative formative is added to the transitive base to yield a change in meaning: *wirāstay* 'to sew' (*wirāz* (prs), *wirāzā* (pst)); *(awa)-rāznay* 'to adorn' ((*awa)-rāzn* (prs); *(awa)-rāznā* (pst)).

Example:

(273) Gorani

Infinitive	Intransitive		Causative	
	present	past	present	past
mář̄īay	mař̌ia	mař̌iā	mář̌	mář̌ā
	'to break'		'to break'	

It is significant that the Iranian causative morphemes in Gorani and Kurdish are also used in agentive intransitive verbs expressing the emission of sound, i.e. unergative verbs. This indicates that the suffixes may also mark agentivity without the increase in valency that is characteristic of the causative. When the causative morpheme is present on the verbs of sound emission, the verb is treated as transitive and the agent is indexed by a pronominal clitic. There are alternative inflections of some verbs of sound emission without the causative morpheme. These are treated as intransitive verbs and the subject is marked by a 3SG zero affix in the past tense.

(274) Gorani
  qēřnāy   'to shout'
  qīžnāy   'to scream'
  gafnā=š, gafā-Ø   'it barked'
  bāřnā=š, bāřā-Ø   '(the sheep) bleated'
  qāřnā=š, qāřā-Ø   '(the goat) bleated'
  sařnā=š, sařā-Ø   'it brayed'
  qūlnā=š   'it crowed'
  hīlnā=š   'it neighed'
  lurnā=š/ nūznā=š   'it howled'

(275) Kurdish
  qāřān=ī   '(the sheep) bleated'
  bālān=ī   '(the goat) bleated'
  sařān=ī   'it brayed'
  čīrān=ī   'it neighed'
  a=y-qūlān   'it crowed'
  a=y-lūrān   'it howled'
  a=y-bořān/qēřān=ī   'he/she shouted'
  qīžān=ī   'he/she screamed'

This extension of a causative morphology to the marking of agentive irrespective of valency is matched by the JSNENA agentive patterns in the past stem and participle. The fact that the agentive/causative vocalic pattern in JSNENA has been levelled across Form I and Form III reflects the breakdown of the Semitic system of derivational forms with distinct vocalic patterns. Instead, a single morphological vocalic pattern is used across the historical vestiges of the derivational forms to express the agentive/causative and a second vocalic pattern is used across the forms to express the unaccusative/passive. This matches the morphological system in the Iranian languages whereby a single morpheme marks agentive/causative and a single morpheme marks unaccusative/passive across the verbal lexicon. In Iranian these morphemes are agglutinative and are not applied regularly across all lexical verbs. In JSNENA the morphological patterns of verbal stems are inflectional and regular. So, we see that JSNENA inflection was matched with a subset of Iranian agglutinative morphemes.

In JSNENA this distinction of semantic role is only available in the past stems and participles. This has been facilitated by the fact that vocalic patterns of these stems are historically different in Form I and in the causative Form III. The vocalic pattern of the present stems of Form I and the causative Form III are the same (*a*—*ə*, e.g. *garəš, madməx*), so no morphological distinctions of agentivity were possible.

5.2.1 Imperatives

In JSNENA stress is placed on the initial syllable of imperative forms. As a result, in some cases only stress position distinguishes the imperative from the present form, e.g.

(276) JSNENA
Imperative Present
màxwē!¹ 'Show!' *maxwḕ¹* 'he shows'

In the Iranian languages of Sanandaj, the imperative/subjunctive prefix *ba-* is stress-bearing. This means that the stress is retracted to the first syllable of the imperative verbal form, in contrast to the final-syllable stress placement in the realis form of present stem verbs.

(277) Kurdish and Gorani
Imperative present indicative
K. *bə̀-nūs-a!¹* 'Write!' K. *a-nūs-î́* 'you write'
G. *bùs-a¹* 'Sleep!' G. *m-ūs-î́* 'you sleep'

The word-initial stress of imperatives of JSNENA, therefore, matches the prosody of the Iranian languages.

5.3 Verbal inflectional suffixes

In JSNENA the present and past verbal stems are inflected with direct person suffixes (see Table 47), and with oblique person suffixes (L-suffixes, see Table 48). Likewise, in Iranian of the Sanandaj region the present and past verbal stems have direct and oblique person inflections.

In JSNENA there is one set of direct suffixes, which are used with both present and past stems. In Iranian there are two sets of direct suffixes according to the stem of the verb. The main difference between the two sets is that the 3SG has a zero suffix in the paradigm that is attached to past stems.

As for their function, the direct suffixes express the subject of all present stem verbs and of the past intransitive unaccusative/passive stem. In Gorani and JSNENA they are also used as inflections of the transitive past stem in order to express the undergoer of the action, while Sanandaj Kurdish uses oblique clitics for this purpose.

Table 47: Direct inflectional suffixes in JSNENA, Gorani, and Kurdish.

	JSNENA	Gorani		Kurdish	
	Present/Past	Present	Past	Present	Past
3SG.M	-Ø	-o	-Ø	-ē, -ā	-Ø
3SG.F	-a		-a		
3PL	-ī	-ā	-ē	-ən	
2SG.M	-ēt	-ī		-ī	
2SG.F	-at				
2PL	-ētun	-dē		-ən	
1SG.M	-ēn	-ū	-ā(nē)	-am	
1SG.F	-an, -ana				
1PL	-ēx, -ēxīn	-mē		-īn	

In JSNENA when the direct suffixes are attached to the present stem, the suffixes are in most cases stressed:

(278) JSNENA
      g-r-š 'to pull'
      3SG.M *garáš-Ø*   'he pulls'
      3SG.F *garš-á*   'she pulls'
      3PL   *garš-í*   'they pull', etc.

2SG.M	garš-ḗt
2SG.F	garš-át
2PL	garš-ḗtun
1SG.M	garáš-na
1SG.F	garš-án, garš-ána
1PL	garš-ḗx, garš-ḗxīn

The stress falls on the stem in the 3SG.M, since the suffix is zero, and in the 1SG.M, since the rule of stressing the suffix is outranked by a rule that the stress must fall on a syllable containing a root consonant (§2.4.3).

When the direct suffixes are attached to the past unaccusative/passive stem, the suffixes are not stressed, but rather the stress falls on the stem throughout the paradigm:

(279) JSNENA
Unaccusative s-m-x 'to stand'

3SG.M	smíx-Ø, sə́mīx-Ø	'he stood'
3SG.F	smíx-a	'she stood'
3PL	smíx-ī	'they stood' etc.
2SG.M	smíx-ēt	
2SG.F	smíx-at	
2PL	smíx-ētun	
1SG.M	smíx-na	
1SG.F	smíx-an, smíx-ana	
1PL	smíx-ēx, smíx-ēxīn	

(280) JSNENA
Passive g-r-š 'to pull'

3SG.M	gríš-Ø, gə́rīš-Ø	'he was pulled'
3SG.F	gríš-a	'she was pulled'
3PL	gríš-ī	'they were pulled', etc.
2SG.M	gríš-ēt	
2SG.F	gríš-at	
2PL	gríš-ētun	
1SG.M	gríš-na	
1SG.F	gríš-an, gríš-ana	
1PL	gríš-ēx, gríš-ēxīn	

The variant in the 3SG.M (sə́mīx, gə́rīš) has the stress on a penultimate syllable of the stem. The vowel in this syllable is in origin an epenthetic. The motivation for this appears to be analogy with the general penultimate stress in most of the rest of the paradigm.

Historically, the direct suffixes on present and past stems in JSNENA are of the same origin. The first and second person suffixes are originally clitic personal pronouns and the third person suffixes are originally nominal inflections (SG.M, SG.F, PL). There is, therefore, no historical reason internal to NENA why there should be a difference in stress placement in present and past stems with direct suffixes. The explanation is that the prosody of JSNENA in these paradigms has converged with that of the Iranian languages of region. In Gorani and Kurdish, the stress falls on the direct suffixes when they are attached to a present stem but on the stem when the suffixes are attached to a past stem:

(281) Gorani Kurdish
Present 'to send'
3SG	kīyān-ó	'he/she sends'		a-nēr-é
3PL	kīyān-á̄	'they send'		a-nēr-ón
2SG	kīyān-í́	'you send', etc.		a-nēr-í́
2PL	kīyān-dé			a-nēr-ón
1SG	kīyān-ú̄			a-nēr-ə́m
1PL	kīyān-mé			a-nēr-ín

(282) Gorani Kurdish
Past 'to die'
3SG.M	márđ-Ø	'he died'		mə́rd-Ø
3SG.F	márđ-a	'she died'		
3PL	márđ-ē	'they died', etc.		mə́rd-ən
2SG	márđ-ī			mə́rd-ī
2PL	márđ-dē			mə́rd-ən
1SG	márđ-ā			mə́rd-əm
1PL	márđ-mē			mə́rd-īn

(283) Gorani Kurdish
Passive 'to kill'
3SG.M	kuš-yá́-Ø	'he was killed'		kož-yá́-Ø
3SG.F	kuš-yá́-(a)	'she was killed'		
3PL	kuš-í́-yē	'they were killed', etc.		kož-yá́-n
2SG	kuš-yá́-y			kož-yá́-y
2PL	kuš-yá́-ydē			kož-yá́-n
1SG	kuš-īá́-ā			kož-yá́-m
1PL	kuš-yá́-ymē			kož-yá́-n

In Iranian there is a historical explanation for this difference in stress position. The lack of stress on the suffixes of past stems has resulted from the fact that these suffixes were originally copula clitics. The suffixes of the present stem, by contrast, were originally personal suffixes and not copulas (Öpengin 2019).

In Gorani and Kurdish oblique clitics are used to mark the agent of past stems in agentive constructions. JSNENA replicates this pattern by oblique L-suffixes to express the agent of agentive past stems. As remarked in §2.4.3, the L-suffixes are not stressed and in JSNENA they correspond prosodically to the Iranian clitics. They are not, however, detachable from the verbal stem, unlike the Iranian clitics, which can be moved and hosted by other constituents in the clause (§5.9). Moreover, in many NENA dialects L-suffixes affect the position of stress in the word and so are prosodically more integrated into the word than clitics (§3.5).

Table 48: Oblique Clitics in Iranian and L-suffixes in JSNENA.

	JSNENA	Gorani	Kurdish
3SG.M	-lē	=š	=y
3SG.F	-la		
3PL	-lū	=šā	=yān
2SG.M	-lox	=t, =d́	=o, =t
2SG.F	-lax		
2PL	-laxun	=tā	=tān
1SG	-lī	=m	=m
1PL	-lan	=mā	=mān

Agentive paradigms:

(284) JSNENA
    g-r-š 'to pull'
    3SG.M *gráš-lē*   'he pulled'
    3SG.F *gráš-la*   'she pulled'
    3PL   *gráš-lū*   'they pulled', etc.
    2SG.M *gráš-lox*
    2SG.F *gráš-lax*
    2PL   *gráš-laxun*
    1SG   *gráš-lī*
    1PL   *gráš-lan*

(285) Gorani
barđ- 'to take'
3SG *barđ=əš*   'he/she took'
3PL *barđ=šā*   'they took'
2SG *barđ=ət*   'you took', etc.
2PL *barđ=tā*
1SG *barđ=əm*
1PL *barđ=mā*

(286) Kurdish
hāwərd- 'to bring'
3SG *hāwərd=ī*   'he/she brought'
3PL *hāwərd=yān* 'they brought'
2SG *hāwərd=o*   'you brought', etc.
2PL *hāwərd=tān*
1SG *hāwərd=əm*
1PL *hāwərd=mān*

The loss of full clitic status of the NENA L-suffixes seems to have come about by analogy with the direct suffixes, which are fully bonded prosodically to the verbal stem. This analogical convergence with direct suffixes is exhibited by a number of properties of L-suffixes in various dialects.[3] In some NENA dialects, for example, the L-suffixes that mark the subject have acquired syntagmatic properties of direct subject suffixes, notably their ability to take a further L-suffix to express the object, and, in the case of the dialect Ch. Hertevin, even assimilation of the subject-marking L-suffixes to the morphological form of direct suffixes when they take an object suffix, e.g.

(287) Ch. Hertevin (Jastrow 1988)
  a. *ḥzē-lē-lī*
     see.PST-OBL.3SG.M-OBL.1SG
     'he saw me'
  b. *ḥzē-lēt-tī* (< *ḥze-lēt-lī*, cf 2SG.M direct suffix *–ēt*)
     see.PST-OBL.2SG.M-OBL.1SG
     'you saw me'
  c. *ḥzē-lēn-nē* (< *ḥzē-lēn-lē*, cf 1SG.M direct suffix *–ēn*)
     see.PST-OBL.1SG-OBL.3SG.M
     'I saw him'

---

3 For further details see Khan (2017).

The use of oblique L-suffixes to mark the subject of only agentive past verbs is a distinctive feature of JSNENA and the neighbouring Jewish trans-Zab dialects of western Iran and Sulemaniyya. In the main body of NENA L-suffixes are used to mark the subject of both transitive past stems and also intransitive unaccusative past stems, e.g.

(288) Ch. Barwar
Agentive, *g-r-š* 'to pull'
3SG.M   *gríš-lē*   'he pulled'
3SG.F   *gríš-la*   'she pulled'
3PL   *gríš-lɛ*   'they pulled', etc.
2SG.M   *gríš-lux*
2SG.F   *gríš-lax*
2PL   *gríš-lēxū*
1SG   *gríš-lī*
1PL   *gríš-lən*
(Khan 2008b)

(289) Ch. Barwar
Unaccusative, *qym* 'to rise'
3SG.M   *qĭm-lē*   'he rose'
3SG.F   *qĭm-la*   'she rose'
3PL   *qĭm-lɛ*   'they rose', etc.
2SG.M   *qĭm-lux*
2SG.F   *qĭm-lax*
2PL   *qĭm-lēxū*
1SG   *qĭm-lī*
1PL   *qĭm-lən*
(Khan 2008b)

In a few dialects on the north-eastern periphery of NENA direct suffixes are used with the past stem of unaccusative verbs to express the present perfect, e.g.

(290) J. Urmi
3SG.M   *qĭm-Ø*   'he has risen'
3SG.F   *qĭm-a*   'she has risen'
3PL   *qĭm-ī*   'they have risen'
(Khan 2008a)

In such dialects L-suffixes mark the subject of the past stem of both transitive and intransitive unaccusative verbs when they express the past perfective, e.g.

(291) J. Urmi
3SG.M *qəm-lē* 'he rose'
3SG.F *qəm-la* 'she rose'
3PL *qə́m-lū* 'they rose'

Some dialects on the north-western periphery of NENA also exhibit the use of direct suffixes on past stems to express the present perfect. In dialects in the Bohtan region direct suffixes are used with both unaccusative intransitive and transitive verbs when denoting the perfect, L-suffixes being used on past stems to express the perfective:

(292) C. Bohtan

		Agentive perfect		Unaccusative perfect
3SG.M	*grī́š-Ø*	'he has pulled'	*qī́m-Ø*	'he has risen'
3SG.F	*grī́š-a*	'she has pulled'	*qī́m-a*	'she has risen'
3PL	*grī́š-ī*	'they have pulled'	*qī́m-ī*	'they have risen'

(Fox 2009)

(293) C. Bohtan

		Agentive perfective		Unaccusative perfective
3SG.M	*grə́š-lē*	'he pulled'	*qə́m-lē*	'he rose'
3SG.F	*grə́š-la*	'she pulled'	*qə́m-la*	'she rose'
3PL	*grə́š-lā*	'they pulled'	*qə́m-lā*	'they rose'

(Fox 2009)

In some dialects of Iraq that have a generalised use of L-suffixes on past stems, a few sporadic examples are attested of direct suffixes on past stems of unaccusative verbs expressing the perfect. In the trans-Zab Jewish Arbel dialect, for example, this is attested in the verb *p-y-š* 'to remain':

(294) J. Arbel
či-hūlā'-ē   la   pīš-ī   gaw
NEG-Jew-PL NEG remain.PST-DIR.3PL Inside
'No Jews have remained in it.'
(Khan 1999, 284–85)

A final piece of evidence for reconstructing the historical background of oblique L-suffixes in JSNENA is that, although L-suffixes are not used, in principle, to mark the subject of past stems of unaccusative verbs, they are used on the past stem of the copula:

(295) JSNENA
    3SG.M   *yē-lē*   'he was'
    3SG.F   *yē-la*   'she was'
    3PL   *yē-lū*   'they were'

This appears to be a vestige of a system like that of the main body of NENA dialects, in which oblique L-suffixes are generalised as markers of the subject of past stems of all verbs.

The use of oblique L-suffixes on both agentive and unaccusative past verbs in the main body of NENA dialects in Iraq correlates with the distribution of oblique clitics in Gorani dialects of Iraq. Although Gorani in Iran uses such clitics to mark the subject only on agentive verbs, in Gorani in Iraq the clitics are used on both agentive and unaccusative past stems. This has been documented, for example, in the Bājalānī variety of Iraqi Gorani (MacKenzie 1956), which exhibits the system of subject markers, represented in Table 49, with oblique clitics on unaccusative verbs in all persons except the 3SG (oblique clitics are shaded):

Table 49: Person suffixes and person clitics in the Bajalani variety of Gorani.

	Present	Past unaccusative	Past agentive
3SG	-ō	-Ø	=š
3PL	-ān	=šā	=šā
2SG	-ī	=t	=t
2PL	-ē	=tā	=tā
1SG	-ī	=m	=m
1PL	-mē	=mā	=mā

Note further that the Kirkuk dialect of Central Kurdish has regularly oblique inflection for past intransitive unaccusative in the 1PL and 2PL and optionally also in the 3PL (cf. Mohammadirad *in review*):

The question arises as to which of the patterns of distribution of direct suffixes and oblique clitics came first. Did the oblique inflection of intransitive unaccusative past verbs, as seen in Iraqi dialects of Gorani such as Bājalānī, historically precede the direct inflection of the intransitive past, as seen in Gorani of Iran and Sanandaj Kurdish?

Data from the late Middle Iranian period show us that oblique suffixes could indeed extend to intransitive verbs. In (296.a) the 1SG subject argument of 'arrive'

Table 50: Person suffixes and person clitics in Kurdish of Kirkuk.

	Present	Past unaccusative	Past agentive
3SG	-ē	-∅	=ī, =y
3PL	-ən	-n, =yān	=yān
2SG	-ī	-ī	=t
2PL	-ən	=tān	=tān
1SG	-m	-m	-m
1PL	-īn	=mān	=mān

is marked by the oblique affix. In (296.b) the unaccusative predicate is *āwēst ēstād* 'be hung'; which agrees with the subject argument 'the souls being punished in hell' by means of a 3PL oblique clitic. In (296.c) the copula is inflected by an oblique clitic.

(296) Middle Persian
  a. *TMH   'YK   ḥwwlšt   PWN   mḥm'nyḥ,   'L   TMH*
     there where   good.work   in   guesthood in   there
     lsytw=m
     arrive.PTPC=1SG
     'There where Good Works (is) resident, thither I arrived.'
     (AWN 9.1, Brunner 1977, 104)
  b. *kē=šān   nigūnsār   andar   dušox   āwēxt   ēstād*
     REL=3PL   upside.down   in   hell   hung   stand.PST.3SG
     '(souls of those wicked) who were hung upside-down in hell'
     (AWN 30.5, Shirtz 2016)
  c. *u=šān   hamāg   an-espās   bē   būd*
     and=3PL   all   grateful   without   COP.PST
     'They were all ungrateful.'
     (mpB 163, Durkin-Meisterernst 2014, 293)

As can be seen, the oblique inflection of the past intransitive and the past copula already started in Middle Iranian. It appears that this distribution of oblique inflection developed by paradigm levelling in Middle Iranian and the same applied to the Iraqi Gorani dialects such as Bājalānī, which probably in turn triggered a shift in the paradigm of intransitive person suffixes of Kirkuk Central Kurdish. Likewise, some Southern Kurdish dialects exhibit cases of oblique inflection of intransitive verbs, especially in the 1PL and 2PL (Mohammadirad 2020a, 97).

The main body of NENA dialects, whose heartland is Iraq, matched the pattern of oblique inflection in Iraqi Gorani. This is likely to be the historically earlier pattern in NENA (Khan 2017; Noorlander 2021). Its appearance in Iraqi Gorani may have been an internal development that possibly was stimulated by contact with NENA. Gorani of Iran (Hawraman region) is more archaic and has retained direct suffix inflection for past intransitive unaccusatives and JSNENA has converged with this. As remarked, in JSNENA there is a vestige of the earlier oblique inflection of intransitives in the inflection of the past stem of the copula by L-suffixes. It appears that extension of direct suffixes to this paradigm was blocked since this would have brought about homophony of the past and present copulas (Khan 2017; 2020a):

(297) JSNENA

	Past copula		Present copula
	L-suffixes	Direct suffixes	Direct suffixes
3SG.M	yē-lē	*yē-Ø	yē
3SG.F	yē-la	*y-a	ya
3PL	yē-lū	*y-ēn	yēn

The emergence of direct inflection of the past stem when expressing the perfect in some dialects on the north-eastern and north-western periphery of NENA, and in a few sporadic cases elsewhere, represent incipient convergence with the Iranian dialects of the region. The process would have involved extension of the direct suffixes from the present and this initially expressed a perfect, which denoted a present state and so was semantically related to the present. The main body of NENA remained resistant to convergence with the Iranian patterns of oblique inflection. In such a system, the oblique infection marks the grammatical relation of the referent of the clitic, i.e. grammatical subject, rather than its semantic role (agent or affectee). This corresponds to the inflection of the present stem with direct suffixes, which index the grammatical subject.

5.4 Inflection of the resultative participles

In JSNENA there are two types of resultative participle, one being used with an agentive active function and the other with an intransitive unaccusative or passive function. These correspond in vocalic pattern to the two corresponding past stems, e.g.

(298) JSNENA
Form I

	Past stem	Resultative participle
Agentive active	gərš-	gərša
Intransitive unaccusative	smīx-	smīxa
Passive	grīš-	grīša

These resultative participles derive historically from the determined state of the passive participle in earlier Aramaic, whereas the the past stems derive from the passive participles in the absolute state. The feminine singular is formed by attaching the ending –*ta* and the plural by attaching the ending –*ē*, which are historically the endings of nominal forms in the determined state. In the case of the agentive participle, the attachment of the feminine suffix involves the rearrangement of the syllable structure:

Form I
g-r-š 'to pull' (agentive active), *s-m-x* 'to stand' (intransitive unaccusative)

(299) JSNENA
    a. Agentive active
        SG.M *gərša*
        SG.F *grəšta*
        PL   *gərše*
    b. Intransitive unaccusative
        SG.M *smīxa*
        SG.F *smīxta*
        PL   *smīxē*
    c. Passive
        SG.M *grīša*
        SG.F *grīšta*
        PL   *grīšē*

The agentive and unaccusative/passive resultative participles are used in compound verbal forms expressing the resultative perfect (§5.11).

In Gorani the resultative participle is, likewise, inflected for gender and number. As discussed in §5.2, a subset of lexical verbs have specific agglutinative morphemes that mark the verb as agentive (-*n*) or unaccusative/passive (-*īa*/-*īā*). The alignment of the patterns of the JSNENA resultative participles, i.e. agentive/causative (*gərša*) and unaccusative/passive (*smīxa*/*grīša*), corresponds to this alignment of morphemes in Gorani:

(300) Gorani
    a. Agentive/causative resultative participle
       sočnāy 'to burn (tr.)'
        SG.M *sočnā*
        SG.F *sočnē*
        PL   *sočnē*

b. Intransitive unaccusative resultative participle
    maṛīāy 'to break' (intr.)
    SG.M   *maṛīā*
    SG.F   *maṛīē*
    PL   *maṛīē*
c. Passive resultative participle
    kūštāy 'to kill'
    SG.M   *kʷšīā*
    SG.F   *kʷšīē*
    PL   *kʷšīē*

In Kurdish of the Sanandaj region, the participle is not inflected for gender and number. Furthermore, as indicated in §5.2, there is no alignment of passive morphology with intransitive unaccusative, as there is in JSNENA and Gorani.

(301) Kurdish
a. Agentive/causative resultative participle
    Infinitive: *šəkān* 'to break'
    Participle: *škānd-əg*
b. Intransitive unaccusative resultative participle
    Infinitive: *hātən* 'to come'
    Participle: *hāt-əg*
c. Passive resultative participle
    Infinitive: *xwārdən* 'to eat'
    Participle: *xor-yā-g*

5.5 Indicative particle

In JSNENA, an indicative particle with the form *k-*, or occasionally its voiced variant *g-*, is prefixed to some verbs derived from the present stem. This expresses the indicative present or the future. The construction is restricted to a set of Form I verbs with /ʾ/ or /h/ as their first radical that includes the following:

(302) JSNENA
ʾ-x-l	'to eat'	*k-xəl-Ø*	'he eats'
		IND-eat.PRS-Ø.3SG.M	
ʾ-m-r	'to say'	*k-mər*	'he says'
ʾ-b-y	'to want'	*g-bē*	'he wants'
h-y-y	'to come'	*k-ē*	'he comes'

ʾ-l-y	'to know'	k-aē	'he knows'
ʾ-z-l	'to go'	g-ēzəl	'he goes'
ʾ-w-l	'to do'	k-ol	'he does'
h-w-y	'to be'	k-wē	'he is'
h-w-l	'to give'	k-wəl	'he gives'

This restricted distribution of the indicative particle is a feature of all trans-Zab Jewish NENA dialects. In many NENA dialects the particle occurs more regularly across all lexical verbs. The form of the particle is *k-* across most dialects in the southern sector of the NENA area. This is likely to be derived from a presentative particle **kā* 'here' (Khan 2007b). In the north-eastern sector of the NENA area this particle is combined with a copula element *ī*, e.g. Ch. Urmi and Ch. Salamas *cī-* (with a palatal /c/). In dialects in the northern sector of the NENA area the *k-* has been elided before the *ī* and the particle has the form *ī̆-*.

In the Kurdish of the Sanandaj region, the corresponding indicative particle has the form *a-*. It has the form *da-* in upper Central Kurdish. The indicative particle in Gorani of the region is *mə-*, which has an adverbial origin (Windfuhr 2009, 26). As with *k-* in JSNENA, present stems of verbs with these prefixes may express the present or the future. There is, therefore, convergence in the domain of TAM in the construction across the languages.

Unlike JSNENA, the particle *a-* in Sanandaj Kurdish occurs with all lexical verbs. Gorani *mə-*, however, appears with only certain verb stems. MacKenzie (1966, 32) notes that "[a]ll verbs with initial *n-*, *z-*, *i-*, and *y-*, and some with initial *d-*, *g-*, *f-*, and *w-*, appear to take the prefix *mə-*. The factors determining which verbs do and which do not take this prefix are not evident." There follows here a sample of verbs which take indicative *m(ə)-* before the present stem in Gorani of the region:

(303) Gorani
m-āč-ū   'I say'
IND-say.PRS-1SG
m-ār-ā   'they bring'
mə-žnās-ū   'I know'
mə-l-ī   'you go'
m-řfān-o   'he abducts'
m-ađ-o   'he gives'

The following present stems do not take indicative *mə-*:

(304) Gorani
> *bar* 'take'
> *kīān* 'send'
> *wāz* 'climb'
> *kēš* 'pull'
> *šor* 'wash'
> *jan* 'mince'
> *čən* 'pick'

Contrary to Kurdish *a-*, the indicative *mə-* of Gorani is restricted to the present tense. It is not used in the realis past and irrealis past.

(305) Gorani
> a. Realis present: *m-aw* 'I come'
>   Realis past: *āy ēnā* 'I was coming'
>   habitual past: *ēnā* 'I used to come'
>   Irrealis past: *ēnā* 'I would come'
> b. Realis present: *mə-l-ū, mə-l-āy mə-l-ū* 'I go, I am going'
>   Realis past: *luāy lwēnā* 'I was going'
>   habitual past: *lūēnā* 'I used to go'
>   Irrealis past: *lūēnā* 'I would go'

It would appear that the indicative marker *m-* in Gorani has only been partially grammaticalised as an inflectional element and so is not used systematically across all lexical verbs. It is possible that the partial distribution of the indicative marker *k-* in JSNENA has been conditioned by convergence with this unsystematic distribution of the corresponding particle in Gorani. In JSNENA the process involves a retrenchment from an originally systematic distribution. The JSNENA *k-* was lost before verbal stems beginning with a consonant and preserved before vowels, so phonetic attrition in consonantal clusters can be identified as the internal cause. This internal development, however, is likely to have been externally catalysed by convergence with the unsystematic distribution in Gorani. The particle was eliminated in contexts where the elision was phonetically facilitated in consonantal clusters (e.g. **k-ṭaləb > ṭaləb* 'he requests') but elimination was resisted where preservation was facilitated before vowels where there were no clusters (e.g. *k-ol* 'he does'). Indeed many of the verbs in Gorani that exhibit the prefix have stems beginning with a vowel. In some JSNENA verbs of this latter category, however, the vowel was subsequently elided, resulting in a cluster (e.g. **k-axəl > k-xəl* 'he eats').

A feature of the partially systematised distribution in Gorani is the fact that it is restricted to present tense verbs. In JSNENA, by contrast, the *k-* is used with present stems that have a past converter morpheme and have past tense reference (habitual or progressive):

(306) JSNENA
  k-mər 'he says' *k-mər-wa* 'he used to say'
  k-ol 'he does' *k-ol-wa* 'he used to do'

Some NENA dialects, in fact, do not use the *k-* with such verbs with the past converter morpheme, e.g.

(307) C. Shaqlawa
  k-axəl 'he eats' *'axəl-wa* 'he used to eat'

It is possible that this was a more archaic distribution in NENA and that the particle was extended by analogy to the past tense in some dialects.

The distribution of *k-* on present stem verbs with initial /ʾ/ and /h/ that is found in JSNENA is common to all Jewish trans-Zab dialects. There is one construction with *k-*, however, that has been documented so far only in JSNENA. This is its prefixing to an infinitive that is combined with a present stem of a verb to express a present progressive. In all cases where this is attested, the verb itself takes *k-*, i.e. it belongs to the set with initial /ʾ/ or /h/ in the root, e.g.

(308) JSNENA
  a. *'axolē* 'to eat'
    k-xolē k-xəl 'he is eating'
  b. *'amorē* 'to say'
    k-morē k-mər 'he is saying'

If the present stem does not take the *k-* particle, the infinitive lacks the particle also, e.g.

(309) JSNENA
  a. *šatoē* 'to drink'
    šatoē šatēna 'I am drinking'
  b. *šaholē* 'to cough'
    šaholē šahəl 'he is coughing'

The model for this construction is Gorani, which expresses the present progressive by a construction consisting of a present verb with *m-* combined with a form that consists of the present stem with the ending *-āy*,[4] e.g.

(310) Gorani
    a. *lūāy* 'to go'
        mə-l-āy mə-l-ū   'I am going'
    b. *wātay* 'to tell'
        m-āč-āy m-āč-dē   'you (pl) are saying'
    c. *ārḍay* 'to bring'
        m-ār-āy m-ār-ā   'they are bringing'

If the verb does not take *m-*, the preceding element ending in *-āy* also lacks the *m-* e.g.

(311) Gorani
    a. *wārday* 'to eat'
        war-āy war-ū   'I am eating'
    b. *vəratay* 'to sell'
        vəraš-āy vəraš-mē   'we are selling'
    c. *barḍay* 'to take'
        bar-āy bar-o   'he is taking'

The combination of an infinitive with a finite verb of the same root as an inner object rather than an affected argument is a construction that is found elsewhere in NENA, e.g.

312 Ch. Urmi
    a. *xá   štằya   ští-lə.*'
        one drink.INF drink.PST-OBL.3SG.M
        'He drank a (great) drinking (= he had a good drink).'
    b. *ḳābŭlə   p̂-ḳàbl-ī   'árxə?*'
        drink.INF FUT-accept.PRS-3PL guests
        'Will they accept guests?' (A 43:14)
        (Khan 2016, vol. 1, 239–240)

---

[4] MacKenzie (1966, 50) refers to this form as an adverb.

In JSNENA this NENA construction with an infinitive expressing an inner object has been matched with Gorani progressive constructions such as *mə-l-ā́y mə-l-ū* 'I am going'. As a result, the indicative prefix is attached to the first element according to the Gorani pattern. As remarked, the first element in the Gorani construction does not have the morphological form of an infinitive but is a form based on a present verbal stem. It is for this reason that it takes an indicative prefix.

Contact with Gorani, therefore, can be said to have reinforced a potential inherited construction in JSNENA and also to have extended it by the application of the indicative particle to the infinitive due to the infinitive being matched with a form that is based on a present stem in a Gorani construction.

Unlike JSNENA and Gorani, the indicative particle *a-* in the Kurdish of Sanandaj is fully grammaticalised and is used systematically with all lexical verbs. Furthermore it is used on past tense verbs formed from the past stem, e.g.

(313) Kurdish
    Present: *a-č-əm*   'I go/ I am going'
              IND-go.PRS-1SG
    Past: *a-čū-m*   'I used to go/ I was going'
              IND-go.PST-1SG

In a few verbs the prefix *a-* (< **da*) has become merged into the verb stem:

(314) Kurdish
    tēm   'I come'   < **da-ē-m*
    tērəm   'I bring'   < **da-ēr-əm*

The use of the indicative particle '*a-* with past tense verbs to express the past imperfective habitual and progressive in Kurdish may have been the model for the use of *k-* in the past in JSNENA. As we have seen, some NENA dialects do not use the particle in the past, like Gorani, and this may be the more archaic situation. The prefixing of the indicative particle to the past stem, which is used in Kurdish (e.g. '*a-čū-m*), however, has no equivalent in JSNENA, or the rest of NENA. In NENA dialects the corresponding construction is formed with a present stem combined with the past converter suffix *-wa*, e.g.

(315) JSNENA
    g-r-š 'to pull'
    3SG.M   *garə́š-Ø-wa*   'he used to pull/was pulling'
    3SG.F   *garš-ā́-wa*   'she used to pull/was pulling'
    3PL   *garš-ī́-wa*   'they used to pull/were pulling', etc.

2SG.M	garš-ḗt-wa
2SG.F	garš-át-wa
2PL	garš-ḗtun-wa
1SG.M	garə́š-na-wa
1SG.F	garš-án-wa
1PL	garš-ḗx-wa

As remarked, when the present stem takes the *k-* indicative particle, this is extended to the past, e.g.

(316) JSNENA
k-ol 'he does'   *k-ol-wa* 'he used to do/was doing'

The NENA verbal system has converged with Iranian to a marked degree. If Kurdish was the model of this convergence, therefore, it is surprising that NENA did not replicate the *a-čū-m* type of construction with a past stem. In Gorani, however, past imperfective (progressive and habitual) is expressed by a construction consisting of the present stem and a past converter morpheme *-ēn*. This is apparently derived from the Old Iranian participle morpheme *-ant*.

(317) Gorani
vraš 'to sell'
3sg	*vraš-ḗ(n)-Ø*	'he used to sell/was selling'
3PL	*vraš-ḗn-ē*	'they used to sell/were pulling', etc.
2SG	*vraš-ḗn-ī*	
2PL	*vraš-ḗn-dē*	
1SG	*vraš-ḗn-ē*	
1PL	*vraš-ḗn-mē*	

As can be seen, in Gorani the person markers of the verb are placed after the past converter particle *-ēn* whereas they are placed before the corresponding particle *-wa* in JSNENA. Furthermore, the person markers are the ones that are attached to past stems rather than present stems and for that reason they are not stressed (see §2.4.3). The construction of the present stem combined with *-wa* is common to all NENA dialects. It is inherited from earlier Aramaic, in which the tense of a participle was shifted to the past by combining it with the past auxiliary verb *hwā* (root *h-w-y* 'to be'), e.g. Syriac :

(318) Syriac
g-r-š 'to drag'

3SG.M	*gāreš-wā* drag.PTCP.SG.M-AUX.3SG.M	'he was dragging'
3SG.F	*gāršā-wāϑ* drag.PTCP.SG.F-AUX.3SG.F	'she was dragging'
3PL.M	*gāršīn-waw* drag.PTCP.PL.M-AUX.3PL.M	'they were dragging'
3PL.F	*gāršān-way* drag.PTCP. PL.F-AUX.3PL.F	'they were dragging'
2SG.M	*gāreš-wayt* drag.PTCP.SG.M-AUX.2SG.M	'you were dragging'
2SG.F	*gāršā-wayt* drag.PTCP.SG.F-AUX.FMS	'you were dragging'
2PL.M	*gāršīn-waytōn* drag.PTCP. PL.M-AUX.2PL.M	'you were dragging'
2PL.F	*gāršān-waytēn* drag.PTCP. PL.F-AUX.2PL.F	'you were dragging'
1SG.M	*gāreš-wēϑ* drag.PTCP.SG.M-AUX.1SG	'I was dragging'
1SG.F	*gāršā-wēϑ* drag.PTCP.SG.F-AUX.1SG	'I was dragging'
1PL.M	*garšīn-wayn* drag.PTCP.PL.M-AUX.1PL	'we were dragging'
1PL.F	*garšān-wayn* drag.PTCP.PL.F-AUX.1PL	'we were dragging'

In Syriac the auxiliary *hwā* was a clitic and lost its initial /h/. In this respect it resembles the NENA particle *-wa*. In NENA, however, the particle has no person inflection, unlike Syriac, where it is inflected for person. The participle stem in Syriac also has gender and number inflection. In NENA gender, number and person markers are all suffixed to the present stem of the verb (erstwhile participle). This has brought about a regularisation of the construction with the present paradigm with regard to the position of the gender and number markers in the construction with the past auxiliary (i.e. Syriac 3SG.F *gāršā-wā*, 1PL.M *gāršīn-wā*):

(319) JSNENA

garš-ī	'they pull'	*garš-ī-wa*	'they used to pull'
garš-ēt	'you (SG.M) pull'	*garš-ēt-wa*	'you (SG.M) used to pull'

As a result, the position of the person inflection in the construction with the -*wa* past converter particle in NENA dialects is different from that of Gorani, which places the persons markers after the corresponding particle. This difference, however, is due to the aforementioned regularisation within NENA. The existence of a construction that shifts a present stem in the past by a suffixed past converter morpheme in Gorani is likely to have facilitated the preservation of the Aramaic construction in NENA. This would reflect the impact of a Gorani substrate on NENA in general. In JSNENA the past converter can be added also to the past stem of verbs. In such constructions the verb generally has a past perfect function.

When it is added to transitive past stems, the particle is placed between the stem and the L-suffix inflectional ending:

(320) JSNENA
g-r-š 'to pull'
3SG.M	*gṛə́š-wā-lē*	'he had pulled'
3SG.F	*gṛə́š-wā-la*	'she had pulled'
3PL	*gṛə́š-wā-lū*	'they had pulled', etc.
2SG.M	*gṛə́š-wā-lox*	
2SG.F	*gṛə́š-wā-lax*	
2PL	*gṛə́š-wā-laxun*	
1SG	*gṛə́š-wā-lī*	
1PL	*gṛə́š-wā-lan*	

When the past stem is intransitive/passive, the *wa* morpheme is added after the direct suffix inflection:

(321) JSNENA
s-m-x 'to stand up'
3SG.M	*smíx-∅-wa*	'he had stood up'
3SG.F	*smíx-ā-wa*	'she had stood up'
3PL	*smíx-ī-wa*	'they had stood up', etc.
2SG.M	*smíx-ət-wa*	
2SG.F	*smíx-at-wa*	
2PL	*smíx-ētun-wa*	
1SG.M	*smíx-na-wa*	
1SG.F	*smíx-an-wa*	
1PL	*smíx-əx-wa*	

(322)   JSNENA
   g-r-š 'to pull'
   3SG.M   gríš-Ø-wa   'he had been pulled'
   3SG.F   gríš-ā-wa   'he had been pulled'
   3PL   gríš-ī-wa   'he had been pulled', etc.
   2SG.M   gríš-ət-wa
   2SG.F   gríš-at-wa
   2PL   gríš-ētun-wa
   1SG.M   gríš-na-wa
   1SG.F   gríš-an-wa

In Gorani the past converter morpheme *ēn* can also be attached to a past stem of verb. This, however, does not have the function of a past perfect but rather a conditional modal expressing a counterfactual condition in the past (protasis):

(323)   Gorani
   3sg   ám(ā)-ē(n)-Ø   '(If) he had come'
   3PL   ám(ā)-ēn-ē   '(If) they had come', etc.
   2sg   ám(ā)-ēn-ī
   2PL   ám(ā)-ēn-dē
   1SG   ám(ā)-ēn-ē
   1PL   ám(ā)-ēn-mē

Examples:

(324)   Gorani Luhon
   agar   hīzī   ām(ā)-ēn-ī   pēwa   wīn-ēn-mē=š
   if   yesterday   come.PRS-PSTC-2SG   together   see.PRS-PSTC-1PL=3SG
   'If you had come yesterday, we could have seen it together'
   (MacKenzie 1966, 59)

In Gorani the past perfect is expressed by the participle and past copula. Such a pattern of construction is not available in JSNENA for reasons explained below (§5.11.2). The construction of the past stem + past converter *wa* originally had the function of past perfect in the history of NENA. In many NENA dialects this function has been mainly taken over by a participle + past copula construction following the model of Iranian contact languages. As a result the past stem + past converter *wa* construction came to be used to express remote past perfective. This convergence with Iranian has not taken place in JSNENA and the past stem + *wa* construction has retained its past perfect function.

5.6 Subjunctive

In JSNENA the verbs that take the particle *k-* in indicative contexts have no prefixed particle when they express the irrealis subjunctive, e.g.

(325) JSNENA

Indicative		Subjunctive	
k-xəl	'he eats'	'axəl	'(that) he eats'
k-wəl	'he gives'	hawəl	'(that) he gives'
k-ol	'he does'	'ol	'(that) he does'

Verbs that do not take *k-* make no morphological distinction between indicative and subjunctive. The lack of marking of the subjunctive with a prefixed particle is the norm throughout NENA.

In the western Iranian languages a subjunctive particle is used with the form of an unstressed *bə-* before the present stem. The use of this as a subjunctive particle was absent, however, in the Middle Iranian period. It was only in the early new Iranian period that it came to develop as a TAM affix, functioning also as the imperative particle in the modern languages (for the development of Iranian *bə-* see Noorlander and Stilo 2015). The Gorani of the region, however, exhibits the older pattern of no subjunctive particle for most of the verbs, e.g.

(326) Gorani

Indicative		Subjunctive	
vəraš-ū́	'I sell'	vəraš-ū́	'(that) I sell'
wāz-mḗ	'we demand'	wāz-mḗ	'(that) I demand'
bar-dḗ	'you take'	bar-dḗ	'(that) you take'
kīyān-ā́	'they send'	kīyān-ā́	'(that) they sell'

The subjunctive particle tends to occur in Gorani before those verbal stems that take the indicative prefix, e.g.

(327) Gorani

Indicative		Subjunctive	
mə-l-ó	'he goes'	bə-l-ó	'(that) he goes'
m-a-ydḗ	'you will give'	b-a-ydḗ	'(that) you give'
m-ār-ū́	'I will bring'	b-ār-ū́	'(that) I bring'

In Kurdish of the Sanandaj region, on the other hand, the subjunctive prefix is used more regularly, e.g.

(328) Kurdish
Indicative   Subjunctive
a-zān-ə́m   'I know'   *bə-zān-ə́m*   '(that) I know'
a-č-ín   'we go'   *bə-č-ín*   '(that) we go'
a-dəz-ḗ   'he/she steals'   *bə-dəz-ḗ*   '(that) he/she steals'
a-xwá-y   'you eat'   *bə-xwá-y*   '(that) you eat'

One exception is in constructions with complex predicates consisting of a noun and a light verb. In this context the subjunctive particle is usually omitted before the light verb:

(329) Kurdish
Indicative   Subjunctive
tuwāšā a-ká   'he/she looks'   *tuwāšā ∅-ká*   '(that) he/she looks'
kār a-ká-m   'I work'   *kār ∅-ká-m*   '(that) I work'
bāng a-ká-yn   'we call'   *bāng ∅-ká-yn*   '(that) we call'

NENA, therefore, again matches more closely Gorani than Kurdish. There is no inherited subjunctive particle in NENA. This lack of marking was conserved by matching NENA subjunctive verbs with the morphosyntax of Gorani, which did not have a fully grammaticalised use of the particle and so did not have a salient regular inflection that could be replicated systematically.

5.7 Deontic particles

Although JSNENA has not replicated the Iranian subjunctive particle, it has borrowed several Iranian deontic particles. Such direct borrowing of morphemes is no doubt motivated by the fact that deontic constructions are used in interactional discourse, which involves subjective emotion. The particles in question include the following:

5.7.1 bā

This has the deontic force of expressing a wish, giving permission or seeking permission and is followed by subjunctive verb forms in both JSNENA and the Iranian languages, where these are morphologically distinguished:

(330) Gorani
    a. *bā bə-l-mē* 'May we go, let us go'
       bā kīyān-ū 'May I send, let me send'
    b. *bā   qə̀sa=y   qaymī=t pay Ø-kàr-ū.*|
       HORT talk=EZ old=2SG for SBJV-do.PRS-1SG
       'Let me tell you about the past.'

(331) Kurdish
    a. *bā b-ē-n* 'May they come, let them come'
       bā b-ēž-əm 'May I say, let me say'
    b. *bā   làm   kēfā   řož*
       HORT in.DEM.PROX mountain-POST day
       na-ka-yn=aw.|
       NEG.SBJV-do.PRS-1PL=TELIC
       'Let us not stay the night in this mountain.'

(332) JSNENA
    bā-šaqəl 'may he buy, let him buy'
    bā-'axəl 'may he eat, let him eat'

5.7.2 magar

The particle *magar* is often contracted into *mār, mar* or *mawr* in the Iranian languages of Sanandaj. It is used to express hope, wish, astonishment, or fear regarding the proposition expressed by the utterance. It is followed by the subjunctive form where this is morphologically distinguished.

(333) Kurdish
    a. *mar   xwằ   bə-zān-ē*|
       maybe God SBJV-know.PRS-3SG
       'Maybe only God knows.'
    b. *mar   nà=m-wət?*|
       PTCL NEG=1SG-say.PST
       'Didn't I say so?'

(334) Gorani
    magar   wè=t   bə-l-ī|
    maybe.only REFL=2SG SBJV-go.PRS-2SG
    'Maybe only you go by yourself.'

In JSNENA the contracted form *mar* is used:

(335) JSNENA
    mar-garəš   'may he pull, let him pull'
    mar-'axəl   'may he eat, let him eat'

5.7.3 dā

The particle *dā* adds immediacy to an imperative verb, e.g.

(336) Kurdish
  a. *dā*   *b-ēs-a*   *b-ēs-à!* |
        PTCL   SBJV-wait.PRS-IMP.2SG SBJV-wait.PRS-IMP.2SG
        'wait! wait!'
  b. *dā*   *bè*|
        PTCL   SBJV.come.PRS.IMP.2SG
        'come!'

(337) Gorani
    dā bo!   come!
    dā war-a! eat!

(338) JSNENA
    dā-gruš!   pull!

5.8 The copula

5.8.1 Present copula

In JSNENA clauses with a predicate that is a nominal or preposition phrase generally contain a copula that is cliticised to the end of the predicate item. This has a stem consisting of the element /y/, see Table 51. The dialect uses a present and past copula. The present copula is inflected for person by verbal direct suffixes (§5.3). The suffixes specifically have the form of so-called final-*y* verbs. These have the weak segment /y/ as their final radical, which contracts in many cases. In what follows the paradigm of the present copula is given together with the paradigm of the present stem of the final-*y* verb *h-w-y* 'to be'. The verb *h-w-y* takes the place of the copula in modal and future contexts:

Table 51: Copula paradigms in JSNENA.

	Enclitic Copula	Verb *h-w-y* 'to be'
3SG.M	=y-ē, =y	haw-ē
3SG.F	=y-a	hawy-a
3PL	=y-ēn	haw-ēn
2SG.M	=y-ēt	haw-ēt
2SG.F	=y-at	hawy-at
2PL	=y-ētun	haw-ētun
1SG.M	=y-ēna	haw-ēna
1SG.F	=y-an	hawy-an
1PL	=y-ēx	haw-ēx

The NENA copula was historically an enclitic pronoun (Khan 2018b; 2022b).

In the main body of NENA, the third person present copulas are inflected with L-suffixes, whereas the first and second person copulas have direct verbal inflection matching that of the verb *h-w-y*, as represented by Ch. Barwar in Table 52.

Table 52: Copula paradigms in Ch. Barwar (Khan 2008b, 180–81).

	Enclitic Copula	*h-w-y*
3SG.M	=ī-lē	hāwē
3SG.F	=ī-la	hawya
3PL	=ī-lē	hāwē
2SG.M	=ī-wət	hāwət
2SG.F	=ī-wat	hawyat
2PL	=ī-wītu	hāwītū
1SG.M	=ī-wən	hāwən
1SG.F	=ī-wan	hawyan
1PL	=ī-wəx	hāwəx

In JSNENA on the eastern periphery of NENA the verbal inflection of the verb *h-w-y* has extended to the third person and the L-suffixes have been eliminated, resulting in the whole paradigm being inflected with verbal direct suffixes. There are, however, a few vestiges of a third person 3SG.M copula with an L-suffix. These occur when the predicate ends in *-ē* or *-o*. In such cases the *ī* stem of the copula has contracted with the preceding vowel, e.g.

(339) JSNENA
    a. 'o   rēša   gārē=lē
        he   on   roof=COP.3SG.M
        'He is on the roof.' (*gārē*)
    b. 'ay   bēla   do=lē
        this house OBL.3SG.M=COP.3SG.M
        'This house is his.' (*do*)

This shows that the extension of direct verbal suffixes to the 3rd person is likely to be a relatively recent development in JSNENA. The loss of the L-suffix was blocked to avoid the 3SG.M inflection being contracted with the final vowel.

The paradigms of the present copula in Gorani and Kurdish of the Sanandaj region are shown in Table 53 and Table 54, respectively. The direct verbal suffixes are given in an adjacent column:

Table 53: Copula paradigm in Gorani in comparison with inflectional person suffixes.

	Present enclitic copula	Present verb inflection
3SG.M	=n-∅, =∅-ā[5]	-o
3SG.F	=n-a	-o
3PL	=n-ē	-ā
2SG	=n-ī	-ī
2PL	=n-dē	-dē
1SG	=n-ā	-ū
1PL	=n-mē	-mē

Table 54: Copula paradigm in Kurdish in comparison with inflectional person suffixes.

	Present enclitic copula	Present verb inflection
3SG	=a-∅, =s-∅	-ē, -ā
3PL	=ən	-ən
2SG	=ī	-ī
2PL	=ən	-ən
1SG	=əm	-əm
1PL	=īn	-īn

---

[5] =*n* is used after vowel-final copula predicates, e.g. *zānā=n* 'he is intelligent' and =*ā* after predicates ending in a consonant, e.g. *zərang=ā* 'he is clever'.

The Gorani present copula forms consist of a stem n and inflectional suffixes. In the 3SG.M the stem n has zero inflection. The variant form of the 3SG.M =$ā$ is likely to be the result of elision of the n. Compare the paradigm of the copula of the Bājalānī dialect of Gorani, spoken in Iraq (Table 55):

Table 55: Copula paradigm in Gorani Bājalānī in comparison with inflectional person suffixes.

	Gorani (Iraq, Bājalānī) (MacKenzie 1956, 423)	
	Present enclitic copula	Present verb inflection
3SG	=(a)n-Ø	-ō
3PL	=(a)n-ē	-ān
2SG	=n-ī	-ī
2PL	=n-ē	-ē
1SG	=n-ī	-ī
1PL	=n-mē	-mē

It is possible that this feature of the n stem of the Gorani paradigm acted as a pivot with which the $ī$ element of the NENA copula was matched.[6] This would have applied to the NENA dialect group as a whole, which can be assumed to have been in contact with a Gorani substrate at some point in history. In Kurdish the copula does not have a stem throughout the paradigm, but rather consists only of inflectional suffixes. The 3SG form of the copula, however, may be the vestige of the original stem of the copula. Compare the forms of the copula in earlier Iranian (Table 56):

Table 56: The copula paradigm in proto-Iranian and Old Iranian.

	Proto-Iranian	Old Iranian
1SG	*as-mi	ah-mi
2SG	*as-ī	ah-ī
3SG	*as-ti	as-ti

The 3SG.M forms in Kurdish, therefore, are represented as =a-Ø and =s-Ø with a zero inflectional element in the tables above. The form =s occurs after a word with a final vowel, e.g.

---

[6] See Khan (2022) for details. For the notion of pivot matching in language contact see Matras and Sakel (2007).

(340) Kurdish
gawra=s
'It is big.'

The inflectional suffixes of the copula in Kurdish exhibit a close correspondence to the present verbal suffixes, which are given in the adjacent columns of the paradigms. The suffixes of the Gorani copula have a less complete correspondence to present verbal suffixes. It is significant, however, that there is correspondence in the first and second persons (complete in Bājalānī Gorani, in all but the 1SG in Hawraman Gorani). The Gorani third person copula endings that do not correspond to the present verbal endings are likely to be clitic pronouns in origin, as is the case with 3rd person copulas in some other Iranian languages (Korn 2011). This split in the paradigm between pronominal third person copulas and verbal first and second person copulas would, therefore, match the split in the paradigm in the present copula in the main body of NENA dialects. If the *n* element of the 3SG.M of the Gorani paradigm is indeed a pronoun in origin, this would be a direct match of the NENA *ī* stem, which is also likely to be originally a third person pronoun (Khan 2022).

The complete levelling of inflection of the present copula with verbal inflection that is found in JSNENA on the eastern periphery of the NENA area matches more closely the profile of the copula in Kurdish than that of Gorani. The presence of the *ī* stem (in the form of the glide /y/) in the JSNENA copula and the vestiges of non-verbal inflection in the form of L-suffixes after vowels (see above *gārē=lē*, *do=lē*), suggests that the JSNENA copula has its roots in the main body of NENA that was formed on the model of Gorani. In more recent times, however, the copula of JSNENA has converged more with the model of Kurdish. The main body of NENA dialects in Iraq have maintained a Gorani type of copula profile despite the fact that also in Iraq Gorani has now been almost entirely replaced by Kurdish.

5.8.2 Further types of copulas

In JSNENA the past copula is formed by the past stem *yē-* and inflected with L-suffixes (Table 57):

Table 57: Past copula paradigm in JSNENA.

3SG.M	=yē-lē
3SG.F	=yē-la
3PL	=yē-lū

Table 57 (continued)

2SG.M	=yē-lox
2SG.F	=yē-lax
2PL	=yē-laxun
1SG	=yē-lī
1PL	=yē-lan

In several other Jewish trans-Zab dialects the past stem of the copula is *wē-*, see Table 58:

Table 58: Past copula paradigm in J. Arbel.

3SG.M	=wē-lē
3SG.F	=wē-la
3PL	=wē-lū
2SG.M	=wē-lox
2SG.F	=wē-lax
2PL	=wē-lxun
1SG	=wē-lī
1PL	=wē-lan

This stem *wē-* is clearly the past stem of the verb *h-w-y*. In JSNENA the initial /w/ has shifted to /y/, probably by analogy with the paradigm of the present copula, which has a stem beginning with /y/.

Most NENA dialects outside the subgroup of Jewish Trans-Zab form a past copula by combining the past converter suffix *-wa* with the present copula (Table 59). In the third person the *-wa* is generally combined with only the stem of the present copula.

Table 59: Past copula paradigm in Ch. Barwar (Khan 2008b, 183–84).

	Present copula	Past copula
3SG.M	=īlē	=īwa
3SG.F	=īla	=īwa
3PL	=īlɛ	=īwa
2SG.M	=īwət	=īwatwa
2SG.F	=īwat	=īwatwa
2PL	=īwētū	=īwētūwa
1SG.M	=īwən	=īwənwa
1SG.F	=īwan	=īwanwa
1PL	=īwəx	=īwəxwa

This is compatible with the normal use of the -*wa* suffix with the present stem of a verb to express an imperfective past (habitual or progressive). In dialects that form the past copula in this way, the past stem of the verb *h-w-y* is used to express a perfective aspect denoting a temporally bounded period or the onset of a period at a specific starting point ('became'), e.g. Ch. Barwar *wē-lē* 'he became' (Khan 2008b, 651–52). In JSNENA the past copula *yēlē* (< *wēlē), by contrast, has a general imperfective sense of a continuing state in the past or a habitual state in the past.

The formation of the past copula from the past stem of the verb *h-w-y* in Jewish trans-Zab replicates the Iranian languages of the region. The closest documented model for the past copula of Jewish Trans-Zab NENA is found in the Bājalānī dialect of Gorani dialect that is now spoken in Iraq. This is inflected with oblique clitics, which correspond to the NENA oblique L-suffixes (Table 60):

Table 60: Past copula paradigm in Gorani Bājalānī (Iraq) (MacKenzie 1956, 424).

	Past copula	Past verb inflection
3SG	*bī-Ø*	*-Ø*
3PL	*bīšān*	*=īšān*
2SG	*bīt*	*=īt*
2PL	*bītān*	*=ītān*
1SG	*bīm*	*=īm*
1PL	*bīmān*	*=īmān*

In Bājalānī the past intransitive stems are inflected like transitive past stems with oblique clitics, though an /ī/ element is added to the clitic in intransitive past forms, as in the column adjacent to the copula in Table 60 (MacKenzie 1956, 421). The Bājalānī past copula can be analysed as a past stem inflected with oblique clitics. The type of generalised oblique inflection of both transitive and intransitive past stems of verbs in Bājalānī corresponds, indeed, to the generalised inflection of transitive and intransitive past stems by L-suffixes in the main body of NENA. As remarked in §5.3, the inflection of the past stems of intransitive verbs with direct suffixes in JSNENA appears to be a later development under the influence of Kurdish and Iranian Gorani. The existence of L-suffixes in the past copula of JSNENA can be regarded as an archaic vestige of the earlier type of generalised oblique inflection of past stems that is found in the main body of NENA dialects. Its replacement by direct suffixes is likely to have been blocked in order to avoid homophony with the present copula (§5.8.1).

5.8 The copula

The formation of the past copula by a combination of a past stem and oblique clitics has been identified also in the Shabaki dialect of Gorani, spoken in the Mosul region.

In addition to the past copyla *yēlē*, JSNENA also uses the verbal form *k-wēwa* to express imperfectively a past state (Khan 2009, §9.7.3). This is formed from the root *h-w-y* with an indicative *k-* prefix and the past converter particle *wa*. It typically has a habitual sense, e.g.

(341) JSNENA
xá-yarxá   bár   'īlānḕ,' 'ənyēxáē̃ ga-fkə́r   kw-ḗn-wa   kḗ
one-month   after   trees   they   in-thought   be.PRS-3PL-PSTC   that
báqa   patīrḗ   má   lāzə́m=yē   tahyà   hol-ī́.'
for   Passover what   necessary=COP.3SG.M   preparation   make.PRS-3PL
'A month after Tu bə-Shvat, they considered what they should prepare for Passover.' (B:14)

JSNENA uses the present stem of the verb *h-w-y* with the indicative prefix *k-* to express the future, e.g. *k-wē* 'he will be'. In some Jewish Trans-Zab dialects *k-wē* can also have a sense of a present predicating a generic or permanent property, e.g.

(342) J. Sulemaniyya
talga   qarda   k-əwy-a
snow   cold   IND.be.PRS-3SG.F
'Snow is cold.'
(Khan 2004, 311)

The present stem form *hawē* without the indicative prefix is used in JSNENA to express the modal subjunctive.

In JSNENA the ingressive sense of 'becoming' is expressed by the verb *x-Ø-r* (present stem: *xar-*, past stem: *xir-*). This is derived historically from the root **x-d-r*, which originally had the sense of 'turning round', as it still does in some NENA dialects, e.g.

(343) JSNENA
  a. nāšḗ   mā́rē   doltá   xìr-ī=ū|
     people   possessors.of   wealth   become.PST-3PL=and
     'People became rich.' (B:56)
  b. kē-'aql-ú   ṣàf   xár-ī|
     that-feet-their   smooth   become.PRS-3PL
     'so that their feet would become smooth' (A:38)

The various copulas in JSNENA can be summarised as follows:

(344) JSNENA
    Present indicative: =yē   present copula
    Past (imperfective):   =yēlē   < *=wēlē, past stem of *h-w-y*
    Past (habitual)   k-wēwa   < *h-w-y*
    Future: k-wē   < *h-w-y*
    Modal subjunctive: hawē   < *h-w-y*
    Ingressive ('become') :   xar   < *x-d-r*

In the Gorani of the Sanandaj region there are two sets of the past copula. One is formed from the past stem of the verb 'to be' and inflected with direct verbal suffixes. The other is formed from the present stem of the verb 'to be' and is inflected with the past converter morpheme *ēn* and direct verbal suffixes (Table 61):[7]

Table 61: Past copula paradigms in Gorani.

	Set 1	Set 2
3SG.M	bī-Ø	b-ē (< *b-ēn)
3SG.F	bī-a	b-ē (< *b-ēn)
3PL	bī-ē	b-ēn-ē
2SG	bī-ay	b-ēn-ī
2PL	bī-ayde	b-ēn-dē
1SG	bī-ā(ē)	b-ēn-ē
1PL	bī-ayme	b-ēn-ē

The paradigm of the first set is the less frequent one (indeed it occurs rarely in our corpus). This copula has an ingressive sense of 'become'. The paradigm of the second set is the more frequent past copula. Mahmoudveysi and Bailey (2018, 551) refer to it as the 'imperfect form of copula'. The use of the *-ēn* morpheme with a present verbal stem is, indeed, generally used elsewhere to express the imperfective past.

Examples: Set 1 of Gorani:

(345)   Gorani Luhon (MacKenzie 1966, 64)
    ganmakē=šā   *hāřā*   *tā*   *wurd-a*   **bī-a**
    wheat.DEF.DIR.F=3PL   grind.PST   till   small-F   COP.PST-3SG.F
    'They ground the wheat until it **was** fine.'

---

[7] A further past copula stem *bo* was attested in the speech of an old woman in Hawraman Takht. It is unclear if this stem is systematically used in Gorani.

Set (2):

(346) Gorani
    mən   *šāngzà-na*   **b-ēn-ē**|
    1SG   sixteen-POST   be-PSTC-1SG
    'I **was** sixteen years old.'

The ingressive set 1 past copula would correspond to JSNENA *xar* and the imperfective set 2 copula to JSNENA *yēlē* and *k-wēwa*. The closest morphological match of the set 2 copula is with JSNENA *k-wēwa*, which is formed from the present stem and the past converter suffix *wa*.

Gorani expresses the generic present and future by the present stem of the verb 'to be' inflected with direct suffixes. This form can also have an ingressive sense of 'become':

(347) Gorani
    3SG   *b-o*   'he is/will be; he becomes/will become'
    3PL   *b-ā*
    2SG   *b-ī*
    2PL   *b-īde*
    1SG   *b-ū*
    1PL   *b-īme*

The past copula in the Kurdish of Sanandaj is formed by the past stem inflected with direct suffixes (Table 62):

Table 62: Past copula paradigm in Kurdish.

3SG	*bū-∅*
3PL	*bū-n*
2SG	*bū-y*
2PL	*bū-n*
1SG	*bū-m*
1PL	*bū-īn*

In the Kurdish of Sanandaj the present stem of the verb *būn* 'be' with the indicative prefix *a-* and direct inflectional suffixes is used to predicate the present or the future. In past discourse it is used also with past time deixis. The construction has the form *a-w-ē* (< *a-b-ē*). This form is used also with an ingressive sense ('becomes, will become'):

(348) Kurdish
 3SG *a-w-ē*
 3PL *a-w-ən*
 2SG *a-w-ī*
 2PL *a-w-ən*
 1SG *a-w-əm*
 1PL *a-w-īn*

Examples:

(349) Kurdish
 a. *nāřāhàt a-w-ē*[|]
   sad   IND-COP.PRS-3SG
   'He becomes sad.'
 b. *a-wēt=a mənā̀ḷ*[|], *a-wēt=a kanīšk-ề.*[|]
   IND-COP.3SG=DRCT child IND-COP.3SG=DRCT girl-INDF
   '(The kidney) turned into a baby, it became a girl.'

It is found in reported discourse at the beginning of narratives:

(350) Kurdish
 a. *pāwšā̀-y aw   šār-a a-w-ē.*[|]
   king-INDF DEM.SG.DIST city-DEM1 IND-COP.PRS-3SG
   'She was the king of that city.'
 b. *šā-yk a-w-ē*[|] *kùř-ēk=ī a-w-ē,*[|]
   king-INDF IND-be.PRS-3SG son-INDF=3SG IND-be.PRS-3SG
   kuř-aka hàf sāḷ pā nā-gr-ē[|]
   son-DEF seven year foot NEG-grab.PRS-3SG
   'There was a king. He had a son. The son was not able to walk for seven years.'

For the expression of irrealis mood, the indicative prefix in *a-w-ē* is replaced by the subjunctive particle, yielding *b-w-ē-*.

(351) Kurdish
 ā yak nafar bə-ř-ề   swār b-w-ē[|]
 INTJ one person SBJV-go.PRS-3SG riding SBJV-be.PRS-3SG
 bəzān-a   aw   du nafar-a bočà
 SBJV-know.PRS-ĪMP.2SG DEM.DIST two person-DEM1 why

*šař=yān=a*¹
fight=3PL=COP.3SG

'May someone go and mount (a horse), see why those two persons are fighting.'

Table 63 compares the various functions of the forms of the copula in JSNENA, Hawraman Gorani and Sanandaj Kurdish:

Table 63: Functions of copula forms in JSNENA, Gorani, and Kurdish.

	JSNENA	Gorani	Kurdish
Present indicative:	=yē	=n	=a, =s
Past (imperfective):	=yēlē	b-ē (< *b-ēn)	bū
Past (habitual)	k-wēwa	b-ē (< *b-ēn)	bū
present/future:	k-wē	b-o	a-w-ē
Modal subjunctive:	hawē	b-o	b-w-ē
Ingressive past (perfective)	xīr	bī	bū
Ingressive present/future:	xar	b-o	a-w-ē
Ingressive modal subjunctive	xar	b-o	b-w-ē

As can be seen, the system of copulas in JSNENA exhibits only partial convergence with the systems of the Iranian languages. JSNENA uses a distinct lexical verb to express 'becoming', whereas the Iranian languages use the same lexical verb to express 'to be' and 'to become'. NENA dialects in general have separate ingressive verbs meaning 'to become'. In most Christian dialects this is the root *p-y-š*, which also means 'to remain'. In the Jewish Trans-Zab dialects *p-y-š* means only 'to remain' and 'to become' is expressed by the root *x-d-r* (JSNENA > *x-Ø-r*), which originally meant 'to go around'. In earlier literary Aramaic there are no obvious antecedents for the use of these verbs in the sense of 'become'. If there has been any external influence on the development of these verbs, this may have come from Arabic in the western sector of NENA and spread eastwards. In the Arabic dialects of the region (known as *qəltu* dialects), as in Classical Arabic, there is a distinct lexical verb for expressing 'become', viz. *ṣār* (root *ṣ-y-r*), which corresponds to a large proportion of the meanings of the NENA ingressive verbs. In NENA dialects in Iran the use of a distinct lexical verb for 'becoming' may have been reinforced by contact with Persian constructions with the verb *šodan* 'to become'.

The JSNENA form *k-wēwa* is a direct structural match of Gorani *b-ē* (< *b-ēn*), both having the past converter morpheme. The JSNENA form, however, is more restricted in use than the Gorani form. The JSNENA form is used only for habitual and generic situations in the past, whereas the Gorani form is used as a general imperfective past.

The JSNENA general past imperfective copula =*yēle* matches closely the structure of the Bājalānī Gorani copula, as discussed above, with a past stem inflected by oblique suffixes. In Bājalānī this appears to be used as a general past imperfective. In Sanandaj the past copula *bū* is, likewise, formed from the past stem and has the function of a general past imperfective. In both Bājalānī and Sanandaj Kurdish, however, these past copulas can also be used with an ingressive sense ('became'), which is not the case with the JSNENA =*yēle*.

5.9 Existential copula

In JSNENA there is a present and past existential copula with the following forms. They are uninflected for number and gender:

(352) JSNENA
hīt 'there is/are'
hītwa 'there was/were'

The initial /h/ has arisen by the common shift of an initial pharyngeal stop *ˁ' to a pharyngeal fricative *ˁīt > hīt (§2.2.2.6).

Possessive constructions are formed by combining the existential copula with the oblique L-suffixes, which express a dative relationship. In the present forms the /l/ of the suffixes is regularly assimilated to the final /t/ and the resulting gemination of the /t/ is weakened according to the usual phonetic process in JSNENA (§2.2.2.12):

(353) JSNENA
hītē 'he has' (lit. 'it exists to him') < *hīttē < *hītlē
hītwālē 'he had' (lit. 'it existed to him)

If the possessor in a clause is an independent noun or pronoun, this is resumed by the oblique L-suffix on the existential copula. It does not take a dative preposition directly, e.g.

(354) JSNENA
ʾaxon-ī̀ dawāxānè-hīt-wā-le.'
brother-my pharmacy-exist-PSTC-OBL.3SG.M
'My brother had a pharmacy.' (A:27)

In Gorani and Kurdish existential copulas are formed by adding copula endings to the stem *ha-*. The third person forms are presented below.

(355) Gorani
    3SG.M   *ha-n*
    3SG.F   *ha-na*
    3PL   *ha-nē*

(356) Kurdish
    3SG   *ha-s*
    3PL   *ha-n*

These predicates express possession in predicative possessive constructions, in which the clitic person markers index the possessor argument. See Mohammadirad (2020b) for an overview of predicative possession across West Iranian languages. Note that in Kurdish the predicate has the invariable 3SG form *has*:

(357) Gorani
ha-n=əm	'I have it (m).' (lit. it is to me)
ha-na=m	'I have it (f)'
ha-nē=m	'I have them'
ha-n=ət	'you have it (m)'
ha-na=ət	'you have it (f)'
ha-nē=t	'you have them'
ha-n=əš	'he/she has it (m)'
ha-na=š	'he/she has it (f)'
ha-nē=š	'he/she has them'
ha-n=mā	'we have it (m)'
ha-na=mā	'we have it (f)'
ha-nē=mā	'we have them'
ha-n=tā	'you have it (m)'
ha-na=tā	'you have it (f)'
ha-nē=tā	'you have them'
ha-n=šā	'they have it (m)'
ha-na=šā	'they have it (f)'
ha-nē=šā	'they have them'

Kurdish

(358) Kurdish
ha-s=əm	'I have (it, them)' (lit. it is to me)
ha-s=ət	'you (s) have (it, them)'
ha-s=ī	'he/she has (it, them)'

ha-s=mān   'we have (it, them)'
ha-s=tān   'you (pl) have (it, them)'
ha-s=yān   'they have (it, them)'

The oblique clitic used here has a dative sense. These Iranian constructions match the JSNENA possessive construction with *hīt* + oblique L-suffix. The JSNENA existential copula does not inflect to agree with the possessed item, which corresponds to the invariable form *has* in the Kurdish construction.

The direct match between the pattern of the JSNENA and Iranian constructions is in the form that occurs in clauses without an independent possessor argument. Whereas the JSNENA L-suffix remains fixed on the existential copula in such cases, in the Iranian languages the oblique clitic moves onto the possessor argument, e.g.

(359) Gorani
a. *mēwa=y   āl-ē=š   ha-nē*
   fruit=EZ   good-DIR.PL=3SG existent-COP.3PL
   'It has good fruit.'
b. *yo   gāya=mā   ha-na*
   each   COW.F.DIR=1PL existent-COP.3SG.F
   'We each have a cow.'

(360) Kurdish
mən   kanīšk-ēk=əm   ha=s
1SG   daughter-INDF=1SG   existent=COP.3SG
'I have a daughter.'

The JSNENA existential copula *hīt* (*īt* in the majority of NENA dialects) is historically independent of the present copula. This differs from the Iranian existential copulas, which contain elements from the present copula paradigm. There is marginal use of another possessive construction in JSNENA consisting of the stem *lā* + L-suffixes:

(361) JSNENA
3SG.M   *lālē*
3SG.F   *lāla*
3PL   *lālū*
2SG.M   *lālox*
2SG.F   *lālax*
2PL   *lālaxun*
1SG   *lālī*
1PL   *lālan*

This copula phrase with L-suffixes has a restricted functional distribution. It is used after the interrogative *m-lēka* 'from where?' in constructions such as the following:

(362) JSNENA
'*āna pūḷē mən-lēka lā-lī haw-na ta dīdox?*
I money from-where EXIST-OBL.1SG give.PRS-1SG to OBL.2SG.M
'From where do I have money to give to you?'

The *lā-* element in the JSNENA dative copula *lālē* appears to be derived historically from a 3SG.F copula with the form **īla*, which is its normal form in the majority of NENA dialects. A number of dialects of the area have the particle *lā* (e.g. Ch. Bədyəl, Ch. Koy Sanjak, J. Arbel, J. Ruwanduz, J. Rustaqa) (Mutzafi 2004b; Khan 1999; 2002b; 2018b). This particle is related in function to the so-called deictic copula of other NENA dialects, which are inflected for person.[8] The inflected deictic copula typically consists of an invariant pronominal element and an inflected copula, e.g.[9]

(363) Ch. Barwar: *holē* < **hā-'aw=īlē* [DEIC-PRO.3SG.M=COP.3SG.M]
Ch. Urmi: *dūlə* < **dī-'ū=īlə* [DEIC-PRO.3SG.M=COP.3SG.M]

The Ch. Sulemaniyya dialect has the invariable form *'ūla*, which functions as an uninflected deictic copula. This appears to have developed from a combination of the pronominal element and the invariable 3SG.F copula, viz. **'ū=īla* [PRO.3SG. M=COP.3SG.F]. The invariable deictic copula *lā* of the NENA dialects mentioned above may have evolved from a form like Ch. Sulemaniyya *'ūla* through the elision of the pronominal element.

The JSNENA dative copula *lālē* would, therefore, be a closer match to the Gorani and Kurdish possessive constructions than the JSNENA construction *hītē*. The closest match would be to Kurdish, since in Kurdish the copula element is invariable. The *ha-* element in the Iranian existential copulas could, indeed, be interpreted as a deictic element, and so this would also correspond closely to the function of *lā* in other NENA dialects. Constructions such *hītē* (< **ītlē*) are found across the whole NENA area. The *lālē* construction, however, is a distinctive feature of JSNENA and can be regarded as the result of closer convergence with Iranian, in which the *hīt* element has been replaced by an element from the present copula paradigm, although in archaic fossilised form. It is significant that the more innovative *lālē* construction is

---

8 See, for example, Ch. Barwar (Khan 2008b, 186) and Ch. Urmi (Khan 2016, vol. 1, 253).
9 For details of the historical development of NENA deictic copulas see Khan (2018b).

restricted to emotionally-charged interactional contexts such as (362), which is likely to have motivated the innovation.

In the past tense of the possessive construction, the Iranian languages use a past copula with oblique dative suffixes. Gorani uses the paradigm that contains the present stem of the verb 'to be' and the past converter *-ēn* morpheme:

(364)   Gorani   Kurdish
      3SG   *bē*   *bū*
      3PL   *bēnē*   *bū*

Examples:

(365)   Gorani: *bēnē=mā* 'we had (them)' (lit. it existed to us')
       Kurdish: *bū=mān*   'we had it' (lit. 'it existed to us')

The corresponding forms in JSNENA have the past converter suffix *wa*, which matches most closely the Gorani construction:

(366)   JSNENA
       hītwālan 'we had'
       lāwālan 'we had'

5.10 Pronominal direct objects on present, imperative and past stem verbs

5.10.1 Pronominal direct objects on present stem verbs

In JSNENA the pronominal direct object of a verb form derived from the present stem may be expressed by oblique L-series suffixes in all persons except the 1SG.M. and 1SG.F., which take simple pronominal suffixes without the /l/ element. The forms attached to a 3SG.M. verb are as follows:

(367)   JSNENA
Object Suffix	3SG.M. verb	
3SG.M	*garǝ́š-lē*	'he pulls him'
3SG.F	*garǝ́š-la*	'he pulls her'
3PL	*garǝ́š-lū*	'he pulls them', etc.
2SG.M	*garǝ́š-lox*	
2SG.F	*garǝ́š-lax*	

2PL	garə́š-laxun
1SG	garə́š-lī
1PL	garə́š-lan

The /l/ of the suffix assimilates to the /t/ of the 2SG.M and 2SG.F forms and the resulting gemination of /t/ is weakened:

(368) JSNENA

Verb	3SG.M Object Suffix		
2SG.M	garšḗt-ē	'you pull him'	< garšet-lē
2SG.F	garšā́t-ē	'you pull him'	< garšat-lē
2PL	garšētū-lē	'you pull him'	

When the L-suffixes are added to a 1PL. verb, an additional /i/ vowel is inserted before the suffix:

(369) JSNENA
    1PL   *garšēxī-lē*   'we pull him'

The 1st person singular verb forms express the pronominal object with the series of pronominal suffixes that are attached to nouns and prepositions (§3.5). The final /a/ of the 1SG.M. subject suffix –*na* is elided before the pronominal object suffix:

(370) JSNENA

Object Suffix	1SG.M verb	
3SG.M	garə́šn-ēf	'I (m.) pull him'
3SG.F	garə́šn-af	'I (m.) pull her'
3PL	garə́šn-ū	'I (m.) pull them'
2SG.M	garə́šn-ox	'I (m.) pull you'
2SG.F	garə́šn-ax	'I (m.) pull you'
2PL	garə́šn-axun	'I (m.) pull you'

With the 1SG.F three variant forms are attested, one retaining the –*an* subject suffix, one reduplicating the suffix and a third eliding the suffix altogether before the object suffix:

(371)

	3SG.M	garšán-ēf	garšánan-ēf	garš-ēf	'I (f.) pull him'
	3SG.F	garšán-af	garšánan-af	garš-af	'I (f.) pull her'
	3PL	garšán-ū	garšánan-ū	garš-ū	'I (f.) pull them', etc.

The motivation to use this alternative set of suffixes to express the pronominal object of first person verbs is likely to be to avoid ambiguity between verbs with 3SG.F and first person subject inflection in verbs from roots ending in final /n/. Due to processes of assimilation and degemination these forms would be identical (Khan 2009, 32–33), e.g.

(372) JSNENA
z-b-n 'to sell'
zabná	'she sells'	zabnā́-lē	'she sells it'
zábna	'I (m) sell'	*zabnā́-lē	'I (m) sell it''
zabnán	'I (f) sell'	*zabnā́-lē	'I (f) sell it'

Attachment of pronominal object suffixes to present stem forms with the past tense enclitic -wa:

(373) JSNENA
3SG.M	garə́š-wā-lē	'he used to pull him'
3SG.F	garšā́-wā-lē	'she used to pull him'
3PL	garšī́-wā-lē	'they used to pull him'
2SG.M	garšḗt-wā-lē	'you (SG.M) used to pull him'
2SG.F	garšát-wā-lē	'you (SG.F) used to pull him'
2PL	garšḗtun-wā-lē	'you (PL) used to pull him'
1SG.M	garā́šna-wā-lēf	'I (M) used to pull him'
1SG.F	garšán-wā-lēf	'I (F) used to pull him'
1PL	garšḗx-wā-lē	'we used to pull him'

The third person singular pronominal suffixes on first person singular verb forms are -lēf (1SG.M) and -laf (1SG.F) by analogy with the suffixes –ēf and –af that are attached to the first person forms in the present.

An alternative means of expressing the pronominal direct object is by a prepositional phrase. Such a prepositional phrase is not bonded to the verb like L-suffixes and may be placed either after or before it. When the pronominal object is fronted before the verb, the object pronoun is typically an information focus, which typically expresses contrast.

Prepositional phrases containing the preposition 'əl- with pronominal suffixes are placed either after or before the verb:

(374) JSNENA
  garə́š 'əlȅf| 'he pulls him'
  garə́š 'əlòx| 'he pulls you'
  'əlȅf garə́š| 'he pulls HIM'
  'əlòx garə́š| 'he pulls YOU'

When the pronominal suffix is fronted before the verb, it may also be expressed by morphologically 'heavier' phrases in which the pronominal element is combined with the preposition by means of an oblique pronoun (§3.6). When used independently of pronominal suffixes, the preposition has the form *həl-* with an initial /h/. Such direct object phrases do not necessarily have narrow focus:

(375) JSNENA
  həl-dīdī garəš   'he pulls me'
  həl-dīdan garəš   'he pulls us'
  həl-dīdox garəš   'he pulls you (SG.M)'
  həl-dīdax garəš   'he pulls you (SG.F)'
  həl-dīdaxun garəš   'he pulls you (PL)'
  həl-do garəš   'he pulls him/her'
  həl-donī garəš   'he pulls them'

The *həl-* preposition may be optionally omitted before the oblique pronoun. This is particularly common before the *dīd-* phrase with first and second person objects:

(376) JSNENA
  dīdī garəš   'he pulls me'
  dīdóx garəš   'he pulls you (SG.M)'
  dīdax garəš   'he pulls you (SG.F)'
  dīdaxun garəš   'he pulls you (PL)'
  do garəš   'he pulls him/her'
  donī garəš   'he pulls them'

In Gorani and Kurdish, pronominal objects can be expressed by either oblique clitic pronouns or by independent pronouns. The bound object pronouns are placed after the verbal person suffixes in Gorani, but in Kurdish they are placed between the indicative particle and the verb stem. The pattern of Gorani, therefore, is the closest match to that of JSNENA, in which the oblique L-suffixes expressing the object are placed after the person suffixes.

(377) Gorani
   vīn 'see' present tense
   Object Suffix   3SG verb
   3SG   *vīn-o=š*   'he/she sees him/her/it'
   3PL   *vīn-o=šā*   'he/she sees them'
   2SG   *vīn-o=-t*   'he/she sees you'
   2PL   *vīn-o=-tā*   'he/she sees you'
   1SG   *vīn-o=m*   'he/she sees me'
   1PL   *vīn-o=mā*   'he/she sees us'

(378) Kurdish
   wēn 'see' present tense
   Object Suffix   3SG verb
   3SG   *a=y-wēn-ē*   'he/she sees him'
   3PL   *a=yān-wēn-ē*   'he/she sees them'
   2SG   *a=w-wēn-ē*   'he/she sees you'
   2PL   *a=tān-wēn-ē*   'he/she sees you'
   1SG   *a=m-wēn-ē*   'he/she sees me'
   1PL   *a=mān-wēn-ē*   'he/she sees us'

The examples below illustrate the attachment of bound pronominal objects to present stem verbs with the accompanying past converter suffix -*ēn*:

(379) Gorani
   vīn 'see' imperfective
   Object Suffix   1PL subject
   3SG   *vīn-ēn-mē=š*   'we were watching him/her/it'
   3PL   *vīn-ēn-mē=šā*   'we were watching them'
   2SG   *vīn-ēn-mē=t*   'we were watching you'
   2PL   *vīn-ēn-mē=tā*   'we were watching you'

This, likewise, would be a close match of the place of object L-suffixes in present stem verbs with the past converter morpheme *wa* in JSNENA after the person marker (*garš-ā-wā-lē* 'she used to pull him'). The only difference is that the Gorani past converter morpheme is before the subject person marker.

As remarked, a peculiarity of the marking of objects on present stem verbs in JSNENA is that nominal possessive suffixes are used after first person singular subject markers. In Gorani the pronominal object after first person singular subjects is marked by oblique suffixes as in the rest of the paradigm. It is significant, however, that the Gorani oblique suffix paradigm is used also as possessive suffixes (§3.5). It is likely, therefore, that the use of possessive suffixes in JSNENA in this context, which was motivated by the need to avoid ambiguity (see above), was facilitated by matching the possessive suffixes with Gorani oblique clitics.

Gorani has case and gender inflection of independent third person pronouns. These can be used to express the pronominal object of a present stem verb. In such constructions the third person pronoun is in the oblique form. This would match the use of oblique independent pronouns in this context in JSNENA:

(380) Gorani
    a. *āḏ*   *āḏīšā*   *vīn-o*
        3SG.DIR.M 3PL.OBL see.PRS-3SG
        'he sees them'
   Gorani
    b. *mən*   *āḏī*   *vīn-ū*
        1SG   3SG.OBL.M see.PRS-1SG
        'I see him'

First and second person pronouns in Gorani have lost case distinction. Therefore, they appear in the bare form when functioning as direct objects of the verb:

(381) Gorani
    a. *mən* *tu*   *vīn-ū*
        1SG   2SG see.PRS-1SG
        'I see you'
    b. *tu*   *mən* *vīn-ī*
        2SG   1SG see.PRS-2SG
        'you see me'

The marking of pronominal objects on present stem verbs in Sanandaj Kurdish is much less like JSNENA than is Gorani. In Kurdish, as remarked, the object oblique clitic is not placed after the subject person marker but after the preverbal mood prefix:

(382) Kurdish
    a=m-wēn-ē   'he sees me'
    a=tān-wēn-ē   'he sees you (pl.)'
    a=y-wēn-ē   'he sees her'
    b=ī-w-a   'take it!'

In Sanandaj Kurdish none of the independent pronouns are inflected for case and gender. They appear in the same form irrespective of the grammatical function they express:

(383) Kurdish
    a. **mən** aw a-wēn-əm
        1SG 3SG IND-see.PRS-1SG
        'I see her/him'
    b. aw **mən** a-wēn-ē.
        3SG 1SG IND-see.PRS-3SG
        'He/she sees me'

5.10.2 Imperative

In JSNENA the pronominal object on imperatives is expressed by L-suffixes. The stress is placed on the initial syllable, e.g.

(384) JSNENA
    a. SG *grúš-lē* 'pull him!'
        PL *grúšmū-lē* 'pull him!'

Likewise, in Gorani and Kurdish the pronominal objects of imperatives appear as clitic pronouns, which correspond to NENA L-suffixes. In Gorani these are placed at the end of the verb, as in JSNENA, but in Kurdish they are placed after the preverbal subjunctive particle:

(385) Gorani
    2SG -a b-ār-a=š 'bring (s) him!'
    2PL -dē b-ār-dē=š 'bring (pl) him!'

(386) Kurdish
    2SG -a b=ī-nūs-a 'write (s) it!'
    2PL -ən b=ī-nūs-ən 'write (pl) it!'

5.10.3 Pronominal direct objects on past stem verbs

In JSNENA third person objects of transitive past stem verbs can be expressed by a direct suffix on the past stem of the verbal form, the subject agent being expressed by an oblique L-suffix. This is ergative alignment, since the direct suffixes are used to expressed the subject of intransitive past stem verbs. JSNENA, therefore, as NENA dialects in general, exhibits split ergativity consisting of ergative alignment with past stems and accusative alignment with present stems.

(387) Gorani
    3SG.M   *grə́š-Ø-lē*   'he pulled him'
    3SG.F   *gərš-ā́-lē*   'he pulled her'
    3PL   *gərš-ī́-lē*   'he pulled them'

The form *grəš-Ø-lē* may, in fact, either express specifically a SG.M undergoer that is anaphorically bound to the context or may be used in a neutral sense without denoting any specific undergoer.

The third person pronominal objects may be expressed in this way also when the past converter particle *wa* is attached to the past stem:

(388) JSNENA
    3SG.M   *grə́š-wā-lē*   'he had pulled him'
    3SG.F   *gərš-ā́-wā-lē*   'he had pulled her'
    3PL   *gərš-ī́-wā-lē*   'he had pulled them'

First and second person pronominal objects are not expressed by direct suffixes. They are rather expressed by independent pronominal prepositional phrases headed by the preposition *'əl-/həl-*. When placed before the verb, this prepositional phrase is optionally replaced by a morphologically heavier phrase containing the oblique pronoun. Third person pronominal objects may also be expressed in this way rather than by direct suffixes on the stem. The full paradigm of pronominal objects expressed in this way is as follows:

(389) JSNENA
    3SG.M   *grəšlē 'əlēf*   *'əlēf grəšlē*   *həl-do grəšlē*
                                                                                                     'he pulled him'
    3SG.F   *grəšlē 'əlaf*   *'əlaf grəšlē*   *həl-do grəšlē*
                                                                                                     'he pulled her'
    3PL   *grəšlē 'əlū*   *'əlū grəšlē*   *həl-donī grəšlē*
                                                                                                      'he pulled them'
    2SG.M   *grəšlē 'əlox*   *'əlox grəšlē*   *həl-dīdox grəšlē*
                                                                                                 'he pulled you (SG.M)'
    2SG.F   *grəšlē 'əlax*   *'əlax grəšlē*   *həl-dīdax grəšlē*
                                                                                                 'he pulled you (SG.F)'

2PL	grəšlē 'əlaxun	'əlaxun grəšlē	həl-dīdaxun grəšlē 'he pulled you (pl)'
1SG	grəšlē 'əlī	'əlī grəšlē	həl-dīdī grəšlē 'he pulled me'
1PL	grəšlē 'əlan	'əlan grəšlē	həl-dīdan grəšlē 'he pulled us'

The *həl-* element before forms with the genitive particle may be dropped, e.g.

(390) JSNENA
 do grəšlē   'he pulled him'
 dīdī grəšlū 'they pulled me'
 dīdox grəšlī 'I pulled you (SG.M)'

In the text corpus of Khan (2009) two cases occur of a 1SG.F undergoer of the action being expressed by a direct suffix on the past stem:

(391) JSNENA
 ləbl-ánan-u   bīmarīstắn-e   Hadasà.|
 take.PST-1SG.F-3PL   hospital-EZ   Hadasa
 'axon-ì   ləbl-ánan-ēf.|
 brother-my   take.PST-1SG.F-3SG.M
 'They took me to Hadasa hospital. My brother took me.' (C:2)

When, however, attempts were made to elicit further forms of undergoers that are not 3rd person expressed in the inflection of the past stem, informants did not accept their grammaticality.

The expression of objects of all persons by direct suffixes on the past stem is a feature of various NENA dialects, which are concentrated in the northern sector of NENA (Khan 2017; Noorlander 2021) In dialects in the southern sector of NENA the expression of objects by direct suffixes is generally restricted to the third person. In some dialects there are signs that the use of direct suffixes for first and second person objects is in the process of decay (Khan 2016, vol. 1, 271–273). It is possible that the isolated occurrence of a first person direct suffix marking an object in (391) is a reflection of such a decay in JSNENA from an original situation in which objects of all persons could be expressed by direct suffixes.

In Gorani of the Sanandaj region pronominal objects of past stem verbs are expressed ergatively by direct suffixes on the stem and the agent is expressed by a following oblique clitic:

(392) Gorani

Object Suffix	3SG subject	
3SG.M	ārd-Ø=əš	'he/she brought him'
3SG.F	ārd-a=š	'he/she brought her'
3PL	ārd-ē=š	'he/she brought them'
2SG	ārd-ī=š	'he/she brought you (sg)'
2PL	ārd-īdē=š	'he/she brought you (pl)'
1SG	ārd-ā=š	'he/she brought me'
1PL	ārd-īmē=š	'he/she brought us'

(393) Gorani

Object Suffix	3PL subject	
3SG.M	bard-Ø=šā	'they took him'
3SG.F	bard-a=šā	'they took her'
3PL	bard-ē=šā	'they took them'
2SG	bard-ī=šā	'they took you (s)'
2PL	bard-īdē=šā	'they took you (pl)'
1SG	bard-ā=šā	'they took me'
1PL	bard-īmē=šā	'they took us'

Ergativity has been lost in Sanandaj Kurdish. This is manifested by the extension of oblique clitics to mark objects in the past tense. This results in a levelling of object indexing by oblique clitics in present and past transitive constructions. The order of agent and patient remains the same as the substrate Gorani, i.e. Verb–Object–Agent (cf. Mohammadirad *in review* for discussion):

(394) Gorani

Object index	3PL subject	
3SG.M	hāwərd=ī=yān	'they brought him'
3PL	hāwərd=yān=yān	'they brought them'
2SG	hāwərd=ət=yān	'they brought you'
2PL	hāwərd=tān=yān	'they brought you'
1SG	hāwərd=əm=yān	'they brought me'
1PL	hāwərd=mān=yān	'they brought us'

In Upper Central Kurdish, however, the ordering of the bound arguments is Verb–Agent–Object, e.g.

(395) Mukri (Upper Central Kurdish)
 hēnā=yān-īn
 bring.PST=3PL-1PL
 'they brought us'

JSNENA matches the Gorani pattern of expression of pronominal objects, except for the fact that in JSNENA the object expressed by the direct suffixes is restricted to third person. The fact that some isolated cases of first person objects have been documented, suggest that at an earlier period, JSNENA matched Gorani exactly with also first and second person objects expressed by direct suffixes. The incipient loss of this ergative construction is likely to have come about due to contact with Kurdish, in which direct suffixes no longer express the object. The first and second person object direct suffixes were eliminated in this decay process, whereas the third person object suffixes have been more resilient. This is likely to be due to the greater markedness of first and second person participants in object position than third person referents and their consequent greater susceptibility to change (Khan 2017). As we have seen, the first and second person objects are expressed by independent prepositional phrases rather than L-suffixes, which are the normal match for the Iranian clitics. It is relevant to note, however, that in fast speech these phrases often loose their stress, which would make them prosodically identical to clitics, e.g.

(396) JSNENA
 grəšlī-lox 'I pulled you (SG.M)' < grəšlī 'əlóx

5.11 Compound verbal forms containing the verb 'to be'

5.11.1 Realis perfect

In JSNENA the realis resultative perfect is expressed by a compound construction consisting of the resultative participle combined with the present enclitic copula. This construction is available for all persons in intransitive or passive verbs, expressed by the intransitive/passive base:

Intransitive

(397) JSNENA
 s-m-x 'to stand up'
 3SG.M smīxá=y 'he has stood up'
 3SG.F smīxtḗ=ya 'she has stood up'

3PL	smīxḗn	'they have stood up', etc.
2SG.M	smīxḗt	
2SG.F	smīxtḗ=yat	
2PL	smīxḗtun	
1SG.M	smīxḗna	
1SG.F	smīxtḗ=yan	
1PL	smīxḗx	

The participle is inflected for gender and number (SG.M *smīxa*, SG.F *smīxta*, PL *smīxē*). In several cases in this paradigm the copula has become contracted with the ending of the participle, e.g. 3PL *smīxḗn* < *smīxē=yēn*, 2SG.M *smīxḗt* < *smīxa=yēt*, 2PL *smīxḗtun* < *smīxē=yētun*, 1SG.M *smīxḗna* < *smīxa=yēna*, 1PL *smīxḗx* < *smīxē=yēx*. In the 3SG.F, 2SG.F and 1SG.F the final -*a* of the SG.F participle *smīxta* becomes -*ē* by assimilation to the /y/ of the copula, e.g. *smīxtḗ=ya* < *smīxta=ya*.

Passive

(398) JSNENA

g-r-š 'to pull'

3SG.M	grīšá=y	'he has been pulled'
3SG.F	grīštḗ=ya	'she has been pulled'
3PL	grīšḗn	'they have been pulled', etc.
2SG.M	grīšḗt	
2SG.F	grīštḗ=yat	
2PL	grīšḗtun	
1SG.M	grīšḗna	
1SG.F	grīštḗ=yan	
1PL	grīšḗx	

With transitive active resultative participles this perfect construction is only available where the agent of the transitive action is third person. The participle and the copula cliticised to the participle do not agree with this agent, but rather with the undergoer of the action, analogously to the inflection of the transitive past stem with direct suffixes (§5.10.3). The alignment of both past constructions with a transitive past stem and perfect constructions with a transitive participle is ergative. However, unlike the construction with the transitive past stem, in which the agent is marked by L-suffixes, the agent in the resultative perfect construction is not marked. There is, therefore, no specific marking of the agent as SG.M, SG.F or PL:

(399) JSNENA
    a. *gərša=y*   'he/she/they has/have pulled (him)'
        grəš-lē   'he pulled him'
    b. *grəštē=ya* 'he/she/they has/have pulled her'
        gərš-ā-lē   'he pulled her'
    c. *gəršēn*   'he/she/they has/have pulled them'
        gərš-ī-lē   'he has pulled them'

As is the case with the 3SG.M transitive past stem, the construction with the SG.M resultative participle and 3SG.M copula *gərša=y* may either express specifically a SG.M undergoer that is anaphorically bound to the context or may be used in a neutral sense without denoting any specific undergoer.

The resultative participle is not combined with the past copula *yēlē* to form the past perfect. The past perfect is formed by the more archaic past perfect construction *grəšwālē, smīxwa* (§5.11.1).

The formation of the perfect in JSNENA, and other NENA dialects, by a construction consisting of resultative participle and a copula is an innovation under the influence of Iranian languages. In many NENA dialects there is only partial convergence with the Iranian model (Khan 2020a). In most NENA dialects that form the perfect with a participle, for example, its alignment in transitive clauses is not ergative but accusative, in contrast to the Iranian model in the various regions. In JSNENA the convergence is greater in this respect, since the alignment of transitive perfect constructions is ergative. It does not, however, replicate all details of the Iranian model.

In Kurdish and Gorani of the Sanandaj region the realis perfect is formed by combining the resultative participle with copula clitics. The intransitive forms of perfect in Gorani are shown below. The participle inflects for gender and number (SG.M *wəta*, SG.F *wətē*, PL *wətē*):

(400) Gorani
    wətay 'to sleep'
    3SG.M   *wəta=n*   'he has slept'
    3SG.F   *wətē=na*   'she has slept'
    3PL   *wətē=nē*   'they have slept', etc.
    2SG.M   *wəta=nī*
    2SG.F   *wətē=nī*
    2PL   *wətē=ndē*
    1SG.M   *wəta=nā*
    1SG.F   *wətē=nā*
    1PL   *wətē=nmē*

This, therefore, is the direct model of the intransitive present perfect paradigm in JSNENA, in which the participle inflects for gender and number (SG.M *smīxa*, SG.F *smīxta*, PL *smīxē*).

The present perfect in the Kurdish dialect of Sanandaj consists of the participle plus copula inflectional clitics. The participle has an invariable form ending in *-əg*:

(401) Kurdish
hātən 'to come'
3SG *hātəg=a*   'he/she has come'
3PL *hātəg=ən*   'they have come', etc.
2SG *hātəg=ī*
2PL *hātəg=ən*
1SG *hātəg=əm*
1PL *hātəg=īn*

The perfect transitive of Gorani has ergative alignment whereby both the participle and the copula clitics agree with the direct object. The transitive agentive subject is indexed by oblique clitic person markers:

(402) Gorani
dīay 'to see'

	Object clitic	3PL Subject	
3SG.M	*dīa=n=šā*	'they have seen him'
3SG.F	*dīē=na=šā*	'they have seen her'
3PL	*dīē=nē=šā*	'they have seen them'
2SG.M	*dīa=nī=šā*	'they have seen you'
2SG.F	*dīē=nī=šā*	'they have seen you'
2PL	*dīē=ndē=šā*	'they have seen you'
1SG.M	*dīa-nā=šā*	'they have seen me'
1SG.F	*dīē=nā=šā*	'they have seen me'
1PL	*dīē=nmē=šā*	'they have seen us'

In some realis perfect and perfective past constructions of Gorani the agent can be left unindexed on the verbal complex. This is the case when an agent argument in the clause is in the oblique case. The oblique case is only preserved on nominal arguments and third person pronouns in Gorani, so this construction is only available for third person agents:

(403) Gorani
    a. **tātà-y=m**   kīāst-a=nā|
        father-OBL.M=1SG   send.PST-PTCP.M=1SG
        'My father has sent me (over).'
    b. màn| tāza **pādšà-y** karḍa-nā   wakēḷ|
        1SG   any.way   king-OBL.M   do.PTCP.M=COP.1SG   advocate
        'Me— anyway the king has given me responsibility [lit. he has made me advocate].'

By contrast, in the Kurdish of Sanandaj ergativity in the perfect construction has decayed. As in constructions with the past stem (§5.3), clitic pronouns now mark the direct object as well as the agent, resulting in a sequence of clitics on the verb. The order of these clitics is Object–Subject, which corresponds to the order of the indexing of arguments in the Gorani perfect construction. The copula appears at the end of the verbal complex in the form of the suffix -*a*, which is an invariable fossilised form of the copula stem:

(404) Kurdish
    a. bərd-əg=mān=yān-a
        take.PST-PTCP=1PL=3PL-PERF
        'they have taken us'
    b. nārd-əg=yān=t-a=(a)   kwḕ?
        send.PST-PTCP=3PL=2SG-PERF=DRCT   Where
        'where have you sent them to?'

5.11.2 Irrealis perfect

In JSNENA an irrealis resultative perfect may be formed by combining the irrealis subjunctive form of the verb *h-w-y* 'to be' (§5.8.2), i.e. *hawē*, with the resultative participle. The final vowel of the participle and the initial /h/ of the inflected form of *h-w-y* are elided when the two forms are bonded together. This construction is available for all persons with intransitive/passive compound forms with intransitive/passive resultative participles. The stress remains on the final syllable of the participle:

(405) JSNENA
Intransitive
3SG.M	smīxáwē	'he may have stood up'
	(< smīxá-hawē)	
3SG.F	smīxtáwya	'she may have stood up'
	(< smīxtá-hawya)	
3PL	smīxáwēn	'they may have stood up'
	(< smīxḗ-hawēn, etc.)	
2SG.M	smīxáwēt	
2SG.F	smīxtáwyat	
2PL	smīxáwētun	
1SG.M	smīxáwēna	
1SG.F	smīxtáwyan	
1PL	smīxáwēx	

(406) JSNENA
Passive
3SG.M	grīšáwē	'he may have been pulled'
3SG.F	grīštáwya	'she may have been pulled'
3PL	grīšáwēn	'they may have been pulled', etc.
2SG.M	grīšáwēt	
2SG.F	grīštáwyat	
2PL	grīšáwētun	
1SG.M	grīšáwēna	
1SG.F	grīštáwyan	
1PL	grīšáwēx	

In constructions with transitive active resultative participles the inflected forms of *h-w-y* agree with the object and they are restricted to the 3rd person. Unlike the realis form of the transitive perfect, however, the agent is explicitly marked in the irrealis form with L-suffixes, as it is in inflections of the past stem. As is the case with the past stem inflection, the L-suffixes mark the agent of all persons:

(407) JSNENA
gəršáwēlē	'he may have pulled (him)'
(< gərša-hawē-lē)	
grəštáwyālē	'he may have pulled her'
(< grəšta-hawya-lē)	
gəršáwēnīlē	'he may have been pulled them'
(< gərše-hawēnī-lē)	

gəršáwēla	'she may have pulled (him)'
grəštáwyāla	'she may have pulled her'
gəršáwēnīla	'she may have pulled them'
gəršáwēlū	'they may have pulled (him)'
grəštáwyālū	'they may have pulled her'
gəršáwēnīlū	'they may have pulled them'
gəršáwēlox	'you (SG.M) may have pulled (him)'
grəštáwyālox	'you (SG.M) may have pulled her'
gəršáwēnīlox	'you (SG.M) may have pulled them'
gəršáwēlax	'you (SG.F) may have pulled (him)'
grəštáwyālax	'you (SG.F) may have pulled her'
gəršáwēnīlax	'you (SG.F) may have pulled them'
gəršáwēlaxun	'you (PL) may have pulled (him)'
grəštáwyālaxun	'you (PL) may have pulled her'
gəršáwēnīlaxun	'you (PL) may have pulled them'
gəršáwēlī	'I may have pulled (him)'
grəštáwyālī	'I may have pulled her'
gəršáwēnīlī	'I may have pulled them'
gəršáwēlan	'we may have pulled (him)'
grəštáwyalan	'we may have pulled her'
gəršáwēnīlan	'we may have pulled them'

In Gorani the irrealis perfect is formed from the resultative participle and the subjunctive form of the verb 'to be'. In the intransitive irrealis perfect the verb 'to be' agrees with the subject:

(408) Gorani
Intransitive

3SG.M	*wəta-b-o*	'he may have slept'
3SG.F	*wətē-b-o*	'she may have slept'
3PL	*wətē-b-ā*	'they may have slept'
2SG.M	*wəta-b-ī*	
2SG.F	*wətē-b-ī*	
2PL	*wətē-b-īdē*	
1SG.M	*wəta-b-ū*	
1SG.F	*wətē-b-ū*	
1PL	*wətē-b-īmē*	

In the transitive irrealis perfect, both the participle and the subjunctive verb 'to be' agree with the object. The agent is expressed by oblique clitics:

(409) Gorani
transitive

Object	3PL Subject	
3SG.M	dīa-b-o=šā	'they may have seen him'
3SG.F	dīē-b-o=šā	'they may have seen her'
3PL	dīē-b-ā=šā	'they may have seen them'
2SG.M	dīa-b-ī=šā	'they may have seen you'
2SG.F	dīē=b-ī=šā	
2PL	dīē=b-īdē=šā	
1SG.M	dīa-b-ū=šā	
1SG.F	dīē=b-ū=šā	
1PL	dīē=b-īmē=šā	

The structure of the JSNENA irrealis perfect matches almost completely these Gorani irrealis perfect constructions. The only difference is that in the Gorani transitive construction the object with which the participle and verb 'to be' agrees can be any person, whereas in JSNENA objects are restricted to third person. This is most likely due to analogy with the transitive past stem construction in JSNENA which, for reasons discussed above, now can take only third person objects.

By contrast, in the irrealis perfect construction in Sanandaj Kurdish the irrealis form of the verb 'to be' has the invariable form *bēt-/bət* or *w(ēt)-*. Moreover, the verb is not in its participle form:

(410) Kurdish
Intransitive

3SG	xaft-w-ē	'he may have slept'
3PL	xaft-w-ən	'they may have slept'
2SG	xaft-w-ī	
2PL	xaft-w-ən	
1SG	xaft-w-əm	
1PL	xaft-w-īn	

(411) Kurdish
Transitive

Object	3PL Subject	
3SG	dī-bēt=ī=yān	'they may have seen him'
3PL	dī-bēt=yān=yān	'they may have seen them'

2SG	dī-bēt=ət=yān	'they may have seen you'
2PL	dī-bēt=tān=yān	
1SG	dī-bēt=əm=yān	
1PL	dī-bēt=mān=yān	

It is clear, therefore, that the JSNENA perfect constructions have developed on the model of Gorani rather than Kurdish. Some deviations from the Gorani model, however, may have been triggered by the influence of Kurdish in more recent times. This applies to the loss of expression of first and second person objects in the transitive constructions.

One surprising deviation from the Gorani model in the realis transitive perfect is the lack of indexing of the agent by oblique L-suffixes in JSNENA where the corresponding Gorani construction indexes these by oblique clitics. The explanation appears to be that this has come about in order to avoid semantic ambiguity. If an L-suffix were added the basic 3SG.M form *gərša=y* (participle + present copula) 'he has pulled', it would run the risk of becoming indistinguishable from a construction consisting of the participle + past copula (*yele*). The past copula typically contracts when attached to a word with a final -*a* vowel thus:

(412) JSNENA
 laxa + *yēlē* > *laxḗlē* 'he was here'

A sequence such as *gərša=y-lē* (participle + present copula + L-suffix) is likely to have contracted to *gəršēlē*, which could have been parsed as participle + past copula, i.e. the past perfect. In order to avoid this potential confusion, the L-suffix was dropped. One consequence of this was that a past perfect could not be formed on the model of Gorani and Kurdish, which expresses this by combining the participle with the past copula. So the more archaic past perfect construction *graš̌wālē* (§5.11.1) was retained in JSNENA for the expression of this meaning. In the irrealis perfect of JSNENA there was no risk of ambiguity with the attachment of L-suffixes, so the Gorani model was replicated with L-suffixes corresponding to the Gorani oblique agent clitics.

The JSNENA realis transitive perfect, which lacks any marking of the agent by L-suffixes, is restricted to clauses that have third person agents as subjects. The subject may be a nominal or independent pronominal argument in the clause (413.a) or a referent that is recoverable from the discourse but not explicitly coded (413.b):

(413) JSNENA
  a. *gor-akē grəštē=ya*
     man-the pull.PTCP.SG.F=COP.3SG.F
     'The man has pulled her.'
  b. *grəštē=ya*
     pull.PTCP.SG.F=COP.3SG.F
     'He/she/they has/have pulled her.'

The restriction of the construction to third person subjects could be explained by the fact that third person is, in fact, unmarked for person, or a non-person (Benveniste 1971, 195–204; Koch 1995), and, therefore, in the absence of explicit subject marking the default interpretation of the identity of the subject would be third person. There is, however, a Gorani model that may have facilitated the use of such JSNENA constructions without indexing of the third person subjects by L-suffixes. In Gorani the indexing of a third person subject agent by an oblique clitic on the verb is omitted in a clause with broad focus on the predicate if there is a oblique third person subject argument. In Gorani, nominals and third person independent pronouns inflect for case. A first or second person independent pronoun, however, does not inflect for case, and when these pronouns are the agent subject an agent clitic is obligatory on the verb:

(414) Gorani
  a. *pīyā-(a)kay kēštē=na*
     man-DEF.OBL.M pull.PTCP.F=COP.3SG.F
     'The man has pulled her.'
  b. *ādī kēštē=na*
     3SG.M.OBL pull.PTCP.F=COP.3SG.F
     'He has pulled her.'
  c. *mən kēštē=na=m*
     1SG pull.PTCP.F=COP.3SG.F=1SG
     'I have pulled her.'
  d. *to kēštē=na=t*
     2SG pull.PTCP.F=COP.3SG.F=2SG
     'You (s) have pulled her.'

JSNENA constructions such as (413) with a third person subject argument and no L-suffix may have been modelled on Gorani constructions such as (414.a-b). The profile of the syntactic pattern is the same, though the oblique inflection of the subject agent argument has not be replicated. There is no Gorani syntactic model with first and second person subjects without an agent clitic on the verb.

In JSNENA, transitive realis perfects with first or second person subjects are expressed by verbal forms with the past stem. First or second person past stem verbs, therefore, express either the past perfective or the perfect. When the subject is third person the past stem verb expresses the past perfective and the perfect is expressed by the innovative construction with the participle and copula:

(415) JSNENA

3SG.M	grəš-lē	'he pulled'
	gəršā=y	'he/she/they has/have pulled'
2SG.M	grəš-lox	'you pulled/have pulled'
2SG.M	grəš-lox	'you pulled/have pulled'
2SG.F	grəš-lax	'you pulled/have pulled'
2PL	grəš-laxun	'you pulled/have pulled'
1SG	grəš-lī	'I pulled/have pulled'
1PL	grəš-lan	'we pulled/have pulled'

The perfect meaning of the past stem is an archaism, since this stem originally expressed the perfect, then came to express the past perfective after a new perfect form developed on the basis of Iranian models. The development of the innovative perfect on the model of Gorani was blocked for transitive constructions with first or second person subjects.

In the Christian NENA dialect of Sanandaj and the neighbouring Christian dialect of Sulemaniyya, the perfect is expressed by combining the past perfective form with the prefixed particle *gī-*, e.g.

(416) Ch. Sanandaj

grəš-lē	'he pulled'	gī-grəš-lē	'he has pulled'
qəm-lē	'he rose'	gī-qəm-lē	'he has risen'

The origin of the particle *gi-* is likely to be the stem of the copula *ī* combined with the indicative particle *g-* < **k-*. The construction, therefore, has some resemblance to the pattern of the Sanandaj Kurdish transitive perfect, which contains the invariable stem of the copula *-a* preceded by the *g* morpheme of the participle, e.g.

(417) Kurdish
kešā-g=y-a
pull.PST-PTCP=3SG-PERF
'he has pulled'

5.11.3 Indirective function of the perfect

In JSNENA the perfect construction formed from a participle and copula (intransitive *smīxa=y*, transitive *gərša=y*) and the past perfective construction formed from the past stem and past converter morpheme *wa* (intransitive *smīxwa*, transitive *grašwālē*) can have an 'indirective' function. When this is the case, they do not refer to resultant states or situations but rather to events in the past from which the speaker is cognitively distanced. This is often because the speaker has not directly witnessed the event, but only heard about it by report, i.e. it is evidential (Aikhenvald 2004). In some cases, however, the speaker may have witnessed the event, but it took place in the distant past. We shall refer to this function as 'indirective', a term that is used by Johansson (2000) for corresponding constructions in the Turkic languages.

This indirective use of the perfect and past perfective is found also in Gorani and Kurdish of the Sanandaj region, with which JSNENA has converged.

For further details and examples of the indirective perfect and past perfect, see §5.11.6.

5.11.4 The perfect of the copula

In JSNENA the perfect of the copula is not formed from the verb *h-w-y* 'to be' but rather from the verb *x-Ø-r*, which in other contexts has the ingressive sense of 'to become'. In the perfect it is suppletive to *h-w-y* and can mean 'has been' or 'has become'. The perfect is formed with the pattern of intransitive perfects with a participle and present copula:

(418) JSNENA
  x-Ø-r
  3SG.M *xirá=y*   'he has been/become'
  3SG.F *xirtḗ=ya*   'she has been/become'
  3PL   *xirḗn*   'they have been/become', etc.
  2SG.M *xirḗt*
  2SG.F *xirtḗ=yat*
  2PL   *xirḗtun*
  1SG.M *xirḗna*
  1SG.F *xirtḗ=yan*
  1PL   *xirḗx*

In Gorani and Kurdish of the region the perfect form of the copula is formed by the participle of the verb 'to be' and the present copula. In Gorani the participle agrees in gender and number with the subject, as in JSNENA. As is the case with all inflections of the verb 'to be' in these Iranian languages, the perfect can refer to a state ('has been') or ingressive change of state ('has become')

(419) Gorani
    3SG.M *bīa=n*   'he has been/has become'
    3SG.F *bīē=na* 'she has been/has become'
    3PL   *bīē=nē* 'they have been/has become', etc.
    2SG.M *bīa=nī*
    2SG.F *bīē=nī*
    2PL   *bīē=ndē*
    1SG.M *bīa=nā*
    1SG.F *bīē=nā*
    1PL   *bīē=nme*

(420) Kurdish
    3SG *būg=a*   'he/she has been/has become'
    3PL *būg=ən* 'they have been/has become', etc.
    2SG *būg=ī*
    2PL *būg=ən*
    1SG *būg=əm*
    1PL *būg=īn*

The fact that the verb 'to be' can be used with an ingressive sense ('become') in Gorani and Kurdish may have facilitated the suppletion of the verb *h-w-y* by *x-∅-r* in the JSNENA paradigm. In the past and present stems *h-w-y* and *x-∅-r* shared the stative and ingressive functions of the Iranian verb 'to be/to become', whereas in the perfect the semantic distinction was collapsed and *x-∅-r* expressed both meanings. A factor in this may be that the perfect of the verb is more marked than the present and past TAM. This semantic markedness is likely to be due to the fact that the perfect of these verbs in both JSNENA and Iranian are frequently used with an indirective function of the perfect. Marked semantic categories typically have a narrower range of morphological distinctions than unmarked categories.[10]

---

[10] Jakobson (1971, 130–47), Lyons (1977, 306–9), Croft (2003).

5.11.5 Indirective past perfect

In JSNENA a further type of perfect construction is available known as the indirective past perfect, which is used to express a past perfect denoting a resultant situation in the past from which the speaker is cognitively distanced, typically because he/she has heard about it by report but has not witnessed it directly (§5.11.3). It is formed by replacing the copula of the realis perfect construction by the perfect form of the verb $x\text{-}\emptyset\text{-}r$.

(421) JSNENA
Intransitive
3SG.M	smīxá-xīra=y	'he had stood up (reportedly)'
3SG.F	smīxtá-xīrtē=ya	'she had stood up (reportedly)'
3PL	smīxḗ-xīrēn	'they had stood up (reportedly)'
2SG.M	smīxá-xīrēt	
2SG.F	smīxtá-xīrtē=yat	
2PL	smīxḗ-xīrētun	
1SG.M	smīxá-xīrēna	
1SG.F	smīxtá-xīrtē=yan	
1PL	smīxḗ-xīrēx	

(422) JSNENA
Passive
3SG.M	grīšá-xīra=y	'he had been pulled (reportedly)'
3SG.F	grīštá-xīrtē=ya	'she had been pulled (reportedly)'
3PL	grīšḗ-xīrēn	'they had been pulled (reportedly)'
2SG.M	grīšá-xīrēt	
2SG.F	grīštá-xīrtē=yat	
2PL	grīšḗ-xīrētun	
1SG.M	grīšá-xīrēna	
1SG.F	grīštá-xīrtē=yan	
1PL	grīšḗ-xīrēx	

(423) JSNENA
Transitive
3SG.M	gəršá-xīra=y	'he/she/they have pulled (him) (reportedly)'
3SG.F	grəštá-xīrtē=ya	'he/she/they have pulled her (reportedly)'
3PL	gəršḗ-xīrēn	'he/she/they have pulled them' (reportedly)

There is no construction in Gorani or Kurdish of Sanandaj that corresponds to this construction. An exact match, however, is a construction in literary Persian that has the structure *karde bude-ast* (do.PTCP be.PTCP-COP.3SG) 'he had done' (Lazard 2000). It is possible, therefore, that this feature of literary Persian influenced the speech of speakers of JSNENA who had a Persian literary education. An equivalent construction occurs in the Christian Urmi dialect of NENA, viz. *viyy=ələ ptīxa* 'he had opened' (be.PTCP=COP.3SG.M open.PTCP.SG.M) (Khan 2016, vol. 2, 218–19), which is also likely to be a replication of the literary Persian construction by speakers educated in Persian.

5.11.6 Summary of direct past, direct perfect and indirective verbal functions

PST= past stem
PRS = present stem
IND = indicative particle
PSTC = past converter suffix
PTCP = resultative participle
COP.PRS = present copula
COP.PST = past copula

(424) JSNENA
(*s-m-x* 'to stand', *g-r-š* 'to pull')

		Direct	Indirective
1	PST *smīx/grəšlē*	perfective past	—
2	IND-PRS-PSTC *saməxwa/garəšwa*	imperfective past	—
3	PTCP-COP.PRS *smīxa=y/gərša=y*	present perfect	perfective past imperfective past
4	PST.PSTC *smīxwa/grəšwālē*	past perfect	perfective past
5	PTCP-PTCP.COP-COP.PRS *smīxa-xīra=y/* *gərša-xīra=y*	—	past perfect

(425)   Gorani
        wətay 'to sleep'

		Direct	Indirective
1	PST	perfective past	—
	wət-īmē		
2	PRS-PSTC	imperfective past	—
	ūs-ēn-mē		
3	PTCP-COP.PRS	present perfect	perfective past
	wətē=nmē		imperfective past
4	PTCP-COP.PSTC	past perfect	perfective past
	wətē bēn-mē		

(426)   Kurdish
        xaftən 'to sleep'

		Direct	Indirective
1	PST	perfective past	—
	xaft-īn		
2	IND-PST	imperfective past	—
	a-xaft-īn		
3	PTCP-COP.PRS	present perfect	perfective past
	xaftəg=īn		imperfective past
4	PTCP-COP.PST	past perfect	perfective past
	xaft-ū=yn		

As can be seen, there is a close match in structure and function between JSNENA and the Iranian languages. The closest structural match of JSNENA is with Gorani, which has the past converter particle (row 2). JSNENA, however, differs from Gorani and Kurdish structurally in row 4, since JSNENA forms the past perfect differently for reasons explained above. Furthermore, JSNENA has replicated the indirective past perfect from literary Persian, whereas this is not the case in Gorani and Kurdish.

5.12 Light verb constructions

JSNENA contains numerous light verb constructions, which consist of a finite inflected verb and a non-finite element (generally a nominal). These are calques from parallel constructions in Persian and Kurdish. The non-finite element is generally retained from the source language with the finite verb being exchanged for an equivalent Aramaic verb. In some cases the light verb construction is from Persian, but the non-finite element has Kurdish pronunciation. This suggests that these light verb constructions were borrowed into NENA from Kurdish and/or Gorani, which in turn borrowed them from Persian. In the majority of cases the verbal element is the light verbs *ʾ-w-l* 'to do' or *x-Ø-r* 'to become', e.g.

(427) JSNENA   Iranian

ʾarz ʾ-w-l	'to say (polite)'	P. *ʾarz kardan*
		K. *arz kərdən*
bāwař ʾ-w-l	'to believe'	K. *bāwař kərdən*
daʿwat ʾ-w-l	'to invite'	P. *daʿwat kardan*
ḥāz ʾ-w-l	'to desire'	K. *haz kərdən*
komak ʾ-w-l	'to help'	P. *komak kardan*
qanāʿat ʾ-w-l	'to be content'	P. *qanāʿat kardan*
tamašā ʾ-w-l	'to observe'	K. *tamašā kərdən*
tahdīd ʾ-w-l	'to threaten'	P. *tahdīd kardan*
wēḷ ʾ-w-l	'to stop'	K. *wēḷ kərdən*
zəndəgī ʾ-w-l	'to live'	P. *zendegi kardan*
ʾāxər x-Ø-r	'to come to an end'	P. *āxar šodan*
ḥālī x-Ø-r	'to understand'	P. *hāli šodan*
		K. *ḥāḷī būn*
hazm x-Ø-r	'to be digested'	P. *hazm šodan*
jamʾ x-Ø-r	'to gather (intr.)'	P. *jam šodan*
pēa x-Ø-r	'to be born'	K. *payā būn*
rad x-Ø-r	'to pass by'	P. *rad šodan*
rawāna x-Ø-r	'to set off'	P. *ravāne šodan*
		K. *řawāna būn*
wārəd x-Ø-r	'to enter'	P. *vāred šodan*

In some cases light verb constructions occur with other verbal elements, e.g.

(428) JSNENA   Iranian

hawa ʾ-x-l	'to breathe'	P. *havā xordan*
taṣmīm d-w-q	'to decide'	P. *tasmim gereftan*
ṭūl g-r-š	'to last'	P. *tul kešidan*
ḥasrat l-b-l	'to envy'	K. *hasrat bərdən*
pāḷ l-p-l	'to lie down (lit. to fall aside)'	G. *pāḷ kawtay*

Occasionally the non-finite element of the source language is calqued with an Aramaic equivalent, e.g.

(429) JSNENA   Iranian
  'ila '-w-l   'to begin' (lit. hand do)   G. *dast karđay*
  rēša d-Ø-y   'to visit' (lit. head hit)   K. *sar dān*
  'ēna d-Ø-y   'to wink' (lit. eye hit)   P. *češmak zadan*

Less frequently, a few Iranian verbs have been integrated into the Semitic non-concatenative root system, e.g. JSNENA: *r-m-y* 'to collapse, to be destroyed' < G. *řəmāy*; K. *řəmīn* (see §11.1.16 for a complete list).

5.12.1 Pronominal direct objects on light verb constructions

In JSNENA a pronominal direct object of light verb constructions is expressed in one of the following ways:

(i) Pronominal possessive suffix on the non-finite component:

(430) JSNENA
  daʿwat-u   *k-ol-a*
  invitation-3PL   IND-do.PRS-3SG.F
  'she will invite them'

(ii) If the verb component has a present stem, the object can appear as a L-suffix on the verb:

(431) JSNENA
  daʿwat   *k-ol-ā-lū*
  invitation   IND-do.PRS-3SG.F-OBL.3PL
  'she will invite them'

(iii) The pronominal object may be an oblique independent pronoun before or after the non-finite component:

(432) JSNENA
  a. *doni*   *daʿwat*   *k-ol-a*
     OBL.3PL   invitation   IND-do.PRS-3SG.F
  b. *daʿwat*   *doni*   *k-ol-a*
     invitation   OBL.3PL   IND-do.PRS-3SG.F
     'she will invite them'

(iv) If the verb component has a past stem, the object can appear as a direct suffix on the verb:

(433) JSNENA
da'wat   wīl-ī-la
invitation   do.PST-3PL-OBL.3SG.F
'she invited them'

In Gorani of the Sanandaj region the pronominal object of light verb constructions is expressed in the following ways:

(i) Pronominal oblique clitic on the non-finite component:

(434) Gorani
xuḷka=š   kar-ū
people=3SG.OBL   do.PRS-1SG
'I shall invite him'

(ii) An oblique pronoun before or after the non-finite component:

(435) Gorani
a. *ādīšā   xuḷka   kar-ū*
3PL.OBL   people   do.PRS-1SG
b. *xuḷk=ū   ādīšā   kar-ū*
people=EZ   3PL.OBL   do.PRS-1SG
'I shall invite them'

(iii) When the verb component has a past stem, the object may be expressed by a direct suffix on the verbal stem:

(436) Gorani
ādē=m   xuḷka   karḍ-ē
3PL.DIR=1SG.OBL   people   do.PST-3PL
'I invited them'

The JSNENA object constructions are a replication of the Gorani constructions. The only apparent lack of correspondence is the JSNENA construction with an L-suffix. It is likely, however, that the JSNENA constructions (i) and (ii) are both replications of the Gorani construction (i). This is because the range of functions of the oblique clitics in Gorani include both the JSNENA possessive suffixes attached to nouns and prepositions and the indexing of the agent of verbs.

In Sanandaj Kurdish there is no case distinction in independent pronouns and objects cannot be expressed as direct suffixes on past verb stems. In light verb constructions the pronominal object is expressed as follows:

(i) An oblique clitic on the non-finite component:

(437) Kurdish
xuḷk=yān   a-ka-m
people=3PL.OBL   IND-do.PRS-1SG
'I shall invite them'

(ii) An independent pronoun. This construction is used with both present stem and past stem verbs:

(438) Kurdish
    a. *awān   xuḷk   a-ka-m*
       3PL   people   IND-do.PRS-1SG
       'I shall invite them'
    b. *awān=əm   xuḷk   kərd*
       3PL=1SG.OBL   people   do.PST
       'I invited them'

5.13 Pronominal indirect object

In JSNENA, a pronominal indirect object of a present stem or imperative verb form is expressed by an L-suffix, so long as there is no pronominal direct object in the same verb phrase:

(439) JSNENA
    a. *k-w-í-lan*
       IND-give.PRS-3PL-OBL.1PL
       'they give us'
    b. *húlmu-lan*
       give.IMP.PL-OBL.1PL
       'give (pl) us!'

First person singular verbs derived from the present stem do not take L-suffixes but rather have the series of pronominal suffixes that is attached to nouns and prepositions, as they do when expressing direct pronominal objects (§5.10.1), e.g.

(440) JSNENA
   a. *k-əw-n-ēf*
      IND-give.PRS-1SG-3SG.M
      'I (m) shall give him'
   b. *k-əw-n-af*
      IND-give.PRS-1SG-3SG.F
      'I (m) shall give her'

This use of suffixes matches Gorani, in which indirect pronominal objects of present stem verbs and imperatives are expressed by oblique clitics after the verb. As discussed in §5.10.1, both the oblique L-suffixes and the adnominal suffixes that are added to the 1st person forms match the Gorani oblique clitics:

(441) Gorani
   a. *m-ē-ydē=mā?*
      IND-give.PRS-2PL=1PL
      'will you give us?'
   b. *má-(a)-ydē=mā?*
      NEG-give.PRS-2PL=1PL
      'won't you give us?'

(442) Gorani
   d-a=m   (*pana*)
   give.PRS-2SG.IMP=1SG   to
   'give me!'

In the corresponding constructions in Kurdish, on the other hand, the pronominal indirect object occurs as a clitic on the pre-stem indicative and negative particles. The bound pronominal clitic is governed by the preposition *=ē* which is cliticised to the verb.

(443) Kurdish
   a. *a=mān-da-n=ē?*
      IND=1PL-give.PRS-2PL=to
      'will you give us?'

b. *nā=mān-da-n=ē?*
   NEG.IND=1PL-give.PRS-2PL=to
   'won't you give us?'

In JSNENA, the indirect pronominal object may also be expressed by a prepositional phrase headed by the prepositions *bāq-* or *'əl-*:

(444) JSNENA
k-w-ī   bāq-ēf
k-w-ī   'əl-ēf
IND-give.PRS-3PL   to-3SG.M
'they will give to him'

This is obligatory when a present stem verb has a pronominal direct object expressed by an L-suffix or when the verb has a past stem:

(445) JSNENA
  a. *k-w-ī-lē   bāq-ēf*
     k-w-ī-lē   'əl-ēf
     IND-give.PRS-3PL-OBL.3SG.M   to-3SG.M
     'they will give it to him'
  b. *hiw-lē   bāq-ēf*
     hiw-lē   'əl-ēf
     give.PST-OBL.3SG.M   to-3SG.M
     'he gave (it) to him'

Likewise, in both Gorani and Kurdish, the pronominal object is sometimes expressed by a prepositional phrase, which usually follows the verb. In Gorani the pronominal clitic that is the complement of the preposition is attached to the verbal complex when the verb has a present stem:

(446) Gorani
m-a-ū=šā   pana
IND-give.PRS-1SG=3PL   to
'I give to them'

(447) Kurdish
a-wa-n   pē=m
IND-give.PRS-3PL   to=1SG

'they give to me'

Prepositional phrases are obligatory when a present stem verb has a direct object:

(448) Gorani
    m-ār-ū=š   *pay=t*
    IND-bring.PRS-1SG=3SG to=2SG
    'I will bring it to you'

(449) Kurdish
    tēr-əm=ī   *bo=t*
    IND.bring.PRS-1SG=3SG to=2SG
    'I will bring it to you'

The prepositional phrase is also obligatory when the verb has a past stem. In Gorani the pronominal complement of the preposition is a direct suffix on the verb, or alternatively an oblique clitic on the preposition when the verb expresses the object as a direct suffix:

(450) Gorani
  a. *sāwī=š*   *dā-(ā)nē*   *pana*
      apple=3SG give.PST-1SG to
      'He gave me apples.'
      Gorani
  b. *d(ā)-ē=š*   *pana=m*
      give.PST-3PL=3SG to=1SG
      'He gave them to me.'

(451) Kurdish
    sēf=ī   *dā*   *pē=m*
    apple=1SG give.PST to=1SG
    'He gave me apples.'

The pattern of the JSNENA construction with a prepositional phrase consisting of a preposition and pronominal complement is closer to Kurdish, which also has the pronominal clitic on the preposition and is not incorporated into the verbal complex.

It is significant that in Gorani, although the pronominal complement of the preposition is incorporated into the verbal complex as a direct suffix on a past stem, an indirect object cannot be expressed by a direct suffix alone without a following preposition. In JSNENA, likewise, a pronominal indirect object cannot be expressed by a direct suffix on the past stem. This contrasts with some NENA dialects, in which this is possible when there is no direct object, e.g.

(452) Ch. Barwar
mīr-ā-lī
say.PST-3SG.F-OBL.1SG
'I said to her'

(453) J. Amedia
hīw-ā-lī
give.PST-3SG.F-OBL.1SG
'I gave to her'

The fact that this is not possible in JSNENA may be due to the fact that there is no Gorani model for it.

5.14 Negation of verbs and copulas

In JSNENA all verbal forms are negated by the particle *la*, which precedes the positive form:

(454) JSNENA
    a. Present stem verbs
        la garəš   'he is not pulling'
        la garəšwa 'he was not pulling'
    b. Past stem verbs
        la grəšlē 'he did not pull'
        la smīx   'he did not stand'
        la grīš   'he was not pulled'
    c. Imperatives
        la gruš!   'do not pull (sg.)!'
        la grušmu(n)! 'do not kill (pl.)!'

The negative particle *la* is combined with preverbal particles that are used before verbs derived from the present stem, viz. the indicative particle *k-* and the deontic particle *mar*. The negator precedes the *k-*, which is closely bonded to the verbal base, e.g.

(455) JSNENA
    la k-mər 'he does not say'

It is, however, placed after the deontic particle, e.g.

(456) JSNENA
    mar la garəš 'may he not pull'

This placement of the negator matches the placement of the negator in the Iranian languages.

Gorani

(457) Gorani
    a. Present stem verbs
        ma-kēš-mē 'we are not pulling'
        na-kēš-ēn-mē 'we were not pulling'
    b. Past stem verbs
        na-kēšt=mā 'we did not pull'
        na-mərḏā-ymē-ra 'we did not stand'
        na-kēšīā-ymē 'we were not pulled'
    c. Imperatives
        ma-kēš-a 'do not pull (sg.)!'
        ma-kuš-dē 'do not kill (pl.)!'

In Gorani the negator before the indicative particle *m-* is *nə-*. The negator is *ma-* for stems that do not take an indicative particle.

(458) Gorani
    nə-m-ār-ū 'I do not bring'
    ma-kēš-mē 'we are not pulling'

(459) Kurdish
    a. Present stem verbs
        nā-kēš-īn 'we are not pulling'
        na=mān-a-kēšā 'we were not pulling'
    b. Past stem verbs
        na=mān=kēšā 'we did not pull'
        na-hastā-yn 'we did not stand'
        na-kēšrā-yn 'we were not pulled'

na=mān-kēšā-w	'we had not pulled'
hāl-na-stā-bū-yn	'we had not stood'
na-kešrā-bū-yn	'we had not been pulled'

c. Imperatives

ma-kēš-a	'do not pull (sg.)!'
ma-kēš-ən	'do not pull (pl.)!'

In JSNENA the present and past copula are likewise negated with *la*, as represented in Table 64:

Table 64: The paradigm of negated copulas in JSNENA.

	Negated Present	**Negated past**
3SG.M	la=y	lá=yēlē
3SG.F	lé=ya	lá=yēla
3PL	lēn	lá=yēlū
2SG.M	lēt	lá=yēlox
2SG.F	lé=yat	lá=yēlax
2PL	létun	lá=yēlaxun
1SG.M	léna	lá=yēlī
1SG.F	lé=yan	lá=yēlī
1PL	lēx	lá=yēlan

The paradigms of the negative copulas in Gorani and Kurdish of the Sanandaj region are shown in Table 65 and Table 66.

Table 65: The paradigm of negated copulas in Gorani.

	Present	**Past set 1**	**Past set 2**
3SG.M	nī́ā	ná-bī́-∅	ná-bē
3SG.F	nī́an-a	ná-bīa	ná-bē
3PL	nī́an-ē	ná-bī-ē	ná-b-ēn-ē
2SG	nī́an-ī	ná-bī-ay	ná-b-ēn-ī
2PL	nī́an-dē	ná-bī-ayde	ná-b-ēn-dē
1SG	nī́an=ā	ná-bī-ān(ē)	ná-b-ēn-ē
1PL	nī́an-mē	ná-bī-ayme	ná- b-ēn-mē

In the paradigms of the negative present copula of Gorani and Kurdish, the negator has the form *nī-* whereas it has the form *na-* before the past copula. In the paradigm of the Gorani negated present copula the form *nīan*, consisting of the negator *nī-* plus the truncated form of the existential stem *han* in 3SG.M, is used as the stem for

Table 66: The paradigm of negated copulas in Kurdish.

	Present	Past
3SG	nī-a	ná-bū
3PL	nī-n	ná-bū-n
2SG	nī-y	ná-bū-y
2PL	nī-n	ná-bū-n
1SG	nī-m	ná-bū-m
1PL	nī-n	ná-bū-yn

the inflections of the rest of the paradigm. This pattern may have been replicated in the paradigm of the JSNENA negated present copula. In the JSNENA paradigm the vowel after the initial /l/ is /ē/ even in forms such as lē=ya (3SG.F), lē=yat (2SG.F) and lē=yan (1SG). It is possible that the /ē/ has arisen by raising through assimilation to the following /y/. Another possibility is that the 3SG.M form la=y has been made the stem of the rest of the paradigm, following the pattern of the Gorani paradigm, thus:

(460) JSNENA
    3SG.M   lay
    3SG.F   lay=ya > lē=ya
    3PL   lay-yēn > lēyēn > lēn

JSNENA compound verbal forms consisting of a resultative participle and a cliticised copula or form of the verb h-w-y (§5.11.4) are negated by placing the particle la before the entire unit rather than before the verb 'to be':

(461) JSNENA
    la smīxa=y   'he has not stood up'
    la grīša=y   'he has not been pulled'
    la gərša=y   'he/she/they has/have not pulled (him)'
    la grīštē=ya   'he/she/they has/have not pulled her'
    la smīxáwē   'he may not have stood up'
    la grīšáwē   'he may not have been pulled'
    la gəršawēlē   'he may not have pulled (him)'
    la grəštawyālē   'he may not have pulled her'
    la smīxá-xīra=y   'he had not stood up (reportedly)'
    la grīšá-xīra=y   'he had not been pulled (reportedly)'
    la gəršá-xīra=y   'he/she/they had not pulled (him) (reportedly)'
    la grəštá-xīrtē=ya   'he/she/they had not pulled her (reportedly)'

This pattern of negation is found in the neighbouring Jewish Trans-Zab dialects of western Iran, in Sulemaniyya and Ḥalabja. It differs, however, from the main body of NENA, in which the negation of compound verbal forms containing a copula is expressed by replacing the positive copula with the negative copula, e.g.

(462) Ch. Barwar
　　　zīlē=lē [go.PTCP=COP.3SG.M] 'he has gone'
　　　lēlē zīla [NEG.COP.3SG.M go.PTCP] 'he has not gone'

The negation of compound verbal forms in JSNENA matches the pattern of the equivalent constructions in Gorani and Kurdish, in which the negator precedes the whole verbal form rather than appearing before the copula:

(463) Gorani
　　　na-wta=n　　　　'he has not slept'
　　　na-kēšīā=n　　　'he has not been pulled'
　　　na-kēšta=n=əš　 'he has not pulled (him)'
　　　na-kēštē=na=š　 'he has not pulled her'
　　　na-wta-b-o　　　'he may not have slept'
　　　na-kēšīā-b-o　　'he may not have been pulled'
　　　na-kēšta-b-o=š　'he may not have pulled him'
　　　na-kēštē-b-o=š　'he may not have pulled her'
　　　na-wta-bē　　　　'he had not slept (reportedly)'
　　　na-kēšīā-bē　　 'he had not been pulled (reportedly)'
　　　na-kēšta-bē=š　 'he had not pulled (him) (reportedly)'
　　　na-kēštē-bē=š　 'he had not pulled her (reportedly)'

(464) Kurdish
　　　na-xaftəg-a　　　'he has not slept'
　　　na-kēšrāg-a　　　'he has not been pulled'
　　　na=y-kēšāg-a　　 'he has not pulled (him)'
　　　na=y-kēšāg-a　　 'he has not pulled her'
　　　na-xaft-bē　　　 'he may not have slept'
　　　na-kēšrā-bē　　　'he may not have been pulled'
　　　na=y-kēšā-bē　　 'he may not have pulled (him)'
　　　na=y-kēšā-bē　　 'he may not have pulled her'
　　　na-xaft-(b)ū　　 'he had not slept (reportedly)'
　　　na-kēšrā-(b)ū　　'he had not been pulled (reportedly)'
　　　na=y-kēšā-(b)ū　 'he had not pulled (him) (reportedly)'
　　　na=y-kēšā-(b)ū　 'he had not pulled her (reportedly)'

5.15 Summary

Table 67: Direct borrowing of verbal morphological features into NENA.

Feature attested in JSNENA	Main contact language	Section
Deontic particle *bā,*	G./ K.	§5.7.1
Deontic particle *magar*	G./ K.	§5.7.2
Deontic particle *dā*	G./ K.	§5.7.3

Table 68: Pattern replication of verbal morphological features into JSNENA.

Feature attested in JSNENA	Main Contact language	Section
L-suffixes replicate Iranian clitics in indexing verbal arguments	G./ K.	§5.3, §5.10
Inflectional patterns of the stems of verbs	G./ K.	§5.2
The alignment of passive morphology with intransitive unaccusative	G.	§5.2
The extension of the causative inflection pattern to agentive verbs in Form I	G.	§5.2
Inflectional direct person suffixes of a transitive past stem expressing direct object	G.	§5.10.3
The use of oblique L-suffixes to mark the subject of only agentive past verbs	G./K.	§5.3
In present progressive the indicative prefix attaches both to the infinitive and the present stem	G.	§5.5
The inflection of the past stems of intransitive verbs with direct suffixes	K./ G.	§5.3
Oblique independent pronouns express the pronominal object of a present stem verb	G.	§5.10.1
Pronominal objects of past stem verbs are expressed ergatively by direct suffixes	G.	§5.10.3
The intransitive present perfect paradigm	G.	§5.3
In the perfect transitive both the participle and the copula clitics agree with the direct object	G.	§5.11.1
In irrealis perfect constructions participle and the verb 'to be' agree with a 3rd person object	G.	§5.11.2
Lack of indexation of 3rd person agents in realis transitive perfect	Gorani	§5.11.1
Indirective past perfect	Literary Persian	§5.11.5
Pronominal direct objects realised on light verb constructions	Gorani	§5.12.1
The expression of indirect object as a clitic on the verb	Gorani	§5.13
The form of negative copula	Gorani	§5.8.1

5.15 Summary

Table 69: Pattern matching of verbal morphological features in NENA with contact languages.

Feature attested in JSNENA	Main Contact language	Section
A single morphological vocalic pattern is used to express the agentive/causative	G./ K.	§5.2
Word-initial stress pattern of imperatives	G. / K.	§5.2.1
The use of oblique L-suffixes on both agentive and unaccusative past verbs	Gorani of Iraq	§5.8.2
The inflection of resultative participle for gender and number	Gorani	§5.4
Partial grammaticalisation of the indicative marker	Gorani	§5.5
Lack of marking of the subjunctive with a prefixed particle	Gorani	§5.6
Complete levelling of inflection of the present copula with verbal inflection	Kurdish	§5.8.1
The copula consists of a stem to which inflectional person exponents attach	Gorani	§5.8.1
k-wēwa form of copula	Gorani	§5.8.2
General past imperfective copula =*yēle*	Bājalānī Gorani	§5.8.2
The existential copula is uninflected for gender and number	Kurdish	§5.9
The *lālē* copula construction	Kurdish	§5.9
The past copula in predicative possessive constructions	Gorani	§5.9
Oblique L-suffixes expressing the object are placed after the person suffixes	Gorani	§5.10.1
The pronominal objects of imperatives appear as clitic pronouns at the end of the verb	Gorani	§5.10.2
Indirect object is expressed by a prepositional phrase consisting of a preposition and a bound pronominal complement	Kurdish	§5.13
Negation of compound verbal forms	G./ K.	§5.14

Table 70: Verbal morphological features of JSNENA reinforced due to contact.

Feature attested in JSNENA	Main contact language	Section
Progressive constructions containing an infinitive expressing inner object plus the same root	Gorani	§5.5
The expression of past imperfective by a construction consisting of the present stem and a past converter morpheme	Gorani	§5.5

Table 71: Verbal morphological features of JSNENA lost due to contact.

Feature attested in JSNENA	Contact language	Section
The incipient loss of ergative construction, especially with 1st and 2nd persons	Kurdish	§5.10.3

6 The syntax of nominals and particles

6.1 Introductory overview

The morphologically non-bound indefinite marker *xa* in JSNENA appears with nominals that refer to a specific referent with some degree of discourse saliency. The Iranian languages generally use a bound indefinite suffix for the same purpose. JSNENA avoids using the indefinite marker with generic, non-specific referents, and those referents that have an incidental role in the discourse. Here the convergence with Iranian remains partial since the indefinite suffix in Iranian exhibits a greater tendency to appear with non-specific human referents.

The JSNENA definite suffix *-akē*, a direct borrowing from Gorani, is used in a similar set of contexts as Iranian definite suffixes. These include anaphoric contexts, bridging contexts (associative anaphora), and at discourse boundaries. This reflects the fact that JSNENA has converged with Iranian in its discourse organisation. Unlike Iranian, however, the definite suffix in JSNENA is not used as a diminutive suffix, since it has inherited diminutive suffixes and is resistant to extending *-akē* to have this function. This is a reflection of how languages avoid borrowing bound morphology unless there is a functional need for it (Weinreich 1953, 33).

Independent demonstrative pronouns are used in both JSNENA and Iranian not only to express physical distance, but also to express emotional engagement with referents, in that protagonists in a discourse are usually referred to by proximate deixis pronouns whereas remote deixis pronouns are generally used to express less salient referents. Likewise, in JSNENA as well as in Iranian the demonstratives can be used in a presentative function as a device for discourse management in order to draw attention to a proposition. JSNENA converges with Kurdish in using deictic pronouns and anaphoric pronouns interchangeably. On the other hand, in Gorani there seems to be a clear division of labour between deictic pronouns and anaphoric pronouns.

The presentative particle *wa* in JSNENA is absent in Iranian languages of Sanandaj, yet is used in the Kurdish of the Sulemaniyya region. This is evidence of the earlier settlement of JSNENA-speakers in the Sulemaniyya region.

In JSNENA numerals above one are combined with plural nouns, which is reinforced by the same feature in Gorani. In Kurdish numerals are always combined with singular nouns.

JSNENA exhibits different layers of convergence with contact languages in the structure of the noun phrase. Attributive adjectives are normally placed after the head noun by simple juxtaposition, as in earlier Aramaic, which matches Kurdish syntax. JSNENA uses simple juxtaposition also of head and dependent nouns in genitive constructions. In this case NENA originally had a genitive linking particle between the two components (*d*), but this has been lost. The model again is Kurdish. Many non-attributive modifiers in JSNENA are followed by the *ezafe* suffix, replicating Gorani and Persian.

6.2 The Expression of indefiniteness

In JSNENA, the cardinal numeral 'one' (*xa*) is often used as an indefinite article that is a grammatical signal of the indefinite status of the nominal, i.e. when the speaker assumes that the hearer is not able to identify the referent of the nominal. This contrasts with its use as a cardinal numeral, in which the speaker extracts one item from a set of items.

The particle *xa* is not used as an indefinite marker with all nominals that have indefinite status on the pragmatic level. Certain general tendencies can be discerned in its usage, though there are no categorical rules. The English indefinite article has a far wider distribution among nouns with indefinite status and it is often appropriate to use the indefinite article in an English translation where no *xa* particle appears in the dialect.

The JSNENA particle *xa* may also be combined with the word *dāna*, a Kurdish word literally meaning 'grain', to express indefiniteness, e.g. *xa-dāna tórta* 'a cow' (A:81).

The Kurdish indefinite suffix *-ēk*, and its shortened form *-ē*, are also marginally attested in JSNENA, in predications expressing exclamation, e.g.

(465) JSNENA
'ajab   bron-ȅk=yē.
wonder son-INDF=COP.3SG.M
'He is a wonderful boy.' (A:17)

In the Kurdish of Sanandaj *-ēk* is used as an indefinite suffix on both singular and plural nouns. It may be combined with the word *dāna* 'grain' to yield the heavy indefinite form *dānay(k)*. In Gorani the indefinite marker is *-ēw* (m.); *-ēwa* (f.), which in some cases reduce to *-ē*.

The cardinal numeral *yak* 'one' is only marginally used in Kurdish with the function of an indefinite article. When it is used in this function, it typically occurs before the human classifier word *nafar*, e.g. *yak-nafar řīš-čarmū* 'an old man (lit. white beard)'.

In what follows we illustrate to what extent the JSNENA and Iranian systems converge with regard to the distribution of the marking of indefiniteness.

6.2.1 Indefinite specific referent with discourse salience

In general, the JSNENA marker *xa* tends to occur with an indefinite specific countable nominal with a referent that is individuated and salient in some way, whereas it tends to be omitted when these features are absent. In narrative and other contexts the specific referents of such indefinite nominals introduced by *xa* often play an important role in the following context, which is reflected by the fact that they are referred to in subsequent clauses. This, therefore, is a factor that further enhances the salience of the referent. Examples:

(466) JSNENA
xa-gorà hīt-wa.│ 'ēa g-ēzəl-wa ga-pliyāw jangàḷ.│
one-man EXIST-PSTC he IND-go.PRS.3SG.M-PSTC in-middle woods
'īlānə̀ gardəq-wa=ū│ k-mè-wā-lū│
trees gather.PRS.3SG.M-PSTC=and IND-bring.PRS.3SG.M-PSTC-OBL.3PL
ga-'aḥra zabə̀n-wā-lū.│
in-town sell.PRS-PSTC.3SG.M-OBL.3PL
'There was **a man**. He used to go to the woods. He used to gather (branches from) trees, bring them back and sell them in the town.' (A:98)

(467) JSNENA
xà šwāwa hīt-wā-lē│ ràba
one neighbour EXIST-PSTC-OBL.3SG.M very
dawlaman=yē-lē.│ tājə̀r=yē-lē.│
rich=COP.PST-3MS.OBL.3SG.M merchant=COP.PST-OBL.3SG.M
'He had **a neighbour**, who was very rich. He was a merchant.' (A:100)

This would correspond to the following examples from Iranian, in which a noun that is introduced into the discourse with the indefinite suffix (*žən-ēk* in (468.a), *dēw-ēk* in (468.b), and *pādš(ā)-ēw* in (469) is referred to in the subsequent clauses.

(468) Kurdish
 a. **žən-ēk** ha=s hā la Kərmāšān-ā
 woman-INDF EXIST=COP.3SG EXIST.3SG in PN-POST
 Tằy=ī nāw=a.│ rož-ē dừ hazār nafar
 PN=3SG name=COP.3SG day-INDF two thousand person
 nānxwar=ī ha=s.│
 bread.eater=3SG EXIST=COP.3SG
 'There is **a woman**. She is in Kermanshah. Her name is Tāy. She feeds two thousand people each day.'

b. sē   dāna   kanìšk a-wē-t   **dẽw-ēk**
   three CLF   girl   IND-be.PRS-3SG   demon-INDF
   a-řö-t   a=yān-dəz-è.| a=yān-wā
   IND.go.PRS-3SG   IND=3PL-steal.PRS-3SG IND=3PL-take.PRS.3SG
   bū   lā=y   xwà=y|
   go   at.the.home=EZ   REFL=3SG
   'Once there were three girls. **A demon** went, stole them, and took them to his home.'

(469) Gorani Luhon
pādš(ā)-ēw bē   ojāxa=š   kora   bē
king-INDF   COP.PST.3SG hearth=3SG   blind.F   COP.PST.3SG
dawḷat-ēw=ī   fəra=š   bē
wealth-INDF=EZ much=3SG   COP.PST.3SG
'There was **a king**; he was childless (his hearth was blind) but he had much wealth.'
(MacKenzie 1966, 66)

6.2.2 Temporal adverbial referring to specific time

In JSNENA an indefinite nominal referring to a period that functions as an adverbial setting the frame of the following discourse is typically combined with the particle *xa* when the reference is to one specific time.

(470) JSNENA
   a. **xa-yoma** zīl   lāg-èf=ū| mìr-ē
      one-day   go.PST.3SG.M   side-his=and   say.PST-OBL.3SG.M
      bāq-ēf| mīr-ē   flànakas| 'āt   ba-day
      to-3SG.M   say.PST-3SG.M so-and-so you.S   in-DEM.OBL
      zəndəgī   ba-kār   māyay-òx   k-xəl?|
      life   in-work   what-you.SG.M   IND-eat.PRS.3SG.M
      '**One day** he went to him (the neighbour). He said to him, he said, "So-and-so, what use is this life to you?"' (A:103)
   b. **xà yoma**| 'ay-baxt-ī   'ata
      one day   this-wife-1SG   now
      ya-xaēt-à| xīy-ằ-lī.|
      REL-see.PRS.2SG.M-OBL.3SG.F   see.PST-3SG.F-OBL.1SG
      '**One day** I saw this wife of mine whom you see (now).' (A:8)

In the corresponding constructions from Kurdish an adverbial is accompanied by the indefinite *-ē* (shortened form of *-ēk*).

(471) Kurdish
žə̀n-ēk=ū   pīyàw-ēk   a-w-ən| mənāḷ=yān
woman-INDF=and man-INDF   IND-COP.PRS-3PL   child=3PL
nà-wē.| bo   xwa=y| **řož-ē**   šū-aka=y
NEG-COP.3SG for   REFL=3SG day-INDF   husband-DEF=3SG
a-yž-ȅ,   mən   a-č-əm   bo   dàšt.|
IND-say.PRS-3SG   1SG   IND-go.PRS-1SG   to   field
'Once there was a couple (lit. woman and man) who did not have a child. Simply put,[1] **one day** her husband said, "I'm going outside."'

6.2.3 Indefinite specific referent without discourse salience

In JSNENA the particle *xa* tends to be omitted before a nominal with a specific referent when this referent plays an incidental role in the text and is not the centre of concern of the speaker. In (9), for example, the 'horse' does not have a central role in the following foreground narrative, but is only a component of the preliminary background.

(472) JSNENA
   a. 'āna   xa-yoma   rēša   **sūsì**=yē-lī.|
       I   one-day   on   horse=COP.PST-OBL.1SG
       'One day I was on a **horse**.'
   b. 'axon-ī   **dawaxānè**-hīt-wā-lē.|
       brother-1SG   pharmacy-EXIST-PSTC-OBL.3SG.M
       'My brother had a **pharmacy**.'
   c. **qaṣāb**   hīt-wā-lan   b-šəma   'Azīz-Xàn.|
       butcher   EXIST-PSTC-OBL.1PL   by-name   PN
       hulàa=yē-le.|
       Jew=COP.PST-OBL.3SG.M
       'We had a **butcher** by the name of Aziz Khan. He was a Jew.' (A:74)

---

[1] It is common in the Kurdish dialects of the region to express the discourse marker 'just, simply' by the addition of the prepositon *bo* 'for' (or its equivalents) to the reflexive form *xway* 'himself' (cf. Bailey 2018, 389 for equivalent in the Gorani dialect of Gawrajo).

The same phenomenon is found in Iranian. In the following examples the words that have an incidental role in the narrative are not introduced by the indefinite suffix.

(473) Kurdish
    a. ēma hāt-īn **madrasà** dərus ka-yn|
       1PL come.PST-1PL school right do.PRS-1PL
       'We came (went) to build a **school**.'
    b. aw fasḷ-a aw=īč **tằwa** at-ēr-ēt=ū
       DEM.SG.DIST time-DEM 3SG=ADD pan IND-bring.PRS-3SG=and
       hı̀lka=y tē a-škən-ē|
       egg=3SG in IND-break.PRS-3SG
       'Then, she brought **a pan** and broke the eggs into it.'

(474) Gorani
    haywān bar-ò| yawà kar-o kīsa=š|
    animal take.PRS-3SG barley do.PRS-3SG sack=3SG
    'He took **an animal** (a horse) and put barley in its saddlebag.'

6.2.4 Non-specific indefinite

In JSNENA there is a tendency to omit the particle when the nominal does not refer to a specific referent but rather to an unspecified representative of the class designated by the nominal, e.g.

(475) JSNENA
    a. **čarčī** ʾò=yē-lē| ya-'aspāḷ matū-wa
       peddler he=COP.PST-OBL.3SG.M REL-goods put.PRS.3SG.M-PSTC
       rēša xmārà|
       on Donkey
       '**A peddler** was somebody who put goods on a donkey.' (A:70)
    b. **jām** k-mē-n-wa ba-qam kalda=ū xətnà.|
       mirror IND-bring.PRS-3PL-PSTC to-before bride=and groom
       'They brought **a mirror** to the bride and groom.' (A:45)
    c. **pəštī** hīt-wā-lan| daē-x-wā-lū
       support EXIST-PSTC-OBL.1PL put.PRS-1PL-PSTC-OBL.3PL
       ba-gūzà.|
       on-wall
       'We had **a back-support**, which we put on the wall.' (A:56)

This matches Iranian, in which nouns with unspecified referents often do not have an indefinite marker:

(476) Kurdish
    a. *haft   bərå̀   a-w-ən*| **xwašk**=*yān   nå̀-wē.*|
        seven brother IND-COP.PRS-3PL sister=3PL NEG-COP.PRS.3SG
        'There were seven brothers, who did not have **a sister**.'
    b. *wət=ī-a   pīyāw **gawj** bə-xwå̀,*| *aw*
        say.PST=3SG-PERF man fool SBJV-eat.PRS.3SG DEM.SG.DIST
        fasḷ-a   ītər   bərsī=yī   nå̀-wē|
        time-DEM no.more hungry=3SG NEG-COP.PRS.3SG
        'He said, "If one eats **a fool**, then, he will not be hungry anymore."'
    c. **asb** *la   sang kày   dros a-w-ē!*|
        horse from stone how right IND-COP.PRS-3SG
        '**A horse** cannot be made of stone!'

(477) Gorani
    maḷā *bar-mè̀*| *žanī   māra   biř-mè̀*|
    mullah take.PRS-1PL woman marriage cut.PRS-1PL
    'We take **a mullah** and marry the woman.'

In certain circumstances, however, nominals with unspecified referents are combined with the indefinite particle in JSNENA. This is found in the following contexts where the referent has some kind of individuation or prominence. The particle often occurs before a nominal with an unspecified referent but one whose description is specified by an adjective.

(478) JSNENA
    a. *mən-taxta   trə̀ṣ-wā-lū,   **xa-taxta   ruwà**.*|
        from-board make.PST-PSTC-OBL.3PL one-board big
        'They made it out of a board, **a large board**.' (A:9)
    b. *lēle   rēš-šāta   **xa-səfra**   šawē-n-wa   **ruwà**,*|
        night head.of=year one-cloth spread.PRS-3PL-PSTC big
        mən-dày-lag   rēš-ay-bēla| *ta-rēš-o-bēla.*|
        from-this.OBL-side on-this-house to-on-that-house
        'On New Year's Eve, we spread out **a large cloth**, from this side, on this (side of) the house, to that (side of) the house.' (A:65)

Likewise, in JSNENA the particle occurs in contexts where the nominal is specified by an adjacent relative clause, e.g.

(479) JSNENA
'ay-bšəlmānè̀| kē-xalwa zabn-ī ta-dīdàn|
DEM-Muslims REL-milk sell.PRS-3PL to-OBL.1PL
'ay-xalwà| mən-dó tortà| yā mən-dó 'ərba
this-milk from-DEM.OBL cow or from-DEM.OBL sheep
dəwqà=y| ga-**xa-patīlà** dəwqa=y|
hold.PTCP.SG.M=COP.3SG.M in-one-container hold.PTCP.3SG.M=COP.3SG.M
kē patīḷ-akē mumkən=yē pəsra
REL container-ART possible=COP.3SG.M meat
bəšla-hawē-lū gà-ēf.|
cook.PTCP.3SG.M-COP.SBJV.3SG.M-OBL.3pl in-3SG.M

'Those Muslims, who sell milk to us, have taken the milk from the cow or from the sheep and have kept it **in a container** in which they may have cooked meat.' (A:64)

In Iranian the distribution of the indefinite suffix -*ēk* on nominals with an unspecified referent appears to be wider than in JSNENA, since it is used with nouns without modifiers as well as those with modifiers.

The indefinite article appears with a bare nominal in (480), (481.a), a compound nominal in (481.b), a nominal modified by an adjective in (481.c) and a nominal modified by a relative clause in (482):

(480) Gorani
hasar-ēwa muqābəḷ=ū māšīn-ēwa īsa-y bē|
mule-INDF.F equivalent=EZ car-INDF.F now-OBL COP.PST.3SG
'In the past, **a mule** was equivalent to a car nowadays.'

(481) Kurdish
a. wawī=yān a-hāwərd| māšīn nà-w| ba
bride=3PL IPFV-bring.PST car NEG-be.PST.3SG with
àsp-ēk a=yān-bərd|
horse-INDF IPFV=3PL-take.PST
'They would bring the bride. There were no cars. They would bring her on **a horse**.'

b. řīš-čarmù̀-**ēk**=ū pūp-čarmù̀-**ēk**=yān
beard-white-INDF=and hair.of.women-white-INDF=3PL
a-hanārd bū xwāzgīnī|
IPFV-send.PST for asking.hand
'They would send **an old man** (lit. a white beard) and **an old woman** (lit. a white hair) to ask for the hand (of a girl).'

c. **dasmāḷ-ē**   **sṳ̀r**=yān a-bast=a   məl=ī-awa|
    kerchief-INDF red=3PL   IPFV-tie.PST=DRCT   neck=3SG-POST
    'They would tie **a red kerchief** to the bride's neck.'

In the following parallel construction the nominal is specified by a relative clause.

(482) Kurdish
    mən   **àsp-ēk**=əm   garak=a   la   sang   dərus=ī
    1SG   horse-INDF=1SG   necessary=COP.3SG   from   rock   right
    ka-y| b=ī-r-īt=ya   sarā=y   həkūmàt|
    do.PRS-2SG SBJV=3SG-bring.PRS-2SG=DRCT home=EZ government
    'I want **a horse** which you must make of rock and bring it to the government building.'

Example (483) contains the Kurdish indefinite particle on a plural noun with an unspecified referent. There is no corresponding feature in JSNENA, which uses the indefinite marking *xa* only on singular nouns:

(483) Kurdish of the Sanandaj region
    aw   waxt-a   **bənz-gal-ē** **řàš**   bū| tāzà
    DEM.DIST time-DEM   PN-PL-INDF   black   COP.PST.3SG   just
    hāt-ū|
    come.PST-be.PST.3SG
    'Back then there were **black Benzes** (brand of bus). They had just arrived.'

6.2.5 Heavy coding for discourse structuring

In (484) from the JSNENA corpus the use of the indefinite particle *xa* with the second mention of the nominal *tʷka* 'place' but not the first is a strategy to add end-weighting to the closure of the passage. The coding of the second mention of the nominal is made even heavier by expressing the attribute as a relative clause rather than an adjective. The nominal does not have a specific referent:

(484) JSNENA
    k-əmrī-wā-lē   qawurmà.| natè̱-n-wā-lē|
    IND-say.PRS-3PL-PSTC-OBL.3SG.M meat.fat   take.PRS-3PL-PSTC-OBL.3SG.M
    ga-tʷka   qarīra   mat-ì-wā-lē.| yaxčāl
    in-place cool   place.PRS-3PL-PSTC-OBL.3SG.M fridge

> lìt-wā-lan xor-o-waxtara.⏐ mat-ī-wā-lē
> NEG.EXIST-PSTC-OBL.1PL still-DEM-time place.PRS-3PL-PSTC-OBL.3SG.M
> ga-**xa-t^wka** qarīrà hawē⏐ pēš ta-sətwà.⏐
> in-one-place cold be.PRS.3SG.M remain.PRS.3SG.M. for-winter
> 'They called this *qawurma*. They took it and placed it in a cool place. We still did not have a fridge at that time. They put it **in a place** that was cool for it to remain until winter.' (A:83)

In the corresponding Kurdish construction (485), the indefinite suffix is used with the second mention of the nominal *dawāy bēhošī* 'anaesthetic drug', although it does not have a specific referent:

(485) Kurdish of the Sanandaj region
> jā aw waxt-a šəmšḕr=ū həmāyēḻ
> well DEM.SG.DIST time-DEM1 sword=and sword.belt
> xwa=m=əm bərd=ū⏐ **dawà̄=y bēhošī=m** bərd.⏐
> REFL=1SG=1SG take.PST=and drug=EZ anaesthesia=1SG take.PST
> **dawā=y bēhošī-yē** hamīša lā=m-awa=w⏐
> drug=EZ anaesthesia-INDF always with=1SG-POST=COP.PST.3SG
> 'Then I took my sword and sword belt and **an anaesthetic drug**. I had always **an anaesthetic drug** with me.'

6.2.6 Cardinal numeral

In JSNENA *xa* is regularly used when functioning as a cardinal numeral (486.a-b) and when combined with units of measure as in (486.c, 487):

(486) JSNENA
a. ga-'Irằn⏐ ya-ga-taṃāṃ=ē mamlakatē kē-xārəj
in-Iran or-in-all=EZ countries which-outside
m-Isrāyēl=yēn⏐ lēlē patīrē trè̄ lēlē=ya.⏐
from-Israel=COP.PRS.3PL night Passover two nights=COP.3SG.F
b-Isrāyēl **xà lēlē=ya.**⏐
in-Israel one night=COP.3SG.F
'In Iran, or in all the countries that are outside of Israel, the night of Passover is two nights, but in Israel it is **one night**.' (A:62)

b. *har-kas*   *g-ēzəl-wa*   *ba-'anāzē nòš-ēf,*|
   every-person   IND-go.PRS.3.SG.M   in-amount-self-3SG.M
   ***xa-nafàr**=yē,*| *trḕ*   *nafar=ēn,*| *təlḥà*   *nafar=ēn,*|
   one-person=COP.3SG.M   two   person=COP.3PL   three   person=COP.3PL
   'arbà-nafar=ēn   *g-o-bēlà*| *ba-'anāzē*   *nóšū*
   four-person=COP.3PL   in-DEM-house   in-amount   self-3PL
   pəsra   *šaql-ī̀-wa.*|
   meat   buy.PRS-3PL-PSTC
   'Everybody went and according to his own requirements, whether he was **one person**, or there were two people, or there were three people, or there were four people in the house, they would buy meat according to their requirements.' (A:74)

c. ***xa***   ***kīlo***   *xēta*   *ho-lī̀,*| *mastà*   *ho-lī̀.*|
   one   kilo   other   give.IMP.SG-OBL.1SG   yoghurt   give.IMP.SG-obl.1sg
   'Give me **one kilo** of such-and-such a thing, give me yoghurt.' (A:79)

(487) JSNENA
xalēt-ēf   ***xa-dasa***   *ləbàs=yē-lē.*|
gift-3SG.M   one-set   clothes=COP.PST-OBL.3SG.M
'His gift was **a set** of clothes.' (A:51)

In Kurdish the indefinite suffix is used with units of measure (488.a)-(488.b):

(488) Kurdish
a. ***kīlò-ē***   *qan=əm*   *b-a-r=ḕ*|
   kilo-INDF   sugar.cube=1SG   SBJV-give.PRS-2SG.IMP=to
   'Give me **one kilo** of sugar cubes.'
   bə-r̀ò   *həkāyat*   *tujār*   *'Ahmàw=əm*   *bo*
   SBJV-go.IMP.2SG   tale   merchant   PN=1SG   for
   bēr-a| *bə-zān-əm*   *awa*   *tujār*
   SBJV.bring-IMP.2SG   SBJV-know.PRS-1SG   DEM.DIST   merchant
   'Ahmàw| *boča*   *gə̀*   *ēwāra-yk*| ***xarwàr-ē***   ***bərənj***
   PN   why   each   evening-INDF   ass.load-INDF   rice
   a-kāt=a   *nāw*   *māšīn-aka=y=ū*| *a=y-wà*
   IND-do.PRS.3SG=DRCT   in   car-DEF=3SG=and   IND-3SG-take.PRS.3SG
   a=y-kāt=a| *nāw*   *bahr=ū*   *t-èt=aw!*|
   IND-3SG-do.PRS.3SG=DRCT   in   sea=and   IND-come.PRS.3SG=TELIC
   'Go and bring the tale of Merchant Ahmad to me, so that I may know why each evening he puts as much as an **ass-load of rice** into his car and pours it into the sea.'

6.2.7 Kurdish yak as indefinite marker

Unlike *-ēk*, the use of *yak* as an indefinite marker is restricted in Kurdish and found only sporadically. The particle *yak* is combined typically with classifiers such as *nafar* 'person' for signalling human referents that have discourse saliency.

(489) Kurdish
    a. **yak-nafàr** řīš-čarmū ha=s l-am šār-aˈ
         one-CLF beard-white EXIST=COP.3SG in-DEM.PROX city-DEM
         kanīšk kāwrā a-xwāz-è̄ dā sāḷ-ēkˈ
         daughter fellow IND-marry-3SG until year-INDF
         'There **is an old man** (lit. white beard) in this city, who marries fellows' daughters for the duration of one year.'
    b. la qarāx šār-aw **yàk nafar** a-ga-yē pēˈ
         in margin city-POST one CLF IND-arrive.PRS-3SG to=3SG
         'In the city suburb he came across **a person**.'

6.2.8 Summary

It can be seen from the examples from Iranian adduced above that the indefinite marker that corresponds to the JSNENA indefinite marking *xa* is in the vast majority of cases the Kurdish indefinite suffix *-ē(k)* and the Gorani indefinite suffix *-ēw*. Structurally JSNENA *xa* corresponds to the Kurdish independent cardinal numeral *yak* rather than the suffix *-ē(k)*. In Kurdish, however, *yak* is only marginally used as an indefinite marker. One may say that the inherited JSNENA cardinal numeral *xa* is matched with both Kurdish *yak* and *-ē(k)*. It does not become a bound suffix like *-ē(k)*. This indicates that the extension of the function of an inherited non-bound construction is preferred over the replication of the pattern of a bound element in Iranian.

6.2.9 Pronominal use of xa

In JSNENA the particle *xa* may be used independently with the function of an indefinite pronoun with specific reference, e.g.

(490) JSNENA

    xa   *'lī-lē-ò*| *xa*   *la*   *'lī-lē-ò*|
    one   know.PST-OBL.3SG.M-TELIC   one   NEG   know.PST-OBL.3SG.M-TELIC
    'One recognised him and another did not recognise him.' (D:14)

In Iranian too, the numeral 'one' can be used pronominally. As in JSNENA, Gorani uses the bare form of numeral 'one', while in Kurdish the numeral 'one' has the indefinite suffix *-ē*. This suggest that JSNENA structurally converges with Gorani rather than Kurdish.

(491) Gorani

  a. *yūa=m*   *màra*   *bəřyē=na*   *sar=ū*   *yaraṣa*   *təmana*|
     one.F=1SG   marriage   cut.PTCP.F=3SG.F   on=EZ   300   Toman
     'I married one (a woman) for 300 tomans of wedding proportion.'

  b. *yo*   *pānṣàt*   *təmanī=šā*   *dā-ym=ē*|
     one.M   five.hundred   toman=3PL   give.PST-1PL=to
     'They gave us each 500 hundred tomans.'

(492) Kurdish

  a. *sēmìn*| *wət=ī*   *roḷà*| *sē*   *dàna*   *dawrīš*   *tē-n*|
     thirdly   say.PST=3SG   dear   three   CLF   dervish   IND.come.PRS-3PL
     yàk-ē   *dāna=y*   *l-aw*
     one-INDF   CLF=EZ   from-DEM.DIST
     kanīš-al=yān-a   *ba-n*   *pē*   *bā*   *b=ī-wà-n*|
     girl-PL=3PL-DEM1   SBJV.give.PRS-2PL   to   HORT   SBJV=3SG-take.PRS-3PL
     'Thirdly, he said, "Dear sons! Three dervishes will come here. Give **each one** of them one of the daughters in marriage, so that they take them."'

  b. *yak-ē*   *kùř-ēk=tān*   *a-w-ē*|
     one-INDF   son-INDF=2PL   IND-COP.PRS-3SG
     'Each one of you will have a son.'

6.2.10 JSNENA xa dana

In JSNENA, the phrase *xa-dana* expresses individuation with heavier morphological coding than the particle *xa* alone. It tends to be used to express a greater degree of distinctness of the referent of the nominal. One context in which it is typically used is where the nominal marked by the phrase has a referent that has particular discourse prominence, in that it plays an important role in what follows:

(493) JSNENA
    a. *har xānawādē ta-nòš-ēf,*[|] *har* ^H*məšpaḥa*^H
        each family   for-self-3SG.M each family
        ta-nòš-ēf,[|]   *g-ēzəl-wa*[|]   **xa-dāna tórta**
        for-self-3SG.M IND-go.PRS.3SG.M-PSTC one-CLF cow
        šaqəl-wā-la.[|]   *k-mē-wā-l-ó*
        take.PRS.3SG.M-PSTC-OBL.3SG.F IND-bring.PRS.3SG.M-PSTC-3SG.F-TELIC
        ga-bēla *nòš-ēf.*[|] *rāb-an* *k-ē-wa*
        in-house self-3SG.M rabbi-1PL IND-come.PRS.3SG.M-PSTC
        dabəḥ-wā-l-ó   *bāq-èf.*[|]
        slaughter.PRS.3SG.M-PSTC-3SG.F-TELIC for-3SG.F
        'Each family, each family went in their turn and bought **a cow**. They would bring it back to their home. Our rabbi would come and slaughter if for them.' (A:81–82)
    b. **xa-dāna lačaga rabta** *ba-rēš-àf=yē-la.*[|]
        one-CLF veil big on-head-3SG.F=COP.PST-OBL.3SG.F
        rēš-af *ksè-wā-la=ū*[|]   *yāwāš mən-rēš-af*
        head-3SG.F cover.PST-PSTC-OBL.3SG.F=and slowly from-head-3SG.F
        gərš-à-lī[|]   *šolt-ā-lī*   *do-làg.*[|]
        pull.PST-3SG.F-OBL.1SG throw.PST-3SG.F-OBL.1SG OBL.DEM-side
        '**A large veil** was on her head. She had covered her head. I slowly pulled it from her head and threw it to one side.' (A:24)

The model of the JSNENA construction *xa-dana* is the Kurdish the phrase *dāna-yk*, *dāna-y*, which, likewise, marks a heavier coding of indefiniteness. The use of *dāna-yk*, *dāna-y* gives prominence to a particular referent that has some role in the ensuing discourse.

(494) Kurdish
    a. *a-řö*[|]   *kàm a-řö*[|]   *fərà a-řö,*[|]
        IND-go.PRS.3SG little IND-go.PRS.3SG long IND-go.PRS.3SG
        a-ga-yt=a   **dāna-y jəftyàr**[|],
        IND-arrive.PRS-3SG=DRCT CLF-INDF farmer
        xarīk=a *jəft* *a-kà.*[|]   *a-yž-è,*[|]
        busy=COP.3SG ploughing IND-do.PRS.3SG IND-say.PRS.3SG
        bo könà a-ř-ī   *bərā?*[|]
        to where IND-go.PRS-2SG brother
        'He went; he went a little (way), he went a lot (a long way). He arrived at **a farmer**, who was busy farming. (The farmer) said, "Fellow! where are you heading?"'

b. čū-m=a   nāw šằr| təmāšằ=m   kərd   čə   dukān|
    go.PST-1SG=DRCT into city watching=1SG do.PST INTJ store
    dāna-y   dằrfərūš   har   bāz=a=w| dārfərūš
    CLF-INDF   timber.seller EMPH   open=COP.3SG=and timber.seller
    har   xarīk=a   māmḷà   a-kā=w| mən=īš   la
    EMPH   busy=COP.3SG bargain   IND-do.PRS.3SG=and 1SG=ADD in
    barāwar   dukān-aka-y-aw   dā-nīšt-ə̀m.| āqībat   kāwrā
    opposite.side   store-DEF=3SG-POST   PVB-sit.PST-1SG finally fellow
    hằt| wət=ī   bərā   čà=y?| čə   kārà=y?|
    come.PST.3SG   say.PST=3SG   brother what=2SG what skilled=COP.2SG
    'I went into the city and saw that the shop (of) **a timber-seller** was still open. The timber-seller was bargaining. I sat down in front of his store. Eventually, the man (timber-seller) came to me and said, "Brother, who are you? What is your job?"'

In JNENA the phrase *xa-dāna* may be used independently of a noun with the function of an indefinite pronoun, e.g.

(495) JSNENA
    a. mangól laxa   là=yē-lē| hēz-ī   **xa-dāna**
        like   here   NEG-COP.PST-OBL.3SG.M go.PRS-3PL one-CLF
        šaql-ī̀.|
        take.PRS-3PL
        'It was not the case that they went to buy **one**, as (they do) here.'
    b. ga-doka   har-knīšta   **xà-dāna** hīt-wā-la.|
        in-there   every-synagogue   one-CLF   EXIST-PSTC-3SG.F
        'There every synagogue had **one**.' (B:80)

Likewise, in Kurdish the phrase *dāna-y*, *dāna-yk* can be used pronominally in the sense of an indefinite pronoun.

(496) Kurdish of the Sanandaj region
    dằna-yk has   wa nāw   Sü-Čāwkāḷ|
    CLF-INDF   exist.3SG   by name PN-light.brown.eye
    sằhər=a=w| fərazằn=a=w,| řafēq=ī   nà-ka-n.|
    magician=COP.3SG=and sly=COP.3SG=and friend=3SG NEG-do.PRS-2PL
    'There is **one (person)** who is called Sü Čāwkāḷ. He is a magician, a sly person. Don't make friends with him.'

6.2.11 Borrowing by JSNENA of Kurdish indefinite suffix -ēk

JSNENA has borrowed the Kurdish indefinite suffix -ēk on nominals that are modified by evaluative adjectives (497.a-b). The predicate in this context expresses an exclamation.

(497) JSNENA
    a. bróna rāba 'ayz-èk=yē-lē.|
        boy very fine-INDF=COP.PST-OBL.3SG.M
        'He was a very fine lad.' (A:14)
    b. 'ajab bron-èk=yē.|
        wonder boy-INDF=COP.3SG.M
        'He is a wonderful boy.' (A:17)

The following examples show the parallel construction in Kurdish.

(498) Kurdish
    a. xānm=īš āzā swār asb-ēk bā̀š a-wē|
        woman=ADD quickly rider horse-INDF fine IND-be.PRS.3SG
        'The lady quickly mounted on a fine horse.'
    b. nā-zān-ī čə̀ kuř-ēk=ū|
        NEG-know.PRS-2SG what rider-IND=COP.PST.3SG
        'You don't realize what a boy he was.'

(499) Gorani
    yāg(a)-ēwa fəra wašà bīyē=na|
    place-INDF.F much pleasant.F be.PST.PTCP.F=COP.PRS.3SG
    'It was a very nice place.'

In JSNENA there are sporadic occurrences of an indefinite suffix with the form –ē, which is a shortened form of the Kurdish suffix –ēk. Compare Kurdish example (501), in which -ēk has been shortened to -ē.

(500) JSNENA
    bāqa 'ay xaṭa'-ī̀| hìt xa jwāb-ē|
    for this fault-1SG EXIST one answer-INDF
    'For this fault of mine I have an answer.' (E:62)

(501) Kurdish
    šaw-ē   kuř-akān=ī   bàng kərd.[|]
    night-INDF boy-DEF.PL=3SG call do.PST
    '**One night** he summoned his sons.'

6.3 The definite article –akē

The Gorani definite suffix *-akē* is used extensively in JSNENA. It does not occur, however, on all nouns that are definite in status. Many nouns whose referents the speaker considers to be identifiable by the hearer do not have the suffix. Just as is the case with the JSNENA indefinite article *xa*, the definite suffix *-akē* in JSNENA tends to be restricted to definite nouns that have some kind of textual salience.

6.3.1 Anaphora

One reflection of this textual salience is that a noun with the *-akē* suffix has usually been mentioned previously in the preceding context. The referent of the noun, therefore, has been explicitly activated in the interaction between speaker and hearer and so the definite marker has an anaphoric function (cf. Becker 2018 for types of definiteness contexts)

(502) JSNENA
    a. 'afsarḕ[|] 'artḕš[|] rakw-ī-wa   sūsī̀.[|]   **sūsī̀**
        officers army ride.PRS-3PL-PSTC horse horse
        k-wī-wā-lū.[|]   xa-nafar=əč mangal nokằr,[|]
        IND-give.PRS-PSTC-OBL.3PL one-CLF=ADD like   servant
        xa-sarbằz,[|] lapəl-wa   ba-šon-ēf   rēša sūsī
        one-soldier fall.PRS.3SG.M-PSTC in-place-3SG.M on   horse
        xḕt.[|] **susy-akē** mən-sarbāzxānē
        other horse-DEF from-barracks
        k-mē-wā-lē   qam   tarà.[|]
        IND-bring.PRS.3SG.M-OBL.3SG.M before door
        'Officers, in the army, would ride on **a horse**. They would give them a horse. Somebody like a servant, a soldier, would, moreover, follow him on another horse. He would bring **the horse** (for the officer) from the barracks to the door.' (A:15–16)

b. *bàr-do*| *g-bē-wa*   *hēz-ī-wa*
after-OBL.DEM IND-need.PRS.3SG.M-PSTC go.PRS-3PL-PSTC
zara   *šaql-ī̀,*| ***zar-akē***   *hamè̠-n-wā-lē-o*|
wheat take.PRS-3PL wheat-DEF bring.PRS-3PL-PSTC-OBL.3SG.M-TELIC
ga-bēla   *dāna*   *dāna*   *gabè̠-n-wā-lē,*|
in-house grain grain sort.PRS-3PL-PSTC-OBL.3SG.M
tamīz   *hol-ī̀-wā-lē.*|
clean   make.PRS-3PL-PSTC-OBL.3SG.M
'Afterwards they had to go and buy **wheat**, bring **the wheat** back, sort it grain by grain in the house, clean it.' (A:58)

Examples (503)-(504) show in Gorani and Kurdish the use of definite markers in similar anaphoric contexts.

(503) Gorani
īsà| *han*   ***dawḷatmàn=ā=w***| *mən* *gadā̀=nā*| *mən*
now   exist.PRS.3SG rich=COP.3SG=and   1SG   poor=COP.1SG 1SG
řamìyā=ū   ***dawḷatmana-(a)ka-y***| *mà-yā-ū=š*   *panē*|
run.PST.1SG=and rich-DEF-OBL.M   NEG-arrive.PRS-1SG=3SG to
'Nowadays, there is **a rich fellow**, and as for me, I am poor. I run (i.e. work) like **the rich (fellow)** but I cannot reach him.'

(504) Kurdish
čàḷ-ēk   *a-kan-ē*| *a-řōt=a*   *nāw*   ***čāḷ-aka***|
hole-INDF IND-dig.PRS.3SG IND-go.PRS.3SG=DRCT   inside hole-DEF
dā-a-nīš-è-ū|
PVB-IND-sit.PRS-3SG=and
'He digs **a hole**, (and) goes into **the hole** (and) sits (there).'

6.3.2 Associative anaphora

On some occasions the *-akē* suffix in JSNENA is attached to a noun that is definite in status due to its association with the situation described in the preceding discourse without it being explicitly mentioned. This is a use of the definite marker to express associative anaphora in what can be described as 'bridging contexts' (Becker 2018). In (505.a) the 'door' is definite since the speaker assumes that the hearer can identify this as the door of the room mentioned in the preceding clause.

In (505.b) the 'house' is definite since it is inferable from the situation described in what precedes.

(505) JSNENA
a. *ə̀rq-ā-la* *zīl-a* *tīw-a* *ga-xa-'otā̀q.*
   flee.PST-3SG.F-OBL.3SG.F go.PST-3SG.F sit.PST-3SG.F in-one-room
   ta-nóšaf **tar-akē** *məzr-a* *ba-rēša-nòšaf.*
   to-self-3SG.F door-DEF close.PST-OBL.3SG.F on-upon-self-3SG.F
   'She fled and sat in a room. She closed **the door** behind her (literally: upon her).' (A:22)

b. *lēlawāē sətwa yat-ềx-wa* *dawrē làxlē.* *lēlē*
   nights winter sit.PRS-1PL-PSTC around each_other night
   sətwa ga-doka yarīxà=yē-lē *qardề=č=yē-la.*
   winter in-there long=COP.PST.OBL.3SG.M cold=ADD=COP.PST.OBL.3SG.F
   bāqa dóa **bēl-akē** *mašxn-ī-wā-lề.* *xa-'əda*
   for OBL.DEM house-DEF heat.PRS-3PL-PSTC-OBL.3SG.M one-number
   buxarî̀ hīt-wā-lū *ba-ṣīwề* *malq-ī-wā-la,*
   stove EXIST-PSTC-OBL.3PL by-sticks ignite.PRS-3PL-PSTC-OBL.3SG.F
   'o-bēla *mašxn-ī̀-wā-lē.*
   DEM-house heat.PRS-3PL-PSTC-OBL.3SG.M
   'During the winter nights we would sit together in a circle. A winter night was long there and it was cold. For this reason they heated **the house**. Some people had a stove, which they would fuel by sticks and they would heat the house.' (A:89)

Parallels to this are found in the Iranian languages of the area. In (506) 'bridegroom' is inferable from the wedding ceremony and is marked by the definite marker. In (507) 'meat' is marked by the definite suffix since it is associated with the ewe.

(506) Gorani
   a *č-ī̀* *Bana-na* *zamāwənà bē*, **pīyā-ka**
   PRSNT in-DEM.PROX PN-POST wedding COP.PST.3SG man-DEF
   zamā-(a)ka *nāmē=š* *'Alī Guḷāḷà bē.*
   bridegroom-DEF.DIR name=3SG PN PN COP.PST.3SG
   'In this village of Bana there was a wedding ceremony. **The man, the bridegroom**'s name was *Ali Gulala*.'

(507) Kurdish
ēma   dawr   dușàw   paz=mān   bū.| am   dusaw   paz-a
1PL   around   200   ewe=1PL   COP.PST DEM.SG.PROX   200   ewe-DEM
gə   sāḷ-ē   du   kaša   a-zả.| **gošt-aka**=mān
each   year-INDF two   time   IPFV.give.birth.PST meat-DEF=1PL
a-dā   tahwīl   Kursàn.|
IPFV-give.PST   delivery PN

'We had around 200 ewes. These 200 ewes would lamb twice a year. We would send **their meat** to Kursan (Sanandaj).'

6.3.3 Marking a discourse boundary

In some cases in the JSNENA corpus the clause is given prominence by the additional coding of the suffix -*akē* not primarily on account of the clause's intrinsic content but rather due to its occurrence at a boundary in the discourse. In (508), for example, the clause in which the heavily-coded noun is used occurs at a point where there is a shift of subject:

(508) JSNENA
mīr-wā-la   Mərza Xanaka   xa-gora   g-bē-lòx.|
say.PST-PSTC-3SG.F   PN   one-man   IND-want.PRS.3SG.M-OBL.2SG.M
la-k-ay-an   màni=yē.| Xanaka=č   mən-**panjar-akē**
NEG-IND-know.PRS-1SG.F who=COP.3SG.M   PN   from-window-DEF
mīn-e-ò| həl-dīdī   xè-lē.|
look.PST-OBL.3SG.M-TELIC to-OBL.1SG   see.PST-3SG.M

'She said, "Mərza Xanaka, a man wants you. I do not know who it is". Xanaka looked from **the window** and saw me.' (A:21)

Likewise, in (509) from Kurdish the heavily-coded noun 'ladder' has not been mentioned earlier. It occurs in a boundary in the discourse where there is a shift of subject.

(509) Kurdish
dwāngza   dawrī̀=m   dā-wərd.| aw=īš   haḷ-sà|
twelve   plate=1SG PVB-take.PST   3SG=ADD   PVB-stand.PST.3SG
payja-ka=y   hāwə̀rd.|
ladder-DEF=3SG   bring.PST

'I took twelve plates, (while) he rose and brought **the ladder**.'

In JSNENA a nominal modified by a demonstrative can additionally be marked with the suffix *-akē*, when it occurs at the boundary of discourse. This heavy coding of the nominal gives more salience to the nominal and this is exploited to indicate the closure of a discourse segment:

(510) JSNENA
k-mər   mà   ho-na?| mīr-ī   'àt| ba-'aqlḕ|
IND-say.PRS.3SG.M   what   do.PRS-1SG.M   say.PST-1SG   you   with-feet
sē   rēša   'ay   jəlḕ.| ba-'aqlē   'ay   jəlē
go.IMP.SG   upon   DEM   clothes   with-feet   DEM   clothes
ùč-lū| úč-lū   'ē-jəl-akḕ| 'ānā=č
trample.IMP.SG-OBL.3PL   trample.IMP.SG-OBL.3PL   DEM-clothes-DEF   I=ADD
'asr-ànān-ū.|
wring.PRS-1SG.F-OBL.3PL
'He says, "What should I do?" I said, "You go onto **the clothes** with your feet. Trample **the clothes** with your feet. Trample **the clothes** and I shall wring them out."' (C:11)

Likewise, in Kurdish the definite suffix can be added to a nominal that is modified by a demonstrative. This typically occurs in contexts where the heavily-coded nominal is in contrast with another nominal. Salience here is used to express contrast.

(511) Kurdish
am   asb-aka=y   tər   l-am
DEM.PROX   horse-DEF=EZ   other   from-DEM.PROX
bē-řang-tər=a
without-colour-CMPR=COP.3SG
'This other horse is weaker than this one (horse).'

6.4 Demonstrative pronouns

6.4.1 Deictic function

The JSNENA demonstratives (§3.3) may be used deictically to point out referents that are visible in the speech situation. In principle the proximate deixis form is used to refer to items near to the speaker and the remote deixis form to refer to items distant from the speaker. Physical distance, however, is not the only factor that conditions the choice between these two sets of demonstrative. Close emotional engagement or interest in a referent can motivate the use of a proximate deixis form to point out a referent that is spatially distant from the speaker.

(512) JSNENA
 mən-laḥāl 'o-xīy-ằ-lī.| mīr-ū 'ēa xaləsta
 from-far DEM-see.PST-3SG.F-OBL.1SG say.PST-OBL.3PL DEM sister
 Xanakè̱=ya.|
 PN=COP.3SG.F
 'I saw her from afar. They said, "This is the sister of Xanaka."' (A:14)

Likewise, in the Iranian languages of Sanandaj the proximate demonstrative indicates emotional engagement with a referent who is physically distant.

(513) Kurdish
 mən čət-ēg=əm la tò garak=a.| agar aw
 1SG thing-INDF=1SG from 2SG be.necessary=COP.3SG if DEM.SG.DIST
 kằr-a anjām bay
 job-DEM accomplish SBJV.give.PRS.2SG
 bə-tān-ī,| a-twān-əm àm žən=t-a
 SBJV.can.PRS-2SG IND-can.PRS-1SG DEM.SG.PROX wife=2SG-DEM
 bēr-m=aw.|
 SBJV.bring.PRS-1SG=TELIC
 'I want something from you. If you can do the task, I can bring **this wife of yours** back.'

(514) Gorani
 a. mən yarè̱ sāḷ-ē ī **bərā=m=a** tūš=ū
   1SG three year-PL.DIR DEM.PROX brother=1SG=DEIC inflicted=EZ
   ī dard-ē=a āmā=n.|
   DEM.PROX illness-FEM.OBL=DEIC come.PST.PTCP.M=COP.3SG
   'As for me, it's been three years that **my brother** is suffering from this illness.'
 b. m-è̱ dil-ū dagē=w| pars-o
   IND-come.PRS.3SG inside-EZ village.OBL.F=and ask.PRS-3SG
   'jarayān čikò=n=ū| ī yāna=w kābrā-y
   story where=COP.3SG.M=and DEM.PROX house=EZ fellow-OBL.M
   kè̱=n=ū| īna kè̱=n=ū'|
   who=COP.3SG.M=and DEM.PROX who=COP.3SG=and
   'He came to the village. He asked, "What's the story? Where is the house of the fellow? Who is **he**?"'

6.4.2 Anaphoric function

In JSNENA demonstrative pronouns can also have an anaphoric function. In this usage they do not point to a referent in the extralinguistic situation but rather signal that the referent of the nominal is identifiable in the surrounding discourse context, typically in what precedes. In JSNENA all sets of demonstratives (independent and attributive) (§3.3 & §3.4), indeed, can be used with either deictic or anaphoric function. In Gorani the attributive demonstratives are used with deictic or anaphoric function but there appears to be a clear division of labour between the independent demonstrative pronouns, which are used only with a deictic function, on the one hand, and the anaphoric pronouns *āđ* (neutral), *aw* (remote), and *īđ* (near), on the other (§3.2). In the Kurdish of Sanandaj, however, several of the demonstrative pronouns are used with either deictic or anaphoric function. This applies to the sets of Kurdish pronouns that correspond structurally to the JSNENA demonstratives (§3.3 & §3.4). It would appear, therefore, that the syntactic usage of the JSNENA demonstratives has matched the usage of the corresponding demonstrative pronouns in Kurdish. In what follows, we shall examine some specific anaphoric uses of the demonstratives that are shared by JSNENA and Iranian.

In JSNENA and Iranian both the proximate and the remote sets of demonstrative pronouns are used for anaphoric reference. In some cases, particularly in expository discourse, near and remote pronouns are used to express contrastive opposition between two anaphors, separating them virtually in the mental space of the discourse. An example from JSNENA is (515):

(515) JSNENA
'*agar ṣoma ṣəhyon lapəl yoma šabàt*⏐ *la*
if fast Zion fall.PRS.3SG.M day Sabbath NEG
doq-èxī-lē.⏐ *mand-ēxī-lē yoma xšābà.*⏐
hold.PRS-1PL-OBL.3SG.M postpone.PRS-1PL-OBL.3SG.M day Sunday
'*agar ṣoma Lēlangè,*⏐ *Purìm,*⏐ *lapəl yoma šabàt,*⏐ *là*
if fast Lelange Purim fall.PRS.3SG.M day Sabbath NEG
doq-ēxī-lē.⏐ *xamšùšab doq-ēxī-lē.*⏐ *ta-ma*
hold.PRS-1PL-OBL.3SG.M Thursday hold.PRS-1PL-OBL.3SG.M for-what
'*ē xamùšab doq-ēxī-lē*⏐ '*ó xšābà?*⏐
this Thursday hold.PRS-1PL-OBL.3SG.M that Sunday
'If the fast of Zion (9th of Ab) falls on a Sabbath, we do not keep it. We postpone it to the Sunday. If the fast of Lelange, Purim, falls on a Sabbath, we do not keep it. We keep it on the Thursday. Why do we hold **this one** on Thursday but **that one** on Sunday?' (B:73)

Example (516) is a parallel to this in Kurdish in which the near and remote pronouns are set up in a contrastive opposition.

(516) Kurdish of the Sanandaj region
ītər àm čan nafar-a wā mən la zəndān
EMPH DEM.PROX some person-DEM1 REL 1SG from prison
məraxas=yān=əm kərd-ü[|] àm a=y-wət[|] bərā
free=3PL=1SG do.PST-COP.PST 3SG.PROX IPFV=3SG-say.PST brother
a-šē da šaw mēwằn mən wī[|] àw
IND-should.PRS.3SG ten night guest 1SG IRR.COP.PRS.2SG 3SG.DIST
a=y-wət[|] pànza šaw mēwān mən wī.[|]
IPFV=3SG-say.PST fifteen night guest 1SG SBJV.COP.PRS.2SG
'These few people whom I had freed from prison. . . . **this one** would say, "You should be my guest for ten nights"; **that one** would say, "You should be my guest for fifteen nights."'

In both JSNENA (517.a-b) and Iranian (518.a-b) proximate forms are used to refer anaphorically to nominals whose referents are the centre of attention at a particular point in the discourse:

(517) JSNENA
a. xà[|] bronà[|] hīyē ba-'olằm[|] kačằl=yē-lē.[|] ...
one boy come.PST.3SG.M in-world bald=COP.PST-OBL.3SG.M
'ay bronà[|] barūxa lìt-wā-lē.[|]
this boy friend NEG.EXIST-PSTC-OBL.3SG.M
'A boy came into the world who was bald. . . . **This boy** (the protagonist of the story) did not have a friend.' (D:1)
b. g-bē hē-t-ó 'ay-brāta
IND-need.PRS.3SG.M come.PRS-2SG.M-TEL this-girl
gor-ēt-à.[|]
marry.PRS-2SG.M-OBL.3SG.F
'You must go back and marry **the girl**.' (A:18)

(518) Kurdish
Sənjər xằn[|] aw-waxta bāwā=y 'ābdìn xān=ū[|] aw-waxta
PN khan well grand.father=EZ PN khan=and well
'azīz xān=ū amānà bū.[|] māḷ=yān la farah-à
PN khan=and DEM.PROX.PL COP.PST.3SG house=3PL at PN-POST

6.4 Demonstrative pronouns — 249

bū.^{|}	řūs-aka	hàt-ū^{|}	**àm**	tanyā	xwa=y
COP.PST.3SG	Russian-DEF	come.PST-COP.PST	3SG.PROX	alone	REFL=3SG
řū^{|}	řūs-aka=y	šəkəs	dà.^{|}		
go.PST.3SG	Russian-DEF=3SG	defeat	give.PST		

'Sinjir Khan, well he was the grandfather of Abdin Khan, Aziz Khan and so forth. Their house was in Farah district. The Russians had come (here). **He went alone and defeated the Russians.**'

(519) Gorani
    a. wa **ìd̃=īč,**[|]   ka   ī   šēx   'usmằn-a[|]
       and 3SG.PROX=ADD COMPL DEM.PROX Sheikh PN-DEM
       ba-farz   m-āč-ā   murafàh bīya=n.[|]
       supposedly IND-say.PRS-3PL well.off be.PST.PTCP.M=COP.3SG.M
       'As for **him**, that is Sheikh Osman, it is said that he was supposedly well-off.'
    b. pādšà-ē[|] wa hākəm=ū mamlakatè-(ē)wa b-o[|]
       king-INDF and ruler=EZ country.OBL.F-INDF be-PRS.3SG
       ī   **pādšā** sāḥəb dasaḷàt b-o[|]
       DEM.PROX king owner power be.PRS-3SG
       'There was a king, a ruler of a country. **This king** was powerful.'

In JSNENA, speakers may use near forms anaphorically to express some kind of emotional engagement with referents, as in (520), in which the demonstratives convey a negative attitude:

(520) JSNENA
    ma kul-yóma g-ēz-ēt **'ay-jangàḷ**[|] **'ay-kule** zāḥamta
    why every-day IND-go.PRS-2SG.M this-wood this-all trouble
    garš-èt-a=ū?[|]
    pull.PRS-2SG.M-OBL.3SG.F=and
    'Why do you go to **the wood** everyday and take **all this trouble**?' (A:105)

Example (521) shows a parallel construction in Gorani, in which the proximate demonstrative conveys negative attitude.

(521) Gorani Luhon
ī   **xarīb-a**   kē=n   ka   č-ī   šār=ū
DEM.PROX stranger-DEM who=COP.3SG.M COMPL in-DEM.PROX city=EZ
mən-a-na   pēsa   nāmdār   bīya=n?
1SG-DEM-POST such famous become.PTCP.M=COP.3SG.M
'(The king said to his viziers), "Who is **this stranger** who has become so famous in **this** city of mine?"'
(MacKenzie 1966, 70)

In JSNENA, the remote demonstratives are used anaphorically in a more neutral sense, without expressing a prominent near perspective. Examples:

(522) JSNENA
   a. malka Šabà   gwīrtē=ya.| **'o=č**   rāba
      queen Sheba marry.PTCP.SG.F=COP.3SG.F that=ADD   very
      dawlamàn   xīrtē=ya.|
      rich   be.PTCP.SG.F=COP.3SG.F
      'He married the Queen of Sheba. **She** also become very rich.' (A:97)
   b. qaṣāb   hīt-wā-lan   b-šəma   'Azīz-Xàn.|
      butcher EXIST-PSTC-OBL.1PL by-name PN
      hūlàa=yē-lē.| **'ó**   pəsr-akē   k-mē-wā-lē
      Jew=COP.PST-OBL.3SG.M that   meat-DEF   IND-bring.PRS-PSTC-OBL.3SG.M
      ga-tʷkanè.|
      in-shops
      'We had a butcher by the name of Aziz Khan. He was a Jew. **He** brought meat to the shops.' (A:74)
   c. nāšē   **'o-bēla**   noš-ū   komak-af   k-ol-ī-wa.|
      people that-house   self-3PL help-3SG.F IND-do.PRS-3PL-PSTC
      'The people of **the house** helped her.' (A:66)

Likewise in Kurdish the remote pronouns are used with neutral anaphoric function:

(523) Kurdish
   a. wət=ī   **àw**   **řaš=a**| màn   čarməg=əm.|
      say.PST=3SG 3SG.DIST   black=COP.3SG   1SG   white=COP.1SG
      'She said, "**He** (the wolf) is black, I am white."'
   b. **awa**   a   awà   bū.|
      DEM.DIST   PRSNT   such   COP.PST.3SG
      '**It** (the situation) was like this.'

Gorani uses neutral third person independent pronouns in these contexts:

(524) Gorani
a. ī   gīyān=ū   qafas=w   sīna=w   min=a   īnà=n|
   DEM.PROX   soul=EZ   cage=EZ   chest=EZ 1SG=DEIC DEM.PROX=COP.3SG.M
   āḍa   lūā̀.|
   3SG.F.DIR go.PST.3SG
   'The soul in my rib cage [that I swore an oath on] was this [sparrow]. It [just] flew away.'
b. āna=šā   zil-tar=ū   āl-tar   b-o   āḍ-ì̀
   DEM.DIST=3PL BIG-CMPR=and   good-CMPR   be.PRS-3SG   3SG-OBL.M
   bar-ā.|
   take.PRS-3PL
   'The one who was bigger and healthier, they took **him**.'

In the JSNENA corpus a remote pronoun is sometimes used as a neutral anaphoric with nouns whose referent has not been explicitly invoked in the preceding discourse but is only associated with it. The speaker assumes the referent is identifiable due to its association with the context. This is the case in (525), where the 'burnt ash' (*qīla*) is associated with the act of burning of the rags:

(525) JSNENA
xór   darmānè̄=č   līt-wa   'o-waxtara   darmāne   dàē-n.|
yet   medicines=ADD   NEG.EXIST-PSTC   that-time   medicines put.PRS-3PL
paroē maql-ī̀-wa| **'o-qīlà,**| qīlē   paroè̌|
rags burn.PRS-3PL-PSTC that-burn.PTCP.3SG.M burn.PTCP.PL rags
mat-ī-wa   rēša 'o-mīḷà.|
put.PRS-3PL-PSTC   on   that-circumcised
'They did not have medicines at that time to apply. They would burn rags and they would put on the circumcision **the burnt ash**, burnt rags.' (A:76)

A related usage is attested in the Kurdish corpus, in which a remote pronoun is used in speech when the speaker has not mentioned the noun 'well' but assumes that the hearer can identify the referent due to its association with fridges in terms of being cold and suitable for preserving meat:

(526) Kurdish
har   yaxačâḷ   na-w| *gošt=yān   a-kēšä̀=w*
EMPH   fridge   NEG-be.PST.3SG   meat=3PL   IPFV-weigh.PST=and
a=yān-xist=a   nāw   aw   čä̀-(a)| *šòř=əž=yān*
IPFV=3PL-throw.PST=DRCT   inside   DEM.DIST   well-DEM   salty=ADD=3PL
a-kərd=aw   dākadē   hàyč=ī   pē   nā-a-hāt|
IPFV-DO.PST=TELIC   so.that   nothing=3SG   to   NEG-IPFV-come.PST.3SG
fēnək=ū|
cold=COP.PST.3SG
'There were no fridges. People would weigh the meat and put it in **the well**. They would add salt to it too. Nothing would happen to it (since) the well was cold.'

In both JSNENA and Iranian a neutral remote demonstrative is frequently used with anaphoric adverbials.

(527) JSNENA
a. ***'o-waxtara**   'āraq   rāba   rasmī̀=yē-la.*|
   that-time   arak   very   legal=COP.PST-OBL.3SG.F
   '**At that time** arak was completely legal.' (A:11)
b. ***'o-lēlē**   xa-šām   mfaṣal   hīw-lū   bāq-àn=ū*|
   that-night   one-dinner   copious   give.PST-OBL.3PL   to-1PL=and
   '**That night** they gave us a copious dinner.' (A:26)

(528) Gorani
*ā   **waxt-ī**   sarbāzī   sàxt   bē.*|
DEM.DIST   time-OBL.M   military.service   difficult COP.PST.3SG
'At **that time** military service was difficult.'

(529) Kurdish of the Sanandaj region
jā   aw   řož-a   xwa=y   a-kāt=a   naxwàš|
well   DEM.DIST   day-DEM1   REFL=3SG   IND-do.PRS.3SG=DRCT   ill
Sü-čāwkāḷ.|
PN-light.brown.eye
'**That day** Sü čāwkāḷ feigned illness.'

In both Kurdish and Gorani the anaphoric adverbial *ā waxtī* (Gorani), *aw waxta* (Kurdish) 'that time' tends to be used as a filler word. This does not seem to be the case in JSNENA.

(530) Gorani
ā waxt-akày| wa'za=mā āl-a nì-ana hāḷāy=ū|
DEM time-DEF-OBL.M situation=1PL good-F NEG=COP.3SG.F now=and
'Anyway, our situation is not good now.'

(531) Kurdish
aw waxt-à| ama kùř=a=w| kanīšk nì=ya.|
DEM.DIST time-DEM 3SG.PROX boy=COP.3SG=and girl NEG=COP.3SG
'Anyway, this is a boy not a girl.'

In JSNENA remote demonstratives can be used on the head of a relative clause to bind its reference to the identifying description of the following subordinate clause rather than to the preceding context. This, therefore, is a cataphoric rather than an anaphoric function:

(532) JSNENA
a. lēlē xlūlà| mən-bē-xətnà| **'o-nāšē** ya-da'wàt
night wedding from-house-groom those-people REL-invitation
kol-ī-wā-lū,| familù̄ yē-lū,|
do.PRS-3PL-PSTC-OBL.3PL relatives COP.PST-OBL.3PL
baruxù̄=yē-lū.|
friends=COP.PST-OBL.3PL
'**The people** whom they invited on the night of the wedding from the family of the groom were relatives, were friends.' (A:42)
b. **'onyēxāē** ya-šī'à=yē-lū|
those REL-Shi'ite=COP.PST-OBL.3PL
'**those** who were Shi'ites' (A:77)

This feature is found also in Kurdish and Gorani:

(533) Kurdish
awà=yān-a wā šalāq=əm dā-w|
DEM.DIST=3PL-NA REL whip=1SG do.PST-COP.PST
'**The one** of them whom I had whipped.'

(534) Gorani
āna=šā zil-tar=ū āl-tar b-o āđ-ì̄ bar-ā.|
DEM.DIST=3PL BIG-CMPR=and good-CMPR be.PRS-3SG 3SG-OBL.M take.PRS-3PL
'**The one** who was bigger and healthier, they took him.'

In narrative contexts near anaphoric demonstratives may be used with all protagonists to express equal prominence, as in (535) from JSNENA, (536) from Gorani, and (537) from Kurdish:

(535) JSNENA
'ay baxta=ū   'ay gorà| baxēḷì labl-ī-wa   l-**day**
this woman=and this man   jealousy take.PST-3PL-PSTC to-OBL.this
gora xēt.|
man   other
'**The woman and the man** were jealous of **the other man**.' (A:103)

(536) Gorani
haḷbatana   ī   **kuř=a**   bə̀ř=əš   dā=wa.|
surely   DEM.PROX   boy=DEIC   LVC=3SG   give.PST.PTCP=TELIC
filfòr| ī   **kināčē=m=a** pay=š mārà   kar-dē.|
immediately DEM.PROX   girl=1SG=DEIC to=3SG marriage do.PRS.IMP-2PL
'Surely, **the boy** has arrived [at the palace]. Marry **my daughter** to him immediately.'

(537) Kurdish
Sənjər xằn| yak-ē   la   bagzāwa-(a)kān   Nařằn bū.|
PN   khan   one-INDF of   son.of.ruler-DEF.PL PN   COP.PST.3SG
aw-waxta   la   zamān řūs-akằ| **àm**   **bəsəḷmān-a**|
DEM.DIST-time-DEM at time   Russian-DEF.POST DEM   musim-DEM
təfàng=ī   haḷ-gərt=ū| sangàr=ī   bast| **àm**
gun=3SG   PVB-take.PST=and   fortress=3SG tie.PST   DEM.PROX
řūs=y-a   šəkān.|
Russian=3SG-DEM   break.PST
'Sinjir Khan was one of the descendants of rulers from Naṛān. At the period of the Russians, **this Muslim** took up guns, built defences around, and defeated **these Russians**.'

The participants are sometimes distinguished by the use of different types of demonstratives, expressing different degrees of perspective. Consider the following from the JSNENA corpus:

(538) JSNENA
mìr-ē	baq-ēf	... 'ó	mīr-ē		tòb.	zīl
say.PST-OBL.3SG.M	to-3SG.M	that	say.PST-OBL.3SG.M	good	go.PST.3SG.M
lāg-èf=ū	mē-lē		mtù-lē=ū		'ay-zīl
to-3SG.M=and	bring.PST-OBL.3SG.M	place.PST-OBL.3PL=and		this
jəns	ləbl-è,		jəns-akē	ləblē	
go.PST.3SG.M	take.PST-OBL.3SG.M	cloth-DEF	take.PST-OBL.3SG.M	
mātū-le		ga-xa	tʷkāna	zabn-è.		'ay=əč
put.PRS.3SG.M-OBL.3SG.M	in-one	shop	sell.PRS-OBL.3SG.M	this=ADD
xīr		mangàl	dó.		
become.PST.3SG.M	like	OBL.that		

'He (the neighbour) said to him . . . **He** (the neighbour) said, "Fine (that is agreed)." He went to him, brought it (the cloth) and put it down (for him). **He** (the family man) went and took the cloth, he took the cloth away to put it in a shop and sell it. **He** (the family man) became like **him** (the neighbour).' (A:105)

In this passage there are two participants, the neighbour and the family man. It is the family man who is the main protagonist and the centre of attention of the narrative and it is he who is referred to by the near pronoun. The neighbour, on the other hand, is referred to by the neutral form.

A similar strategy of marking participants is seen in the following passage from Kurdish. The main protagonist is referred to by a proximate demonstrative, but her friends are referred to by the neutral remote demonstrative form.

(539) Kurdish
xulāsa,	qàw	a-kā	la rafēq-akān=ī=ū
in.short	voice	IND-do.PRS.3SG	at friend-DEF.PL=3SG=and
haḷ-a-sə̀-n	čày	a-xwa-n=ū	čāy-aka
PVB-IND-stand.PRS-3PL	tea	IND-eat.PRS-3PL=and	tea-DEF
a-xwà-n=ū	**awə̀n**	a-xaf-ən=aw	**àm**
IND-eat.PRS-3PL=and	3PL.DIST	IND-sleep.PRS-3PL=TELIC	DEM.PROX
har	xaw=ī	pē-ā	nā-kaf-ē.
EMPH	sleep=3SG	to-POST	NEG-fall.PRS-3SG

'Anyway, she called her friends. They woke up, and drank tea. Again, **they** went to sleep, (but) **she** did not fall sleep.'

In Gorani, by contrast, anaphoric pronouns are used to express the degrees of salience given to the participants.

(540) Gorani
ìd̀=īč lūā=w| **àw**=īč lūā.|
3SG.PROX=ADD go.PST.3SG=AND 3SG.DIST=ADD go.PST.3SG
'**He** (the child whom I took with me) died; **he** (the child whom I left behind) too died! (Lit. This one went; that one too went.)'

JSNENA and Iranian both frequently use a proximate demonstrative to express the notion of 'so forth'.

(541) JSNENA
ba-xá dasá jəlē zìl=ū| ga-pəlga nāš-akē
in-one suit clothes go.PST.3GM.M-and in-middle people-DEF
tìw=ū| ḥqē-lē mən-un=ū 'èxà=ū|
sit.PST.3SG.M=and speak.PST-OBL.3SG.M with-3PL=and this=and
'He went in a suit and sat among the people and spoke to them, and **so forth**.' (D:16)

(542) Gorani
ī kināčē waš-à bī-ē=na=w īnīšà|
DEM.PROX girl well-F be.PST-PTCP.F=COP.3SG.F=and DEM.PRX.PL
'This girl is cured and **so forth**.'

(543) Kurdish
bāwā=y 'ābdìn xān=ū| aw-waxta 'azīz xān=ū
grand.father=EZ PN khan=and well PN khan=and
amānà bū.|
DEM.PROX.pl COP.PST.3SG
'He was the grandfather of Abdin Khan, Aziz Khan, and **so forth**.'

6.4.3 Demonstratives with cardinal numeral 'one'

The JSNENA independent demonstrative pronouns may be combined with a *xa* element (§3.3). This can be identified as the cardinal numeral 'one'. The original meaning of *xa* is clear in the singular forms, which are used in a speech situation to pick out one referent from a set that is given in the speech situation or discourse.

(544) JSNENA
    a. 'óxa barūx-ī̀=yē| wālē 'óxa barūx-ī là=y.|
        that friend-1SG=COP.3SG.M but that friend-1SG NEG=COP.3SG.M
        'That one is my friend, but that (other) one is not my friend.'
    b. 'ēxa barūxī̀=yē| wālē 'ēxa barūxī là=y.|
        this friend-1SG=COP.3SG.M but this friend-1SG NEG=COP.3SG.M
        'This one is my friend, but this (other) one is not my friend.'

In the Iranian languages of the region there are corresponding sets of independent demonstratives incorporating the cardinal 'one' or singular classifier element *dāna*, e.g. Kurdish *amaka* (< *am=yak-a*) 'this one', *awaka* (< *aw=yak-a*) 'that one', Gorani *ī-yo* 'this one', *ī-dāna* 'this one', *ā yo* 'that one', *ā dāna* 'that one'. In Kurdish there is also a set of attributive demonstratives with the cardinal 'one' element, which is suffixed to the nominal, e.g. *aw mənāl-ak-a* 'that (one) child'. The sequence *-ak-a* should not be mistaken for a definite marker.

The function of these sets of demonstratives in Iranian is the same as that of the JSNENA demonstratives of the corresponding structure, viz. they extract one referent from a set that is given in the speech situation or discourse, e.g.

(545) Kurdish
    čū-m   bo lā=y   **aw-yàk-a=y**   tər| čə
    go.PST-1SG to at.the.place.of=EZ DEM.DIST-INDF-DEM=EZ other INTJ
    àm   asb-aka=y   tər   l-am   bēřang-tər=a.|
    DEM.PROX horse-DEF=EZ other of-3SG.PROX pale-CMPR=COP.3SG
    'I went to the other one (the other horse) and saw that this horse is weaker than **the other one**.'

6.4.4 Discourse presentative function of demonstratives

In JSNENA an independent demonstrative may be used as a device for discourse management to draw particular attention to a proposition, as in constructions such as (546):

(546) JSNENA
    'ēa   xabra ḥaqè-n-ox.|
    this word   tell.PRS-1SG.M-OBL.2SG.M
    'Now (listen), I shall tell you a story.' (B:60)

In Kurdish the demonstratives *ama* and *awa*, and in Gorani demonstrative *īna* and *āna* are used with a similar discourse management function, as seen in the following examples:

(547) Kurdish
    a. kura bərằ,ˈ   awa   čwằr dāna   līra=t   pē   a-wa-m.ˈ
        VOC   brother DEM.DIST four   clf   lira=2SG to   IND-give.PRS-1SG
        'Brother, look, I am giving you four liras (unit of currency).'
    b. awa   čà   a-ka-n?ˈ
        DEM.DIST what   IND-do.PRS-2PL
        'What are you doing?'
    c. ama   čùn   hāt-ī?ˈ
        DEM.PROX why   come.PST-2SG
        'Why did you come (here)?'

(548) Gorani
    a. īna   mən   nằn=əm   ārd-ē.ˈ
        DEM.PROX.3SG.M 1SG   bread=1SG   bring.PST-3PL
        'Look, I have brought bread.'
    b. m-āč-o,   'mə̀nˈ   īna   jaryān=əm
        IND-say.PRS-3SG 1SG   DEM.PROX.3SG.M story=1SG
        ačīnà=n.'ˈ
        in.this.manner=COP.3SG.M
        'He said, "I—my story is like this."'

In (549) the speaker uses the demonstrative *awa* to draw attention to the proposition in order to correct a belief of the hearer:

(549) Kurdish
     awa   nằn   hā   la-bar   das=m-ā.ˈ
     DEM.DIST bread exist.3SG in.front hand=1SG-POST
     a-yž-ī   šarm   Ø-kà-m!ˈ
     IND-say.PRS-2SG shame   SBJV-do.PRS-1SG
     'There is food in front of me (contrary to what you believe). Are you saying that I'm being shy!'

6.5 Presentative particles

JSNENA uses a number of presentative particles to draw attention to referents or situations.

6.5.1 JSNENA wā

The deicitic presentative particle *wā*, which is combined with the remote deixis demonstrative pronouns, is used to draw attention either to a referent or to a situation in the extralinguistic environment, e.g.

6.5.1.1 Referent

(550) JSNENA
    a. *wā*   *'òa.*|
        PRSNT that
        'There he is.'
    b. *wā*   *'onyḕ.*|
        PRSNT those
        'There they are.'
    c. *wā*   *'ó*   *nāšḕ.*|
        PRSNT those people
        'There are those people.'
    d. *wā*   *'axon-ī̀.*|
        PRSNT brother-1SG
        'There is my brother.'

6.5.1.2 Situation

(551) JSNENA
    a. *wā*   *'oà=y.*|
        PRSNT that=COP.3SG
        'Look it is him.'
    b. *wā*   *'ó*   *raxə̀š.*|
        PRSNT he walk.PRS.3SG.M
        'Look he is walking.'

c. *wā   'onī   raxš-ì.*|
   PRSNT those   walk.PRS-3PL
   'Look they are walking.'
d. *wā   maṭè-xīn.*|
   PRSNT arrive.PRS-1PL
   'Look we are arriving.' (= 'We are about to arrive')

6.5.2 Iranian wā

The corresponding particle in the Iranian languages of the Sanandaj region, viz. *wā*, does not have significant presentative function. In Sanandaj Kurdish *wā* rather functions as an adverbial deictic 'thus, this way/direction':

(552) Kurdish
   a. *wā   dīyar=a.*
      SIM   visible=COP.3SG
      'It seems thus.'
   b. *mən   tìr-ē   wā   a-xa-m,*| *yàk-ē   wā*
      1SG   arrow-INDF   DEIC   IND-throw.PRS-1SG one-INDF DEIC
      a-xa-m,| *yàk-ē   wā   a-xa-m.*|
      IND-throw.PRS-1SG   one-INDF   DEIC   IND-throw.PRS-1SG
      'I shot one arrow in this direction, one in this direction, and another in this direction.'

In the Kurdish dialect of Sulemaniyya, however, *wā* can be used as a presentative particle to draw attention to a situation.

(553) Sulemaniyya Kurdish
   a. *wā   gàyšt-ən.*|
      PRSNT arrive.PST-3PL
      'Look they have arrived.'
   b. *wā   nān   a-xò-m.*|[2]
      PRSNT bread IND-eat.PRS-1SG
      'Look, I am eating (a) meal.'

---

[2] Presentative *wā* is differentiated from the deictic *wā* meaning 'such, thus'. The latter takes stress, e.g. *wà axom* 'I eat like this' (see McCarus 1958, 35).

c. wā   čú̀-m.ˈ
    PRSNT   go.PST-1SG
    'I'm going, I'm about to go.'
d. wā   xarīk=əm   à-mr-əm.ˈ
    PRSNT   busy=COP.1SG   IND-die.PRS-1SG
    'I'm about to die.'

The close similarity between the function of the particle *wā* in JSNENA and that of the corresponding particle *wā* in the Kurdish of Sulemaniyya, which differs from its function in the Iranian languages of Sanandaj, could be interpreted as evidence of the migration of the Jewish community from the Suleimaniya region at an earlier period.

6.5.3 JSNENA ʾayānē

In JSNENA, the form *ʾayāne* is a presentative particle that is used to draw attention to a referent (554.a), or a situation (554.b):

(554) JSNENA
    a. ʾayānē   ʾaxon-ī̀.ˈ
        PRSNT   brother-1SG
        'There is my brother.'
    b. ʾayānē   ʾaxon-ī   hì̀yē.ˈ
        PRSNT   brother-1SG   come.PST.3SG.M
        'Look my brother has come.'

This particle appears to have been formed by the combination of the proximate demonstrative *ʾay* and the augment element *-ānē*. This augment element is found elsewhere in JSNENA in the interrogative spatial adverbial particle *lēkānē* 'where', which is a variant of the basic form *lēka* 'where?' It is found in other NENA dialects on spatial adverbials, which are also usually variants of basic forms without the augment, e.g. J. Arbel *laxxa* ~ *laxxānē* 'here', Ch. Hassana *ʾaxxa* ~ *ʾaxxānē*, Ch. Urmi ⁺*tamma* ~ ⁺*tammānē* 'there'. This augment in NENA may be an imitation of the Kurdish ending *-āna*, which is used on some adverbials, e.g. *šaw-āna* 'at night', *pīyāw-āna* 'in a manly fashion'.

6.5.4 JSNENA hā

In JSNENA this presentative particle is combined with the copula in constructions such as the following:

(555) JSNENA
  a. *ga-laxa   xa-našà   hā=y.*|
     in-here   one-person   PRSNT=COP.3SG.M
     'There is somebody here.'
  b. *'ay-tara   hūlēf-ò,*| *xa   nā̌sà-hā=y.*|
     this-door do.IMP.SG-3SG.M.-TEL   one   person-PRSNT=COP.3SG.M
     'Open the door, there is somebody there.'
  c. *'ó   laxa   hà̀=y-a.*|
     it.SG.F here   PRSNT=COP-3SG.F
     'It (SG.F) is here.'
  d. *hā=y-a   ga-laxḕ=y-a.*|
     PRSNT=COP-3SG.F   in-here= PRSNT=COP-3SG.F
     'Here, it (SG.F) is here.'
  e. *nā̌šē   başór   ga-laxà   hā=ē-n.*|
     people few   in-here   PRSNT=COP-3PL
     'There are a few people here.'
  f. *čəkma   šənē   ga-Sanandàj   hā=yē-lox?*|
     how_many   years   in-PN   PRSNT=COP.PST-OBL.2SG.M
     'How many years were you in Sanandaj?'

The same particle has a presentative function in Sanandaj Kurdish (*hā*). It combines with the present copula or a spatial adverbial or spatial interrogative particle:

(556) Kurdish
  a. *sə̀   dāna   kanīšk   hā=n=a   aw   bar-aw.*|
     three CLF   girl   PRSNT=COP.3PL=DRCT   DEM.DIST   front-POST
     'Three girls are on the other side.'
  b. *mə̀n*| *šwằn=əm=ū*| *hā=m=a   lā=y   řằn=ū*|
     1SG   shepherd=COP.1SG=and   PRSNT=COP.1SG=DRCT   by=EZ flock=and
     'I am a shepherd. I am by my flock.'
  c. *hā=n=a   ērà.*|
     PRSNT=COP.3PL=DRCT   here
     'They are here.'
  d. *hā   kwò̀   gurg-aka?*|
     PRSNT.3SG   where   wolf-DEF
     'Where is the wolf?'
  e. *hā   l-ērà.*|
     PRSNT.3SG   in.here
     'He is here.'

f. *hā   l-önà.*|
    PRSNT.3SG   in.there
    'He is there.'

Kurdish *hā* can also be used to draw attention to a situation (557.a) and to express prospective aspect (557.b). JSNENA uses constructions with *wā* for this latter function, cf. (553.d):

(557) Kurdish
   a. *žən-aka=y   wət=ī   hā   kā   čonarī   hằt=aw.*|
      wife-DEF=3SG   say.PST=3SG INTJ   Mr.   PN   come.PST.3SG=TELIC
      'His wife said, "Look! Mr. Chonari has come back (home)."'
   b. *hā   kàft!*|
      PRSP   fall.PST.3SG
      'He is about to fall.'

Kurdish uses the particle *hā* and also the similar sounding attention drawing particle *ā* in compound demonstrative pronouns to draw attention to visible referents that are far away from the interlocutors (§3.3):

(558) Kurdish
   wət=ī   day   aysà   hā   kwö   gurg-aka?| *wət=ī   ā*
   say.PST=3SG   well   now   PRSNT   where   wolf-DEF   say.PST=3SG   PRSNT
   awa   *hā   čūg=as=a*   *nằw   sawzaḷānī-aka*| *xwa=y*
   DEM.DIST   PRSNT   go.PTCP=COP.3SG=DRCT   inside meadow-DEF   REFL=3SG
   dərèž=aw   kərd-g=as=aw.|
   long=TELIC   do.PST-PTCP=COP.3SG=TELIC
   '(The mother) said, "Where is the wolf now?" (The kid-goat) replied, "Look **over there**. He has gone into the meadow (and) has lain down there."'

6.6 Pronominal suffixes on adverbials

In JSNENA several adverbial expressions have a 3rd person singular suffix, which refers anaphorically to the situation in the preceding context. This is normally the 3sg.m suffix *–ēf*, though sporadically the 3sg.f. suffix *–af* is used, e.g.

(559) JSNENA
    a. *lēl-ēf   daʿwat-àn   wī-lū.*|
       night-3SG.M invitation-1PL do.PST-OBL.3PL
       'That night they invited us.' (A:26)
    b. *'axr-ēf   ba-zór   mīy-à-lun=u*|
       end-3SG.M in-force bring.PST-3SG.F-OBL.3PL=and
       'In the end they brought her by force.' (A:23)
    c. *bàr-do*| *lēl-èf-o*| *daʿwat wī-lū   mən-famīl-àn*|
       after-OBL.that night-3SG.M-TEL invitation do.PST-OBL.3PL from-family-1PL
       'Then, in the evening, they invited our family.' (A:26)
    d. *'ē   m-'awaḷ-àf.*|
       this from-first-3SG.F
       'This (is what happened) at first.' (A:32)

Parallel constructions from Kurdish are given below:

(560) Kurdish
    a. *duwāra swār   asb-ē   tər   a-w-è̄   hən*
       again   mounting horse-INDF other IND-COP.PRS-3SG EZ.PRO
       šaw   duwum=ī.|
       night second=3SG
       'Again, he mounts on another horse, the one from the second night.'
    b. *āxər=ī   bēčằra=y=o   kərd.*|
       end=3SG wretched=3SG=2SG do.PST
       'Eventually, you made him wretched.'

6.7 Attributes

6.7.1 Adjectives

In JSNENA attributive adjectives are normally placed after the head noun, e.g. *bēla ruwa* 'big house'. On some occasions the Persian *ezafe* particle –*ē* connects the head to the modifying adjective. This is used after both nouns with an Aramaic nominal inflectional ending and also unadapted loanwords.

(561) JSNENA
    a. *ləbās=ē   xarāb   lòš-wa.*|
       cothing=EZ bad wear.PRS.3SG.M-PSTC
       'He wore ragged clothes.' (A:108)

b. *k-ól-wā-lē*   *ba-lēša*   *ga-pliyāw*
    IND-do.PRS.3SG.M-PSTC-OBL.3SG.M   in-dough   in-middle
    xa-ṭašt=ē   *mēsî.*|
    one-bowl=EZ   copper
    'He made it into dough in a copper bowl.' (B:19)

In Persian nominal phrases, the *ezafe* particle links the noun to modifiers, e.g. *lebās-e xarāb* 'ragged clothes'; *ye dust-e xub* 'a good friend'.

In JSNENA a pronominal suffix is placed on the adjective rather than the head noun, e.g.

(562) JSNENA
    'axona   *ruw-ì*|
    brother   big-1SG
    'my elder brother'

This is a replication of the pattern of pronominal suffix attachment in the Iranian languages of the Sanandaj region:

(563) Gorani
    *kətēb-a*³   *sīyāw-akay=m*
    book-CPM   black-DEF.OBL=1SG
    'my black book'

(564) Kurdish
    xwašk-a   *gawra-(a)ka=m*
    sister-CPM   big-DEF=1SG
    'my elder sister'

In some isolated cases in the JSNENA corpus the adjective is placed before the head. This is found where the adjective is evaluative, i.e. expressing the subjective evaluation by the speaker rather an objective description of the head, e.g.

(565) JSNENA
    'ayza   *kasbī*   *hùl*   *ta-noš-ox.*|
    good   earning   give.IMP.SG   to-self-2SG.M
    'Take the good earnings for yourself.' (A:103)

---

3 The morpheme *-a* is a linker used in the structure of what MacKenzie (1961a) calls "open compound NP". For *-a* to occur the head noun must be definite.

Likewise, in Kurdish an evaluative adjective can appear before the noun.

(566) Kurdish
gawra māḷ 'big family, the house of a well-known man'
juwān-a žən 'beautiful woman'

6.7.2 Adverbial modifiers

6.7.3 Modifiers of active participles

In JSNENA an active participle may be modified by a noun expressing the undergoer of the activity it relates to. This noun is regularly placed before the participle, e.g.

(567) JSNENA
xola garšāna 'rope puller'
syāmē tarṣāna 'maker of shoes'

These replicate the pattern of corresponding constructions in Iranian:

(568) Kurdish
saʿāt sāz 'watchmaker'
čopī kēš 'figure dancer' [lit. one who pulls figure dancing]

6.7.4 Non-attributive modifiers

6.7.4.1 kulē

This quantifier is used with plural or singular head nouns with the sense of 'all'. The particle may be used without any nominal being directly dependent on it. In most cases it has 3pl. reference, e.g. (569.c):

(569) JSNENA
   a. *kúlē hūlāē lā-làxlē yē-lū.*|
       all Jews side-each_other COP.PST-OBL.3PL
     'All the Jews were (living) side by side.' (A:44)
   b. *ʾata kúlē ʿolām xīrtē=ya pūḷè.*|
       now all world become.PTCP.SG.F=COP.3SG.F money
     'Now the whole world has become money.' (A:55)

c. *kúlē màst=yē-lū.*|
   all   drunk=COP.PST-OBL.3PL
   'They were all drunk.' (A:54)

Example (570) shows the use of an identical sounding quantifier with a plural noun in Kurdish. In Kurdish *kull=ē* should be analysed as the quantifier plus the Persian *ezafe* particle *=ē* (cf. Persian *koll=ē*). This seems to be a loan from Persian, which in turn borrowed it from Arabic. It is possible that the JSNENA quantifier, which is of Aramaic etymology, is imitating the pattern of this Persian construction with *ezafe*. Evidence for this is the fact that the final *-ē* in the JSNENA is not stressed, as is the case in the Persian construction. Several NENA dialects have a final *-ē* or *-ə* vowel on this quantifier and it has been argued that this is a fossilised vestige of a 3sg.m pronominal suffix, e.g. Ch. Urmi *cullə* (Khan 2016, vol. 1, 243). The suffix of JSNENA form *kúlē* may have had the same historical background but has now been reanalysed as the *ezafe* linking particle. The Persian *ezafe* is used with several other JSNENA particles.

(570) Kurdish
   kull=ē hamro-akān rəžyà   bān zawī.|
   all-EZ pear-DEF.PL pour.PST.3SG on   earth
   'All the pears were spread on the earth.'

6.7.4.2 tamām 'all'

This loanword from Persian, ultimately of Arabic origin, is used before definite singular nouns with the sense of 'the whole of' or plural definite nouns with the sense of 'all'. It is normally connected to the noun by the Persian *ezafe* particle, e.g.

(571) JSNENA
   tamām=ē *ʿolằm*| *ḥasrat-ềf   ləbla=y.*|
   whole=EZ   world envy-3SG.M take.PTCP.SG.M=COP.3SG.M
   'The **whole** world became envious of him.' (A:97)

The corresponding particle in Kurdish appears without an *ezafe* particle and exhibits a shift of *m > w*, which is a feature of Kurdish historical phonology. This further indicates that JSNENA *tamām* is a loan from Persian, in which it is used with *ezafe*.

(572) Kurdish
   tuwāw *mantaqa jàm   a-ka-n.*|
   whole   region   addition IND-do.PRS-3PL
   'They gather **all** the people from that region.'

6.7.4.3 xēt 'other'

The invariable modifier *xēt* of JSNENA is used to express 'other' both in the sense of 'different' and in the sense of 'additional'. The form *xēt* can also be used adverbially, e.g. (575.c):

(573) JSNENA
    a. xa-nafar-**xēt**   šər-wā-la   bāqa   'axon-àf⌐
       one-CLF-other   send.PST-PSTC-3SG.F to   brother-3SG.F
       'She sent **another** person to her brother.' (A:18)
    b. xa-'axóna   **xēt**-àf⌐   čəkma   šoġlè   hīt-ē.⌐
       one-brother   other-3SG.F several jobs   EXIST-OBL.3SG.M
       '**Another** brother of hers has several jobs.' (A:6)
       là   šóq-wa   **xēt**   ẓólm   hol-ī̀-lēf.⌐
       NEG   allow.PRS.3SG.M-PSTC other   injustice do.PRS-3PL-OBL.3SG.M
       'He did not allow him **any more** to suffer injustice.' (A:109)

As indicated in §4.10.1, the invariable form of JSNENA *xēt* is likely to have arisen by it being matched with the invariable Kurdish modifier *tər*. This Kurdish modifier has the sense of 'different', and 'additional'.

(574) Kurdish
    dāna=y   **tər**   tè̀,⌐   har   pāwšà̀-yk,⌐   àw=īš
    CLF=EZ   other IND.come.PRS.3SG EMPH king-INDF   3SG.DIST=ADD
    a-kož-ē⌐
    IND-kill.PRS-3SG
    '**Another** person comes, another king, he kills him too.'

When, however, the Kurdish word is used adverbially, it has an augment and has the form *ītər* (575). JSNENA has not replicated this bound augment prefix but has rather extended the meaning of the inherited form *xēt* to include the meaning of *ītər*. This is a case, therefore, of a preference being given to extension of meaning of unbound inherited elements in JSNENA over the replication of bound elements in the model Iranian language.

(575) Kurdish
    ītər   nà-tānē   bēt=a
    no.longer   NEG-can.PRS-3SG SBJV.come.PRS.3SG=DRCT
    am   bar-aw⌐
    DEM.PROX front-POST
    'He can **no longer** come to this side.'

6.7.4.4 har, har čī 'each, every'

In JSNENA the Iranian particle *har* is occasionally used as a modifier of singular nouns with the sense of 'each', e.g.

(576) JSNENA
har   xānawādē   ta-nòš-ēf,| har   ᴴməšpaḥaᴴ   ta-nòš-ēf,|
each family   for-self-3SG.M each family   for-self-3SG.M
g-ēzəl-wa| xa-dāna   tórta   šaqə̀l-wā-la.|
IND-go.PRS.3SG.M-PSTC   one-CLF   cow   take.PRS.3SG.M-PSTC-OBL.3SG.F
'Each family, each family went in their turn and bought a cow.' (A:81)

The phrase *har-čī* is also used as a quantifier with the same sense, e.g.

(577) JSNENA
har-čī   məltè| ḥasràt   ləbla=y   bā-ēf.|
each   nations   jealousy take.PTCP.SG.M=COP.3SG.M   in-3SG.M
'Each of the nations became jealous of him.' (A:95)

The particle *har* in JSNENA is also used in various other contexts as a phasal aspect marker 'still' and as an emphatic particle that can generally be translated as 'just', e.g.

(578) JSNENA
a. ta pəlgà-lēlē| xa-sā'at bar   pəlga-lēle yatù-wa,| har
   to half-night   one-hour   after half-night sit.PRS.3SG.M-PSTC still
   qàrē| har   'ay-ḥasàb   k-ól-wā-lē.|
   read.PRS.3SG.M   still this-accounting IND-do.PRS.3SG.M-PSTC-OBL.3SG.M
   'He would sit until midnight, an hour after midnight, still reading and doing the accounts.' (A:100)
b. har-'axa   tamāšà   k-ol-əx-wa.|
   just-here look   IND-do.PRS-1PL-PSTC
   'We were just looking.' (A:12)
c. har   mangol dòa|
   just   like   OBL.that
   'just like that one' (B:51)

Kurdish *har* has a similar range of functions, including, for example, the quantifier 'each', phasal aspect particles with the senses of 'only', 'no longer' (with negated verbs), 'still', and an emphatic particle in various contexts (579.b) and (579.c). When the particle was introduced into JSNENA, therefore, it retained most of the functions that it had in Iranian:

(579) Kurdish
    a. *har ēwāra-y dawrēš-ē tē.*|
        each evening-INDF dervish-INDF IND.come.PRS.3SG
        'Every evening a dervish comes.'
    b. *hàr Waḷkna waryā=s.*|
        EMPH PN conscious=COP.3SG
        'Only Waḷkna is awake.'
    c. *dawḷamàn=t a-kāt=aw*| *har šwānì̀=š*
        rich=2SG IND-do.PRS.3SG=TELIC EMPH shepherdhood=ADD
        ma-ka.|
        PROH-do.IMP.2SG
        'That will make you rich. Do not shepherd sheep anymore.'
    d. *harčì̀ kār-a a-zān-am.*|
        each job-DEF? IND-know.PRS-1SG
        'I know (can do) every job.'

6.7.4.5 čəkma 'how much/many?' 'several'

The JSNENA quantifier *čəkma* is used interrogatively in the sense of 'how much/many?' (580.a). It can also be used as a non-interrogative indefinite quantifier with the sense of 'some', 'several' (580.b).

(580) JSNENA
    a. *čəkmà šanē ga-dóka xīrè̀=n?*|
        how_many years in-there be.PTCP.PL=COP.3PL
        'How many years were they there?' (B:1)
    b. *čəkma 'aksē ntē-nì-lan.*|
        some photographs take.PST-3PL-OBL.1PL
        'We took some photographs.' (A:29)

The equivalent quantifier in Gorani is *čən* /*čənna*. This can be used both as an interrogative quantifier and indefinite quantifier meaning 'some', 'several'. In (581.d) the quantifier has an exclamatory sense.

(581) Gorani
    a. *čən řò-ē zamāwana=d bē?*|
        how.many day-PL.DIR wedding=2SG COP.PST.3SG
        'How many days did your wedding last?'

b. *mārayī čənnà bē?*
   mariage.portion how.much COP.PST.3SG
   'How much was the marriage portion?'
c. *čən nafar-ē àmē lā=m.*
   several person-PL.DIR come.PST.3PL to=1SG
   'Some people came to me.'
d. *čənnà dasaḷāt=ē dunyāyī=š bē!*
   so.much power=EZ worldly=3SG COP.PST.3SG
   'So much worldly power he had!'

In Kurdish the cognate form *čan* is used with the same range of meanings.

(582) Kurdish
a. *čan-ē poḷ=ū māḷ=m=o xwàrd!*
   so.much-INDF money=and property=1SG=2SG eat.PST
   'You pillage my wealth so much!'
b. *haḷ-a-sē čan řož-ē wa řē-yā a-řò.*
   PVB-IND-stand.PRS-3SG some day-INDF in road-POST IND-go.PRS.3SG
   'He rose and took the road for several days.'

JSNENA *čəkma* appears to be a fusion of Gorani *čən* + native Aramaic *kma* 'how much' (*čən-kma* < *čəkma*). Most other NENA dialects outside of the Jewish Trans-Zab subgroup use the native particle *kma* (or phonetic variations thereof). So the native particle *kma* has not been replaced by a loanword but rather enhanced by fusion with it. The motivation for this may have been related to the emotional subjective sense of the particle in exclamatory contexts. The native particle had its salience enhanced by bonding together NENA and Iranian.

6.7.4.6 xančī 'some, a little'

The JSNENA quantifier *xančī* expresses the meaning 'some, a little'. It can also be used adverbially.

(583) JSNENA
a. *xančī 'àràq šatē-n-wa.*
   some arak drink.PRS-3PL-PSTC
   'They drank some arak.' (A:10)
b. *xančī nóš-ū doq-ī̀-wā-la.*
   a_little self-3PL hold.PRS-3PL-PSTC-OBL.3SG.F
   'They held themselves back a little.' (A:31)

The equivalent Iranian quantifiers are *čək-ē* in Kurdish and *kuč-ē* in Gorani, which are formed by the addition of the indefinite suffix *-ē* to the particles *čək*, and *kuč*. These particles are used in the same contexts as JSNENA *xančī*. It is likely that the initial *xa-* syllable in JSNENA *xančī* is the indefinite particle *xa*. The indefinite *xa* appears as the first syllable of various equivalent quantifiers attested in the NENA dialects, e.g. *xakma* (Ch. Ankawa, etc.), *xamka* (J. Amedia, etc.), *xapča* (J. Betanure, etc.), *xačča* (Ch. Urmi, etc.), *xa-čəkka* (Ch. Billin), *xa-qəṣṣa* (Ch. Peshabur, etc.), *xanawa* (Ch. Qaraqosh). The JSNENA form *xančī* may have arisen from a fusion of *xa* + Gorani *čən* and subsequent metathesis, i.e. *xačən* > *xančī*. This would correspond to the pattern of *xakma* (*xa* + *kma*), since Gorani *čən* corresponds to Aramaic *kma* as we have seen in §6.7.4.5. Some NENA dialects have the metathesised form *xamka*.

(584) Kurdish
    a. *čək-ē*   *nān-a*   *řàq=ī*   *dar*   *hāwərd.*|
        a.bit-INDF bread-CPM stiff=3SG PVB bring.PST
        'He took out a little stiff bread.'
    b. *baškam*   *čək-ē*   *kằr*   *Ø-ka-m.*|
        perhaps bit-INDF work SBJV-do.PRS-1SG
        'Perhaps I'll work a little bit.'

6.7.4.7 hīč

This Iranian particle is used as a negative modifier in constructions such as the following:

(585) JSNENA
     hīč   *məndīx*   *xēt*   *là*   *k-əxl-ēx-wa.*|
     nothing thing other NEG IND-eat.PRS-1PL-PSTC
     'We did not eat anything else.' (B:29)

It is found in the loaned phrase *hīč-kas* 'nobody', and may be used without any nominal being directly dependent on it:

(586) JSNENA
    a. *hīč-kas*   *šrāta*   *lìt-wā-lē.*|
        none-person lamp NEG.EXIST-PSTC-OBL.3SG.M
        'Nobody had a lamp.' (B:45)

b. 'aġlab=ē| təqna-xwārè̀| kē-hīč-mən-ū   la
   most=EZ beard-white REL-none-from-3PL NEG
   pīš-ī-wà| k-àē-wā-lū-o.|
   remain.PST-3PL-PSTC IND-know.PRS.3SG.M-PSTC-OBL.3PL-TELIC
   'He knew most of the old folk, none of whom were alive
   (by that time).' (B:63)

Likewise, in Iranian *hīč* is used either as a modifier of a nominal, or without the nominal.

(587) Kurdish
    a. *hīč* *bərā-yk*   *ītər*   *garak=ī*   *nà̀-wē.*|
       no   brother-INDF no.longer   be.necessary=3SG NEG- SBJV.COP.3SG
       'No brother wants him anymore.'
    b. *hīč*   *ma-yž-à!*|
       nothing PROH-say.PRS-IMP.2SG
       'Do not say anything!'
    c. *dərgā* *bo* *hīčka*   *bāz*   *nà-ka-n!*|
       door   for no.one   open   proh-do.PRS-2PL
       'Do not open the door to anybody!'

6.8 Comparative constructions

6.8.1 bīš

In JSNENA comparative constructions are generally formed by placing the particle *bīš* before an adjective or adverb. The item with which it is compared, if this is mentioned, is introduced by the preposition *mən* or *ta-*, e.g.

(588) JSNENA
    a. *'axon-ī*   *mən-xaləst-ī*   *bīš-ruwà=y.*|
       brother-1SG than-sister-1SG   more-big=COP.3SG.M
       'My brother is bigger than my sister.'
    b. *'ay* *xamušta* *ta-do*   *xamušta* *bīš-rabtè̀=y-a.*|
       this apple   than-OBL.that apple   more-big=COP-3SG.F
       'This apple is bigger than that apple.'

The particle *bīš* does not occur in the current state of the Iranian languages of the Sanandaj region. It is, however, abundant in classical Gorani poetry, where it has the forms *bīš*, *fēš*. The particle still occurs in a few contexts in the Gorani dialect of Gawrajū, spoken near Kermanshah, where its function is unclear.

(589) Gawrajū Gorani
ē bīš,   alāna na   dūstdāštan wan=ē.
INTJ CMPR? Now   NEG.COP.3SG love   in=3SG
'Eh, there was, there is no love in it (their marriage).'
(Mahmoudveysi et al. 2012, 171)

6.8.2 bīš-zoa, bī-zoa

In JSNENA the modifier *zoa* is combined with the comparative particle *bīš* or *bī*, which is a contracted form of *bīš*. The form *zoa* is a contracted form of *zoda* (< *zawda*). The /d/, which has weakened by the Zagros /d/ effect in JSNENA, is preserved in other dialects, e.g. J. Arbel *bī-zoda*, Ch. Barwar *bīz-zawda*, Ch. Urmi *buš zoda*. JSNENA *bī-zoa* matches Kurdish *ba-zīyāw* 'more' in function and is similar in phonetic form.

JSNENA *bī-zoa* is placed either before or after nouns. When placed before nouns it has the sense of 'more of' the quantity expressed by the nominal, e.g.

(590) JSNENA
bīš-zoa nāšē   ʾəstəqbāl   k-ol-ī-wa   ta-laxà.|
more   people acceptance IND-do.PRS-3PL-PSTC   than-here
'More people used to accept (this) than here.'

When the modifier is placed after the noun in JSNENA, it has the sense of 'more of', 'more than' or 'more by' the quantity expressed by the nominal. This pattern is the pattern of the corresponding construction with *ba-ziyāw* in Kurdish:

(591) JSNENA
ʾagar kiló   bī-zóa xar-ā-wa   mast-akḛ̀,| là
if   kilo   more   become.PRS-3SG.F-PSTC   yoghurt-DEF NEG
darē-wā-l-ó   tʷk-àf.|
pour.PRS.3SG.M-OBL.3SG.M-TELIC   place-3SG.F
'If the yoghurt turned out to be more than a kilo, he did not pour it back.'
(A:79)

(592) Kurdish
kīlo-ē ba-zīyāw gòšt=ī sand-ū.|
kilo-INDF in-extra meat=3SG buy.PST-be.PST
'He had bought more than a kilo of meat.'

6.9 Conjoining of phrases

In JSNENA nominal phrases are normally conjoined by the particle *ū*, which is typically cliticised to the end of the first nominal. In lists of more than two items, the conjunctive particle is often attached to each item, e.g.

(593) JSNENA
'Astàxr=ū| *'Asfahằn=ū*| *Golpayagằn=ū*| *Hamadằn,*| *ənyēxāē*
PN=and PN=and PN=and PN=and these
pāētaxtè| *Kurēš=e Kabìr xīrē=n.*|
capitals PN PN be.PTCP.PL=COP.3PL
'Istakhr, Isfahan, Golpayagan and Hamadan, these were the capitals of Cyrus the Great.' (B:1)

The Iranian languages use a phonetically identical clitic with the same patterns of distribution:

(594) Kurdish
čărwā-(a)kà-yān=ū| *asḷahà=yān=ū*| *lībàs=yān*| *tēr-èt=ī*|
animal-DEF=3PL=and gun=3PL=and clothes=3PL IND.bring.PRS-3SG=3SG
la màḷ-ā dā=y-a-n-ē.|
at house-POST PVB=3SG-IND-put.PRS-3SG
'Their horses, guns, and clothes— he brings them (it) and puts them (it) in the house.'

On some occasions the particle is attached also to the final item in the list, which gives a sense of open-endedness, e.g.

(595) JSNENA
a. *jwanqē=ū pīrē=ū 'ənšē=ū gūrē=ū 'amēta kúlē*
young=and old=and women=and men=and together all
naqḷ-ī-wa.|
dance.PRS-3PL-PSTC
'Young and old, women and men all danced together.' (A:54)

b. *mēwa=ū   šīrnī=ū   'ēxa kúlē mtū-lū   rḗša*
   fruit=and sweets=and   this all   place.PST-OBL.3PL on
   mèz=ū|
   table=and
   'They laid out on the table fruit, sweets and so forth.' (D:26)

(596) Gorani
   mən   zāro-ḷà   b-ēn-ē,| ətə   hamīšay   p-ā
   1SG   child-DIM   be-PSTC-1SG well   always.OBL   in-DEM.DIST
   kaš=ū   ko-na   šwàna   b-ēn-ē=ū| pāḷē
   mountain=and mountain-POST   shepherd be.PRS-PSTC-1SG=and shoes
   dəřyè=ū| gəjī-la=ū   bē-gəjī=ū.|
   torn.F=and   shirt-DIM=and   without-shirt=and
   '(When) I was a small child, I was a shepherd in those mountains, wearing torn shoes and small shirt, and shirtless.'

Alternatively, the open-endedness of the list may be expressed by using a proximate demonstrative pronoun at the end, e.g.

(597) Kurdish
   šằm   xor-yā=ū| kārakàr=ū| nūkàr=ū| kəlfàt=ū|
   dinner eat.PRS-PASS.PST=and worker=and servant=and maid=and
   amānà| hìčka   na-mā.|
   DEM.PL.PROX   no.one   NEG-remain.PST.3SG
   'The dinner was eaten. None of the workers, servants, maids, and so forth remained in the palace.'

The JSNENA conjunction *ū* has an Aramaic etymology (*w-*). In earlier Aramaic, however, this conjunctive particle was a proclitic attached to the front of words, e.g. Syriac *w-malkā* 'and the king'. The pattern of enclisis at the end of words developed through a process of matching it to the Iranian conjunction and its prosodic patterns.

Note the grammatical subject agreement of the conjoined phrase in (598), in which the tightly-knit phrase 'drum and pipe' is treated as singular:

(598) JSNENA
   dohól=ū   zorna   lapl-ā-wa   qàmē.|
   drum=and   pipe   fall.PRS-3SG.F-PSTC in_front
   'The drum and pipe went in front.' (A:10)

Likewise, the tightly-knit phrase 'pipe and drum' and other tightly-knit phrases have 3sg agreement in the Iranian languages (599–600). The conjunction *ū*, however, is usually absent in such phrases:

(599) Gorani
ēmà¹ sərnā duhoḷ=mā harằm=ā.¹
1PL pipe drum=1PL taboo=COP.3SG
'We—pipe and drum are taboo for us.'

(600) Kurdish
nằnčāy=mān xwārd.¹
bread.and.tea=1PL eat.PST.3SG
'We ate breakfast.' (*nānčāy* <*nān=ū čāy* 'bread and tea')

6.10 Numerals

In JSNENA, numerals above 'one' are combined with plural nouns.

(601) JSNENA
yāla trèsar šənē,¹ xamsar šənē dòq-wā-lē.¹
boy twelve years fifteen years hold.PRS.3SG.M-PSTC-OBL.3SG.M
'A boy twelve years old (and one) fifteen years old would observe it (the fast).' (B:44)

In Gorani numerals above 'one' are, likewise, combined with plural nouns.

(602) Gorani
a. yàrē řo-ē=ū,¹ dəvè řo-ē=ū,¹ pànja řo-ē=ū¹
three day-PL.DIR=and two day-PL.DIR=and five day.PL.DIR=and
'ənnà zamāwənē kar-ēn-mē.¹
this.much wedding.PL.DIR do.PRS-PSTC-1PL
'Three days, two days, five days . . . we used to hold wedding ceremonies this long.'
b. pànj řo-ē hurpř-ēn-mē.¹
five day-PL.DIR dance.PRS-PSTC-1PL
'We would dance for five days.'

In Kurdish, however, a singular noun occurs after numerals, e.g.

(603) Kurdish
haft kanìšk a-w-ən.⎪
seven girl   IND-be.PRS-3PL
'They were seven girls.'

The existence of the pattern of using plural nouns after numerals above 'one' in Gorani helped preserve the JSNENA pattern, which was inherited from earlier Aramaic, although it differed from that of Kurdish.

6.11 Adverbial expressions

6.11.1 Temporal adverbials

In JSNENA several nominals are used with the function of adverbials without an explicit marking of their relation by a preposition. These are mainly temporal expressions, some of which are presented below.

(604) JSNENA
a. 'āna xa-yoma rēša sūsì=yē-lī.⎪
   I   one-day   on   horse=COP.PST-OBL.1SG
   'One day I was on a horse.' (A:17)
b. 'āna 'o-lēlē   la-zì-na-o   bēla.⎪
   I   that-night NEG-go.PST-1SG.M-TELIC house
   'I did not go back home that night.' (A:26)
c. lēlawāē k-ē-wa-ò.⎪
   nights   IND-come.PRS.3SG.M-PSTC-TELIC
   'He would return in the evenings.' (A:99)

Similarly, in the Iranian languages of Sanandaj temporal expressions are used adverbially without explicit marking of their relation by a preposition.

(605) Kurdish
a. šaw-ē   kuř-akān=ī   bàng kərd.⎪
   night-INDF boy-DEF.PL=3SG   call do.PST
   'One night he summoned his sons.'

b. ēwāra   tḕ-n=aw| kanīšək-al   das
   evening IND.come.PRS-3PL=TELIC   girl-PL   hand
   a-ka-n=a   gì̄rī.|
   IND-do.PRS-3PL=DRCT   cry
   'In the evening when they returned, the girls started to cry.'
c. jā   aw   řož-a   xwa=y   a-kāt=a   naxwàš|
   well DEM.DIST day-DEM1 REFL=3SG   IND-do.PRS.3SG=DRCT   ill
   'That day he feigned illness.'

6.11.2 Spatial adverbials

In JSNENA the spatial adverbs *laxa* 'here' and *doka* 'there' can themselves take the spatial preposition *ga-* 'in', e.g. *ga-laxa, ga-doka*.

Similarly, the Kurdish spatial adverbs *ēra* 'here', *öna* 'there' can take the spatial preposition *l-* 'in', e.g. *l-ēra, l-öna*.

The spatial adverbs in Gorani are *ēga* 'here', *āga* 'there'. They can, likewise, take the spatial preposition *č-* 'in', e.g. *č-ēga, č-āga*. Alternatively, to express spatial adverbs 'here' and 'there' in Gorani, the preposition *č-* 'in' attaches to the proximate and remote demonstrative: *čē* 'here', *čā* 'there'.

6.11.3 Destinations

In JSNENA nominals without prepositions sometimes occur with verbs of movement to express the place of destination.

(606) JSNENA
a. nāšē   g-ēz-ī-wa-o   bēlà=ū|
   people IND-go.PRS-3PL-PSTC-TELIC   house=and
   'The people went back home.' (A:49)
b. nóš-ū   labl-ī-wā-lē   'orxèl.|
   self-3PL take.PRS-3PL-PSTC-OBL.3SG.M   mill
   'They would themselves take it to the mill.' (A:58)

Similarly in the Iranian languages destinations are often not marked by prepositions (607–608):

(607) Gorani
 lūā-ymē   Kərmāšǎn.|
 go.PST-1PL PN
 'We went to Kermanshah.'

(608) Kurdish
 a-gayt=a   məḷk   pəḷə̀ng.|
 IND-reach.PRS.3SG=DRCT property Leopard
 'He arrives at the territory of the leopard.'

6.11.4 Manner adverbials

In JSNENA some adjectives are used adverbially to express the manner of action. This applies especially to the evaluative adjective ʾayza 'well', e.g.

(609) JSNENA
 ḥašt-akē   ʾayzà   wīl-ā-lox.|
 done-DEF   good   do.PST-3SG.F-OBL.2SG.M
 'You have done the job well.'

Likewise, in the Iranian languages of the Sanandaj region an evaluative adjective can be used adverbially to express the manner of action (613–614).

(610) Gorani
 ʾāl   wē=š   čàrma   kard=o.|
 well   REFL=3SG white   do.PST=TELIC
 'He whitened himself well.'

(611) Kurdish
 mən   čāw=əm   xās   hanà̀   nā-kā|
 1SG   eye=1SG   well   vision   NEG-do.PRS.3SG
 'I can't see well.'

6.12 Summary

The syntax of nominals in JSNENA exhibits a high degree of convergence with Iranian, summarised in Table 72:

6.12 Summary

Table 72: Nominal syntax of JSNENA and the type of convergence it shares with contact languages.

Feature attested in JSNENA	Type of convergence with Iranian		Section
	Gorani	Kurdish	
Indefinite specific referent with discourse salience is marked by the indefinite marker	total	total	§6.2.1
Temporal adverbials referring to specific time are marked by the indefinite marker	total	total	§6.2.2
Indefinite specific referent without discourse salience is not marked by the indefinite marker	total	total	§6.2.3
Non-specific indefinite is not usually coded by the indefinite marker	partial	partial	§6.2.4
Heavy coding of nominal with the indefinite marker to mark discourse salience	total	total	§6.2.5
The indefinite marker is used with units of measure	total	total	§6.2.6
The indefinite suffix -ēk is used on nominals that are modified by evaluative adjectives	partial	total	§6.2.11
Numeral 'one' can be used pronominally	total	partial	§6.2.9
The definite marker is used in anaphoric contexts	total	total	§6.3.1
The definite marker is used in associative contexts	total	total	§6.3.2
The definite marker marks a discourse boundary	total	total	§6.3.3
Demonstrative pronouns have a discourse presentative function	total	total	§6.4.4
Demonstrative pronouns can be used in both deictic and anaphoric functions		total	§6.4
Proximate demonstrative forms mark main protagonists	total	total	§6.4.2
Remote pronouns are used with neutral anaphoric function	total	total	§6.4.2

Finally, the syntax of attributive and non-attributive modifiers in JSNENA exhibits different layers of convergence with Iranian languages, summarised in Table 73.

Table 73: The syntax of attributive modifiers in JSNENA and its convergence with similar phenomena in contact languages.

Features attested in JSNENA	Main contact language	Section
Use of 3SG pronominal suffix on adverbials	G./K./P.	§6.6
Occasional use of ezafe -ē on noun-adjective combinations	Persian	§6.7.1
A pronominal suffix is placed on the adjective rather than the head noun	G./K./P.	§6.7.1
Occasional placement of adjectives before nouns in NPs	G./K.	§6.7.1

Table 73 (continued)

Features attested in JSNENA	Main contact language	Section
The non-attributive modifier *kulē* has the structure *kul* + *ezafe* -*ē*	Kurdish	§6.7.4.1
The non-attributive modifier *tamām* is used with the *ezafe* particle	Persian	§6.7.4.2
The invariable modifier *xēt* expresses 'other' both in the sense of 'different' and 'additional'	G./K.	§6.7.4.3
The particle *har* expressing phasal aspect marker 'still' and being emphatic	G./K.	§6.7.4.4
čəkma 'how much, how many' being used also in the sense of 'several'	G./K./P.	§6.7.4.5
The particle *bīš*	Gorani	§6.8.1
Numerals above 'one' are combined with plural nouns	Gorani	§6.10
The spatial adverbs 'here' and 'there' can take spatial preposition *ga*- 'in'	G./K.	§6.11.2

7 The syntax of verbs

7.1 Introductory overview

The verb forms in JSNENA match closely in their function those of the corresponding forms in the Iranian contact languages. In both JSNENA and Iranian the realis form of present-stem verbs expresses (i) imperfective aspectual functions such as progressive and habitual, (ii) perfective aspectual uses such as narrative present and performative and (iii) future tense reference (deontic and predictive future).

In JSNENA the irrealis form of the present-stem verb matches Iranian in its functions. It can, moreover, be combined with the Iranian particles *bā* and *baškam* to express speaker-oriented modality and epistemic modality respectively.

A conspicuous feature of mutual convergence between JSNENA and Gorani in the realm of verbal syntax is the combination of present-stem verbs with past-converter particles (*-wa* in JSNENA and *-ēn* in Gorani) to express past realis forms denoting aspectual meanings such as progressive and habitual. The combination of the past converter suffix with irrealis present-stem forms is used in a wider range of contexts in JSNENA than in Gorani.

Another area of convergence between JSNENA and Iranian, and indeed with Turkic languages of Western Asia, is the 'indirective' function of the perfect, i.e. its functional extension to express perfective events in the past which the speaker has not witnessed or which occurred in the remote past.

The passive is formed morphologically in JSNENA, Gorani and Kurdish. In a few cases, JSNENA replicates the formation of the passive in Persian by combining the inflected ingressive auxiliary 'become' with the resultative participle. As for the distribution of passive constructions, in JSNENA as well as in Gorani and Kurdish they are restricted to verbs in which the grammatical subject of the passive verb is an affectee of the action and undergoes a clear change of state. In addition, JSNENA matches Iranian in expressing the passive by the use of an active construction with an impersonal 3pl. subject.

In JSNENA telicity distinctions of verbs are expressed by the post-verbal particle *-o*. This morpheme and its function are borrowed from Gorani.

JSNENA partially matches Gorani in patterns of differential object marking (DOM). In JSNENA DOM occurs with both present-stem and past-stem verbs through either cross-indexing on the verb or flagging the direct object by the preposition *hal*. In Gorani DOM is limited to present-stem constructions and is expressed by inherited case suffixes on the direct object. In both JSNENA and Gorani DOM occurs on maximally salient objects, i.e. definite human objects or inanimate objects that have discourse salience.

7.2 The function of verb forms derived from the present stem

In JSNENA the irrealis of present-stem verbs is unmarked. The realis is distinguished from the irrealis by the addition of the prefixed particle *k-*, but this is restricted to a small number of verbs with weak initial radicals in their root. Many JSNENA verbs do not distinguish formally between moods (§5.5 & §5.6)

In the Iranian languages of the region, present-stem verb forms distinguish realis and irrealis moods by different prefixed particles. The particle expressing realis mood is *(d)a-* in Kurdish and *m-* in Gorani. Unlike Kurdish *(d)a-* the use of *m-* is not regularised in Gorani, i.e. only a subset of verbs take it (cf. §5.5). The particle expressing irrealis mood is *b-* in both languages. Here again, the use of *b-* is not regularised in Gorani (cf. morphology section §5.6). In principle, therefore, no formal distinction between moods is available for a considerable number of Gorani verbs. Furthermore, in Kurdish the irrealis particle *b-* does not usually appear on the light verb of a complex predicate, e.g. *ka kār Ø-kāt* 'that he work'.

7.2.1 Function of irrealis forms

In general terms, it can be said that an irrealis present-stem form in JSNENA expresses an action that has not been realised in the perception of the speaker but is only potential or an action whose reality is not fully asserted by the speaker. It is used in a variety of contexts. Most of its occurrences are found in syntactically subordinate clauses, though it is occasionally also used in main clauses. It is neutral as to aspect, in that it expresses either a perfective aspect, referring to one punctual event, or an imperfective aspect, referring to an unbounded situation.

7.2.1.1 Speaker-oriented modality in main clauses

When the form occurs in main clauses, it usually expresses 'speaker-oriented modality', according to the terminology of Bybee et al. (1994, 177–79), i.e. it expresses some kind of directive imposing the will of the speaker on addressees. These include, for example, requests for permission, hortative expressions encouraging somebody to action, and optative expressing a wish or hope of the speaker. Such verbs can be used in all persons. The Iranian particle *bā* is optionally used before the JSNENA irrealis form to express speaker-oriented modality.

(612) JSNENA
    a. *bā-'āna   hēz-n-o   bāqa   Farànsa.*ˈ
        HORT-1SG   go.PRS-1SG.M-TELIC   to   PN
        'Let me go back to France.' (B:62)
    b. *hēz-ēx   dokà.*ˈ
        go.PRS-1PL   there
        'Let us go there.'
    c. *bā-laxa   zəndəgî   hol-ēt.*ˈ
        HORT-here   life   do.PRS-2SG.M
        'May you live a life here.' (A:107)

In the Iranian languages of the Sanandaj region, the irrealis mood also expresses speaker-oriented modality in main clauses. The particle *bā* often appears in such constructions.

(613) Gorani
    a. *bā   qəsa=y   qaymî̀=t   pay   Ø-kar-ū.*ˈ
        HORT   talk=EZ   old=2SG   for   SBJV-do.PRS-1SG
        'Let me tell you about the past.'
    b. *bā   ì̀   gozā   waš-ē   Ø-kar-ū.*ˈ
        HORT   DEM.PROX   pot.PL.OBL   nice-PL   SBJV-do.PRS-1SG
        'Let me make these (into) nice pots.'

(614) Kurdish of the Sanandaj region
     bā   làm   kēfā   řož
     HORT   in.DEM.PROX   mountain-POST   day
     *na-ka-yn=aw.*ˈ
     NEG.SBJV-do.PRS-1PL=TELIC
     'Let us not stay the night in this mountain.'

First person verbs in such constructions can be used as a self-hortative in situations where the speaker is alone. This applies, for example, to (613.b) above.

    In JSNENA, this speaker-oriented modal form is found in prayer formula expressions such as the following:

(615) JSNENA
    a. *'əlha   manìx-le.*ˈ
        God   grant_rest.PRS.3SG.M-OBL.3SG.M
        'May God grant him rest.' (A:14)

b. *'əlha šoq-la ta-dāak-èf.*|
   God keep.PRS.3SG.M-OBL.3SG.F to-mother-3SG.M
   'May God preserve his mother.' (A:17)

Similar prayer formulas in Iranian with the irrealis form are the following:

(616) Kurdish
   xwā 'àfw=ī Ø-kā bāwk=əm|
   god pardon=3SG SBJV-do.PRS.3SG father=1SG
   'My father, may God pardon him . . .'

(617) Gorani
   hasūrà=m,| *xwā 'afwa=š Ø-kar-à'*| *wāč-ì̀.*|
   father.in.law=1SG god pardon=3SG SBJV-do-IMP.2SG say.PRS.2SG
   'My father-in-law—God, may you pardon him—whom you talk about.'

(618) Gorani Luhon
   řoḷa xuđā ja mən=ət bə-sān-o!
   child god from 1SG=2SG SBJV-take.PRS.3SG
   'Child! May God take you from me!'
   (MacKenzie 1966, 66)

In JSNENA the irrealis form is used in some main clause questions with speaker-oriented modality inviting permission from the addressee, e.g.

(619) JSNENA
   a. *mà ho-na?*|
      what do.PRS-1SG.M
      'What should I do?' (C:11)
   b. *hēz-an-ò?*|
      go.PRS-1SG.F-TELIC
      'Should I go back?' (C:12)

Parallel constructions from Iranian are:

(620) Kurdish
   day ča b-kà-yn?|
   well what SBJV-do.PRS-1PL
   'What should we do then?'

(621) Gorani Luhon
ətər   ba   čēš   bə-žīw-mē?
now   with   what   SBJV-live.PRS-1PL
'Now, what shall we live on?'
(MacKenzie 1966, 68)

7.2.1.2 Epistemic modality in main clauses

In some contexts the irrealis form of a present-stem verb in JSNENA has epistemic modality, indicating that the speaker is not fully committed to the truth of what the verb is expressing. This is the case, for example, after the particle *baškam/baška* 'perhaps':

(622) JSNENA
  a. baškam   līšān-an   la-hē-la   qaṭè.
     perhaps   language-1PL   NEG-come.3SG.M-OBL.3SG.F   cut.PRS.3SG.M
     'Perhaps our language will not become extinct.' (E:75)
  b. xa   brāta   ma'arəfì   wīl-ā-lū   bā-ēf¹
     one   girl   acquaintance   do.PST-3SG.F-OBL.3PL   to-3SG.M
     kè¹   baška   xlūlà=č   hol.¹
     REL   perhaps   wedding=ADD   do.PRS.3SG.M
     'They introduced a girl to him, whom he could perhaps marry.' (D:17)

Likewise in Iranian, the particles *baška* 'perhaps, if only', *baḷkū* 'maybe', *gās* 'maybe' combine with the verb in the irrealis mood to express epistemic modality.

(623) Gorani
  baškom   ī   kənāčè̌=m-a¹   dəḷ=əš   bə-lo
  perhaps   DEM.PROX   girl.OBL.F=1SG-DEM1   heart=3SG   SBJV-go.PRS.3SG
  yū-i̯=šā.¹
  one-OBL.M=3PL
  'Perhaps my daughter would fall in love with one of them.'

(624) Gorani Luhon
  baḷkū   xuđā   zāroḷēw=ət   bə-đo   pana.
  perhaps   god   kid.INDF=2SG   SBJV-give.PRS.3SG   to
  'Perhaps God will give you a child.'
  (MacKenzie 1966, 66)

(625) Kurdish
    a. *baškam   čək-ē   kār   Ø-kà-m.*ˈ
        perhaps bit-INDF work   SBJV-do.PRS-1SG
        'Perhaps I'll work a little bit.'
    b. *gàs   b-ē-m.*ˈ
        AUX   SBJV-come.PRS-1SG
        'I may come.'

Note also the idiomatic usage of the irrealis form in JSNENA in constructions with the verb *'-m-r* 'to say', such as (626), which express a possible rather than a real event:

(626) JSNENA
    *ga-dokà*ˈ   *rāba   nāšȅ*ˈ   *rāba   hamr-ēt   dawlaman*
    in-there   many   people   many   say.PRS-2SG.M   rich
    *hawȅ-n,*ˈ   *dawlaman   là=yē-lū.*ˈ
    be.PRS-3PL   rich   NEG=COP.PST-OBL.3PL
    'There you would say that many people were rich, but they were not rich.' (A:55)

A parallel to this construction is found in the following example from Gorani. The irrealis form of the verb 'to say' appears in a construction which conveys a possible event.

(627) Gorani
    *mumkə̀n=ā*ˈ   *to   kas-ē   payà   Ø-kar-ī*
    possible=COP.3SG   2SG   person-INDF   visible SBJV-do.PRS-2SG
    *Ø-wāč-ī*ˈ   *ja   tāyfa=w   naqšbandī   b-ò.*ˈ
    SBJV-say.PRS-2SG from   family=EZ   PN   be.SBJV-3SG
    'It is possible that you will find someone (and) say he is from the family of Naqshbandi.'

7.2.1.3 Generic relative clauses

In JSNENA and Iranian the irrealis form is used in relative clauses qualifying heads that have generic reference rather than specific referents. This can be classified as epistemic modality, since the speaker is not committed to the truth of the existence of a member of the set of entities denoted by the head for the relative clause.

(628) JSNENA
    a. *har-kas*   *hē*   *laxa* *pūḷḕ*
       every-person come.PRS.3SG.M here money
       k-əw-n-ēf.|
       IND-give.PRS-1SG.M-3SG.M
       'I shall give money to whomsoever comes here.'
    b. *ba-tafawot=ē*   *nāš-akḕ,*| *čəkma*
       in-difference=EZ people-DEF how_many
       nafarē-hīt-wā-lū   *xāla* *'axl-ī̀.*|
       people-EXIST-PSTC-OBL.3PL food eat.PRS-3PL
       'According to the different (numbers) of people, how many people they had who eat food.' (B:17)

(629) Kurdish of the Sanandaj region
    har-kà   *bə-ř-ē*   *Sü* *čāwkāḷ*
    whoever SBJV-go.PRS.3SG PN light.brown.eye
    a=y-kož-ē|
    IND=3SG-kill.PRS.3SG
    'Sü Chawkal will kill whoever goes (there).'

(630) Gorani
    har-kàz   *bə-l-o*| *Ø-war-ò*| *hìč-kas* *ma-wāč-o*
    whoever SBJV-go.PRS-3SG SBJV-eat.PRS-3SG no.one NEG-say.PRS-3SG
    čēš   *Ø-kar-ī?*|
    what IND-do.PRS-2SG
    'Whosoever goes there, (and) eats (from the fruit), nobody is going to ask "What are you doing (here)?"'

7.2.1.4 Subordinate complements

The irrealis form in JNENA and Iranian occurs in subordinate clauses that are complements of various verbs and expressions when the action of the verb in the subordinate clause is as yet unrealised relative to the time of the main verb. The form is used not only with present tense main verbs, but also with main verbs that have past time reference, in which the form takes the past reference of the main verb as its deictic centre.

In a number of cases the subordinate clause with the irrealis verb is a complement of a verb or expression expressing some kind of deontic modality (wish, intention, permission, obligation). This would fall into the category of 'agent-oriented modality' according to the terminology of Bybee et al. (Bybee, Perkins, and Pagliuca

1994, 177), which involves the existence of internal or external conditions on the agent with respect to the completion of the action, e.g.

(631) JSNENA
    a. g-bē-n   dasgīrān-ỉ   šarbat   hamy-a   bāq-ī.ˈ
       IND-want.PRS-1SG.M betrothed-1SG sherbet bring.PRS-3SG.F to-1SG
       'I want my betrothed to bring sherbet to me.' (A:23)
    b. ḥāz   k-ol-ī-wa   hē-n   bēla   dīdan
       desire IND-do.PRS-3PL-PSTC come.PRS-1SG.M house OBL.1PL
       yat-ỉ   ʾonyēxāē.ˈ
       sit.PRS-3PL they
       'They wanted to come to our house and sit.' (A:80)
    c. k-əm-na   ta-roxàˈ   laxà   hamy-ā-lax.ˈ
       IND-say.PRS-1SG.M to-wind here bring.PRS-3SG.F-OBL.2SG.F
       'I shall tell the wind to bring you here.' (E:49)

(632) Gorani
    ēmē   garak=mā   bay-mē   ī
    1PL be.necessary=1PL SBJV.come.PRS-1PL DEM.PROX
    kināčē=t-a   Ø-wȧz-mē.ˈ
    girl.F.OBL=2SG-DEM1 SBJV-marry.PRS-1PL
    'We would like to come and ask for your daughter's hand in marriage.'

(633) Kurdish
    bənyāwəm   hàz   a-kāˈ   tuwāšā=y   juwānỉ   māyīn-aka
    human.being liking IND-do.PRS.3SG watching=EZ beauty mare-DEF
    Ø-kā.ˈ
    SBJV-do.PRS.3SG
    'One would like to watch the beauty of the mare.'

(634) Gorani
    haz   na-kar-ēn-ē   pēsa   mə̀n   Ø-wīn-ī.ˈ
    liking NEG-do.PRS-PSTC-1SG such 1SG SBJV-see.PRS-2SG
    'I did not want you to see me like this.'

In JSNENA, deontic necessity is often expressed by the impersonal verbal expression *g-bē* 'it is necessary' or its past form *g-bēwa* 'it was necessary'. In such impersonal constructions the agent-oriented modality is transferred to the subject of the embedded complement clause, e.g.

(635) JSNENA
 a. *g-bē*   *hē-t-o*   *bāqa*   *'aḥrà.*
    IND-want.PRS.3SG.M   come.PRS.2SG.M   to   town
    'You must come back to the town.' (A:6)
 b. *g-bē*   *xlūlà*   *hol-ī.*
    IND-want.PRS.3SG.M   wedding   do.PRS-3PL
    'They must marry.' (A:31)

This JSNENA construction matches the Kurdish invariable 3s auxiliary *a-šē* and the cognate Gorani invariable form *mə-šo*:

(636) Kurdish
  mən   *a-š-ē*   *bə-ř-əm*   *àm*   *šans*   *xwa=m-a*
  1SG   IND-AUX-3SG   SBJV-go.PRS-1SG   DEM.PROX   fortune   REFL=1SG-DEM
  payā   *Ø-ka-m.*
  visible   SBJV-do.PRS-1SG
  'I should go to find my fortune.'

(637) Gorani
  šəma   *mə-š-ò*   *bə-l-dē*   *pay*   *Kaljī.*
  2PL   IND-should.PRS-3SG   SBJV-go.PRS-2PL   to   PN
  'You should go to Kalji.'

It should be noted, however, the corresponding impersonal construction in the Kurdish of the Sulemaniyya region is *a-bē*, which is phonetically more similar to JSNENA *g-bē*.

Similarly the irrealis form of the verb in JSNENA and Iranian is used to express deontic possibility (permission), e.g.

(638) JSNENA
 a. *là*   *šoq-wa*   *xēt*   *ẓolm*   *hol-ī-l-ēf.*
    NEG   allow.PRS.3SG.M-PSTC   other   harm   do.PRS-3PL-to-3SG.M
    'He did not allow them to harm him any more.' (A:109)
 b. *'ījāza*   *hul-mu*   *kē-'axnī*   *xlūlà*   *hol-ēx*
    permission   give.IMP-PL   that-we   wedding   do.PRS-1PL
    'Give permission for us to hold the wedding.' (A:31)

(639) Gorani Luhon
    m-āz-ū   *bə-l-ī*   *pay*   *yāna-y=šā.*
    IND-let.PRS-1SG   SBJV-go.PRS-2SG   to   house-OBL=3PL
    'I permit you to go to their house.'
    (MacKenzie 1966, 60)

The irrealis form is used in clauses expressing purpose. In some cases these are introduced by subordinating particles such as JSNENA *kē* (borrowed from Persian) and *bāqa* and Kurdish *bā*. Indeed JSNENA *bāqa* can be regarded as a direct formal and functional match of Kurdish *bā* (see §5.7.1). In many cases purpose clauses are placed after the clause on which they are dependent without a linking conjunction, e.g.

(640)   JSNENA
     a.   *lēl-ēf-o*   *zīl-ēx*   *bāqà*ˈ   *šīrīnì*   *hamē-x-o.*ˈ
         night-3SG.M-TELIC   go.PST-1PL   to   sweets   fetch.PRS-1PL-TELIC
         'On that very night we went to fetch the sweets.' (A:19)
     b.   *tor*   *matə-x-wa*   *ba-dawrē*   *qàt*ˈ
         net   put.PRS-1PL-PSTC   in-around   bed
         kē   *paša*   *là*   *hē*   *loʿa.*ˈ
         that   mosquito   NEG   come.PRS.3SG.M   inside
         'We would put a net around the bed so that mosquitoes did not come inside.'

(641)   Kurdish
     a.   *b-ē-n*   *bā*   *bə-č-īn*   *kīšì*   *qawr-aka=y*
         SBJV-come.PRS-2PL   OPT   SBJV-go.PRS-1PL   guard   tomb-DEF=3SG
         *b-a-yn.*ˈ
         SBJV-give.PRS-1PL
         'Come, so that we go to guard his tomb.'
     b.   *bḕ*ˈ   *bə-xaf-à*   *bā*
         SBJV.come.PRS.2SG   SBJV-sleep.PRS-IMP.2SG   OPT
         mən   *bə=t-xwà-m.*ˈ
         1SG   SBJV=2SG-eat.PRS-1SG
         'Come, lie down so that I can eat you.'

(642)   Gorani
     Ø-mərḍ-a   *bā*   *màč-ēwa=t*   *Ø-kar-ū!*ˈ
     SBJV-wait.PRS-2SG.IMP   OPT   kiss-INDF.F=2SG   SBJV-do.PRS-1SG
     'Wait, so that I may give you a kiss!'

The irrealis form is also used in a variety of other subordinate complement clauses in which the action or situation expressed in the subordinate clause is potential in relation to the main verb rather than one that actually exists. It is commonly attested, for example, in clauses that are the complement of expressions of ability, which are formed in JSNENA by the verb 'to come' and L-suffixes (*kē-lī* 'I am able', *kē-wā-lī* 'I was able' etc.):

(643) JSNENA
    a. *k-ē-lī*   *hè̱-na.*|
        IND-come.PRS.3SG.M-OBL.1SG   come.PRS-1SG.M
        'I can come.'
    b. *'ò*   *k-ē-wā-lan*   *'axl-ēx.*|
        that   IND-come.PRS.3SG.M-PSTC-OBL.1PL   eat.PRS-1PL
        '*That* we could eat.' (B:29)
        'axnī noš-an là k-ē-wā-lan|
        we   self-1PL   NEG   IND-come.3SG.M-PSTC-OBL.1PL
        xalw-akē hamè̱-xī-lē.|
        milk-DEF   bring.PRS-1PL-OBL.3SG.M
        'We could not fetch milk ourselves.' (A:63)

This JSNENA construction matches the pattern of a corresponding Kurdish construction in which ability is expressed by combining the preposition *lē* 'in, from' with the verb 'to come'.

(644) Kurdish
    a. *lē=m*   *nā-yē*   *bə-ř-əm.*|
        at=1SG   NEG.IND-come.PRS.3SG   SBJV-go.PRS-1SG
        'I cannot go.' [lit. it does not come to me to go]
    b. *lē=t*   *tē*   *wā*   *Ø-kà-y.*|
        at=2SG   IND.come.PRS.3SG   DEIC   SBJV-do.PRS-2SG
        'You are able to do such.'

The Iranian languages also use an inflected verb to express ability:

(645) Kurdish
     a-twān-əm   *àm*   *žən=t-a*   *bēr-m=aw.*|
     IND-can.PRS-1SG   DEM.SG.PROX   wife=2SG-DEM1   SBJV.bring.PRS-1SG=TELIC
     'I can bring this wife of yours back.'

(646) Gorani
  mà-tāw-o   hīč=šā   pana   wāč-o.|
  NEG-can.PRS-3SG   nothing=3PL   to   SBJV.say.PRS-3SG
  'He couldn't say anything to them.'

The irrealis form is used in complements of expressions of 'fearing', e.g.

(647) JSNENA
  'ana   zadē-na   la-bā   hḕ.|
  I   fear.PRS-1SG.M   lest   come.PRS.3SG.M
  'I fear lest he come.'

(648) Kurdish
  la   nāw   am   āsyāw-a   dā-∅-niš-əm| na-wā
  in   inside   DEM.PROX   mill-DEM   PVB-SBJV-sit-1SG   lest
  jānawar-ē   čət-ē   b-ē   bə=m-xwả.|
  animal-INDF thing-INDF   SBJV-come.PRS.3SG   SBJV=1SG-eat.PRS.3SG
  'I shall stay in this mill lest an animal, a thing, comes and eats me.'

The particle used in such constructions in JSNENA *la-bā* 'lest' appears to be a replication of the corresponding Kurdish particle. In Sanandaj Kurdish this has the form *na-wā*. In Sulemaniyya Kurdish, however, it has the form *na-bā*, which may have been the model for JSNENA when the ancestors of the JSNENA-speakers were in the Suleminayya region. In JSNENA the Iranian negator *na* has been replaced by the JSNENA negator *la*, resulting in the form *la-bā*.

The irrealis form is used after the temporal conjunctions with the sense of 'before' or 'until' in clauses describing an event that has not yet happened from the perspective of the main clause, e.g.

(649) JSNENA
  qamē   do=č   xlúla   hol-ī́| kúlē   bē
  before   OBL.3SG.M=ADD   wedding   do.PRS-3PL   all   without
  batūlà=yēn.|
  virgin=COP.3PL
  'Before they marry, they are all non-virgins.' (A:50)

(650) Kurdish
  bar   la-(a)wa   b-ḕ-n| a-yž-ə̀n   pē=mān.|
  before   of-DEM.DIST   SBJV-come.PRS-3PL   IND-say.PRS-3PL to=1PL
  'Before they come, they will tell us.'

7.2.1.5 Conditional constructions

In JSNENA and Iranian the irrealis present stem form is sometimes used in the protasis and/or the apodosis of conditional sentences, which refer to possible rather than real situations, e.g.

(651) JSNENA
   a. 'agar   mən-day   ləxma   'axl-ětun,ˈ   kās-axún
       if   from-OBL.this   bread   eat.PRS-2PL   stomach-2PL
       bazy-à.ˈ
       burst.PRS-3SG.F
       'If you eat any of this bread, your stomach will burst.' (B:23)
   b. 'agar   hē-t   bēl-iˈ   ləxmà   k-əw-n-ox.ˈ
       if   come.PRS-2SG.M   house-1SG bread   IND-give.PRS-1SG.M-2SG.M
       'If you come to my house, I shall give you bread.'

(652) Kurdish
   agar   aw   kằr-a   anjām   bayˈ
   if   DEM.SG.DIST   job-DEM   accomplish   SBJV.give.PRS.2SG
   bə-tān-ì̀,ˈ   a-twān-əm   àm   žən=t-a
   SBJV.can.PRS-2SG   IND-can.PRS-1SG   DEM.SG.PROX   wife=2SG-DEM
   bĕr-m=aw.ˈ
   SBJV.bring.PRS-1SG=TELIC
   'If you can do the task, I can bring this wife of yours back.'

(653) Gorani
   žənya-bē=š   ka   agar   gač
   hear.PST.PTCP.M-be.PSTC=3SG   COMPL   if   chalk
   Ø-war-òˈ   dang=əš   nāsək-tàr   Ø-b-o=wa.ˈ
   SBJV-eat.PRS-3SG   voice=3SG   soft-CMPR   IND-be.PRS-3SG=TELIC
   'He had heard that if he ate chalk, his voice would be softer.'

7.2.2 Realis form of the present-stem verbs

The realis form of a verb has a number of converging functions in JSNENA and Iranian, which we discuss in what follows.

7.2.2.1 Progressive

The realis form may express an imperfective progressive aspect, i.e. an activity that is taking place in the present or, in the case of stative verbs, a state that holds at the present moment ('actual present'), e.g.

(654) JSNENA
    a. *'ata   k-xəl.*|
       now   IND-eat.PRS.3SG.M
       'Now he is eating.'
    b. *lēka   g-ēz-ə̀t?*|
       where   IND-go.PRS-2SG.M
       'Where are you going?'
    c. *xa-gora   g-bē-lòx.*|
       one-man   IND-want.PRS.3SG.M-OBL.2SG.M
       'A man wants (to see) you.' (A:20)

(655) Kurdish
    bo   könà   a-ř-ī   bərā?|
    to   where   IND-go.PRS-2SG   Brother
    'Fellow, where are you heading?'

(656) Gorani
    a. *čī̀   Ø-gəraw-ī?*|
       why   IND-cry.PRS-2SG
       'Why are you crying?'
    b. *čə̀š   m-āč-ī?*|
       what   IND-say.PRS-2SG
       'What are you saying?'
    c. *Rahmān-ī   mə-žnās-ū.*
       PN-OBL.M   IND-know.PRS-1SG
       'I know Rahman.'

In JSNENA when the realis form expresses the progressive, it is sometimes preceded by the infinitive of the verbal root of the verb:

(657) JSNENA
    šatoē   šatə̀-na.|
    drink.INF   drink.PRS-1SG.M
    'I am drinking.'

As remarked already in §5.5, this replicates the pattern of a progressive construction in Gorani in which an inflected realis form is preceded by a form composed of the present stem and the ending -*āy*. This is not the same form as the infinitive, but its ending resembles that of infinitives, which end in -*āy* or -*ay*, and it has been matched with the JSNENA infinitive in the progressive construction.

(658) Gorani
mə-řamāy   mə-řam-ū.
IND-run.ADV   IND-run.PRS-1SG
'I am running.'

(659) Gorani Luhon
har   ja   īsa-wa   wārāy   wār-o.
EMPH   from   now-POST   rain.ADV   rain.PRS-3SG
'It is raining already (even from now).'
(MacKenzie 1966, 50)

7.2.2.2 Habitual

The realis form in JSNENA and Iranian may express an imperfective habitual aspect, presenting a characteristic property of the subject referent. As is the case with habituals cross-linguistically (Carlson 2012; Boneh and Doron 2013; Boneh and Jędrzejowski 2019), this usage of the realis form typically expresses repeated eventualities. These constitute a set of an unspecified number of eventualities that occur at unspecified points of time. The speaker/writer does not have in mind specific events bound to specific points in time. It rather expresses a characteristic property of the subject. In principle the habitual has present tense reference, i.e. the deictic centre of the tense is the time of speaking, e.g.

(660) JSNENA
a. 'ay   šwāwa   dīdàn| g-ēzəl   șīwē
this   neighbour   OBL.1PL   IND-go.PRS.3SG.M   branches
mən-jangaḷ   k-mē   zabən-u.|
from-wood   IND-bring.PRS.3SG.M   sell.PRS.3SG.M-OBL.3PL
'This neighbour of ours goes and brings branches of wood from the woods and sells them.' (A:102)
b. Lēlangè̩   k-əmr-ex   'àxnī.|
PN   IND-say.PRS-1PL   we
'We say Lelange (for Purim).' (A:57)

c. *xa-məndìx=yē* | *kē pərčē komà*
one-thin=COP.3SG.M that hair Black
k-ol-ű. |
IND-do.PRS.3SG.M-OBL.3PL
'It is a thing that makes hair black.' (A:40)

(661) Gorani
a. *awaḷē-na doē žanī Ø-kīyān-à.* |
first.F-ADP two woman IND-send.PST-3PL
'First, they (i.e. the family of the boy) send two women (to the family of the girl).'
b. *ap-ī harī-a hamīša bàr Ø-bar-o*
with-DEM.PROX donkey.OBL.M-DEM1 always load IND-take.PRS-3SG
pay šār-ī=ū | *šār-ana Ø-wəraš-ò=š.* |
to city-OBL.M=and city-POST IND-sell.PRS-3SG=3SG
'Using this donkey, (the trader) keeps taking stuff to the city, and sells it in the city.'

(662) Kurdish
bafər bahār zū a-tāw-ềt=aw. |
snow spring quickly IND-melt.PRS-3SG=TELIC
'The spring snow melts quickly.'

It is used in JSNENA and Iranian with this aspect also to express the persistence of a habitual situation in constructions such as (663) and (664), which would be rendered in English by a perfect:

(663) JSNENA
ḥaq-ēx b-ay līšānà | *mən-dawra=ū dawrằn.* |
speak.PRS-1PL in-this language from-generation=and generations
'We have been speaking in this language for many generations.' (E:7)

(664) Kurdish
īmšaw dū-ằn=a | *ēma wa taraštà=w* | *wa kotàk* |
tonight two-PL=COP.3SG 1PL with cudgel=and with stick
a-wằ-yn la to. |
IND-give.PRS-1PL at 2SG
'It has been two nights that we have been beating you with cudgels and sticks.'

The realis form may take the past time reference of an adjacent past verb as its deictic centre. This is often the case in subordinate clauses, where the main clause has a past verb form, e.g.

(665) JSNENA
'ay baxta=ū 'ay gorà' baxēḷì labl-ī-wa l-day
this woman=and this man jealousy take.PRS-3PL-PSTC to-OBL.this
gora xēt kē' ba-day jora zəndəgī k-òl.'
man other who in-OBL.this way life IND-do.PRS.3SG.M
'The woman and the man were jealous of the other man who lived in this way.' (A:103)

(666) Kurdish
la awaḷ-aw wa=y zānī a-wà-n lē.'
at first-POST such=3SG know.PST IND-give.PRS-3PL at.3SG
'At the beginning he thought they would beat him.'

7.2.2.3 Narrative present

The realis form in JSNENA may be used to denote foreground events in a narrative. In such cases it presents the events as punctual with a perfective aspect and with their deictic temporal centre in the surrounding discourse. This type of construction typically occurs after the past time reference has been established by a preceding past verb form. It is particularly commonly used with verbs of 'saying', e.g.

(667) JSNENA
a. dāak-ī hīy-a Taràn' k-əmr-a ...
mother-1SG come.PST-3SG.F PN IND-say.PRS-3SG.F
'My mother came to Tehran and says ...' (A:5)
b. 'āna xa-yoma rēša sūsì=yē-lī' 'ay=ū
I one-day on horse=COP.PST-OBL.1SG she=and
xaləst-af rad xar-ì,' xaləst-af
sister-3SG.F passing become.PRS-3PL sister-3SG.F
k-əmr-a bāq-àf'
IND-say.PRS-3SG.F to-3SG.F
'One day I was on a horse. She and her sister pass by and her sister says to her ...' (A:17)

In Iranian the realis form of present stem verbs is frequently used to express sequential perfective events in narratives:

(668) Kurdish
ēwāra   tḕ-n=aw| kanīšək-al   das
evening IND.come.PRS-3PL=TELIC   girl-PL   hand
a-ka-n=a   gìrī.|
IND-do.PRS-3PL=DRCT   cry
'In the evening they returned (and) the girls started to cry.'

(669) Gorani
dubāra gḙl-ò=wa=w| har-akay   wəz-o
again   go.PRS-3SG=TELIC=and   donkey-DEF.OBL.M   put.PRS-3SG
tawḕḷa-(a)ka=w| čā   'əsrāhàt   kar-on| tā   sawày.|
stable-DEF=and   there rest   do.PRS-3SG till   tomorrow.morning
'Again, (the man) comes back (home) and puts the donkey in the stable. It rests there until the next day.'

The historical present is a development of the habitual usage of the realis form. As remarked, the habitual form expresses an unspecified number of repeated eventualities at unspecified points in time. These are repeated perfective, i.e. temporally-bounded, eventualities. The lack of specification allows a habitual form to express a single specific event at a specific point in time in narrative. In such cases the narrative context, typically a preceding past perfective verb, specifies the variables of number and time location, coercing its interpretation as a narrative form expressing a single specific event. This usage resembles the English historical present. It is important to note that this narrative realis form does not have present tense nor does it have imperfective aspect. Rather it is a past perfective, conditioned by the context. The same, it can be argued, applies to the English historical present, which is a simple present resembling a habitual rather than a progressive, and to the historical present used in narrative in other languages (Wolfson 1979; Schiffrin 1981; Carruthers 2012, 307), e.g. *John came home exhausted. He sits down and eats his dinner.* Since the aspect and tense of the narrative realis form are specified by the context, one of the effects of the use of the form in narrative is to express dependency on and cohesion with the verbal forms that express specific events in their semantic structure.

7.2.2.4 Performative
Another perfective use of the realis form in JSNENA and Iranian is to express the performative present, i.e. the action denoted by the verb is performed by the act of uttering it. These constructions are compatible, therefore, with the addition of 'hereby' in their translation into English, e.g.

(670) JSNENA
'āna   da'wat   k-o-n-ox   lēlē   patīrē
I   invitation IND-do.PRS-1SG.M-OBL.2SG.M   night   Passover
hal   laxà!|
until   here
'I (hereby) invite you to come here on the eve of Passover!' (A:57)

(671) Kurdish
a. à=w-ka-m=a   šā!|
    IND=2SG-do.PRS-1SG=DRCT   King
    'I (hereby) make you king!'
b. gəràw=tān   tak-ā   a-ka-m!|
    bet=2PL   with-POST   IND-do.PRS-1SG
    'I (hereby) bet against you.'

This also can be regarded as a development from the habitual semantics of the realis form expressing an unspecified set of eventualities. As with the narrative form discussed in the previous section, the context of use of the performative specifies the event variable and coerces it to be referring to a single time-bound event in the present. One may say that the event variable is specified by the act that is performed by the utterance of the speaker and witnessed by the hearer.

7.2.2.5 Future

The realis form in JSNENA and Iranian may be used with a future tense reference. In such cases it may have a perfective or imperfective aspect. Most cases attested in the text corpora are perfective and refer to a single specific event. It may be a deontic future expressing the intention of the speaker (672.a-c) or a predictive future with a third person subject (672.d):

(672) JSNENA
a. 'āna   k-ē-na   bāqa   'Isràyəl.|
    I   IND-come.PRS-1SG.M   to   PN
    'I shall come to Israel.' (C:3)
b. moraxaṣî   šaq-na=ū,| k-e-n-ò.|
    permission take.PRS-1SG.M=and   IND-come.PRS-1SG.M.-TELIC
    'I shall take leave and shall come back.' (A:7)
c. 'āna   jəns   k-əw-na   ba-'īl-òx|
    I   cloth   IND-give.PRS-1SG.M to-hand-2SG.M
    'I shall give to you some cloth.' (A:103)

d. *k-w-ī-lē*   *ʾəl-ĕf.*
   IND-give.PRS-3PL-obl.3sg.m   to-3SG.M
   'They will give it to him.'

(673) Kurdish
   a. *a-ř-əm*   *šans*   *xwà=m*   *xawar*   *a-ka-m=aw.*
      IND-go.PRS-1SG   luck   REFL=1SG   news   IND-do.PRS-1SG=TELIC
      'I will go away (and) awake my fortune.'
   b. *jā*   *mardəm*   *pē=mān*   *a-kàn-ən.*
      INTJ people   to=1PL   IND-laugh.PRS-3PL
      'People will laugh at us.'

(674) Gorani
   mə-l-o   *Hawrāmằn-ī.*
   IND-go.PRS-3SG   PN-OBL.M
   'He will go to Hawraman.'

7.2.3 Present-stem verbs with past converter suffix

In JSNENA the past converter suffix *-wa* is added to present-stem verbs to derive a number of past tense constructions, which have both realis past and irrealis past functions.

The past converter *-wa* of JSNENA is closely matched structurally and functionally by the Gorani past converter suffix *-ēn* (apparently derived from the Old Iranian participle ending *-ant*), which is attached to present-stem verbs in order to form a number of past tense constructions (§5.5).

7.2.3.1 Realis

7.2.3.1.1 Progressive
A realis present-stem form with the past converter suffix in JSNENA may be used to express an imperfective progressive aspect in the past. This is the case in (675) where the act of 'looking' is circumstantial and temporally overlapping with the actions expressed by the following perfective verbs:

(675) JSNENA
har-'ăxa   tamāšà   k-ol-əx-wa.| ... mən-lăḥāl
just-thus look   IND-do.PRS-1PL-PSTC   from-afar
'o-xīy-ā̀-lī.| mīr-ū   'ēa   xaləsta   Xanakḕ=ya.|
3SG-see.PST-3SG.F-OBL.1SG say.PST-OBL.3PL this   sister   PN=COP.3SG.F
'We were just looking on. . . . I saw her from afar. They said, "That is the sister of Xanaka."' (A:12–14)

In the following Gorani sentence the realis form of the verb with the past converter suffix -ēn combined with a non-finite form of the present stem expresses an imperfective progressive aspect in the past.

(676) Gorani
haḷāy   kalašīr-ē   wanāy   wan-èn-ē| 'ànna
still   rooster-DIR.PL   crow.ADB   crow-PSTC-3PL   that.much
zū   lūā.|
early   go.PST.3SG
'He went so early [to the garden] that the roosters were still crowing.'

7.2.3.1.2 Habitual
The realis present-stem form with the past converter suffix in JSNENA is most commonly used in the text corpus to refer to habitual actions in the past, e.g.

(677) JSNENA
a. g-ēz-ī-wa   bāqa   ḥamằm.|
   IND-go.PRS-3PL-PSTC   to   bath
   'They would go to the bath.' (A:36)
b. rāba   fāmīl   da'wat   k-ol-ī-wā-lē.|
   much   family   invitation   IND-do.PRS-3PL-PSTC-obl.3sg.m
   'They would invite a lot of family.' (A:33)

Likewise in Gorani the verb form in -ēn expresses a habitual action in the past:

(678) Gorani
a. pànj   řo-ē   hurpř-ēn-mē.|
   five   day-PL.DIR   dance.PRS-PSTC-1PL
   'We would dance for five days.'

b. mən=īč   frà   wē=m   gēr-ēn-ē=ū| fra
    1SG=ADD very   REFL=1SG   grab.PRS-PSTC-1SG=and very
    fīs-ē   kar-ə̀n-ē.|
    pretention-PL   do.PRS-PSTC-1SG
    'I used to boast about myself and show off.'

7.2.3.2 Irrealis

7.2.3.2.1 Main clauses

In JSNENA an irrealis present-stem form with the past converter suffix (*garəšwa*) is used to express a counterfactual situation in the past, generally expressing deontic modality, e.g.

(679) JSNENA
    a. mar   hə̀-x-wa.|
        HORT   come.PRS-1PL-PSTC
        'Let us suppose we had come.'
    b. maḥnəq-nà-wā-l-ēf!|
        throttle.PRS-1SG.M-PSTC-OBL-3SG.M
        'I could have throttled him!'

Likewise, in Gorani an irrealis form in *-ēn* is used to express a counterfactual situation in the past.

(680) Gorani
    ašyē   lu-ēn-ī.
    AUX.PST   go.PRS-PSTC-2SG
    'You should have gone.'

7.2.3.2.2 Conditional constructions

In JSNENA the irrealis present-stem form with the past converter suffix is used in conditional constructions referring to a habitual situation in the past. This usage of irrealis does not occur in Gorani.

(681) JSNENA
    'agar   xa-nafar   hēzəl-wa   ... bāqa   mārē   t^wkāna
    if   one-person   go.PRS.3SG.M-PSTC   to   owner   shop
    hamə̀r-wa| xa   kīlo   xēta   hol-ī̀,| mastà   hol-ī̀.|
    say.PRS-3SG.M-PSTC   one   kilo   other   do.PRS-3PL yoghurt do.PRS-3PL

'agar kīlo bī-zoa xar-ā-wa   mast-akẹ̀,ˡ là
if   kilo more   become.PRS-3SG.F yoghurt-DEF NEG
darē-wā-l-o   tʷk-àf.ˡ
pour.PRS.3SG.M-PSTC-3SG.F-TELIC place-3SG.F

'If somebody went . . . and said to a shop owner,
"Give me a kilo of such-and-such a thing, give me yoghurt," if the yoghurt
turned out to be more than a kilo, he did not pour it back.' (A:79)

The form is used also in counterfactual conditional constructions relating to the past, e.g.

(682) JSNENA
'agar 'alē-nā-wa   'āt   ga-laxè̱=t,ˡ
if   know.PRS-1SG.M-PSTC   you.SG in-here=COP.2SG.M
'āna dēr-nā-wa-ò.ˡ
I   return.PRS-1SG.M-PSTC-TELIC
'If I had known that you were here, I would have returned.'

In Gorani a counterfactual conditional construction is formed by the addition of the -ēn to the past stem.

(683) Gorani
āy   agar mən   'anna   laqà=m=əm
INTJ if   1SG   that.much   kick=1SG=1SG
na-gērt-ēn=ē   wano.ˡ
NEG-take.PST-COND=COP.3PL at
'Oh, only if I had not have cavilled at them that much.'

7.2.3.2.3 Generic relative clause
The JSNENA irrealis form is used in relative clauses that qualify heads with generic reference. This function of irrealis is not attested in Gorani.

(684) JSNENA
har-kas   hē-wā-lè̱ˡ
every-person come.PRS.3SG.M-PSTC-OBL.3SG.M
'whoever was able . . .' (A:57)

7.2.3.2.4 Subordinate complements

The JSNENA past irrealis is most commonly attested in subordinate clauses that are complements of past tense verbs and express actions that are unrealised at the time referred to by the main verb. The various types of irrealis function in this context parallel those of the *garəš* form.

(685) JSNENA
    a. *pīrè*[|]   *g-bē-wa*   *'emzà*   *hol-ī-wā-la.*[|]
        elders   IND-need.PRS.3SG.M-PSTC   signature   do.PRS-3PL-PSTC-OBL.3SG.F
        'The elders had to make a signature.' (A:48)
    b. *g-bē-wa*   *hēzəl-wa*   *ga-doka*
        IND-need.PRS.3SG.M-PSTC   go.PRS.3SG.M-PSTC   in-there
        noš-ēf   *dabəḥ-wā-lū-ò.*[|]
        self-3SG.M   slaughter.PRS.3SG.M-PSTC-OBL.3PL-TELIC
        'He had to go there and slaughter them himself.' (A:73)

The following example shows the parallel construction in Gorani.

(686) Gorani
        pīr-akē   *mə-šyēm*   *zū*   *wət-ēn-è.*[|]
        old-DEF.PL.DIR   IND-should.PST   early   sleep.PST-COND-3PL
        'The elders had to sleep early.'

In conclusion, the JSNENA irrealis is wider in function than the Gorani irrealis. For example, the JSNENA irrealis present-stem form with the past converter suffix is used in conditional constructions expressing counterfactual conditions whereas in corresponding Gorani constructions the past stem with -*ēn* is used (§7.3.2). Unlike JSNENA, Gorani does not use the past irrealis form for expressing habitual past (§5.5) and in relative clauses with generic heads (§7.2.3.2.3).

7.3 The function of verb forms derived from past stems

7.3.1 Past-stem forms without the past converter affix

7.3.1.2 Past perfective

In JSNENA verb forms derived from past stems without the past converter affix (e.g. *grəš-lē* transitive 'he pulled', *smīx-Ø* intransitive 'he stood') are most commonly used in the text corpus to refer perfectively to specific time-bound events at a particular time in the past. They are typically used to express the sequential events of a narrative, e.g.

(687) JSNENA
    a. *ʾərq-ā-la*   *zīl-a*   *tīw-a*   *ga-xa-ʾotằq.*|
        flee.PST-3SG.F-OBL.3SG.F   go.PST-3SG.F   in-a-room
        ta-noš-af   *tar-akē*   *məzr-a*   *ba-rēša*
        to-self-3SG.F   door-DEF   close.PST-OBL.3SG.F   on-head
        nòš-af.|
        self-3SG.F
        'She fled and sat in a room. She closed the door behind her (literally: upon her).' (A:22)
    b. *zīl*   *lāg-èf=ū*| *mē-lē*
        go.PST.3SG.M   side-3SG.M=and   bring.PST-OBL.3SG.M
        mtù-lē=ū|
        put.PST-OBL.3SG.M=and
        'He went to him, brought it (the cloth) and put it down (for him).' (A:105)

Similarly, in the following Gorani example the past forms are past perfectives expressing sequential events.

(688) Gorani
     bard-ằ=šā   *āḷəf*   *kanē.*| *dřè̱=šā*   *pana*   *kan-ā,*|
     take.PST-1SG=3PL   fodder   mow.INF   prickle=3PL   by   pluck.PST-1SG
     āḷə̣f=šā   *pana*   *pēt-ā*| *dəmằ=w*   *ānay*|
     fodder=3PL   by   gather.PST-1SG   after=EZ   DEM.DIST.OBL.SG
     jằ   *žan-ēkī=šā*   *dā-(ā)nē=ū.*| *àrd-a=m.*|
     then   woman-INDF.OBL=3PL   give.PST-1SG=and   bring.PST-3SG.F=1SG
     'They took me to mow the grass. They made me cut down prickles. They made me gather the fodder. Only then did they give me a woman (my wife) and I took her.'

The form may express a single event that had an inception and an end in the past but had a duration that extended over a long period of time. This applies, for example, to the event 'we worked together' in (689) which would have lasted several weeks:

(689) JSNENA

> hīyē-n-o zī-na tīwna lāg-èf=ū|
> come.PST-1SG.M-TELIC go.PST-1SG.M sit.PST-1SG.M side-3SG.M=and
> bəxlē ḥašta wīl-àn=ū| ḥašt-an 'ayztà=yē-la=ū|
> together work do.PST-OBL.1PL=and work-1PL good=COP.PST-3SG.F=and
> rāba 'ayztà=yē-la=ū.|
> very good=COP.PST-3SG.F=and
> 'I went back and stayed with him. We worked together. Our work (together) was good, very good.' (A:28)

This usage of past perfective is found also in Gorani, as seen in the following example:

(690) Gorani

> dəwè sāḷ-ē luwā-yme sarwàzī=mā karḍ.|
> two year-PL.DIR go.PST-1PL military.service=1PL do.PST
> 'We went away for two years (and) did military service.'

The extended period may overlap with other events described in the surrounding discourse. In (691), for example, the adverbial clause 'when I got married' is intended to set the temporal frame for the period of all the events relating to the wedding that are narrated in the subsequent discourse:

(691) JSNENA

> 'āna waxt=ē xlūla wīl-ì| ga-Taràn=yē-lī
> I time=EZ wedding do.PST-OBL.1SG in-PN=COP.PST-obl.1sg
> noš-ī.| dāak-ī hīy-a Taràn| k-əmr-a...
> self-1SG mother-1SG come.PST-3SG.F PN IND-say.PRS-3SG.F
> 'When I married, I myself was in Tehran. My mother came to Tehran and said...' (A:5)

A corresponding construction with the past perfective in Gorani is shown in example (692):

(692) Gorani

> waxt=ē žànī=m ārd-a| yawāšē yāna=m
> when=EZ woman=1SG bring.PST-3SG.F well house=1SG
> nà-bē| jīyà bī-ānē.| ja zəmsàn bē
> NEG-COP.PST.3SG separate be.PST-1SG in winter COP.PST.3SG

jīyā	bī-ā|	luwā-(ā)nē	hìč=əm	na-bē|,
separate	be.PST-1SG	go.PST-1SG	nothing=1SG	NEG-COP.PST.3SG
čanū	žanī	luā-ymē	yānà=mā	gērt kərāha.|
with	woman	go.PST-1PL	house=1PL	take.PST rent

'When I got married (I took a wife), well, I didn't have a house. I left the house of my father (lit. I became separate). It was winter. I left the family of my father and I went away. I did not have anything. Together with my wife, we rented a house.'

In (693.a-b) the past perfective is used to express a completed event that sets the frame for a following habitual action:

(693) JSNENA
  a. bar-dèa| 'ay-marāsəm   tǐm,| nāšē
     after-OBL.that this-ceremony   finish.PST.3SG.M people
     g-ēz-ī-wa-o   bēlà=ū|
     IND-go.PRS-3PL-PSTC-TELIC   house=and
     'After that, when the ceremony had finished, people went home.' (A:49)
  b. 'o-lēlè̀=č| pəsra tǐm,| məšxà
     that-night=ADD meat   finish.PST.3SG.M dairy_food
     k-əxl-ī-wa.|
     IND-eat.PRS-3PL-PSTC
     'On that night (when) the meat was finished, they used to eat dairy food.' (A:63)

A corresponding construction in Gorani is seen in the following example:

(694) Gorani
  yawāšē wahằr   āmā| ətə   lu-ēn-ē   kār
  well   spring   come.PST.3SG   then   go.PRS-PSTC-1SG   work
  kar-èn-ē.|
  do.PRS-PSTC-1SG
  'Then Spring came and I would go (and) work.'

7.3.2 Past-stem forms with the past converter affix

7.3.2.1 Past perfect

In JSNENA the most common function of past-stem forms with the past converter affix *wa* (e.g. *grəš-wā-lē* transitive, *smīx-∅-wa* intransitive) is to express a state that held in the past as a result of a prior action remoter in the past. Such past perfect constructions are used to present a resultant state as the background of a past action or situation, perfective or imperfective, in the adjacent context.

(695) JSNENA
    a. *xəmē=ū*   *xmālè*⎮   *həl-kald-ū*
        fathers-in-law=and mothers-in-law OBL-bride-3PL
        la-xaē-n-wa   *'əqrà,*⎮   *yani*   *kald-akē*   *hamēša*
        NEG-see.PRS-3PL-PSTC so_much it_means bride-DEF always
        rēš-af   *ksè̄-wā-la.*⎮
        head-3SG.F cover.PST-PSTC-3SG.F
        'The fathers-in-law and mothers-in-law did not see their bride very much, because the bride had always covered her head.' (A:3)
    b. *tʷkānē* *ràba*   *hīt-wā-lē*⎮   *hī-wā-lē*
        shops   many EXIST-PSTC-OBL.3SG.M give.PST-PSTC-OBL.3SG.M
        ba-'ijārà.⎮
        in-rent
        'He had many shops, which he had rented out.' (A:7)

This usage in JSNENA differs from the Iranian languages of the region, in which the past perfect is expressed by a resultative participle and past copula, which contains the past converter *-ē(n)* in Gorani (§5.11.6):

(696) Gorani Luhon
    a. *čūn xāsa=š*   *karda-bē*   *īsa*   *maxloq=īč*
        as   goodness=3SG do.PTCP.M-be.PRS.PSTC now people=ADD
        čanī=š   *xās*   *b-ē.*
        with=3SG good be.PRS-PSTC
        'As he had done good, so the people were good to him.'
        (MacKenzie 1966, 74)
    b. *č-āwaḷ*   *pādšā zāna-bē=š*   *ka*
        from-beginning king know.PSTP-be.PRS.PSTC =3SG COMP
        kənāčakē=š   *dəḷ=əš*   *īnā*   *ba hama-y-o.*
        girl-DEF.F=3SG heart=3SG exist.PTCL to PN-OBL.M-POST
        'From the beginning the king had known that his daughter's heart was set on Hama.'
        (MacKenzie 1966, 74)

(697) Kurdish
döšaw   am   ān-ayl-a   dāyk=əm   čằy-k=ī
last.night DEM.PROX   time-PL-DEM1   mother=1SG   tea-INDF=3SG
dam   kərd=ū| čāy=mān   a-xwȧrd.|
mouth   do.PST=COP.PST   tea=1PL   IPFV-eat.PST

'Last night around this time my mother had diffused tea. We would drink tea.'

If an intransitive verb expresses a non-dynamic state or a telic actionality, i.e. one that expresses an action with an inherent non-dynamic endpoint, the JSNENA past perfect is used to express an enduring state in the past that is an observable property of the subject of the verb. This is seen in (698), which contains past perfects of the verbs *p-y-š* 'to remain, to remain alive' (non-dynamic state) and *s-m-x* 'to stand up' (telic with non-dynamic endpoint). These enduring states typically overlap temporally with other actions in the surrounding context:

(698) JSNENA
'o-waxtara   Xanaka   pĭš-wa.|
that-time   PN   remain.PST.3SG.M-PSTC

'At that time Xanaka was alive.' (A:15)

'axnī   jwanqē   smīx-əx-wa   ga-ḥawšà.| xa-'əda   jwanqē,
we   youngsters   stand.PST-1PL-PSTC   in-courtyard a-few   youngsters
barūxawāl-ī,   smīx-əx-wa   ga-ḥawšà.| har-'axa   tamāšà
friends-1SG   stand.PST-1PL-PSTC   in-courtyard just-thus   look
k-ol-əx-wa.| xa-'əda   blānè̀| smĭx-ī-wa.| . . . mən-laḥāl
IND-do.PRS-1PL-PSTC   a-few   girls   stand.PST-3PL-PSTC   from-afar
'o-xīy-ȧ-lī.|
3SG-see.PST-3SG.F-OBL.1SG

'We youngsters were standing in the courtyard. We, a few youngsters, my friends, were standing in the courtyard. We were just looking. A few girls were standing there. . . . I saw her from afar.' (A12–14)

Corresponding past perfect constructions in the Iranian languages in the region are expressed by a resultative participle and past copula, as in (700), which denotes an enduring state:

(699) Gorani Luhon
kənāčē   ja   marāq=ū   hama-y-ana   rangzard-a   w   za'îf-a
girl   from longing=EZ   PN-OBL.M-POST   pale-F   and weak-F
bīē-bē.
be.PST.PTCP.F-be.PRS.PSTC.3SG
'The girl had become pale and weak from longing for Hama.'
(MacKenzie 1966, 74)

7.3.2.2 Indirective

In a number of cases the JSNENA *grəšwālē* or *smīxwa* forms express a past perfective action rather than an enduring resultant state. Such a perfective action may be sequential to a preceding action. The *grəšwālē* or *smīxwa* forms are used in this way in contexts where the speaker has not directly witnessed the action in question but has only received a report about it, i.e. they are evidential in function. Here the term 'indirective' is used for this phenomenon (see §5.11.3). This is exemplified in (700), in which the speaker narrates a conversation between his future wife and her sister which he himself did not hear but must have been reported to him later:

(700) JSNENA
k-əmr-a   bāqa   baxt-ỉ| k-əmr-a   'ēa   brona
IND-say.PRS-3SG.F   to   wife-1SG   IND-say.PRS-3SG.F   this   son
Jahàn=yē.| xīra=y   ba-'afsàr.| 'ay=əč
PN=COP.3SG.M   become.PTCP=COP.3SG.M to-officer   son=ADD
mīr-wā-la   'əlha šoq-la   ta-dāak-èf| 'ajab
say.PST-PSTC-3SG.F God   keep.IMP.SG-3SG.F to-mother-3SG.M   wonder
bron-èk=yē.| 'ajab   zarîf=yē.|
boy-INDF=COP.3SG.M   wonder   handsome=COP.3SG.M
'She said to my wife, she said, "That is the son of Jəhān. He has become an officer." **She (I am told) said**, "May God preserve his mother, he is a wonderful boy, he is wonderfully handsome."' (A:17)

A similar use of the past perfect (expressed by a participle, and past copula which contains the past converter affix) in Gorani is seen in example (701). The speaker describes how it was reported to him that a decision had been made that he should go to the military service.

(701) Gorani
    zamāna=w šā-y, mən=ū hasan-ĩ⎪ tāza mən sənh=əm
    period=EZ PN-OBL.M 1SG=and PN-OBL.M just 1SG age=1SG
    šāngzà-na bē.⎪ īna čayxanà bē;⎪
    sixteen-POST COP.PST.3SG DEM.PROX.DIR tea.house COP.PST.3SG
    īna gə̀rd=əš čāyxana bē⎪ duaṣa yaraṣà
    DEM.PROX.DIR all=3SG tea.house COP.PST.3SG 200 300
    nafar-ē=š lu-ē-(ē)n=a.⎪ **wāta-bē=šā**...
    person-PL.DIR=3SG go.PRS-PSTC-3PL=to say.PTCP.M- be.PRS.PSTC=3PL
    fəḷān=ū fəḷa̍n⎪ Bāqī=ū ḥasan yò=šā gēl-mē
    such=and such PN=and PN one=3PL roll.PRS-1PL
    bə-l-o sarwāzī.⎪
    SBJV-go.PRS-3SG military.service
    'In the period of the Shah, Hasan and I . . . I had just turned sixteen. Here there were a lot of teahouses where 200, 300 people would gather. **They said (according to what was reported to me)**, "Bāqī or Hasan, we will send one of them to go to the military service."'

In (702) the Gorani narrator uses a past perfective at the beginning of the narrative for an event that he has witnessed or knows to be true. When, however, he relates the discussion between the participants for which he has no direct evidence, he switches to past perfects.

(702) Gorani
    dā=šā vana lūēn=a ogà⎪ **wāta-bē=šā**
    give.PST=3PL at go.PST.3PL=DRCT there say.PTCP.M-be.PRS.PSTC=3PL
    īna jarayà̀n=ā!⎪ ādī=č **wāta-bē**
    DEM.PROX.DIR story=COP.3SG OBL.3SG.M=ADD say.PTCP.M- be.PRS.PSTC
    day mə̀n Ø-tāw-ū.⎪
    well 1SG IND-can.PRS-1SG
    'They set off (and) went there. **They said (according to report)**, "The story is such." **He said (according to report)**, "Well, I am able (to help you)."'

7.4 The imperative

The imperative form is typically used perfectively to command a particular action to be undertaken or, with the negator, prohibits a particular action to be undertaken, e.g.

(703) JSNENA
    a. *mastà   ho-lī!*
       yoghurt give.IMP.SG-OBL.1SG
       'Give me yoghurt!' (A:79)
    b. *'ijāza   hul-mū   kē   'axnī   xlūlà   hol-ēx.*
       permission give.IMP-PL that we wedding DO.PRS-1pl
       'Give permission for us to hold the wedding.' (A:30)
    c. *la   škḕ!*
       NEG move.IMP.SG
       'Don't move!'

The imperative has the same function in Iranian languages of Sanandaj:

(704) Gorani
    a. *kar-à=š=va!*
       do.PRS-IMP-2SG=3SG=TELIC
       'Open it!'
    b. *mà-don-a=m!*
       PROH-talk.PRS-2SG=1SG
       'Don't talk to me!'

(705) Gorani Luhon
    lu-a   āga!
    go.PRS-IMP.2SG there
    'Go there!'
    (MacKenzie 1966, 61)

In JSNENA an imperative may be given added immediacy by combining it with the particle *dā-/də-*, e.g.

(706) JSNENA
    a. *dā-mar   xàē-na!*
       PTCL-say.IMP.SG see.PRS-1SG
       'Now tell (me), let me see!' (B:63)
    b. *də-maʿīn-ò!*
       PTCL-see.IMP.SG-TELIC
       'Look!' (B:82)

This is a borrowing from Kurdish, in which the particle *dā* adds immediacy to the imperative.

(707) Kurdish
    a. *dā*   *kučk-ē*   *bə-n-a*   *nāw*   *məšt=o!*
       PTCL   stone-INDF   SBJV-put.PRS-IMP.2SG   inside   fist=2SG
       'Put a stone into your fist!'
    b. *dā*   *bēsa*   *bēsà!*
       PTCL   SBJV-wait.PRS-IMP.2SG   SBJV-wait.PRS-IMP.2SG
       'Wait! Wait!'

The JSNENA imperative form is used also to command iterative perfective events, e.g.

(708) JSNENA
    se-bāqa   *jangàḷ,*   *ʾīlān-akè*   *mē-lū,*
    go.IMP.SG-to   woods   trees-DEF   bring.IMP.SG-OBL.3PL
    zàbn-ū!
    sell.IMP.SG-OBL.3PL
    'Go to the woods. Bring pieces of wood and sell them!' (A:107)

7.5 The copula

7.5.1 The present copula

Predicates with the present copula express a state in the present. This may be a state that is a permanent property of a subject or a state that is a contingent property, i.e. one that is observable at the present moment but is not a permanent characteristic of the subject. The boundary between these two categories is often not clear-cut and depends on the subjective judgement of the speaker. In all cases the predication is indicative in that it refers to a real situation. Examples:

(709) JSNENA
    a. *ʾēa*   *brona*   *Jahằn=yē.*
       this   son   PN=COP.3SG.M
       'That is the son of Jahān.' (A:17)
    b. *ʾēa*   *xaləsta*   *Xanakè=ya.*
       this   sister   PN=COP.3SG.F
       'That is the sister of Xanaka.' (A:14)
    c. *fāmīl-ừ*   *rāba*   *ʿayza=y.*
       family-3PL   very   good=COP.3SG.M
       'Their family is very good.' (A:6)

d. *talga xwartḕ=ya.*|
   snow white=COP.3SG.F
   'Snow is white.'
e. *šwāw-an ga-bēlà=y.*|
   neighbour-1PL in-house=COP.3SG.M
   'Our neighbour is at home.'

Likewise, in Iranian the present copula expresses permanent states. Examples are from Gorani:

(710) Gorani
   mən kuř=ū Rahmān-ĭ=nā.|
   1SG son=EZ PN-OBL.M=3SG
   'I am Rahman's son.'

(711) Kurdish
   ama mantaqa=y šḕr=a.|
   DEM.PROX.3SG region=EZ lion=COP.3SG
   'This is the territory of the lion.'

(712) Gorani Luhon
   āđē kuř-ē=nē.
   3PL.DIR son-DIR.PL=COP.3PL
   'They are boys.'
   (MacKenzie 1966, 35)

Contingent states are expressed by default through an existential construction, consisting of a deictic particle (in Gorani) or the existential particle (in Kurdish) combined with the copula, cf. (713)-(714). In (715) from the Gorani corpus a present copula expressing a continguent state is attached directly to the predicate in an interrogative sentence.

(713) Gorani
   īnā=n yānà.|
   DEIC=COP.3SG.M home
   'He is at home.'

(714) Kurdish
    hā=m=a   mằḷ.|
    EXIST=COP.1SG=DRCT home
    'I am at home.'

(715) Gorani
    čə-kò=ndē| zāroḷa-kằ?|
    in-where=COP.2PL child-DEF.PL.OBL
    'Children, where are you?'

In past contexts the JSNENA present copula is sometimes used to express a state in the past. Here, as is the case with the present-stem form, the copula has a relative tense and takes the past reference of the adjacent verbs as its deictic centre.

(716) JSNENA
    'onī là   k-aē-n-wa   ma=yēn.|
    they NEG IND-know.PRS-3PL-PSTC what=COP.3PL
    'They did not know what they were.' (A:87)

Likewise, in the following Gorani examples the present copula has past time reference.

(717) Gorani
    ēma har   nà-zānā=mā   jaryān čēš=ā.|
    1PL   EMPH NEG-know.PST=1PL story   what=COP.3SG
    'We could not understand what the story was (what was going on).'

7.5.2 Past copula

Predicates with the JSNENA past copula express a state in the past. This may have an imperfective aspect expressing a state that was permanently in existence in the past without the connotation of inception and end, e.g.

(718) JSNENA
    a. 'axon-af   duktər kākề=lē.|
         brother-3SG.F doctor teeth=COP.3SG.M
         'Her brother was a dentist.' (A:6)

b. *šəma   'axon-af   Xanakḕ=yē-lē.*|
   name   brother-3SG.F   PN=COP.PST-OBL.3SG.M
   'The name of her brother was Xanaka.' (A:14)
c. *bātē   ntòē=yē-lū.*|
   houses   high=COP.PST-OBL.3PL
   'Houses were high.' (A:12)
d. *xa-pašor   kēpa   komtà=yē-la.*|
   one-foot_washer stone   black=COP.PST-OBL.3SG.F
   'A "foot washer" was a black stone.' (A:38)

The past copula is used with the same functions in Iranian.

(719) Gorani Luhon
*ganmakē=šā   hằrằ   tā   wurd-a   **bī-a**.*
wheat.DEF.DIR.F=3PL grind.PST   till   small-F   COP.PST.3SG.F
'They ground the wheat until it **was** fine.'
(MacKenzie 1966, 64)

(720) Gorani
*mən   šāngzà-na   **b-ēn-ē**.*|
1SG   sixteen-POST   be.PSTC-1SG
'I **was** sixteen years old.'

(721) Kurdish
*mardəm   la   xwašî̀-yā   **bū-∅**.*|
people   in   happiness-POST   be.PST-3SG
'People **were** happy [lit. in happiness].'

7.6 The existential particle

The JSNENA existential particle (*hīt, hītwa*) generally expresses permanent, continuous existence or at least an existence that the speaker wishes to present as being permanent. The corresponding negative form (*līt, lītwa*) expresses the lack of this.

(722) JSNENA
    a. *mawad=ē tabīʾī=yē*[|]   *la mangal day rangē*
       substance natural=COP.3SG.M   NEG like OBL.these colours
       ya-ʾata hìt.[|]
       REL-now EXIST
       'It is a natural substance, not like the colours that there are nowadays.' (A:40)
    b. *ḥawəš hìt-wa.*[|]
       courtyard EXIST-PSTC
       'There was a courtyard.' (A:54)
    c. *baṣīrē ràba hīt-wa ga-ḥawša nāšē.*[|]
       grapes many EXIST-PSTC in-courtyard people
       'There were many grapes in the courtyard of people.' (A:72)

The corresponding existential construction in Sanandaj Kurdish is *has* and in Gorani is *han*. They consist of the deictic/existential particle *ha-* combined with the copula stem, which is *-s* in Sanandaj Kurdish and *-n* is Gorani. In the past tense the particle *ha-* is omitted and the past copula replaces the 3SG present copula. In some Central Kurdish dialects *ha-* occurs before the past copula, thus *habū* 'there was'. The particle *hā* without a copula stem is also used in Sanandaj Kurdish to express existence. As in JSNENA, these existential constructions generally express permanent, continuous existence:

(723) Kurdish
    žən-ēk ha-s,[|]   *hā la Kərmāšàn-ā.*[|] *Tāī=y*
    woman-INDF PTCL-COP.3SG EXIST in PN-POST PN=3SG
    nàw=a.[|]
    name=COP.3SG
    'There is a woman, (who) is in Kermanshah. She is called Tay.'

(724) Gorani
    bīs sī xānəwàdēwa b-ēn-ē[|] *lū-ēn-ē pay*
    twenty thirty family.INDF be-PSTC-3PL go-PSTC-3PL to
    šārazūr-ī pamačìay.[|]
    PN-OBL.M cotton-harvesting.INF
    'There were twenty, thirty families who would go to Sharazur for cotton-harvesting.'

7.7 The JSNENA verb h-w-y

The JSNENA verb *h-w-y* is conjugated in the present stem *garəš* and *garəšwa* forms (§5.8.2). A morphological distinction is made between the realis with a *k-* prefix (*k-wē*, *k-əwya*, etc.) and the irrealis that lacks this (*hawē*, *hawya*, etc.).

The uses of this verb are suppletive to those of the copula and existential particle. They may be classified as follows:

7.7.1 k-wē

This is used to express the future, e.g.

(725) JSNENA
    a. *'āna=č barūxawālē k-wè̱-lī.|*
       I=ADD friends   IND-be.PRS.3SG.M-OBL.1SG
       'I shall have friends.' (D:6)
    b. *xa-yoma k-wè̱| 'ānà| da'wat-ī̀ k-ol-ī̱.|*
       one-day IND-be.PRS.3SG.M I   invitation-1SG IND-do.PRS-3PL
       'A day will come when they will invite me.' (D:8)

7.7.2 hawē

This form expresses irrealis. It is found in both main and subordinate clauses in the same contexts as the irrealis *garəš* form of other verbs is used (§10.2.1.1.).

7.7.2.1 Speaker-oriented modality in main clauses
It is typically used with optative speaker-oriented modality, expressing a wish of the speaker that something come about:

(726) JSNENA
    a. *'ēl-ox   hawy-a   brīxtà.|*
       festival-2SG.M be.PRS-3SG.F blessed
       'May your festival be blessed.' (B:50)
    b. *'ēla=ū rēš-šāt-ox   hawē-n   brīxè̱.|*
       festival head-year-2SG.M be.PRS.3PL blessed
       'May your festival and New Year be blessed.' (B:33)

7.7.2.2 Conditional constructions

(727) JSNENA
wa-'agar čanānčē xa-nāša na-rāḥatī hawḕ-lē,|
and-if if one-person grievance be.PRS.3SG.M-OBL.3SG.M
'àlē bā-ēf.|
know.PRS.3SG.M about-3SG.M
'If a person had a grievance, he would know about it.' (A:108)

7.7.2.3 Generic relative clauses
The irrealis form is used in relative clauses that qualify heads with generic reference, e.g.

(728) JSNENA
a. mat-ī-wā-lē ga-xa-t^wka qarīrà hawē.|
put.PRS-3PL-PSTC-OBL.3SG.M in-one-place cool be.PRS.3SG.M
'They put it in a place that was cool.' (A:83)
b. kúlē məndīx kḕ| ... xəlyà-hawē.|
every thing REL sweet-be.PRS.3SG.M
'Everything that is sweet.' (A:33)

7.7.2.4 Subordinate complements
The form occurs in subordinate clauses that are complements of various verbs and expressions when the action of the verb in the subordinate clause is as yet unrealised relative to the time of the main verb:

(729) JSNENA
kúlē nāšē ḥāz k-ol-ī-wā-lē bēl-ù|
all people desire IND-do.PRS-3PL-PSTC-OBL.3SG.M house-3PL
'īlānē baṣīrḕ hawē.|
trees grapes be.PRS.3SG.M
'Everybody wanted there to be grape vines in their home.' (A:72)

7.8 Iranian *w-/ b-* copula

In the Iranian languages of the Sanandaj region the stem of the verb 'to be' realised as *w-* in Sanandaj Kurdish and *b-* Gorani Takht is used as a copula and existential verb. It is conjugated like regular verbs. Unlike Kurdish and JSNENA, in Gorani the copula is not preceded by the indicative affix, which means that JSNENA *k-we* matches more closely the Kurdish form *a-wē*. The form is used with both realis and irrealis functions. The irrealis functions correspond to the irrealis functions of JSNENA *h-w-y*. It is significant that there is also a phonetic resemblance between the JSNENA irrealis stem *hawē* and the Kurdish stem *wē-*.

7.8.1 Realis functions of the *w-/ b-* copula

When used in a realis function, the copula *w-/ b-* occurs especially at the beginning of fictional narratives in order to set the scene. It can take present or past time reference.

(730) Kurdish
    a. *pì̀yāw-ēk*   ***a-w-ḕ*** ...   *du*   *žə̀n=ī*   *a-w-ḕ.*
        man-INDF   IND-be.PRS-3SG   two   woman=3SG   IND-be.PRS-3SG
        'There **was** a man, who had two wives.'
    b. ***a-w-ēt=a***   *yàk*   *pāwšā-yk,*   *žə̀n-ēk=ī*
        IND-be.PRS-3SG =DRCT   one   king-INDF   woman-INDF=3SG
        a-w-ē,   *žə̀n-aka*   *parīzāw*   *čəl*   *gì̀s*
        IND-be.PRS-3SG   woman-DEF   fairy   forty   plait.of.hair
        a-w-ḕ.
        IND-be.PRS-3SG
        'There **was** a king. He had a wife. The wife **was** a fairy with forty plaits of hair.'
    c. *haft*   *bərā*   *a-w-ən*   *xwašək=yān*
        seven   brother   IND-be.PRS-3PL   sister=3PL
        nà̀-w-ē.
        NEG-be.PRS-3SG
        'There were seven brothers who did not have a sister.'

(731) Gorani
    a. *āna=šā*   *zil-tar=ū*   *āl-tar*   ***b-o***   *āđ-ì̀*
        DEM.DIST=3PL   BIG-CMPR=and   good-CMPR   be.PRS-3SG   3SG-OBL.M
        bar-ā.
        take.PRS-3PL
        'The one who was bigger and healthier, they took him.'

b. *pādšā̃=w mīsrī*   *kinā̃čē=š*   *b-o*   *falajà*
king=EZ Egypt-OBL.M girl.INDF=3SG be.PRS-3SG disabled
b-o.|
be.PRS-3SG
'The king of Egypt had a daughter who was disabled.'

The *w-/ b-* copula also conveys the inchoative meaning 'become', as in the following examples:

(732) Kurdish
  a. ***a-w-ēt=a***   *mənāḷ,*| ***a-w-ēt=a***   *kanīšk-ẻ.*|
IND-be.PRS-3SG=DRCT child IND-be.PRS-3SG=DRCT girl-INDF
'(The kidney) **turned into** a baby, it **became** a girl.'
  b. *aw=īž*   ***a-w-ēt=a***   *bàhr-ē.*|
3SG.DIST=ADD IND-be.PRS-3SG=DRCT sea-INDF
'That **becomes** a sea.'

(733) Gorani
b-o   *ba*   *tāqat=ē*   *xaḷk-ỉ.*|
be.PRS-3SG to support=EZ people-OBL.M
'He **became** a support for people.'

7.8.2 Irrealis functions of the *w-/ b-* copula

When used in the irrealis mood, in Kurdish either the bare form *w-* is used or the copula is preceded by the subjunctive *b-*. In Gorani, only the bare form *b-* is used. The irrealis form expresses most of the functions of the NENA irrealis form *hawē*.

7.8.2.1 Speaker-oriented modality in main clauses

(734) Kurdish
  a. *sāḷ*   *tāzà=tān*   *muwārak*   *Ø-w-ē.*|
year new=2PL blessed SBJV-be.PRS-3SG
'May your New Year be blessed.'
  b. *àmānat=tān*   *lē*   *farz*   *Ø-w-ē.*|
trust=2PL to obliged SBJV-be.PRS-3SG
'May it be a task for you!'

(735) Gorani
    a. *mubārak=ū   sāhēb-ì̄=š   Ø-b-o.*|
       happy=EZ   owner-OBL.M=3SG SBJV-be.PRS-3SG
       'May she be happy with her owner [i.e. father].'
    b. *āđ=īč   hukm=əš   dā   wàt=əš,*| *'žanē*
       3SG=ADD order=3SG give.PST say.PST=3SG woman.PL.DIR
       lamapařa   mà-bo   Ø-b-o.'|
       pregnant   NEG.SBJV-be.PRS-3SG SBJV-be.PRS-3SG
       'He issued an order [and] said, "There shall be no pregnant women."'

7.8.2.2 Conditional constructions

(736) Kurdish
    agar xwā kūmak=əm Ø-w-ề| *haq   xwa=m*
    if   God help=1SG   SBJV-be.PRS-3SG right REFL=1SG
    a-sàn-m=aw.|
    IND-grab.PRS-1SG=TELIC
    'If God helps me, I shall reclaim my right.'

(737) Gorani
    agar Ø-b-o   m-ār-ū̀=t   pay.|
    if   SBJV-be.PRS-3SG IND-bring.PRS-1SG=2SG for
    'If there will be (enough food), I will bring you [some].'

7.8.2.3 Generic relative clauses

(738) Kurdish
    la-bar   ark   šāhī-ā   hāwār=ī   kə̀rd:| *kas-ē   kār*
    in.front.of palace royal-POST shout=3SG do.PST person-INDF work
    duktàr=ī   Ø-bē| *kas-è*| *nàsāx   Ø-w-ē,*|
    doctor=3SG SBJV-be.PRS.3SG person-INDF unhealthy SBJV-be.PRS-3SG
    kas-ē   naxwàš   Ø-w-ē.|
    person-INDF ill   SBJV-be.PRS-3SG
    'He shouted in front of the royal palace: "Is there anybody who needs a doctor, anyone who is unhealthy, anyone who is sick?"'

(739) Gorani
  yāna=w   hačkasī   b-ā   čwår   b-ā| pànj   b-ā.|
  house=EZ   each.one   be.PRS-3PL   four   be.PRS-3PL   five   be.PRS-3PL
  'No matter whose house they (the officers) were [guests] at; [no matter whether] they were four or five [guests].'

7.8.2.4 Subordinate complements

(740) Kurdish
  tàza   garak=y=a   jwān   Ø-w-ē.|
  now   be.necessary=3SG=COP.3SG   young   SBJV-be.PRS-3SG
  'It is now that she wants to be young again.'

(741) Gorani
  mən   čı̀w-ēw=əm   nī=yā=rē   lāyəq=ū
  1SG   thing-INDF=1SG   NEG=COP.3SG=POSTV   deserved=EZ
  ī   pādšāzaya   Ø-b-o.|
  DEM.PROX   princess   SBJV-be.PRS-3SG
  'I have nothing which would be up to the standards of this princess.'

7.9 JSNENA resultative participle + copula

7.9.1 Present perfect

The JSNENA compound forms consisting of the resultative participle and the copula (gərša=y, smīxa=y) generally have a present perfect function. This expresses a state in existence in the present that has come about as the result of a previous action. It is the resultant state of an action that is the focus of the verb rather than the action itself, e.g.

(742) JSNENA
  a. bron-akē   rəwyà=y,| brāt-akē
     boy-DEF   grow.PTCP.SG.M=COP.SG.M   girl-DEF
     rwītḕ=ya=ū| g-bē   xlūlà   hol-ī.|
     grow.PTCP.SG.F=COP.SG.F=and   IND-need.PRS.SG.M   wedding   do.PRS-3PL
     'The boy has grown up and the girl has grown up. They must marry.'
     (A:31)

b. čəkma 'aksē   ntē-nĭ-lan,| 'onyēxāē
   some   photographs take.PST-3PL-OBL.1PL they
   pīšē=n   bāqa yādgarĭ.|
   remain.PTCP.PL=COP.3PL   for reminder
   'We took a few photographs and they have remained as a reminder (of the event).' (A:29)

c. 'ay-bšəlmānè| kē-xalwa zabn-ī   ta-dīdàn| 'ay-xalwà|
   these-Muslims REL-milk sell.PRS-3PL to-OBL.1PL this-milk
   mən-do   tortà| yā-mən-do   'ərba
   from-OBL.that   cow   or-from-OBL.that sheep
   dəwqà=y| ga-xa-patīlà   dəwqa=y|
   keep.PTCP.SG.M=COP.SG.M   in-one-container   keep.PTCP.SG.M-COP.3SG.M
   kē   patīl-akē   mumkən=yē   pəsra
   REL container-DEF   possible=COP.3SG.M meat
   bəšla-hawē-lū   gà-ēf.|
   cook.PTCP.SG.M-be.PRS.3SG.M-OBL.3PL   in-3SG.M
   'Those Muslims, who sell milk to us, have taken the milk from the cow or from the sheep and have kept it in a container in which they may have cooked meat.' (A:64)

The form may be used to express 'experiential perfects', i.e. events that are part of the speaker's life experience, e.g.

(743) JSNENA
      'arbà-karat ziltē=yan   Farànsa.|
      four-times   go.PTCP.SG.F=COP.1SG.F PN
      'I have gone to France four times.' (C:13)

7.9.2 Indirective

The JSNENA perfect form may be used to express perfective events in the past from which the speaker is cognitively distanced. In some cases this is due to the fact that the speaker has not directly witnessed the event and relies only on a report of it. The perfect can, however, be used also when the speaker has witnessed or experienced the event but is cognitively distanced from it due to its occurrence in the remote past. We have adopted here the term 'indirective' for this overarching function of cognitive distancing. This term was used by Johansson (2000) for corresponding constructions in the Turkic languages. This expression of cognitive distancing has parallels with the expression of what Botne and Kershner (2008) term the 'dissociative cognitive domain' in the Bantu verbal system.

7.9.2.1 Reports of past events
The JSNENA perfect form may be used to express perfective events in the past that are presented as reported to the speaker but not directly witnessed by him/her,[1] i.e. it has an evidential function, e.g.

(744) JSNENA
*xaṭraṭē   noš-ēf   ḥqḕ-lē   bāq-an*ˈ *kē-dàx*
reminiscences   self-3SG.M   tell.PST-OBL.3SG.M   to-1PS   that-how
*hīya=y   bāqa 'Īrằn.*ˈ *'o ga-zamān=ē   Mozafar-dīn*
come.PTCP.SG.M=COP.3SG.M   to   PN   he   in-time-EZ   PN
*Šằh.*ˈ *hīya=y   bāqa 'Īrān   bāqa   tasīs=ē*
PN   come.PTCP.SG.M=COP.SG.M   to PN   to   foundation=EZ
*madrasa   'aliằns.*ˈ
school   PN
'He told us his reminiscences as to how he came to Iran. He came to Iran in the time of Mozafaredin Shah in order to found the school of the Alliance.' (B:61)

7.9.2.2 Folktales and legends
The compound form is used in fictional folktales and legends to express imperfective habitual activities and perfective events. This also can be identified as an evidential function, expressing legendary events that the speaker has heard about only from reports, e.g.

(745) JSNENA
  a. *šāta   zīla=y   lā   xà   baxt-ēf.*ˈ
     year   go.PTCP.SG.M=COP.3SG.M   side   one   wife-3SG.M
     'He went to one of his wives (once) in a year.' (A:94)

---

[1] In many languages present perfect verb forms have developed this evidential function. This is due to the fact that it does not present an event directly but only through its results (Comrie 1976, 108–110; Aikhenvald 2004, 112–115). For the use of the perfect as a narrative form characteristic of fictitious narrative in other NENA dialects see Khan (2008b, 669–77; 2012; 2020a).

b. zīlà=y| ṭalaba   malka   Šabà.| malka   Šabà
go.PTCP.SG.M=COP.3SG.M seeking queen PN   queen   PN
gwīrtē=ya.|
marry.PTCP.SG.F=COP.3SG.F

'He went and sought the hand of the Queen of Sheba. He married the Queen of Sheba.' (A:97)

7.9.2.3 Remote past

A related usage of the perfect is to express perfective events and imperfective situations in the remote past. These may be before the lifetime of the speaker and so could be identified as an evidential type function, in that the speaker has not directly witnessed the events and situations (746.a-c). The construction, however, can be used by speakers also in the first person to narrative events the speaker has experienced in his/her remote past (746.d):

(746) JSNENA
a. qamē   doa   'āna   b-'olām   hē-nà,| hulaē   waxt=ē
   before   OBL.that I   in-world   come.PRS-1SG.M   Jews   time=EZ
   zīlē=n   waryà,| maxṣūṣan   ga-yomawāē   naxlà,|
   go.PTCP.PL=COP.3PL   outside   especially on-days   rain
   g-bē-wa   xa-parča   zayra   daē-n
   IND-need.PRS.3SG.M-PSTC   one-cloth yellow   put.PRS-3PL
   ba-laxà-ū| b-lā   sang-ù| kē   'alē-n   'ənyēxāē
   in-here-3PL   in-side   chest-3PL   that   know.PRS-3PL   they
   hulaè=n.|
   Jews=COP.3PL

   'Before I was born, when the Jews went outside, especially on rainy days, they had to put a patch of yellow here, on their chest so that they (the Muslims) knew that they were Jews.' (A:78)

b. zilē=n   bāqa   Rūsìya,| zīlē=n   bāqa
   go.PTCP.PL=COP.3PL   to   PN   go.PTCP.PL=COP.3PL   to
   Turkìya.| jàns   šəqla=y,| mīya=y
   PN   goods   buy.PTCP.SG.M=COP.3SG.M   bring.PTCP.SG.M=COP.3SG.M
   ga-Kurdəstān   zəbnà=y.|
   in-PN   sell.PTCP.SG.M=COP.3SG.M

   'They went to Russia, they went to Turkey. They bought goods, brought them to Kurdistan and sold them there.' (B:6)

c. Šīrāz ’o-waxtara ba-šəma ʾƷstàxr xīrtē=ya.
   PN   that-time   by-name PN   be.PTCP.SG.F=COP.3SG.F
   'Shiraz at that time was (known) by the name of Istakhr.' (B:1)
d. ’āna hītē=yan   laxa qam=ē   ’əštī šnè̠.
   I   come.PTCP.SG.F=COP.1SG.F   here before=EZ sixty years
   'I came here (i.e. to this country) sixty years ago.'

7.10 Iranian resultative participle + copula

The corresponding Iranian construction has a similar range of functions.

7.10.1 Present perfect

It may express a present perfect, i.e. it denotes a state in existence in the present that has come about as the result of a previous action, e.g.

(747) Gorani
wāt=šā,   ʿAlī Guḷāḷa zamā̀wəna kar-o,   daʿwat=əš
say.PST=3PL PN   PN   wedding   do.PRS-3SG invitation=3SG
kàrdē=ndē.'
do.PST.PTCP.PL=2PL
'They said, "Ali Gulala is having a marriage ceremony. He has invited you."'

(748) Kurdish
nằn=əm   hāwərd-g=a   bo=tān.
bread=1SG   bring.PST-PTCP=PERF   for=2PL
'I have brought you food.'

7.10.2 Indirective

7.10.2.1 Reports of past events
The perfect form of the verb expresses perfective events which have not been witnessed by the speaker but are rather a hearsay or an inference, conveying thus an evidential function.

(749) Gorani
Pīr   šalīyàr[|]   nām=əš   say   məsafà=n[|]
religious.leader PN   name=3SG   PN   PN=COP.3SG.M
ađā=š=ū   tātà=š[|]   fàwt=šā   karda=n[|]
mother=3SG=and   father=3SG death=3PL   do.PST.PTCP.M=COP.3SG.M
hatìm   bīya=n.[|]
orphan   COP.PST.PTCP.M=COP.3SG.M
'Pir Shaliar, his [true] name was Say Mustaffa. His parents passed away. He was an orphan.'

(750) Kurdish
aw   sằḷ-a   ā   muḥamaw   zā-w=a[|]
DEM.DIST year-DEM   mr.   PN   give.birth.PST-PTCP=PERF
kuř-aka=y   bù-w=a[|]   ēma   àm   zawī=mān-a
son-DEF=3SG   be.PST-PTCP=PERF   1PL   DEM.PROX   land=1PL-DEM
baš   kərdē=a.[|]
portion   do.PST.PTCP=PERF
'We divided this land in the year when Mr. Muhammad gave birth and had a son.'

7.10.2.2 Folktales and legends

(751) Gorani
jā   pāđšā-kay   vằta=n   ba   lālo=w   kənāča-kē.[|]
DSCM king-DEF.OBL.M say.PST.PTCP.M=COP.3SG.M   to   uncle=EZ   girl-DEF.OBL.F
'Well, the king said to the girl's uncle.'

(752) Kurdish of the Sanandaj region
a-yž-ən   pāwšằ-yk   bī-w=a   la   zamān
IND-say.PRS-3PL king-INDF   be.PST-PTCP=COP.3SG.PERF   in   time
qayīm-ā.[|]   àm   pāwšā[|]   sè   kuř=ī   bī-w=a=w
old-POST   DEM.PROX.3SG   king   three   son=3SG   be.PST-PTCP=PERF=and
sē   kanìšk.[|]   řīš=ī   čarmù   kərdē=ya=w[|]   'amr=ī
three   girl   beard=3SG   white   do.PST.PTCP=PERF=and   age=3SG
pìr   bī-w=a=w[|]
old   be.PST-PTCP=COP.3SG.PERF=and
'It is said that there was a king in the olden days. The king had three sons and three daughters. He aged (lit. his beard grew white); he grew old.'

7.10.2.3 Remote past

In Gorani the perfect is used to express perfective events and imperfective situations in the remote past. In some cases these are experienced by the speaker and narrated in the first person

(753) Gorani
    a. ēma   bè-dəḷī   šū=ma   karda=n.|
       1PL   unwillingly husband=1PL do.PST.PTCP.M=COP.3SG.M
       'We got married unwillingly.'
    b. mən   žàn-ē=m   māra   bəřyē=na   sar=ū   ṣa
       1SG woman-INDF=1SG marriage cut.PTCP.F=COP.3SG.F on=EZ 100
       təmanà.| yūa=m   màra   bəřyē=na   sar=ū   yaraṣa
       toman   one.F=1SG marriage cut.PTCP.F=COP.3SG.F on=EZ 300
       təmana,| īna   har   pay   wè=m.| yūà=yč=m
       toman   DEM.PROX EMPH for   REFL=1SG one.F=ADD=1SG
       māra   bəřyē=na   har   pay wē=m| yarē, ba
       marriage cut.PTCP.F=COP.3SG.F EMPH for REFL=1SG three by
       yaraṣà   təman-ī.|
       300   toman-OBL.M
       'I married (a) woman for 100 tomans (i.e. the bride price). I married another woman for 300 tomans, it was for me. I married another, again for myself. This makes it three (women) for 300 tomans.'
    c. qayīm ā   banna-na duē   gàlē=š   čana
       past   DEM.DIST PN-POST two herd.PL.DIR=3SG in
       bīē=nē;| ī   dagā=y   ēma   yàrē
       be.PST.PTCP.PL=COP.3PL dem.prox village=EZ 1pl three
       galē=š   čana   bīyē=nē;| īsa   duē
       herd.PL.DIR=3SG now be.PST.PTCP.PL=COP.3PL now two
       yānè   heywān=šā ha-n.|
       house.DIR.PL animal=3PL PTCL=COP.3SG.M
       'In the past, the village of Banna had two herds; our village had three herds; now, only two households have (tame) animals.'

(754) Kurdish
    ēma la dēhāt-ā   māḷ=a   gawrà bū-g=īn|
    1PL in village-POST house=CPM big   be.PST-PTCP=PERF
    hudùd| ḥaftà   sar haywān=mān   bū-g=a.|
    around seventy CLF animal=1PL   be.PST-PTCP=PERF
    'We were a big family in the village. We had around seventy animals.'

In (755)-(756) the perfect is used to describe a chain of events used habitually in the far past.

(755) Gorani
ēma   'ənnà=mā   zānā=n| latarē=mā
1PL   this.much=1PL   know.PTCP.M=COP.3SG.M   spindle=1PL
rəsīyà=n=ū| gorawē=mā   čənīyà=n=ū|
spin.PST.M=COP.3SG.M=and   sock=1PL   knit.PTCP=COP.3SG.M=and
jājəm=mā   dīyà=n=ū|
tapis=1PL   see.PTCP.M=COP.3SG.M=and
'We knew (only) these things: we would spin the wool, knit socks, and we saw tapis.' (The speaker refers to things they used to do in the past)

(756) Kurdish
ēma   la   dēhàt-ā   bū-g-īn.| kār
1PL   in   village-POST   be.PST-PTCP-1PL job
kašāwarzì̄=mān   kərd-g=a.| dāmdārì̄=mān
agriculture=1PL   do.PST-PTCP=PERF   animal.husbandry=1PL
kərd-g=a.|
do.PST-PTCP=PERF
'We used to live in villages. We used to farm. We used to do animal husbandry.'

7.11 Morphological coding of transitivity

Past stems and resultative participles in JSNENA fall into two sets, which have been labelled as 'transitive' and 'intransitive' (§5.2 & §5.4). Whereas this characterisation captures the functional distinction between the two sets of forms in broad terms, the distribution of the forms is not wholly predictable. Crucially the use of a transitive form is not restricted to clauses that have an explicit direct object complement.

Verbs that frequently occur without a specified direct object complement but that could, nevertheless, take one are generally conjugated with transitive forms, e.g.

(757) JSNENA
'-x-l   'to eat'   xīlē   'He ate.'
š-t-y   'to drink'   štēlē   'He drank.'
l-w-š   'to dress'   lwəšlē   'He dressed.'
š-l-x   'to undress'   šləxlē   'He undressed.'

m-q-l-b	'to vomit'	*məqləblē-o*	'He vomited.'
q-n-š	'to sweep'	*qnəšlē*	'He swept.'
q-r-y	'to read, to study'	*qrēlē*	'He studied.'
x-l-p	'to win'	*xləplē*	'He won.'

With object complements:

(758)

xāla xīlē	'He ate food.'
maē štēlē	'He drank water.'
jəlēf ləwšīlē	'He put on his clothes.'
jəlēf šəlxīlē	'He took off his clothes.'
xāla məqləblē-o	'He vomited food.'
ḥawša qənšālē	'He swept the yard.'
hulaūla qəryālē	'He studied Judaism.'
pūḷē xəlpīlē	'He won the money.'

The use of the transitive inflection for these verbs, therefore, can be explained by the fact that there is an implied 'latent' affectee of the action, although this is not necessarily specified.

The transitive coding is conditioned also by the properties of the subject, crucially the agent properties of the subject as controller and instigator of the action. These properties of the subject are in some cases relevant for the transitivity coding of verbs with direct object complements. Consider (759.a-b)

(759) JSNENA
    a. *'o rāba məndīxānē yəlpà=y.*|
       he many things   learn.PTCP.SG.M=COP.3SG.M
       (transitive coding) 'He has learnt many things.'
    b. *'o rāba məndīxānē ylīpà=y.*|
       he many things   learn.PTCP.SG.M=COP.3SG.M
       (intransitive coding) 'He has learnt many things.'

Example (759.a), which has a transitive compound verb, implies that the subject referent learnt the things at his own instigation and under his own control, by himself. By contrast the intransitive coding of (759.b) implies that the subject lacks these properties of control and instigation and is typically used to describe a situation where the subject learnt more passively by being taught by somebody else.[2]

This helps us to understand the transitive coding of a further set of verbs in the JSNENA dialect, namely verbs expressing an emission of sound or speech. Such verbs are not generally used with an explicit object complement, but nevertheless are widely coded as transitive, e.g.

(760) JSNENA

ʾ-m-r	'to say'	mərē	'He said.'
ḥ-q-y	'to speak'	ḥqēlē	'He spoke.'
z-m-r	'to sing'	zəmrē	'He sang.'
d-ʿ-y	'to pray'	dʿēlē	'He prayed.'
m-w-m-y	'to utter an oath'	momēlē	'He swore.'
n-w-x	'to bark'	nwəxlē	'It barked.'
s-r-p	'to slurp'	srəplē	'He slurped.'
b-ʿ-y	'to bleat'	ʾərba bʿēla	'The sheep bleated.'
m-ʿ-y	'to bleat'	ʾəza mʿēla	'The goat bleated.'
n-h-m	'to roar'	nhəmlē	'It roared.'
s-r-y	'to bray'	xmāra srēlē	'The donkey brayed.'
m-k-r-z	'to crow'	kalašēr məkrəzlē	'The cock crowed.'
š-h-l	'to cough'	šəhlē	'He coughed.'
t-p-l	'to sneeze'	təplē	'He sneezed.'

The subject of such verbs is the instigator rather than the affectee. This is the profile of transitive predicates and it is for this reason that the verb is coded as transitive. The subject need not be in control of the event, as in the verbs 'to cough', 'to sneeze', but is still the cause.

Events of emission of sound that do not have an animate instigator may be coded as intransitive with the subject referent being presented as the affectee of the event, e.g.

---

[2] This would be consistent with the broad notion of transitivity that was proposed by Hopper and Thompson (1980). According to this approach, the existence of an object participant in the clause is only one parameter of transitivity. Another parameter is the extent to which the subject has properties characteristic of an agent, i.e. the extent to which the subject referent is the controller and instigator of the action rather than the affectee.

(761) JSNENA
'ēwa gərgìm⌐
cloud thunder.PST.3SG.M
'The cloud thundered.'

In reality it is not always possible to establish an objective dividing line between the concepts of instigator and affectee, in that, in principle, in an event involving the emission of sound the subject referent could be viewed as being affected by or undergoing the event. Indeed the coding of transitivity of verbs of sound emission in neighbouring Jewish NENA dialects is sometimes different from what is found in JSNENA. For a discussion of this issue relating to J. Urmi and J. Sulemaniyya see Khan (2004, 300; 2008a, 266). We present here some cross-dialectal variations by way of illustration:

Table 74: Transitive vs. intransitive coding of sound emission verbs across NENA.

	Transitive	Intransitive
š-h-l 'to cough'	J. Sanandaj (šəhlē)	J. Qar Hasan (šhīl)
	J. Sulemaniyya (šhallē)	J. Bokan (šhīl)
	J. Tikab (šhallē)	
	J. Kerend (šhallē)	
t-p-l 'to sneeze'	J. Sanandaj (taplē)	J. Bokan (tpīl)
	J. Sulemaniyya (tpallē)	J. Qar Hasan (tpīl)
	J. Tikab (tpallē)	J. Urmi (tpīl)
	J. Kerend (tpallē)	
n-w-x 'to bark'	J. Sanandaj (nwaxlē)	J. Urmi (nwīx)
	J. Sulemaniyya (nwaxlē)	
	J. Qar Hasan (noxlē)	
	J. Kerend (noxlē)	
p-h-r 'to yawn'	J. Sanandaj (pahrē)	J. Urmi (phīr)
	J. Sulemaniyya (phərrē)	
	J. Kerend (phərrē)	

Note also that in J. Urmi 'to dance' is coded morphologically as transitive, presenting the 'dancer' as the instigator of the action, whereas in other dialects the 'dancer' is presented as the undergoer of the action and the verb is coded as intransitive:

(762) J. Urmi

	Transitive	Intransitive
r-q-l 'to dance'	J. Urmi (rqīlē)	J. Sanandaj (nqīl)
		J. Sulemaniyya (rqīl)

Some lexical verbs in JSNENA are coded as transitive or intransitive by the presence or absence respectively of an impersonal 3sg.f object suffix:

(763) JSNENA

	Intransitive	**Transitive**
'-r-q 'to run'	rīq	'ərqālē
g-x-k 'to laugh'	gxīk	gəxkālē

In the case of *'ərqālē—rīq*, the transitive form puts more focus on the purposiveness of the subject ('He fled') whereas in the intransitive form the focus is on the affectedness of the subject referent ('He ran').

The distinction between *gəxkālē* and *gxīk* is not primarily one of agentivity but rather discourse prominence. The intransitive form *gxīk* is typically used to express an event of laughing that is incidental to another activity, e.g.

(764) JSNENA
g-ay ḥašta gxīk
in-this job laugh.PST.3SG.M
'He laughed in the course of this job.'

The transitive form *gəxkālē*, on the other hand, is used, in principle, to refer to an independent foreground event in its own right and not incidental to another event. This may have developed from proto-typical association of foreground events with transitive clauses.

There is a residue of a few verbs of perception that are treated grammatically as agentive in JSNENA although the subject cannot be felicitously classified as semantically agentive, e.g. *x-z-y* 'to see', *š-m-y* 'to hear'. They are, however, transitive in that they typically have a direct object, which is the prototypical construction of agentive verbs.

The distribution of transitive and intransitive verbal stems in the Iranian languages of the region follows similar principles. It is the agentivity of subject that is the crucial factor for the selection of a transitive form rather than the existence of a direct object in the clause. As in JSNENA, there is some degree of variation of encoding the transitivity of some lexical stems and this can sometimes be linked to differences in the context of their usage. There is, moreover, some variation between Gorani and Kurdish.

The examples from Kurdish (765a) and (765b) correspond to the JSNENA constructions (759a) and (759b) above. As in JSNENA a difference in transitivity is encoded according to whether the subject is the agentive instigator of the action or not, i.e. whether the subject 'learnt by himself' (transitive) or 'learnt passively' (intransitive). It is important to note, however, that this is expressed in Kurdish by different lexical light verbs in a light-verb construction (with the non-finite element *fēr* 'learned') rather than morphological alternation within the stem of a single verb as in the JSNENA examples:

(765) Kurdish
    a. *xwa=y=ī*   *fēr*   *sàz*   *kərd.*|
        REFL=3SG=3SG learned musical.instrument do.PST
        'He learned (to play) the *sāz* (musical instrument) by himself.'
    b. *ba-lāy*   *məʿaləm-à*   *fēr*   *sāz*   *bū.*|
        at.the.place.of teacher-POST learned PN COP.PST.3SG
        'He learned (to play) the *sāz* (musical instrument) through a teacher.'

In Gorani of Hawraman there is variation in the coding of verbs expressing sound emission of animals as transitive or intransitive. The transitive counterpart contains the agentive suffix *-n* in the verb stem.

(766) Gorani

'to bark'	*gafā* (intr.)	'It barked.'
'to bleat'	*bā́řyā-va* (intr.), *bā́řnā=š-va* (tr.)	'It bleated.'
'to bleat'	*qā́řyā-va* (intr.), *qā́řnā=š-va* (tr.)	'It bleated.'
'to bray'	*sarā* (intr.), *sarnā=š* (tr.)	'It brayed.'
'to howl'	*nūzyā-va* (intr.), *nūznā=š-va* (tr.)	'It howled.'
'to crowed'	*qūlnā=š* (tr.)	'It crowed.'
'to neigh'	*hīlyā-va* (intr.), *hīlnā=š-va* (tr.)	'It neighed.'
'to meow'	*mīyāwnā=š* (tr.)	'It meowed.'

In both Kurdish and Gorani, verbs of emission of animal sounds that are made by humans are always transitive because they must be intentional:

(767) Gorani
     āḍa   *nūznā=š*
     3SG.DIR whine.PST=3SG
     'She whined.'

(768) Kurdish
    a. *sařān=ī*
        shout.PST=3SG
        'He shouted.'

b. *kar-aka*   *saṛān=ī*
    donkey-DEF   bray.PST=3SG
    'The donkey brayed.'

This variation of transitivity of verbs expressing the emission of animal sounds in the Iranian languages may have given rise to the cross-dialectal variation of the coding of the transitivity of such verbs across Jewish NENA in the area. As seen in Table 74, this applies to the Jewish NENA verb 'to bark' (*n-w-x*).

The verbs 'to cough' and 'to sneeze' are intransitive in Gorani of Hawraman:

(769)   Gorani
        āđ qozā   'He/she coughed.'
        āđ pižmā   'He/she sneezed.'

This intransitivity corresponds to the intransitive coding of these verbs in some Jewish NENA dialects of the area, but not JSNENA, which codes them as transitive.

In Sanandaj Kurdish these verbs could be either transitive or intransitive depending on the intensity and repetition of the action. Thus, the difference between the following pair lies in the fact that in (770.a) the speaker coughed continually, while in (770.b) the action is unintentional.

(770)   Kurdish
        a. *a=y-qozā*
            IPFV=3SG-cough.PST
            'He/she coughed.' (tr.)
        b. *a-qozā-∅*
            IPFV-cough.PST-3SG
            'He/she coughed.' (int.)

Table 75 summarises the correspondences in the encoding of transitivity in verbs of sound emission between JSNENA and Iranian.

Table 75: Encoding transitivity in JSNENA, Gorani, and Kurdish, compared.

	JSNENA	Gorani	Kurdish
bark	tr.	intr.	tr., intr.
bleat	tr.	tr., intr.	tr.
bray	tr.	tr., intr.	tr.
laugh	tr., intr.	intr.	intr.

Table 75 (continued)

	JSNENA	Gorani	Kurdish
cough	tr.	intr.	intr., tr.
sneeze	tr.	intr.	intr., tr.
thunder	intr.	tr.	tr.
yawn	tr.	tr.	tr.
slurp	tr.	tr.	tr.
dance	intr.	intr.	intr.
give birth	intr.	intr.	intr.
shout	tr.	tr.	tr.
dare	tr.	tr.	tr.

This indicates that there is a considerable degree of convergence but this is not total. There is, furthermore, variation across the various Jewish dialects of the area. Moreover, Gorani and Kurdish exhibit internal variation, sometimes linked to semantic distinctions, which does not exist in JSNENA or other Jewish NENA dialects. All this suggests that the Jewish NENA dialects have replicated the general principles of the encoding of transitivity from Iranian but have applied them internally within the NENA dialects in different ways. In some cases variation in Iranian gives rise to dialectal diversity in NENA. In other cases variation has arisen in NENA that does not match any corresponding variation in Iranian.

7.12 Expression of the passive

7.12.1 Passive past stem

In JSNENA transitive verbs that inflect a past transitive stem with L-suffixes may form a past perfective passive by inflecting a past intransitive stem of the verb with direct suffixes. In such cases the undergoer object of the active transitive construction is made the grammatical subject of the passive construction. In strong verbs and some categories of weak verb distinct transitive and passive past stems are employed (§5.2), e.g.

(771)   JSNENA
        traṣ-lē   'He built (it).'   *trīṣ*   'It was built.'
        tərṣī-lē 'He built them.'   *trīṣī* 'They were built.'

In practice, however, past perfective passives are not formed from all verbs of the lexicon that are coded as transitive in the past perfective active. The passive form tends to be restricted to constructions in which the grammatical subject of the passive is the affectee of the action and undergoes a change of state. In such cases the verb has telic actionality with an inherent stative endpoint, e.g.

(772) JSNENA
 *māmī qṭīl*ˈ 'My father was killed.'
 *knīšta trīṣa*ˈ 'The synagogue was built.'
 *bəza zmiṭ*ˈ 'The hole was filled.'

The passive of the past stem tends to be avoided with verbs which in the active form take grammatical objects that are not direct affectees of the action, such as verbs of perception (e.g. *x-Ø-y* 'to see') and are non-telic without a stative endpoint. The passive is also not available for verbs with objects that are the affectees of the action but do not necessarily undergo a change of state. Such a verb is *d-Ø-y* 'to hit', since the act of hitting does not necessarily produce a change of state in the undergoer. Such verbs are also in principle non-telic. So telic actionality with an inherent stative endpoint appears to be a condition for passive construction formation.

In Kurdish and Gorani a passivising affix is added to the present stem in order to form a passive stem.

(773) Gorani
 košt=šā *koš-ī(ā)-ē*
 kill.PST=3PL kill.PRS-PASS.PST-3PL
 'They killed.' 'They were killed.'

(774) Kurdish
 košt=yān *kož-yā-n*
 kill.PST=3PL kill.PRS-PASS.PST-3PL
 'They killed.' 'They were killed.'

As in JSNENA, in Gorani and Kurdish the passive is most commonly used with telic verbs, in which the grammatical subject is an affectee of the action and undergoes a clear change of state (775–776). The passive of verbs of perception (e.g. 'see', 'hear') is not attested in our corpus.

(775) Kurdish
 dā-nīšt *hatākadē* *šằm* *xor-yā.*ˈ
 PVB-sit.PST.3SG until dinner eat.PRS-PASS.PST
 'He remained (lit. sat) until the dinner was eaten.'

(776) Gorani
ja   šwāna-y   bəř-yā-(ā)nē   kard-ā=šā
from   shepherd-NOML   cut.PRS-PASS.PST-1SG   do.PST-1SG=3PL
wəḷāxdâr.
donkey.breeder
'(When) I got stopped shepherding (lit. I was cut from shepherding), they made me donkey-breeder.'

7.12.2 Passive resultative participle

In JSNENA a passive perfect may be formed with an intransitive resultative participle and copula (or suppletive *h-w-y*). The distribution of passive constructions with resultative participles is wider than with past-stem verbs. The explanation is likely to be that the resultative participle of all verbs in principle expresses a state, whereas in past-stem forms only telic verbs have a stative component.

Such constructions may be formed for both telic and non-telic verbs, e.g.

(777) JSNENA
    a. Telic
        qṭīla=y   'He has been killed.'
        trīṣa=y   'It has been built.'
        qṭīla=yēlē   'He had been killed.'
        trīṣa=yēlē   'It had been built.'
        qṭīla hawē   'He may have been killed.'
        trīṣa hawē   'It may have been built.'
    b. Non-telic
        xīya=y   'He has been seen.'
        dīya=y   'He has been hit.'
        xīya=yēlē   'He had been seen.'
        dīya=yēlē   'He had been hit.'
        xīya hawē   'It may have been seen.'
        dīya hawē   'He may have been hit.'

In the Iranian languages of the area, likewise, passive perfects can be formed with participles of both telic and non-telic verbs to which the appropriate forms of the copula are added, e.g.

(778) a. Telic

Gorani		Kurdish
koš-yā=n	'He has been killed.'	kož-yā-g=a
waš kər-yā=n	'It has been built.'	dros kəryā-g=a
koš-yā bē	'He had been killed.'	kož-yā=ū ~ kož-yā bū
waš kər-yā bē	'It had been built.'	dros kər-yā=ū ~ dros kər-yā bū
koš-yā bo	'He may have been killed.'	kož-yā-g bēt
waš kər-yā bo	'It may have been built.'	dros kər-yā bēt

b. Non-telic

Gorani		Kurdish
vīnīā=n	'He has been seen.'	bīn-yā-g=a
dər-yā=n vana	'He has been hit.'	lē dər-yā-g=a
vīn-īā bē	'He had been seen.'	bīn-yā bū
dər-yā bē vana	'He had been hit.'	lē dər-yā bū
vīn-īā bo	'It may have been seen.'	bīn-yā bēt
dər-yā bo vana	'He may have been hit.'	lē dər-yā bēt

7.12.3 Passive formed with an ingressive auxiliary

In JSNENA, when the verb has telic actionality, another construction is available to express the passive, in which a resultative participle is combined with the ingressive verb *x-Ø-r* 'to become'. The construction expresses an event with a stative endpoint, e.g.

(779) JSNENA
    a. *qṭīla*   *xīr*
        kill.PTCP.SG.M become.PST.3SG.M
        'He was killed.'
    b. *qṭīla*   *xar*
        kill.PTCP.SG.M become.PRS.3SG.M
        'He will be killed.'

There is no clear corresponding construction in Gorani or Kurdish of Sanandaj to this periphrastic passive in JSNENA. It corresponds closely, however, to the Persian passive construction, which is formed by the combination of the auxiliary verb *šod* 'become' with the past participle, e.g.

(780) Persian
 košt-e šod
 kill.PST-PTCP become.PST.3SG
 'He was killed.'

The likelihood that the JSNENA construction is replicating this Persian construction is increased by the fact that similar constructions occur in other Jewish NENA dialects in Iran spoken by communities in contact with Persian, e.g. J. Urmi (Khan 2008a, 293–94) but not in Jewish dialects spoken outside of the Persian area in Iraq.

7.12.4 Impersonal 3pl. subject

Another method of expressing an action without specifying the agent is to use an active construction with an unexpressed subject argument and impersonal 3pl. subject marking on the verb. This is rendered idiomatically by an English passive, e.g.

(781) JSNENA
 ga-tēlēvīzyon mʾīn-wā-lē xa-nafar mən-day
 in-television watch.PST-PSTC-OBL.3SG.M one-person from-OBL.these
 'ayānè˩ maləkˈ=yē-lē˩ qṭəl-wā-lū.˩
 dignitaries king=COP.PST-OBL.3SG.M kill.PST-PSTC-OBL.3PL
 'On the television he saw that one of the dignitaries who was a landlord had been killed (literally: they had killed one of the dignitaries . . .).' (C:9).'

This occurs also in the Iranian languages of the Sanandaj region.

(782) Gorani
 hàngūrī bē,˩ har č-āy=š war-ī=nē
 grape COP.PST.3SG EMPH from-3SG.OBL=3SG eat.PRS-PASS=COP.3PL
 har č-āy=š nā, kàr-ēn-ē=š haškočī.˩ marwè
 EMPH from-3SG.OBL=3SG no do.PRS-PSTC-3PL=3SG raisins pear-PL.DIR
 bē˩ har č-āy=š war-ī=nē har
 COP.PSTC.3SG EMPH from-3SG.OBL=3SG eat.PRS-PASS=cop.3pl EMPH
 č-āy=š nā wašk=əš kàr-ēn-ē.˩
 from-3SG.OBL=3SG no dry=3SG do.PRS-PSTC-3PL

'(Among the fruit produced here) was grapes. It continued to be eaten, and whatever remained of it would be turned into raisins (lit. they would make it into raisins). There were also pears. It continued to be eaten, and whatever remained of it would be dried (lit. they would dry it).'

7.13 Labile verbs with transitive—unaccusative alternation

In JSNENA several verbs exhibit an alternation of transitive and unaccusative intransitive usage. Such 'labile verbs' can be used transitively with a volitional subject and an object complement that is the undergoer of the action or alternatively can be used intransitively with the non-volitional undergoer being made the grammatical subject. Unlike passive constructions, such unaccusative intransitive alternants of transitive verbs are not restricted to past stems and resultative participles but include also inflections of the present stem, e.g.

(783) JSNENA
    a. *pyāḷakē torīla*   'They **will break** the glass.'
       pyāḷakē tora   'The glass **will break**.'
    b. *ləxma parčəkīlē*   'They **will crumble** the bread.'
       ləxma parčək   'The bread **will crumble**.'
    c. *bēla ṭapēlē*   'He **will destroy** the house.'
       bēla ṭapē   'The house **will collapse**.'

The past stems and resultative participles of such labile verbs exhibit morphological distinctions between transitive and intransitive, according to the regular coding of transitivity differences in past stems and participles:

(784) JSNENA
    a. *pyāḷakē təwrālū*   'They **broke** the glass.'
       pyāḷakē twīra   'The glass **broke**.'
    b. *pyāḷakē twərtē=ya*   'They **have broken** the glass.'
       pyāḷakē twīrtē=ya   'The glass **has broken**.'

In Gorani one pattern for deriving transitive stems from their unaccusative counterpart is through a change in the vowel of the stem. This is found in a few verbs, e.g. 'break', 'pour'. Such a pattern of Umlaut is also attested in Middle Persian, e.g. *-ahram* 'go up' vs. *-ahrām* 'lead up' (tr.) (cf. Skjærvø 2009, 220). Note further that the intransitive stem is also used as the passive stem for these Gorani verbs.

(785) Gorani
    a. *pyāḷaka **marī**-o*   'The cup **will break**.'
       *pyāḷakay **mǎř**-ū*   'I **will break** the cup.'
    b. *pyāḷaka **maryā**-∅*   'The cup **broke**.'
       *pyāḷaka=m **mǎřǎ***   'I **broke** the cup.'
    c. *āwī **məjī**-o*   'The water **will pour**.'
       *āwī **məj**-o*   'He **will pour** the water.'
    d. *āwī **məjyā**-(a)*   'The water **poured**.'
       *āwī=š **mət**-a*   'He **poured** the water.'

This encoding of transitivity by Umlaut may have facilitated the development of the encoding of transitivity differences in JSNENA past stems and resultative participles, which manifests itself principally in differences in vowels, e.g. *twər-* 'broke' (trans. past stem) vs *twīr-* 'broke' (intrans. past stem). This was achieved by reallocating vocalic patterns internal to JSNENA morphology (see §5.2 for more details). Distinct vocalic patterns were internally not available for the present stem so the Gorani model of Umlaut was not replicated in the present stem. The convergence, therefore, was partial.

In Gorani the more regular pattern for the derivation of a transitive causative stem from an unaccusative stem is through the addition of the causative affix *-n* to the unaccusative stem.

(786)   a. *yāna **wuř**-o*   'The house **will collapse**.'
         *yānakay **wuř-n**-o*   'He **will destroy** the house.'
    b. *yanaka **wuř**-ā*   'The house **collapsed**.'
       *yānaka=š **wuř-n**-ā*   'He **destroyed** the house.'

These derivational changes to the stems could also have acted as a model for the JSNENA differences in encoding transitive and intransitive, though the model was formally less close than the Umlaut system of vowel alternation. In both cases JSNENA has replicated the distribution of the transitivity coding of Gorani in so far as this has been possible using internal JSNENA resources, which, as remarked, had the result of it being restricted to the past stem and resultative participle.

In Sanandaj Kurdish transitivity distinctions are not made with Umlaut but only by the addition of the causative suffix *-n* (present), *-n(d)* (past) to the unaccusative stem to derive the transitive counterpart.

(787) Kurdish
*āw **a-rəž-ē*** 'The water **pours**.'
*āw **a-rəž-n-ē*** 'He **pours** the water.'
*āw **rəjyā-Ø*** 'The water **poured**.'
*āw=ī **rəjā-nd*** 'He **poured** the water.'

So far the discussion has concerned morphological causatives of intransitive verbs, whereby the subject of an intransitive verb is made the object of a causative transitive verb. JSNENA and the Iranian languages of the Sanandaj region can apply morphological causatives also to transitive verbs. In English the agent of the transitive verb is made the object of the causative verb, e.g. 'I cut down the prickles' > 'He made me cut down the prickles'. In JSNENA and the Iranian languages there is a different typology, whereby the object of the transitive verb is made the object of the causative verb and the agent of the transitive verb (i.e. the causee) is expressed by a prepositional phrase, e.g.[3]

(788) JSNENA
jəl-af ləwš-ī̀-la.ǀ
clothes-3SG.F wear.PST-3PL-OBL.3SG.F
'She put on her clothes.'
ʾonī jəl-af məlbəš-ī-lū ə̀l-af.ǀ
they clothes-3SG.F cause_to_wear.PST-3PL-OBL.3PL on-3SG.F
'They caused her to put on her clothes.'

(789) Gorani
dřè̠=šā pana kan-ā.ǀ
prickle=3PL by pluck.PST-1SG
'They made me cut down prickles.'

(790) Kurdish
nān=ī pē=m a-kə̀rd.ǀ
bread=3SG by=1SG IPFV-do.PST
'She would make me cook bread.'

The non-causative versions of the sentences above are as follows:

---

[3] For the typology of the causative of transitive verbs cross-linguistically see Dixon (2000, 48). The typology of JSNENA and the Iranian languages of Sanandaj is an areal feature of many languages of Western Asia (Khan 2016 vol. 1, 397–436).

(791) Gorani
 dřȅ=m   kan-ē.|
 prickle=1SG pluck.PST-3PL
 'I cut down prickles.'

(792) Kurdish
 nằn=əm   kərd.|
 bread=1SG do.PST
 'I made bread.'

In JSNENA and Iranian, however, such morphological causatives of transitive verbs are not very productive. In JSNENA periphrastic constructions are more frequently used, such as

(793) JSNENA
 a. 'o   ʾəbē-lē   mən-af   zar-akē
    he   want.PST-OBL.3SG.M   from-3SG.F wheat-DEF
    taxn-ằ-lē.|
    grind.PRS-3SG.F-OBL.3SG.M
    'He wanted/required her to grind the wheat (= He made her grind the wheat).'
    'o   ʾəbē-lē   mən-af   kēp-akē
    he   want.PST-OBL.3SG.M   from-3SG.F stone-DEF
    manty-ằ-la.|
    lift.PRS-3SG.F-OBL.3SG.F
    'He wanted/required her to lift the stone (= He made her lift the stone).'

7.14 The post-verbal particle -o

The post-verbal particle *-o* (< *-āwa*) is widely used in JSNENA. In principle it takes the stress, e.g. *kēnwa + o > kēnwa-ó* 'They used to come back' and it is connected to what precedes by a hyphen in the transcription of JSNENA. It, nevertheless, has properties of a clitic according to criteria such as its regular peripheral position and the freedom of its host selection (cf. Bickel and Nichols 2007, 174–75). As we shall see (§7.14.5), it also occurs on non-verbal hosts.

A vowel preceding it is sometimes elided, e.g. *dīrna + o > dīrn-ó* 'I returned'.

This particle is a loan from the Iranian languages of Sanandaj, where it takes the form =*aw*, =*awa* in Kurdish, and =*o*, =*wa*, =*va* in Gorani of Hawraman, all of which are clitics that are never stressed. This particle is apparently related to Middle Iranian *abāz* 'back, again'. It is generally referred to as a particle marking telicity distinctions. The JSNENA form *-o* could be directly borrowed from Gorani.

JSNENA has also replicated the functional range of this particle in the Iranian languages of the region.

7.14.1 'again, back'

In some cases the particle is used in JSNENA to express the sense of 'returning back', 'restoring' or 'repetition':

(794) JSNENA
    a. *lēlawāē   k-ē-wa-ò.*|
       evenings   IND-come.PRS.3SG.M-PSTC-TELIC
       'He would return in the evenings.' (A:99)
    b. *k-mē-wā-l-o   ga-bēla   nòš-ēf.*|
       IND-bring.PRS.3SG.M-PSTC-OBL.3SG.M-TELIC   in-house   self-3SG.M
       'He would bring it back to his house.' (A:81)

This meaning of the particle in Kurdish and Gorani is seen in the following examples:

(795) Gorani
    āmà̱-(ā)nē=wa.|
    come.PST-1SG=TELIC
    'I came back.'

(796) Kurdish
    a. *šèr-ēk   hāt=aw.*|
       lion-INDF   come.PST.3SG=TELIC
       'A lion returned (to the mill).'
    b. *a=y-tèr-m=aw   bo=t.*|
       IND=3SG-bring.PRS-1SG=TELIC   for=2SG
       'I will bring her back to you.'

7.14.2 Telicity

In many cases the particle *-o* in JSNENA expresses simply that the action has an endpoint, which is not necessarily a point of return. The action, therefore, is marked as telic, i.e. it contains a dynamic component and an endpoint (*telos*) attained by the completion of the event, rather than being a homogeneous state or durative activity, e.g.

(797) JSNENA
    a. ’ara   pēx-a-ò.ǀ
       ground cool.PRS-3SG.F-TELIC
       'The ground will cool down (completely).'

Contrast:

    b. ’ara   pex-à.ǀ
       ground cool.PRS-3SG.F
       'The ground will cool (but not necessarily reach the endpoint of being totally cool).'

(798) JSNENA
    a. *talga* *pašr-a-ò.*ǀ
       snow   melt.PRS-3SG.F-TELIC
       'The snow will melt (and completely disappear).'

Contrast:

    b. *talga* *pašr-à.*ǀ
       snow   melt.PRS-3SG.F
       'The snow will melt (but not necessary completely).'

The telic function of particle in the Iranian of Sanandaj is seen in the following examples.

(799) Kurdish
    *kanīšk pāwšā xwaš a-w-èt=aw.*ǀ
    girl   king   good IND-COP.PRS-3SG=TELIC
    'The princess will be healed.'

(800) Gorani Luhon
    yax-aka garmā-y   tāwnā=wa
    ice-DEF   heat-OBL.M melt.PST=TELIC
    'The heat melted the ice.'
    (MacKenzie 1966, 51)

7.14.3 'opening'

In JSNENA the particle is used in combination with the verb ʾ-w-l 'to do' to express the sense of 'to open'. When the construction is intransitive, the verb ʾ-w-l 'to do' is replaced by x-∅-r 'to become', e.g.

(801) JSNENA
    a. *tara*   *k-o-n-ēf-ò.*ˈ
        door   IND-do.PRS-1SG.M-3SG.M-TELIC
        'I am opening the door.'
    b. *wardē*   *xar-ī-ò.*ˈ
        flowers become.PRS-3PL-TELIC
        'The flowers are opening.'

The transitive construction is a direct calque of a corresponding construction in the Iranian languages:

(802) Kurdish
    mard *səfra-(a)ka=y* *xwà=y=ī*   *kərd=aw.*ˈ
    PN   cloth-DEF=EZ   REFL=his-3SG do.PST=TELIC
    'Mard opened his cloth.'

(803) Gorani
    kara=š=va!
    do.PRS-IMP.2SG=3SG=TELIC
    'Open it!'

The intransitive construction has a parallel in Kurmanji, though note the preverbal position of the particle.

(804) Kurmanji
    gul   *va=d-b-ən.*
    flower TELIC=IND-be.PRS-3PL
    'The flowers are opening.'

7.14.4 Combination with other verbal affixes

The position of the particle *-o* in the JSNENA verbal form replicates that of the Iranian languages in that it is always placed at the end of the verbal form, after all other affixes such as pronominal suffixes or the enclitic copula.

(805) JSNENA
    a. heštan   baxt-ēf   la   thītē=ya-ò.|
        yet   wife-3SG.M   NEG   find.PTCP.3SF.F=COP.3SG.F-TELIC
        'He has not found his wife yet.'
    b. sē-lox-o   ba-šon-àf!|
        go.IMP.SG-OBL.2SG.M   in-place-3SG.F
        'Go back after it!' (E:35)

(806) Gorani
    kard=īč=š=o.
    do.PST=ADD=3SG=TELIC
    'He opened it too.'

(807) Kurdish
    awān   a-xàf-n=aw.|
    3PL   IND-sleep.PRS-3PL=TELIC
    'They sleep again.'

7.14.5 On adverbials

In JSNENA the particle *-o* is found on spatial adverbs such as *tēx-o* 'below', which may have been motivated by its usage with the cognate verb *t-y-x-o* 'to go down', *rēš-o* 'again' (literally: 'back to the head') and *laḥal-o* 'into the distance', e.g.

(808) JSNENA
    a. xa   ṭabaqa   xèt=əč   xīrē-n| bīš   tēx-ò.|
        one level   other=ADD   be.PTCP.PL-COP.3PL more low-TELIC
        'There was another class (of people), (who were)
        lower down.' (B:6)

b. *xmār-akē   mən-pliyaw   o   dašta   laḥal-o*
   ass-DEF   from-middle that field   far-TELIC
   *mrə̀q-lū.*ǀ
   cause_to_flee.PST-OBL.3PL
   'They made the ass run from the field into the distance.'

It seems that here JSNENA replicates the Kurdish postposition *-aw*, which is homophonous with the aspectual particle *-aw*. In the following examples the postposition *-aw* forms a circumposition with the directional particle *=a* (a reduced form of preposition *ba* in origin) on the verb and appears on the spatial adverbs 'down', and 'this side'.

(809) Kurdish
 a. *Nāmard=ī   hāwərd=a   xwār-àw.*ǀ
    PN=3SG   bring.PST=DRCT   down-POST
    '(The lion) brought Namard down.'
 b. *kanīšk   nàwo=yš   tēr-ēt=a   am   war-aw.*ǀ
    girl   middle=ADD   IND.bring.PRS-3SG=DRCT DEM.PROX   front-POST
    'He brings the middle girl to this side too.'

7.15 Direct object

7.15.1 Present stem verbs and imperatives

In JSNENA when a present stem verb or imperative has a direct object that is an independent nominal or pronominal phrase various types of syntactic construction are used. There may be no grammatical marking of the object (§7.15.1.1) or there may be grammatical marking in the form of a pronominal object copy on the verb or a preposition on the object nominal (§7.15.1.2).

In Gorani when a present stem verb or imperative has a direct object nominal, the direct object nominal may be inflected with case marking in some circumstances. There is no corresponding case marking in Kurdish.

7.15.1.1 No grammatical marking of object
In JSNENA when the object nominal is indefinite, there is no grammatical marking of the object either on the nominal or on the verb in the form of a pronominal suffix. This includes cases where the object is combined with the indefinite particle *xa* (810.a-b) and were the particle is absent (810.c-e), e.g.

(810) JSNENA
- a. xa-waxtara tāt-ī yatū-wa| **xa ḥakayat**
  one-time father-1SG sit.PRS.3SG.M-PSTC one story
  ḥaqē-wa bāqàn.|
  tell.PRS.3SG.M-PSTC to-us
  'Once my father sat and told us **a story**.' (A:98)
- b. lēlē rēš-šāta **xa-səfra** šawē-n-wa ruwà.|
  night head-year one-cloth spread.PRS-3PL-PSTC big
  'On New Year's Eve they spread out **a large cloth**.' (A:65)
- c. **jām** k-mē-n-wa ba-qam kalda=ū xətnà.|
  mirror IND-bring.PRS-3PL-PSTC to-before bride=and groom
  'They brought **a mirror** to the bride and groom.' (A:45)
- d. šamaš=ē knīštà| g-ēzəl-wa **sūsì**
  beadle=EZ synagogue IND-go.PRS.3SG.M-PSTC horse
  k-mē-wa.|
  IND-bring.PRS.3SG.M-PSTC
  'The beadle of the synagogue went to fetch a horse.' (A:43)
- e. **mastà** ho-lī.|
  yoghurt give.IMP.SG-OBL.1SG
  'Give me yoghurt!' (A:79)

Likewise, in Gorani direct object nominals that are indefinite are generally left unmarked for case marking. This includes cases where the object has the indefinite suffix -ēw (811.a-b–812.a) and where it lacks the suffix (812.b–d):

(811) Gorani Luhon
- a. ay padšāzād **gıraw-ew** kar-me.
  VOC prince wager-INDF do.PRS-1PL
  'O prince, let us make **a wager**.'
  (MacKenzie 1966, 80)
- b. **baʿezē-(ē)w āḷəf=īč** paydā kar-ū pay
  some-IND fodder=ADD visible do.PRS-1SG for
  asp-aka-y=m.
  horse-DEF-OBL.M=1SG
  'And also I procure **some fodder** for my horse.'
  (MacKenzie 1966, 78)

(812) Gorani
    a. Ø-lū-a   čan-ēwa=w   bāzē   bàn=əm
       SBJV-go.PRS-IMP.2SG needle-INDF=and some thread=1SG
       pay   b-ār-a.|
       for   SBJV-bring.PRS-IMP.2SG
       'Go (and) bring me a **needle and some thread**.'

    b. **das**   măč   Ø-kar-mē=ū| dəmā ānày,| **maḷå̀**
       hand kiss IND-do.PRS-1PL=and after DEM.OBL.M mullah
       Ø-bar-me,| **žanī**   mára   Ø-bəř-mè̌=ū.|
       IND-take.PRS-1SG woman marriage IND-cut.PRS-1SG=and
       '(As for the marriage customs) we kiss the **hands** (of elders) (lit. a hand),
       take **a mullah**, marry **women** and so on.'

    c. **zamāwəna**=š pay   Ø-gēr-òn.|
       wedding=3SG for   IND-take.PRS-3SG
       'He throws **a wedding ceremony** for her.'
       yò   taqn-a   bə-zān-a   jūab=ət
       one   shot.PRS-IMP.2SG SBJV-know.PRS-IMP.2SG answer=2SG
       ha-n.|
       PTCL-COP.3SG
       'Shoot **one** (bullet), see if there is an answer.'

    d. 'awal-ē-na   **duē žanī**   Ø-kīān-å̀.|
       first-PL.DIR-in two woman.DIR.PL IND-send.PRS-3PL
       'First, they will send **two women** (to the house of the bride).'

7.15.1.2 Grammatical marking of object

In JSNENA a direct object may be indexed by a co-referential pronominal direct object suffix on the verb. This construction is used when the object nominal is definite, e.g.,

(813) JSNENA
    a. xwān-akē   k-mē-n-wā-là=ū|
       table-DEF   IND-bring.PRS-3PL-PSTC-OBL.3SG.F=and
       'They delivered the table and ..'
       g-bē   hē-t-o   'ay-brāta
       IND-need.PRS.3SG.M come.PRS-2SG.M this-girl
       gor-ēt-à.|
       marry.PRS-2SG.M-OBL.3SG.F
       'You must go back and marry that girl.' (A:18)

b. *'ay-zarà*ˡ   *taxn-ỉ-wā-lē.*ˡ
this-wheat   grind.PRS-3PL-PSTC-OBL.3SG.M
'They used to grind the wheat.' (A:59)

A pronominal copy is also used with some indefinite objects. This occurs where the indefinite object plays a prominent role in the immediately succeeding discourse. Indefinite nominals with this prominent discourse status are typically marked by the indefinite marker *xa dana* (§6.2.10) or at least by *xa* (§6.2.1), e.g.

(814) JSNENA
xa-dāna put ḥalabī doq-wā-la
one-CLF can Aleppan hold.PRS.3SG.M-PSTC-OBL.3SG.F
*ba-'ĭl-èf=ū*ˡ   *daēl-wa*   *gà-af=u*ˡ
in-hand-3SG.M=and beat.PRS.3SG.M-PSTC in-3SG.F=and
'He would hold a metal can in his hand and beat it (like a drum).' (A:99)

An alternative means of marking a direct object nominal in JSNENA is to attach the preposition *həl-* to the object nominal without cross-indexing it by a co-referential pronominal suffix on the verb. This construction is attested with definite object nominals that have human referents, e.g.

(815) JSNENA
*'ay-bronà*ˡ   *həl-day brāta g-bè.*ˡ
this-boy OBL-this girl IND-love.PRS.3SG.M
'The boy loves the girl.' (A:18)

It is also used where the object is an independent pronominal phrase with a human referent, e.g.

(816) JSNENA
susy-akē mən-sarbāzxānē k-mē-wā-lē
horse-DEF from-barracks IND-bring.PRS.3SG.M-PSTC-OBL.3SG.M
*qam-tarà,*ˡ   *həl-dīdī*   *markû-wa.*ˡ
before-door OBL-OBL.1SG cause_to_mount.PRS.3SG.M-PSTC
'He would bring the horse from the barracks to the door and would mount me (on it).' (A:15–16)

In Gorani definite object nominals have oblique marking when they are definite human referents (817.a) or when they have the definite suffix *-aka* (817.b-e):

(817) Gorani
    a. *lāla   Hasan-ī   mə-žnās-ù̇,*ˈ   *Rahmān-ī mə-žnās-ù̇.*ˈ
       uncle PN-OBL.M IND-know.PRS-1SG PN-OBL.M IND-know.PRS-1SG
       'I know uncle Hasan, I know Rahman.'
    b. *kənāč-akē=š   Ø-čər-ò.*ˈ
       daughter-DEF.F.OBL=3SG IND-call.PRS-3SG
       *šāzāda-(a)ka-y=č   Ø-čərò.*ˈ
       prince-DEF-OBL.M=ADD IND-call.PRS-3SG
       '(The king) summoned her daughter. He summoned the prince too.'
    c. *har-aka-y   Ø-wəz-o   tawè̦la-(a)ka=w*ˈ
       donkey-DEF-OBL.M IND-put.PRS-3SG stable-DEF=and
       'He puts the donkey in the stable.'
    d. *məro-akā   dà̦na   dāna   Ø-čən-o.*ˈ
       pear-DEF.OBL.PL CLF CLF IND-pick.PRS-3SG
       'He plucks the pears one by one.'
    e. *čāwlāy   kāwř-akā   m-ār-ã̀*ˈ
       afterwards sheep-DEF.OBL.PL IND-bring.PRS-3PL
       *č-ā   sara   Ø-bəř-ã̀.*ˈ
       IN-DEM.DIST head IND-cut.PRS-3PL
       'Then they bring the sheep and butcher them there.'

An independent pronoun object has oblique marking:

(818) Gorani
     *ād̠-ī   Ø-wìn-ū.*ˈ
     3SG-OBL.M IND-see.PRS-1SG
     'I see him.'

In Gorani, however, specific indefinite objects are not oblique-marked, as seen above in §7.15.1.1.

The distribution of grammatical coding of object nominals in JSNENA and Gorani, therefore, is to a large extent parallel. Whereas in Gorani, however, there is one exponence of coding, in the form of oblique case-marking, in JSNENA there are two types of exponence, viz. a preposition on the nominal or a pronominal copy on the verb. The two exponents of object coding in JSNENA have historical roots in earlier Aramaic. The preposition *həl-* is a reflex of the oblique preposition *l-*. Both this preposition and pronominal object copies on the verb are object marking strategies in earlier eastern Aramaic varieties such as Syriac and Jewish Babylonian Aramaic (Nöldeke 1904, 226–34; Bar-Asher Siegal 2016, 201–2). The oblique preposition *həl-* on the object nominal in JSNENA can be regarded as the closest structural match of the two JSNENA strategies to the oblique case marking on the nominal in Gorani. It is significant that this match occurs on maximally salient objects, i.e. definite human objects. The matching, therefore, has been triggered by salience. Although the distribution of grammatical marking in JSNENA matches the distribution in Gorani, only a subset of the marking of JSNENA objects matches the Gorani marking structurally. This is a case, therefore, of partial structural convergence, in which a salient subset undergoes convergence.

7.15.2 Past stem verbs

The expression of pronominal direct objects of past stem verbs has been described in §5.10.3.

In JSNENA the pronominal object of all persons may be expressed by prepositional phrases. When the pronominal direct object is 3rd person, it may alternatively be expressed by the number and gender inflection of the past stem. This corresponds to the direct person suffixes that are used to express the subject of intransitive past stems and may be identified as 'ergative' syntax:

(819) JSNENA–Ergative
    a.   *grəš-Ø-lē* 'He pulled him.'
         pull.PST-3SG.M-OBL.3SG.M
    b.   *gərš-ā-lē* 'He pulled her.'
         pull.PST-3SG.F-OBL.3SG.M
    c.   *gərš-ī-lē* 'He pulled them.'
         pull.PST-3PL-OBL.3SG.M

In Gorani all persons can be grammatically indexed by means of direct person affixes on the past stem of the verb.

(820) Gorani
    a.   *bàrd-ā=šā*   *āḷəf*   *kanē.*
         take.PST-1SG=3PL fodder mow.INF
         'They took me to mow the grass.'
    b.   *tāta-y=m*   *kīāst-īdē.*
         father-OBL.M=1SG send.PST-2PL
         'My father sent you (pl).'

c. *bard-īmē=šā.*
   take.PST-1PL=3PL
   'They took us.'

In Sanandaj Kurdish no trace of object direct suffixes is left on past stem verbs. Rather direct objects are marked on the verb by oblique clitics:

(821) Kurdish
   a. *bə̀rd=yān=mān.*
      take.PST=3PL=1PL
      'We took them.'
   b. *hāwə̀rd=mān=o.*
      bring.PST=1PL=2SG
      'You brought us.'

In the ergative construction of JSNENA, the 3rd person pronominal object may be expressed in addition by an independent pronoun in its direct form, without any object marker:

(822) JSNENA – ergative
   a. *'o grəš-Ø-lē*   'He pulled him.'
      3SG pull.PST-3SG.M-OBL.3SG.M
   b. *'o gərš-ā-lē*   'He pulled her.'
      3SG pull.PST-3SG.F-OBL.3SG.M
   c. *'onī gərš-ī-lē*   'He pulled them.'
      3PL pull.PST-3PL-OBL.3SG.M

Likewise, in the ergative construction of Gorani, a pronominal object may be expressed by an independent pronoun in addition to the person affix. In such cases third person pronouns, which inflects for case, are in the direct case, as in JSNENA:

(823) Gorani
   a. *mən āḍa=m   dī-a.*
      1SG 3SG.F.DIR=1SG see.PST-3SG.F
      'I saw her.'
   b. *mən āḍē=m   dī-ē.*
      1SG 3PL.DIR=1SG see.PST-3PL
      'I saw them.'

c. *mə̀n=šā karḍ-ā ba šwāna.*
1SG=3PL do.PST-1SG to shepherd
'They made me into shepherd.'

In JSNENA when a verb that is treated as transitive and inflected with oblique L-suffixes does not have a specific object, the past stem is in the neutral 3SG.M form, e.g.

(824) JSNENA
šəhlē 'He coughed.' < **šhəl-lē*
təplē 'He sneezed.' < **tpəl-lē*
mīrē 'He said.' < **mīr-lē*
momēlē 'He swore.'

Similarly, in corresponding forms in Gorani 3SG.M inflection is the unmarked form of the stem, which in addition to expressing a 3SG.M object, is used neutrally without marking any specific object.

(825) Gorani
vāt=əš
say.PST=3SG
'He said.'

In JSNENA, when the direct object is a definite full nominal, the past stem agrees with this so long as the nominal is in its direct form, without any object marker. This agreement is only distinguishable with SG.F and PL objects:

(826) JSNENA
  a. *gor-akē grəš-Ø-lī*
     man-DEF pull.PST-3SG.M-OBL.1SG
     'I pulled the man.'
  b. *baxt-akē gərš-ā-lī*
     woman-DEF pull.PST-3SG.F-OBL.1SG
     'I pulled the woman.'
  c. *barūxawāl-ī gərš-ī-lī*
     friends-1SG pull.PST-3PL-OBL.1SG
     'I pulled my friends.'

Examples from the text corpus:

(827) JSNENA
   a. ga-doka   madrasa   'Aliáns   tərṣ-ằ-lē.|
      in-there school   PN   build.PST-3SG.F-OBL.3SG.M
      'The Alliance built the school there.' (B:12)
   b. qīm-ēx   zəbn-ī́-lan   bēl-akē|
      rise.PST-1PL sell.PST-3PL-OBL.1PL   house-DEF
      'We sold the houses.' (C:8)

Likewise, in Gorani the verb agrees with direct-marked definite direct object nominals:

(828) Gorani
      dāna   dāna   wara-(a)kē=š   bar   ằrd-ē.|
      CLF   CLF   lamb-DEF.PL.DIR=3SG   out   bring.PST-3PL
      'She took out the lambs one by one.'

(829) Gorani Luhon
      kənāčē   padšā=š   dī-a.
      daughter   king=3SG   see.PST-3SG.F
      'He saw the king's daughter.'
      (MacKenzie 1966, 72)

In JSNENA the past stem agrees also with an indefinite object with a specific referent that plays a prominent role in the immediately following discourse. Such nominals are typically marked by the indefinite particles *xa* or *xa dāna*, when singular, and *čəkma*, when plural:

(830) JSNENA
   a. xa   brāta   ma'arəfi̊   wīl-ā-lū
      one   girl   acquaintance   make.PST-3SG.F-OBL.3PL
      bā-ēf| kè̩| baška   xlūlà=č   hol.|
      to-3SG.M   REL   perhaps   wedding=ADD   do.PRS.3SG.M
      'They introduced a girl to him, whom he could perhaps marry.' (D:17)
   b. xa   xlūla   rāba   mojalàl   dəwq-ā-lē
      one   wedding   very   grand   hold.PST-3SG.F-OBL.3SG.M
      bāq-af   tāt-akē.|
      for-her   father-DEF
      'The father arranged a very grand wedding for her.' (D:27)

In this feature JSNENA matches Gorani, as shown by the following examples, in which the verbs agree with salient indefinite objects.

(831) Gorani
    a. mən žàn-ē=m   ārd-a.|
       1SG woman-INDF=1SG bring.PST-3SG.F
       'I took a wife.'
    b. bāzē tawanī=š wə̀st-ē   dəl=ē   lama=w warga-(a)kē.|
       some stone=3SG put.PST-3PL inside=EZ belly=EZ wolf.F-DEF.F.OBL
       'She put some stones inside the wolf's belly.'

In JSNENA a definite object nominal may optionally have the preposition *həl-* prefixed to it. This functions as a direct object marker. When the definite object has this explicit object marking, the past stem is always in the neutral 3SG.M form and does not agree with the object nominal:

(832) JSNENA
    a. həl-gor-akē   grəš-lī.
       OBL-man-DEF pull.PST-OBL.1SG
       'I pulled the man.'
    b. həl-baxt-akē   grəš-lī.
       OBL-woman-DEF pull.PST-OBL.1SG
       'I pulled the woman.'
    c. həl-barūxawāl-ī grəš-lī.
       OBL-friends-1SG pull.PST-OBL.1SG
       'I pulled my friends.'

Example from the text corpus:

(833) JSNENA
    hìt-wa| bron-akē həl-brāt-akē
    EXIST-PSTC boy-DEF OBL-girl-DEF
    la-xē-wā-lē   ba-ʿamr-èf.|
    NEG-see.PST-PSTC-OBL.3SG.M in-life-3SG.M
    'Sometimes the boy had never seen the girl in his life.' (A:2)

Gorani does not favour the use of oblique-marked nominal direct objects with past tense of verbs, since it would be a violation of ergativity in the past tense. No example of oblique-marked direct objects of past-stem verbs were found in the text corpus of Gorani. The following example with an oblique-marked nominal direct object comes from elicited data. Here the verb carries a 1SG direct suffix which expresses an external possessor.

(834) Gorani
zaroḷa-kā=šā   bard-ā.
child-DEF.OBL.PL=3PL   take.PST-1SG
'They took away my children.'

In Kurdish of the Sanandaj region, a past-stem verb never agrees with a direct object argument.

7.15.2.2 Compound verbal forms

As with the past stem, the compound verbal forms consisting of a resultative participle and a copula in JSNENA can be used in ergative or accusative type constructions. In the ergative type of construction, the resultative participle + copula phrase agrees with a 3rd person undergoer. There is no coding of the 3rd person agent in the verbal phrase corresponding to the L-suffixes of the past-stem construction:

(835) JSNENA
    a. *'onī gərša=y*
       3PL   pull.PTCP.SG.M=COP.3SG.M
       'They have pulled him.'
    b. *'onī graštē=ya*
       3PL   pull.PTCP.SG.F=COP.3SG.F
       'They have pulled her.'
    c. *'o   gəršē=n*
       3SG pull.PTCP.PL=COP.3PL
       'He/she has pulled them.'

It is also possible to express the pronominal object by an independent pronominal prepositional phrase. In such cases, the construction has an accusative type syntax. Here the compound verb always has the 3SG.M form used neutrally, without agreeing with the undergoer. The marking of the object is expressed only by the prepositional phrase. The agent must be 3rd person but still has no coding on the verb. The undergoer, which in such constructions is not referentially bound to the compound verb, may be any person:

Accusative

(836) JSNENA
   a. *tāt-ī*   *həl-do*   *gəršā=y*
       father-1SG OBL-OBL.3SG.M pull.PTCP.SG.M=COP.3SG.M
       tāt-ī   *gəršā=y*   *'əl-ēf*
       father-1SG pull.PTCP.SG.M=COP.3SG.M OBL-3SG.M
       'My father has pulled him.'
   b. *həl-dīdox*   *gəršā=y*
       OBL-OBL.2SG.M pull.PTCP.SG.M=COP.3SG.M
       gəršā=y   *'əl-ox*
       pull.PTCP.SG.M=COP.3SG.M OBL-2SG.M
       'He/she/they has/have pulled you (sg.m).'
   c. *həl-dīdī*   *gəršā=y*
       to-OBL.1SG pull.PTCP. SG.M=COP.3SG.M
       gəršā=y   *'əli*
       pull.PTCP.SG.M=COP.3SG.M to-OBL.1SG
       'He/she/they has/have pulled me.'

In Gorani the ergative construction is used with compound verbal forms. The resultative participle and the copula agree with the undergoer and the object nominal has direct case inflection.

(837) Gorani
   a. *mən*   *žan-ē=m*   *māra*   *bəřyē=na*
       1SG   woman.DIR.F-INDF=1SG marriage cut.PTCP.F=3SG.F
       sar=u *ṣa*   *təmanà.*|
       on=EZ 100 Toman
       'I married (a) woman for 100 tomans (unit of currency) of wedding proportion.'
   b. *Alī Guḷāḷa zamàwəna kar-o,*| *da'wat=əš*   *kàrdē=ndē.*|
       PN PN   wedding   do.PRS-3SG invitation=3SG do.PST.PTCP.PL=2PL
       'Ali Gulāla is having a marriage ceremony. He has invited you.'

(838) Gorani Luhon
tā āro p-ī jora juan-ē
till today in-DEM.PROX kind-DEM1 youth-DIR.PL
basazuan-ē=š sarnugum kardē=nē
helpless-DIR.PL=3SG overthrow do.PST.PTCP.PL=3PL
'(but this mistress of yours), who till today has overthrown (so many) helpless youths in this way.'
(MacKenzie 1966, 82)

In constructions with a compound verb JSNENA exhibits the following features that differ from Gorani:
(i) There is no coding of the agent by an oblique pronominal affix.
(ii) An agent nominal is not marked as oblique.
(iii) A direct object expressed by a direct pronominal affix is restricted to the 3rd person.
(iv) A direct object nominal or independent pronoun may be in an oblique form (expressed by the preposition həl-).

7.16 The infinitive

7.16.1 Nominal function

In various constructions in JSNENA the infinitive occupies the position of a nominal in the clause. These include the following.

7.16.1.1 Complement of a preposition

This is most frequently attested where the infinitive is the complement of expressions of 'beginning' such as *šərū' '-w-l ba-* 'to make a start at, to begin to' or *'īla d-Ø-y ba-, 'īla h-w-l ba-, 'īla '-w-l* 'to put a hand to, to begin', which are calques of the Kurdish and Gorani compound verb *das kirdin ba* 'to put a hand to' (see below), e.g.

(839) JSNENA
  a. šərū' wī-lē ba-'axolē.
     beginning do.PST-OBL.3SG.M in-eat.INF
     'He began to eat.'
  b. 'īla dī-lē ba-garošē.
     hand put.PST-OBL.3SG.M in-pull.INF
     'He began to pull.'

c. ʾīla   hīw-lē   ba-čaqoē.
   hand   give.PST-OBL.3SG.M   in-dig.INF
   'He began to dig.'

In (840) from the text corpus the preposition *ba-* is omitted before the infinitive *băxoe*.

(840) JSNENA
ʾīl-ī   wī-lī   baxoḕ.
hand-1SG   do.PST-OBL.1SG   weep.INF
'I began to weep.' (C:4)

If there is a direct object nominal, this is usually placed between the preposition and the infinitive, in conformity with the normal placement of objects before the verb in clauses:

(841) JSNENA
   a. šərū'   wī-lī   ba-mēwa   'axolē.
       beginning do.PST-OBL.1SG   in-fruit eat.INF
       'I began to eat fruit.'
   b. ʾīla   hīw-lī   ba-xola   garošē.
       hand   give.PST-OBL.1SG rope   pull.INF
       'I began to pull the rope.'

In Kurdish and Gorani of Sanandaj, an infinitive is used after the expression *das kirdin ba* 'to put a hand to'. In Kurdish the infinitive occurs often with the cliticised form of the preposition *ba-* on the verb, viz. *=a* (842), but in Gorani the preposition has its full form *ba-* (843.a). Alternatively, the preposition is elided in Gorani (843.b). This suggests that the corresponding constructions in JSNENA *ʾīla d-∅-y ba-, ʾīla h-w-l ba-, ʾīla '-w-l* replicates the construction in Gorani rather than the one in Kurdish.

(842) Kurdish
kanīšk-al   das   a-ka-n=a   gīrìn.
daughter-PL hand   IND-do.PRS-3PL=DRCT   cry.INF
'The girls start to cry.'

(843) Gorani
   a. das   kar-ā   ba   məro   wằrday=ū   gāḷta   karday.
       hand   do.PRS-3PL to   pear   eat.INF=and   joking   do.INF
       'They started to eat pears and to joke.'

b. *das   kar-o   gərawə̀y.*|
   hand   do.PRS-3SG   cry.INF
   'She started to cry.'

The expression of beginning *šəruʿ-w-l ba-* 'to make a start at, to begin to' in JSNENA is a calque of Persian *šoru kardan*, which has probably been borrowed through Sanandaj Kurdish.

7.16.1.2 Complement of a nominal

In JSNENA the infinitive may be a complement of a preceding nominal in an annexation relationship. This is found in (844), in which the infinitive expresses a transitive event with a direct object constituent placed before it:

(844) JSNENA
   'āna   ḥawṣala=ē   'ara   tarošḕ   līt-ī=ū|
   I   patience=EZ land   build.INF   NEG.EXIST-OBL.1SG=and
   'I do not have the patience to build (on) the land.' (C:6)

A parallel Gorani construction is seen in (845):

(845) Gorani
   duē   sāḷ-ē,   yar-ḕ   sāḷē   ēn-ē
   two   year-DIR.PL   three   year-DIR.PL   come.PSTC-3PL
   āmošo   kar-ēn-ē=ū   lū-ēn-ē=wa| *ətə*
   visiting do.PRS-PSTC-3PL=and   go.PRS-PSTC-3PL=TELIC   well
   tā   waxt=ū   bàrday=ū   žanī.|
   until   time=EZ   take.INF=EZ woman
   'They would come to visit (the family of the bride) for two, three years until it was the time to take the woman (the bride).'

In (846) the infinitive in JSNENA is the complement of the adjective *ḥarīk* 'busy'. This has a parallel in the Gorani sentence in (847), in which the infinitive is the complement of the adjective *xarīk* 'busy'.

(846) JSNENA
   'o-trē   ḥarīkē   šyākà=yē-lū.|
   those-two   busy   wrestle.INF=COP.PST-OBL.3PL
   'The two of them were busy wrestling.'

(847) Gorani
　　　xarīk=ū　čənyày　məro-akā=n.|
　　　busy=EZ　pluck.INF　pear-DEF.OBL.PL=COP.3SG.M
　　　'He is busy plucking pears.'

7.16.1.3 Nominal arguments in copula or existential clauses

In JSNENA an infinitive can be the head of a nominal argument in a copula or existential clause. In such constructions, the infinitive is treated as either masculine or feminine in gender. Nominals that are the complement of the infinitive are placed before it, e.g.

(848) JSNENA
　　a.　'ēa　'īla　dwaqà=yē-la.|
　　　　this　hand　join.INF=COP.PST-OBL.3SG.F
　　　　'This is "the joining of hands."' (A:35)
　　b.　'ēa　ḥamām　zālu=yē-lē.|
　　　　this　baths　go.INF=COP.PST-OBL.3SG.M
　　　　'That was (the description of) their going to the baths.' (A:38)

The following sentences exhibit parallel constructions in Gorani.

(849) Gorani
　　a.　hurpřày　bīa=n=ū　　　　　　šīrīnī　wàrday
　　　　dance.INF　be.PST.PTCP.M=COP.3SG=and　sweet　eat.INF
　　　　bīa=n.|
　　　　be.PST.PTCP.M=COP.3SG
　　　　'(Among the customs of marriage) were dancing and pastry eating.'
　　b.　faqat　mən　kār=əm　žan　taḷàq　dāy
　　　　only　1SG　job=1SG　woman　divorce　give.INF
　　　　bē=ū|　　　　　　hìjbī　　　karday　bē.|
　　　　COP.PST.3SG=and　match.making　do.INF　COP.PST.3SG
　　　　'My job was taking care of divorces (woman-divorcing) and marriages (acting as intermediary for asking the hand of woman).'

7.16.2 Verbal functions

7.16.2.1 Placement before finite verb

In JSNENA the infinitive may be placed before a realis present stem form of the same verb to reinforce the function of the verb in some way. This strategy of 'heavy coding' is often used when the verbal form has a progressive function. When the present-stem verbal form has the realis prefixed particle *k-/g-*, this particle is attached also to the infinitive, e.g.

(850) JSNENA
    a. *šatoē   šatē-na.*
       drink.INF drink.PRS-1SG
       'I am drinking.'
    b. *'aroqē   'arəq-na.*
       run.INF run.PRS-1SG.M
       'I am running.'
    c. *zbot-ī   'aroē   'ary-a.*
       finger-1SG freeze.INF freeze.PRS-3SG.F
       'My finger is freezing.'
    d. *k-xolē   k-əx-na.*
       IND-eat.INF IND-eat.PRS-1SG.M
       'I am eating.'
    e. *k-morē   k-əm-na.*
       IND-say.INF IND-say.PRS-1SG.M
       'I am saying.'

As remarked already in §7.2.2.1, this replicates the pattern of a progressive construction in Gorani in which an inflected realis form is preceded by a form composed of the present stem and the ending *-āy*. This is not the same form as the infinitive, but its ending resembles that of infinitives, which end in *-āy* or *-ay*, and it has been matched with the JSNENA infinitive in the progressive construction, e.g.

(851) Gorani
    wārāy wār-o   'It is raining.'
    mə-lāy məl-ū   'I am going.'
    mə-řamāy mə-řam-ū 'I am running.'
    lūāy lūē-nā   'I was going.'
    ay ēnā   'I was coming.'

In JSNENA the heavy coding resulting from the combination of an infinitive with a finite verb may also be used to express some kind of discourse prominence. This is the case in (852) from the text corpus where it is combined with a present stem verb form that is used with habitual aspect. Its purpose is to draw particular attention to the merriment of the neighbours, which contrasts with the boring life style of the speaker's husband.

(852) JSNENA
xa-rēza   ləxma=ū   gupta   šaqəl   bāqa
one-little bread=and   cheese   buy.PRS.3SG.M   for
yāl-èf=u| g-ay-pút   daēl   naqòḷē
children-3SG.M=and   in-this-tin   hit.PRS.3SG.M dance.INF
naql-ī   bāq-èf.| 'àt   ma-k-ol-ēt?|
dance.PRS-3PL   to-3SG.M   you   what-IND-do.PRS-2SG.M
'He buys a little bread and cheese for his children. He drums on the tin and they dance to it. What do you do?' (A:102)

In the following Gorani example, the corresponding heavy construction is used to express a surprising event.

(853) Gorani
haḷāy kalašīr-ē   wanāy   wan-èn-ē| 'ànna   zū   lūā.|
still rooster-DIR.PL   call.INF call-PSTC-3PL   that.much early   go.PST.3SG
'He went so early to the garden that the roosters were still crowing.'

7.16.2.2 Placement after finite verb
In JSNENA an infinitive may be placed after a finite verb to modify the event expressed by the verb in some way. In such cases the infinitive is typically from a different verbal root. It may elaborate on the event by expressing other activities that were circumstantial to it, as in (854):

(854) JSNENA
ga-doka   nāšē   yatw-ī-wa| 'āraq   šatoè=ū|
in-there   people   sit.PRS-3PL-PSTC   arak   drink.INF=and
mašrūb   šatoè=u|
drink   drink.INF=and
'People would sit there, drinking arak, drinking drink.' (B:32)

It is sometimes used to express the purpose of an action, especially that of a verb of movement, e.g.

(855) JSNENA
'āṣər   k-ē-n-wa-ò| 'āraq   šatoè̱=ū|
evening IND-come.PRS-3PL-PSTC-TELIC arak drink.INF=and
kēf   wālà.|
merriment   do.INF
'In the evening they would come back in order to drink arak and make merry.' (B:43)

The purpose function may be explicitly marked by a subordinating particle, e.g.

(856) JSNENA
zīl   ta-čay   šatoè̱.|
go.PST.3SG.M to-eat   drink.INF
'He went to drink tea.'

The following examples show parallel purposive constructions in Gorani. In both examples the infinitive is a complement of a verb of movement.

(857) Gorani
  a. sa'āt panj=ū   səbḥ-ī̀| wər-m-ēz-ā
     hour   five=and morning-OBL.M   PVB-IND-take.PRS-3PL
     m-əl-ā   pay   āḷəf   kanay.|
     IND-go.PRS-3PL for   fodder   mow.INF
     'They wake up at five in the morning (to) go to harvest the grass.'
  b. bàrd-ā=šā   āḷəf   kanē.|
     take.PST-1SG=3PL   fodder   mow.INF
     'They took me to mow grass.'

7.17 Summary

The functions of verbal forms derived from present-stem verbs in JSNENA converge closely with the functions of the corresponding forms in the Iranian languages of the Sanandaj region. This convergence includes the borrowing by JSNENA of Iranian grammatical particles. For example, the irrealis form of the present-stem verb in JSNENA combines with the Iranian particles *bā* and *baškam* to express speaker-oriented modality (§7.2.1.1) and epistemic modality (§7.2.1.2), respectively. Likewise, expressions of fearing and negative purpose ('in order not ..', 'lest') are conveyed by combining the irrealis form of the verb with the particle *la-bā* in JSNENA, which is a replication of Kurdish *na-bā ~ na-wā* (§7.2.1.4).

Table (76) summarises a selection of the convergences of JSNENA with Iranian in the syntax of verb forms derived from present-stem verbs.

Table 76: Convergence of JSNENA with Iranian in the function of present-stem verbal forms.

Feature in JSNENA	Contact languages	Section
The particle *bā* combines with the verb in the irrealis mood to express speaker-oriented modality	G./K.	§7.2.1.1
The particle *baškam* combines with the verb in the irrealis mood to express epistemic modality	G./K.	§7.2.1.2
Expressions of 'ability' by the verb 'to come' and L-suffixes	Kurdish	§7.2.1.4
The particle *la-bā* is used in complements of expressions of 'fearing' and negative purpose.	Kurdish	§7.2.1.4
The present progressive is formed by the realis form of the verb preceded by the infinitive of the verbal root of the verb.	Gorani	§7.2.2.2
The realis form of the verb may be used with a future tense reference without an additional morpheme.	G./K.	§7.2.2.5
The realis form of the verb can express persistence of a habitual situation, rendered by a perfect in English.	G./K.	§7.2.2.2
The realis form of a present-stem verb in a subordinate clause can take the past time reference of a past tense verb in the main clause	G./K.	§7.2.2.2

Present-stem verbs in JSNENA may combine with the past converter suffix *-wa* to yield a number of past tense constructions. Similarly, Gorani adds the past converter *-ēn* to present-stem verbs. Table 77 summarises convergences between JSNENA and Gorani in the use of past converter suffixes with present-stem verbs. As can be seen, the JSNENA irrealis with the past converter suffix is wider in function than the Gorani irrealis with the past converter suffix. The convergence, therefore, is only partial in the function of these verbal forms in the two languages.

Table 77: The function of past-converter suffixes in JSNENA and Gorani.

Function of present-stem verbs with a past converter suffix	JSNENA	G.	Section
Realis form expressing progressive	yes	yes	§7.2.3.1.1
Realis form expressing habitual	yes	yes	§7.2.3.1.2
Irrealis form expressing deontic modality	yes	yes	§7.2.3.2.1
Irrealis form in counterfactual conditionals	yes	no	§7.2.3.2.2
Irrealis form is used in generic relative clauses	yes	no	§7.2.3.2.3
The irrealis form is used in subordinate clauses	yes	yes	§7.2.3.2.4

Constructions with past-stem verbs and resultative participles in JSNENA exhibit some degree of convergence with the corresponding constructions in the Iranian languages, see Table 78 and Table 79. In a number of constructions, however, JSNENA uses past-stem verbs where Iranian uses resultative participles. Constructions with resultative participles are innovations in JSNENA and so the retention of past-stem verbs in these cases of lack of convergence is an archaism. The convergence has been blocked due to constraints on the use of the oblique agent marking L-suffixes on constructions with resultative participles in JSNENA, as has been discussed in this chapter.

Table 78: Convergence of JSNENA with Iranian in the function of past-stem verbal forms.

Past-stem verbs	JSNENA	G./K.	Section
Past perfective	yes	yes	§7.3.1.2
Present perfect	yes	no	§7.9.1
Past-converter suffix is used in the formation of past perfect and indirective perfective	yes	no	§7.3.2

Table 79: Convergence of JSNENA with Iranian in the function of constructions with resultative participles.

Constructions with resultative participles	JSNENA	G./K.	Section
Present perfect	yes	yes	§7.9.1 & §7.10.1
Indirective past perfective	yes	yes	§7.10.2
Indirective past imperfective	yes	yes	§7.10.2.3
Past perfect (with past copula)	no	yes	§7.3.2.1

Other features in the syntax of verbs are listed in Table 80. In some features JSNENA converges with both local Kurdish and Gorani dialects, yet the number of JSNENA features converging only with Gorani outnumbers those features in which JSNENA converges only with Kurdish. The periphrastic expression of passive using an auxiliary in JSNENA, which is not found in Gorani or Kurdish, appears to be an imitation of Persian syntax.

Table 80: Convergence of JSNENA with Iranian in other features of verbal syntax.

Feature in JSNENA	type of convergence with contact languages		section
	Gorani	Kurdish	
The present copula clause expresses contingent states	partial	not relevant	§7.5.1
The copula verb *h-w-y*	partial	total	§7.7
Morphological coding of transitivity	partial	partial	§7.11
Morphological coding of passive	total	total	§7.12
The coding of transitive-unaccusative alternation by umlaut	partial	not relevant	§7.13
Use and function of the post-verbal particle *-o*	total	total	§7.14
Periphrastic expression of the passive	not relevant	not relevant	§7.12.3
Differential object marking	partial	not relevant	§7.15
The past perfective past-stem verb agrees with a third person direct object argument.	partial	not relevant	§7.15.2
Morphosyntax of transitive present perfect constructions	partial	not relevant	§7.15.2.2

8 The Clause

8.1 Introductory overview

This chapter investigates the syntax of different types of main clauses. The syntax of the clause in JSNENA has converged to a large degree with the Iranian languages of the Sanandaj region.

In copula clauses, following the Kurdish model, and unlike Gorani, the copula clitic is fixed at the end of the clause and is impervious to the effects of changes in information structure in the clause. This differs from many other NENA dialects, in which the copula moves around the clause onto focused items.[1]

In inchoative predicates with the verb 'to become' in Kurdish and Gorani the adjectival complement is rigidly to the left of the predicate, whereas the nominal complement is overwhelmingly to the right of the predicate. JSNENA has partially converged with this syntax of 'become'. Thus adjectival complements of the verb 'to become' in JSNENA regularly occur pre-predicatively, while about 50% of nominal complements of the verb occur post-predicatively.

The existence in Kurdish and Gorani of existential particles in predicative possessive constructions has presumably reinforced the use of the existential particle in corresponding possessive constructions in JSNENA.

With regard to word order, JSNENA has diverged from the more conservative NENA dialects, which have predominantly VO word order, and converged with Iranian languages in adopting OV as the basic word order. The existing corpus counts reveal that nominal objects occur only rarely in the post-verbal position in JSNENA, suggesting a high degree of convergence with the contact languages in Sanandaj. The closest statistical match is with the word order patterns of Gorani. The few cases of VO syntax in JSNENA and Iranian have the function of giving prominence to a newly introduced object or of marking the cohesion of the clause with the preceding discourse.

JSNENA matches the Iranian contact languages in the ordering of arguments expressing goals of the verb, e.g. goals of verbs of movement and goals of verbs of caused movements, recipients. These arguments show high propensity to occur post-predicatively, yielding OVX (where X stands for a goal arguments) as the basic word order configuration of languages in Sanandaj region.

Constructions of naming in JSNENA are formed by an impersonal 3pl. form of the verb 'to say' ('they say to X such-and-such'). This exactly matches Gorani, but Kurdish uses the compound verb *nāw nān* 'put a name' in such constructions.

---

[1] See, for example, Khan (2008b, 634–35; 2016, vol. 2, 296).

In JSNENA and the Iranian languages of Sanandaj, interrogative particles are generally placed immediately before the verb.

8.2 The copula clause

8.2.1 Preliminary remarks

In both JSNENA and Iranian, the present and past copulas are placed after the predicate of the clause. They are used to form ascriptive clauses, e.g. (858.a-b)-(859)-(860) and equative clauses, e.g. (861)-(862)-(863). In both types of clauses the copula is regularly placed after the predicate regardless of the information structure of the predicate or the subject. The nuclear stress typically falls on the predicate.

(858) a. JSNENA
 šwāw-an kpīnà=y.|
 neighbour-1PL hungry=COP.3SG.M
 'Our neighbour is hungry.'
 b. rāba rāzì=yē-lē.|
 very content=COP.PST-OBL.3SG.M
 'He was very content.'

(859) Kurdish
 kām=tān wəryà=n?|
 which=2PL aware=COP.2PL
 'Which one of you is awake?'

(860) Gorani
 īsa-tè̱| wa'za waš-à=na.|
 now-NA situation good-F.DIR=COP.3SG.F
 'Now, the situation is good.'

(861) JSNENA
 'o-gora màni=yē?| 'o-gora šwāw-àn=yē.|
 that-man who=COP.3SG.M that-man neighbour-1PL=COP.3SG.M
 'Who is that man?' 'That man is our neighbour.'

(862) Kurdish
ama   mantaqa=y   šə̀r=a.|
DEM.PROX.3SG region=EZ   lion=COP.3SG
'This is the territory of the lion.'

(863) Gorani
mən   kuř=ū   Ràhmān-ī=nā.|
1SG   son=EZ   PN-OBL.M=COP.1SG
'I am Rahman's son.'

In some contexts, however, ascriptive copula clauses may have a different information structure, whereby the subject item is the focus of new information and the item expressing the property expresses presupposed information. In such cases the copula remains in its position after the property item. The syntactic structure of the clause, therefore, does not change and from a syntactic point of view the property item should still be regarded as the predicate. The nuclear stress, however, is placed on the subject rather than on the predicate. The focus may be corrective contrastive focus, as in (864). In such cases the speaker wishes to correct a misunderstanding by strongly asserting that one particular referent should be selected for the role in question rather than the one currently entertained by the hearer. Other types of focus are possible, such as non-contrastive 'completive focus' according to the terminology of Dik (1981, 60) as in (865). Such constructions are typically responses to constituent questions ('Who was a Jew?'). It specifies a variable in the presupposition triggered by the constituent question word without contrasting it with any other specific candidates that the speaker assumes the hearer may be entertaining for the role in question. The presupposition triggered by the question here is 'somebody was a Jew'. Completive focus can be regarded as involving selection from an open set of alternatives.

(864) JSNENA
bron-ī   bēlà=y?| *brāt-òx*
son-1SG   home=COP.3SG.M   daughter-2SG.M
bēla=ya.| *bron-ox   bēla   là=y.*|
home=COP.3SG.F son-2SG.M   home   NEG=COP.3SG.M
'Is my son at home? 'YOUR DAUGHTER is at home. Your son is not at home.'

(865) Kurdish
 àw   mūsāī=ū-Ø.|
 3SG   jew=COP.PST-3SG
 'HE was (a) Jew.'

In Gorani, by contrast, copula clauses that have focus on the subject constituent can result in the mobility of the copula. In (866.a-b) the subject has corrective contrastive focus.

(866) Gorani
 a. mən=nā   kuř=ū   mīr-ī.|
    1SG=COP.1SG son=EZ   prince-OBL.M
    'I am the prince's son.'
 b. īnà=n   žīwāy
    DEM.PROX=COP.3SG live.INF
    'THIS is life.'

8.2.2 Subject constituents

If the subject of the clause is referred to by a nominal or independent pronoun, it is generally placed before the predicate. In most cases the subject is uttered in the same intonation group as the predicate and the nuclear stress is on the final element of the predicate:

(867) JSNENA
 a. 'axon-af   xa-duktàr=yē.|
    brother-3SG.F   one-doctor=COP.3SG.M
    'Her brother is a doctor.' (A:6)
 b. šəma   'axon-af   Xanakè=yē-lē.|
    name   brother-3SG.F PN=COP.PST-OBL.3SG.M
    'The name of her brother was Xanakē.' (A:14)

(868) Gorani
 īna   řafèq=m=ā.|
 DEM.PROX.3SG.DIR.M friend=1SG=COP.3SG.M
 'This is my friend.'

(869) Kurdish
mardəm la xwašî-ya bū-Ø.|
people at happiness-ADP COP.PST-3SG
'People were happy.'

The subject is given nuclear stress when the speaker wishes to give it particular prominence. In (870) the subject has the nuclear stress since it is newly introduced and is more informative than the remainder of the clause, which is a repeated predicate frame:

(870) JSNENA
famīl-ŭ rāba ʾayza=y.|
family-3PL very good=COP.3SG.M
'Their family is very good.' (A:6)

In both JSNENA and Iranian, when the predicate is a long phrase, the copula is placed after the head of the phrase rather than at the end.

(871) JSNENA
čarčī ʾò=yē-lē| *ya-ʾaspāḷ matū-wa rēša*
peddler that=COP.PST-OBL.3SG.M REL-goods put.PRS.3SG.M-PSTC on
xmārà| *rēša maxṣūṣan parčānè̩,*| *labl-ī-wā-lū*
donkey on especially fabrics take.PRS-3PL-PSTC-OBL.3PL
sūsī| *ga-mālawằē*| *zabn-ī-wā-lū.*|
horse in-villages sell.PRS-3PL-PSTC-OBL.3PL
'A peddler was somebody who put goods on a donkey or on a horse, especially fabrics, and took them to the villages to sell them.' (A:70)

(872) Kurdish
ama kuř-akà=s wā pā=y nà-w-Ø!?|
DEM.PROX.3SG boy-DEF=COP.3SG REL leg=3SG NEG-COP.PST-3SG
'Is this the (same) boy who could not walk!?' [lit. who did not have legs].

8.2.3 Postposing of subject constituent

In JSNENA the subject nominal in a predication is occasionally placed after the predicate resulting in the order *predicate—copula—subject*. In the attested examples the postposed subject has a referent that has been evoked previously or is at least anchored to a previously evoked referent by means of a pronominal suffix.

The construction typically occurs when there is some type of close semantic connection between the clause and what precedes. The construction in (873a), for example, supplies information that is supplementary to the main point that the speaker is making in the preceding clause, viz. that the rooms in Sanandaj were high, by specifying how high they were. In (873b) and (873c) the postposition of the independent demonstrative pronominal subject occurs in clauses that are final tags at the end of a section of discourse:

(873) JSNENA
    a. ʾo-waxtara   bātē   mangal-laxa kəryē là=yē-lū.|
       that-time   houses   like-here   short   NEG=COP.PST-OBL.3PL
       bātē   ntòē=yē-lū.| ʾay-ʾotāqà| ʾəqra košta
       houses high=COP.PST-3PL   this-room   thus   low
       là=yē-la.| trē-ʾəqrà=yē-la   ʾotāq-af.|
       NEG=COP.PST-OBL.3SG.F   two-thus=COP.PST-OBL.3SG.F   room-3SG.F
       'At that time houses were not low like here. Houses were high. The room there was not as low as this. A room there (literally: its room) was twice (the height).' (A:12)
    b. xa   provə̀rb=yē-lē   ʾēa.|
       one proverb=COP.PST-OB.3SG.M this
       'This was a proverb.' (B:65)
    c. ba-ʾənyāxāē ʾalē-tun.| ʾənyāxằē| masòret=yēn.|
       in-these   know.PRS-2PL   these   tradition=COP.3PL
       ga-halaxa=č   klīwà=y   ʾēa.|
       in-halakah=ADD   write.PTCP.SG.M=COP.3SG.M this
       'You should know these things. These things are tradition. It is also written in the *halakha*.' (B:73)

Likewise in the Iranian languages of the region the subject can be postposed if its referent has already been evoked in the preceding discourse, see (874.a-b). The construction in (875) with a postposed subject is a response to a question as to whether speaking between a bride to-be and grooms was allowed.

(874) Kurdish of the Sanandaj region
    a. *mằyn-īk=ī ha=s| wa nāw māyīn sḕ ləng.|*
       mare-INDF=3SG EXIST=COP.3SG by name mare three leg
       sāhēr=ū bahrì=a māyīn sē ləng=ū.|
       enchanter=and aquatic=COP.3SG mare three leg=and
       'He has a mare, which is called "the three-legged mare". The three-legged mare is supernatural and aquatic.'
    b. *gaī=ya dìw-ēk=ū| wət=ī=ya*
       arrive.PST.3SG=DRCT demon-INDF=and say.PST=3SG=DRCT
       dềw| wət=ī, 'arē ēwa quwà=tān
       demon say.PST=3SG DISC 2PL power=2PL
       ha=s?| quwaàr=ən ēwa?|
       EXIST=COP.3SG powerful=COP.2PL 2PL
       'He bumped into a demon, and said to the demon, "Hey, do you have strength? Are you powerful?"'

(875) Gorani
    mamnò'a bī qəsa karḍ-ay.|
    forbidden COP.PST.3SG talk do.PST-INF
    'Speaking was forbidden.'

8.2.4 Postposing of predicate

In JSNENA the predicate is occasionally placed after the irrealis form of the verb *h-w-y* in constructions with subject-oriented modality. This was no doubt facilitated by the fact that this verb was not a clitic. The Kurdish construction in (877), which is the equivalent to the JSNENA construction (876), is also characterised by the postposing of the predicate. In Kurdish the preposition *ba-* is cliticised on the verb in the form of a directional particle.

(876) JSNENA
    a. *'ēla=ū rēš-šāt-ox hawē-n brixḕ.|*
       festival=and head-year-2SG.M be.PRS-3PL blessed
       'May your festival and New Year be blessed.' (B:33)
    b. *'arz hawē ba-xzəmt-òx.|*
       petition be.PRS.3SG.M in-service-2SG.M
       'May a petition be for your service (= Let me tell you).' (A:70)

(877) Kurdish
'arz   Ø-b-ēt=a   xəzmàt=o.|
petition SBJV-be.PRS-3SG=DRCT   service=2SG
'May a petition be for your service (= Let me tell you).'

8.2.5 Omission of copula

In JSNENA and in the Iranian languages of the region, the copula is omitted in a number of contexts. This is found in clauses that are closely bound semantically with a copula predication in an adjacent clause with a parallel structure, e.g.

(878) JSNENA
  a. bšəlmānē trè̀ jorē=n.| xa šī'a xa sunnì=yē.|
     Muslims two kinds=COP.3PL one PN one PN=COP.3SG.M
     'Muslims are of two kinds, one is Shi'ite and the other Sunni.' (A:77)
  b. fāmīl-ù̀   rāba 'ayza=y| 'axon-àf   'ayza.|
     family-3PL   very good=COP.3SG.M   brother-3SG.F   good
     'Their family is very good. Her brother is good.' (A:6)

(879) Kurdish
  a. wət=ī̀,   'bərà̀!| mən   xwàšək=m=ū   tu   bərà̀.|
     say.PST=3SG   brother   1SG   sister=1SG=and   2SG   Brother
     '(The woman) said, "O brother, I am (your) sister, and you (are my) brother."'
  b. mən nāw=əm   Karî̀m,| xaḷk   Ahmaà̀wā.|
     1SG name=1SG PN   people PN
     'My name (is) Karim, I (am) from Ahmadabad.'

8.2.6 Interrogative predicates

In JSNENA and in the Iranian languages of Sanandaj, when the predicate is an interrogative particle, the copula is placed immediately after this particle, in accordance with the regular syntax of copula clauses. If the subject of the clause is a nominal or independent pronoun, it is normally placed before the predicate phrase, e.g.

(880) JSNENA
  a. 'ay   mà=yē?|
     this   what=COP.3SG.M
     'What is this?' (B:81)

b. *ḥašt-ox   mà=ya?*|
   work-2SG.M what=COP.3SG.F
   'What is your work?' (D:19)
c. *xwān   mà=yē-lē?*|
   table   what=COP.PST-OBL.3SG.M
   'What was a "table"?' (A:9)
d. *ḥamām=ē   turkī   mà-jor=yē-la?*|
   bath=EZ   Turkish what-type=COP.PST-OBL.3SG.F
   'What was a Turkish bath like?' (A:37)
e. *hulāē   Kurdəstàn*| *čəkmà=yē-lū?*|
   Jews   Kurdistan   how_many=COP.PST-OBL.3PL
   'How many were the Jews of Kurdistan?' (B:1)

(881) Gorani
   a. *xāzā=w   zəmsān-ī=tā   čèš̀=ā?*|
      food=EZ   winter-OBL.M=2PL what=COP.3SG.M
      'What is your winter food?'
   b. *mārayī   čənnà   bē?*|
      marriage.portion how.much be.PSTC.3SG
      'How much was a marriage portion?'

(882) Kurdish
   a. *aw   bēška   čà=s?*|
      DEM.DIST barrel   what=COP.3SG
      'What is that barrel?'
   b. *to   həkāyat=o   čà=s?*|
      2SG adventure=2SG   what=COP.3SG
      'What is your adventure?'
   c. *mardəm am   āwāyī-a   čòn=ən?*|
      people DEM.PROX village-DEM   how=COP.3PL
      'What are the people of this village like?'

8.2.7 Predicative complements of the JSNENA Verb x-Ø-r

Unlike JSNENA, the verb 'to become' has the same stem as the verb 'to be' in the Iranian languages of Sanandaj. Nonetheless, the verbs meaning 'to become' have the same syntactic properties across the languages spoken in the Sanandaj region. The predicative complement of 'to become' is placed before the verb if it is an adjective. This is further borne out by frequency counts of adjective complements of 'to become' in the corpora of JSNENA (cf. Noorlander (2022) and Sanandaj Kurdish (cf. Mohammadirad 2022b), in both of which adjective complements occur in 100% of cases before the verb.²

(883) JSNENA
a. k-mē-n-wā-la ga-txēla 'aql-ǔ|
IND-bring.PRS-3PL-PSTC-OBL.3SG.F in-bottom feet-3PL
kē-'aql-ū ṣằf xar-ī.|
that-feet-3PL smooth become.PRS-3PL
'They applied it to the bottom of their feet so that they would become smooth.' (A:38)
b. rāba xoš-ḥằl xar-əx-wa=ū|
very happy become.PRS-1PL-PSTC=and
'We became very happy.' (B:33)

(884) Gorani
zāmdằr b-o.|
wounded become.PRS-3SG
'He became wounded.'

(885) Kurdish
šằkat a-w-ən| a-č-ən=a āsyāw=a kona-yk-àw.|
tired IND-be.PRS-3PL IND-go.PRS-3PL=DRCT mill=EZ old-IND-ADP
'They became tired (and) went to an old mill.'

The predicative complement of 'to become' is, however, placed after the verb if it is a noun. The post-verbal noun is preceded by the preposition ba- in both JSNENA and the Iranian languages. In Kurdish this is cliticised to the verb in the form =a. The use of the non-cliticised form of the preposition ba- in JSNENA matches Gorani rather than Kurdish.

(886) JSNENA
a. 'o-pəsra qalḕ-n-wā-lē| xar-wa ba-čokḕ.|
that-meat fry.PRS-3PL-PSTC-OBL.3SG.M become.PRS.3SG.M to-čokē
'They would fry meat and it would become čokē.' (A:86)

---

2 On the other hand, in the neighbouring Gorani dialect of Gawrajo (West Iran), adjective complements of 'to become' exhibit 10% post-verbal realisation (cf. Mohammadirad 2022a).

b. *xira=y*   *ba-'afsàr.*ǀ
    become.PTCP.SG.M   to-officer
    'He has become an officer.' (A:17)

(887) Gorani Luhon
ḥama bī   ba   pādšā.
PN   become.PST.3SG   to   king
'Hama became king.'
(MacKenzie 1966, 78)

(888) Gorani
*bo   ba   tāqàt=ē   xałk-ī̀.*ǀ
become.PRS.3SG   to   support=EZ   people-OBL.M
'He became a support for people.'

(889) Kurdish
*a-w-ēt=a   mənằḷ,*ǀ *a-w-ēt=a   kanīšk-ề.*ǀ
IND-be.PRS-3SG=DRCT   child   IND-be.PRS-3SG=DRCT   girl-INDF
'(The kidney) turned into a baby, it became a girl.'

Note further that in JSNENA 50% of nominal complements of 'to become' occur after the verb (Noorlander 2022) whereas the figure is 97% for Sanandaj Kurdish (Mohammadirad 2022b), and 86% for the Gorani dialect of Gawrajo (Mohammadirad 2022a). JSNENA thus converges partially with the syntax of 'to become' of Kurdish and Gorani.

8.3 Clauses with existential particles

8.3.1 Existential clauses

The existential particles in JSNENA are *hīt* (present) 'there is/are', *hītwa* (past) 'there was/were'. In Kurdish and Gorani the corresponding construction is formed from the particle *ha* and the copula in the present. In the past tense the copula alone is used to express existence (890). The nominal complement of these expressions, i.e. the term whose existence is being asserted, is normally placed before the expressions. The nuclear stress is generally placed on the nominal complement.

(890) JSNENA
   a. šērē màē-hīt-wa.|
      taps water-EXIST-PSTC
      'There were water taps.' (A:37)
   b. ṭabaqē ruwḕ hīt-wa.|
      trays big EXIST-PSTC
      'There were big trays.' (A:33)
   c. ga-dokà| kul yoma pəsrà-hīt-wa.|
      in-there every day meat-EXIST-PSTC
      'There, every day there was meat.'

(891) Kurdish
   roḷà,| čapka guḷ-èk ha=s.|
   child bouquet flower-INDF EXIST=COP.3SG
   'Child, there is a bouquet of flower.'

(892) Gorani
   a. duē žanī̀ ha=nē.|
      two woman.DIR.PL EXIST=COP.3PL
      'There are two women (in the yard).'
   b. bīs sī xānəwàdēwa b-ēn-ē.|
      twenty thirty family.PL.DIR.INDF be-PSTC-3PL
      'There were twenty, thirty families.'

In the following Gorani example the nominal complement is placed after the existential expression.

(893) Gorani
   īsa| ha=n dàwlatman=ā=w| mən gadā̀=nā|
   now EXIST=COP.3SG.M rich=COP.3SG.M=and 1SG poor=COP.1SG
   'Nowadays, there is a rich fellow, and as for me, I am poor.'

In JSNENA, a complement nominal consisting of a head and a modifier may be split by placing the existential particle immediately after the head, especially when the modifier is an attributive prepositional phrase or a relative clause (894.a-b)-(895). Parallel constructions are found in Iranian.

(894) JSNENA
    a. *gūrānì-hīt-wa   b-šəma   ḥanabandàn.*|
       song-EXIST-PSTC with-name PN
       'There was a song called ḥanabandan.' (A:41)
    b. *başīrē ràba hīt-wa   ga-ḥawša nāšē.*|
       grapes many EXIST-PSTC in-courtyard people
       'There were many grapes in the courtyard of people.' (A:72)

(895) Kurdish
    yak-nafar rīščarmù has   lam   šār-a|
    one-person old.man EXIST=COP.3SG in.DEM.PROX city-DEM
    'There is an old man in this city.'

8.3.2 Possessive constructions

In JSNENA, possession is expressed by existential constructions in which a pronominal suffix of the L-series is attached to the existential particle. As in other existential constructions, the nominal complement is normally placed before the particle with the nuclear stress on the nominal:

(896) JSNENA
    a. *t^{w}kānē ràba hīt-wā-lē.*|
       shops   many EXIST-PSTC-OBL.3SG.M
       'He had many shops.' (A:7)
    b. *xa 'ambar rāba rabtà hīt-wā-lē.*|
       one warehouse very big   EXIST-PSTC-OBL.3SG.M
       'He had a big warehouse.' (A:7)
    c. *pəštì   hīt-wā-lan.*|
       back-support EXIST-PSTC-OLB.1PL
       'We had a back-support.' (A:56)

In the Iranian languages of Sanandaj, the predicative possessive constructions are similar to those of JSNENA in that the nominal is placed before the verb and it receives the nuclear stress. The only difference from JSNENA lies in the mobility of the dative clitic, which indexes the subject-like argument in Iranian.

(897) Gorani
 mēwa=y āl-ḕ=š ha=nē.
 fruit=EZ good-PL.DIR=3SG EXIST=COP.3PL
 'It has good fruit.'

(898) Kurdish
 mən kanīšk-èk=əm ha=s.
 1SG daughter-INDF=1SG EXIST=COP.3SG
 'I have a daughter.'

On some occasions the nominal is split, the particle being placed after the head noun and a modifier postposed after the particle, e.g.

(899) JSNENA
 qaṣāb hīt-wā-lan b-šə̀ma 'Azīz-Xằn.
 butcher EXIST-PSTC-OBL.1PL with-name PN
 'We had a butcher by the name of Aziz Khan.' (A:74)

(900) Kurdish
 mằyn-īk=ī ha=s wa nāw māyīn sè̀ lə̀ng.
 mare-INDF=3SG EXIST=COP.3SG by name mare three leg
 'He has a mare by the name of "three-legged mare."'

8.4 Verbal clauses

8.4.1 Direct object constituent

8.4.1.1 Object—verb

JSNENA matches Iranian of Sanandaj in having SOV as default word order. The frequency counts show that OV is the preferred order for 95% of total direct objects in JSNENA (cf. Noorlander 2022). In Sanandaj Kurdish 99% of total direct objects are placed before the verb (cf. Mohammadirad 2022b). A study of the neighbouring Gorani dialect of Gawrajo has revealed that 96% of direct objects are placed before the verb (cf. Mohammadirad 2022a).

In the OV order, the nuclear stress is generally placed on the object if it is indefinite with a newly introduced referent:

(901) JSNENA
   a. ləbās=ē   dawrēšî̀   loš-wa.|
      clothes=EZ beggary   wear.PRS.3SG.M-PSTC
      'He would wear clothes of a beggar.' (A:108)
   b. mastà   ho-lī.|
      yoghurt give.IMP.SG-OBL.1SG
      'Give me yoghurt!' (A:79)
   c. gā-ēf   šīrı̀n   mat-ī-wa,| ləbā̀s   mat-ī-wa,|
      in-3SG.M sweets   put.PRS-3PL-PSTC clothes   put.PRS-3PL-PSTC
      jəlē   'ayzè   mat-ī-wa.|
      clothes good   put.PRS-3PL-PSTC
      'They put sweets in it, they put clothes in it, they put fine clothes in it.' (A:9)
   d. xa-čày   šatē-n-wa=ū| xančī̀   'āràq   šatē-n-wa.|
      one-tea   drink.PRS-3PL-PSTC=and some   arak   drink.PRS-3PL-PSTC
      'They drank tea and they drank some arak.' (A:10)

(902) Gorani
   a. hēḷà=w   řon-ē   war-ēn-ē=w   lū-ēn-ē=wa.|
      egg=and oil-INDF eat.PRS-PSTC-3PL=and   go.PRS-PSTC-3PL=TELIC
      'They would eat fried eggs and return.'
   b. panjšamà-y| waywà   ār-ēn-ē.|
      thursday-OBL.M bride   bring.PRS-PSTC-3PL
      'They would bring brides on (a) Thursday.'

(903) Kurdish
   waxt=ē   soḥ   hàḷ-a-s-ən| čə   dāna=y
   when=EZ morning PVB-IND-lift.PRS-3PL   INTJ CLF=EZ
   əfrı̀t=ī   topā-(ā)n=a.|
   dragon=3SG hit.PST-CAUS=PERF
   'When they woke up in the morning, [they saw that] he had killed a dragon.'

In JSNENA as well as in the Iranian languages of Sanandaj, if the object constituent is definite and refers to a referent that has been introduced in the preceding discourse, the nuclear stress is generally placed on the verb, e.g.

(904) JSNENA
   a. ḥamām-akē   mašxn-ī-wā-là.|
      bath-DEF   heat.PRS-3PL-PSTC-OBL.3SG.F
      'They used to heat the bath.' (A:37)

b. *ləxm-akē   k-ol-ā-wā-lḕ-o.*|
   bread-DEF   IND-do.PRS-3SG.F-PSTC-OBL.3SG.M-TELIC
   'She opened out the bread (dough).' (A:66)

c. *xwān-akē   k-mē-n-wā-là=ū*|
   table-DEF   IND-bring.PRS-3PL-PSTC-OBL.3SG.F=and
   'They delivered the table.' (A:11)

d. *xāl-ēf   k-xəl-wā-lḕ.*|
   eat-3SG.M   IND-eat.PRS.3SG.M-PSTC-OBL.3SG.M
   'He used to eat his food.' (A:101)

(905) Gorani

a. *čāwlāy   kāwř-akā   m-ār-ằ*| *čā*
   from.then.on sheep-DEF.PL.OBL   IND-bring.PRS-3PL   there
   sara   bəřằ.|
   head   cut.PST
   'They bring the sheep (and) butcher (them) there.'

b. *sī-panj   řoē   zəmsān   man-ò,*|
   thirty-five day-PL.DIR   winter   remain.PRS-3SG
   wazakā   baxš-n-ằ.|
   walnut.DEF.PL   donate.PRS-CAUS-3PL
   'Thirty-five days before winter ends, they donate the walnuts.'

(906) Kurdish

a. *šaw-ē   kuř-akān=ī   bàng   kərd.*|
   night-INDF   boy-DEF.PL=3SG   call   do.PST
   'One night he summoned his sons.'

b. *kanīšk   gawra   a-wā-t=a   bərằ=y   gawra=y.*|
   girl   big   IND-give.PRS-3SG=DRCT   brother=EZ   big=3SG
   'He gives the eldest girl to his eldest brother.'

8.4.1.2 Verb—object

Occasionally an object constituent is placed after the verb. In both JSNENA and Iranian post-verbal objects make up less than 10 percent of all direct objects. The data from Table 81 extracted from copora of JSNENA (cf. Noorlander 2022), and Sanandaj Kurdish (cf. Mohammadirad 2022b) indicate that JSNENA exhibits a slightly greater tendency than Kurdish for having postverbal objects, most commonly with definite nominals. Relevant percentages are shown for the corpus of the Gorani dialect of the Gawraju (Mohammadirad 2022a), spoken to the south of Sanandaj. It can be seen that Gorani Gawraju and JSNENA have similar tendencies in the post-predicate realisation of direct objects, especially definite direct objects, but also indefinite ones. The post-verbal position of objects was the historically earlier default position of objects in NENA and development of preverbal object placement was the result of convergence with Iranian languages. This historical shift in word order has taken place in varying degrees in the eastern sector of NENA. It is most advanced in the trans-Zab Jewish dialects (Khan 2020a, 398–401). The statistics suggest that JSNENA has converged most closely with word order patterns of Gorani.

Table 81: Percentage of post-predicate objects across JSNENA, Kurdish, and Gorani.

	JSNENA	Kurdish	Gorani Gawraju
rate of post-predicate direct objects, all forms	0.05	0.01	0.04
rate of post-predicate direct objects, nominal	0.05	0.01	0.05
rate of post-predicate direct objects, pronominal	0.00	0.00	0.00
rate of post-predicate direct objects, nominal, definite	0.13	0.02	0.06
rate of post-predicate direct objects, nominal, indefinite	0.03	0.00	0.02

In JSNENA the placement of an object after the verb is sometimes used to give prominence to an indefinite noun with a newly introduced referent that plays a role in the ensuing discourse, e.g.

(907) JSNENA
    a. *rasm*   *dè̱=ē-lē*| *'afsarè̱*|
        custom   OBL.this=COP.PST-OBL.3SG.M   officers
        'artě̱š| *rakw-ī-wa*   *sūsī̱.*|
        army   ride.PRS-3PL-PSTC   horse
        'It was the custom that officers, in the army, would ride on a horse.' (A:15)
    b. *k-mē-n-wa*   *xà*   *nafar.*|
        IND-bring.PRS-3PL-PSTC   one   person
        'They brought somebody.' (B:17)

The following Gorani examples match JSNENA in (907.a-b) in that a newly-introduced object is given extra-prominence by being placed after the verb.

(908) Gorani
    a. *āḍ-īč*   *Ø-čəř-o*   *Alī Ašraf xàn ū*
        3SG.DIR.M   IND-call.PRS-3SG   PN   PN   khan and
        Yāwar jafar xànī.ǀ sarlaškar-è   *b-ēn-ē.ǀ*
        PN   PN   khan   major.general-PL.DIR   be.PRS-PSTC-3PL
        'He summons Ali Ashraf Khan and Yawar Jafar Khan. They were major generals.'
    b. *Ø-tàw-ū*   *kīyān-ū*   *dawḷat.ǀ*
        IND-can.PRS-1SG   send.PRS-1SG   government
        'I can send the government (to quell the unrest).'

In JSNENA an object is also postposed after the verb when its referent is bound anaphorically to the preceding discourse, either by explicit mention or by association. The construction in this case is used in clauses that are closely connected in some way to what precedes. In (909), for example, the act of going up to the people and listening to what they say are presented as aspects of the same overall event and not independent events:

(909) JSNENA
    g-ēzəl-wa   *masalan*   *xa-'əda*   *nāšē*   *kē-ga-xa*
    IND-go.PRS-PSTC   for_example   one-number   people   REL-in-one
    meydān smīxè=nǀ   *xabra ḥaqè-n,ǀ*
    square   stand.PTCP.PL=COP.3PL   word   speak.PRS-3PL
    maṣīl-wa   *xabr-ù.ǀ*
    listen.PRS.3SG.M-PSTC   word-3PL
    'He would go, for example, to a group of people who were standing in a square speaking and listening to what they said.' (A:109)

Example (910) illustrates a parallel in Kurdish, in that a postposed direct object is bound to the explicit mention of its referent in the preceding discourse:

(910) Kurdish
a-yž-ē, 'yārīya=m b-a bā àma
IND-say.PRS-3SG aid=1SG SBJV.give.IMP.2SG OPT DEM.PROX.SG
šā=s| la-žēr àm čārwā dar=ī
king=COP.3SG at-under DEM.PROX.3SG horse out=3SG
b-ēr-īn.'| dàr=ī t-ēr-ən| har jor
SBJV-bring.PRS-1PL out=3SG IND-bring.PRS-3PL each manner
a-w-ē dàr=ī t-ēr-ən šā.|
IND-be.PRS-3SG out=3SG IND-bring.PRS-3PL king

'He said, "Help me so that—this is a king. Let's pull him out from under this animal." They pulled him out. In any way possible they pulled the king out.'

In (911) the construction with a postposed object in JSNENA is used in a clause that recapitulates the content of what precedes rather than advancing the discourse:

(911) JSNENA
ba-'aqlē 'ay jəlē 'uč-lū.| 'uč-lū
with-feet these clothes trample.IMP.SG-OBL.3PL trample.IMP.SG-OBL.3PL
'ē-jəl-akè,| 'ānā=č asr-ànān=ū.|
these-clothes-DEF 1SG=ADD wring.PRS-1SG.F-OBL.3PL

'Trample the clothes with your feet. Trample the clothes and I shall wring them out.' (C:11)

In a parallel construction below in Kurdish the postposed object həkāyat 'tale' appears in a clause that recapitulates the content of the preceding clause.

(912) Kurdish
Tāyī=š wə̀t=ī| ay ama čūn ā àm
PN=3SG say.PST=3SG INTJ DEM.PROX.SG how PTCL DEM.PROX
həkāyat-yal=t-a hāwərd=as=aw tu!?| wət=ī, 'ītər
tale-PL=2SG-DEM bring.PST-PERF=TELIC 2SG say.PST=3SG anyway
hàwərd-u=m=as=aw tāza həkāyat.|
bring.PST-PTCP=1SG=PERF=TELIC anyhow tale

'Tay said, "How were you able to return from those places and bring back all these tales with you in your memory (lit. how were you able to bring back all these tales)?" He said, "Well, anyhow I have brought back the tales."'

8.4.1.3 Predicative complements and expressions of content

In JSNENA, when a verb takes a second complement in addition to a direct object of the type illustrated in (913.a-b), this second complement is generally placed after the verb:

(913) JSNENA
    a. *k-ol-ī-wā-la*   *xa*   *'otāqa*   *ḥasabī̀=ū.*|
        IND-do.PRS-3PL-PSTC-OBL.3SG.F one room proper=and
        'They would make it into a proper room.' (B:76)
    b. *pyāḷ-akē*   *zmaṭ-lē*   *màē.*|
        glass-DEF fill.PST-OBL.3SG.M water
        'He filled the glass with water.'

In (913.a) the post-verbal argument without a preposition can be analysed as a predicative complement. It is a non-referential nominal phrase that ascribes a resultant quality to the direct object argument that it acquires through the change of state brought about by the verb 'to make'. This may be termed a 'predicative complement' in that it express a semantic predicate.³ In (913.b) the argument 'water' without a preposition expresses the resultant content of the changed state undergone by the direct object. The post-verbal arguments, therefore, are not second direct objects.

Similarly, in Gorani, predicative complements or expressions of content in parallel constructions follow the verb without a preposition:

(914) Gorani
    a. *č-ā*   *Ø-kar-ā=š*   *šəwāna=w*   *hàywān-ī̀.*|
        in-DEM.DIST IND-do.PRS-3PL=3SG shephard=EZ animal-OBL.M
        'There, they make him into a shepherd.'
    b. *parđāx-aka=š*   *pəř*   *kard-Ø*   *āwì.*|
        glass-DEF.DIR.M=3SG fill do.PST-3SG.M water
        'He filled the glass with water.'

In Kurdish, however, the corresponding form of complement is preceded by a preposition, which is cliticised to the verb:

---

3 For the term and an analysis of these constructions in English see Huddleston and Pullum (2002, 251–66).

(915) Kurdish
    a. *lēwān-aka=y   pəř   kərd=a   åw.*|
       glass-DEF=3SG fill do.PST=DRCT water
       'He filled the glass with water.'
    b. *a=w-ka-m=a   šằ.*|
       IND=2SG-do.PRS-1SG=DRCT king
       'I will make you into a king.'

JSNENA, therefore, matches the syntax of Gorani rather than that of Kurdish, since unlike in Kurdish no directional particle is added to the verb in such constructions in Gorani.

8.4.2 Subject constituent

8.4.2.1 Subject—(Object)—verb

In JSNENA, if the clause has a subject nominal constituent, this is normally placed before the verb and before a direct object nominal:

(916) JSNENA
    a. *kald-akē   hamēša rēš-af   ksẽ-wā-la.*|
       bride-DEF   always head-3SG.F cover.PST-PSTC-OBL.3SG.F
       'The bride had always covered her head.' (A:3)
    b. *yāl-ēf   naqḷ-ì-wa=ū*| *baxt-ēf*
       children-3SG.M dance.PRS-3PL-PSTC=and wife-3SG.M
       naqḷ-ằ-wa=ū|
       dance.PRS-3SG.F-PSTC=and
       'His children danced and his wife danced.' (A:99)
    c. *dāak-ī   hīy-a   Taràn.*|
       mother-1SG come.PST-3SG.F Tehran
       'My mother came to Tehran.' (A:5)

Subject—Verb constructions may have the pragmatic structure of categorical sentences or thetic sentences. Categorical sentences are bipartite in that they announce a base of predication and then make a statement about this. A thetic sentence presents a unitary situation rather than stating something about the subject (Sasse 1987). Thetic sentences are typically used for 'discourse management' such as presenting the preliminary grounds for what follows in the discourse (Kaltenböck, Heine, and Kuteva 2011). Constructions such as (916.b), which express a parallel between two juxtaposed subjects, are most easily interpreted as categorical sentences. The speaker announces a base of predicate then makes a statement about, after which another base of predication is announced and a statement is made about that one. An example such as (916.c) could be interpeted as a thetic sentence. The speaker presents the situation of his mother coming to Tehran, as grounds for what follows in the discourse.

The subject nominal is sometimes separated from the rest of the clause by an intonation group boundary. In such cases the prosody explicitly signals that the construction is a bipartite categorical sentence, e.g.

(917) JSNENA
 'ay-bronà⎮ həl-day brāta g-bḕ.⎮
 this-boy OBL-OBL.this girl IND-love.PRS.3SG.M
 'The boy loves the girl.' (A:18)

In the Iranian languages of Sanandaj the subject constituent likewise occurs by default before the object and the verb.

(918) Gorani
 ēma ənnà=mā zānā.⎮
 1PL this.much=1PL know.PST
 'We know this much [about life].'

(919) Kurdish
 ēwāra paḷəng t-ḕ-t=aw.⎮
 evening leopard IND-come.PRS-3SG=TELIC
 'In the evening the panther returns (home).'

Bipartite categorical sentences may be explicitly marked in the prosody by placing an intonation group boundary after the subject constituent:

(920) Gorani
 īsa   kuř-akày| vàt   ba   kənāčakḕ,
 now boy-DEF.OBL.M say.PST to   girl.DEF.OBL.F
 'garaka=m=nī=ū'| *kənāčakè̀| vàt,*
 be.necessary.F=1SG=COP.2SG=and gir.DEF.OBL.F say.PST
 'garak=əm=nī'| *ītər   adā-ū   tātē=ū*
 be.necessary.M=1SG=COP.2SG then mother=and father=and
 čīw   pār-ēw   mà-kar-o.|
 thing money-INDF NEG-do.PRS-3SG
 'Nowadays, (if) the boy said to the girl, "I want you", and if the girl said, "I want you", then the word of parents and so-and-so does not count [lit. does not make money].'

The nuclear stress is placed on the subject if the speaker wishes to give it particular focus, as in (921)-(922), where the subject is given contrastive focus:

(921) JSNENA
 hūlaà   la   k-aē-wa.|
 Jew   NEG   IND-know.PRS.3SG.M-PSTC
 'A Jew (as opposed to a Muslim) did not know.' (B:20)

(922) Gorani
 pīr   šalīyàr   zāyənda=w   ēga-y=n.|
 spiritual.guide   PN   born=EZ   here-OBL.M=COP.3SG.M
 'Pir Shaliyar was born here (i.e. he should be included in the set of people born here, contrary to what others assume about his religion and origin).'

8.4.2.2 Object—subject—verb
The subject is occasionally placed after the object constituent. This construction may be used to put particular focus on the subject referent, in contexts such as (923a) and (923b). Here the remainder of the proposition is presupposed to be known but the identity of the subject referent in the proposition is new information:

(923) JSNENA
 a. *'ēa   hūlằē   trəṣtē=ya.|*
    this   Jews   make.PTCP.SG.M=COP.3SG.F
    'The Jews made this.' (B:83)

b. 'ē   maṣṣāē[|] baxta mārē bēl-akè,[|]
these matzos woman owner house-DEF
yā 'o-baxta=ē ləxm-akè
or that-woman=EZ bread-DEF
k-ol-ā-wā-lē-o,[|]   tarṣ-à-wā-lū.[|]
IND-do.PRS-3SG.F-PSTC-OBL.3SG.M-TELIC make.PRS-3SG.F-PSTC-OBL.3PL
'The mistress of the house or the woman who made the bread would make these matzos.' (B:22)

Likewise, in Gorani the OSV order occurs when the object is topical and the subject is given focal prominence:

(924) Gorani
       a. axḷab=ū žan-ā   mən hījbī
           most=EZ woman-PL.OBL 1SG formal.engagement
           kar-ēn-ē=ū[|]   axḷab=īč=šā mən taḷāq d-ēn-ē.[|]
           do.PRS-PSTC-1SG=and most=ADD=3PL 1SG divorce give.PRS-PSTC-1SG
           'It was me who was in charge of registering marriages. It was also me who was also in charge of divorces.' (lit. I would ask permission for marrying most women, and I would divorce most of them too).'
       b. nān=īč wè=tā pač-ēn-dē?[|]
           bread=ADD REFL=2PL bake.PRS-PSTC-2PL
           'Did you use to bake bread yourselves?'

In such OSV constructions the topical object is treated syntactically like a prototypical topical subject and the focal subject is treated like a prototypical focal object in a SOV construction.

8.4.2.3 Verb—subject
In JSNENA the subject constituent is postposed after the verb in certain circumstances. This occurs when the subject is either definite or indefinite. When the subject is indefinite, the function of the postposition is to give added prominence to a newly introduced referent that plays a role in the subsequent discourse, e.g.

(925) JSNENA
       a. patīrē 'əwìr-a,[|]   k-y-ā-wa   'aṣàrta.[|]
           Passover pass.PST-3SG.F IND-come.PRS-3SG.F-PSTC Pentecost
           '(After) Passover was over, Pentecost came.' (B:37)

    b. *bar-do k-y-ā-wa lēlē rēša šātà.*|
       after-OBL.that IND-come.PRS-3SG.F-PSTC eve head year
       'Then came New Year's Eve.' (A:63)

The JSNENA examples (925.a-b) are directly parallel to the following sentence in Gorani, which comes at the beginning of a folk song.

(926) Gorani
    āmā=wa wahàr.|
    come.PST.3SG=TELIC spring
    'The spring came again (returned).'

In Kurdish, VS order is typical of clauses with a copula verb expressing the onset of a temporal season, as in the JSNENA and Gorani examples above, or the existence of a newly introduced referent. Note, however, that the postposed subject is treated like a goal argument in (927.b), since it comes after a directional clitic. There is no parallel to this in JSNENA and Gorani.

(927) Kurdish
    a. *a-w-ā nawròz.*|
       IPFV-be.PST-IPFV? PN
       The new Year came.' [lit. it would be the New Year.']
    b. *a-w-ēt=a yàk pāwšā-yk,*| *žən-ēk=ī*
       IND-be.PRS-3SG=DRCT one king-INDF woman-INDF=3SG
       a-w-ē,| *žən-aka parīzāw čəl gìs*
       IND-be.PRS-3SG woman-DEF fairy forty plait.of.hair
       a-w-ē.|
       IND-be.PRS-3SG
       'There was a king. He had a wife. The wife was a fairy with 40 plaits of hair.'

In JSNENA, when the subject is definite and is not an information focus, the effect of the postposition of the subject is to bind the clause closely with what precedes. In (928.a), for example, the clause with the postposed subject *knīšta* is presented as a supplementary comment on what precedes. In (928.b) the statement that the Jews did not eat meat over a certain period is tagged on as an afterthought giving explanatory background to what is said at the beginning of the passage:

(928) JSNENA
    a. 'ēa tìm-a| lēlè̩| kulē 'amādè̩,| xāla
       this finish.pst-3sg.f evening all ready food
       k-əxl-í-wa| g-ēz-ī-wa bāqa knīštà.|
       ind-eat.prs-3pl-pstc ind-go.prs-3pl-pstc to synagogue
       ga-knīštà| mənḥà=yē-la=ū|
       in-synagogue evening.prayer=cop.pst-obl.3sg.f=and
       'arbìt=yē-la=ū| mūsaf=ē 'arbīt
       night_prayer=COP.PST-3SG.F=and Musaf=EZ night.prayer
       qarè̩-n-wā-la=ū,| ta-sa'at 'əsra=ū pəlgè̩,| xēsar
       read.prs-3pl-pstc-obl.3sg.f=and to-hour ten=and half eleven
       ṭūl garš-ā̀-wa knīšta,| lēlē kəpùr.|
       length pull.prs-3sg.f-pstc synagogue night atonement
      'When this finished, in the evening, when they were all ready, they ate food and went to the synagogue. In the synagogue there were evening and night prayers. They read the Musaf for the night prayers. The synagogue service lasted until half past ten or eleven o'clock on the night of the Day of Atonement.' (B:72)

    b. 'ằṣər| har xar-ā-wa qarwa
       evening just become.prs-3sg.f-pstc near
       mənḥà,| xēt-'o-waxtàra| mutằr=yē-lē
       evening.prayer again-that-time permitted=COP.PST-OBL.3SG.M
       bāqēf| šaḥīṭà k-ol-ī-wa.| tmanyà yomē|
       to-3SG.M slaughter IND-do.PRS-3PL-PSTC eight days
       'ē=č tmanya yomē mən-yomà| ṣəhyòn,|
       this=ADD eight days from-day Zion
       mən-yoma rēš-yarx=ē 'Àb| ḥata yoma ṣəhyòn|
       from-day head-month=EZ PN until day Zion
       pəsrà la k-əxl-ī-wa hūlaē.|
       meat NEG IND-eat.PRS-3PL-PSTC Jews
      'In the evening, just as it was getting near evening prayer, it was then again permitted to perform slaughtering. For eight days, for the eight days from the day of Zion, the day of beginning of Ab until the day of Zion the Jews did not eat meat.' (B:47)

The placement of a definite subject nominal before the verb typically sets up a new topic or re-identifies an existing topic for the clause and often for the ensuring section of discourse. This, therefore, forms a boundary in the discourse. When a definite non-focal subject is placed after the verb, this does not set up a topic but rather maintains an existing topic.

A parallel construction with a postposed definite subject is used in the Iranian languages of the region, which is illustrated by (929) from Kurdish. As in JSNENA, the function of the postposing of the non-focal definite subject is to bind the clause to the preceding discourse.

(929) Kurdish of the Sanandaj region
wət=əm,   'xằḷū,ǀ   bār   sē   wəḷāx-aka   xà
say.PST=1SG uncle load three donkey-DEF throw.IMP.2SG
am   war-aw.'ǀ bār   sē   wəḷāx-aka=y
DEM.PROX side-ADP load three donkey-DEF=3SG
xəst=a   am   wàr-aw   xāḷū=m.ǀ
throw.PST=DRCT DEM.PROX side-ADP uncle=1SG
'I said, "Uncle, send me over as much as three loads of asses to this other side." My uncle sent me over as much as three loads of ass to this other side.'

8.4.2.4 Subject Verb Agreement
In the following Gorani example, the existential verb agrees with the nominal subject which is closer to it.

(930) Gorani
haywān=šā, gằwa=šā   ha=na.ǀ
animal=3PL cow=3PL EXIST=COP.3SG.F
'(People) have animal(s), and cow(s).'

In (931) a 1sg. Subject followed by a comitative expression takes 1pl. agreement on the verb, referring both to the subject and to the complement of the comitative preposition. Example (932) presents a parallel to this from Gorani:

(931) JSNENA
'āna məntak=ē   tāt-ī   hīyē-x   bāqàǀ   'Isrằyəl.ǀ
I   with   father-1SG come.PST-1PL to   PN
'I came to Israel with my father.' (B:60)

(932) Gorani
hīzī   čanū   bərā-kay=m   lūā-ymē   bàr.ǀ
yesterday with brother-DEF.OBL.M=1SG   go.PST-1PL   out
'Yesterday I went out together with my brother.'

8.4.2.5 Independent subject pronouns

Pronominal reference to the subject of a clause is expressed by inflectional elements on the verb and by independent pronouns. The constructions with independent pronouns exhibit a 'heavier' coding of the content of the clause. The pronouns are generally placed before the verb.

An independent subject pronoun is used when the pronominal referent is a contrastive focus marked by the nuclear stress, e.g.

(933) JSNENA
 àt g-ēz-ēt sē-o.| 'āna là g-ēz-an.|
 your IND-go.PRS-2SG.M go.IMP.SG-TELIC I NEG IND-go.PRS-1SG.F
 '*You* (not me) go back. I shall *not* go.' (C:12)

Here the pronoun *àt* 'you' is in replacing contrastive focus (Dik 1981), i.e. it is uttered against the background of a presupposition that 'we shall both go'. The focus on the subject pronoun is corrective in that it signals that the subject argument in the presupposition should be replaced.

The use in Kurdish of independent subject pronouns with nuclear stress to express contrast is seen in (934).

(934) Kurdish
 àw gorānī=ī a-wət=ū| *mə̀n* dozala=m a-žan.|
 3SG song=3SG IPFV-say.PST=and 1SG flute=1SG IPFV-play.PST
 '*He* would sing songs, and *I* would play flute.'

This is a 'contrastive topic' construction in which a contrastive parallel is set up between two subjects (Dik 1981, 47; Lambrecht 1994, 291–291). Each clause consists of two domains of focus, viz the subject and the predicate. In the first domain the focus selects the subject from an accessible set of two ('he' and 'I'). In the second domain the predicate is selected from an accessible limited set of activities within the domain of musical performance. The type of focus, therefore, is different from the JSNENA example (933). In both cases, however, the subject pronouns are in focus, i.e., the focus selects one item from a presupposed set of alternatives (Krifka 2008), and there is some kind of contrastive opposition between the subject and another referent.

Where there is no contrastive focus on the pronoun, the heavily-coded constructions with an independent pronoun before the verb generally mark boundaries of some kind between sections of the discourse, signalling the onset a section.

An independent pronoun is used in JSNENA at the beginning of direct speech, e.g.

(935) JSNENA
 a. mīr-ē   'ānà⎸ baxtà   gəwr-ī.⎸
   say.PST-OBL.3SG.M   I   woman   marry.PST-OBL.1SG
   'He said, "I have married."' (C:11)
 b. mīr-ī   'āna šarbat   mən-'īla   dīdax
   say.PST-OBL.1SG   I   sherbet   from-hand   OBL.2SG.F
   là   šatē-na.⎸
   NEG   drink.PRS-1SG.M
   'I said, "I shall not drink sherbet from your hand."' (A:23)
 c. mīr-ū   ròḷa⎸   'āt   sarwatmànd=yē-t.⎸
   say.PST-OBL.3PL   dear_boy   you   rich=COP-2SG.M
   'They said, "Dear boy, you are rich."' (D:9)

Likewise, in the following examples from the Iranian languages of the region the independent subject pronoun marks the beginning of speech:

(936) Kurdish
  a-gà-yt=a   bar⎸ a-r-ö   a-yž-ē,
  IND-arrive.PRS-3SG=DRCT   front   IND-go.PRS-3SG   IND-say.PRS-3SG
  'mən a-š-ē   bə-ř-əm⎸   àm
  1SG   IND-AUX-3SG   SBJV-go.PRS-1SG   DEM.PROX
  šans   xwa=m-a   payā   Ø-ka-m.'⎸
  fortune   REFL=1SG-DEM   visible   SBJV-do.PRS-1SG
  'He arrived (at the gates of the city), went (to the guards) and said, "I shall go (and) find this fortune of mine."'

(937) Gorani
  wāta-bē=šā   īnà   jarayān=ā⎸
  say.PST.PTCP.M-be.PSTC.3SG=3PL   DEM.PROX.3SG.M.DIR   situation=COP.3SG
  ādī=č   wāta-bē,   'day mən⎸
  3SG.OBL.M   say.PST.PTCP.M-be.PSTC.3SG   DISC   1SG
  Ø-tāw-ù⎸   īsa   mà-tāw-ā.'⎸
  IND-can.PRS-1SG   now   NEG-can.PRS-1SG
  'They had said, "The situation is like this." He had said, "Well [normally] I can [be of help], [but] now I cannot."'

In JSNENA, an independent pronoun is often used when there is a change in subject referent and the attention is shifted from one referent to another. A parallel to this from Kurdish is seen in (939).

(938) JSNENA
'ay   bxḕ=ū| 'āna   bəxy-àn.|
this   weep.PST.3SG.M=and   I   weep.PST-1SG.F
'He wept and I wept.' (C:11)

(939) Kurdish
a-yž-è̀   tu   xwā   řēza-y   law
IND-say.PRS-3SG   2SG   god   a.little-INDF   from.DEM.DIST
āwər=m-a   pē   a-wa-y?| aw=īš   a-yž-è̀
fire=1SG-DEM   to   IND-give.PRS-2SG   3SG=ADD   IND-say.PRS-3SG
bān   čāw   a-wa-m   pē=t.|
top   eye   IND-give.PRS-1SG   to=2SG
'(The little girl) said, "Would you please give me a bit of that fire?" **She** (the demon) said, "Yes, gladly (lit. on eyes). I will give you."'

In JSNENA, on some occasions an independent subject pronoun occurs when there is no shift in subject referent, but there is a re-orientation on some other level of the discourse. In (940), for example, the pronoun occurs in a clause that marks a shift from an introductory section, which introduces the referent, to a foreground section that narrates his activities.

(940) JSNENA
xà   šwāwa   hīt-wā-lē| ràba   dawlaman=yē-lē.|
one   neighbour   EXIST-PSTC-OBL.3SG.M   very   rich=COP.PST-OBL.3SG.M
tājər=yē-lē.| 'o   lēlawāē   k-ē-wa-o
merchant=COP.PST-OBL.3SG.M   he   evenings   IND-come.PRS.3SG.M-PSTC-TELIC
bēlà,| g-bē-wa   yatū-wa   hasāb=ū
home   IND-need.PRS.3SG.M-PSTC   sit.PRS.3SG.M-PSTC   accounts=and
ktàbē   hol-ū.|
books   do.prs.3gs.m-obl.3pl
'He had a neighbour, who was very rich. He was a merchant. He would return home in the evenings and had to sit and do the accounts and books.' (A:100)

Similarly, in the Kurdish example (941) an independent subject pronoun occurs at the beginning of a clause that introduces the foreground after a preliminary background section.

(941) Kurdish
*Sənjər xàn*ǀ *aw-waxt-a* *bāwà=y* *'ābdīn*
PN khan DEM.DIST-time-DEM grand.father=EZ PN
*xān=ū*ǀ *aw-waxt-a* *'azīz xān=ū* *amānà*
khan=and DEM.DIST-time-DEM PN khan=and DEM.PROX.PL
*bū.*ǀ *māḷ=yān* *la farah-ằ bū.*ǀ *řūs-aka*
COP.PST.3SG house=3PL at PN-POST COP.PST.3SG Russian-DEF
*hāt-ù*ǀ **àm** *tanyā xwa=y*
come.PST-COP.PST 3SG.PROX alone REFL=3SG
*řū-Ø*ǀ *řūs-aka=y* *šəkə̀s dā.*ǀ
go.PST-3SG Russian-DEF=3SG defeat give.PST
'Sənjər Khan, well he was the grandfather of Abdin Khan, Aziz Khan and so forth. Their house was in Farah district. The Russians had come (here). **He** went alone and defeated the Russians.'

In (942) from a JSNENA narrative a subject pronoun is used in a clause that constitutes a disjunction from what precedes in that it offers an evaluative comment on the foregoing sequence of events:

(942) JSNENA
'ay-zīl *jəns ləbl-ề,*ǀ *jəns-akē*
this-go.PST.3SG.M cloth take.PST-OBL.3SG.M cloth-DEF
ləbl-ē *matū-lē* *ga-xa t^wkāna*
take.PST-OBL.3SG.M put.PRS.3SG.M-OBL.3SG.M in-one shop
*zabn-ề.*ǀ *'ay=əč xīr*
sell.PRS.3SG.M-OBL.3SG.M this=ADD become.PST.3SG.M
*mangàl do.*ǀ
like OBL.3SG.M
'He went and took the cloth, he took the cloth away to put it in a shop and sell it. He became like him (the neighbour).' (A:105)

A parallel function of an independent subject pronoun in Gorani is seen in (943), where the clause with the subject pronoun presents an evaluation of the foregoing event.

(943) Gorani
lūwā-ymē-ra   Tāqwasàn.│ yo   bəlīt-ē=mā   gərt
go.PST-1PL-POST pn   one.M   ticket-INDF=1PL take.PST
yo-ē   duwè   təman-ē.│ yawāšē   lūwā-ymē
one.M-?   two   PN-PL.DIR then   go.PST-1PL
hàwz-ē   čā   bē│   qāyə̀q=əš   čanē.│
pond-INDF in.DEM.DIST be.PRS.PSTC.3SG   boat=3SG   in
ēma   har   qāyəq=mā   nà-yīa-bē!│
1PL   at.all boat=1PL   NEG-see.PST.PTCP.m-be.PSTC.3SG
yawāšē   qāyəqswārī̀   kar-ēn-ē   xuḷk.│
well   boating   do.PRS-PSTC-3PL people

'We went towards Taq Bostan. We each bought a ticket. Each cost two Tomans. Then we went (inside). There was a pond there. There were boats in it. **We** had never seen a boat. People would go boating.'

On some occasions independent subject pronouns are placed after the verb. In this case the clause is presented as having a closer connection with what precedes and does not mark the onset of a new section. In (944) from JSNENA and (945) from Kurdish the postposed pronoun is not contrastive and does not bear the nuclear stress. In constructions of this nature the heavy coding of the pronoun is exploited as end-weighting to mark closure.

(944) JSNENA
ʾaxnī   k-ē-n-wa   bēl-an   yat-ì-wa.│
we   IND-come.PRS-3PL-PSTC   house-1PL   sit.PRS-3PL-PSTC
ḥāz   k-ol-ī-wa   hē-n   bēla   dīdan
desire   IND-do.PRS-3PL-PSTC   come.PRS-3PL   house   OBL.1PL
yat-ì̀   ʾonyēxāē.│
sit.PRS-3PL   they

'They would come to our house and sit. They wanted to come to our house and sit.' (A:80)

(945) Kurdish
Tāyī=š   wə̀t=ī│   ay   ama   čūn   ā
PN=3SG   say.PST=3SG   INTJ   DEM.PROX.SG   how   PTCL
àm   həkāyat-yal=t-a   hāwərd=as=aw   tu!?│
DEM.PROX   tale-PL=2SG-DEM   bring.PST-PERF=TELIC 2SG

[Hatam wrote his tales too, and brought them to Tay] Tay said, "How were you able to bring back all these tales (with you)?"

8.4.3 Prepositional phrases

8.4.3.1 Verb—prepositional phrase

In JSNENA, a prepositional phrase expressing an indirect object or some other complement of the verb is normally placed after the verb. Table 82 summarizes the rate of post-predicate realisation for different types of indirect objects. The ratios are extracted from datasets of JSNENA (Noorlander 2022) and Central Kurdish of the Sanandaj region (Mohammadirad 2022b).

Table 82: Rate of post-predicate realisation of nominal indirect objects in JSNENA and Kurdish.

	JSNENA	Kurdish
Addresses	0.100	0.93
Location	0.100	0.100
Goals of verbs of movement, e.g. 'go'	0.93	0.93
Goals of verbs of caused movement, e.g. 'put'	0.87	0.98
Recipients of 'give'	0.100	0.80

According to the data in Table 82 Kurdish and JSNENA closely match with regard to the word order profile of indirect objects, resulting as VOX (where X stands for indirect objects) as the basic word order. These tendencies reflect structural convergence.

If the prepositional phrase constitutes the end of the clause, it generally bears the nuclear stress. The nuclear stress in such cases typically expresses a broad focus that includes both the prepositional phrase and the verb.

(946) JSNENA
    a. *k-əmr-a*   *bāqa* *baxt-ı̀*ˈ
        IND-say.PRS-3SG.F to   wife-1SG
        'She says to my wife ...' (A:18)
    b. *g-bē*   *hē-t-o*   *bāqa* *'aḥrà.*ˈ
        IND-need.PRS.3SG.M come.PRS-2SG.M-TELIC to   town
        'You must come back to the town.' (A:6)
    c. *g-ēz-ī-wa*   *bāqa* *bēla*   *nòš-ū.*ˈ
        IND-go-3PL-PSTC to   house self-3PL
        'They delivered the table, then went to their homes.' (A:11)
    d. *xa-jām*   *daēl-wa*   *qam*   *bābēn-èf.*ˈ
        one-mirror put.PRS.3SG.M-PSTC before forehead-3SG.M
        'He put a mirror in front of its forehead.' (A:43)

e. 'axnī   jwanqē   smīx-əx-wa   ga-ḥawšà.ˈ
    we   youngsters stand.PST-1PL-PSTC   in-courtyard
    'We youngsters were standing in the courtyard.' (A:12)

Similar prosodic patterns of post-verbal prepositional phrases are found in Kurdish and Gorani:

(947) Kurdish
      āqàˈ   a-řū-n   bū   řåw.ˈ
      man   IND-go.PST-3PL   to   hunting
      'Well, they went hunting.'

(948) Gorani
      wēžankàr-ē   b-ēn-ēˈ   salàm
      gum.tragacanth.worker-DIR.PL   be.PRS-PSTC-3PL   advance.selling
      kar-ēn-ē.ˈ   lu-ēn-ē   lā   dawḷatman-à.ˈ
      do.PRS-PSTC-3PL   go.PRS-PSTC-3PL   to   rich-PL.OBL
      'There were people who distilled gum (from trees). They would sell in advance (their product). They would go to the rich.'

8.4.3.2 Prepositional phrase—verb

On some occasions the prepositional phrase in JSNENA is placed before the verb. This construction is generally used when the phrase contains a referent that has some kind of prominence in the discourse. Sometimes the referent is newly introduced into the discourse and it is marked as an information focus by the nuclear stress. In such cases the speaker may draw particular attention to it on account of its importance. In (949.a) the speaker wishes to draw special attention to the fuel of the oven. In (949.b) the 'board' is the essential distinctive feature of the object in question, which is given further salience by repeating it at the end of the clause:

(949) JSNENA
      a. tanūr-akē   ba-ṣīwè̀   malq-ī-wā-la.ˈ
         oven-DEF   with-wood   heat.PRS-3PL-PSTC-OBL.3SG.F
         'They heated the oven with wood.' (A:67)

b. xwān mà=yē-lē?| mən-taxtà
   table what=COP.PST-OBL.3SG.M from-board
   trəṣ-wā-lū,| xa-taxta ruwà.|
   make.PST-PSTC-OBL.3PL one-board big
   'What was a 'table'?. They made it out of board, a large board.' (A:9)

In the Iranian languages of Sanandaj the placing of a prepositional phrase immediately before the verb likewise is generally a strategy for giving the phrase prominence:

(950) Gorani
ēma=yč pay kalūpalî̀ lūē b-ēn-mē.|
1PL=ADD for merchandise go.PST-PTCP.PL be.PRS-PSTC-1PL
'We had gone for merchandise.'

(951) Kurdish
pēsa-ka=y=mān bo gāwə̀z garak=a.|
skin-DEF=3SG=1PL for leather.bottle necessary=COP.3SG
'We will need its (cow's) skin for (making) leather bottle(s).'

Prepositional phrases are occasionally fronted before the verb when the nominal in the phrase has already been evoked in the immediately preceding context and so is topically bound to it. The nominal in such cases does not bear the nuclear stress. These constructions are used when not only the referent of the prepositional phrase is bound to the foregoing discourse but also the proposition expressed by the clause as a whole has a close connection to what precedes. In (952), for example, the statement that the peddlers lived in the villages is presented as an elaborative supplement to the statement that they would make commercial trips to the villages:

(952) JSNENA
g-ēz-ī-wa bāqa mālawāè̀.| ga-malawāē
IND-go.PRS-3PL-PSTC to villages in-villages
zəndəgî k-ol-ī-wa.|
life IND-do.PRS-3PL-PSTC
'They (the peddlers) went to the villages. They lived in the villages.' (B:4)

Similarly, in the following narrative 'mountain' has been evoked in the preceding discourse and does not bear the nuclear stress. The clause coheres with what precedes.

(953) Kurdish of the Sanandaj region
bərà̀ | bāwk=əm wasəyàt=ī kərdē=ya | bā
brother father=1SG will=3SG do.PST.PTCP=PERF hort
lam kēf-ā řož nà-ka-yn=aw! |
in.DEM.PROX mountain-ADP day NEG.IMP-do.PRS-1PL=TELIC
'Brother, my father had made a will [for us]. Let's not stay the night in this mountain!'

8.4.3.3 Nominal complements expressing goals after verbs of movement

When a nominal without a preposition is used with a verb of movement to express a goal, this is normally placed after the verb. The nuclear stress is usually placed on the nominal expressing broad information focus that includes both the nominal and verb:

(954) JSNENA
    a. bar-do k-ē-n-wa-o bē-kaldà. |
       after-OBL.that IND-come.PRS-3PL-PSTC-TELIC house-bride
       'Afterwards they would come back to the
       house of the bride.' (A:39)
    b. noš-ū labl-ī-wā-lē 'orxèl. |
       self-3PL take.PRS-3PL-PSTC-OBL.3SG.M mill
       'They would themselves take it to the mill.' (A:58)
    c. ma kul-yoma g-ēz-ēt 'ay-jangàḷ? |
       why every-day IND-go.PRS-2SG.M this-wood
       'Why do you every day go to the wood?' (A:104)
    d. 'āna 'o-lēlē la-zì-na-o bēla |
       I that-night NEG-go.PRS-1SG-TELIC home
       'I did not go back home that night.' (A:26)
    e. zīl-ēx dokà=ū |
       go.PST-1PL there=and
       'We went there.' (A:20)

A goal may be also be expressed by a prepositional phrase, e.g.

(955) JSNENA
    g-ēz-ī-wa bāqa bēla nòš-ū. |
    IND-go.PRS-3PL-PSTC to house self-3PL
    'They went to their homes.' (A:11)

Similarly, in the Iranian languages of Sanandaj the goals of verbs of movement are generally placed after the verb. The postposed nominal usually takes the nuclear stress. In Gorani, as in JSNENA, a goal may be expressed by a bare nominal (956.a-c) or by a prepositional phrase (956.d):

(956) Gorani
    a. *lūā-ymē*   *Kərmāšа̀n.*
        go.PST-1PL   PN
        'We went to Kermanshah.'
    b. *yawà*   *Ø-kar-o*   *kīsa=š.*
        barley   IND-do.PRS-3SG   sack=3SG
        'He put barley into his sack.'
    c. *āmà-(ā)nē*   *Tārа̀n.*
        come.PST-1SG   PN
        'I came to Tehran.'
    d. *lū-ēn-ē*   *pay*   *šārazūr-ī*   *pama*   *čənī-ày.*
        go.PRS-PSTC-3PL   to   PN-OBL.M   cotton   pick.PST-INF
        'People would go to Sharazoor for cotton herding.'

In Kurdish, on the other hand, there is not such a close match with JSNENA, since a goal is expressed by a prepositional phrase or by a nominal preceded by a directional particle on the verb.

(957) Kurdish
    a. *a-hāt-Ø*   *bo*   *lāy*   *bāwk=əm.*
        IPFV-come.PST-3SG   to   place.of.EZ   father=1SG
        'He would come to my father.'
    b. *šàkat*   *a-w-ən*   *a-č-ən=a*   *āsyāw=a*   *kona-yk-àw.*
        tired   IND-be.PRS-3PL   IND-go.PRS-3PL=DRCT   mill=EZ   old-IND-ADP
        'They got tired (and) went to an old mill.'

In clauses with a goal argument, therefore, JSNENA has converged more with Gorani than with Kurdish.

In JSNENA, occasionally a nominal expressing a goal is fronted before the verb. In (958) a demonstrative pronoun that refers to a set of goals is placed before the verb. This is a recapitulatory statement that is tagged onto what precedes. Example (959) presents a parallel from Iranian:

(958) JSNENA
    ʾənyēxāē   kulē   g-ēz-ī̀-wa.|
    these   all   IND-go.PRS-3PL-PSTC
    'They went to all of these.' (B:43)

(959) Kurdish
    ama bàz| *harkà   bo   am   mantaqa*
    DEIC falcon whoever to   DEM.PROX region
    hātē-Ø=ya| *kòšt=ī=ya.*|
    come.PST.PTCP-3SG=PERF kill.PST=3SG=PERF
    'The falcon has killed whoever came to this region.'

8.4.3.4 Nominal complements of verbs of naming

In JSNENA, the name of referents may be expressed by a construction consisting of an impersonal 3pl. form of the verb *'-m-r* 'to say', with the named item marked by an L-suffix. The nominal complement of this construction is generally placed after the verb, e.g.

(960) JSNENA
    a. *k-əmr-ī-le*   *pā-gošà.*|
         IND-say.PRS-3PL-OBL.3SG.M leg-stretching
         'It is called "stretching of the leg."' (A:26)
    b. *k-əmr-ī-wā-lē*   *īla   dwāqà.*|
         IND-say-3PL-PSTC-OBL.3SG.M hand joining
         'It was called "the joining of hands."' (A:34)
    c. *k-əmr-ī-wā-lū*   *čarčì.*|
         IND-say-3PL-PSTC-OBL.3PL   peddler
         'They were called "peddlers."' (A:70)

The expression of a nominal complement of verbs of naming in JSNENA matches the equivalent construction in Gorani, where the verb 'to say' is used, and the nominal complement is placed after the verb, e.g. (961.a-b). Occasionally, a preposition comes before the nominal, e.g. (961.c), which is more characteristic of the speech of the younger generation.

(961) Gorani
- a. šàxs-ē=mā   ha=n| m-āč-mē   šālīyār   sīyà.|
     person-INDF=1PL EXIST=COP.3SG.M IND-say.PRS-1PL PN   PN
     'We have a saint (whom) we call "Shaliar Siya."'
- b. šaxs-ē   tàr=mā   ha=n| m-āč-ā=š
     person-INDF other=1PL EXIST=COP.3SG.M IND-say.PRS-3PL=3SG
     Pīr   Xāłè.|
     spiritual.guide PN
     'We have another saint; he is called "Pir Xale."'
- c. m-āč-ā=š   pana tasawùf.|
     IND-say.PRS-3PL=3SG to   sufism
     'It is called "Sufism."'

On the other hand, in Kurdish the compound verb *nāw nān* 'put a name' is used in similar contexts:

(962) Kurdish
- a. nāw=ī   a-n-ən-a   wəḷkənà.|
     name=3SG IND-put.PRS-3PL=DRCT   PN
     'She is named "Wilkna."'
- b. nāw=ī   a-n-ən-a   āsn=a   sar-à.|
     name=3SG IND-put.PRS-3PL=DRCT   iron=EZ   head-DEF
     'He is named "iron-head."'

It can be seen that in this construction JSNENA corresponds to Gorani rather than Kurdish.

8.4.3.5 Interrogative clauses

In JSNENA and the Iranian languages of Sanandaj, interrogative particles are generally placed immediately before the verb, e.g.

(963) JSNENA
- a. mànī   g-bē-t?|
     who   IND-want.PRS-2SG.M
     'Whom do you want?' (A:20)
- b. mà   k-ol-ī-wa   ga-patīrē?|
     what IND-do.PRS-3PL-PSTC   at-Passover
     'What did they do at Passover?' (B:14)

c. *'ənšē   ga-bēla   ma   k-ol-ī-wa?*|
women   in-house   what   IND-do.PRS-3PL-PSTC
'What did the women do in the house?' (B:40)

d. *'ə̀t   ma-k-ol-ēt?*|
you   what-IND-do.PRS-2SG.M
'What do you do?' (A:102)

(964) Gorani
čī̀   kušt-∅=ət?|
why   kill.PST-3SG.M=2SG
'Why did you kill him?'

(965) Kurdish
a. *l-ēra   čà̀   a-ka-y?*|
in-here   what.INTJ   IND-do.PRS-2SG
'What are they doing here?'

b. *bočà   hāt-ī?*|
why   come.PST-2SG
'Why did you come (here)?'

c. *Tāyī=š   wə̀t=ī*| *ay   ama   čūn   ā*
PN=3SG   say.PST=3SG   INTJ   DEM.PROX.SG   how   PTCL
àm   həkāyat-yal=t-a   hāwərd=as=aw   tu!?|
DEM.PROX   tale-PL=2SG-DEM   bring.PST-PERF=TELIC   2SG
'Tay said, "How were you able to return from those places and bring back all these tales with you in your memory (lit. how were you able to bring back all these tales)?"'

8.5 Negated clauses

8.5.1 Negator before verb

In JSNENA, the usual way to negate a verbal clause is to place the negative particle *la* before the verb. This is either stressed or unstressed. When stressed, it takes either the nuclear or non-nuclear stress, depending on the prominence that the speaker wishes to give to the negator.

8.5.1.1 Unstressed negator

(966) JSNENA
    a. *la-k-ay-an*   *màni=yē.*[|]
        NEG-IND-know.PRS-1SG.F   who=COP.3SG.M
        'I do not know who it is.' (A:21)
    b. *'āna 'o-lēlē*   *la-zǐ-na-o*   *bēla.*[|]
        I   that-night   NEG-go.PST-1SG.M-TELIC   home
        'I did not go back home that night.' (A:26)

8.5.1.2 Negator with non-nuclear stress

(967) JSNENA
    a. *rājə'   ba-ḥanabandàn   la   ḥqē-lī   bāq-ox.*[|]
        referring to-henna_ceremeony NEG tell.PST-OBL.1ST to-2SG.M
        'I have not told you about the henna ceremony.' (A:39)
    b. *nāšē   rāba   taqālà   la   daē-n-wa.*[|]
        people much attempt NEG put.PRS-3PL-PSTC
        'People did not exert themselves.' (A:55)
    c. *xa-mdī   la   mīr-ī   bāq-òx.*[|]
        one-thing NEG say.PST-OBL.1SG to-2SG.M
        'One thing I did not tell you.' (A:77)

8.5.1.3 Negator with nuclear stress

One type of situation in which this occurs is where the adversative force of the negator is made salient by its contradiction of what would be expected from a statement in the precding context:

(968) JSNENA
    a. *pas   har-čī   'əṣrār   wīl-ū*
        then however_much insistence make.PST-OBL.3PL
        là   hīy-a.[|]
        NEG come.PST-3SG.F
        'Then, however much they insisted, she did not come.' (A:23)

b. 'agar   kīlo   bī-zoa   xar-ā-wa   mast-akȅ,ǀ
    if   kilo   more   become.PRS-3SG.F-PSTC   yoghurt-DEF
    là   darē-wā-l-o   tʷk-àf.ǀ
    NEG   pour.PRS.3SG.M-PSTC-OBL.3SG.F-TELIC   place-3SG.F
    'If the yoghurt turned out to be more than a kilo, he did not pour it back
    (as you might expect).' (A:79)

8.5.1.4 Negated verb with nouns negated by hīč

The verb is negated with *la* when a nominal participant in the clause is modified by the negative particle *hīč*, which denies the existence of referents of the class denoted by the nominal, e.g.

(969) JSNENA
   a. hȋč-kas   la-hīyē.ǀ
       nobody   NEG-come.PST.3SG.M
       'Nobody came.' (D:7)
   b. hȋč-kas   barūx-ȅf   la   xar-wa.ǀ
       nobody   friend-3SG.M   NEG   become.PRS.3SG.M-PSTC
       'Nobody became his friend.' (D:1)

8.5.2 Negated clauses in Iranian

In Kurdish and Gorani, the negator morpheme takes different forms depending on the verb form. This is summarised in Table 83.

Table 83: Negator formatives in Gorani and Kurdish.

	Gorani	Kurdish
Present copula	nīan <nī + an 'be'	nī-
Present indicative	ma-~ na-	nā-
Imperative/ Present subjunctive	ma-~ na-	na- ~ ma-
Past tense	na-	na-

The following sub-sections list the stress-pattern of negator prefixes in Kurdish and Gorani and how they match the JSNENA patterns that are described above.

8.5.2.1 Unstressed

(970) Gorani
bàrd-ā=šā, ka ba hayằt=əm ālf=əm
take.PST-1SG=3PL SBRD in life=1SG grass=1SG
na-kana=n, bàrd-ā=šā āḷəf kan-ay.
NEG-mow.PST.PTCP.M=COP.3SG take.PST-1SG=3PL grass mow.PST-INF
'They took me—I have never mowed grass in my life—they took me to mow grass.'

(971) Kurdish
bā làm kēf-ā řož na-ka-yn=aw.
hort in.DEM.PROX mountain-POST day NEG.SBJV-do.PRS-1PL=TELIC
'Let us not stay the night in this mountain.'

8.5.2.2 Stressed with non-nuclear stress

(972) Kurdish
bə-zā šů̀=m pē ná-kā!
SBJV-know.IMP.2SG husband=1SG to NEG-do.PRS.3SG
'See if she marries me!'

8.5.2.3 Stressed with nuclear stress

(973) Gorani
āđī=č wāta-bē, 'day mə̀n
3SG.OBL.M say.PST.PTCP.M-be.PSTC.3SG DISC 1SG
Ø-tāw-ǜ īsa mà-tāw-ā.'
IND-can.PRS-1SG now NEG-can.PRS-1SG
'He had said, "Well [normally] I can [be of help], [but] now I cannot."'

(974) Kurdish
jā dawrề š hakāyat mə̀n hīčka
INTJ dervish tale 1SG no.one
nà=y-wərdē=ya dayšt-aw!
NEG-take.PST.PTCP=PERF field-ADP
'Well! Dervish, my tale—nobody has taken it out.'

8.5.2.4 Negated verb with nouns negated by hīč

(975) Kurdish
   a. *am   hamka   kör-à,ˈ   pāwšā   hawāḷ   la*
      DEM.PROX.SG all   blind-DEF   king   news   at
      hìčka   nā́-pərs-ēt.ˈ
      no.one   NEG-ask.PRS-3SG
      'All these blind people, (and) the king does not ask of anybody.'
   b. *hīč   mà-zān-mēˈ   har   ānày   Ø-zān-mē.ˈ*
      nothing   NEG-know.PRS-1PL   only   DEM.DIST.OBL.M   IND-know.PRS-1PL
      'We know nothing. We only know that [much].'

8.5.2.5 Negator before other elements in the clause

The negative particle is placed before an argument of a clause where this is one of a list of items that are presented over two or more adjacent clauses. The clauses usually share the same verb and the focus of information, which is expressed by the nuclear stress, is on the clause argument rather than the negator:

(976) JSNENA
   xēt   la   zàrb   daēl-wa   ʾəl-af=ūˈ   la   ba-pūt-akè̀
   more   NEG   blow   hit.PRS.3SG.M-PSTC   on-3SG.F=and   NEG   on-can-DEF
   daēl-waˈ   ʾu-la yal-ēf   naqḷ-ī̀-wa.ˈ
   hit.PRS.3SG.M-PSTC   and-NEG-children-3SG.M   dance.PRS-3PL-PSTC
   'He no longer played on the drum, he did not beat the can and his children did not dance.' (A:107)

A corresponding construction in Gorani with negators before clause arguments is shown in (977):

(977) Gorani
   taḷā   nà-bīya=n   zamān-ē   mən
   gold   NEG-be.PST.PTCP.M=COP.3SG.M   when-OBL.F   1SG
   šū=m   karda=n.ˈ   na   taḷà̀
   husband=1SG   do.PST.PTCP.M=COP.3SG.M   no   gold
   bīyan,ˈ   na   habātà-y   bīyanˈ
   be.PST.PTCP.M=COP.3SG.M   no   gift-OBL.M   be.PST.PTCP.M=COP.3SG.M
   hīč   nabīyan.ˈ
   nothing   NEG-be.PST.PTCP.M=COP.3SG.M
   'When I got married there was **neither** gold **nor** gift(s). There was nothing.'

Elsewhere a negator before an adjective negates the adjective rather than the predicate, e.g.

(978) JSNENA
    a. *'ēa là xar-wa 'o-la*
       this NEG become.PRS.3SG.M-PSTC it-NEG
       qrīxa hawè.|
       whitened be.PRS.3SG.M
       'It could not be unwhitened' (B:19)
    b. *šišmē la qlīwè|*
       sesame NEG clean
       'uncleaned sesamed' (B:27)

Iranian languages of Sanandaj also allow a negator before an adjective.

(979) Kurdish
    la-bar ark šāhī-ā hāwār=ī kə̀rd|
    in-front.of palace royal-POST shout=3SG do.PST
    kas-ē kār duktàr=ī Ø-b-ē| kàs-ē|
    person-INDF work doctor=3SG SBJV-be.PRS-3SG person-INDF
    nàsāx Ø-wē|, kas-ē naxwàš Ø-w-ē.|
    unhealthy SBJV-be.PRS-3SG person-INDF unwell SBJV-be.PRS-3SG
    'He shouted in front of the royal palace, "Is there anybody who needs a doctor? Anyone who is unhealthy? Anyone who is sick?"'

8.5.3 Idiomatic usage

A negative predicate is sometimes combined in parallel with a positive predicate as an idiomatic way of expressing a lack of certainty, e.g.

(980) JSNENA
    bāqa do 'alè| ... nāš-èf,| nāšē
    to OBL.3SG.M know.PRS.3SG.M people-3SG.M people
    'ay mamlakatà| dàx zəndəgī k-ol-ī|
    this kingdom how life IND-do.PRS-3PL
    dàx la k-ol-ī.|
    how NEG IND-do.PRS-3PL
    'In order that he might know how his people, the people of his kingdom lived.' (A:108)

This idiomatic use of the negator in Kurdish expresses an incomplete action, which is only in its onset phase:

(981) Kurdish
xwar-aka   kaft=ū   nà-kaft|
sun-DEF   fall.PST.3SG=and   NEG-fall.PST.3SG
dằ=y=a   nāw   āsyāw-aka.|
give.PST=3SG=DRCT   inside   mill-DEF
'(When) the sun had just risen (lit. it fell and it didn't fall) and broken into the mill.'

8.6 Extrapositional constructions

The structure of extraposition involves placing a nominal or independent pronoun in syntactic isolation in clause initial position and resuming it by an anaphoric pronominal element later in the clause. The extraposed item is accessible from the speech situation or preceding discourse. The construction is categorical, in that the extraposed item sets up the base of predication and the following clause expresses a predication about it (Sasse 1987). Extraposition constructions typically coincide with some kind of boundary in the discourse.

In JSNENA, a speaker sometimes opens a speech turn with a topic referent that is accessible to the hearer in the speech situation. If this is not the subject of the clause, it stands in extraposition.

(982) JSNENA
  a. *bar-xa-mudat-xēt   dāak-ī   hīy-a*
     after-one-period-other   mother-1SG   come.PST-3SG.F
     ba-šon-ī   'axa   k-òl-a| *'āt*
     in-after-1SG   here   IND-do.PRS-3SG.F   you
     taḥṣīl-ox   tīmà=y| *g-bē*
     studies-2SG.M   finish.PTCP.SG.M=COP.3SG.M   IND-need.PRS.3SG.M
     hē-t-ò| *lāga   'axon-òx.*|
     come.PRS-2SG.M-TELIC   to   brother-2SG.M
     'After a while my mother came after me and says, "You—your studies are finished, you must return to your brother."' (A:27)
  b. *mīr-ē   'āt   ḥašt-ox   mà=y-a?*|
     say.PST-OBL.3SG.M you   work-2SG.M   what=COP-3SG.F
     'He said, "What is your job?"' (D:20)

In the extraposition constructions of Kurdish and Gorani, a nominal stands in clause-initial position and is resumed by a clitic pronoun. In Gorani, which inflects for case, the extraposed nominal is always in the direct case. In (983)-(984)-(985) the resumptive pronoun is a possessive clitic. In (985) the resumptive pronoun resumes the extraposed nominal. These examples of extraposition occur at the beginning of a speech turn:

(983) Gorani
    faqat mən kār=əm īsḷāhkarḋ-ày=ū xuḷk-ī bē.|
    only 1SG job=1SG reform.do.PST-INF=EZ people-OBL.M be.PSTC.3SG
    'I—my job was only giving advice to people.'

(984) Kurdish of the Sanandaj region
    a. *mən čằw=əm xās hanằ nā-kā.*|
       1SG eye=1SG well vision NEG-do.PRS.3SG
       'I—my eyes don't function properly.'
    b. *mə̀n*| *'ahmaw=əm nằw=a.*|
       1SG PN=1SG name=COP.3SG
       'I—my name is Ahmaw.'
    c. *mə̀n*| *ā awa jor-a wā=m-a*
       1SG PTCL DEM.DIST manner-DEM DEIC=1SG-DEM
       pē hằt.|
       to come.PST.3SG
       'I—in this manner, such happened to me.'

(985) Gorani
    kāwř-akē kè mə-ḋ-o=ā?|
    Sheep-DEF.PL.DIR who IND-give.PRS-3SG=3PL
    'The sheep—who donates them?'

In (986) from JSNENA the extrapositional clause coincides with a shift to background description after a narrative event:

(986) JSNENA

> m-zamå̀n=ē| Kurēš=ē Kabı̀r| hīyē=n   bāqa
> from-time=EZ PN=EZ PN   come.PTCP.PL=COP.3PL to
> Hamadå̀n,| 'Asfahå̀n,| Golpayagå̀n.| 'ay təlḥa
> PN   PN   PN   these three
> tʷkē   hūlāē ràba xīrē=n   ga-ū.|
> places   Jews   many be.PTCP.PL=COP.3PL   in-3PL

'At the time of Cyrus the Great, they came to Hamadan, Isfahan and Golpayagan. These three places—there were many Jews in them.' (B:1)

In (987) the extrapositional construction with the initial 1st person pronoun, which is topical from the speech situation, constitutes an explanatory supplement to what precedes:

(987) JSNENA

> 'arba xamša nafarē pīl-ēx   'orxà=ū|
> four   five   people fall.PST-1PL way=and
> zīl-ēx   dokà,| məntak=ē dāak-ì.| 'āna
> go.PST-1PL there   with   mother-1SG I
> tāt-ī   mən-'olām   zı̀l-wa.|
> father-1SG from-world   go.PST.3SG.M-PSTC

'We set off, four or five people (in all) and went there, with my mother. My father had passed away three years previously.' (A:19)

In (988)-(989) from the Iranian languages the extrapositional construction provides background information for the adjacent discourse.

(988) Gorani

> mə̀n| tāza   pād̂šä̀-y   kard̂a-nā   wakēḷ.|
> 1SG   any.way   king-OBL.M do.PTCP.M=COP.1SG   advocate

'Me—anyway the king has given me responsibility [lit. he has made me advocate].'

(989) Kurdish
mən döšaw am ằn-ayl-a| dằyk=əm|
1SG last.night DEM.PROX time-PL-DEM mother=1SG
hīlkà=w řon=ī bo=m dəros a-kərd.|
egg=and oil=3SG for=1SG right IPFV-do.PST
'I—last night around this time, my mother was cooking fried-eggs for me.'

A further usage of extraposition is found in (990), where the extraction of the nominal at the front creates a structural balance between the two items *xa-tīkaf . . . xa-tikaf*, which are set up in opposition:

(990) JSNENA
'ay 'arà| xa-tīk-af 'axtǔ ntūmū| xa-tīk-af 'àxnī.|
this land one-piece-3SG.F you take.IMP.PL one-piece-3SG.F we
'This land—one piece of it you take, one piece of it we (shall take).' (C:5)

A corresponding usage of extraposition in Kurdish is seen in (991) where the construction creates a balance between *kut-ēk . . . kut-ēk* 'half . . . . half'.

(991) Kurdish
sīnì māmər-aka| kut-ēk=ī dā Nāmàrd=ū|
breast hen-DEF half-INDF=3SG give.PST PN=and
kut-ēk=īš=ī bo xwà=y gəl-aw dā.|
half-INDF=3SG for REFL=3SG turn-ADP give.PST
'The hen breast—he gave half of it to Namard and left the other half for himself.'

In JSNENA, in possessive constructions consisting of an existential particle or the verb *h-w-y* combined with an L-suffix, a nominal or independent subject pronoun referring to the possessor is obligatorily extraposed:

(992) JSNENA
 a. 'axon-ī dawaxānè-hīt-wā-lē.|
    brother-1SG pharmacy-EXIST-PSTC-OBL.3SG.M
    'My brother had a pharmacy.' (A:27)
 b. kulē nāša bēla jyà hīt-wā-lē.|
    every person house separate EXIST-PSTC-OBL.3SG.M
    'Everybody had a separate house.' (A:71)

c. *'axnī̀ fàrš rāba hīt-wā-lan.*|
   we bedding much EXIST-PSTC-OBL.1PL
   'We had a lot of bedding.' (A:56)
d. *xa-'əda buxārī̀ hīt-wā-lū.*|
   one-amount stove EXIST-PSTC-OBL.3PL
   'Some people had a stove.' (A:89)

Likewise, in Iranian the possessor phrase in predicative possessive constructions precedes the co-indexing bound clitic.

(993) Gorani
màn| *panj šaš bəz-ề=m ha=nē=ū*|
1SG five six goat-PL.DIR=1SG EXIST=COP.3PL
haywằn=əm ha=n.|
animal=1SG EXIST=COP.3SG.M
'I have five, six goats. I have animals.'

(994) Kurdish
a. *mə̀n=īš*| *mənà̦l=əm bū-w-Ø=a.*|
   1SG=ADD child=1SG be.PST-PTCP-3SG=PERF
   'I've had a baby.'
b. *mən bərà̦=m bū-Ø?*|
   1SG brother=1SG be.PST-3SG
   'Did I have any brother(s)?'

On some occasions the extraposed item is placed at the end of the clause. Such constructions are more cohesively bound with what precedes than constructions with an initial nominal, e.g.

(995) JSNENA
'aṣlan na-raḥatī lı̀t-wā-lū 'o-nāšē.|
in_principle uneasisness NEG.EXIST-PSTC-OBL.3PL those-people
'The people were not ill at ease.' (A:76)

8.7 Placement of adverbials

8.7.1 In clause initial position

Temporal or spatial adverbials that stand at the front of a clause and are given prominence by presenting them in a separate intonation group typically mark a new orientation or section in the discourse and set the temporal or spatial frame for what follows. This frame often incorporates a series of clauses, e.g.

(996) JSNENA
    a. xà-lēlē| rāba   xàrj   wīl-ē| rāba
         one-night   much   spending   do.PST-OBL.3SG.M   much
         xālà   trəṣ-lē.|
         food   do.PST-OBL.3SG.M
         'One night he spent a lot of money and made a lot of food.' (D:3)
    b. bəqatà=č| g-bē   pāxasū| hēz-à|
         morning=ADD   IND-need.PRS.3SG.M   inspector   go.PRS.3SG.F
         'ay-stāčē   bakāràt=ē| day-kaldà|
         these-sheets   virginity=EZ   OBL.this-bride
         labl-ā-lū   bāqa   tāt=ū-dāakà.|
         take.PRS-3SG.F-OBL.3PL   to   father=and-mother
         'In the morning the 'woman inspector' had to go and take the 'sheets of virginity' of the bride to the father and mother.' (A:50)

(997) Gorani
    a. sa'àt   čūwār=ū   saʿb-ē| hur-m-ēz-ā
         hour   four=EZ   morning-OBL.F   PVB-IND-rise.PRS-3PL
         mə-l-ā   pay   hīn-ì| pay   Banan-ì|
         IND-go.PRS-3PL   to   thing-OBL.M   to   PN-OBL.M
         mə-l-ā   pay   'ələf   kanày.|
         IND-go.PRS-3PL   grass   grass   mow.INF
         'At four o clock in the morning, they wake up (and) go to thingy [place]; to Banan, they go to Pir Yara; [they go to] mow grass.'
    b. īsa-tə̀| wa'za   waš-à=na.|
         now-NA   situation   good-F.DIR=COP.3SG.F
         'Now, the situation is good.'

Initial adverbials that set the temporal or spatial frame for the following discourse section are sometimes incorporated into the intonation group of the clause, e.g.

(998) JSNENA
 a. *xa-yoma zīl lāg-èf=ū¹ mìr-ē bāq-ēf¹*
  one-day go.PST.3SG.M to-3SG.M=and say.PST-OBL.3SG.M to-3SG.M
  'One day, he went to him (the neighbour) and said to him . . .' (A:103)
 b. *bəqata 'āṣər g-ēzəl-wa¹ jəns*
  morning evening IND-go.PRS.3SG.M-PSTC cloth
  zabən-wa=u¹ kalù-wā-lē.¹
  sell.PRS.3SG.M-PSTC=and write.PRS.3SG.M-PSTC-OBL.3SG.M
  'Morning and evening he would go and sell cloth and write down (what he had sold).' (A:105)

(999) Gorani
 čūwār=ū sə̀b-ī mə-l-ā¹ panj=ū
 four=EZ morning-OBL.M IND-go.PRS-3PL five=EZ
 yaragà-y m-ēnē=wa.¹
 afternoon-OBL.M IND-come.PRS.3PL=TELIC
 'They leave [home] at four in the morning, and come back at five in the afternoon.'

(1000) Kurdish
 šaw-ē kuř-akān=ī bằng kərd.¹
 night-INDF boy-DEF.PL=3SG call do.PST
 'One night he summoned his sons.'

8.7.2 At the end or in the middle of a clause

When the adverbial is placed after the subject constituent or at the end of the clause, the clause generally does not involve a major spatio-temporal break from what precedes. This applies, for example, to (1001), in which the second clause with the adverbial after the subject pronoun occurs in the same temporal frame, viz. 'that night', as the preceding clause:

(1001) JSNENA
'o-lēlē   xa-šām   mfaṣal   hīw-lū
that-night one-dinner copious give.PST-OBL.3PL
bāq-àn=ū| 'āna   'o-lēlē   la-zì-na-o
to-1PL=and   I   that-night   NEG-go.PST-1SG.M
bēla,| ga-doka   gnè-na.|
home   in-there sleep.PST-1SG.M
'That night they gave us a copious dinner. I did not go back home that night but rather I slept there.' (A:26)

A parallel construction from Kurdish is seen in (1002.a-b).

(1002) Kurdish
a. mən   döšaw   am   àn-ayl-a| dàyk=əm|
   1SG   last.night DEM.PROX time-PL-DEM mother=1SG
   hīlkà=w   řon=ī   bo=m   dəros   a-kərd.|
   egg=and   oil=3SG   for=1SG right   IPFV-do.PST
   'I, last night around this time, my mother was cooking fried-eggs for me.'
b. hatānē   šaw=īč   dà-a-nīšt-ən   řafēq-al.|
   even   night=ADD PVB-IPFV-sit.PST-3PL friend-PL
   'Friends would gather in the evenings.'

In (1003) the clause with the postposed adverbial repeats the description of the situation expressed by what precedes and does not advance the discourse.

(1003) JSNENA
'o   lēlawāē   k-ē-wa-o   bēlà,|
he   evenings   IND-come.PRS.3SG.M-PSTC-TELIC home
g-bē-wa   yatū-wa   ḥasāb=ū   ktàbē
IND-need.PRS.3SG.M   sit.PRS.3SG.M-PSTC accounts=and books
hol-ū.| ...'ay   yatū-wa   lēlè.|
do.PRS.3SG.M-OBL.3PL   this   sit.PRS.3SG.M-PSTC night
'He would return home in the evenings and had to sit and do the accounts and books. . . . He would sit at night.' (A:100–101)

Example (1004) from Kurdish exhibits a similar construction with a postposed adverbial, which, likewise, does not express a spatio-temporal re-orientation:

(1004) Kurdish
    dà̀-a-nīš-ē=ū   löna   šaw.│
    PVB-IND-sit.PRS-3SG=and   there   night
    'He remained (lit. sat) there at night.'

8.8 Summary

The features in JSNENA that exhibit total convergence with both Kurdish and Gorani are word order properties and the internal structure of the clause, see Table 84. Though, as seen, the syntactic structure of ascriptive copula clauses matches Kurdish rather Gorani (cf. §8.2.1).

Table 84: Features in JSNENA showing total convergence with Kurdish and Gorani contact languages.

Feature attested in JSNENA	Section
Postposing of the subject of the copula	§8.2.3
Omission of copula in clauses that are closely bound semantically with a copula predication in an adjacent clause	§8.2.5
Preverbal ordering of adjectival complement of 'become'	§8.2.7
Ordering of nominal complement of existential particle	§8.3.1
Default SOV order	§8.4.1.1
Negators	§8.5
Extrapositional constructions	§8.6
Placement of Adverbials	§8.7

As represented in Table 85, There are features in JSNENA that exhibit total convergence with Gorani but not with Kurdish. These can be divided into two types.

The first type includes features that show closer structural similarities with Gorani in certain syntactic constructions. This concerns nominal goal complements of verbs of movement and the syntactic pattern of predicative complements and expressions of content. In these constructions both Gorani and JSNENA may put a complement after the verb without any accompanying preposition, whereas Kurdish requires a full form of the preposition 'to' or a cliticised form of it, i.e. =a. Likewise JSNENA and Gorani use the full form of preposition *ba* 'to' with a nominal complement of the verb 'become' whereas Kurdish uses the cliticised form.

The second type of features are features in JSNENA that seem to be syntactic calques of Gorani. This concerns the nominal complement of verbs of naming. Here, JSNENA like Gorani uses the verb 'to say' and the bare nominal appears after the verb. Kurdish, on the other hand, uses a different verb, and requires the nominal to appear in a prepositional phrase.

Table 85: Features showing different convergence patterns with Contact languages.

Feature attested in JSNENA	Type of convergence with contact languages		Section
	Gorani	Kurdish	
Non-mobility of the copula clitics in ascriptive copula clauses	---	total	§ 8.2.1
Post-verbal ordering of nominal complement of 'become'	total	partial	§ 8.2.7
Post-verbal realisation of predicative complements and expressions of content	total	partial	§ 8.4.1.3
Nominal complements of verbs of movement	total	partial	§ 8.4.3.1
Nominal complements of verbs of naming	total	none	§ 8.4.3.4

9 Clause sequences

9.1 Introductory overview

JSNENA and Iranian use the same strategies for clause coordination. One strategy is to connect clauses asyndetically. Another is to link clauses by the clitic particle *=ū*. The coordinating particle *wa* is also used, especially in the formal register.

JSNENA has borrowed the additive particle *=əč* from Gorani. The functions of the particle in JSNENA exhibit direct parallels in the Iranian languages of the region. These functions can be classified broadly into those in which the focus of the particle has scope over a clause constituent and those in which it has scope over the proposition as a whole. When taking scope over a constituent the particle expresses inclusive focus, scalar additive focus, and establishes a new topic. When taking scope over a proposition, the particle is used in thetic clauses and concessive clauses.

Another area of convergence of JSNENA with Iranian is the demarcation of intonation group boundaries. For instance, a clause that has a close semantic connection with one that precedes is frequently combined with the first clause in the same intonation group.

JSNENA matches Iranian in the technique of advancing the discourse through the repetition of a preceding clause, referred to as 'incremental repetition', in order to act as the grounds for the new information in the following clause.

9.2 Expression of co-ordinative clausal connection

9.2.1 Asyndetic connection

In both JSNENA and Iranian, when main clauses are linked together co-ordinatively, they are often combined asyndetically without any connective element. This applies both to series of clauses that express sequential actions and also to those that express temporally overlapping actions or situations.

9.2.1.1 Sequential actions
(1005) JSNENA
    a. *g-ēz-əx-wa*   *bē-kaldà.* | *kalda*
       IND-go.PRS-1PL-PSTC house-bride bride
       k-mē-n-wā-la   *tə̀x.*|
       IND-bring.PRS-3PL-PSTC-OBL.3SG.F below

        markw-ī-wā-la　　　　　　　həl-do　　sūsì.¦
        mount.PRS-3PL-PSTC-OBL.3SG.F　on-OBL.that　horse
        'We would go to the house of the bride. They brought the bride down. They mounted the bride on the horse.' (A:46)

   b. xīr-a　　　　　　ba-dasgīrānì,¦　bəqat-ēf-o　　　　qīm-na
      become.PST-3SG.F　to-betrothal　morning-3SG.M-TELIC　rise.PST-1SG.M
      zī-na　　　　　dokà.¦　hīy-a
      go.PST-1SG.M　there　come.PST-3SG.F
      ga-ᴴbalkon-akè̱,ᴴ¦　k-əmr-a　　　　　　　bāq-ì̱.¦
      in-balcony-DEF　IND-say.PRS.3SG.F　to-1SG
      'She became my betrothed, the next morning I went there. She came onto the balcony and said to me ... ' (A:20)

   c. dāak-ī　　　hīy-a　　　　　　Tāràn¦　k-əmr-a
      mother-1SG　come.PST-3SG.F　PN　　IND-say.PRS-3SG.F
      'My mother came to Tehran and said ... ' (A:5)

   d. šamāš=ē　knīštà¦　　g-ēzəl-wa　　　　　　　sūsì
      beadle=EZ　synagogue　IND-go.PRS-3SG.M-PSTC　horse
      k-mē-wa.¦
      IND-bring.PRS.3SG.M-PSTC
      'The beadle of the synagogue would go and fetch a horse.' (A:43)

(1006) Kurdish

   a. gà-yək　　sar　　a-wř-ən,¦　　　　qasāwī　　　a-kà-n¦
      cow-INDF　head　IND-cut.PRS-3PL　butchering　IND-do.PRS-3PL
      a-rö　　　　　wəḷk-aka=y　　　　　tēr-èt=aw.¦
      IND-go.PRS.3SG　kidney-DEF=3SG　IND.bring.PRS-3SG=TELIC
      'They slaughtered a cow and butchered it. She went and brought its kidney home.'

   b. awàḷ　waxt¦　dawrèš-ē　　　gardən　kuluft　hāt¦
      first　time　dervish-INDF　neck　thick　come.PST.3SG
      baš　　　xwà=yī　　bərd.¦
      portion　REFLX=3SG　take.PST
      'Early in the morning an unholy Dervish came, (and) took his share.'

(1007) Gorani
     ēma　zàř　barēnmē¦　　　lū-èn-mē¦　　　ba　　zàř
     1PL　money　take.PRS-PSTC-1PL　go.PRS-PSTC-1PL　with　money
     čīw　　sān-mē.¦
     thing　buy.PRS-1PL
     'We would take money, (and) go (to Iraq). We would buy stuff with money.'

9.2.1.2 Temporally overlapping actions or situations

(1008) JSNENA
   a. *'ay-sūsī   qašang   marzən-wā-lē-ò.*|
      this-horse beautiful decorate.PRS.3SG.M-PSTC-OBL.3SG.M-TELIC
      yāraq   daèl-wa   bā-ēf.| *parčānē   'ayzē   daēl-wa*
      cover   put.PRS.3SG.M on-3SG.M materials good   put.PRS.3SG.M-PSTC
      ba-susī-akè.| *qašang   marzən-wā-lē-ò.*|
      on-horse-DEF beautiful decorte.PRS.3SG.M-PSTC-OBL.3SG.M-TELIC
      xa-jām   daēl-wa   qam   bābēn-èf.|
      one-mirror put.PRS.3SG.M-PSTC before forehead-3SG.M
      'He decorated the horse beautifully. He put a decorative cover on it. He put fine materials on the horse. He decorated it beautifully. He put a mirror in front of its forehead.' (A:43)
   b. *har-kas   hē-wā-lè̇*| *ga-bēla*
      every-person come.PRS.3SG.M-OBL.3SG.M in-house
      yatù-wa| *tamīsì   doq-wa.*|
      sit.PRS-3SG.M-PSTC cleaning hold.PRS.3SG.M-PSTC
      'Everybody who could, would stay in the house and do cleaning.' (A:57)
   c. *duxwà   tarṣ-ī-wa.*| *halwà   tarṣ-ī-wa.*|
      duxwa   make.PRS-3PL-PSTC sweets make.PRS-3PL-PSTC
      xurma-u-rùn   tarṣ-ī-wa.| *dūšà   mat-ī-wa.*|
      dates_and_egg make.PRS-3PL-PSTC honey put.PRS-3PL-PSTC
      karà   mat-ī-wa.| *guptà   mat-ī-wa.*|
      butter put.PRS-3PL-PSTC cheese put.PRS-3PL-PSTC
      'They made *duxwa*. They made sweets. They made dates and egg. They put out honey. They put out butter. They put out cheese.' (A:65)

(1009) Kurdish
   a. *tīrkāwản=yān   hāwərd.*| *wət=ī̄,   mən   tīr-è̇*
      bow-and-arrow=3PL bring.PST say.PST=3SG 1SG bow-INDF
      wā   a-xa-m,| *yàk-ē   wā   a-xa-m,*|
      DEIC IND-throw.PRS-1SG one-INDF DEIC IND-throw.PRS-1SG
      yàk-ē   wā   a-xa-m.|
      one-INDF DEIC IND-throw.PRS-1SG
      'They brought bow-and-arrow. He said, "I shot one bow in this direction, I shot one in this direction, and I shot another in this direction."'

b. hàšt   nū-k=yān| a=yān-a-wərd   pəř=yān
   eight   nine-INDF=3PL   IPFV=3PL-IPFV-take.PST   full=3PL
   a-kərd   la   àw| a=yān-a-hāwə̀rd=aw.|
   IPFV-do.PST of   water   IPFV=3PL-IPFV-bring.PST=TELIC
   'Eight, nine of them would take it (the leathern bottle), fill it with water and bring it back.'

(1010) Gorani
   gorānīwàč-ē   ār-ēn-mē| hēḷay=šā   pay   kar-ēn-mē
   singer-PL.DIR   bring-PSTC-1PL   egg=3PL   for   do.PRS-PSTC-1PL
   pīnay   dang=šā   nà-gīr-o| āw   dāx=šā
   for.DEM.PROX.M.OBL   voice=3PL   NEG-tie.PRS-3SG water   hot=3PL
   d-ēn-mē   pīnay   dang=šā   wàr   Ø-b-o.|
   give.PRS-PSTC-1PL   for.DEM.PROX.M.OBL   voice=3PL   front   SBJV-be.PRS-3SG
   'We used to bring singers (for our weddings). We would give them egg lest their voice be hoarse. We would give them hot water for their voice to be clear.'

9.2.2 The co-ordinating particle *ū*

Main clauses are sometimes linked by the co-ordinating particle *ū*. This has the same form in JSNENA and in the Iranian languages, although it has a different internal etymology in Semitic and Iranian. JSNENA *ū* derives historically from the co-ordinating particle *w* of earlier Aramaic and general Semitic. The particle in the Iranian languages is derived from Old Iranian **uta/*utā*. In the modern Iranian languages it is realised as an enclitic form =*ū* or =*o*. This is generally attached to the last item of a clause before an intonation group boundary, though on some occasions it occurs after an intonation group boundary at the onset a clause. This prosodic pattern of the particle has been replicated by JSNENA, in which the particle is likewise normally an enclitic, although this was not the case in earlier Aramaic.

In JSNENA, a long variant form *ūnū* is sporadically used. This appears to have developed by false analogy with the sequence of 3pl. pronominal suffix + *ū*, viz. –*ūn*=*ū* (< *-*hun*=*ū*).

The particle may link a series of clauses that express sequential actions and also clauses that express temporally overlapping actions or situations.

9.2.2.1 Sequential actions

(1011) JSNENA
    a. *moraxaṣī̀   šaq-na=ū,ˈ   k-ē-n-ò.ˈ*
       permission take.PRS-1SG.M IND-come.PRS-1SG.M-TELIC
       'I'll take leave and come back.' (A:7)
    b. *xa-yoma zīl   lāg-èf=ūˈ mìr-e   bāq-ēfˈ*
       one-day go.PST.3SG.M to-3SG.M say.PST-OBL.3SG.M to-3SG.M
       'One day he went to him and said to him.' (A:103)
    c. *xwān-akē k-mē-n-wā-là=ūˈ   g-ēz-ī-wa*
       table-DEF IND-bring.PRS-3PL-PSTC-OBL.3SG.F=and IND-go.PRS-3PL-PSTC
       bāqa bèla   nòš-ū.ˈ
       to   home   self-3PL
       'They delivered the table and went to their homes.' (A:11)
    d. *'axr-ēf   ba-zor   mīy-å-lūn=ūˈ   mīr-ī*
       end-3SG.M with-force bring.PST-3SG.F-OBL.3PL=and say.PST-OBL.1SG
       là   šatē-n-af   'āna.ˈ
       NEG drink.PRS-1SG.M-3SG.F I
       'In the end they brought her by force and I said, "I shall not drink it."'
       (A:23)

(1012) Kurdish
    a. *gaī=ya   dìw-ēk=ūˈ   wət=ī=ya   dèwˈ*
       arrive.PST.3SG=DRCT demon-INDF=and say.PST=3SG=DRCT demon
       wət=ī   arē   ēwa   quwà=tān   ha=s?ˈ
       say.PST=3SG DISC 2PL power=2PL EXIST=COP.3SG
       'He bumped into a demon and said to the demon, "Hey, do you have strength?"'
    b. *aw   wàxt=aˈ,   wa   swarī=k   xàsˈ   haftā   dāna*
       DEM.DIST time=DEM with ride=INDF good seventy CLF
       līr-aka=y   hāwə̀rd=ūˈ   hāt   bo-lā=y
       liret-DEF=3SG bring.PST=and come.PST.3SG to-the.place.of=EZ
       šwān-akà.ˈ
       shephard-DEF
       'Then riding on a good horse, he brought the seventy coins of lira and came to the shephard.'

(1013) Gorani

   das   *mằč*   *Ø-kar-mē=ū*|
   hand   kissing   IND-do.PRS-1PL=and   after=EZ   DEM.3SG-OBL.M
   dəmā=w   *ānà-y*|
   maḷằ   *Ø-bar-mē*| *žanī*   *māra*   *Ø-bəř-mè̱=ū*|
   mulla   IND-take.PRS-1PL   woman   marriage   IND-cut.PRS-1PL=and
   '(As for the marriage customs) we will perform "hand-kissing" and afterwards, we will take a mullah, marry the girl and so on.'

In a series of more than two clauses expressing sequential events, the co-ordinating particle generally connects the final two clauses, e.g.

(1014) JSNENA

 a.   *g-ēz-ī-wa*   *bē-kaldà.*| *yat-ı̇̄-wa.*| *xa-čày*
   IND-go.PRS-3PL-PSTC   house-bride   sit.PRS-3PL-PSTC   one-tea
   šatē-n-wa=ū| *xančī*   *'àràq*   *šatē-n-wa.*|
   drink.PRS-3PL-PSTC=and   some   arak   drink.PRS-3PL-PSTC
   'They went to the house of the bride and sat down. They drank tea and they drank some arak.' (A:10)

 b.   *bəqata*   *'āṣər*   *g-ēzəl-wa*| *jəns*
   morning   evening   IND-go.PRS.3SG.M-PSTC   cloth
   zabə̀n-wa=ū| *kalù̱-wā-lē.*|
   sell.PRS.3SG.M-PSTC=and
   'Morning and evening he would go and sell cloth then write down (what he had sold).' (A:105)

(1015) Kurdish

   ā   *amà*   *təfang-aka,*| *fišak=ī*   *tē*   *a-xà-m.*|
   PTCL   DEM.SG.PROX   gun-DEF   bullet=3SG   in   IND-throw.PRS-1SG
   hakāyat-aka=m   *a-yž-ə̀m=ū*| *la*   *āxər-aw*   *a=t-kù̱ž-əm.*|
   tale-DEF=1SG   IND-say.PRS-1SG=and   at   end-POST   IND=2SG-kill.PRS-1SG
   'This (is) the gun. I'll put some bullets in it, I'll tell you the tale, and in the end, I'll kill you.'

Since the particle is typically associated with the end-boundary of a sequence, it also expresses a degree of prominence. When speakers wish to give particular prominence to all clauses of a connected sequence, they sometimes link each one with the *ū* particle, e.g.

(1016) JSNENA

    pàs¦ g-ēz-ī-wa bāqa dokà=ū¦ har bēlà¦ zara=ē
    then IND-go.PRS-3PL-PSTC to there=and every house wheat=EZ
    bēla noš-ēf matū-wa rēša xa ta'na xmārà=ū¦
    house self-3SG.M put.PRS.3SG.M-PSTC on one load donkey=and
    lābəl-wā-lē ga-dokà.¦
    take.PRS.3SG.M-PSTC-OBL.3SG.M in-there
    'Then they would go there. Every family put its own wheat on the back of a donkey and took it there.' (B:16)

Similarly, in the Kurdish narrative (1017) the particle is repeated on a series of clauses expressing foreground sequential events. It also expresses open-endedness by appearing after the last clause.

(1017) Kurdish

    aw=īš čāw=ī a-kaf-ēt=a bərằ,¦ xwašī xwašī
    3SG=ADD eye=3SG IND-fall.PRS-3SG=DRCT brother happily happily
    tḕt=ū¦ bāwš=ī pē-yā a-kằ=w,¦
    IND.come.PRS-3SG=and hug=3SG to-POST IND-do.PRS.3SG=and
    a=y-wā-t=a māḷ-awà=w¦
    IND-take.PRS.3SG=DRCT home-POST=and
    'She too, as her eyes clapped on (her) brother, she came happily, cuddled him, took him home, and so on.'

9.2.2.2 Temporally overlapping actions or situations

(1018) JSNENA

    'onī=č xa-başor k-əmr-ī-wa hằya=ū¦ xančī
    they=ADD one-little IND-say.PRS-3PL-PSTC early=and somewhat
    noš-ū doq-ī̀-wā-la.¦
    self-3PL hold.PRS-3PL-PSTC-OBL.3SG.F
    'They would say, "It is a little too soon" and would be rather reluctant.' (A:31)

(1019) Kurdish

    àw gorānī=yī a-wət=ū¦ mə̀n dozala=m a-žan.¦
    3SG song=3SG IPFV-say.PST=and 1SG flute=1SG IPFV-play.PST
    'He would sing songs, and I would play the flute.'

In (1020) and (1021) the clause following the particle supplies background information about circumstances of the events narrated in what precedes:

(1020) JSNENA
xlūlà   wīl-an=ū| g-o   waxtàra=č| tanha
wedding   do.PST-OBL.1PL=and in-that   time=ADD   only
xà   ʿakās   hīt-wa|
one   photographer   EXIST-PSTC
'We held the wedding, at that time there was only one photographer.' (A:29)

(1021) Gorani
mən   hawrāmī̀=nā=ū| ā   waxtē   yāna=mā
1SG   PN=COP.1SG=and   DEM.DIST   time.OBL   home=1PL
nà-bīya=n   Hawrāmān|
NEG-be.PST.PTCP.M=COP.3SG.M   PN
'I am a Hawrami (speaker). At that time our house was not in Hawraman.'

If there is a series of temporally overlapping events, the particle is sometimes repeated and connects each of the events of the series, e.g.

(1022) JSNENA
a. xa-ʾəda   jwanqē   daʿwat   k-ol-ī̀-wa| məntak=ē
   one-amount   youths   invitation IND-do.PRS-3PL-PSTC   with
   xətn-akē   ta-yoma   yat-ī̀-wa,| naql̥-ī̀-wa=ū
   groom-DEF   for-day   sit.PRS-3PL-PSTC dance.PRS-3PL-PSTC=and
   nandè-n-wa=ū,| dēārà   daē-n-wa   ʾəl-ēf=ū,|
   jig.PRS-3PL-PSTC=and   tambourine   hit.PRS-3PL-PSTC on-3SG.M=and
   šabūbà   da-ē-n-wā-lē,| ta-yomà.|
   pipe   hit.PRS-3PL-PSTC-OBL.3SG.M   for-day
   'They would invite several young men and they would sit with the groom for the day, dance and jig. They would beat the tambourine and play the pipe for a day.' (A:35)
b. bar-dèa| ʾay-mārāsəm   tìm,| nāšē
   after-this   this-ceremony   finish.PST.3SG.M   people
   g-ēz-ī-wa=o   bēlà=ū| har-kas-ū
   IND-go.PRS-3PL-PSTC=TELIC   home   each-person-3PL
   g-ēzəl-wa   bēla   nòš-ēf=ū| kalda=ū
   IND-go.PRS.3SG.M-PSTC   house   self-3SG.M=and   bride

> xətna   pīš-ī̀-wa.|
> groom   remain.PST-3PL-PSTC
>
> 'After that, when the ceremony had finished, people went home. Each person went to his own home. The bride and groom remained.' (A:49)

The following Gorani narrative exhibits a parallel usage of the particle in a series of temporally overlapping events:

(1023) Gorani
> yawāšē   lūānē   Hawrāmàn-ī=ū| yānà=m   na-bē=ū|
> then   go.PST.1SG PN-OBL=and   house=1SG   NEG-be.PST.3SG=and
> čāga   yāna=m   gērt   kərāhà=ū| žanī=m   ārd-à=ū|
> there   house=1SG take.PST   rent=and   woman=1SG   bring.PST-3SG
> yarē   čwār   sāḷ-ē   Hawrāmàn   bī-yā.|
> three   four   year-DIR.PL   PN   be.PST-1SG
>
> 'Then I went to Hawraman. I didn't have a house. I rented a house. I got married, and I stayed in Hawraman for three, four years.'

9.2.3 The co-ordinating particle *wa*

In JSNENA, clauses are occasionally connected by the co-ordinating particle *wa-*, which is attached to the front of a clause, generally after an intonation group boundary. It is typically placed before the final clause in a series, e.g.

(1024) JSNENA
> rab-àn| rab=ē   knīšt-àn| ham-ràb=yē-lē,| ham
> rabbi-1PL   rabbi=EZ   synagogue-1PL   also-rabbi=COP.PST-OBL.3SG.M also
> torà   qarē-wa,| ham   mīl̀à   k-ol-wa,|
> Torah   read.PRS.3SG.M-PSTC also circumcision   IND-do.PRS.3SG.M-PSTC
> wa-ham   šoḥèṭ=yē-lē.|
> and-also   PN=COP.PST-OBL.3SG.M
>
> 'Our rabbi, the rabbi of our synagogue—he was a rabbi, he also read the Torah, he also performed circumcisions, and he also was a *šoḥeṭ* (ritual slaughterer).' (A:73)

In the Iranian languages of Sanandaj, the particle *wa* is used typically in a formal register. As in JSNENA, it is placed before the final clause in a series.

(1025) Gorani
'asl=ū   tarīqat=ū   tasawof-ī   ānà=n| ka   kābrā
basis=ēz Doctrine=ēz sufism   DEM.DIST=COP.3SG.M COMPL man
'ǝlm=ǝš   ha=n,| 'amaḷ   Ø-kar-o   ba
knowledge=3SG EXIST=COP.3SG.M act   IND-do.PRS-3SG   to
'ǝlm-akày=š,| **wa** ba   ǝxlàs-o   'amaḷ=ǝš
Jnowledge-DEF.OBL.M=3SG and with virtuoisity-POST act=3SG
pana   Ø-kar-o.|
to   IND-do.PRS-3SG
'The basic principle of Sufiism is that man has knowledge (about his faith), he fulfils that knowledge, and he fulfils it by virtuosity.'

9.3 =əč

This particle is cliticised to words. If the word ends in a vowel the /ə/ vowel is elided, e.g. 'āna=č (< 'āna+ =əč). The particle has an incremental function that may be proposition-orientated or constituent-orientated.

The corresponding particle in Gorani is =īč. If the word ends in a vowel, the particle either changes to =yč, e.g. ēma=yč 'we too', or the /ī/ vowel of the particle is elided. Likewise, the particle is =īč in the Kurdish dialect of Sanandaj, in contrast to general Central Kurdish =īš. This reflects the Gorani substrate in the Kurdish dialect of Sanandaj. JSNENA, therefore, has borrowed the particle from Gorani.

The generic function of the particle is to express some kind of additive focus. The various functions can be classified broadly into those in which the focus of the particle has scope over a clause constituent and those in which it has scope over the proposition as a whole.[1]

9.3.1 Scope over a constituent

9.3.1.1 Inclusive focus ('too')

Such constructions assert that an item should be included in a set of items with similar properties that is inferable from the context. The constituent in focus typically takes the nuclear stress in the intonation group:

---

[1] For a cross-linguistic typological study of additive markers, see Forker (2016). We use some of her categories, but introduce a number of additions and modifications.

(1026) JSNENA
dūbāra   'ò=č   šar-wa   bāqa dīdī   dēa.|
then   he=ADD   send.PRS.3SG.M-PSTC to   OBL.1SG OBL.this
'Then he also would send that to me.' (B:51)

(1027) Gorani
āđà=yč   m-ē.|
3SG.DIR=ADD   IND-come.PRS.3SG
'She comes by too.'

(1028) Kurdish
dāna=y   tər   tè̱,| har   pāwšà̱-yk,| àw=īč
CLF=EZ   other   IND.come.PRS.3SG   EMPH   king-INDF   3SG.DIST=ADD
a-kož-ē.|
IND-kill.PRS-3SG
'Another person comes— [another] king—he kills him too.'

9.3.1.2 Scalar additive focus ('even')

In such cases the inclusion of the focus constituent in the proposition is unexpected in that it is at the negative extreme in the scale of what is expected when compared to other alternatives. The constituent in focus typically takes the nuclear stress in the intonation group:

(1029) JSNENA
nāšē   g-ēz-ī-wa   warya   ba-talgà=č.|
people   IND-go.PRS-3PL-PSTC outside   in-snow=ADD
'People would go outside even in the snow.' (A:81)

(1030) Kurdish
harčē   dā-a-nīš-è̱| tanānà| mardəm
no.matter   PVB-IND-sit.PRS-3SG   even   people
kārīgarì̱=č=ī   pē   nā-wa-n.|
labour.job=ADD=3SG   to   NEG-give.PRS-3PL
'No matter how long he waits, people do not give him even a job as a labourer.'

(1031) Gorani
hatā   kār-ē   xarà̱b-ē=č=əš   kardē=nē.|
even   job-PL.DIR bad-PL.DIR=ADD=3SG   do.PST-PTCP.PL=COP.3PL
'She would even do bad things.'

9.3.1.3 Establishing a new topic

When used with this function, the particle signals a change in topic constituent, which is typically a subject nominal or pronoun. This can be classified as a usage with scope over a constituent. Such constructions can be analysed as having two domains of focus. In the first domain the topic of construction is selected from a set of alternatives. The process of selection from alternatives is the generic characteristic function of focus (Krifka 2008). In the second domain an assertion is made about this topic. The additive particle operates in the first domain with scope of the topic constituent, in that it adds a new topic by selecting it from a set of alternatives. Constructions of this type should be analysed as bipartite categorical constructions (Sasse 1987). Their bipartite structure is reflected by the fact that the initial topic may be separated from the remainder of the clause by an intonation group boundary:

(1032) JSNENA
    a. k-əmr-a   bāq-ì| ba-līšāna   bšəlmānè̀| kè̀=t
       IND-say.PRS-3SG.F to-1SG   in-language   Muslims   who=2SG
       garak=a?| yānī   mànī   g-bē-t?| 'ana=č
       need=COP.3SG means who IND-need.PRS-2SG.M I=ADD
       mìr-ī| Mərza Xanaka   ga-bēlà=y?|
       say.PST-OBL.1SG PN   PN   in-house=COP.3SG.M
       'She said to me in the language of the Muslims kḕ=t garak=a?, i.e. "Whom do you want?" I said, "Is Mərza Xanaka at home?"' (A:20)

    b. ma'ləm=ē   knīšta   rabtà| bāqa   sākənìn=ē   knīšta
       rabbi=EZ   synagogue big   to   congregation=EZ synagogue
       noš-èf,| ahalī=ē   knīšta   noš-èf| manorà
       self-3SG.M people=EZ synagogue self-3SG.M menora
       maždər-wa.| . . . **mārē bēl-akè̀=č**| ba-tafāwòt|
       send.PRS.3SG.M-PSTC   owner   house-DEF=ADD in-difference
       pùl| k-wəl-wa.|
       money IND-give.PRS.3SG.M-PSTC
       The rabbi of the big synagogue would send a *menora* to the congregation of his synagogue, the people of his synagogue. . . . . **The householder** would give money in varying amounts. (B:51)

(1033) Kurdish
       nana=m   hāt   qāwərma   dar   Ø-ēr-ē
       grandma=1SG come.PST.3SG chopped.meat PVB SBJV-bring.PRS-3SG
       la-nāw   dēzà| **mə̀n=īč**| ču-m   wət=əm,   'nanà|
       in-middle pot.POST 1SG=ADD go.PST-1SG say.PST=1SG grandma

```
pàl-ēk=əm       ba                    pē.
leaf-INDF=1SG   SBJV.give.2SG.IMP     to
```
'My grandmother went (lit. came) to take out stuffed meat from the pot. I went and said, "Grandma, give me a piece."'

(1034) Kurdish of the Sanandaj region
```
bā      mə̀n    řēza-y          bə-xaf-əm        tò=yš       ā
hort    1SG    a.little-INDF   SBJV-sleep.PRS-1SG   2SG=ADD    PTCL
bàm                  tazbēh-a   tazbēh-ằn   ka          bā      xaw=o
with.DEM.PROX        bead-DEM   bead-PL     do.IMP.2SG  HORT    sleep=2SG
pē-ā        nà-kaf-ē.
to-POST     NEG.SBJV-do.PRS-3SG
```
'I shall sleep a little bit. **You** play with these beads lest you fall asleep.'

(1035) Gorani
```
dā=šā           vana    lūēn=a               ogà         wāta-bē=šā
give.PST=3PL    at      go.PST.3PL=DRCT      there       say.PTCP.M-be.PRS.PSTC=3PL
īna              jarayằn=ā!       ādī=č              wāta-bē
DEM.PROX.DIR     story=COP.3SG    3SG.M.OBL=ADD      say.PSTCP.M-be.PRS.PSTC
day     mə̀n    Ø-tāw-ū.
well    1SG    IND-can.PRS-1SG
```
'They set off (and) went there. They said (according to report), "The story is such." **He** said (according to report), "Well, I am able (to help you).'"

9.3.2 Scope over the proposition

9.3.2.1 Thetic clauses

In some cases the additive particle is attached to a subject constituent when there is no change in subject in the discourse, as in (1036):

(1036) JSNENA
```
'o      mīr-ē                 tòb.       zīl             lāg-èf=ū
he      say.PST-OBL.3SG.M     good       go.PST.3SG.M    to-3SG.M=and
mē-lē                     mtṳ̀-lē=ū                     'ay-zīl              jəns
bring.PST-OBL.3SG.M       put.PST-OBL.3SG.M=and        this-go.PST.3SG.M    cloth
ləbl-è̀,                  jəns-akē     ləbl-ē
take.PST-OBL.3SG.M       cloth-DEF    take.PST-OBL.3SG.M
```

matū-lē		ga-xa	t^wkāna	zabn-ḕ.ǀ
put.PRS.3SG.M-OBL.3SG.M		in-one	shop	sell.PRS.3SG.M-OBL.3SG.M
'ay=əč	*xīr*		*mangàl*	*do.*ǀ
this=ADD	become.PST.3SG.M		like	OBL.that

'He (the merchant) said, "Fine (we are agreed)". He went to him, brought it (the cloth) and put it down (for him). He (the family man) went and took the cloth, he took the cloth away to put it in a shop and sell it. **He** (the family man) became like him (the merchant).' (A:105)

In (1036) the particle does not select a new topic, as in the construction described in §9.3.1.3 The construction here consists of one domain of focus and the focal additive particle takes the whole proposition within its scope. The clause can be analysed as a thetic clause rather than a categorical clause, i.e. it presents a situation rather than asserting something about a topic (Sasse 1987). From a cognitive point of view the subject referent can be considered to be the pivot of the situation that stands as the figure against the ground of the situation. This subject is not, however, a topic about which something is asserted.[2] The function of such thetic sentences is typically discourse management rather than advancement of the foreground of the discourse (Sasse 1987; Kaltenböck, Heine, and Kuteva 2011). In the JSNENA example (1036) presented above, the thetic sentence presents an evaluative comment on what precedes. The additive particle has the function of adding the presentation of the situation in the sentence to what precedes for the sake of discourse management.

In (1037) a series of two clauses follow each other with the same initial element marked with the additive particle, the first an extraposed pronoun and the second a subject pronoun. These also can be interpreted as thetic clauses and the particle has scope over the entire proposition. Their function is to evaluate what precedes.

(1037) JSNENA

kulē	*'āṣər*	*dīdán*	*da'wàt*	*k-ol-ī.*ǀ		*hàr*	*'āṣər*ǀ
every	evening	OBL.1PL	invitation	IND-do.PRS-3PL		every	evening
xa-nāša		*da'wat*	*hol-àn*ǀ		*noš-ēf*	*trē*	*yarxē*
one-person		invitation	do.3SG.M-OBL.1PL		self-3SG.M	two	months
ṭūl		*garḕš.*ǀ		*'āna=č*	*barūxawālē*	*k-wḕ-lī*ǀ	
duration		pull.PRS.3SG.M		I=ADD	friends	IND-be.PRS.3SG.M-OBL.1SG	

---

[2] For this approach to thetic sentences in Biblical Hebrew, see Khan (2019) and Khan and van der Merwe (2020).

```
'āna=č     xoš-ḥàl    xar-na              'ēxa.
I=ADD      happy      become.PRS-1SG.M    this
```
'They will invite us every evening. Each evening for two months somebody will invite us (lit. It will last for two months (that) every evening somebody will invite us.). I shall have friends. I shall be happy,' and so forth.' (D:6)

Similar uses of the additive particle with scope over the proposition in Gorani can be seen in (1038.a-b). In (1038.a) the clause-initial item is a subject whereas in (1038.b) the clause-initial items are objects. These can be interpreted as thetic clauses that give evaluative or supportive background on the surrounding discourse.

(1038) Gorani
```
a. lūā-ymē        Kərmāšàn   wuḷāhī    tanā     dokān-ē     bàz
   go.PST-1PL     PN         by.god    only     store-INDF  open
   na-bī          ēma=yč     pay       kalūpàl-ī            lūwāy
   NEG-be.PST.3SG 1PL=ADD    for       goods-OBL.M          go.PST.PTCP
   b-ēn-mē.
   be.PRS-PSTC-1PL
```
'We went to Kermanshah (K. *Kirmaşan*): indeed there was not even one shop open. **We** had gone there to buy goods.'
```
b. harmān-akē    yanà̀=č=əm          kard-ē=na
   work-DEF.F    house=ADD=1SG       do.PST-PTCP.F=COP.3SG.F
   xīyātì=č=əm               kard-a=n                kəḷằš=īč=əm
   tailoring=ADD=1SG         do.PST-PTCP.M=COP.3SG.M shoe=ADD=1SG
   čənīya=n
   weave.PST.PTCP.M=COP.3SG.M
```
'I used to do all my **home tasks**. I used to **sew**. I used to **weave shoes**.'

9.3.2.2 Concessive clauses ('even if')

This is related to the scalar additive function of the particle when it has scope over a constituent (§9.3.1.2). Here it expresses a scalar additive focus with scope over the proposition of the clause. Again, these are best analysed as thetic clauses.

(1039) JSNENA
```
'agar=əč    kpīná      hawè-wa,           'ixāla   là
if=ADD      hungry     be.PRS.3SG.M-PSTC  food     NEG
xilá=y.
eat.PTCP.SG.M=COP.3SG.M
```
'Even though he was hungry, he has not eaten the food.'

(1040) Gorani

    īsa   hatīmbằr=īč   Ø-b-o| har
    now one.who.has.orphans=ADD SBJV-be.PRS-3SG EMPH
    dawḷàt   ūsān-o   řā   pay=š.|
    government grab.PRS-3SG road for=3SG
    'Now, even if one was a person caring for orphans, the government will help him.'

(1041) Kurdish

    agar   ītəfāqan   awa=yč=t=a   nà-kərd,| čū-y
    if   accidentally DEM.DIST=ADD=2SG=DEM NEG-do.PST go.PST-2SG
    gay-īt=a   jəftyār-akà| b-ēža   du   homà   līra
    reach.PST-2SG=DRCT farmer-DEF SBJV-say.PRS.IMP two jug PN
    hā   la-žēr   dāna-y   la   kaḷaka-kān=y-ā.|
    EXIST at-under CLF-INDF of rock-DEF.PL=3SG-POST
    'Even if you happen not to do that, (and) you go and reach the farmer, (still) tell (him) that two jugs of liras lies under one of his rocks.'

9.4 Intonation group boundaries

In both JSNENA and Iranian, independent clauses that present actions as separate events are generally uttered in separate intonation groups, e.g.

(1042) JSNENA

    a. *'ēa   g-ēzəl-wa   ga-plīyaw jangàḷ.| ʾīlānè*
        this IND-go.PRS.3SG.M-PSTC in-middle wood trees
        gardəq-wa=ū| k-mè-wā-lū|
        gather.PRS.3SG.M-PSTC=and IND-bring.3SG.M-PSTC-OBL.3PL
        ga-'aḥra zabə̀n-wā-lū.|
        in-town sell.PRS.3SG.M-PSTC-OBL.3PL
        'He used to go to the wood. He used to gather (branches from) trees, bring them back and sell them in the town.' (A:98)
    b. *g-ēz-əx-wa   bē-kaldà.| kalda*
        IND-go.PRS-1PL-PSTC house-bride bride
        k-mē-n-wā-la   tèx.|
        IND-bring.PRS-3PL-PSTC-OBL.3SG.F below
        'We would go to the house of the bride. They brought the bride down.' (A:46)

(1043) Gorani
bàrd-ā=šā āḷəf kanē.│ dřə̀=šā pana kan-ā,│
take.PST-1SG=3PL fodder mow.INF prickle=3PL by pluck.PST-1SG
āḷə̀f=šā pana pēt-ā│ də̀mā=w ānay│ jà
fodder=3PL by gather.PST-1SG after=EZ DEM.DIST.OBL.SG then
žan-ēkī=šā dā-(ā)nē=ū.│ àrd-a-m.│
woman-INDF.OBL=3PL give.PST-1SG=and bring.PST-3SG.F=1SG
'They took me to mow the grass. They had me cut down prickles. They had me gather the fodder. Only then, they gave me a woman (my wife) and I took her.'

A clause that has a close semantic connection with one that precedes, on the other hand, is frequently combined with the first clause in the same intonation group. This is found where the second clause is a subordinate complement or purpose clause:

(1044) JSNENA
a. *g-bē-n xlūlà hol-ī.│*
IND-want.PRS-3PL wedding do.PRS-3PL
'They want to hold the wedding.' (A:30)
b. *ḥāz k-ol-ī-wa hē-n bēla dīdan*
desire IND-do.PRS-3PL-PSTC come.PRS-3PL house OBL.1PL
yat-ī̀ 'onyēxāē.│
sit.PRS-3PL they
'They wanted to come to our house and sit.' (A:80)
c. *là šoq-wa xēt ẓolm hol-ī̀-l-ēf.│*
NEG allow.PRS.3SG.M-PSTC more harm do.PRS-3PL-on-3SG.M
'He did not allow them to harm him any more.' (A:109)

Likewise in Iranian, subordinate clauses are generally bound to the same intonation group as the main clause.

(1045) Gorani
a. *ēma garak=mā b-ē-ymē ì̀*
1PL be.necessary=1PL SBJV-come.PRS-1PL DEM.PROX.3SG
kənāčē=t=a Ø-wāz-mē.│
girl.OBL.F=2SG=DEM SBJV-ask.PRS-1PL
'We would like to ask for your daughter's hand in marriage.'

b. *āwat=mā   na-bē   hangūrì   Ø-wəraš-mē.*|
   custom=1PL   NEG-be.PST.3SG   grape   SBJV-sell.PRS-1PL
   'It was not customary for us to sell grapes.'

(1046) Kurdish
   nà=mān-a-hīšt   hīčka   bə-xaf-ē.|
   NEG=1PL-IPFV-let.PST   no.one   SBJV-sleep.PRS-3SG
   'We wouldn't let anybody sleep.'

A clause that expresses a situation that is circumstantial to the action of another verb is typically kept in the same intonation group, e.g.

(1047) JSNENA
   a. *xēt   ṣalmē   lìt-wā-lā   samx-a   lāga*
      more   faces   NEG.EXIST-PSTC-OBL.3SG.F   stand.PRS-3SG.F   by
      dīdī   'āna   xaè-n-af.|
      OBL.1SG   I   see.PRS-1SG.M-3SG.F
      'She no longer had confidence to stand by me, whilst I could see her.' (A:22)
   b. *syamē   là   loš-ī-wa   k-ē-n-wa   knīšta.*|
      shoes   NEG   wear.PRS-3PL-PSTC   IND-come.PRS-3PL-PSTC   synagogue
      'They came to the synagogue (while) they were not wearing shoes.' (B:46)

(1048) Kurdish
   a. *hāwār   a-ka-n   čə   bərā-yl=īš   nì-n=a*
      shout   IND-do.PRS-3PL   INTJ   brother-PL=ADD   NEG-COP.3PL=DRCT
      māḷ-ā.|
      home-POST
      'They (the sisters) shouted while the brothers were not home.'
   b. *harčì=m   kərd   na=m-gərt.*|
      whatever=1SG   do.PST   NEG=1SG-take.PST
      'No matter how much I tried, I couldn't grab him.'

Clauses are sometimes linked in the same intonation group also where there is no grammatical dependency between them. In such cases the actions expressed by the clauses are presented as closely related, as if they were aspects of the same overall event. The first clause often contains a verb expressing some kind of movement, such as 'to go', 'to come', 'to rise', e.g.

(1049) JSNENA
    a. *k-ē-n-o*   *xàē-n-af.*|
        IND-come.PRS-1SG.M-TELIC   see.PRS-1SG.M-3SG.F
        'I'll come back and see her.' (A:7)
    b. *bəqat-ēf-o*   *qīm-na*   *zī-na*   *dokà.*|
        morning-3SG.M-TELIC   rise.PST-1SG.M   go.PST-1SG.M   there
        'The next morning I got up and went there.' (A:20)
    c. *'ərq-ā-la*   *zīl-a*   *tīw-a*   *ga-xa-'otằq.*|
        flee.PST-3SG.F-OBL.3SG.F   go.PST-OBL.3SG.F   sit.PST-3SG.F   in-a-room
        'She fled and sat in a room.' (A:22)
    d. *hīyē-n-o*   *zī-na*   *tīw-na*   *lāg-èf=ū*|
        come.PST-1SG.M-TELIC   go.PST-1SG.M   sit.PST-1SG.M   with-3SG.M=and
        'I came back and went and stayed with him' (A:28)
    e. *zīl*   *noš-ēf*   *ga-plīyaw*   *kaštī-akē*
        go.PST.3SG.M   self-3SG.M   in-middle   boat-DEF
        ṭəšy-ā-lē-ò.|
        hide.PST-3SG.F-OBL.3SG.M-TELIC
        'He went and hid himself in the boat.' (B:77)
    f. *qīm*   *zȉl.*|
        rise.PST.3SG.M   go.PST.3SG.M
        'He got up and went.' (D:16)

Similar prosodic patterns are found in the Iranian languages:

(1050) Kurdish
    a. *tē*   *law*   *āw-a*   *a-xwằ-t=aw.*|
        IND.come.PRS.3SG   from.DEM.DIST   water-DEM   IND-eat.PRS-3SG=TELIC
        'She comes out and drinks from that water.'
        a-řˇ-əm   *šans*   *xwa=m*   *payằ*   *a-ka-m.*|
        IND-go.PRS-1SG   luck   REFL=1SG   visible   IND-do.PRS-1SG
        'I go and find my luck.'

(1051) Gorani
    a. *luē*   *bar-aka=šā*   *kàrd=o.*|
        go.PST.3PL   door-DEF.M.DIR=3PL   do.PST=TELIC
        'They went (and) opened the door.'
    b. *mə-l-o*   *ḥaywằn*   *Ø-bar-o.*|
        IND-go.PRS-3SG   animal   IND-take.PRS-3SG
        'He goes (and) takes (a) mule (lit. animal).'

c. kāwř-akā   m-ār-ā   čā   sara   Ø-bəř-à.ǀ
   sheep-DEF.PL.OBL IND-bring.PRS-3PL there head   IND-cut.PRS-3PL
   'They bring the sheep and butcher them there.'

9.5 Incremental repetition

Speakers of JSNENA sometimes present sequences of clauses such as those exemplified in (1052.a-b), in which a clause is repeated before the following clause is presented. The repeated clause acts as the grounds for the new information in the following clause, which advances the discourse. This has the effect of marking a boundary in the discourse and splitting the discourse into sections:

(1052) JSNENA
a zīl-ēx   dokà=ū̀ǀ   šīrīnī hīw-lū   bāq-ànǀ   'ū-xēt
  go.PST-1PL   there=and   sweets give.PST-OBL.3PL to-1PL   and-other
  xīr-a   ba-dasgīrāni̇̀.ǀ   xīr-a
  become.PST-3SG.F to-betrothal   become.PST-3SG.F
  ba-dasgīrāni̇̀,ǀ bəqat-ēf-o   qīm-na
  to-betrothal   morning-3SG.M-TELIC   rise.PST-1SG.M
  zī-na   dokà.ǀ
  go.PST-1SG.M   there
  'We went there and they gave us sweets and then **she became my betrothed. She became my betrothed** and the next morning I went there.' (A:20)
b. 'ərq-ā-la   zīl-a   tīw-a   ga-xa-'otằq.ǀ
   flee.PST-3SG.F-OBL.3SG.F go.PST-3SG.F   sit.PST-3SG.F in-a-room
   ta-noš-af   tar-akē   **məzr-a   ba-rēša nòš-af.ǀ**
   to-self-3SG.F   door-DEF   close.PST-OBL.3SG.F in-upon self-3SG.F
   tara məzr-a   ba-rēša nòš-afǀ   zīl-a-wa
   door close.PST-OBL.3SG.F in-upon self-3SG.F   go.PST-3SG.F-PSTC
   tīw-a   ga-dokà.ǀ
   sit.PST-3SG.F in-there
   'She fled and sat in a room by herself. She **closed the door behind her (literally: upon her). She closed the door behind her** and went and sat there.' (A:22)

In Iranian, incremental repetition is commonly used in stories, where it has the same function as in JSNENA.

(1053) Kurdish
pàšā a-w-ēt=a žēr asb-aka=w¦ **pāšā**
king IND-be.PRS-3SG=DRCT under horse-DEF=and **king**
a-mr-è¦ **pāšā a-mr-è¦** wazīr=īš
IND-die.PRS-3SG king IND-die.PRS-3SG vizier=ADD
dasāwpəl dà-a-xoz-ē.¦
quickly PVB-IND-jump.PRS-3SG
'The king fell under the horse and **the king died. The king died.** The vizier got off hastily (from his horse).'

(1054) Gorani
xaḷk hur-př-ēn-ē¦ ēma har nà-zānā=mā jaryān
people PVB-jump.PRS-PSTC-3PL 1PL EMPH NEG-know.PST=1PL story
čēš=ā¦ žànī hur-př-ēn-ē īnīšā¦
what=COP.3SG.M woman PVB-jump.PRS-PSTC-3PL DEM.PROX.PL.OBL
har nà-zānā=mā tā **luā-ymē kərmāšān¦ luā-ymē**
EMPH NEG-know.PST=1PL until go.PST-1PL PN go.PST-1PL
kərmāšàn¦ wuḷāhī tanā dukān-ē bàz na-bī-∅.¦
PN by.god only store-INDF open NEG-be.PST-3SG
'People were dancing. We didn't know what was going on. The women were dancing and so forth. We didn't know what was going on until **we went to Kermanshah. We went to Kermanshah**: indeed, there was not even one shop open.'

9.6 Summary

It is generally held that grammatical structures larger than the clause are susceptible to substratum effects. These include in particular strategies for clause linking (Mithun 2011, 108). JSNENA clearly exhibits convergence with the Iranian languages in the way that larger units than the clause are structured. The strategies used are asyndetic coordination, employed typically when series of clauses express sequential or overlapping actions, and syndetic coordination using the connective particle -ū (homophonous in JSNENA and Iranian), generally associated with the end-boundary of a series of clauses.

JSNENA also exhibits convergence with Iranian languages of the Sanandaj region in the functional domain of the additive focus particle =əč/=īč. The additive particle =əč/=īč has been borrowed from Gorani in both JSNENA and Sanandaj Kurdish. In the main body of central Kurdish, by contrast, the particle has the form -īš, which has been borrowed by the neighbouring NENA dialects in this form. It has been shown that =*īč* is used with the same functions in JSNENA and Iranian, including those in which it has focal scope over a clause constituent and those in which it has focal scope over a proposition. This reflects a high degree of convergence between the languages in contact.

Another area of convergence is the organisation of discourse into intonation group boundaries. In both JSNENA and the Iranian languages, independent clauses that present actions as separate events are generally uttered in separate intonation groups, while a clause that has a close semantic connection with one that precedes, is frequently combined with the first clause in the same intonation group. Another instantiation of discourse organisation is the use of incremental repetition (cf. §9.5), which divides the discourse into units as it advances.

10 Syntactic subordination of clauses

10.1 Introductory overview

Subordinating particles are frequently borrowed in language contact situations (Matras 2007). This applies to JSNENA, which has borrowed numerous subordinating particles from Iranian. It is noteworthy, however, that Standard Persian has influenced the structure of subordination in JSNENA more than Gorani and Kurdish.

It is notable, however, that JSNENA corresponds to Kurdish and Gorani, rather than Persian, when asyndetic strategies are used for the subordination of clauses.

10.2 Relative clauses

10.2.1 Syndetic relative clauses

Three relative particles occur in JSNENA. These include *ya*, *kē*, and *=ē*. The particle *kē* has been borrowed from Standard Persian, reflecting the sensitivity of subordinate clauses to standard languages.

The particle *ya* is used predominantly when the head nominal is definite. Occasionally, the *ya* particle follows an indefinite head (1055.a-b), a pronominal head (1055.c), and an adverbial head (1055.d)

(1055) JSNENA
   a. *'o-nāšē   ya-da'wàt   k-ol-ī-wā-lū*|
       those-people   REL-invitation   IND-do.PRS-3PL-PSTC-OBL.3PL
       'the people whom they invited' (A:42)
   b. *xa-qəṭa   mən-ləxma=ē   ḥāmḕṣ   doq-wa,*| *zatyē*
       one-piece from-bread=EZ leaven   hold.PRS.3SG.M-PSTC   pittas
       ya-tarṣ-ī-wā-lū   *ga-bēla*   *bàr-do.*|
       REL-make.PRS-3PL-PSTC-OBL.3PL   in-house   after-OBL.3SG.M
       'He would hold a piece of leavened bread, (the type known as) pitta breads, which they made in the house afterwards.' (B:33)
   c. *zargàr   rāba   hīt-wā-lan,*| *zargàr,*| *'onyēxāē*
       goldsmith many   EXIST-PSTC-OBL.1PL   goldsmith   those
       ya-dēwà| *pašr-ī-ò,*| *dēwa*   *tarṣ-ì.*|
       REL-gold   melt.PRS-3PL-TELIC   gold   make.PRS-3PL
       'We had many goldsmiths—goldsmiths, those people who would smelt gold and make gold.' (A:70)

d. 'ata   ya-da'wat-ī   wīlà=y|
   now   REL-invitation-1SG do.PTCP.SG.M=COP.3SG.M
   ba-mà-jor   hēz-na   bēl-ū?|
   by-what-means   go.PRS-1SG.M   house-3PL
   'Now that they have invited me, how shall I go to their house?' (D:15)

The particle *ya* does not occur in the Iranian of the Sanandaj region. The Kurdish dialect of Sulemaniya has a particle with the form -*ī/-y* that is used used as a relative particle. In (1056) the particle occurs after a pronominal head, which has indefinite reference.

(1056) Kurdish Sulemaniya
       am   bəzmār=a   awāna-y   dərust=yān   kərdū=wa
       DEM.PROX   nail   3PL-REL   right=3PL   do.PST.PTCP=PERF
       xərāp=yān   dərus   kərdū=wa.
       bad=3PL   right   do.PST.PTCP=PERF
       'The people who made this nail made it badly.'
       (MacKenzie 1962, 78, 186)

This particle combines with *ka* in order to relativize a definite head qualified by a demonstrative pronoun in a restrictive relative clause.

(1057) Kurdish Sulemaniya
       ka   nəzīk=ī   māḷ=ī   xo=yān   bū   am   čwār
       when   near=EZ   home=EZ   REFL=3PL   be.PST.3SG   DEM.PROX   four
       kuř=a-y   ka   la   māḷ-awa   na-hāt-ən   lagal=ī-ā
       son=DEM-REL   REL   in   home-POST   NEG-come.PST-3PL with=3SG-POST
       ba   šəmšēr-awa   palāmār=ī   bāwk=yān   dā.
       by   sword-POST   attack=3SG   father=3PL give.PST
       'When he approached his own home these four sons, who had not come from home with him, set upon their father with swords.'
       (MacKenzie 1962, 12)

JSNENA uses *ya* in more contexts than -*ī/-y* is used in Sulemaniya Kurdish. The Jewish NENA dialect of Sulemaniyya has a relative particle with the form *ga* or *ka* (Khan 2004, 414–15). This is clearly a borrowing from Iranian, the source being either Sulemaniyya Kurdish *ka* or Gorani of the region, which also used *ka* as a relative particle, though less frequently than Kurdish. It is possible that JSNENA *ya* is a weakened form of Iranian *ka*.

In examples (1058.a) and (1058.b) from Sulemaniya Kurdish *ka* is used without the particle *-ī,-y* after a definite nominal qualified by a demonstrative pronoun in restrictive relative clauses.

(1058) Kurdish Sulemaniya
    a. *aw kas=a=m a-wē ka dāxəḷ ba*
       DEM.DIST person=DEM=1SG IND-want REL entering in
      bāx=əm-ā bū-w=a.
      garden=1SG-POST be.PST-PTCP=PERF
      'I want the person who has entered my garden.'
      (MacKenzie 1962, 52, 125)

    b. *ka mādam wā=ya baw xwā=ya ka to*
       since case DEIC=COP.3SG by.DEM.DIST God=DEM REL 2SG
      cū-yt=a lā=y, nā-řo-yt tā harčī-yak=əm
      go.PST-2SG=DRCT to=3SG NEG-go.PRS-2SG until every.thing=1SG
      ha=ya nīwa=y na-ba-yt la řā=y xwā.
      EXIST=COP.3SG half=3SG NEG-take.PRS-2SG in road=EZ God
      'In that case, by that God whom you have been to see, you shall not go until you take a half of everything I have.'
      (MacKenzie 1962, 66, 166)

Example (1059) shows the use of *ka* after a definite nominal head in a non-restrictive relative clause.

(1059) Kurdish Sulemaniya
    yak šət=əm a-wē la to, hanār=ī
    one thing=1SG IND-want.PRS.3SG from 2SG pomegranate=EZ
    bax=ī fāzuḥur bo bāwk=əm ka naxoš=a.
    garden=EZ PN for father=1SG REL ill=COP.3SG
    'There is one thing I want from you, pomegranates from the garden of Fazuhur for my father, who is ill.'
    (MacKenzie 1962, 113, 46)

Also in Gorani, as remarked, *ka* functions as a relative marker. It occurs with indefinite (1060.a) and definite (1060.b) nominal heads in restrictive relative clauses.

(1060) Gorani

a. kābrā=yč-a   ka   wāč-ē   màn¹ panj   šaš
   man=ADD-DEM   REL   say.PRS-PSTC.3SG   1SG   five   six
   bəzè=m   ha=nē=ū¹   haywàn=əm   ha=n,¹
   goat.PL.DIR=1SG   EXIST=COP.3PL=and   animal=1SG   EXIST=COP.1SG.M
   lu-ē   lā=y   ā   kābrā=y   dawḷatmàn-ī.¹
   go.PRS-PSTC.3SG   to=EZ   DEM.DIST   man=EZ   rich-OBL.M
   'A guy who would say, "I have five, six goats; I have household animals" would go to a rich man.'

b. Ø-yāw-ā   lā   kābrā-y   ka   mərū-akā
   IND-arrive.PRS-3PL   to   man-OBL.M   REL   pear-DEF.OBL.PL
   Ø-takn-ò.¹
   IND-shake.PRS-3SG
   'They reach out to the guy who is picking pears.'

In the Kurdish of Sanandaj the relative particle is *wā*, which is originally a deictic particle (cf. §6.5.2). This is used only after a definite nominal head.

(1061) Sanandaj Kurdish

a. ama   kuař-aka=t=a   wā   pà̀=y   na-w?¹
   DEM.PROX   son-DEF=2SG=COP.3SG   REL   foot=3SG   NEG-COP.PST.3SG
   'Is this your (same) son who couldn't walk?'

b. kotər   sayī-aka   wā   hātē=ya   qəsa=yān
   dove   holy-DEF   REL   come.PTCP.3SG=PERF   talk=3PL
   bo   a-kà.¹
   for   IND-do.PRS.3SG
   'The holy dove who had come there talked to them.'

If JSNENA *ya* is indeed a weakened form of *ka*, it parallels most closely the distribution of *ka* in Gorani, since JSNENA *ya* and Gorani *ka* are used after both definite and indefinite nominal heads, but in Sulemaniya Kurdish it is used only after definite heads.

10.2.1.1 kē

JSNENA uses the Persian relative *kē* after definite (1062.a) and indefinite nominal heads (1062.b):

(1062) JSNENA
    a. *xaē-wa   'ay-ḥaywān kē*
       see.PRS.3SG.M-PSTC this-animal REL
       dabḥ-ī-lē-ò| *ṭarēfa   là   hawē.*|
       slaughter.PRS-3PL-OBL.3SG.M-TELIC unkosher NEG be.PRS.3SG.M
       'He would see that the animal that they slaughtered was not unkosher.'
       (A:73)
    b. *xa-məndìx=yē*| *kē   pərčē komà k-ol-ū.*|
       one-thing=COP.3SG.M REL hair   black   IND-do.PRS.3SG.M-OBL.3PL
       'It is a thing that makes hair black.' (A:40)

This distribution of the particle matches that of Persian, where *kē* is also used after definite and indefinite heads. JSNENA, however, does not match the linking particle *-ī*, which is used in Persian relative constructions:

(1063) JSNENA
    'ay-ḥaywān kē   dabḥ-ī-lē-ò|
    this-animal REL slaughter.PRS-3PL-OBL.3SG.M-TELIC
    'the animal that they slaughtered' (A:73)

(1064) Persian
    heyvān-ī   ke   zabh   mi-kard-and
    animal-PTCL REL slaughter IND-do.PST-3PL
    'the animal that they slaughtered'

The Persian relative *kē* particle in JSNENA, therefore, has the syntax of the JSNENA particle *ya*, which in turn matches that of Gorani *ka*, rather than the syntax of the Persian relative construction.

In the Jewish NENA of Urmi (Khan 2008a, 353–57) and in the Jewish NENA of Kerend the relative particle has the form *kī*, which may be a phonetic development of Persian *kē*.

10.2.1.2 =ē

On some sporadic occasions the Iranian enclitic particle *=ē* is attested on head nouns of relative clauses in JSNENA. This is found on both indefinite and definite heads, e.g.

(1065) JSNENA
    a. *nāša=ē   hawḕ-lē,| xa-karxàna*
       man=EZ be.PRS.3SG.M-OBL.3SG.M one-factory
      hawē-lē| yā-xa   mo'asasà hawē-lē|
      be.PRS.3SG.M-OBL.3SG.M or-one institution be.PRS.3SG.M-OBL.3SG.M
      'a man who had a factory or who had an institution' (B:12)
    b. *'o-baxta=ē   ləxm-akḕ   k-ol-ā-wā-lē-o|*
      that-woman=EZ bread-DEF IND-do.PRS-3SG.F-PSTC-OBL.3SG.M-TELIC
      'the woman who opened out the bread' (B:22)

In Kurdish and Gorani of Sanandaj, this particle *=ē* occurs on definite and indefinite nominal heads of relative clauses. This apparently derives historically from the Old Iranian relative particle *haya*:

(1066) Kurdish
    la-bar   ark   šāhī-ā   hāwār=ī   kə̀rd:| kas-ē   kār
    in.front.of palace royal-POST shout=3SG do.PST person-INDF work
    duktar=ī Ø-b-ē| kas-ḕ| nàsāx   Ø-w-ē|,
    doctor=3SG SBJV-be.PRS-3SG person-INDF unhealthy SBJV-be.PRS-3SG
    kas-ē   naxwàs Ø-w-ē?|
    person-INDF ill   SBJV-be.PRS-3SG
    'He shouted in front of the royal palace, "Is there anybody who needs a doctor, anyone who is unhealthy, anyone who is sick?"'

(1067) Gorani
    taḷā   nà-bīya=n   zamān-ē   mən   šū=m
    gold   NEG-be.PST.PTCP.M=COP.3SG.M time-INDF 1SG husband=1SG
    karda=n.|
    do.PST.PTCP.M=COP.3SG.M
    'The time I got married there was no gold.'

10.2.2 Asyndetic relative clauses

Relative clauses in JSNENA are sometimes asyndetic, with no connective particle. In the majority of cases the head noun is indefinite. On some occasions this has a non-specific referent and the relative clause is restrictive. The verb in such clauses is typically in the irrealis subjunctive form, e.g.

(1068) JSNENA
   a. *mat-ī-wā-lē*   *ga-xa-tʷka*   *qarīrà*   *hawē.*|
      put.PRS-3PL-PSTC-OBL.3SG.M in-one-place cool be.PRS.3SG.M
      'They put it in a place that was cool.' (A:83)
   b. *ba-tafāwot=ē*   *nāš-akè̀,*| *čəkma*   *nafarē-hīt-wā-lū*
      in-difference=EZ people-DEF how_many people-EXIST-PSTC-OBL.3PL
      xāla   *ʾaxl-ī̀.*|
      food eat.PRS-3PL
      'According to the different (numbers) of people, how many people they had who eat food.' (B:17)

Generally, however, where an asyndetic construction corresponds to a relative clause in an idiomatic English translation, the relative clause is non-restrictive. The head noun may have a specific (1069.a) or non-specific (1069.b) referent, e.g.

(1069) JSNENA
   a. *xa*   *ʾambar*   *rāba*   *rabtà*   *hīt-wā-lē*|
      one warehouse very big EXIST-PSTC-OBL.3SG.M
      zmằṭē=la| *tīr-ʾāhằn.*|
      full=COP.3SG.F beam-metal
      'He had a big warehouse, which was full of metal beams.' (A:7)
   b. *xa-ʾəda*   *būxārì̀*   *hīt-wā-lū*| *ba-ṣīwè̀*
      one-number stove EXIST-PSTC-OBL.3PL with-wood
      malq-ī-wā-la.|
      heat.PRS-3PL-PSTC-OBL.3SG.F
      'Some people had a stove, which they would heat by wood.' (A:89)

Sporadically the head of an asyndetic restrictive relative clause is a definite nominal, e.g.

(1070) JSNENA
   ʾē   *har*   *ʾo*   *brona*   *kačal-akē=lē*   *daʿwat-àn*
   this just that boy bald-DEF=COP.3SG.M invitation-1PL
   wīl-wā-lē?|
   do.PST-PSTC-OBL.3SG.M
   'Is this the same bald boy who invited us?' (D:14)

Similarly, asyndetic relative clauses occur in the Iranian languages of the Sanandaj region. As in JSNENA, the head noun can be indefinite (1071.a-b) or definite (1072):

(1071) Gorani
    a. *bīs   sī   xānəwådēwa b-ēn-ē| lū-ēn-ē*
       twenty thirty family.INDF be-PSTC-3PL go-PSTC-3PL
       pay šārazūr-ī pamačìay.|
       to   PN-OBL.M   cotton-harvesting.INF
       'There were twenty, thirty families who would go to Sharazur for cotton-harvesting.'
    b. *šàxs-ē   tar=mā ha=n| m-āč-ā=š*
       person-INDF other=1PL EXIST=COP.3SG.M IND-say.PRS-3PL=3SG
       Pīr Xạḷè.|
       PN   PN
       'We have another person (i.e. saint) who is called Pir Khale.'

When the head noun is definite, the asyndetic relative clause is restrictive.

(1072) Kurdish of the Sanandaj region
     awa   žən   mə̀n=īwa   bərd=ī=ya.|
     DEM.DIST wife 1SG=be.PST.PTCP.PERF take.PST=3SG=PERF
     'It was my wife whom he took away.'

10.2.2.1 har-čī, har-kas

The generic pronominal heads 'whoever/anybody who' or 'whatever/everything that' are expressed in JSNENA by the Iranian constructions *har-kas* and *har-čī* respectively, e.g.

(1073) JSNENA
    a. *har-kas bī-zoa hawē-lē   bīš   'ayzà=y.|*
       every-one more be.PRS.3SG.M-OBL.3SG.M more good=COP.3SG.M
       'Anybody who has more is (considered) better.' (A:55)
    b. *har-čī   'āt k-əmr-àt| 'āna matū-na*
       every-what you IND-say.PRS-2SG.F I   put.PRS-1SG.M
       ba-rēš 'ēn-ì.|
       in-upon eye-1SG
       'Everything that you say, I am willing to do (lit. I put on my eye).' (A:18)

These particles can head a generic relative clause also in the Iranian languages of Sanandaj.

(1074) Kurdish
  a. *ama bằz¦ harkà bo am mantaqa*
     PTCL falcon whoever to DEM.PROX region
     hātē=ya košt=ī=ya.¦
     come.PST.PTCP=PERF kill.PST=3SG=PERF
     'The falcon has killed anyone who has entered this region.'
  b. *hàrčēk=ət garak=a¦ mən*
     whatever.INDF=2AG be.necessary=COP.3SG 1SG
     a-yà-m pē=t.¦
     IND-give.PRS-1SG to=2SG
     'I will give you whatever you need.'

(1075) Gorani
  harkàs¦ sawāy āmā dəl=ē kāx-akề¦
  whoever tomorrow come.PST inside=EZ palace-DEF.F.OBL
  māra=t Ø-bəř-ù̀ pay=š.¦
  marriage=2SG IND-cut.PRS-1SG for=3SG
  'I will marry you to anyone who comes (first) to the palace tomorrow.'

In JSNENA the generic pronominal heads may be connected to the clause by the relative particles *ya* and *kē* respectively:

(1076) JSNENA
  a. *har-čī ya-hīyề-lan¦ dwəq-lan ba-'īlề.¦*
     every-what REL-come.PST.3SG.M-OBL.1PL hold.PST-1PL in-hands
     'We held in our hands everything that we could.' (E:12)
  b. *la guptà,¦ la mastà¦ har-čī kē*
     NEG cheese NEG yoghurt every-what REL
     mən-xalwa=yē-lē la k-əxl-ềx-wā-lē.¦
     from-milk.COP.PST-OBL.3SG.M NEG IND-eat.PRS-1PL-PSTC-OBL.3SG.M
     'We did not eat cheese, yoghurt or anything that was made from milk.'
     (A:68)

It seems that such JSNENA constructions with following relative particles are motivated by corresponding constructions in Standard Persian, in which *har-kas, har-čī* can be connected with the relative particle *kē*:

(1077) Persian
    a. *az   harkas   ke   be-tun-am   bāhā=š   hàrf*
       from   whoever   REL   SBJV-can.PRS-1SG   with=3SG   talk
       be-zan-am   xoš=am   mi-ād.|
       SBJV-hit.PRS-1SG   nice=1SG   IND-come.PRS.3SG
       'I'm fond of anybody I can really talk to.'
    b. *harčī   ke   niyāz   dār-am   injā=st.*
       whatever   REL   necessary   have.PRS-1SG   here=COP.3SG
       'Whatever I need is here.'

JSNENA matches the Persian model rather than the Kurdish one. The question arises as to why JSNENA would be influenced by Persian and not by Kurdish here? It seems that the formal education of speakers in Persian has been the vector of influence.

10.3 Cleft constructions

A cleft construction involves the splitting of a simple clause into two components that are linked in a predicative relationship, with part of the contents embedded in a subordinate clause. The purpose is to put particular focus on one constituent. This is attested in JSNENA in (1078), which puts contrastive focus on the subject constituent of the first clause. The remainder of the clause is not introduced by any explicit subordinating conjunction, so the construction is best characterised as 'quasi-cleft':

(1078) JSNENA
    'o   bšəlmantḕ=ya   ləxma   day-ā-wa   ba-tanūra.|
    that   Muslim.F=COP.3SG.F   bread   put.PRS-3SG.F-PSTC   in-oven
    hulāà   la   k-aē-wa.|
    Jew   NEG   IND-know.PRS.3SG.M-PSTC
    'It was a Muslim (not a Jew) who put the bread in the oven. A Jew did not know (how to do it).' (B:20)

Cleft constructions are rare in our corpus of Iranian Sanandaj. One is exemplified in (1079), in which focus and nuclear stress are placed on the complement of the copula. As in JSNENA, the non-focal component of the clause is not introduced by a subordinating conjunction:

(1079) Kurdish of the Sanandaj region
 awa žən mə̀n=īwa bərd=ī=ya.|
 DEM.DIST wife 1SG=be.PST.PTCP.PERF take.PST=3SG=PERF
 'It was my wife whom he took away.'

10.4 Modifier clauses

Clauses expressing a wish such as 'əlha manīxle 'May God grant him peace' may be placed as an asyndetic non-restrictive modifier before or after a nominal head in JSNENA, e.g.

(1080) JSNENA
 a. 'əlha manīx-le 'Awlē saqəzī nòš-ēf|
  God cause_to_rest.PRS.3SG.M-OBL.3SG.M PN PN self-3SG.M
  ham 'èč-wā-lē| ham
  also knead.PRS.3SG.M-PSTC-OBL.3SG.M also
  daē-wā-lē ba-tanūrà.|
  put.PRS.3SG.M-PSTC-OBL.3SG.M in-oven
  ''Awle from Săqəz, may God give him rest, would himself both knead it and also put it into the oven.' (B:21)
 b. ḥqē-lī-o bāqa tāt-ī 'əlha manīxà.|
  tell.PST-OBL.1SG-TELIC to father-1SG God cause_to_rest.PTCP.SG.M
  'I told my father, may God give him rest.' (B:61)

Functionally and syntactically parallel constructions containing wishes addressed to God are found in Kurdish and Gorani, though with the lexical verb 'pardon' rather than 'give rest' in (1080.a–b). In (1081) the non-restrictive wish clause is placed before the nominal head. In (1082) the clause is placed between the object and the verb.

(1081) Kurdish
 xwā 'afw=ī Ø-kà| bāwk=m=ū bāwā=mằn
 God pardon=3SG SBJV-do.PRS.3SG father=1SG=and grand.father=1PL
 a=yān-gařān=aw.|
 IPFV=3PL-narrate.PST=TELIC
 'May God pardon him, my father and my grandfather would narrate (this).'

(1082) Gorani
hasūrà=m,| xwā 'afwà=š Ø-kar-a, wāč-ī.|
father.in.law=1SG God pardon=3SG SBJV-do-IMP.2SG say.PRS-2SG
'My father-in-law—God pardon him—whom you talk about.'

10.5 Indirect questions

Various subordinate clauses that are introduced by interrogative particles may be classified as indirect questions. These are embedded under verbs such as 'to know', 'to say', 'to ask', 'to see', 'to understand', e.g.

(1083) JSNENA
   a. la-k-ay-an mànī=yē.|
      NEG-IND-know.PRS-1SG.F who=COP.3SG.M
      'I do not know who it is.' (A:21)
   b. la k-aē-na ma ho-nà.|
      NEG IND-know.PRS-1SG.M what do.PRS-1SG.M
      'I do not know what I should do.' (D:2)
   c. k-mər-wa xətna čəkma k-wəl
      IND-say.PRS.3SG.M-PSTC groom how_much IND-give.PRS.3SG.M
      bāqa kald-akè̱,| kald-akē mà hīt-a.|
      to bride-DEF bride-DEF what EXIST-OBL.3SG.F
      'He would say how much the groom would give to the bride and how much the bride had.' (A:48)
   d. 'onī là k-aē-n-wa ma=yēn.|
      they NEG IND-know.PRS-3PL-PSTC what=COP.3PL
      'They did not know what they were.' (A:87)

Likewise, in the parallel constructions from Kurdish and Gorani the interrogative particle introduces a subordinate clause and usually takes nuclear stress.

(1084) Gorani
   a. wāt=mā bā bə-zān-mē ī māšīn-ē
      say.PST=1PL HORT SBJV-know.PRS-1PL DEM.PROX car-DEM.PL
      kò mə-l-ā.|
      where IND-go.PRS-3PL
      'We said, "Let's see where these cars head."'

b. *ətə   hoš=əm   nī=yā   bə-zān-ū*
   anymore intelligence=1SG NEG=COP.3SG SBJV-know.PRS-1SG
   čēš   tàr   bī.
   what else COP.PST.3SG
   'I don't know what else there was (of ceremonies).'

(1085) Kurdish of the Sanandaj region
   a. *bə-zān-əm   la   kwè̱-yā   xaftē=ya.*
      SBJV-know.PRS-1SG in   where-POST sleep.PST.PTCP=PERF
      'I shall find out where he has slept.'
   b. *qūrbān a-zān-ī   čà   a-ka-y.*
      sir   IND-know.PRS-2SG what IND-do.PRS-2SG
      'Sir, you know what you shall do.'

Indirect polar questions are embedded without any introductory particle in both JSNENA and the Iranian languages of the region, e.g.

(1086) JSNENA
   maˈlùm-la=y| 'āt   hūlāē=t   yā bšəlmanè=t.
   known-NEG=COP.3SG.M you Jew=COP.2SG.M or Muslim=COP.2SG.M
   'It is not known whether you are a Jew or you are a Muslim.' (B:25)

(1087) Gorani
   yò   taqn-a   bə-zān-a   jūab=ət
   one.m   shoot-IMP.2SG   SBJV-know.PRS-2SG.IMP answer=2SG
   ha=n.
   EXIST=COP.3SG.M
   'Shoot one (bullet), see if there is an answer.'

(1088) Kurdish
   ītər nà=y-zān-ī   aw   Mard=a   yā Nāmard=a.
   well NEG=3SG-know.PRS-2SG 3SG PN=COP.3SG or PN=COP.3SG
   '(The king) didn't know whether he was Mard or Namard.'

In JSNENA sometimes an embedded constituent question is preceded by the subordinating particle *kē*, e.g.

(1089) JSNENA

a. 'ənyēxāē   ga-fkər   k-wē-n-wa   kē   bāqa   patīrē
   they   in-thought   IND-be.PRS-3PL-PSTC   SBRD   for   Passover
   ma   lāzəm=yē   tahyà   hol-ī.
   what   necessary=COP.3SG.M   preparation   do.PRS-3PL
   'They considered what they should prepare for Passover.' (B:14)

b. 'o   k-àē-wa   kē-tā-ma   la
   he   IND-know.PRS.3SG.M-PSTC   SBRD-for-what   NEG
   k-əmrēt-ē.
   IND-say.PRS-2SG.M-OBL.3SG.M
   'He knew why you did not say (it) to him.' (B:46)

The use of the subordinate particle *kē* in these constructions is a loan from Persian, especially the colloquial register.

(1090) Persian
ne-mi-dunest-am   ke   ki=an.
NEG-IPFV-know.PST-1SG   SBRD   who=COP.3PL
'I didn't know who they were.'

In JSNENA indirect constituent questions and polar questions may be introduced by the Kurdish particle *daxom*, (1092.a-b), which replicates structures such as (1093.a-b) in Kurdish:

(1091) JSNENA

a. mʾīn-ī   ga-dawràn   xaē-na   mà
   look.PST-OBL.1SG   in-around   see.PRS-1SG.M   what
   xīra=y   rēša   'ay-qawm-ī̀   daxom   mà
   become.PTCP.SG.M=COP.3SG.M   on   this-people-1SG   Q.PTCL   what
   zīla=y.
   go.PTCP.SG.M=COP.3SG.M
   'I looked around to see what had happened, what had become of my people.' (E:23)

b. bəqr-ī   mən-yāl-àn   daxom   là
   ask.PST-OBL.1SG   from-children-1PL   Q.PRTL   NEG
   xīya=y.
   see.PTCP.SG.M=COP.3SG.M
   'I asked our children whether they had seen it (our language).' (E:26)

(1092) Kurdish
  a. wət=ī   ama   dāxəm   jaryān=ī   čà=s.
     say.PST=3SG   DEM.PTCL   I.wonder   story=3SG   what=COP.3SG
     'He said, "I wonder what the story is."'
  b. nā-zān-əm   dāxom   řāzī=t   lē=m.
     NEG-know.PRS-1SG   Q.PTCL   satisfied=COP.2SG   at=1SG
     'I don't know whether you're satisfied with me (or not).'

10.6 Subordinate content clauses

A variety of subordinate clauses that are embedded as components of a higher clause will be brought together in this section under the broad classification of 'content clauses'. These function either as subject or direct object complements of a verb or are governed by clausal conjunctions consisting of prepositions, adverbials and quantifiers.

10.6.1 kē

In JSNENA the Persian particle *kē* without any other clausal conjunction introduces the following types of content clause.

10.6.1.1 Factive complement content clauses

Clauses of assumed factual content that function as nominal constituents in the main clause are sometimes introduced by *kē*.

When functioning as object, they are typically complements of verbs such as 'to say' and 'to know', and follow the main verb, e.g.

(1093) JSNENA
  xa-nafar-xēt   šər-wā-la   bāqa   'axon-àf|
  one-person-other   send.PST-PSTC-OBL.3SG.F   to   brother-3SG.F
  hamər   kèˈ| 'ay-bronàˈ| həl-day   brāta   g-bè.ˈ|
  say.PRS.3SG.M   SBRD   this-boy   OBL-OBL.this   girl   IND-love.PRS.3SG.M
  'She sent somebody else to her brother to say that the boy loves the girl.'
  (A:18)

By contrast in Kurdish and Gorani factual content clauses are normally expressed by asyndetic constructions (1094). JSNENA has imitated the Persian syndetic construction of subordinate content clauses with the particle *ke* (1095).

(1094) Kurdish
wət=ī   mardəm am   āwāyī-a   bə̀š=ən.
say.PST=3SG people DEM.PROX village=dem   good=COP.3PL
'He said that the people of this village are good.'

(1095) Persian
mi-g-e   ke   mi-ād.
IND-say.PRS-3SG   COMPL   IND-come.PRS.3SG
'He says that he is coming by.'

In (1096.a–b) the complement clause functions as an elaborative apposition to a nominal or demonstrative phrase:

(1096) JSNENA
a. *qamē   dīdì̭   hīč-kas   'ay-ḥašta   la-wīl-ā-wā-lḙ̀*
    before OBL.1SG no-person   this-thing   NEG-do.PST-3SG.F-PSTC-OBL.3SG.M
    kē   lačaga ba-rēša   dasgīrān-ī   natḙ̀-n-ēf-o
    SBRD   veil   in-on   betrothed-1SG take.PRS-1SG.M-TELIC
    'Before me nobody had done such a thing, namely that I should take away the veil from the head of my betrothed.' (A:25)
b. *tarz=ē   qədūš   'axà=yē-lē| kē-xa-dāna*
   method=EZ consecration   thus=COP.PST.OBL.3SG.M   SBRD-one-CLF
   parda   doq-i̭-wa=ū|
   curtain hold.PRS-3PL-PSTC=and
   'The method of consecration was as follows, (namely) that they would draw a curtain.' (A:47)

A corresponding sentence from Persian is given:

(1097) Persian
jorm=eš   in   bud   ke   be   harf-ā=yē   unā
guilt=3SG   DEM.PROX   be.PST.3SG COMPL to   speech-PL=EZ 3PL
e'teqād   na-dāšt.
belief   NEG-have.PST.3SG
'His crime was that he did not believe in their words.'

In Gorani the suborinating particle *ka*, corresponding to Persian *ke*, is used to introduce various types of elaborative appositions or parenthetical clauses:

(1098) Gorani
  a. *wa   èd̄=īč| ka   ī   šēx   'osmằn-a|*
     and   3SG.PROX=ADD   SBRD DEM.PROX sheikh PN-DEM
     ba-farz   m-āč-ā   murafàh   bīya=n.|
     by-assumption   IND-say.PRS-3PL   well.off   be.PST.PTCP.M=COP.3SG.M
     'And he, namely Sheikh Osman, it is supposed that he was well off.'
  b. *bàrd-ā=šā,| ka   ba   hayằt=əm   ālf=əm*
     take.PST-1SG=3PL   SBRD in   life=1SG   grass=1SG
     na-kana=n,| bàrd-ā=šā   āḷəf   kan-ē.|
     NEG-uproot.PST.PTCP.M=COP.3SG   take.PST-1SG=3PL   grass   mow.PST-INF
     'They took me—I have never mowed grass in my life—they took me to mow the grass.'

On numerous occasions in JSNENA factual complement clauses are asyndetic without any connective particle, e.g.

(1099)   JSNENA
  a. *k-əmr-ī-wa   basīrē   'aṣlan   barāxà   hīt-ū.|*
     IND-say.PRS-3PL-PSTC   grapes   in_particular   blessing   EXIST-OBL.3PL
     'They would say that grapes in particular had blessing.' (A:72)
  b. *rāba nāšē   da'wàt   k-ol-ī-wa,| čun*
     many people   invitation   IND-do.PRS-3PL-PSTC   because
     k-əmr-ī-wa   qāla   mīḷa   šamoē
     IND-say.PRS-3PL-PSTC   voice   circumcision   hear.INF
     maṣwà   hīt-ē.|
     good_deed   EXIST-OBL.3SG.M
     'They would invite many people, because they said that it was a good deed to hear the cry (of the baby) at circumcision.' (A:75)
  c. *ga-dokà| rāba   nāšè̀| rāba   hamr-ēt*
     in-there   many   people   many   say.PRS-2SG.M
     dawlaman   hawè̀-n.|
     rich   be.PRS-3PL
     'There you would say that many people were rich.' (A:55)

As remarked, the basic pattern for Kurdish and Gorani complement clauses is asyndetic:

(1100) Gorani
     vāt=əš   tāta=š   īnā   yānà-na.|
     say.PST=3SG father=3SG DEIC home-POST
     'He said that his father was home.'

(1101) Kurdish
    a. *wət=ī   fəlānakàs*| *a-yž-ən   kanı̀šk=ət*
        say.PST=3SG so.and.so IND-say.PRS-3PL daughter=2SG
        ha=s| *b=ī-yà   pē=m.*|
        EXIST=COP.3SG SBJV=3SG-give.IMP.2SG to=1SG
        'He said, "O such-and-such person, (people) say that you have a daughter. Give her to me (in marriage)."'
    c. *wā-zān-ē   a=y-xwà.*|
        DEIC-know.PRS-3SG IND=3SG-eat.PRS.3SG
        'He thought that it (the wolf) would eat him.'

In Gorani and in Kurdish dialects of Sulemaniyya and Mukri, *ka* can also mean 'when'. In this usage it acts as an adverbial subordinator and introduces a temporal clause. This usage does not seem to be used in JSNENA.

(1102) Gorani
     ka   dokāndằr   b-ēn-ē| *mən   lu-ēn-ē*
     when shop.keeper be.PRS-PSTC-1SG 1SG go.PRS-PSTC-1SG
     pay   Kərmāšān-ì̇.|
     to   PN-OBL.M
     'When I was a shop owner, I would go to Kermanshah (and bring fruit and such).'

10.6.1.2 Non-factive complement

In JSNENA the particle *kē* on some occasions introduces a complement clause expressing an activity that is as yet unfulfilled or only potential from the viewpoint of the main verb, e.g.

(1103) JSNENA
    a. *'ı̏jāza   hùl-mū*| *kē-'axnī   xlūlà   hol-ēx.*|
        permission give.IMP-PL SBRD-we wedding do.PRS-1PL
        'Give permission for us to hold the wedding.' (A:31)

b. hīt-wa   xa-šāta   ṭùl   garəš-wa   kē|
   EXIST-PSTC   one-year   length   pull.PRS.3SG.M-PSTC   SBRD
   g-bē-n   xlūlà   hol-ī.|
   IND-want.PRS-3PL   wedding   do.PRS-3PL
   'Sometimes a year would pass before they wanted to hold the wedding.'
   (A:30)

The use of *kē* to introduce a non-factive complement clause is a replication of (colloquial) Persian syntax, see (1104). Kurdish uses the particle *bā* in such constructions (1105).

(1104) Persian
        ejāze   be-d-in   ke   mā   be-r-im.
        permission   SBJV-give.PRS-3PL   COMPL   1PL   SBJV-go.PRS-1PL
        'Give permission for us to leave.'

(1105) Kurdish
        ījāza=y   mən   bà| bā   mən   b-řo-m
        permission=EZ   1SG   SBJV.give.IMP.2SG   COMPL   1SG   SBJV.go.PRS-1SG
        wa   das   xwà=m   haq   tu   lam   bərāžən
        with   hand   REFL=1SG   right   2SG   from.DEM.PROX   sister.in.law
        xwa=m=a   bə-sēn-m=aw.|
        REFL=1SG=DEM   SBJV-take.PRS-1SG=TELIC
        'Give me permission to go and reclaim your right from my sister-in-law with my own hands.'

10.6.1.3 Purpose

In JSNENA a clause introduced by *kē* often expresses purpose. The use of *kē* for expressing purpose is a borrowing from Persian.

(1106) JSNENA
        wa-maxw-ī-wā-la   nāšē   xēt=əč
        and-show.PRS-3PL-PSTC-OBL.3SG.F   people   other=ADD
        kē-ga-dokḕ=n| kē-'alē-n   'ay-brātà|
        REL-in-there=COP.3PL   SBRD-know.PRS-3PL   this-girl
        batūlà   xīrtē=ya.|
        virgin   be.PTCP.SG.F=COP.3SG.F
        'They would show it to other people who were there so that they would know that the girl had been a virgin.' (A:50)

(1107) Persian
      donbāl=e   dozd   raft-an   ke   be-gir-an=eš
      after=EZ   thief   go.PST-3PL   COMPL   SBJV-grab.PRS-3PL=3SG
      'They went after the thief in order to catch him.'

10.6.2 tā-

10.6.2.1 'when'

In JSNENA when the particle *tā-* introduces a subordinate clause that is placed before the main clause, it has the sense of 'when', e.g.

(1108) JSNENA
      tā-'axa   mīr-ē   bāq-àf¦   'ay   'ərq-ằ-la.¦
      when-thus say.PST-OBL.3SG.M to-3SG.F this flee.PST-3SG.F-OBL.3SG.F
      'When he said this to her, she fled.' (A:22)

This can be identified with the Kurdish particle *tā*, which is sometimes realised as *dā*. In the following example *dā* introduces a subordinate temporal 'when'-clause as in the JSNENA example above.

(1109) Kurdish
      mār   tò   na=w-wət¦   dā   t-ḕ-m=aw¦
      Q.PTCL 2SG   NEG=2SG-say.PST   SBRD   IND-come.PRS-1SG=TELIC
      mənāḷ=o   na-w-ē   a=w-kož-əm.¦
      child=2SG   NEG-be.PRS-3SG   IND=2SG-kill.PRS-1SG
      'Didn't you say, "When I'm back, I will kill you (if) you don't have a child!"'

10.6.2.2 'until'

In JSNENA when the subordinate clause introduced by *tā* is placed after the main clause, the particle has the sense of 'until', e.g.

(1110) JSNENA
      mən-bēla   xəmḕ,¦   mən-bēla   xətn-akḕ,¦   g-ēz-ī-wa
      from-house father-in-law from-house groom-DEF IND-go.PRS-3PL-PSTC
      ba-dohol   'ū-zorna   mən-day   kujī=ū   maḥalḕ¦
      with-drum   and-pipe   from-OBL.this lane=and street

dēy-ā-wa	ʾəl-ēf	tā-g-ēz-ī-wa	bē-kaldà.ˈ
beat.PRS-3SG.F-PSTC	on-3SG.M	until-IND-go.PRS-3PL-PSTC	house-bride

'From the house of the father-in-law, the house of the groom, they went with drum and pipe through the lanes and streets, playing (the instruments) until they arrived at the house of the bride.' (A:10)

In (1111) *tā* is connected to the clause by the subordinating particle *gē-*, a variant of *kē-*:

(1111) JSNENA

g-ēz-ēx-wa	bāqa	sahra	tā-gē	ˈarbìt
IND-go.PRS-1PL-PSTC	to	fields	until-time	evening_prayer
xar-ā-wa.ˈ				
become.PRS-3SG.F-PSTC				

'We would go into the fields until it was time for evening prayers.' (B:32)

The subordinating particle *gē* is attested also in the phrase *tā-gē* before nominals denoting periods of time.

(1112) JSNENA

bəqata	g-ēz-ēx-wa	knīštàˈ	xēt	là
morning	IND-go.PRS-1PL-PSTC	synagogue	again	NEG
k-ēx-wa-o	bēlaˈ	har-tā-gē	lēlè.ˈ	
IND-come.PRS-1PL-PSTC-TELIC	home	just-until-time	night	

'In the morning we went to the synagogue and we did not come back home again until night.' (B:74)

The following examples show parallels from the Iranian languages of Sanandaj. In (1113) *tā* has the sense of until and is placed after the main clause. In (1114) the variant *hatā* is connected to *ka* and the non-analysable *dē*. In (1115) *tā* is used before a nominal denoting period of time.

(1113) Gorani

har	nà-zānā=mā	tā	lūā-ymē	Kərmāšǎ̀n.ˈ
EMPH	NEG-know.PST=1PL	until	go.PST-1PL	PN

'We didn't figure (it) out until we arrived at Kermanshah.'

(1114) Kurdish
dā-nīšt-∅   hatākadē   šằm   xor-yā-∅.
PVB-sit.PST-3SG   until   dinner   eat.PRS-PASS.PST-3SG
'He waited (lit. sat) there until the dinner was eaten.'

(1115) Gorani
walāhī   čā   bī-ymē   tā   yằrē   řo-ē.
indeed   there   be.PST-1PL   until   three   day-PL.DIR
'Indeed, we were there for a period of three days.'

10.6.2.3 Purpose

The preposition *tā* is used in JSNENA and Kurdish before a content clause to express purpose, e.g.

(1116) JSNENA
mar-hē   tā-lab-n-axun   doka   lāg-èf.
PTCL-come.PRS.3SG.M   COMPL-take.PRS-1SG.M-2PL   there   to-3SG.M
'Let him come so that I may take you there to him.' (B:60)

(1117) Kurdish
b-ēs-a   tā   māč-èk=ī   ∅-ka-m=aw!
SBJV-stay-IMP.2SG   COMPL   kiss-INDF=3SG   SBJV-do.PRS-1SG=TELIC
'Wait so that I may give her a kiss!'

10.6.2.4 Result

In JSNENA a subordinate clause introduced by *tā* placed after the main clause may also express result, e.g.

(1118) JSNENA
'ənyēxāē   'əqra   șorèr=yē-lū   tā-'əlhà-hamər
they   so   enemy=COP.PST-OBL.3PL   COMPL-God-say.PRS.3SG.M
malē!
be_enough.PRS.3SG.M
'They were so hostile (to the Jews) that God said, "That is enough!"' (A:77)

This use of *tā* has a parallel in Persian, where the particle *tā* followed by the demonstrative *in* (or *inke*) is used in such contexts.

(1119) Persian
    enqadr   nāšokri   kard   tā   in   balā
    so.much ingratitude do.PST.3SG COMPL DEM.PROX disaster
    sar=eš   āmad
    head=3SG come.PST.3SG
    'He was so ungrateful that such a disaster happened to him.'

10.7 Temporal clauses

In JSNENA temporal 'when'-clauses are expressed by constructions consisting of temporal adverbial expressions connected to a content clause by the enclitic particle =ē.

10.7.1 waxt=ē

(1120) JSNENA
  a. waxt=ē šoma kipūr fəṭr-an-ò,| ma'ləm
     time=EZ fast atonement break.PST-OBL.1PL-TELIC rabbi
     k-ē-wa   bēlà.|
     IND-come.PRS.3SG.M-PSTC house
     'When we had broken the fast of the Atonement, a rabbi would come to the house.' (B:76)
  b. 'āna waxt=ē xlūla wīl-ì|
     I   time=EZ wedding do.PST-OBL.1SG
     ga-Tārằn=yē-lī   noš-ī.|
     in-Tehran=COP.PST-OBL.1SG self-1SG
     'When I married, I myself was in Tehran.' (A:5)

An adverbial head with the same lexical form and the same connecting enclitic *ezafe* particle =ē is use used in temporal 'when'–clauses in the Iranian languages of Sanandaj:

(1121) Gorani
    waxt=ē žànī=m ārd-a| yawašē yānà=m
    time=EZ woman=1SG bring.PST-3SG.F well house=1SG
    na-b-ē.|
    NEG-be.PRS-PSTC.3SG
    'When I got married (lit. I brought a wife), well, I didn't have a house.'

(1122) Kurdish
waxt=ē soḥ ḥàḷ-as-ən[|] čə dāna-y
time=EZ morning PVB-IND.rise.PRS-3PL INTJ seed-INDF
əfrìt=ī topān=a.[|]
demon=3SG kill.PST=PERF
'When they woke up in the morning, he had killed a demon.'

In JSNENA the subject of the 'when'-clause may be extraposed in front of the adverbial particle, e.g.

(1123) JSNENA
qam=ē doa 'āna b-'olām hē-nà,[|] hūlāē
before=EZ OBL.that I in-world come.PRS-1SG.M Jews
waxt=ē zīlē=n waryà,[|] maxṣūṣan ga-yomawāē
time=EZ go.PSTCP.PL=COP.3PL outside especially in-days
nəxlà,[|] g-bē-wa xa-parča zayra daē-n
rain IND.need.PRS.3SG.M-PSTC one-patch yellow put.PRS-3PL
ba-laxà-ū[|] b-lā səng-ū̀[|] kē 'alē-n 'ənyēxāē
in-here-3PL in-side chest-3PL COMPL know.PRS-3PL they
hūlāḕ=n.[|]
Jews=COP.3PL
'Before I was born, when the Jews went outside, especially on rainy days, they had to put a patch of yellow here on them, on their chest so that they (the Muslims) knew that they were Jews.' (A:78)

Similar extrapositional constructions are found in Kurdish:

(1124) Kurdish
tò[|] waxt=ē čū-ìt=aw[|], ga-yt=a
2SG time=EZ go.PST-2SG=TELIC arrive.PRS-2SG=DRCT
àw šār=a[|]
DEM.DIST city=DEM
'When you returned and arrived at that city...'

In JSNENA on some occasions the head adverbial is connected to the clause also by the particle kē, e.g.

(1125) JSNENA
*waxt=ē   kē   mām-ī   hīyē   bēl-àn,*ǀ
time=EZ   SBRD   uncle-1SG   come.PST.3SG.M   house-1PL
*'āna   ga-ḥaštà   yē-lī.*ǀ
I   in-work   COP.PST-OBL.1SG
'When my uncle came to our house, I was at work.'

This is a pattern borrowed from Persian, in which the adverbial 'when' in temporal clauses can be connected to the particle *kē* (1126). Note that the adverbial head in Persian has the enclitic particle *=i*, which corresponds to the *=ē* clitic of Gorani, Kurdish and JSNENA. Both *=i* and *=ē* appear to be derived historically from the Old Iranian relative particle *haya*:

(1126) Persian
vaqt=i   ke   mord,   hatā yek nafar   ham
time-RESTR   SBRD   die.PST.3SG   even one person either
tu=ye   mahale=ye   mā   nārahat na-šod.
in=EZ   neighbourhood=EZ   1PL sad   NEG-become.PST
'When he died, not even one person became sad in our neighbourhood.'

10.7.2 ba-mudat=ē kē

(1127) JSNENA
*ba-mudàt=ē   kē*ǀ   *bəxlē   dasgirə̀n=yē-lū,*ǀ   *bāz-ham   rāba*
at-period=EZ   SBRD   together   betrothed=COP.PST-3PL   still-also   very
*bāsòr   ləxlē   xaē-n-wa.*ǀ
little   each_other   see.PRS-3PL-PSTC
'When they became betrothed, they still saw each other very little.' (A:3)

This adverbial head of a temporal clause in JSNENA is a hybrid form blending the Persian expression *dar modat=i ke* and its calque in Sanandaj Kurdish *ba modat=ē ka*. JSNENA *ba-mudat=ē kē* is borrowed through Kurdish, but the Persian relative particle *kē* substitutes for Kurdish *ka*. This conforms to the tendency of JSNENA to use the Persian relative particle *kē* in various contexts (§10.6.1).

10.7.3 zamān=ē ke

(1128) JSNENA
    hamēša xa-čačàw ba-rēš-af=yē-lè⌐   *yā lačagà*
    always one-robe on-head-3SG.F=COP.PST-OBL.3SG.M or veil
    ba-rēš-àf-yē-la,⌐   *tā-zamān=ē kē-'anà*
    on-head-3SG.F=COP.PST-OBL.3SG.F until-time=EZ SBRD-I
    xlūla wīl-ī.⌐
    wedding do.PST-OBL.1SG
    'There was always a robe on her head or there was a veil on her head, at the time that I married.' (A:4)

This particle is a loan from Persian *zamān=i ke*. The Persian relative particle *=i* has, however, been replaced by the relative particle *=ē*, which is form of the particle used in Kurdish and Gorani of the Sanandaj region and also elsewhere in JSNENA.

10.7.4 čun

In JSNENA temporal 'when'-clauses may also be introduced by the Iranian particle *čun*, e.g.

(1129) JSNENA
    čun tātē=ū dāak-akè⌐ k-əmr-ī-wa   *'ēa*
    when fathers=and mothers-DEF IND-say.PRS-3PL-PSTC this
    'astè=ya?⌐ bron-akē=č qabùl k-ol-wa.⌐
    good=COP.3SG.F boy-DEF=ADD acceptance IND-do.PRS.3SG.M-PSTC
    'When the fathers and mothers would say, "Is she good?", the boy would accept.' (A:2)

The particle *čun* is used as a causal conjunction ('because') in Kurdish and Gorani, but not as a temporal conjunction. The temporal use of *čun* originates from Classical Persian.

(1130) Classical Persian
    čon be xalvat mi-rav-and kār=e digar mi-kon-and.
    when to seclusion IND-go.PRS-3PL job=EZ other IND-do.PRS-3PL
    'When they go into their seclusion, they do other things.'

10.7.5 Asyndetic temporal constructions

In some cases in JSNENA a temporal clause is not introduced embedded under a temporal adverbial but is rendered idiomatically into English by a 'when'-clause. This includes clauses containing a perfective verb expressing a completed event that sets the frame for a following habitual action, e.g.

(1131) JSNENA
    a. *'ēa tīm-ā̀-wa,| bar-do xāl-ū*
       this finish.PST-3SG.F-PSTC after-OBL.that food-3PL
       k-əxl-ī-wā-lē=u| g-ēz-ī-wa
       IND-eat.PRS-3PL-PSTC-OBL.3SG.M=and IND-go.PRS-3PL-PSTC
       ba-šon-ḥašt-ū̀.|
       in-after-work-3PL
       '(When) this had finished, then they ate the food and went to get on with their work.' (B:69)
    b. *'o-lēlḕ=č| pəsra tìm,| məšxà*
       that-night=ADD meat finish.PST.3SG.M dairy_food
       k-əxl-ī-wa.|
       IND-eat.PRS-3PL-PSTC
       'On that night (when) the meat was finished, they used to eat dairy food.' (A:63)

Similar asyndetic temporal constructions are found in Sanandaj Kurdish.

(1132) Kurdish
    a. *bīs=ū haft rož-aka tūwằw bū*
       twenty=and seven day-DEF finished be.PST.3SG
       hāt=aw.|
       come.PST.3SG=TELIC
       '(When) twenty-seven days passed, he returned.'
    b. *aw šaw=a aw qəsa kə̀rd=mān| harka*
       DEM.DIST night=DEM DEM.DIST talk do.PST=1PL whoever
       bū göčkà=y lē bū.|
       be.PST.3SG ear=3SG at be.PST.3SG
       'That night (when) we said those words, (somebody)—whoever it was—listened to it.'

10.8 Conditional constructions

10.8.1 Constructions with the particle ʾagar

In JSNENA conditional constructions consist of a subordinate clause expressing the condition (protasis) and a main clause expressing the consequent (apodosis). The protasis is generally introduced by the Iranian particle ʾagar 'if' (1133), which also introduces protases in the Iranian languages of the Sanandaj region (1134)–(1135). For the use of irrealis verbal forms in conditional constructions, see §7.2.1.5:

(1133) JSNENA
 ʾagar hē-t bēl-īˈ ləxmà k-əw-n-ox.ˈ
 if come.PRS-2SG.M house-1SG bread IND-give.PRS-1SG.M-2SG.M
 'If you come to my house, I shall give you bread.'

(1134) Kurdish
 agar xwā kūmak=əm Ø-w-èˈ haq xwa=m
 if God aid=1SG SBJV-be.PRS-3SG right REFL=1SG
 a-sàn-m=aw.ˈ
 IND-take.PRS-1SG=TELIC
 'If God helps me, I shall reclaim my right.'

(1135) Gorani
 agar m-āč-dē bā Ø-kīyān-ù.ˈ
 if IND-say.PRS-2PL HORT SBJV-send.PRS-1SG
 'If you say (so), then I shall send (for the government).'

10.8.2 Clauses introduced by ʾagar čanānčē

On some occasions in JSNENA the two Iranian particles ʾagar and čanānčē are combined at the head of a protasis clause (1136). This compound particle has its origin in formal Persian (1137).

(1136) JSNENA
 ʾagar čanānčē xa-nāša na-rāḥatī hawè-lē,ˈ
 if in.case one-person grievance be.PRS.3SG.M-OBL.3SG.M
 ʾàlē bā-ēf.ˈ
 know.PRS.3SG.M about-3SG.M
 'If a person had a grievance, he would know about it.' (A:108)

(1137) Standard Persian
  agar čenānče rāyāne-i az xod dār-id
  if in.case computer-INDF from REFL have.PRS-2PL
  mi-tavān-id az system=e interneti=ye bi-sim=e
  IND-can.PRS-2PL from system=EZ of.internet=EZ without-wire=EZ
  ketābxāne estefāde Ø-kon-id.
  library use SBJV-do.PRS-2PL
  'If you have a (portable) computer of your own, you can use the free wireless internet of the library.'

10.8.3 Asyndetic conditional constructions

Some clauses that are not introduced by subordinating conditional particles have a function equivalent to a protasis clauses. In many cases they have irrealis verb forms, e.g.

(1138) JSNENA
 a. *'al-nā-wa ga-laxḕ=t,│ k-ē-nằ-wa.│*
   know.PRS-1SG.M-PSTC in-here=COP.2SG.M IND-come.PRS-1SG.M-PSTC
   'If I had known that you were here, I would have gone to visit you.'
 b. *'āt g-ēz-ət-wa tʷkānà,│ 'axon-ox doka*
   you IND-go.PRS-2SG.M-PSTC shop brother-2SG.M there
   yē-lḕ,│ là k-əmr-ət-wa bāq-ēf
   COP.PST-OBL.3SG.M NEG IND-say.PRS-2SG.M-PSTC to-3SG.M
   šalom 'alēxēm.│
   greetings to.you
   'If you went to a shop and your brother was there, you would not say to him, "Greetings to you."' (B:46)

Parallel constructions in Kurdish and Gorani are shown below:

(1139) Gorani
  haz Ø-kar-ī bās=ū ằ tawan-ā
  liking IND-do.PRS-2SG talk=EZ DEM.DIST rock-PL.OBL
  Ø-kar-a│
  SBJV-do.PRS-2SG.IMP
  '(If) you like, talk about those rocks.'

(1140) Kurdish
mār tò na=w-wət dā t-è̠-m=aw|
Q.PTCL 2SG NEG=2SG-say.PST SBRD IND-come.PRS-1SG=TELIC
mənāḷ=o na-w-ē a=w-kož-əm.|
child=2SG NEG-be.PRS-3SG IND=2SG-kill.PRS-1SG
'Didn't you say, "When I'm back, I will kill you (if) you don't have a child!"'

10.9 Concessive constructions

In JSNENA a concessive sense may be given to a clause by using the expression *ba-wajūd=ē kē*, which is based on Persian *bā-vujūd=i ke* (lit. 'with the existence of that'), the basic meaning of which is 'with (despite) the existence of the fact that', e.g.

(1141) JSNENA
ba-wajūd=ē kē xastè̠=na,| ḥaštà k-o-na
although=EZ SBRD tired=COP.1SG.M work IND-do.PRS-1SG.M
tā-pəlga lēlè̠.|
to-half night
'Although I am tired, I shall work until midnight.'

A conditional 'even if' construction is related, in that it indicates that the situation of the main clause is not expected to follow from the condition but nevertheless will do so. The difference from a concessive construction is that the truth of the protasis is not certain. In JSNENA this is expressed by an inclusive construction with the enclitic additive particle =əč attached to the relative particle *'agar* (1142.a-b):

(1142) JSNENA
a. 'agar=əč xastà hawē-na,| ḥaštà k-o-na.|
if=ADD tired be.PRS-1SG.M work IND-do.PRS-1SG.M
'Even if I were tired, I would work.'
b. 'agar=əč kpīna hawè̠-wa,| ʾīxāla là
if=ADD hungry be.PRS.3SG.M-PSTC food NEG
xīla=y.|
eat.PTCP.SG.M=COP.3SG.M
'Even if he was hungry, he did not eat the food.'

No examples of the concessive use of the corresponding conditional and additive particles were found in Kurdish and Gorani. In (1143) *agar=īč* is rather a clausal connective introducing a conditional construction that is parallel to what precedes.

(1143) Kurdish of the Sanandaj region
agar xaftö=yī wa xàw b=ī-wēn-a.|
if sleep.PTCP=COP.2SG by sleep SBJV=3SG-see.PRS-IMP.2SG
agar=īč xabar=ī wa čȧ̀w b=ī-wīn-a.|
if=ADD awake=COP.2SG by eye SBJV=3SG-see.PRS-2SG.IMP
'If you're asleep, see it in your dream; if you're awake see it with your eyes.'

It seems that the JSNENA concessive use of *'agar=əč* is an imitation of the syntax of Persian *agar ham* 'even if', substituting the Persian additive particle *ham* by the Gorani particle *=əč*.

The Persian particle *magar* 'perhaps' may be in JSNENA used to form concessive constructions, e.g.

(1144) JSNENA
magar rāba naxòš xīr-awē| yā rāba na-raḥàt
even.if very ill be.PTCP.SG.M-be.PRS.3SG.M or very unwell
xīr-awē| hūlāē kulē doq-ī-wa.|
be.PTCP.SG.M-be.PRS.3SG.M Jews all hold.PRS-3PL-PSTC
'Even if somebody was very ill or was very unwell, nevertheless all the Jews observed (the fast).' (B:44)

10.10 Summary

In JSNENA syndetic strategies of subordination involve borrowing of particles and patterns from Standard Persian. This reflects the sensitivity of subordination to the model of standard languages. The spoken Iranian languages of the region, Gorani and Kurdish, by contrast, exhibit more asyndetic strategies. Table 86 summarises the sources for subordinating particles in JSNENA:

Table 86: Subordinating and other particles in JSNENA and their origin.

Type of Subordinator	Form	Main Contact Language
relative particle	kē	Persian
relative particle	ya	< Sulemaniya Kurdish *ka* ?
relative particle	=ē	Kurdish, Gorani
factive/ non-factive complementiser	kē	Persian

Table 86 (continued)

Type of Subordinator	Form	Main Contact Language
temporal adverbialiser	waxt=ē	Kurdish/ Gorani
conditional particle	'agar	Kurdish/ Gorani/Persian
conditional particle	'agar čanānčē	Persian
conditional 'even if'	'agar=ač	Persian (calque)
concessive expression	ba-wajūd=ē kē	Persian
temporal particle 'until'	har-tā-ge	Kurdish hatā-ka-dē 'until'
indirect polar question particle	daxom	Gorani/ Kurdish

11 Lexicon

In this chapter we shall investigate loanwords in JSNENA and their origin. The loanwords in JSNENA originate both from languages in the current contact region of Sanandaj and also from languages outside of the current contact region. The source languages in the Sanandaj region include Gorani, Sanandaj Kurdish, and to a lesser extent Persian. The source languages outside of the Sanandaj region include the Central Kurdish variety of the Sulemaniyya region and the Bahdini Kurmanji variety of northern Iraq. The existence of loanwords in JSNENA from this latter group of source languages can be taken as evidence for the trajectory of migration of the ancestors of JSNENA-speakers from northern Iraq.

There are differences in the number of loanwords that have been transferred to JSNENA from each of the various source languages. Moreover, the type of lexicon transferred from each of the source languages differs. Most loanwords belonging to the basic lexicon that have entered JSNENA come from Gorani rather than Kurdish. This is a reflection of the history of the language situation in Sanandaj. Although the principal contact language for recent generations of speakers of JSNENA has been Kurdish, at an earlier period the principal contact language must have been Gorani.

11.1 Loanwords from Gorani and Sanandaj Kurdish

11.1.1 Introductory remarks

In what follows we present a characterisation of loanwords in JSNENA according to various lexical fields. The majority of loanwords are from Gorani rather than Kurdish. This is the result of the language shift from Gorani to Kurdish in Sanandaj at an earlier period. We may say that JSNENA has preserved a record in its lexicon of the language situation before this shift from Gorani to Kurdish. It should be noted that some loanwords are shared by Gorani and Kurdish. In some such cases, however, the Kurdish word may ultimately be a loan from Gorani.

Lexical borrowing is a universal property of languages. In what follows we present some findings on crosslinguistic lexical borrowing derived from a study of loanwords in 1460 items across 41 languages (Haspelmath and Tadmor 2009). Languages differ with respect to borrowability across different word classes and borrowability across different semantic fields. As for the former, it is generally expected that content words are borrowed more than function words (though see Tadmor 2009, 59 for some exceptions). Likewise, nouns exhibit a higher proportion of borrowing than verbs. This is reflected in statistical data from 41 languages, where the rate of borrowability for nouns is 31%, compared to 14% for verbs. The semantic fields with the highest proportion of borrowing are, in descending order 'religion and belief', 'clothing and grooming', 'the house', and 'law'. The semantic fields that are the least affected by borrowing are 'sense perception', 'spatial relations', 'the body', and 'kinship' (Tadmor 2009, 64–65).

On the basis of the percentage of loanwords in 1460 items, Tadmor (2009) divides languages across a scale of borrowing as 'very high borrowers', 'high borrowers', 'average borrowers', and 'low borrowers'. Thus, Selice Romani with a borrowing rate of over 50% is considered a 'very high borrower', whereas Mandarin Chinese with a borrowing rate of less than 10% is a 'low borrower'. Tadmor (2009, 58) draws on sociolinguistic factors as possible motivations for the radically different rates of borrowing between Selice Romani and Mandarin Chinese. Selice Romani is characterised by the multilingualism of all its speakers, its minority language status, and the socio-politically marginalised status of its speakers. Mandarin Chinese, on the other hand, is the opposite in these respects: there is almost no bilingualism among its speakers, it is a majority language and is socio-politically dominant. Matras (2012) notes that the issue is more complicated, as there is a whole set of social factors that motivate or inhibit borrowing. As for JSNENA, although no comparative list has been studied, as will be seen below, it exhibits properties of a very high borrower language, with loanwords extending to the cross-linguistically least borrowable semantic fields such as 'body part', and 'kinship' terms.

11.1.2 Kinship terms

Several of the loanwords in JSNENA belong to the semantic fields of kinship and body parts, which are considered to constitute part of basic vocabulary. In the literature on language contact, kinship terms are considered an interesting case study of the continuous nature of borrowing. Often, languages retain the inherited word for kin closest to the speaker in age in degree or relatedness, e.g. members of the nuclear family in either childhood or adulthood, while they borrow words for extended kin. English, for example, has retained inherited words for nuclear family members, but borrowed words for extended kin terms from French (see Matras 2009, 169–172). As will be seen below, a roughly similar pattern occurs in JSNENA as well, except that in the nuclear family inherited Aramaic lexicon is retained for speakers that are closest in age to the speaker.

Borrowed kinship terms in JSNENA include the following.

(1145)		JSNENA	Gorani/Kurdish
father	*tāta*	G. *tāta*
mother	*dāaka*	K. *dāyka* (vocative)
mother! (vocative)	*dāe*	K. *dāya*
step-father	*bāwa pyāra*	G./K. *bāwa pyāra*
maternal uncle	*lāla*	G. *lāla, lālo*
paternal uncle	*māma*	G. *māmo*; K. *māma*
wife of paternal uncle	*māmožna*	K. *māmožən*; G. *māmožanī*
betrothed	*dasgīrān*	G. *dasgīrān* (Sulemaniyya K. *dasgīran*; Sanandaj K. *dazūrān*)
grandson	*nawāga*	K./G. *nawa*
granddaughter	*nawagta*	K./G. *nawa*
great grandchildren	*nawšārē*	K./G. *nawazā*

These loanwords in JSNENA include members of the core family unit. A feature that many of them have in common is that they refer to family members who are senior from the perspective of the speaker ('father', 'mother', 'step-father', 'uncle', 'wife of uncle'). Kinship terms that refer to family members equal in seniority from the perspective of the speaker have not been replaced by borrowing in JSNENA, e.g. 'brother' (*'axona*), 'sister' (*xaləsta*). The motivation for borrowing in such cases is likely to increase the formality in social interaction to express politeness. From an anthropological point of view, the expression of formality in a social situation is linked to the increased structuring of discourse that links it to norm and tradition (Irvine 1979). From a language contact point of view, this formal structuring of discourse would involve JSNENA speakers adopting the linguistic norms of the socially dominant Iranian community. The loanword 'betrothed' (*dasgīrān*) in JSNENA also falls in the category of expression of formality, since it is associated with a ceremony.

The term borrowed by JSNENA for 'mother' is a vocative form in Kurdish. Likewise, the terms borrowed for 'father', 'paternal uncle', and 'maternal uncle' by JSNENA can be used in the vocative in Gorani. This is likely to have arisen due to the high frequency of the vocative forms of the words in day-to-day conversation in the source languages.

The borrowing of words for 'grandson' and 'great grandchildren' must have a different motivation. This may be the association of these words with emotion. The process could involve the attempt to make the words more expressive of emotion by replacement by innovative terms through borrowing. The ending -*āga* on *nawāga* 'grandson' is a dimunitive suffix, which is likely to be an expression of endearment rather than diminutive size.

Likewise, terms of endearment, which are associated with emotion, are borrowed by JSNENA from Iranian.

(1146) | | JSNENA | Gorani/Kurdish
my dear (lit. soul) | | *gīyāna* | G./K. *gīyān*
dear (addressed to children) | | *roḷa* | G./K. *roḷa*
my dear (addressed to children) | | *'azīzakam* | K. *'azīzakam*

The term 'pregnant' in JSNENA is expressed by a phrase that literally means 'two souls'. The word 'two' in the phrase is the inherited Aramaic form, but the word for 'soul' is borrowed from Iranian. This, therefore, is a loanblend (cf. Winford 2003, 45 for this terminology).

(1147) | JSNENA | Gorani/Kurdish
pregnant | *trē gyānē* | G. *dəva gīyāna*; K. *dū gīyān*

Some kinship terms in JSNENA are loanblends and others are complete calques (loan translations) from the Iranian contact languages:

(1148) | | JSNENA | Gorani/Kurdish
grandfather (lit. big father) | | *tāta ruwa* | G. *tāta gawra*[1]
grandmother (lit. big mother) | | *dāaka rabta* | K. *dāya gawra*
baby (lit. small child) | | *yāla zora* | G. *zaroḷa wərda*
 | | | K. *mənāḷa wərda*

11.1.3 Body parts

Body parts constitute a universal semantic domain that is highly resistant to borrowing. Generally considered to be a closed semantic class and diachronically stable (Holman et al. 2008; Tadmore 2009), body-part terms resist borrowing due to their being basic vocabulary.

In what follows we present a list of body-part items in JSNENA that are Iranian loanwords. It can be seen that salient body parts such as 'arm', 'breast', 'tail', 'wing' have been borrowed into JSNENA from Gorani or Kurdish, even though the terms for some of these salient external organs, such as 'arm', 'breast', 'tail', have been shown by the study of Tadmor (2009) of basic vocabulary to exhibit a low tendency cross-linguistically to be borrowable into another language (see Tadmor 2009, 71, Leipzig-Jakarta list of basic vocabulary).

---

[1] In conservative Gorani dialects the more common term for 'grandfather' is *bābā*, which has been borrowed into Sanandaj Kurdish as *bāwā*.

The word for 'breast' in JSNENA consists of an Iranian loanword combined with an inherited Aramaic diminutive ending. In Iranian the word is combined with an Iranian diminutive ending, so the JSNENA diminutive is a loan translation.

(1149)

	JSNENA	Gorani/Kurdish
upper arm	qoḷa	G. qoḷ (upper arm)
breast	mamona	G. mama G./K. mamka, makoḷa
wing	bāḷa	G./ K. bāḷ
tail	dūčka	K. dūčka (G. qlīčka)

Many less salient body parts have been borrowed into JSNENA. These include both external organs and internal organs. Note that the loanword qlapī in JSNENA has undergone semantic modification.

External organs

(1150)

	JSNENA	Gorani/Kurdish
index finger	gəlka (pl. gəlke)	G. gʊlka
lock (of hair)	čīn	G. čīn
armpit	hangəḷta	G. hangəḷ; Sul. K. bənhangaḷ
feather	paṛa	G. paṛa; K. paṛ; P. par
beak (of bird)	dandūka	Mukri dəndūk; G. dənūk; Sanandaj K. danūk
moustache	səmbēḷē	G./K. səmēḷ
body	laša	G./K. laš
side, flank	kaḷaka	G./ K. kalaka
(bare) foot	qlapī	G./K. qulāpa 'ankel'; K. qolapē
cheek	gupa	K. gob; G. gəp
clitoris	baḷūka	G. baloka; K. balūka
penis of young boy	guna	G./K. gun
thigh	rāna (pl. rānē)	G./K. řān, P. rān

Internal organs

(1151)

	JSNENA	Gorani/Kurdish
rib	parāsū	G./ K. parāsū
pupil	gəlka 'ēna	G. glēna; K. glēna-y čāw
vein	řag	G./K. řag
small intestine	ma'da	G./K. <A. ma'da
yolk	zardēna	G. K. zardēna

An interesting observation is that human body parts, e.g. 'index finger', 'lock (of hair)' tend to be borrowed from Gorani, whereas animal body parts, e.g. 'tail', 'beak', are borrowed from Kurdish. This could be interpreted as a reflection of the fact that Gorani is an older layer of contact-induced lexical replacement in JSNENA.

Some body parts have been borrowed due to social factors such as association with emotion, cultural formality and taboo.

'Cheek' is associated with baby-talk in Kurdish and is used as an expression of endearment when an adult touches a baby's face. 'Pupil' is used in the affectionate expression 'the pupil of my eye', which is equivalent to the English expression 'the apple of my eye',. The association with emotion may apply also to the loanword *mamona* 'breast' in JSNENA, which contains a diminutive suffix expressing endearment.

The term 'penis of young boy' may have been borrowed due to its association with the ceremony of circumcision. This would be a case of linguistic formality linked to ceremonial being achieved by borrowing from the dominant Iranian culture.

Taboo seems to be the factor triggering the borrowing of 'clitoris'.

The borrowing of these body parts shows that while there is a cross-linguistic constraint against the borrowability of body parts, factors such as expression of emotion, social formality and taboo often outrank linguistic inhibitions against their borrowing (Pattillo 2021).

The terms for body parts in JSNENA have in some cases been calqued on the model of the Iranian contact languages. Examples of direct calques are as follows:

(1152)

	JSNENA	Gorani/Kurdish
eyelid (lit. back of eye)	xāṣa 'ēna	K. pəšt čāw, Gor. pəštū čamī, pēḷūē
nostril (lit. hole of nose)	bəza poqa	G. waḷa lūta; K. konā lūt
earlobe	lāga/narma nahāla	G. narma-w gošī; K. narma-y göčka
back of the neck	bar-pqāra	G. boqat-ū malī; K. pəšt məl
top of head	tapoqa rēša	G. toq-ū sarī; K. tapḷ sar
elbow	qatra qola	K. qořānīsk, qəñ-a bāḷ; G. aražno
thumb	zbota rabta	G. gulka gawrē; K. qāmka gawra

Some derivative body parts in JSNENA, e.g. 'palm of the hand', 'the skin of the hand' are loanblends, in which the derivative part, i.e. 'palm', 'skin', is borrowed from the Iranian contact languages, and the basic part, i.e. hand, is an inherited item. Note that the derivative part in 'palm of hand' is usually used in the source languages in combination with the head. The use of *toqa* with *ʾīla* in JSNENA is thus a case of semantic modification.

(1153) JSNENA   Gorani/Kurdish
       toqa 'īla   'the skin of hand'   cf. G. *toqa sar* 'top of head'
       nawrəsta 'īla 'the palm of hand'   K. *nāwrās das*

Another area of convergence is constituted by idiomatic expressions involving body parts. Here JSNENA copies the phraseology of the Iranian source languages.

It is not to (the liking) of my heart
The expression 'It is not to (the liking) of my heart' is used to express that the speaker does not like something or someone:

(1154) JSNENA: *ba-ləb-ī līt*
       Gorani: *ba-dəḷ=əm nīy=ā*
       Kurdish: *ba-dəḷ=əm nīya.*

On my eyes
The idiomatic expression 'on my eyes' expresses one's willingness to do something.

(1155) JSNENA: *ba-rēš 'ēn-ī*
       Gorani: *sar-ū čam=əm*
       Kurdish: *(ba)-sar čāw=əm*

On one's head
The idiomatic expression 'on one's head' is used to take an oath in all the three languages.

(1156) JSNENA: *ba-rēš-ox*   '(I swear) on your head'
       Gorani: *ba-sar=ət*
       Kurdish   *ba-sar=o*

It hit someone's head
This expression in JSNENA is a calque from Persian. It is used to express that someone has gone mad.

(1157) JSNENA: *ba-rēš-ox dīya=y?* 'Are you mad?' (lit. 'Has it hit your head?')
       Persian: *zad-e be-sar=et?*

11.1.4 Cultural objects

Words for inanimate cultural objects comprise another semantic field that exhibits borrowing from in JSNENA.

(1158)

	JSNENA	Gorani/Kurdish
spoon	čamča	G. čamča, čəmča
cushion	sarīna	G. sarīna, sarəngā
reel, spool (for thread)	groḷī	G. groḷē
loofah	ləfka	G. ləfka
earrings	gošwārē	G. gošawāra
churn	maška	K. maška; vs. G. haḷīza
spindle	tašī (m.)	K. tašī
knife	kārd	G./K. kārd
bread bin	nāndān	G. nānadāna; K. nāndān
large sieve (for sieving earth)	sarand	K. sarang; G. hēḷaka
grindstone	hāra	G. hāřa, K. hāř
quilt	laʿēfa	G. lēfa; K. lāf
plate	dawrī	G./K. dawrī
fork	čəngāḷ	G./K. čəngāḷ
small pot	gozala	G. gozaḷē; K. gozaḷa
small pot for dry produce	humba	G./K. huma
clothes	jəl	G./K. jəl
rag	paro	G./K. pařo
carpet	qāḷī	G./K. qāḷī
net	tor	G. tořa; K. toř
stove	sompa	G. sompa; K. sompā
ladder	payja	G. payja; K. payja, pəlakān
mirror, glass	jām	G./K. P. jām
bag	torqa	G. toraka; K. tūraka
sword	šəmšēr	G./K. šəmšēr
ceramic container	kūzī	G./K. kūzī
container, can	pūt	K. pūt

As can be seen, basic cultural objects exhibit a greater tendency to be borrowed from Gorani than from Kurdish. The loanword from Gorani čamča 'spoon' is found in most NENA dialects. The variant čamčok means 'large spoon' in some Kurmanji dialects.

In JSNENA, the word for 'water tap' is a loanblend composed of Iranian šēr 'tap' and JSNENA māē 'water'.

(1159)   JSNENA   Gorani/Kurdish
water tap   *šēr=ē māē*   P. *šir-e āb*; K. *šēr āw*

11.1.5 Names of locations

Names of locations are another semantic field where loanwords are frequently found in JSNENA. As can be seen from the list below, JSNENA has borrowed names of locations more from Gorani than from Kurdish. In the case of the loanword *komanj*, there has been a semantic modification in its meaning in JSNENA ('steps leading onto a roof') from its meaning in Gorani ('chamber on the roof').

(1160)

	JSNENA	Gorani/Kurdish
chicken coop	*hūlēna*	G. *hēlyānī*
nest (of bird); hammock	*jolāna*	G. *jolānē*
steps leading onto a roof	*komānj*	G. *komānja* (chamber on the roof)
field	*dašta*	G. *dašta*; K. *dašt*
foundation	*bənāġat*	G./K. *bənāġa*
pharmacy	*dawāxāne*	K. *dawāxāna*
courtyard	*ḥafša, hawša*	G./K. *hawš*; G. *havš*
well	*bīra*	G. *bīrī*; K. *bīr*
shop	*tʷkāna*	G. *dūkān*; K. *dukān*
clin	*kūra*	K. *kūra*; G. *korē*
stream	*joga*	G. *jūa*; K. *jo*
river	*roxāna*	G./K. *roxāna*; K. *čam*
hole (in the ground)	*čāl*	K. *čāḷ*; G. *čāḷī*
lane	*kūjī*	K. *kūjī*; Gor. *kūjīya*

11.1.6 Spatial and temporal terms

Words denoting spatial relations exhibit low rates of borrowability cross-linguistically (cf. Tadmor 2009, 64–65). Nevertheless, it can be seen from the list below that some spatial and temporal terms in JSNENA have been borrowed from Iranian.

(1161)

	JSNENA	Gorani/Kurdish
contrary, opposite	*čapawāna*	G. *čapawānay*
side	*dīm*	G. *dīm*; K. *dēw*
middle	*nāwrəsta*	K. *nāwrās*
around	*dawrāndawr*	G./ K. *dawrāndawr*

side, by side of	*lā*	G./K. *lā*
after	*ba-šon*	K. *ba-šon*
time, occasion	*waxtara*	K. *waxtār*; G. *waxtār*
week	*hafta*	G./ K. *hafta*
spring	*bahār*	K. *bahār*
autumn	*pāyīz*	G./K. *pāyīz*

With regard to the names of the seasons, it is worth noting that inherited Aramaic words are retained in JSNENA for the seasons 'summer' (*qēṭa*) and 'winter' (*sətwa*). These are the two salient seasonal extremes. Iranian loanwords are used for the intermediate seasons of 'Spring' and 'Autumn'.

11.1.7 Food and fruit

Many lexical items relating to food in JSNENA are loanwords. These represent items of Iranian culture that have been adopted by speakers of JSNENA together with their names.

(1162)

	JSNENA	Gorani/Kurdish
date	*qasp*	G. *qasp* (a kind of date)
nut kernel	*tome*	G./K. *tom*
apricot	*šīḷanta* (f.)	G. *šēḷānē* (f.); K. *šēḷāna*
vegetable, herb	*sawzī*	G./K. *sawzī*
yoke (of egg)	*zardēna*	G./K. *zardēna*
pepper	*'ālat*	G./K. *hāḷat*
cracked wheat'	*parəšt*	G./K. *pařəšt*
peach	*štāḷwa*	G. *haštāḷūī*; K. *haštāḷo*
orange	*burtaqāḷ*	G./K. *pərtaqāḷ*
melon	*kāḷaka*	G./K. *kāḷak*
yoghurt water	*doē*	G./K. *do*
a kind of herb	*gīlāxa*	G./K. *gīlāxa*
onion pastry	*kalanta*	G. *kēlānē*; K. *kalāna*
sweet pastry	*pərsaxra*	K. *bərsāq*
small cake	*šəlkēna*	K. *šəlkēna*; G. *šəlkīnē*
edible herb	*šəng*	G. *šəngī*; K. *šəng*
sweet porridge made from flour	*haḷwa*	G./K. *haḷwā*; P. *halvā*
dish made from dates and eggs	*xurma=ū rūn*	K. *xurmā=ū ron*
dish made from bulgur and yoghurt	*duxwa*	K. *dūxwā*; G. *doxawā*

dish made of apricots	qaysūron	K. qaysūron 'dried apricot and oil'
cheese left after churning yoghurt	sīrāj	G. sīrājī

11.1.8 Animals and insects

The high number of loanwords in JSNENA for animals and insects, as well as their appurtenances, may reflect that these did not have a significant role in the life of the urban speech community. The majority of the animals in the list below are undomesticated. The words for most domesticated animals found in towns such as 'donkey' (xmāra), 'horse' (sūsī) and 'dog' (kalba), however, are inherited Aramaic terms.

(1163)

	JSNENA	Gorani/Kurdish
fox	řēwī	K. řēwī; G. řūāsa
a small bird	mrīčī	G. mrīčḷē
ant	mroča	G./K. mroča
lion	šēr	G./K. šēr
rooster	kaḷašer	K. kaḷašer; G. kaḷašīr
cock's comb	popwāna	G. popawāna; G. K. popa
owl	bāyaqūš	G. baīqūš; K. bāyaqūš
bee	hanga	G./K. hang
sheep's dung	pəškaḷe	G./K. pəškaḷ
frog	qurbāqa	K. qurwāqa; G. qurwāqī
chick	jūja, jujka	K. jūja, jūjka; G. jūjūḷē
dove	kotər	K. kotər
bird	mal	G./K. mal
locust	sīsərka	K. sīsərka
hornet	zardawāḷa	G./K. zardawāḷa

11.1.9 Abstract, Intangible and mass nouns

(1164)

	JSNENA	Gorani/Kurdish
match-making by intermediary	həjbī	G. hījbī
angel	frīšta	G./K. frīšta
pretext, excuse	byankē	K. bayānək
disgust	qīz	K. qīz; cf. Gor. qīzī

language	zwān	G./K. zwān
kind	jor	G./K. jor
rush	palapal	G./K. palapal
so-and-so	flānakas	K. flānakas
relating to a dervish/beggar	dawrēšī	G./K. dawrēš
advice	mšurta	G. mšūrat
mark, sign	nīšān	G./K. nīšān
pain	žān	G./K. žān
steam	buq	G./K. boq
spittle	təf	G./K. təf
square	čwārgoš	K. čwārgoš
seeing	dīyanī	K. dīyanī
good news; surprise	mazgānī	G. məzānī, K. məzgēnī
share, lot	pəšk	K. pəšk
spark, burning heat	qərča	K. qərča
shame, scandal	šūra	G./K. šūray
a loud bang sounded (in sky)	trəšqa	G./K. trīšqa

11.1.10 Plants

(1165)

	JSNENA	Gorani/ Kurdish
bud	mlago	G. məlagoē
leaf	gaḷa	G./K. gaḷā
fruit	mēwa	G. mēwa; K. mēwa, mīwa
dry grass	pūš	G./K. pūš

11.1.11 Natural world

(1166)

	JSNENA	Gorani/ Kurdish
fog	šawnam	G./K. šawnəm
lightning	bərqa	G. bərq
iron	ʾāsən	G./K. āsən
coal	zoxāḷ	K. zuxāḷ; G. suxāḷ
straw	pūšē	G./K. pūš
dust	toz	G./K. toz

11.1.12 Professions

(1167)
	JSNENA	Gorani/ Kurdish
work colleague	hawkār	K. hāwkār
woman inspector	pāxasū	K. pāxasū
mullah; rabbi	maḷa	G./K. maḷā

11.1.13 Fabrics

(1168)
	JSNENA	Gorani/ Kurdish
material, fabric	pārča	G./K. pārča; P. pārče
curtain	parda	G./K. parda; P. parde
thread (on fringe of carpet)	frēt	G./K. frēt

11.1.14 Clothing

(1169)
	JSNENA	Gorani/ Kurdish
'woman's cover'	čāčaw	G./K. čāšēw
'woman's head cover'	lačaga	G.K. lačka/ lačək

11.1.15 Adjectives and adverbs

Several adjectives and adverbs in JSNENA are loanwords. These have their source in Gorani and Kurdish in roughly the same proportion. The loanword *hāḷa* 'sour, unripe' exhibits semantic extension compared to the source word.

(1170)
	JSNENA	Gorani/Kurdish
sour, unripe	hāḷa	G. *hāḷ* 'unripe fruit, especially grape'
mixed	'āmēta	G. āmēta; Sanandaj K. āwēta
good	'ayza	K./G. < Arab. *'azīz* 'dear, good'
deep	qūl, qola	G./K. qūl
dirty	čaḷkən	G./K. čəḷkən
fast	gurj, gwərj	G./K. gurj
heavy	qurs	G./K. qurs
fresh	tāza	G./K. tāza
rich	dawlaman	G./K. dawlaman
poor	gā	K. gā; Gor. gađā

cheap	*harzān*	G./K. *harzān*; P. *arzān*
hot	*dāx*	G./ K. *dāx*
perhaps	*baška*	K. *baška*; G. *baška, baškom*
on one side, separate	*jya*	G./K. *jīyā*
blind	*kwər*	K. *kwēr, kör*; G. *kor*
curly (hair)	*lūl*	G./K. *lūl*
ill	*naxoš*	K. *naxoš*
twisted	*pīčyāw*	K. *pīčyāw*
old	*pīr*	G./K. P. *pīr*
stiff	*řaq*	G./K. *řaq*
crippled	*šal*	G./K. *šal*
destroyed	*wērān*	G./K. *wērān*
slowly	*laqalaq*	G./K. *laqalaq*

Some of the non-basic colours have been borrowed from Gorani or Kurdish. The inherited Aramaic terms are retained for the basic, cognitively more salient, colours:

(1171)

	JSNENA	Gorani/Kurdish/Persian
white	*xwāra* (Aramaic)	G. *čarma*; K. *čarməg*
black	*koma* (Aramaic)	G. *sīyāw*; K. *řaš*
red	*smoqa* (Aramaic)	G./K. *sūr*
green	*yarūqa* (Aramaic)	G./K. *sawz*
light yellow	*zayra*	G. *zar*; K. *zard*
turquoise	*qənya*	G./K. *pīroza*
brown'	*qaway*	K. < A. *qāwayī*
blue	*'ābī*	P. *ābī*

11.1.16 Verbs

A few verbal roots in JSNENA have been extracted from Gorani or Kurdish verbs, listed in (1172). These Iranian verbs have been integrated into the Semitic non-concatenative root system.

(1172)

	JSNENA	Gorani/Kurdish
to choose	*p-s-n*	G. *pasnāy*
to bray	*s-r-y*	G. *sař-āy, sařnāy*; cf. K. *sařānd-ən*
to low (cattle)	*b-w-r*	G. *bořyāy*; K. *bořāndən*
to decorate	*m-r-z-n*	G. *rāzyāyo*; K. *rāzānawa*

to protect, to preserve	p-r-ḥ-z	G. pārēznāy (pārēzn); K. pārāstən (pārēzn)
to collapse, to be destroyed	r-m-y	G. řəmāy; K. řəmīn
to shatter (intr.)	p-r-t-x	K. pətərkîn
to make a mistake	x-ḷ-ṭ	G. xaḷatyāy (xaḷat); K. xaḷatān < Arab.
to move	š-k-y intr. m-š-k-y tr.	K. šakīn (šak) intr.; šakāndin (šakēn) tr. 'to shake'
to destroy, to be destroyed	ṭ-p-y	K. topīn (top) intr. 'to be destroyed'
to hit	d-∅-y	K. dān
to beseech	l-w-l-y	G. lāḷyāy, K. lāḷīn

The meaning of the Kurdish verb *dān* includes 'to hit' and 'to give'. The JSNENA verbal root *d-∅-y* that has been extracted from this has undergone a semantic restriction and means only 'to hit'. The inherited root *h-w-l* is retained with the meaning of 'to give'. The verb 'to make a mistake' (*x-ḷ-ṭ*) is ultimately of Arabic origin, though it may have been borrowed into JSNENA through Iranian.

The verb 'to suck' in JSNENA has an Aramaic etymology but resembles the corresponding Iranian verb phonetically. This is no doubt since the form of the verb in both JSNENA and Iranian has arisen through onomatopoeic sound symbolism.

(1173)   JSNENA   Gorani/Kurdish
 to suck   *m-y-ṣ*   G./K. *məžīn*

The verb *g-r-g-m* 'to thunder' is found across NENA. In Kurdish *gərma* means 'loud noise'. Here the direction of the loan is not clear.

(1174)   JSNENA   Gorani/Kurdish
 to thunder   *g-r-g-m*   K. *hawra-gərma* 'thunder cloud'

Several Iranian light verb constructions consisting of a nominal element and a light verb have been borrowed into JSNENA (see §5.12). In most cases the Iranian nominal element is borrowed directly whereas the light verb is an Aramaic calque of the Iranian light verb:

(1175)
	JSNENA	Gorani/Kurdish
to believe	*bāwař '-w-l*	K. *bāwař kərdən*
to be born	*pēa x-∅-r*	G. *pīyā bīyay*
to envy	*ḥasrat l-b-l*	K. *ḥasrat bərdən*
to lie down (fall aside)	*pāḷ l-p-l*	G. *pāḷ kawtay* (lit. fall aside)

Constructions with the Kurdish light verb *dān* 'to hit' are replicated in JSNENA with the Iranian nominal element and the verbal root *d-Ø-y*, which has been extracted from the Iranian verb:

(1176)		JSNENA	Gorani/Kurdish
	to slap	*čapāla d-Ø-y*	K. *čapāḷa lē dān*
	to sting (of insect)	*čəza d-Ø-y*	K. *čəza lē-dān*

The NENA verb *š-q-l* originally meant 'to take', but in JSNENA its meaning has been extended to include both 'to take' and 'to buy'. This is a calque on the model of the Gorani verb *sanāy* 'to take, to buy' (replicated also in K. Sanandaj). Such a semantic extension of *š-q-l* is common to most Jewish Trans-Zab dialects. In other NENA dialects, the meaning of *š-q-l* is restricted to its historical meaning of 'to take' and 'to buy' is expressed by a different root, e.g. Ch. Barwar: *š-q-l* 'to take', *z-w-n* 'to buy'. This parallels the Northern Kurdish model: *sətāndin* 'to take'; *kəřīn* 'to buy'.

11.1.17 Prepositions

Prepositions are generally resistant to borrowing due to their being function words. It is noteworthy, therefore, that prepositions have been borrowed into JSNENA both in basic and compound forms. The borrowed basic prepositions *ba* and *tā* have a slightly different range of meanings from those of the Iranian source terms:

(1177)		JSNENA	Gorani/Kurdish
	without	*bē*	G.K. *bē*
	between	*bayn*	G. *bayn*; K. *la-bayn*
	in, at, with (instr)	*ba*	G.K. *ba* 'in, to, by, at, with'
	to, for, at (time), until	*tā*	G/K. *tā* 'until'
	like	*mangol*	literary Gorani: *mangor*

Compound prepositions are a combination of a basic preposition and a nominal:

(1178)		JSNENA	Gorani/Kurdish
	after	*ba-šon*	K. *ba-šon*; G. *(ba)-šon*
	around	*dawr, ba dawr*	G. *dawr*; K. *ba-dawr*

Some prepositions in JSNENA appear to be calques of Iranian forms.

(1179) 　　　　　　JSNENA　Gorani/Kudish
　　on　　　　　　　rēša　　G. sar
　　instead of　　　tʷkā　　G.K. jīyātī (lit. place of)
　　within, among　ga-plīyaw　K. la-nāw (lit. at-middle)

Some prepositions are loanblends. This applies to the following:

(1180) over　　　　　　　ba-rēša　　K. ba-sar
　　　　with (comitative)　mən-tak　　K. la-tak

11.1.18 Indefinites and interrogatives

Indefinite pronouns are commonly borrowed in JSNENA. (1181) lists the most common borrowings in this semantic field.

(1181) 　　　　　　　　　　　　　JSNENA　　Gorani/Kurdish/Persian
　　whoever, anybody who　　　har-kas　　G./K. har-ka(s); P. har-kas
　　everybody　　　　　　　　　har-nafar　P. har nafar
　　nobody　　　　　　　　　　hīč-kas　　G./K. hīč-ka(s); P. hīč-kas
　　all　　　　　　　　　　　　kul　　　　K./ P. kul
　　none　　　　　　　　　　　 hīč　　　　G./K./P. hīč
　　whatever, everything that　har-čī　　　G./K./P. har-čī
　　a few (from a group)　　　　xā ʼəda　　P. ʼədē-ī
　　always　　　　　　　　　　 hamēšā　　G./K. hamēša; P. hamīšē

Some indefinite pronouns are loanblends.

(1182) 　　　　　JSNENA　　　Gorani/Kurdish
　　nothing　　hīč-məndīx　G. hīč čīwē; K. hīč čətē

Calques are also attested. The difference between the JSNENA form and the relevant Iranian forms in (1183) is that the former has replicated the bound Iranian indefinite -ē, -ī using a free form indefinite particle xa.

(1183) 　　　　　　JSNENA　　Iranian
　　something　　xa-mdi　　G. čīw-ē; K. čət-ē; P. čīz-ī

By contrast, interrogative pronouns resist borrowing, as shown in (1184), in line with crosslinguistic tendencies (Matras 2009). It is, however, notable that the terms for 'why' and 'how' are created on the model of the Iranian, through calquing or loanblend.

(1184)

		JSNENA	Iranian
	who	*manī*	G./K. *kē*
	what	*mā*	G. *čēš*; K. *čī*
	which	*hēmā*	G./K. *kām*
	how	*mā-jor*	P. *čē-jūr*
	why	*tā-mā, bāqā mā*	G. *pay čēš*; K. *bo-ča*

11.1.19 Conjunctions

Conjunctions are almost entirely borrowed from Iranian languages. In most cases, it is hard to determine the exact source language from which conjunctions have been borrowed, since the same forms are used across Iranian languages of Sanandaj. However, the borrowed conjunctions are often closer in phonological form to Gorani and Kurdish, rather than the cognate forms in Persian, indicating that JSNENA has borrowed them from Gorani and/or Kurdish (see § 4.16 for list of borrowed particles).

(1185)

	JSNENA	Gorani/Kurdish
co-ordinating particle 'and'	=*ū*	G./K. =*ū* ; P. =*o*
	wa	G./K. *wa*; P. *va*
additive clitic	=*īč*	G. =*īč*
disjunctive conjunction 'or'	*yā*	G./K./P. *yā*
alternative conjunction 'both, also'	*ham*	G./K./P. *ham*
but	*walē*	G./K. *walē*; P. *valī*

As for the complex connectives, 'either – or' and 'both – and' are borrowed from Iranian, however, 'neither – nor' is not borrowed.

(1186)

	JSNENA	Gorani/Kurdish
both – and	*ham – ham*	G./K./P. *ham – ham*
either – or	*yā – yā*	G./K./P. *yā – yā*
neither – nor	*lā – lā*	G./K./P. *na – na*

11.2 Loanwords from Persian

Contrary to loanwords originating from Gorani and Kurdish, the words borrowed from Persian do not generally form part of the basic vocabulary of NENA. Persian loans are rather typically abstract nouns, objects and concepts relating to the modern world, government administration or the wider world.

11.2.1 Nouns

(1187)

	JSNENA	Persian
sugar candies	ʾābnabātē	ābnabāt
mixed nuts	ʾajīlē	ʾajil
booth, sukkah	ʾālunak	ālunak
warehouse	ʾambār	anbār
uncle	ʾamu	ʾamu
army	ʾartēš	arteš
trouble, disturbance	ʾazyat	ʾazyat
ill fortune	bad-baxtī	badbaxti
desert	bīyābān	biābān
stove	būxārī	boxāri
abacus	čort	čortke
property	dārāī	dārāyi
sea	darya	daryā
crack, chink	darz	darz
story	dāstān	dāstān
villager	dēhātī	dehāti
mattress	došak	došak
pool	ʾəstaxr	estaxr
army commander	farmand=ē laškar	farmānde-ye laškar
pressure	fəšār	fešār
cart	gārī	gāri
nothing	hīčī	hiči
war	jang	jang
scale (on vessel), incrustation	jerm	jerm
cabbage	kalam	kalam
big traders	kāsəbē ʾomdē	kasebe ʾomde
boat	kaštī	kašti
man	mard	mard
square (of town)	meydān	meydān

servant	*nokar*	*nokar*
room	*'otāq*	*otāq*
capital	*pāētaxt*	*pāytaxt*
scissors	*qayčī*	*qayči*
secret	*rāz*	*rāz*
joy	*šādī*	*šādi*
servant	*šāgərd*	*šāgerd*
king	*šāh*	*šāh*
police	*šahrbānī*	*šahrbāni*
barber	*salmānī*	*salmāni*
dinner	*šām*	*šām*
chair	*sandali*	*sandali*
soldier	*sarbāz*	*sarbāz*
barracks	*sarbāzxānē*	*sarbāzxāne*
difficulty	*saxtī*	*saxti*
construction	*saxtmānī*	*sāxtemāni*
wire	*sīm*	*sim*
skewer	*sīx*	*six*
bitterness, bitter hardship	*talxī*	*talxi*
bowl	*ṭašt*	*tašt*
metal beam	*tīr-'āhān*	*tir-'āhan*
food	*xorak*	*xorāk*
ice	*yax*	*yax*
goldsmith	*zargar*	*zargar*
life	*zəndəgī*	*zendegi*

Kurdish also has borrowed many words from Persian. In Kurdish the Persian words have become adapted to Kurdish phonology and morphosyntax. Many of the Persian loanwords in JSNENA have the form of this Kurdish adaptation of the words. This suggests that JSNENA acquired such words through Kurdish rather than taking them directly from Persian. Examples of these adapted loanwords are as follows. Morphosyntactic adaptation can be seen in the words 'camera' and 'livelihood'.

(1188)		JSNENA	Kurdish	Persian
	brick	*'ājūr*	*ājūr*	< P. *ājor*
	public	*'amūmī*	*'amūmī*	<P. *'omumi*
	spinach	*'asfanāj*	*'asfanāj*	<P. *esfenāj*
	knapsack	*buqča*	*buqča*	<P. *boxče*
	barrel	*būška*	*būška*	<P. *boške*

11.2 Loanwords from Persian

wrinkle	črūk	črūk	<P. čoruk
team, group	dasa, dasta	dasa	<P. daste
to invite	daʿwat ʾ-w-l	daʿwat	<P. daʿvat
camera	dūrbīn ʿakāsī	dūrbīn ʿakāsī	<P. durbin=e ʿakāsi
second	dūwom	dūwam, dūwom;	< P. dovom
livelihood	ʾəmrār maʿāš	ʾəmrār maʿāš	<P. ʾəmrār=e mă̄ʿāš
immediately	fawrī	fawrī	<P. fori
advantage	fāya	fāya	<P. fāyede
always	hamēša	hamīša	<P. hamiše
never	har-la-gīz	hargīz	<P. hargez
by air (travel)	hawāī	hawāī	<P. havāi
airplane	hawāpayma	hawāpayma	<P. havāpaymā
patience	ḥawṣala	hawsaḷa	<P. hosale
to rent	ʾījāra ʾ-w-l	ʾījāra	<P. ejārē
forest	jangaḷ	jangaḷ	<P. jangal
dispute	janjāḷ	janjāḷ	<P. janjāl
butter	kara	kara	<P. kare
factory	karxāna	kārxāna	<P. kārxāne
cobbler	kawšdoz	kawšdoz	<P. kafšduz
kidney	kulya (pl. kulye)	kulya	<P. kolye
pipe	lūla	lūla	<P. lule
spatula	māḷa	māḷa	<P. māle
lunch	nahār	nahār	<P. nāhār
window	panjara	panjara	<P. panjare
mosquito	paša	paša	<P. paše
saucepan	qāblama	qāblama	<P. qāblame
teapot	qorī	qorī	<P. quri
fenugreek	šambalīla	šambalīla	<P. šambalile
rich	sarwatmand	sarwatman	<P. servatmand
branch	šāxa	šāxa	<P. šāxe
potato	sēbzamīnī	sēbzamīnī	<P. sibzamini
pillar	stūn	stūn	<P. sotun
mouse trap	tala	tala	<P. tale
bathtub	wān	wān	<P. vān
tired	xasta	xasa	<P. xaste
bell	zanguḷa	zangoḷa	<P. zangule
earthquake	zəlzəla	zəlzəla	<P. zelzele

11.2.2 Adjectives and adverbs

(1189)

	JSNENA	Persian
blue	'ābī	ābi
ready	'āmādē	'āmāde
acquaintance, friend	'āšna	āšnā
permitted; free	'āzād	āzād
international	bēnulmalal	beynolmelal
round	gərd	gerd
seventh	haftom	haftom
in a bad mood	harasān	harasān
sufficient	kāfī	kāfi
dirty	kasīf	kasif
drunk, inebriated	mast	mast
made of copper	mēsī	mesi
beautifully	qašang	qašang
bright, clear	rošan	rošan
smooth	ṣāf	sāf
hard	səft	seft
fortunate, happy	xoš-baxt	xošbaxt

It is noteworthy that the adjectives borrowed from Persian include the non-basic colour 'blue'.

11.2.3 Verbs

A small number of verbs in JSNENA are loans from Persian. These include verbal roots extracted from Persian words and light verb constructions (§5.12) in which the nominal component has been borrowed from Persian.

(1190)

	JSNENA	Persian
to forgive, to pardon	b-x-š	baxšidan
to turn, to rotate, to orbit	č-r-x	čarxidan
to order; to give (polite)	f-r-m-n	farmudan
to pass	'ubur '-w-l	'obur kardan
to help	komak '-w-l	komak kardan

11.2.4 Particles

(1191)

	JSNENA	Persian
subordinating particle	ʾɪnkē	inke
let it be so	bāšē	bāše
yet, still, also	bāz, bāz-ham	bāz, bāz-ham
if, whether	čanānčē	čenānče
also the same	ham-čonīn	hamčenin
perhaps	šāyad	šāyad
apart from	ġēr az	ġeyr az

11.3 Loanwords from the Kurdish of the Sulemaniyya region

A few of the loanwords in JSNENA originate in the Kurdish dialect of the Sulemaniyya region. This is likely to be a reflection of the migration of the JSNENA-speakers from the Sulemaniyya region at an earlier period. The Kurdish loanwords in question include the following:

(1192)

	JSNENA	Sulemaniyya K.	Sanandaj K.
jaw, chin	čanāga	čanāga, čanāka	čənāka
chest	sənga	səng, sīng	sīna
watermelon	šwətya	šūtī, G. šūtī	hanī
basement	žērxan	žērxān 'a room in the basement'	žērzawī
small barrel	bastūla	bastū	bēška
hail	tarzaka	tarza	təgər
camel	ḥuštər	ḥuštər	wəštər
ill	naxoš	naxoš	naxwaš
cow's dung	harzālē	harzāḷa 'a place for gathering cow's dung'	lās

11.4 Loanwords from Bahdini Kurdish

Surprisingly, a number of loans, mostly verbs, in JSNENA originate in Bahdini Kurmanji Kurdish. The existence of these loans could be interpreted as evidence that the JSNENA-speakers ultimately originated in Iraq to the east of the Zab river in the Soran-Arbil region where there would have been contact with Bahdini. Some other trans-Zab Jewish NENA dialects were spoken in this region down to modern times, e.g. the Jewish NENA dialects of Arbel, Koy Sanjak and Ruwanduz. These areas represent the farthest extent of Gorani in Iraq. It is possible that the Jews were exposed to Bahdini Kurdish when the Bahdini speakers moved south. It is generally assumed that the heartland of Kurdish was in the Bahdinan region, from where some groups moved southward and converged with Gorani. The result of this was the emergence of the Central Kurdish dialects (cf. MacKenzie 1961b).

(1193)

	JSNENA	Bahdini Kurmanji
hair (collective)'	pərčē	pərč
problem	tašqəlta	tašqala
wide	fərya	fərah
to crumble	p-r-č-k	parčəqīn. pərčəqīn
to tear	č-r-p	čərīn (vi), čəřandən (vt)
to scratch	j-l-x	jalxāndən 'to crack, to fissure'
to uproot; to dig out; to pick	č-q-y	čaqādən 'to pull, to loose'

11.5 NENA loanwords in Kurdish and Gorani

It is significant that a small number of NENA words have been borrowed by the Iranian languages of the Sanandaj region. In some cases, the motivation for the loan appears to be to replace a word that is taboo in Iranian. Examples:

(1194)

Kurdish/Gorani		JSNENA	
K. ʾāšərma	fundament of horse/donkey	šərma	fundament
G. šarmgā	pubis	šərma	'fundament'
K. rūt-ū qūt	naked	qūṭa	'vagina'
K. nāw-nītka	curse	nīta ʾ-w-l	'to swear'
G. dəm	penis	dəma	'blood'

The NENA word jorē 'urine' may come ultimately from Armenian jur 'water', although an etymology from Arabic jry 'to flow' is also possible. In Kurdish the NENA word combines with the native mīz/mēz 'urine' to express 'a stream of urine'.

(1195)

Kurdish/Gorani		JSNENA
K./G. čořē mēz	'stream of urine'	< NENA jorē 'urine'

Other possible borrowings of JSNENA words in Iranian languages of the Sanandaj region include the following:

(1196) Kurdish/Gorani | | JSNENA
K. *kākīla* (*kāka* + dimunitive *-īla*) molar teeth | *kāka* 'tooth'
G./K. *sumāq* | red spice | *smoqa* 'red'
G./K. *'alā-hīda, 'alā-hada* | special | *əlha hīwa* 'God-given'
'aqraw | scorpion | *'aqəwra*
K. *kəlēḷ*; G. *krēḷ* | key | *qlīla*
G. *swāq dāy*; K. *swāq dān* | to become red, to become brown | *s-m-q* 'to become red'

Note also the following possible borrowing of a NENA verb in Sulemaniyya Kurdish:

(1197) Sulemaniyya K. | J. Sulemaniyya NENA
rūwān; P. *rūīdan* 'to grow (plant)' | *r-w-y* 'to grow'

In the Bahdini variety of northern Kurdish there are several lexical items that are likely to have been borrowed from NENA.

(1198) Bahdini Kurdish | | NENA (Ch. Barwar, northern Iraq)
Bah. *qalīn* (intr.); *qalāndin* (tr.) | to fry | *q-l-y*
Bah. *paqīn* (intr.), *paqāndin* (tr.) 'to explode' | to burst (intr.), to explode (intr.) | *p-q-'*
mērg; CK. *mērw;* G. *mara* | meadow | *marga*

Moreover, some compound kinship terms in Bahdini Kurdish exhibit closer parallels in their pattern to the corresponding terms in NENA than in Central Kurdish, such as Sanandaj Kurdish.

(1199) Bahdini Kurdish | | Ch. Barwar NENA | Sanandaj Kurdish
žən-bāb | step-mother | *baxtət-bāba* | *bāwa-žən*
žən-bərā | wife of brother | *baxtət xona* | *bərā-žən*
kuř-mām | son of paternal uncle, i.e. paternal cousin (m.) | *bronət māma* | *'āmo-zā*
kəč-mām | daughter of paternal uncle, i.e. paternal cousin (f.) | *brātət māma* | *'āmo-zā*

This shows that the lexical borrowing from NENA is a widespread feature across the NENA area. A full investigation of NENA loanwords in Kurdish awaits further research (cf. Chyet 1997 for a preliminary study).

11.6 Summary

JSNENA exhibits extensive lexical borrowing from Iranian. This includes items of the basic lexicon, e.g. kinship terms, body-part terms and terms for spatial and temporal relations, which reflects an intense degree of contact by JSNENA-speakers with speakers of Iranian languages in the region. Thomason and Kauffman (1988, 77) propose a scale of borrowability based on the intensity of contact. In this scale the borrowing of non-basic vocabulary occurs at stage (3):

(1) casual contact
(2) slightly more intense contact
(3) more intense contact
(4) strong cultural pressure
(5) very strong cultural pressure

The fact that items of the basic lexicon are borrowed by JSNENA indicates that the contact situation is at stage (4) or (5) of the borrowability scale.

A study of the loanwords in JSNENA reveals various historical layers. Most loanwords belonging to the basic lexicon that have entered JSNENA come from Gorani. This indicates that there was intense contact between speakers of JSNENA and Gorani at an earlier period. Most of the Kurdish loanwords are likely to have been borrowed by JSNENA in more recent times, after the language shift from Gorani to Kurdish in the region.

Some social and psychological factors can be proposed for why specific items of basic JSNENA vocabulary underwent lexical replacement by an Iranian loanword. These include a motivation to increase formality in the case of names of senior members of a family or terms relating to ceremonies by adopting the linguistic norms of the socially dominant Iranian community. Some words were replaced due to their association with emotion. The process involved an attempt to make the words more expressive of emotion by replacement by innovative terms through borrowing. This applies to some kinship terms such as 'grandson', 'granddaughter', 'great grandchildren', and some body parts such as 'cheek' and 'pupil'. Sexual taboo appears to have been a motivation for replacement of words such as 'clitoris' by a loanword. Human body parts tend to be borrowed from Gorani whereas animal body parts, e.g. 'tail', 'beak', are borrowed from Kurdish. This correlates with the fact that the terms for body parts of humans are from a human-centric point of view more basic and salient than animal body parts. There is a high number of loanwords in JSNENA for undomesticated animals and insects, which may reflect that these did not have a significant role in the life of the urban speech community. Cognitive salience seems also to have played a role in loans elsewhere in the lexicon. In the field of colour terms, for example, the inherited Aramaic terms are retained for the basic, cognitively more salient, colours, but the terms for the less basic colours have been borrowed. There is resistance to borrowing of the two salient seasonal extremes 'summer' and 'winter', but the borrowing of the less salient intermediate seasons 'spring' and 'autumn'.

JSNENA also contains numerous loanwords from Persian, many of which, it seems, have been borrowed through Kurdish rather than directly from Persian. Unlike loanwords originating from Gorani and Kurdish, the words borrowed from Persian do not generally form part of the basic vocabulary of NENA. Rather they typically denote abstract nouns, objects and concepts relating to the modern world, government administration or the wider world. This reflects the fact the Persian was a modern layer of the language situation of JSNENA-speakers, associated with modern education.

A few Iranian loanwords in JSNENA have their origin outside of the Sanandaj region. Some can be identified as originating in the Kurdish of the region of Sulemaniyya. A few originate further afield in Bahdini Kurdish. This can be interpreted as reflecting the path of migration of the JSNENA speakers from northern Iraq at an earlier period.

The majority of loanwords in JSNENA from Iranian are nouns, but they include also other grammatical categories, such as adjectives, adverbs, prepositions, particles, and verbs. In JSNENA several verbal roots have been extracted from Iranian verbs.

Loanwords in JSNENA have in some cases undergone semantic extension or semantic restriction in relation to the meaning in the source language. In addition to material loans, there are numerous calques and also loanblends, consisting of inherited and loan material.

12 Conclusion

12.1 Preliminary remarks

In this concluding chapter we shall bring together and summarise a selection of the themes that have been discussed in detail in the preceding chapters. We shall first review the various layers of contact that have been operative on JSNENA at various stages of its history. Then we go on to discuss the typology of the processes that have resulted in the various types of contact-induced change. Finally, we examine various explanatory models of contact linguistics for the development of the current profile of JSNENA.

12.2 Layers of contact

The foregoing chapters have revealed the impact of various Iranian languages on JSNENA. These have had different degrees of influence. The two Iranian languages that have had the greatest influence are the dialects of Gorani and Kurdish of the Sanandaj region. Standard Persian has also had a conspicuous impact in some levels of the language. The study has shown that the source of some marginal influence can be identified in the Kurdish dialects of Iraq, including the Kurdish of the Sulemaniyya region and even Bahdini Kurmanji Kurdish.

The contact with these various Iranian languages took place at various historical periods. The languages of the Sanandaj region with which speakers of recent generations of JSNENA-speakers were in contact are Sanandaj Kurdish and Standard Persian. The speakers of JSNENA whom Khan consulted for his grammar (Khan 2009) had no knowledge of Gorani. The contact of JSNENA with Gorani took place at an earlier period before the language shift in Sanandaj from Gorani to Kurdish. Gorani and Kurdish, therefore, represent two different historical layers of influence in the current state of JSNENA. The influence of Iraqi varieties of Kurdish on JSNENA are easiest to interpret as reflections of an earlier migration history of the JSNENA-speakers from Iraq and so must also be earlier historical layers in the language. The existence of features originating in Bahdini Kurmanji suggest that the ancestors of the JSNENA-speakers may have lived in a region where they could have had contact with Bahdini. This could have been the region where the Jewish trans-Zab NENA dialects of Arbel, Koy Sanjak and Ruwanduz were spoken down to modern times. These areas represent the farthest extent of Gorani in Iraq. It is possible that the Jews were exposed to Bahdini Kurdish when the Bahdini speakers moved south. It is generally assumed that the heartland of Kurdish was in the

Bahdinan region, from where some groups moved southward and converged with Gorani.[1] The features in JSNENA that have their origin in the Kurdish of Sulemaniyya, which is nearer to Sanandaj, presumably entered the dialect at a more recent period. The speakers of JSNENA who are alive today have no memory of Jewish families from Sulemaniyya in Sanandaj. The contact with Sulemaniyya Kurdish, therefore, is likely to have taken place during the migration of the ancestors of the JSNENA-speaking community from Iraq before the threshold of communal memory.

The influence of Persian is associated in particular with the use of Persian in school education, which is a relatively recent phenomenon in the region.

12.2.1 Gorani

Our study has shown that Gorani has had a deeper influence on JSNENA than Kurdish. This must have been due to a longer period of exposure to Gorani than to Kurdish. JSNENA-speakers were evidently in intense contact with Gorani for many centuries, whereas intense contact with Kurdish began only in more recent times following the language shift to Kurdish in the region after the end of the Ardalan dynasty in the late 19th century. The deep influence of Gorani on JSNENA is reflected in particular by the impact of Gorani on the core lexicon of JSNENA and some core areas of morphology and morphosyntax.

Most loanwords belonging to the basic lexicon that have entered JSNENA come from Gorani. These include semantic fields such as body parts, kinship terms and spatio-temporal terms, which exhibit low rates of borrowability cross-linguistically (cf. Tadmor 2009, 64–65). Indeed the majority of loanwords in JSNENA have their source in Gorani. Many of these words are shared also by the Kurdish dialect of Sanandaj, but these are likely to have their source in the Gorani substrate of Kurdish.

In the domain of morphosyntax, innovative oblique case inflection has developed in the 3rd personal pronouns of JSNENA, which matches the oblique case inflection of 3rd person Gorani pronouns (§3.6).

Gorani has had an impact on the morphology of verbal stems in JSNENA (§5.2). This has resulted in the development in JSNENA of different past stems and resultative participles for transitive agentive verbs, on the one hand, and intransitive unacusative or passive verbs on the other. This is an innovation in NENA and appears

---

[1] According to MacKenzie (1961b), this merging of Bahdini with Gorani resulted in the emergence of the Central Kurdish dialects. MacKenzie's theory, however, is now not widely accepted by scholars.

to have come about through convergence with the morphological patterns of the verbal categories of Gorani.

The indexing of arguments on verbs in JSNENA corresponds more closely to the pattern of Gorani rather than Kurdish. JSNENA, for example, matches the Gorani pattern of expression of pronominal objects ergatively by direct suffixes on past stem verbs, except for the fact that in JSNENA the object expressed by the direct suffixes is restricted to third person (§5.10.3).

The JSNENA perfect constructions with the resultative participle and copula have developed on the model of Gorani rather than Kurdish (§5.11).

JSNENA has borrowed a number of key grammatical morphemes from Gorani, such as the definite article suffix -akē (§4.5), the additive particle =ač (§9.3) and the post-verbal particle -o together with its functions of marking telicity distinctions (§7.14).

In the domain of clausal and supra-clausal syntax many of the Iranian patterns that are replicated by JSNENA are found in both Gorani and Sanandaj Kurdish. This is no doubt since Kurdish has a Gorani substrate. There are, however, a number of features of JSNENA syntax that match Gorani rather than Kurdish. JSNENA matches Gorani rather than Kurdish, for example, in patterns of differential object marking on verbs (§7.15). The closest statistical match of JSNENA word order patterns is with the word order patterns of Gorani (§8.4.1 & §8.4.3). Constructions of naming in JSNENA are formed by an impersonal 3pl. form of the verb 'to say' ('they say to X such-and-such'). This exactly matches Gorani, but Kurdish uses the compound verb nāw nān 'put a name' in such constructions (§8.4.3.4).

As remarked, the deep extent of Gorani influence on JSNENA reflects a long period of contact between the two languages. In fact, the direction of this influence may not have been only from Gorani to JSNENA. A number of features of Gorani that resemble JSNENA are unusual in the Western Iranian languages. This applies, for example, to the Gorani past converter suffix on present-stem verbs (§5.5). Another case is the pattern of direct object clitics on present-stem verbs in Gorani after the subject person suffixes (§5.10). The expression of the progressive with a constituent resembling an infinitive preposed before the verb is a further feature that resembles JSNENA. Another possible candidate is the Gorani plural ending -ē on nouns and adjectives in the direct case. This is identical phonetically to the NENA plural ending -ē. All of these features are found throughout NENA and have a clear background in earlier Aramaic. The Gorani constructions could be explained as inner Iranian developments, but their existence in Gorani could have been induced or at least reinforced by contact with NENA, causing Gorani to differ from developments in other western Iranian languages. Indeed, a number of loanwords from NENA can be identified in Gorani. If the hypothesis that NENA had an impact on the structure of Gorani is correct, then the most likely explanation would be that that there was a language shift of many NENA-speakers to Gorani at some period.

It is significant to note in this context that the use of oblique person markers on both transitive and intransitive past-stem verbs that has been documented in Gorani varieties in Iraq, such as Bājilānī and Shabakī (§5.3) is also an unusual profile within the western Iranian languages but is normal in the main body of NENA dialects in Iraq. Also this feature, therefore, may have developed in these varieties of Gorani through contact with NENA. Again one would have to assume that this came about by a major language shift of NENA speakers to Gorani at some point in history. This is likely to have been associated with conversion of Christians and Jews of the region to Islam, a phenomenon that is historically documented (Soane 1912, 186).

12.2.2 Kurdish

In some cases of contact-induced change in JSNENA, the influence of Kurdish can be shown to be a later layer than that of Gorani.

Most of the Kurdish loanwords, for example, are likely to have been borrowed by JSNENA in more recent times, after the language shift from Gorani to Kurdish in the region. Kurdish has not made inroads into the basic lexicon. Rather Kurdish loanwords tend to be restricted to more peripheral domains of vocabulary. Whereas human body parts, for example, tend to be borrowed from Gorani, animal body parts, e.g. 'tail', 'beak', are borrowed from Kurdish (§11.1.3). This correlates with the fact that the terms for body parts of humans are from a human-centric point of view more basic and salient than animal body parts.

A case of change induced by contact with Kurdish is the loss of gender distinction in the 3rd person singular pronouns of JSNENA (§3.2). This matches the pronominal system of Kurdish. Gorani has retained gender distinction in the 3rd person pronouns. There is evidence, however, from literary works composed in the Jewish NENA dialects of Western Iran that these dialects retained a gender distinction in 3rd person singular pronouns until recent times, so the loss of distinction appears to be a recent development.

In the main body of NENA in Iraq the present copula has verbal inflection in the 1st and 2nd person but not in the 3rd person. This follows the pattern of Gorani. In JSNENA and related Jewish NENA dialects on the eastern periphery of the NENA area, however, also the 3rd person copula has verbal inflection. This matches more closely the profile of the copula in Kurdish than that of Gorani. There are, however, some vestiges of the non-verbal inflection of the 3rd person copula in certain constructions, suggesting that verbal inflection of the 3rd person is a recent phenomenon (§5.8.1).

JSNENA matches the Gorani pattern of expression of pronominal objects ergatively by direct suffixes on past stem verbs. In the current state of JSNENA, the object expressed by the direct suffixes is restricted to third person (§5.10.3). This can be considered to be a reflection of the incipient loss of the ergative construction induced by contact with Kurdish, in which direct suffixes no longer express the object.

A few features of morpho-syntax that are replications of Kurdish patterns do not exhibit vestiges of earlier Gorani patterns. These include the lack of a genitive particle linking the head and dependent noun in genitive constructions in JSNENA (§4.8). This matches Sanandaj Kurdish rather than Gorani, which uses *ezafe* in genitive constructions. The use of the invariable form *xēt* 'other' without gender or number distinction matches Kurdish rather than Gorani (§6.7.4.3).

12.2.3 Persian

Contrary to loanwords originating from Gorani and Kurdish, the words borrowed from Persian in JSNENA do not generally form part of the basic vocabulary (§11.2). Persian loans are rather typically abstract nouns, objects and concepts relating to the modern world, government administration or the wider world. This indicates that Persian is a later layer of influence and that JSNENA-speakers did not have such an intense contact with it as they did with Gorani and Kurdish. As shown by the profile of Persian loanwords, the source of Persian influence was from the realm of education and learned discourse. This is shown by the fact that it tends to be found in complex structures. It is significant that JSNENA has borrowed many subordinating particles from Persian and many subordination constructions are based on the model of Persian rather than Gorani or Kurdish (§10). This applies also to the occasional use of the Persian *ezafe* particle =*ē* in JSNENA noun phrases and on prepositions, which can be classified as a subordinating particle. It is notable, however, that JSNENA corresponds to Kurdish and Gorani, rather than Persian, when asyndetic strategies are used for the subordination of clauses. The periphrastic expression of passive using an auxiliary in JSNENA, which is not found in Gorani or Kurdish, appears to be an imitation of Persian syntax (§7.12). In some cases it can be shown that the Persian model for a JSNENA construction is specifically literary Persian rather than colloquial Persian. This applies, for example, to the JSNENA Indirective Past Perfect (§5.11.5), which is based on the model of a construction in literary Persian that has the structure *karde bude-ast* (do.PTCP be.PTCP-COP.3SG) 'he had done' (Lazard 2000). This feature of literary Persian influenced the speech of speakers of JSNENA who had a Persian literary education.

12.2.4 Sulemaniyya Kurdish

A few of the loanwords in JSNENA originate in the Kurdish dialect of the Sulemaniyya region. This is likely to be a reflection of the migration of the JSNENA-speakers from the Sulemaniyya region at an earlier period (§11.3). In addition to lexical items, the loans include grammatical particles. These include the presentative particle *wā* (§6.5.2). Another example is a particle meaning 'lest'. In JSNENA this has the form *la-bā*, which seems to be a replication of the Sulemaniyya Kurdish form *na-bā*, with substitution of the Kurdish negator element *na* by the NENA negator *la*. In Sanandaj Kurdish this particle has the form *na-wā* (§7.2.1.4).

12.2.5 Kurmanji Kurdish

A number of loanwords, mostly verbs, in JSNENA originate in Bahdini Kurmanji Kurdish (§11.4). The existence of these loans could be interpreted as evidence that the JSNENA-speakers ultimately originated in Iraq to the east of the Zab river in the Soran-Arbil region, where there would have been contact with Bahdini. Another feature that may reflect contact with Bahdini is the structure of the names of days of the week (§4.12). In JSNENA these names exhibit the truncation of the final inflectional vowel *-a*. This is the case also in other Jewish dialects through the NENA area. It is a feature of Kurmanji rather than the Iranian languages of the Sanandaj region.

12.3 Processes

In this section we shall summarise the processes that have resulted in contact-induced change in JSNENA.

12.3.1 Matter borrowing

Matter borrowing (Matras and Sakel 2007; Matras 2009) involves the transfer of lexical, morphological, or phonetic material from the Iranian source languages to JSNENA. These can be categorised as 'nonsystemic' elements (Hickey 2010b, 11). In many cases the Iranian material that is borrowed undergoes some kind of change in JSNENA, involving adaptation in morphological inflection, morphosyntax and meaning.

12.3.1.1 Loanwords

The clearest case of matter borrowing by JSNENA is constituted by loanwords. These include both lexical and grammatical words. The distribution and motivation for these loanwords have been examined in detail in chapter 11. In many cases they have replaced native JSNENA words, but in some cases they have enriched the JSNENA lexicon in some way, e.g. through filling lexical gaps or by expressing finer semantic distinctions. Even where the borrowing of loanwords results in lexical replacement in JSNENA, in many cases this could be regarded as a form of enrichment, since such loanwords often introduce added connotations, such as formality or emotive association (§11.1.2 & §11.1.3). This can be seen as arising from the model of bilingualism proposed by Matras (2009; 2010), who argues that bilinguals have a single enriched linguistic system at their disposal rather than two separate systems.

The loanwords undergo various degrees of morphological integration in JSNENA. Most do not acquire JSNENA singular nominal inflection but are inflected with a JSNENA plural morpheme, e.g.

(1200) JSNENA Gorani/Kurdish
'thimble' 'askuk (SG), 'askūk-ē (PL) G. 'askūk
lock of hair čīn (SG), čīn-ē (PL) G./K. čīn

Only a minority of loanwords acquire JSNENA singular nominal inflection, e.g.

(1201) JSNENA Gorani/Kurdish
middle nawrəs-ta K. nāwrās
time, occasion waxtar-a K. waxtār; G. waxtār

Another type of adaptation is the assignment of gender in JSNENA to loanwords from Persian and Kurdish, which do not have gender distinctions (§4.2.1).

Many Persian loanwords in JSNENA appear not to have been borrowed directly from Persian but rather through Kurdish. This is reflected in the phonological and morphosyntactic adaptation of the Persian words to Kurdish patterns (§11.2.1).

In some cases an Iranian loanword has undergone semantic modification, by processes of semantic restriction or extension. For example, the Gorani/Kurdish word qulāpa has the meaning of 'ankle'. This does not replace the native JSNENA word for 'ankle' 'aqolta. It has been borrowed, however, in the JSNENA phrase 'aqla qlapī 'barefoot', presumably since the ankle is exposed when a person walks barefoot. The Gorani word komānja means 'chamber on a roof'. This has been borrowed into JSNENA but has the meaning 'steps leading to the roof', presumably by a process of semantic restriction to designate a part of the entity. The Gorani word *toqa* is used in the Gorani phrase *toqa sar* with the meaning of 'top (surface) of the head'. The Iranian word is used in JSNENA in a wider range of contexts to express the surface of the skin of the body, e.g. *toqa ïla* 'the skin of the hand'. In such cases the semantic modification results in lexical enrichment of JSNENA rather than replacement of native lexical items.

12.3.1.2 Borrowed bound morphemes

In a number of cases JSNENA has borrowed bound affixes and clitics from Iranian languages. These include the definite article suffix *-akē* (§4.5), the additive clitic *=ač* (§9.3), and the Iranian preverbal particle *bā-*, which is optionally prefixed before the JSNENA irrealis verbal forms to express speaker-oriented modality (§5.7.1). These elements relate to what may broadly be described as interactional discourse management.[2] Their distribution is essentially the same as in the Iranian languages, except that the suffix *-akē* has a slightly more restricted range of meanings. In Iranian *-akē* is used with both the sense of a definite article and of a diminutive suffix. In JSNENA *-akē* is not used as a diminutive suffix. This may be because JSNENA has its own native morphological marking of diminutives. Languages are highly resistant to borrow bound morphology unless there is a ready function for it (Weinreich 1953, 33). It is likely, however, that the discourse management function of *-akē* was more easily transferred to JSNENA than its lexical-level function of marking the diminutive.

A notable feature of these borrowed bound particles is that they remain peripheral in JSNENA words and they do not exhibit the same degree of morphological integration as is found in some cases in the Iranian languages.

One may compare these borrowed particles to 'early system morphemes' in the code-switching model of Myers-Scotton (1993; 2002; 2006). These typically have a discourse interactional function, such as determiners, and are often transferred from a source language into the matrix language in codeswitching. By contrast 'late system morphemes', such as agreement markers, which convey grammatical relationships between constituents are rarely transferred in code-switching.

With regard to the borrowed modal particle *bā-*, which is used in requests, a further dimension of discourse interaction may be politeness. It has been remarked by lingusts working on code-switching that the switch to another language by bilinguals can be used as a politeness strategy in requests. It acts to attenuate the direct-

---

[2] For the high susceptibility for borrowing of discourse interactional elements see Matras (2010, 80–81).

ness of a request and, therefore, does not impose such an immediate obligation on the hearer (Gardner-Chloros 2010, 200).

A further feature that we identified with regard to the borrowing of the definite suffix *-akē* (§4.5) is that JSNENA-speakers were exposed to various inflections of this particle in Gorani and the form that was chosen was the one that was used most frequently.

12.3.1.3 Loanblends

Another bound particle that has been borrowed by JSNENA from Iranian is the telicity particle *-o*, which is attached to a variety of native JSNENA verbal forms (§7.14). Unlike the other bound particles discussed above, the telicity particle is a lexical-level component. It appears to have entered JSNENA by a process of imitation of an Iranian verbal construction. This has resulted in what may be called a loanblend (cf. Winford 2003, 45 for this terminology), in which the Iranian telicity particle of the source construction has been retained but the lexical verbal form has been translated into a JSNENA form, e.g.

(1202) Gorani
kara=š=va
do.PRS.IMP.2SG=3SG=TELIC
'Open it!'

(1203) JSNENA
wul-lē-o
do.IMP.SG-OBL.3SG.M-TELIC
'Open it!'

Loanblends may, conversely, involve the transfer of the lexical core of a word from Iranian and the replacement of an Iranian affix by a corresponding native JSNENA affix. An example of this is the word for 'breast' in JSNENA, which consists of an Iranian loanword combined with an inherited Aramaic diminutive ending *-ona* replacing the Iranian diminutive affix *-ka* in the source word.

(1204)   JSNENA   Gorani/Kurdish
         breast   *mam-ona*   G./K. *mam-ka*

The phenomenon of loanblends can be identified in various phrasal constructions. These include light verb constructions, in which the non-verbal element is retained from Iranian and the light verb is translated into JSNENA, e.g.

(1205)   JSNENA   Kurdish
'to observe'   tamāša '-w-l   tamāšā kərdən

As with the telicity constructions, it is the verbal form that is the native JSNENA component of the blend.

Some examples of loanblends with non-verbal elements are as follows, e.g.

(1206)   JSNENA   Iranian
       grandfather (lit. big father)   tāta ruwa   G. tāta gawrē; K. bāwa gawra
       water tap   šērē māē   P. šir-e āb; K. šēr āw
       pregnant   trē gyānē   G. dəva gīyāna; K. dū gīyān
       how?'   ma-jor   Persian če-jur
       with   mən-tak=e   K. la-tak

Some cases of loanblends replace historical NENA lexemes with the same meaning. Many of them, however, result in an enrichment of the lexicon. This may be by supplying an expression for which historical NENA had no equivalent.

Another form of enrichment is the formal distinction between different meanings of a polysemous word. An example of the latter is the preposition *mən-tak=ē* (§4.15.9). The motivation for the formation of this hybrid preposition in JSNENA is that the NENA preposition *mən* in most NENA dialects is polysemous, meaning both 'from' and 'with'. JSNENA has replicated the pattern and part of the material of a form in the Iranian contact language that unambiguously means 'with' (*la-tak*) to make a morphological distinction between the two meanings.

12.3.1.4 Hybrid loanwords

A different type of blending of JSNENA and Iranian elements is where the JSNENA construction is not a replication of an Iranian model with substitution of one the components but rather JSNENA combines an Iranian element with a JSNENA element that corresponds to the Iranian element.

This is the case with the JSNENA preposition *bāqa* 'to' (§4.15.2). The JSNENA element in the word historically had a broader meaning than the Iranian element: *qa(m)* 'to, before'. The addition of the Iranian element that corresponded to only part of this range of meanings (*ba-* 'to') restricted the JSNENA element to this narrower meaning. This type of hybrid blend, therefore, had the function of lexical enrichment.

Another case of hybrid blend is the JSNENA interrogative and exclamatory particle *čəkma* 'how much?/!' This appears to be a fusion of Gorani *čən* + native Aramaic *kma* 'how much' (*čən-kma* > *čəkma*). So the native particle *kma* has not been replaced by a loanword but rather enhanced by fusion with it. The motivation in this case may have been related to the emotional subjective sense of the particle in exclamatory contexts. The native particle had its salience enhanced by bonding together NENA and Iranian.

12.3.1.5 Phonetic matching

A phenomenon that is associated with matter borrowing is the process where an innovative form in JSNENA develops by a matching of the phonetic form of a JSNENA word with that of an Iranian model.

In some cases the morphological material has a native NENA etymology and this is reshaped to correspond more closely to the Iranian model. Some possible cases of this were discussed in the section on the morphology of pronouns (§3.3).

In other cases the phonetic matching takes place by the borrowing by JSNENA of an Iranian form that has the same or similar phonetic shape as the native NENA form. JSNENA, for example, has borrowed the Iranian preposition *bayn* 'between', which replaces the phonetically similar native form *bēn* (§4.15.3). Likewise JSNENA has borrowed the Iranian preposition *ba-* 'in', which is used alongside the native NENA preposition *b-* of similar phonetic shape (§4.15.1).

Some of the derivational affixes of JSNENA are phonetically similar to Iranian derivational affixes with a related function. It is possible that the Iranian affixes have reinforced the use of the JSNENA affixes. The process would have involved the reinforcement of the choice of one particular derivational strategy in JSNENA rather than possible alternatives due to matching of one particular affix with an Iranian affix. An example of this is the JSNENA active participle affix *-āna*, which matches in function and form with the Iranian affix *-ana* (§4.3).

It is relevant to note that in bilingual mixed languages a hierarchy of morphological structural borrowing can be identified. According to Matras (2003), in such cases the first layer consists of structural elements such as derivational affixes, which have come into the borrowing language with loanwords. A second layer includes free structural elements such as personal pronouns and deictics. The examples of phonetic reshaping in JSNENA described above include mainly these categories.

12.3.1.6 Borrowed phonemes

Several consonants have been borrowed by the JSNENA phonological system from the Iranian languages, mostly in loanwords. These include /č/ [tʃʰ], /f/ [f], /j/ [dʒ], /ř/ (trilled rhotic), /ž/ [ʒ], and /ġ/ [ʁ]. These are only marginal phonemes in JSNENA (§2.2.1). It is noteworthy, however, that some of these consonants have developed through sound shifts in native JSNENA words. This applies, for example, to the affricate /č/ (§2.2.2.9). The process can be compared to that of phonetic matching described above. In the case of /č/, this developed in particular from historically pharyngealised sibilants in native JSNENA words, which were matched perceptually with the Iranian /č/ with its strong onset.

12.3.2 Pattern replication

This process involves the replication by JSNENA of patterns in the Iranian source language(s) without the borrowing of Iranian material.

12.3.2.1 Phonology

The phonological system of JSNENA has extensively replicated those of the contact Iranian languages by matching JSNENA phonemes with Iranian phonemes and adopting the patterns of distribution of the Iranian phonemes (see chapter 2). This has resulted in innovative developments in the distribution of native NENA phonemes. In some cases native NENA phonemes have been lost if they do not appear in the matching Iranian system, e.g. the original interdental consonants of NENA (§2.2.2.7). In other cases an innovative phonemic distinction developing within NENA has been reinforced by matching with a parallel distinction in the Iranian phonological system, e.g. the case of /ṛ/ vs /r/ (§2.2.2.4).

The quality and pattern of distribution of the JSNENA vowels in the vowel space replicate those of the Iranian languages in contact (§2.3).

JSNENA also extensively replicates Iranian patterns of prosody (§2.4). The position of the stress in JSNENA matches in most cases that of Iranian in the corresponding grammatical forms. In such cases there is generally a historical explanation for the position of the stress in Iranian but not in JSNENA. The JSNENA co-ordinating particle ū replicates the prosody of the corresponding Iranian particle as an enclitic, which differs from historical Aramaic, in which the particle was a proclitic (§9.2.2).[3]

12.3.2.2 Morphosyntax

JSNENA has replicated many Iranian morphosyntactic patterns. As remarked above (§12.2.1), the source language of the majority of these patterns is Gorani rather than Kurdish. A significant feature of many cases of such morphosyntactic pattern replication is that the process results only in partial convergence rather than complete

---

[3] For the phenomenon of prosody matching of replicated structures see Salmons (1992) and Hickey (2010a, 158).

replication. These constraints in replication are due to various factors, including blocking factors internal to the morphosyntactic system of JSNENA, preference for matching of discrete words rather than bound morphemes, imperfect matching of elements, and the overlay of later Kurdish influence. There is a greater tendency, moreover, for morphosyntactic pattern matching to occur in certain grammatical categories than others. In what follows we shall focus on some selected cases of such partial or skewed convergence and examine the factors involved.

12.3.2.3 Impact of internal exponence of JSNENA

In JSNENA there has been an innovative development of different past stems and resultative participles for transitive agentive verbs, on the one hand, and intransitive unaccusative or passive verbs on the other (§5.2). This has come about through convergence with the morphological patterns of the verbal categories of Gorani. In Gorani the morphological marking of distinctions in transitivity has not been fully systematised and they occur only in a subset of lexical verbs. In JSNENA, on the other hand, the morphological distinctions are systematic. This difference in distribution has arisen from the differences in morphological exponence. In Gorani the morphology in question consists of agglutinative derivative affixes. The corresponding morphological exponents in JSNENA, however, are non-concatenative vocalic patterns that are integrated with non-concatenative verbal roots. This different morphological exponence in JSNENA has conditioned a different degree of distribution of the Iranian pattern, viz. a systematisation to all lexical verbs. Such a situation reflects the replication of an external grammatical category but not the exponence, i.e. manner of expression, of the category in the external language.[4] Rather, the internal JSNENA exponence is maintained.

JSNENA has generally replicated the patterns of distinct subject inflection for transitive and intransitive verbs in past constructions with the past stem and perfect constructions with the resultative participle. This is an innovation in JSNENA in relation to the main body of NENA, in which both transitive and intransitive past verbs and perfects have the same subject inflection (L-suffixes for past stems and copulas agreeing with the subject in perfects). One exception in JSNENA is the inflection of the intransitive past copula, which continues to index the subject with L-suffixes (§5.8.2). The explanation appears to be that elimination of the L-suffixes from this paradigm would have made it identical to that of the present copula. Replication of the Iranian pattern, therefore, is blocked in this paradigm in JSNENA to maintain semantic distinctions.

---

4 For this phenomenon in language contact, see Hickey (2010b, 11; 2010a, 154).

The JSNENA perfect constructions with the resultative participle and copula have developed on the model of the morphosyntactic patterns of Gorani (§5.11.1). The replication of the Gorani patterns, however, are only partial. In the transitive indicative present perfect, for example, JSNENA does not have an oblique subject index corresponding to the oblique subject clitics of Gorani. The cause of the lack of correspondence in subject indexing is internal to JSNENA. The use of oblique L-suffixes to mark the subject would have created an inflection identical to the past copula, thus confusing the construction with a past perfect. In order to avoid this ambiguity, the use of the L-suffix subject index has been blocked. This has had the consequence of restricting the transitive perfect construction based on resultative participles to 3rd person subjects. Zero-marking of 3rd person subjects is tolerated but not of 1st and 2nd person subjects. This, therefore, has resulted in a further difference from the Iranian model, which uses the transitive perfect with subjects of all persons.

Another way in which the internal system of JSNENA can bring about a less than exact replication of Iranian patterns is the process whereby a feature that has been copied from Iranian takes on a life of its own within JSNENA. An example of this is the fact that JSNENA and other Jewish NENA dialects have replicated the general principles of the encoding of transitivity from Iranian but have applied them internally in different ways across the verbal lexicon. As a result variation has arisen in the verbal lexicon of the NENA dialects regarding the distribution of transitivity encoding that does not match any corresponding variation in Iranian (§7.11).

Another example of this phenomenon is the process of replication by JSNENA of Gorani patterns of differential object marking. In Gorani an object of a present-stem verb is in the oblique case when it is human or it is non-human but has the definite article suffix *-aka* or alternatively when the nominal is definite but is not marked with *-aka*. This oblique marking of the object is replicated in JSNENA by the oblique marking prefixed particle *hǝl-*. In JSNENA, however, only human objects have this oblique marking (§7.15.1.2). This can be regarded as another example of how JSNENA has replicated the general principle of an Iranian morphosyntactic pattern, but has applied a slightly different distribution of this feature internally.

12.3.2.4 Impact of Preference for Matching a Discrete Word

JSNENA exhibits a preference to replicate the morphosyntax of unbound words rather than bound elements. The replication of the pattern of a bound element is sometimes avoided and as a result the use of a related unbound element is extended within JSNENA. Examples of this are as follows.

JSNENA has replicated morphosyntactic patterns of Iranian demonstrative pronouns (§6.4). The Iranian pronouns occur as independent forms or, when used adnominally, as discontinuous forms with a preposed element before the noun and a postposed element after it. JSNENA replicated the patterns only of the independent forms. Evidently, matching with a single discrete word was easier than matching with a complex discontinuous morpheme. This resulted in a partial convergence with the Iranian morphosyntactic patterns of demonstratives.

JSNENA has replicated the use of the morphosyntactic pattern of the invariable Kurdish adjectival form *tər* 'other' by the invariable form *xēt*. When in Kurdish *tər* is used adverbially, it has an augment, resulting in the form *ītər*. JSNENA has not replicated this bound augment prefix but has rather extended the meaning of the form *xēt* to include the meaning of *ītər* (§6.7.4.3). This is a case, therefore, of a preference being given to extension of meaning of unbound inherited elements in JSNENA over the replication of bound elements in the model Iranian language.

A further example is seen in the replication by JSNENA of the pattern of Iranian indefinite markers. In Iranian, indefinite nouns are marked either by suffixed indefinite markers (Kurdish *-ē(k)*, Gorani *-ēw*). The unbound cardinal numeral *yak* 'one' is used as an indefinite marker in Kurdish only in restricted contexts to express discourse saliency. JSNENA replicates the pattern of distribution of both the bound indefinite suffixes and the unbound *yak* by the unbound JSNENA cardinal *xa* (§6.2). Structurally JSNENA *xa* corresponds to the Kurdish independent cardinal numeral *yak* rather than the suffix *-ē(k)*. It does not, however, become a bound suffix like *-ē(k)*. This indicates that the extension of the function of an inherited non-bound construction is preferred over the replication of the pattern of a non-bound element in Iranian.

12.3.2.5 Impact of imperfect matching

Another type of partial replication is seen in the JSNENA progressive construction *k-xolē k-ǝx-na* 'I am eating' (§5.5). This replicates the pattern of a progressive construction in Gorani in which an inflected realis form is preceded by a form composed of the present stem and the ending *-āy*. This is not the same form as the infinitive, but its ending resembles that of infinitives, which end in *-āy* or *-ay*. This can be identified, therefore, as a case of imperfect matching, in that the Iranian form has been matched with the inherited JSNENA infinitive in the progressive construction. This is similar to the process in contact phonology described by Blevins (2017) as the 'perceptual magnet effect', whereby speakers of a language match a sound in their L1 with a sound that is perceived to be similar, even if not objectively identical.

12.3.2.6 Impact of a later overlay of Kurdish

JSNENA matches the Gorani pattern of expression of pronominal objects ergatively by direct suffixes on past stem verbs. The Kurdish of the region does not express objects ergatively. In JSNENA, however, the replication of the Gorani pattern is not complete, since the expression of the object by the direct suffixes is restricted to the third person (§5.10.3). In this case the restriction of the replication is likely to have had an external factor, namely the impact of Kurdish overlaying the Gorani pattern. As remarked, ergativity has decayed in the Kurdish of the region. This has resulted in partial decay in JSNENA with the marking of the 1st and 2nd person objects by direct suffixes being eliminated. Another factor in this process, impacting on both Kurdish and JSNENA, may have been the greater markedness, i.e. difficulty of learning, of 1st and 2nd person objects expressed by direct suffixes (Khan 2017, 880; Thomason 2010, 43)

12.3.2.7 Impact of grammatical category

Verbs vs Nouns

In general, our study has shown that there is greater convergence of JSNENA with Iranian in verbal morphosyntax than in nominal morphosyntax. There has been convergence of the core inflectional patterns of the verbal stems of JSNENA and NENA as a whole with those of Iranian verbs, which has brought about a major restructuring of the historical Aramaic verbal system. The nominal morphosyntax of JSNENA has not undergone such major restructuring. This is seen, for example, in the different degrees of convergence of the morphosyntax of person indexes on verbs and nouns. JSNENA replicates the pattern of Iranian oblique clitic pronouns only in their function of verbal arguments. It retains the inherited possessive pronominal suffixes on nouns and prepositions (§3.5). A further reflection of lack convergence of nominal morphosyntax in JSNENA and Iranian is the lack of convergence of gender assignment of JSNENA and Gorani nouns (§4.2.1). JSNENA has retained the historical gender of nouns or has undergone change through internal processes rather than through replication of the gender of Gorani nouns of a corresponding meaning. This is in line with typological findings that systems of gender assignment are stable, and thus resistant to borrowing (Wichmann and Holman 2009).

Realis vs Irrealis

The various verbal forms that are derived from present stems include those that express realis and those that express irrealis. Our study has shown that the replication by JSNENA of the function and distribution of Iranian realis verbal forms is greater than it is of Iranian irrealis verbal forms (§7.17). There are several cases where the distribution of irrealis verbal forms in JSNENA and Iranian do not match.

12.3.2.8 Calques

Pattern replication includes also calques, i.e. loan translations, of various kinds. This may involve replication of idiomatic phrases, e.g.

(1207) JSNENA Iranian
 eyelid (lit. back of eye) xāṣa 'ēna K. pəšt čāw, G. pəštū čamī, pēḷūē
 baby (lit. small child) yāla zora G. zaroḷa wərda; K. mənāḷa wərda
 you are able (lit. it comes to you) k-ē-lox K. lē=t tē

Another form of calque is the extension of the meaning of a single JSNENA word in imitation of the meaning and pattern of distribution of a corresponding Iranian word. The word *rēša* in Aramaic, for example, originally meant 'head'. The corresponding Gorani word is *sar*, which can mean 'head' or be used adverbially in the sense of 'upon'. In JSNENA the word *rēša* has now acquired the additional meaning of a preposition denoting 'upon' by replication of the pattern of distribution of *sar*. This is a clear case of grammaticalisation induced by contact.[5]

Entire idiomatic clauses may be calqued (§11.1.3), e.g.

(1208) JSNENA: *ba-rēš-ox dīya=y?* 'Are you mad?' (lit. Has it hit your head?)
 Persian: *zad-e be-sar=et?*

12.3.2.9 Replication of syntactic and discourse patterns

The syntax of the clause in JSNENA has converged to a large degree with the Iranian languages of the Sanandaj region. In the case of word order, the closest statistical match is with the word order patterns of Gorani. For instance, direct object arguments occur with the same frequency of occurrence in the preverbal position (cf. §8.4.1).

JSNENA clearly exhibits convergence with the Iranian languages in the way larger units than the clause are structured. This includes strategies of clause coordination and discourse cohesion (chapter 9).

As remarked above (§12.2.3), JSNENA has replicated Standard Persian syndetic patterns of subordination rather than those of Gorani and Kurdish. This has involved the borrowing of many Persian subordinating particles. It is notable, however, that JSNENA replicates Kurdish and Gorani patterns, rather than Persian, when asyndetic strategies are used for the subordination of clauses.

---

[5] Language contact often brings about grammaticalisation. See, in particular, Heine and Kuteva (2003; 2005).

12.4 Metatypy and communal identity

We have seen that JSNENA has undergone extensive influence from the Iranian languages of the region. This has resulted in the replication of Iranian patterns in much of the morpho-syntax and syntax, the convergence of the phonological system with Iranian and the incorporation of numerous Iranian loanwords. Such massive change has resulted in a shift in typology of JSNENA, or metatypy, to use a term coined by Ross (1996; 2001; 2003). JSNENA and other closely related Jewish NENA dialects of the surrounding region can be said to have acquired their distinctness or 'speciation' (according to the terminology of Mufwene 2001; 2007) through language contact. This shift in typological profile has replaced many of the typological features of historical Aramaic. Some historical distinctions were lost, if there was not a corresponding distinction in Iranian, e.g. the loss of gender in third person singular pronouns (§3.2). JSNENA has, however, also been enriched with a variety of innovative features and distinctions that did not exist in earlier Aramaic but existed in Iranian, such as the indirective (evidential) use of the perfect (§7.9.2). This reflects the fact that language contact can bring about both simplification and complexification (Trudgill 2010, 306; 2011).

The Semitic heritage of JSNENA is, nevertheless, preserved in the morphology and the inherited elements of the lexicon. This retained inventory of inherited morphemes and lexemes is sufficient to make JSNENA an emblem of community identity (cf. Matras 2010, 76).

The vast number of Iranian loanwords in JSNENA indicates there was no attempt at lexical exclusion. This could be regarded as a reflection of the rapprochement of the community identity of the Jews with that of the surrounding Iranian communities or even a mixed identity. A relevant comparison is with Alsatian–French bilinguals in Strasbourg who perceive language mixing and code-switching as a reflection of their community identity and so are more tolerant of borrowing. The speakers of French and Dutch in Brussels, on the other hand, mix their languages much less, since they perceive themselves as distinct communities (Treffers-Daller 1994; 1999). Another case is the mixed language of the second-generation Portuguese in France, know as *immigrais*, which is regarded by young members of the immigrant community as an emblem of their mixed identity (Gardner-Chloros 2010, 193).

Several cases have been documented of a community consciously excluding loanwords from a language in contact for the sake of maintaining a distinct community identity. It was suggested in Khan (2020a, 389) that the absence of Armenian loanwords in the Christian NENA dialect of the Urmi region despite the close contact between NENA and Armenian speakers may have been motivated by a desire to keep a clearly distinct identity. A similar phenomenon of conscious lexical exclusion in Amazonia has been identified by Epps and Stenzel (2013, 36), Floyd (2013) and Aikhenvald (2003).

The contrast between the lexical exclusion of Armenian loanwords in NENA and the incorporation of numerous Iranian loanwords in Sanandaj may have related to the different relationships between the various community identities involved. The Armenian Christians in the Urmi region and the NENA-speaking Christians shared the same religion. Many Armenians, moreover, married NENA-speaking Christians. There would have been a particular need, therefore, to preserve NENA group identity in such a situation of intimate social connection and cultural homogeneity between the two groups, in which the boundaries between group identities were particularly under threat. In the Sanandaj region, however, there was a clear group demarcation between the Jews and their Muslim Iranian-speaking neighbours in their distinct religions. This religious distinction meant that the boundaries between the two groups was not under threat and there was a lesser need to mark communal distinctions by lexical exclusion or indeed the avoidance of eventual language shift. The effect of language contact, therefore, is more closely tied to social ideologies and perception of identity than the nature of the contact itself (cf. Hazen 2000, 126; Fought 2010, 285).

12.5 Theoretical models of language contact

In this section, we shall examine the sociolinguistic and psychological processes by which the deep influence of Iranian on JSNENA may have taken place.

In the theoretical literature on language contact it is generally recognised that there are two main processes of linguistic influence. One of these has been termed 'borrowing' and the other is generally termed 'interference' or 'imposition' (Thomason and Kaufman 1988, 37; Van Coetsem 1988; 1995; 2000; Winford 2005; 2010). In what follows we shall use the term 'imposition', proposed by Van Coetsem, rather than 'interference' for the second process.

Borrowing is the incorporation by the recipient language (RL) of features from the source language (SL) typically without further changes to the RL beyond these incorporated features. This process involves primarily the acquisition by the RL of vocabulary from the SL without any impact on the structure of syntax or the system of phonology. Imposition, on the other hand, primarily involves the transfer of syntactic patterns and phonological features from the SL to the RL and not vocabulary.[6] The distinction between borrowing and imposition is based, crucially, on which of the languages spoken by a bilingual speaker is the linguistically dominant one. This is the language in which the speaker is most proficient and most fluent, though not necessarily the native language of the speaker (Van Coetsem 1995, 70). Linguistic dominance should be distinguished from social dominance, which refers to the social or political status of a language. The agency of the influence is rooted in the knowledge by the speaker of the linguistically dominant language. When the process involves borrowing by the RL, the RL is the linguistically dominant language and features of the SL are imported into the RL by the agency of the RL. When the process involves imposition, the SL is the linguistically dominant language and features are transferred to the RL by the agency of the SL.

One common situation in which imposition occurs is where there is a language shift by speakers and speakers of the language that is for them linguistically dominant (i.e. the SL) acquire through imperfect learning a second language (i.e. the RL), which is less dominant. The dominant SL in such situations is termed the substrate language and the less dominant RL the superstrate language. In the process of this imperfect learning syntactic structures and the phonological system of the dominant SL are typically imposed by speakers on the acquired language, without necessarily a transfer of vocabulary from the SL.

This is not, however, the only situation in which imposition may occur. Imposition may occur through the agency of a linguistically dominant language in a bilingual situation where this dominant language is not a substrate in a language shift to a less dominant language. This is typically the case where the RL is a maintained ancestral language of a small community and the dominant SL that has the agentivity is an external language of the wider society that exerts cultural pressure on the smaller community.[7] There is a sharing of patterns across the languages in contact. In such cases of imposition it has, indeed, been claimed that bilingual speakers organize their communication in both languages in a single linguistic system (Matras 2010). Such a situation lies behind the development of a linguistic area (*Sprachbund*), in which two or more languages have become structurally similar, as is the case with the languages in the Balkans (Joseph 1983; 2010) and the Indo-Ar-

---

[6] Ross (1996; 2001) coined the term 'metatypy' to describe such a process in Melanesian languages whereby organisational structures are transferred but not concrete words. According to Ross, a factor bearing on this process is that social attitudes disfavour the replication of concrete word forms whose origin in another language is easily identifiable.

[7] For examples of this see especially Winford (2005). Another example is the Dutch community of Iowa where English was the linguistically dominant language while Dutch was still maintained (Smits 1998).

yan and Dravidian languages in India (Emeneau 1956; 1980). Ross (2003, 183) points out that that in almost all case studies of linguistic areas there is a one-sided process whereby one language, in our terms the RL, adopts the structures of another, in our terms the SL. This, therefore, is imposition through SL-agentivity. Imposition and the development of linguistic areas are facilitated by open and flexible attitudes toward community boundaries and identity (Matras 2010, 72).

We have seen in our study that JSNENA has acquired a wide range of syntactic and morphosyntactic patterns from Iranian, and also acquired the phonological system of Iranian. Within the model described above, this should be regarded as the result of the imposition of features from the Iranian SL, which is linguistically dominant in the bilingual speech situation, onto JSNENA, which is less dominant. There is no evidence, however, that the Jews of Sanandaj were in a process of language shift from Iranian to JSNENA in the 20th century before the community dispersed to a diaspora outside Iran.

Rather, there is evidence that the Jews of the region were in a process of language shift from NENA to Iranian. Evidence for this is the fact that in several villages in the Sanandaj region in the 20th century the Jews spoke only Kurdish. It is likely that the ancestors of these Jews originally spoke some form of NENA, especially since the Jews of the region seem to have migrated to Iran from Iraq. Other possible evidence of a language shift from NENA to Iranian is constituted by some structures of Gorani that resemble NENA structures (see §12.1.2 above) and may have arisen by imposition of NENA syntactic patterns on Gorani through language shift from NENA to Gorani at an earlier historical period.[8] Indeed, language shift is a common outcome of asymmetrical bilingualism cross-linguistically where an external language is dominant (Thomason 2001, 9; Romaine 2010, 320).

The JSNENA-speakers who were the informants for Khan's description of the dialect acquired JSNENA as a native language at home. From an early age, however, they became bilingual in Kurdish. There were Kurdish-speaking servants in most Jewish homes with whom young children communicated. The bilingualism appears, therefore, to have been native, or near-native. JSNENA-speakers, therefore, would have acquired Kurdish long before the 'critical threshold' of age for perfect language acquisition (Lenneberg 1967; Labov 1972; Trudgill 2010, 310). Children used Kurdish to communicate with their Kurdish neighbours when playing with them. As adults, JSNENA-speakers, in particular the men, used only Kurdish in their professional and social interactions with Kurds throughout the day. This, no doubt, resulted in

---

[8] Several cases of grammatical replication proceeding in both directions when two languages are in contact have been documented in the literature, see, e.g., Heine and Kuteva (2010, 100–101). The sociolinguistic model as to how such a situation takes place is not, however, always clarified.

the linguistic dominance of Kurdish in at least the adult men of the Jewish community. JSNENA was spoken by Jewish adults, at least the men, as a maintained heritage language and the linguistically dominant Iranian language had the agency of change. This resulted in the imposition of syntactic and phonological features on JSNENA. If the process began with adult men, it would have quickly spread to other speakers through the close-knit social networks of the Jewish community.[9] The trajectory of this situation of imposition on the RL by the agentivity of the SL in a bilingual would have been towards the loss of the maintained RL language, which, as remarked, appears to have happened in some Jewish communities in the region. This linguistic dominance of Kurdish is likely to have come about by intense contact and cultural pressure, enhanced by the cordial relationship between Jews and Muslims in Sanandaj, which no doubt boosted a positive attitude towards Kurdish.[10]

A complicating issue with regard to this proposed model is the presence of a large number of Iranian loanwords in JSNENA. As remarked, loanwords are typically transferred to a RL through a process of borrowing in which the RL is the linguistically dominant language. Loanwords are not expected in a process of imposition through the agency of a linguistically dominant SL. One way of explaining this may be to regard all Iranian features in JSNENA to have been transferred by a process of borrowing through RL agency. It would have to be assumed that due to the proficiency of the JSNENA-speakers in Iranian, the borrowing process went beyond the transfer of vocabulary and included also syntax and phonology. An analogous case of an ancestral language undergoing extensive influence in lexicon and grammatical structure from a politically dominant external language that has been studied in the literature is Asia Minor Greek (Dawkins 1916). Thomason and Kaufman (1988, 45, 215) regard this to be a case of borrowing by the Greek dialects, which was so intense that it included all levels of language. Winford (2005, 402–9; 2010, 181), on the other hand, argues that such a wholesale transfer of features must have taken place through the process of imposition by Turkish-dominant bilinguals, i.e. by SL agentivity. This would explain, he argues, why the lexical loans include many items of basic vocabulary, which is 'not normally associated with borrowing alone'. Winford (2005, 408), nevertheless, contends that the process that brought about the changes in Asia Minor Greek involved both types of agentivity with Greek-dominant bilinguals implementing RL agentivity, and Turkish-dominant bilinguals implementing SL agentivity. He apparently means that much of

---

[9] For the role of close-knit social networks in the spread of linguistic innovations see e.g. Milroy (1987).
[10] See Thomason (2010, 38–39) and Matras (2010, 72) for the way speakers' attitudes facilitate or block contact-induced change.

the lexical borrowing resulted from RL agentivity, though he does not state this explicitly.

The situation of JSNENA is similar to Asia Minor Greek in that speakers have historically gradually lost competence in their ancestral language as they become linguistically dominant in a language they have acquired later. As remarked above, this is an incipient language shift to the external language, i.e. Iranian in the case of JSNENA and Turkish in the case of Asia Minor Greek. Indeed many of the Greek-speaking villages shifted completely to Turkish and, as remarked above, there is evidence of a complete shift of some NENA-speaking communities in western Iran to Iranian.

If we apply Winford's model for Asian Minor Greek to JSNENA, we would have to assume that the process that brought about the contact-induced changes in JSNENA involved both NENA-dominant bilinguals implementing RL agentivity, and Iranian-dominant bilinguals implementing SL agentivity. This would mean, in effect, that there was a fine balance and tension between the dominance of the two languages. Such a scenario could perhaps have arisen in a situation in which some components of the community (e.g. women and children) were dominant in NENA and other components (e.g. adult men) were dominant in Iranian.

A possible alternative model would be to take a diachronic perspective. It is significant that the majority of Iranian loanwords in JSNENA are from Gorani rather than Kurdish. This would mean that most of the lexical borrowing took place at an earlier historical period, before the shift to Kurdish in the population of the region at the end of the nineteenth century. If the NENA dialects of the region were on a trajectory of language shift to Iranian, this would have involved a shift in dominance in the languages of bilinguals. It can be hypothesised that at an earlier period the bilingual NENA-speaking communities were NENA-dominant and this gave rise to the borrowing of vocabulary from Gorani. In some regions NENA-speakers appear to have remained NENA-dominant to modern times (see below). As we have discussed (§12.3.1.1), there is often a functional motivation for the borrowing of basic vocabulary in JSNENA, e.g. the expression of formality in the naming of senior members of the family or the association of words with emotion. This selection of loanwords for the sake of lexical enrichment would seem to be a feature of RL agentivity. At a later period, the linguistic dominance of NENA would have given ground to the dominance of Iranian. As a consequence imposition of Iranian features would have taken place through SL agentivity. As we have seen, many of the syntactic and morpho-syntactic patterns that were imposed on JSNENA were specifically those of Gorani, which suggests that this process of Iranian-dominant SL agentivity had begun while Gorani was still widely spoken in the region. A number of syntactic and morphosyntactic features of JSNENA, however, have been shown to have their origin in Kurdish rather than Gorani. This shows that the Iranian-dominant agentivity of imposition continued down to modern times. The borrowing of vocabulary from Kurdish through NENA-dominant agentivity does not seem to have so evident in this more recent period.

Unlike in a language shift situation, the dominance of a maintained heritage language by an external language in a bilingual situation also appears to have brought about an increase in the number of loanwords in the maintained language from the dominant language. Although the process of incorporating loanwords may have begun by borrowing through RL agentivity, when the dominance shifts to the external language in such bilingual situations the scale of the transfer of loanwords is likely to increase.

There are other possible scenarios in which imposition may have taken place on JSNENA.

Before the foundation of the town of Sanandaj, the Jews in the region lived in small villages. They may have had Gorani-speaking Muslim neighbours in the same village. In such small village communities it is possible that the Gorani-speakers learnt some of the NENA of their Jewish neighbours. We are aware of some cases in small village communities of speakers of an external language learning NENA. This has been observed by Khan, for example, in villages in Armenia where native speakers of Armenian learn NENA to communicate with their NENA-speaking neighbours. If the Gorani-speaking inhabitants in the villages learnt NENA, this is likely to have been imperfect learning, which would have resulted in the imposition of features from the linguistically dominant Gorani language. This could have resulted in the diffusion of Gorani syntactic and phonological features into NENA.

Another possible route for the imposition of Iranian features on JSNENA may have been through the migration of Iranian-speaking Jews from villages into Sanandaj. If these Jews learnt JSNENA, this, again, is likely to have been imperfectly and, therefore, be the vector of imposition of Iranian features on JSNENA. Indeed, there are reports that in the twentieth century Jews who spoke Kurdish rather than NENA in villages migrated to Sanandaj and learnt to speak JSNENA. These Jews are said to have spoken JSNENA with an 'accent', suggesting that they learnt the language imperfectly.

So, we see that although it is reasonably clear that there must have been imposition of Iranian features on JSNENA by the agentivity of a linguistically dominant Iranian SL, it is not possible to establish with complete certainty how this imposition took place. It is, in fact, possible that several of the vectors of imposition described above were operative on JSNENA at various stages of its development.

Finally, how does the incorporation in JSNENA of features from Persian fit into these models? It has been shown that some Iranian loanwords in JSNENA are from Persian (§11.2). Also several subordinating particles have been borrowed from Persian (§10).

Many of the Persian loanwords in JSNENA have undergone morphological and phonological adaptation to Kurdish, which suggests that they entered JSNENA through Kurdish. They do not belong to the basic vocabulary but are rather typically abstract nouns, objects and concepts relating to the modern world, government administration or the wider world. They, therefore, fill a lexical gap in JSNENA. It is likely, therefore, that they entered JSNENA through imposition by Kurdish-dominant agentivity. This differs from replacement of basic NENA vocabulary by Iranian loanwords, often for functional purposes, which happened at an earlier period and can be considered to have taken place by a process of borrowing through NENA-dominant agentivity.

The formation of subordinate syntactic constructions with Persian subordinating particles appears to involve a different process. Such constructions are replications of Standard Persian constructions learned by JSNENA-speakers at school. They are associated, therefore, with a high register of educated language. All of Khan's JSNENA-speaking informants attended Persian-speaking schools.

It is relevant to note that although JSNENA-speakers use Persian subordination particles, the subordinate constructions do not always replicate the exact structure of corresponding Persian syntactic constructions. This is seen, for example, in JSNENA relative clauses that use the Persian subordinating particle *kē* but do not replicate the Persian linking particle *-ī* on the head noun. It is possible, therefore, that the Persian subordinating particles entered JSNENA by a process of borrowing, whereby for JSNENA-speakers JSNENA was linguistically dominant vis-à-vis Persian. This would explain why words were borrowed, rather than structures.

An alternative explanation of the lack of full correspondence between the structure of JSNENA and Persian relative clauses is that the Persian linking particle *-ī* was not replicated because it was a bound element. The process could have been one of imposition of a syntactic structure from Persian, but there was a constraint on the replication of bound elements. This constraint on replication of bound elements has been observed in other areas of grammar (e.g. indefinite marking §6.2). The subordinate constructions with Persian particles in JSNENA reflect the replication of the high register of the literary Persian language. When JSNENA-speakers use asyndetic constructions, these follow the pattern of Kurdish and Gorani rather than Persian (§10.2.2 & §10.7.5 & §10.8.3) and can be regarded as belonging to a lower register of JSNENA speech. If the incorporation of Persian subordinating particles in JSNENA is the result of imposition on JSNENA from Persian, the latter must be assumed to have been linguistically dominant in high register speech. Khan's informants, however, must be assumed to be Kurdish-dominant, following the discussion above. This means that there would have been a complex dominance relationship between three languages in the speech of JSNENA-speakers in the twentieth century. There was the basic dominance of Kurdish and this was supplemented by the dominance of Persian for constructions associated with high register speech.

The NENA dialect spoken by the Christian community in Sanandaj differed radically from JSNENA. This book has not compared JSNENA systematically with Christian NENA of Sanandaj, mainly on account of the fact that the Christian dialect has still not been documented in any detail. Furthermore, due to the radical differences between the Jewish and Christian dialects, the Jews communicated with the Christians in Kurdish. This means that the Jewish NENA-speakers did not have contact with the Christian NENA dialect. The Christian NENA dialect, therefore, did not play a role in the language networks of the Jews and did not, as far as we can see, have any influence on JSNENA. It is worth drawing attention, however, to a distinction between JSNENA and the Christian NENA of Sanandaj with regard to the imposition of Iranian structures. It would appear from what is known of the Christian dialect that it has converged to a lesser extent with Iranian structures than JSNENA. This can be illustrated by a feature in the phonology and a feature in the morphosyntax.

In JSNENA, several words exhibit a non-etymological pharyngeal, which has developed by segmentalisation of flat resonance. The model for this process is found in the Iranian phonological system (see §2.2.2.5 for details). Such non-etymological pharyngeals do not occur in the Christian dialect, e.g.

(1209) **Non-Etymological Pharyngeals**

	Jewish Sanandaj	Christian Sanandaj	Historical flat resonance in Jewish Sanandaj
'town'	'aḥrá	'ásra	< *'aḥra < *'aθrā
'three'	təlḥá	ṭlása	<*tḷaha < *tlāθā
'day before yesterday'	lá-ḥmal	lá-təmal	< *lahəṃmaḷ < *lāθəmmal
'ears'	naḥāḷḗ	nasyásē	< *nahāḷē < *nāθāθā

In the inflection of past stems of verbs, JSNENA uses oblique subject indexes on transitive verbs and direct subject indexes on intransitive verbs. This matches the pattern of inflection of Iranian. The Christian NENA dialect, on the other hand, uses oblique indexes for both transitive and intransitive verbs, as is the case in the main body of NENA:

(1210) JSNENA
Transitive   grəš-lū   'they pulled'
             pull.PST-OBL.3PL
Intranstive qīm-ī   'they arose'
             rise.PST-DIR.3PL

(1211) Sanandaj Kurdish
Transitive   kēṣā=yān   'they pulled'
             pull.PST=OBL.3PL
Intranstive haḷ-sā-n   'they arose'
             pvb-rise.PST-3PL

(1212) Christian Sanandaj NENA
Transitive   grəš-lū   'they pulled'
             pull.PST-OBL.3PL
Intranstive qəm-lū   'they arose'
             rise.PST-OBL.3PL

These differences suggest that there was a difference in the balance of linguistic dominance of NENA and Iranian in the Jewish community from that of the Christian community. It would appear that Iranian was linguistically dominant in the Christian community. This is shown by the fact that the phonology has lost features that do not appear in Iranian, e.g. the interdentals *θ and *ð, which are realised as /s/ and /d/ respectively. Moreover the language has replicated many Iranian syntactic structures, such as clause-final word order. There has been, therefore, an imposition of Iranian patterns on Christian NENA of Sanandaj. The degree of the linguistic dominance and the extent of the imposition, however, appears to have been less than is the case with JSNENA. This suggests that linguistic dominance is scalar.

The greater linguistic dominance of Iranian in the Jewish community of Sanandaj than in the Christian community is likely to have a sociolinguistic explanation. As stated above (§12.4), the effect of language contact is more closely tied to social ideologies and perception of identity than the nature of the contact itself. One could see this, therefore, as a reflection of a greater rapprochement between the communal identity of the Jews and that of the Muslim Iranians than was the case between identities of the Christian community and the Muslim Iranians. Using the terminology of Hazen (2000), it could be said that the Jews had a more 'expanded identity' than the Christians.

When investigating the various possible models of processes of contact-induced change that took place in JSNENA, it is helpful to take into account how these models can be applied to the development of the NENA dialect group as a whole.

In modern times, NENA dialects that are still spoken in Iraq and Iran are in contact with a variety of external languages. In the main body of NENA various dialects of Kurdish constitute the main contact language. In the region of the Mosul plain, the main contact language is Arabic. In the Urmi region of north-western Iran the main contact languages are Azeri Turkish and Persian. This is reflected in loanwords from these various external languages in the dialects in these respective regions. The phonological systems of many NENA dialects exhibit adaptations to match the phonological systems of the contact languages. The morphosyntax and syntax of the NENA dialects also include various imitations of patterns found in contact languages.

It is a complex task to attempt to apply the model of borrowing and imposition to the various dialects of the NENA group. One complicating factor is that the external contact languages have changed diachronically. Also the relative dominance of the external languages has changed diachronically. Moreover, there appear to have been various historical layers of language shift. In the Urmi region, for example, the main contact vernacular language is now Azeri Turkish and this is reflected by the presence of hundreds of Azeri loanwords in the NENA dialects of the region. Embedded in these dialects, however, one may find an earlier layer of Kurdish loanwords, which have been fully adapted to NENA morphology (Khan 2016, vol. 1, 1–2). Nowadays speakers of NENA in the Urmi region have little contact with Kurdish, but the Kurdish loanwords suggests that Kurdish was a major contact language at an earlier period. The same applies to the dialects of the Mosul plain, such as Ch. Qaraqosh, which contains various Kurdish loanwords, but in modern times the main contact language of NENA-speakers of Qaraqosh has been Arabic. In some cases in modern times there was only limited bilingualism. Many NENA-speakers in the remote mountain villages of the Ṭyare region, for example, did not speak the Kurdish of the Muslims of the region.[11]

The verbal system of all NENA dialects reflects a radical restructuring of the verbal system of historical Aramaic by imitation of the patterns of the Iranian verbal system. As discussed in §5.2, this involved the loss of the historical Aramaic finite verbal forms and their replacement with participles. A similar radical restructuring of the verbal system took place in the neighbouring Ṭuroyo group of Neo-Aramaic dialects west of the Tigris. Such a thoroughgoing transfer of morphosyntactic patterns is the kind of change that would be expected to have taken place through imposition rather than borrowing. Since this is a feature of all NENA dialects, although there are variations in the details across the dialects, and is also a feature of Ṭuroyo, it must be an ancient development.

As remarked, this radical change must have occurred through imposition by Iranian-dominant bilinguals. This could have arisen in a language situation such as the one we have described in Sanandaj, where an ancestral NENA dialect had ceded linguistic dominance to Iranian. As we have seen, in such a situation the NENA-speaking community would have been on a trajectory of language shift to

---

[11] The authors are grateful to Hezy Mutzafi and Shabo Talay for clarifying the language situation of the NENA-speakers in the Ṭyare region in modern times.

Iranian. There is, indeed, some evidence that NENA-speaking communities shifted to Iranian. Some of the Jewish communities in mountain villages in Iraq and Turkey spoke only Kurdish in modern times. Counterevidence to this model, however, is that the NENA dialects have survived and have remained robustly vital for many centuries and do not appear to have been on an inexorable trajectory to language shift to Iranian. Indeed some dialects in modern times, such as those of the Urmi region and the Mosul plain, are not in intense contact with Iranian. Moreover some dialects in remote mountain villages, such as those in the Upper and Lower Ṭyare regions, appear to have had only limited contact with Kurdish.

Another model for explaining the radical restructuring of the NENA and Ṭuroyo verbal system is that there was a language shift of Iranian-speaking communities to Aramaic some time in antiquity when Aramaic was widely spoken in the Middle East. The Iranian morphosyntactic patterns would, therefore, have entered Aramaic by imperfect learning by Iranian-dominant speakers, i.e. by a process of imposition. In such a situation, Iranian would have been a substrate language. The shift must have been from some kind of Middle Iranian, in which the syntactic patterns of the verbal system that are parallel with NENA had developed. It is likely that speakers of also other languages shifted to Aramaic at some point in the past and left their mark on NENA. This applies, for example, to Armenian. There are some clear parallels in structure between the present verbal forms of Eastern Armenian and Western Armenian and NENA present forms, i.e. the use of locative constructions for the present in Eastern Armenian and the use of preverbal particles, in some cases with a *k-* element, in Western Armenian (Khan 2018a, 39–40). Such forms are innovations in NENA in comparison with historical Aramaic and are likely to have entered NENA by Armenian-speakers shifting to Aramaic. Unlike the basic re-organisation of the NENA verbal system into a system based on participles, which is general to NENA, the introduction of these Armenian patterns differs across the various geographical areas of NENA. This suggests that the shift from Armenian is likely to have taken place at an earlier period.

It is significant that NENA dialects contain relatively few loanwords that can be identified as coming from Middle Iranian or earlier. The vast majority of Iranian loanwords are from local Kurdish or Gorani dialects from a later period. Likewise there are few Armenian loanwords in NENA dialects. This lack of loanwords would be expected in a situation of language shift.

At some point after these language shifts to Aramaic, the Aramaic language gradually became less widely spoken in the region. This certainly would have been the case after the rise of Islam and the spread of Arabic. The ancestor dialects of NENA survived in the Christian and Jewish minority groups mainly, it seems, since they came to be an emblem of their distinct cultural identity. These NENA dialects were initially the linguistically dominant language of their speakers and contact with external local languages resulted in borrowing of loanwords. In some communities the linguistic dominance of the NENA dialects continued down to modern times. This applies, for example, to the Ṭyare dialects. The speakers of these dialects in the isolated mountain villages had only limited contact with the Kurdish dialects of the region in modern times. As expected, therefore, they are among the most archaic NENA dialects, preserving archaisms in phonology and Aramaic lexicon. The speakers of many other dialects, however, were in more intense contact with external languages, which gradually acquired linguistic dominance due to cultural pressure. This resulted in the imposition of the phonology of the external languages and features of their syntax, as well as an increase in loanwords.

In the NENA-speaking communities where the linguistic dominance of an external language had developed, this linguistic dominance was of varying degrees. These differences in degree of dominance are reflected, in particular, by different degrees of levelling of syntactic patterns and different proportions of loanwords. The dominance of the external language appears to have been particularly advanced in the case of the Jewish communities speaking the Trans-Zab dialects. This is seen in the fact that the syntax of the Jewish Trans-Zab dialects has acquired the patterns of Iranian to a greater extent than other subgroups of NENA, one conspicuous feature being near-regular clause-final word order. They also contain a larger quantity of loanwords than other NENA dialects. Within the Jewish Trans-Zab subgroup, the dialects on the south-eastern periphery of NENA in the region of Suleimaniyya and western Iran, including JSNENA in Sanandaj, exhibit the greatest assimilation to the syntax and morpho-syntax of Iranian. It follows, therefore, that in these communities the dominance of the external Iranian languages was particularly advanced. According to the model that we are adopting here, therefore, these dialects would have been furthest along the trajectory towards language shift to the external language.

Since JSNENA, and indeed many other NENA dialects, are now on the verge of extinction due the displacement of the speakers, this drift towards language shift will not be completed. If our model is correct, however, the dialect would have probably become extinct eventually due to language shift even if there had not been such a population displacement.

Appendix

Glossed texts

JSNENA

This text is a folktale narrated by Victoria Amini, who was born in Sanandaj in the 1930s. It was recorded in Israel in 2007 by Geoffrey Khan and appears in the text corpus of Khan (2009, 480–87). Its transcription here has been adapted to the system used in this volume.

(1) xà˩ bronà˩ hīyē ba-ʿolàm˩ kačàl=yē-lē.˩ məsta
one boy come.PST.3SG.M in-world bald=COP.PST-OBL.3SG.M hair
lɨ̀t-wa ba-rēš-ēf.˩
NEG.EXIST-PSTC on-head-3SG.M
'A boy came into the world who was bald. He did not have a hair on his head.'

bar-do xarā̀ē˩ ʾay bronà˩ barūxa lɨ̀t-wā-lē.˩
after-OBL.that later this boy friend NEG.EXIST-PSTC-OBL.3SG.M
'Later (in his life) he did not have a friend.'

hīč-kas barūx-èf la xar-wa.˩
nobody friend-3SG.M NEG become.PRS.3SG.M-PSTC
'Nobody became his friend.'

rə̀wē, ˩ rə̀wē˩ tā-ʾɨnkē xɨ̀r˩ ba-xa
grow.PST.3SG.M grow.PST.3SG.M until-SBRD become.PST.3SG.M at-one
bronà˩ taqrīban ʾəsrī šənē.˩
boy approximately twenty years
'He grew and grew until he became a boy about twenty years old.'

ʾay brona bē-čāra hīč-kas līt-wā-lē.˩
this boy without-remedy no-person NEG.EXIST-PSTC-OBL.3SG.M
'This helpless boy had nobody.'

(2) xa-yoma tīw məntak=ē dāak-èf˩ ḥqē-lē
one-day sit.PST.3SG.M with mother-3SG.M speak.PST-OBL.3SG.M
mɨ̀r-ē˩ dàyka˩ ʾānà˩
say.PST-OBL.3SG.M mother I

hìč barūxa līt-ī| wa-la k-aē-na
any friend NEG.EXIST-OBL.1SG and-NEG IND-know.PRS-1SG.M
ma honà.|
what do.PRS-1SG.M
'One day he sat with his mother, spoke and said, "Mother, I do not have any friend and I do not know what to do."'

hằ-lax| tamām 'ay dawruwar-àn| da'wàt
come.IMP.SG-OBL.2SG.F all those around-1PL invitation
ho-n-ū| baška 'āšna xa-dāna màn-ūn=ū|
do.PRS-1SG.M-3PL perhaps acquaintance one-CLF from-3PL=and
bəxlē zəndəgî hol-ēxīn.|
together life do.PRS-1PL
'"Come, I shall invite everybody around us, perhaps I shall become acquainted with one of them and we can spend time[1] together."'

(3) xà-lēlē| rāba xàrj wīl-ē| rāba xālà
one-night much expenditure make.PST-OBL.3SG.M much food
trəṣ-lē.|
make.PST-OBL.3SG.M
'One night he spent a lot of money and made a lot of food.'

xālà| ga-ḥafšà| rēša 'ara məndề-lē=ū| nāšē
food in-courtyard upon ground lay.PST-OBL.3SG.M=and people
kulē tìw-ī=ū| xāla ràba trəṣ-lē.|
all sit.PRS-3PL=and food much do.PST-OBL.3SG.M
'He laid out the food in the courtyard on the ground and all the people sat down. He made a lot of food.'

mīr-ē 'àna,| ta-dāak-èf mīr-ē,| 'āna
say.PST-OBL.3SG.M I to-mother-3SG.M say.PST-OBL.3SG.M I
'ay-xāla tarəṣ-n-èf|
this-food make.PRS-1SG.M-3SG.M
'He said, "I"—he said to his mother—"I shall make this food."'

---

[1] Literally: life.

'āna   k-àē-na| bar-do   xarā̀ē| 'ay   čakma
I   IND-know.PRS-1SG.M after-OBL.that   afterwards   these   some
nāšḕ| har-lēlē   xa-nāša   da'wat   dīdī   k-òl,|
people each-night   one-person   invitation   OBL.1SG   IND-do.PRS.3SG.M
kē   'āna   g-ēz-na   ga-pəlg-ừn=ū| 'ānà| barūxawālē
SBRD   I   IND-go.PRS-1SG.M   in-middle-3PL=and   I   friends
dòq-na.|
hold.PRS-1SG.M

"'I know that afterwards each night one of these people will invite me, since I shall go among them and make friends.'"

(4) wàlē| ēa   zi̇̀l=ū| nāš-akē   'àṣər   xi̇̀l-ū|
    now   this   go.PST.3SG.M=and   people-DEF   evening eat.PST-OBL.3PL
    'Now, he went (to make the preparations) and the people ate in the evening.'

    nāšē   kulē   hı̄yē-n   dokà=ū| xālà| rāba
    people   all   come.PST-3PL   there=and   food   much
    trə̀ṣ-wā-lē=ū| yaxnī   saqātà=ū| kačāwè̀,| yaprāġè̀,|
    make.PST-PSTC-OBL.3SG.M=and   soup   offal   rissoles   vine_leaves
    rəzzà   xwāra=ū| rəzzà   yarūqa=ū| kùlē   jor   trə̀ṣ-wā-lē
    rice   white=and   rice   green=and   every   kind   make.PST-PSTC-OBL.3SG.M
    bāqa   nāšē.|
    for   people

    'The people all came there. He had made a lot of food—offal soup, rissoles, stuffed vine leaves, white rice, green rice. He made every kind (of food) for the people.'

(5) 'ay-nāšē   kulē   hi̇̀yē-n| 'ay-xāla   kulē   xi̇̀l-ū.|
    those-people   all   come.PST-3PL   this-food   all   eat.PST-OBL.3PL
    'The people all came and ate all the food.'

    kulē   xi̇̀l-ūn=ū| rāba   mtừ-lūn=ū|
    all   eat.PST-OBL.3PL=and   much   serve.PST-OBL.3PL=and
    ḥqè-lūn=ū| gxi̇̀k-ī=ū| pṣi̇̀x-ī=ū| 'o=č
    speak.PST-OBL.3PL=and   laugh.PST-3PL=and   be_merry.PST-3PL=and   he=ADD
    rāba   xoš-ḥằl   xīr=ū|
    very   happy   become.PST.3SG.M=and

    'They all ate, served themselves a lot, spoke, laughed, made merry, and he was happy.'

mən-ū	kulē	ḥqḛ̀-lē		baška	ʾəlhà=y		ʾənyēxāē
with-3PL	all	speak.PST-OBL.3SG.M		perhaps	God=COP.3SG.M		they

barūx-ēf xar-ḭ̀ wa he-lū
friends-3SG.M become.PRS-3PL and come.PRS.3SG.M-OBL.3PL
daʿwat-èf hol-ī́ kē-hēzəl ga-pəlga nāšḛ̀, hawē
invitation-3SG.M COMPL go.PRS.3SG.M in-middle people be.PRS.3SG.M
ga-pəlga nāšḛ̀=ū ʾalē-nī-lē-ò.
in-middle people=and know.PRS-3PL-OBL.3SG.M-TELIC

'He spoke with them all, so that perhaps, God willing, they would become his friends and would be able to invite him, so that he could visit people,[2] be among people and become acquainted with them.'

(6) ʾay bronà daʿwat-akē wīl-ằ-lē=ū ta-sāʿat-ē
    this boy invitation-DEF do.PST-3SG.F-OBL.3SG.M=and to-hour-EZ
    trēsàr lēlē dokà-yē-lūn=ū
    twelve night there=COP.PST-3PL=and

'The boy held the party[3] and they were there until twelve o'clock at night.'

dāna dāna kulē zīl-ī-ò. tīw m-dāak-ēf
CLF CLF all go.PST-3PL-TELIC sit.PST.3SG.M with-mother-3SG.M
ḥqḛ̀-lē.
speak.PST-OBL.3SG.M

'One by one they went away. He sat down and spoke with his mother.'

mīr-ē dàyka ʾāt noš-ax hāzə̀r hūl-a.
say.PST-OBL.3SG.M mother you self-2SG.F ready make.IMP.SG-OBL.3SG.F
jəlē ʿayzē=č xṵ̀ṭ, jəlē ʿayzē hawḛ̀-lax,
clothes good=ADD sew.IMP.SG clothes good be.PRS.3SG.M-OBL.2SG.F
kulē ʾāṣər dīdan daʿwàt k-ol-ī.
every evening OBL.1PL invitation IND-do.PRS-3PL

'He said, "Mother, prepare yourself, sew fine clothes, get some fine clothes, they will invite us every evening."'

---

2 Literally: go among people.
3 Literally: made the invitation.

hàr   'áṣər| xa-nāša   da'wat   hol-àn| noš-ēf
every evening one-person   invitation   do.PRS.3SG.-OBL.1PL self-3SG.M
trē   yarxē   ṭūl   garèš.|
two   months length pull.PRS.3SG.M

'"Each evening for two months somebody in turn will invite us."'[4]

'āna=č barūxawālē k-wè-lī| 'āna=č xoš-ḥằl
I=ADD   friends   IND-be.PRS.3SG.M-OBL.1SG I=ADD   happy
xar-na   'ēxa.|
become.PRS-1SG.M this

'"I shall have friends. I shall be happy," and so forth.'

(7) walè| kulē   'āṣər| tīw   ga-qam-tarà=ū| muntazər
    but   every evening sit.PST.3SG.M in-before-door=and   expecting
    xīr| baška   da'wat-èf   hol-ī.| hìč-kas
    become   perhaps invitation-3SG.M do.PRS-3PL   nobody
    la-hīyē.|
    NEG-come.PST.3SG.M

'But, every evening he sat outside, he waited hoping they would invite him, and nobody came.'

xà   yoma,| trè yomē,| təlḥà   yomē,| xīr   xà
one   day   two days   three   days   become.PST.3SG.M one
yarxa| hìč-kas da'wat-ēf   la   wīl-è.|
month   nobody   invitation-3SG.M NEG do.PST-OBL.3SG.M

'One day, two days, three days (went by), a month passed, nobody invited him.'

dāak-ēf   mīr-a   xè-lox?| 'āt   'ay   ḥašta
mother-3SG.M say.PST-OBL.3SG.F see.PST-OBL.2SG.M   you   this   work
wīl-à-lox,| 'ay   kulē pūḷē   xərj-ī-lox|
do.PST-3SG.F-OBL.2SG.M   this   all   money spend.PST-3PL-OBL.2SG.M
hìč kasī   da'wat-ox   la   wīl-è.|
no   person invitation-2SG.M NEG do.PST-OBL.3SG.M

'His mother said, "Do you see? You have done this work, you have spent all this money, and nobody has invited you."'

---

4 Literally: It will last for two months (that) every evening somebody will invite us.

(8) mīr-ē   dàyka| 'əlha ruwà=y| 'àt| xafàt
    say.PST-OBL.3SG.M mother God   great=COP.3SG.M   you   worry
    la-xul.| bəl'àxərà| xa-yoma   k-wè| 'ānà| da'wat-ī̀
    NEG-eat.IMP.SG in_the_end   one-day   IND-be.3SG.M I   invitation-1SG
    k-ol-ī.|
    IND-do-3PL
    'He said, "Mother. God is great. Don't worry. In the end, a day will come when they will invite me."'

    zīl   bāzàr=ū| 'o-nāšē   kulē   da'wat
    go.PST.3SG.M   market=and   those-people   all   invitation
    wīl-ī-wā-lè| kulē   dūbāra   šālòm   drē-lū
    do.PST-3PL-PSTC-OBL.3SG.M   all   again   greeting   put.PST-OBL.3PL
    'əl-ēf=ū|
    on-3SG.M=and
    'He went to the market. The people whom he had invited all greeted him again.'

    ḥqè-lē   mən-ūn=ū| mīr-ē   mà'īn| 'ānà|
    speak.PST-OBL.1SG   with-3PL-and   say.PST-OBL.3SG.M look.IMP.SG I
    da'wat=ē   didaxūn   wīl-ī̀| kē   hè-tūn| bēl-ī
    invitation=EZ   OBL.2PL   do.PST-OBL.1SG   SBRD   come.PRS-2PL   house-1SG
    mēmānī   wīl-ī   bāq-axùn.|
    hosting do.PST-OBL.1SG   for-2PL
    'He spoke to them and said, "Look, I invited you to come and I hosted you in my house."'

    'axtū   ta-mà   dīdī=ū   dāak-ī   da'wat   la
    you   for-what   OBL.1SG=and   mother-1SG invitation   NEG
    k-ol-ētun,| kē   'āna=č   hē-na   ga-pəlg-axùn?|
    IND-do.PRS-2PL SBRD   I=ADD   come.PRS-1SG.M in-middle-2PL
    '"Why do you not invite me and my mother, so that I can visit you?"'

(9) mīr-ū   ròḷa| 'āt   sarwatmànd=yēt| kē   'àt| pūḷè
    say.PST-OBL.3PL   child   you   rich=COP.2SG.M   SBRD   you   money
    rāba   hīt-ox   kē   'ay   mēmānī   dəwq-ằ-lox.|
    much   EXIST-OBL.2SG.M SBRD   this   hospitality hold.PST-3SG.F-OLB.2SG.M
    'axnī   là   k-ē-lan   mēmānī   'axa   doq-ēxīn.|
    we   NEG   IND-come.PRS.3SG.M-OBL.1PL   hospitality thus   hold.PRS-1PL
    'They said, "Dear boy, you are rich, since you must have a lot of money to have offered that hospitality. We cannot offer such hospitality."'

hīyē-o	*bēlà=ū*	*ta-dāak-ēf*	*mìr-ē*
come.PST.3SG.M-TELIC	home=and	to-mother-3SG.M	say.PST-OBL.3SG.M
dāak-ēf=əč	*rāba*	*noš-af*	*na-raḥat wīl-ằ-la.*
mother-3SG.M=ADD	very	self-3SG.F	upset make.PST-3SG.F-OBL.3SG.F

'He came back home and told his mother. His mother became very upset.'

mìr-a	*xafàt*	*la-xul*	*'əlhà*	*ruwa=y.*
say.PST-OBL.3SG.F	worry	NEG-eat.IMP.SG	God	great=COP.3SG.M
bəl'āxərà	*xa-mdī*	*xàr*	*'əlha xà*	*tara bāqa*
in_the_end	one-thing	become.PRS.3SG.M	God one	door for
dīdan=əč	*k-ol-ò.*			
OBL.1PL=ADD	IND-do.PRS.3SG.M-TELIC			

'She said, "Don't worry. God is great. In the end something will happen. God will open a door for us."'

(10)
xa-yoma	*tīwa*	*ga-bēlà*	*'ēxà=ū*	*xē-lē xà*
one-day	sit.PTCP.SG.M	in-house	this=and	see.PST-OBL.3SG.M one
gora tara	*dì-lē=ū.*		*ḥāl-èf*	*bəqr-ū*
man door	hit.PST-OBL.3SG.M=and		condition-3SG.M	ask.PST-OBL.3PL
mīr-ē	*dàx=yētū*	*'ēxa=ū?*		
say.PST-OBL.3SG.M	how=COP.2PL	this=and		

'One day he was sitting in the house and so forth, and he saw a man knock on the door. They asked after his health. He said, "How are you?" and so forth.'

mīr-ē	*wala*	*ṭòb=yēna.*	*'ànà*	*'axa mēmānī*
say.PST-OBL.3SG.M	indeed	good=COP.1SG.M	I	thus hospitality
dwə̀q-lī=ū		*hìč-kas*	*da'wat-ī*	*la*
hold.PST-OBL.1SG=and		no-person	invitation-1SG	NEG
wīl-ē-ò.				
do.PST-OBL.3SG.M-TELIC				

'He said, "I am well. But, I held a party and nobody invited me back."'

wa-là	*k-aē-na*	*m-qam*	*dēa*	*'ànà pərčè*
and-NEG	IND-know.PRS-1SG.M	from-before	OBL.this	I hair
līt-ī,		*kačàl=yēna*	*yā šəmà līt-ī*	*'ēxa.*
NEG.EXIST-OBL.1SG		bald=1SG.M	or name NEG.EXIST-OBL.1SG	this

'"I don't know whether it was because I do not have any hair and am bald, or whether I am not well known," and so forth.'

(11) mīr-ē   là| 'āna xa ḥašta k-əw-na   bāq-òx.|
    say.PST-OBL.3SG.M no I one thing IND-give.PRS-1SG.M for-2SG.M
    sē-lox   xà| ksīla pərčē matù̱.|
    go.IMP.SG-OBL.2SG.M one hat   hair put.IMP.SG
    'He said, "No, I'll sort something out for you. Go and put on a wig."'

   ksīla pərčē matù̱| wa-sè̱| noš-ox   'ayza
   hat   hair put.IMP.SG and-go.IMP.SG self-2SG.M good
   trùṣ-la| sē   ga-pəlgāwa nāšē dūbàra.|
   make.IMP.SG-OBL.3SG.F go.IMP.SG in-middle people again
   '"Put on a wig and go and make yourself look good, then go and visit people again."'

   mīr-ē   lēka hēz-nà?| rāhnamāī
   say.PST-OBL.3SG.M where go.PRS-1SG.M guidance
   wìl-ē=ū,| mīr-ē   sē   flān
   do.PST-OBL.3SG.M=and say.PST-OBL.3SG.M go.IMP.SG such_and_such
   tʷkà,| salmānī kē pərčē tarəṣ,| 'oa hīt-è̱.|
   place   barber REL hair do.PRS.3SG.M he EXIST-OBL.3SG.M
   'He said. "Where should I go?" He guided him and said, "Go to such-and-such a place, a barber who makes hair, he has one."'

(12) zīl   dòka.| xančī pūḷē pas-andāz
    go.PST.3SG.M there some money saving
    wīl-ì-wā-lē| hīw-ī-lē   bāq-èf=ū|
    make.PST-3PL-PSTC-OBL.3SG.M give.PST-3PL-OBL.3SG.M to-3SG.M=and
    'He went there. He had saved some money and gave it to him.'

   mīr-ē   mà'īn| 'āna g-bè-na| xà| ksīla
   say.PST-OBL.3SG.M look.IMP.SG I   IND-want.PRS-1SG.M one hat
   pərčē mat-ət   bāqa dīdī̱| kē   'āna hè-lī|
   hair place.PRS-2SG.M for   OBL.1SG SBRD I   come.PRS.3SG.M-OBL.1SG
   ga-pəlga nāšē   hawè-na| nāšē   xoš-ū   hē
   in-middle people be.PRS-1SG.M people wellbeing-3PL come.PRS.3SG.M
   mən-ì̱.|
   with-1SG
   'He said, "Look, I want you to make a wig for me so that I can be among people and people will like me."'

mīr-ē　　　　　ṭòv.|　qìm|　　　　ksīl-akē　tərṣ-ằ-lē
say.PST-OBL.3SG.M　good　rise.PST.3SG.M　hat-DEF　make.PST-3SG.F-OBL.3SG.M
bāq-ēf=ū|　　　　　mìr-ē|　　　　　xa　čəkma　yomē　xēt　hal
for-3SG.M=and　say.PST-OBL.3SG.M　a　few　days　more　come.IMP.SG
bāq-àf.|
for-3SG.F
'He said, "Fine." He made the wig for him. He said, "In a few more days come for it."'

(13) čəkma　yomē　muntazər　xīr=ū|　　　　　　　hīyē=ū
a_few　days　waiting　become.PST.3SG.M=and　come.PST.3SG.M=and
zìl=ū|　　　　　　hīyē=ū　　　　　　zìl|　　　　ta-ìnkē|　　'ay
go.PST.3SG.M=and　come.PST.3SG.M=and　go.PST.3SG.M　until-SBRD　this
ksīla　trīṣ-à.|
hat　make.PST-3SG.F
'He waited for a few days. He came and went, came and went, until the wig was finished.'

mət-ā-lē　　　　　　　　rēš-èf=ū|　　　　　dūbāra　zīl
put.PST-3SG.F-OBL.3SG.M　head-3SG.M=and　then　go.PST.3SG.M
ga-bāzằr=ū|　　ga-nāšē　kē　da'wàt　wīl-ī-wā-lē,|
in-market=AND　in-people　REL　invitation　make.PST-3PL-OBL.3SG.M
šalòm|　xèta　wīl-ē　　　　　　'èxa.|
greeting　other　do.PST-OBL.3SG.M　this
'He put it on his head, then he went to the market and greeted the people whom he had invited, and so forth.'

(14) mīr-ū　　　　　'ē　'òa=y?|　　　　'ē　har　'o　brona
say.PST-OBL.3PL　this　that=COP.3SG.M　this　just　that　boy
kačāl-akē=le　　　　da'wat-àn　　wīl-wā-lē?|
bald-DEF=COP.3SG.M　invitation-1PL　do.PST-PSTC-OBL.3SG.M
'They said, "Is it him? Is it the same bald boy who invited us?"'

xa   'lī-lē-ò| xa   la   'lī-lē-ò.|
one   know.PST-OBL.3SG.M-TELIC   one   NEG   know.PST-OBL.3SG.M-TELIC
'axr-ēf   bəqr-ù   mən-ēf| mìr-ē| 'ì| 'āna
end-3SG.M   ask.PST-OBL.3PL from-3SG.M say.PST-OBL.3SG.M yes   I
'òē=na.|
that=COP.1SG.M
'One recognised him and another did not recognise him. In the end they asked him. He said, "Yes, it is me."'

(15) wà| bar   xa-čəkma yomē xə̀t| k-ē-n   dāna   dāna
      and   after one-few   days other IND-come.PRS-3PL   CLF   CLF
      tara   daè̱-n=ū| da'wat-èf   k-ol-ī.|
      door   knock.PRS-3PL=and   invitation-3SG.M IND-do.PRS-3PL
      'Then, after a few more days, they came one by one and knocked on the door, and invited him.'

      mìr-ē| 'ata mà-ho-na?| 'ata   ya-da'wat-ī
      say.PST-OBL.3SG.M now what-do.PRS-1SG.M   now   REL-invitation-1SG
      wīlà=y| ba-mà-jor   hēz-na   bēlū?|
      do.PTCP.SG.M   in-what-way   go.PRS-1SG.M   house-3PL
      'He said, "Now what should I do? Now that they have invited me, how shall I go to their house?"'

(16) qīm   zìl| mən-xa   t^wkāna jəlē   krà
      rise.PST.3SG.M go.PST.3SG.M from-one   shop   clothes rent
      wīl-ē=ū| har   'ə̣ṣər| ta-har-kas   da'wat-ēf
      do.PST-OBL.3SG.M=and   every evening to-every-person   invitation-3SG.M
      wìl-ē| ba-xa   dasa jəlē   zìl.|
      do.PST-OBL.3SG.M   in-one   suit clothes go.PST.3SG.M
      'He went and hired clothes from a shop. Each evening he went in a suit to each one who had invited him.'

      ba-xa   dasa jəlē   zìl=ū| ga-pəlga   nāš-akē
      in-one suit clothes go.PST.3SG.M=and   in-middle   people-DEF
      tìw=ū| ḥqē-lē   mən-ūn=ū   'ēxà=ū|
      sit.PST.3SG.M=and   speak.PST-OBL.3SG.M   with-3PL=and   this=and
      'He went in a suit and sat among the people and spoke to them, and so forth.'

yawằš| yawằš| wārəd xīr=ū| wa-nāšē
slowly slowly entering become.PST.3SG.M=and and-people
'lī-lū-ò-'əl-ēf.|
know.PST-OBL.3PL-TELIC-on-3SG.M
'Gradually he entered (into their circle) and people became acquainted with him.'

(17) 'lī-lū-ò-'əl-ēf=ū| xa brāta ma'arəfī
know.PST-OBL.3PL-TELIC-on-3SG.M=and one girl acquaintance
wīl-ā-lū bā-ēf| kḕ| baška xlūlà=č
do.PST-3SG.F-OBL.3PL to-3SG.M SBRD perhaps wedding=ADD
hol| 'ēa zəndəgī-ēf bīš-'ayza xàr.|
do.PRS.3SG.M this life-3SG.M more-good become.PRS.3SG.M
'They became acquainted with him and introduced a girl to him, whom he could perhaps marry and so his life would become better.'

xa mən-barūxawāl-ḕf| kē barūxà xīr-wa=ū|
one from-friends-3SG.M REL friend become.PST.3SG.M-PSTC=and
da'wat-ḕf wīl-ē dūbāra=ū| zīl doka
invitation-3SG.M do.PST-OBL.3SG.M again go.PST.3SG.M there
'ēxà.|
this
'One of his friends, (somebody) who had (already) become his friend, invited him again and he went there (to his home) and so forth.'

mīr-ē xa brāta 'axà hīt| 'āna k-mḕ-n-af|
say.PST-OBL.3SG.M one girl thus EXIST I IND-bring.PRS-1SG.M-3SG.F
'āt 'əlū-la-ò| šāyad hē-laxūn
you know.IMP-OBL.3SG.F-TELIC perhaps come.PRS.3SG.M-OBL.2PL
bàxlē| xlūla hol-ḕtū.|
one_another wedding do.PRS-2PL
'He (the friend) said, "There is a such a girl (here), I shall bring her and you can get to know her, perhaps you can marry one another."'

(18) brāt-akē hīy-a=ū 'èxà=ū| xè̱-la| 'ì| brona
girl-DEF come.PST-3SG.F=and this see.PST-OBL.3SG.F yes boy
'àyz-èk=yē=ū| xa čəkma mudàtē| hīyē-n=ū zìl-ī.|
fine-INDF=COP.3SG.M=and one few times come.PST-3PL=and go.PST-3PL
'The girl came and so forth. She saw that, yes, he was a fine boy. They came and went a few times.'

brāt-akè̱| mīr-a g-bē hē-t
girl-DEF say.PST-OBL.3SG.F IND-need.PRS.3SG.M come.PRS-2SG.M
xāstgārī lā tāt-ī=ū dāak-ì̱.|
courtship side father-1SG=and mother-1SG
'The girl said, "You must come to ask for my hand in marriage from my father and mother."'

mīr-ē bà̱š=a.| 'āna dāak-ī
say.PST-OBL.3SG.M good=COP.3SG.M I mother-1SG
k-mè̱-n-af=ū| k-ē-na xāstgārì̱.|
IND-bring.PRS-1SG.M-3SG.F=and IND-come.PRS-1SG.M courtship
'He said, "So be it." I shall bring my mother and I shall ask for your hand."'

(19) qīm-a dāak-è̱f| həjbì̱-af hol-a|
rise.PST-3SG.F mother-3SG.F intermediary-3SG.F do.PRS-3SG.F
hīy-a zīl-a həjbì brāt-akē.| zīl
come.PST-3SG.F go.PST-3SG.F intermediary girl-DEF go.PST.3SG.M
lā tāta dāak-àf=ū|
side father mother-3SG.F=and
'His mother went to act as intermediary to ask for the hand of the girl. He then went to her father and mother.'

mìr-ē| ḥašt-ox mà=ya? 'èxa| mīr-ē
say.PST-OBL.3SG.M work-2SG.M what=COP.3SG.F this say.PST-OBL.3SG.M
wàlla| 'āna tā-'ata ḥašta=ē xa-ba-jor-ī laxa
by_God I until-now work=EZ one-in-kind=INDF here
lìt-ī=ū| g-bē-na hēz-na ḥaštà
NEG.EXIST-OBL.1SG=and IND-want.PRS.1SG.M go.PRS-1SG.M work
yaləp-na kē| ḥašta 'ayza dòq-na.|
learn.PRS-1SG.M SBRD work good hold.PRS-1SG.M
'He (the father) said, "What is your work?" and so forth. He said, "By God, I have not any particular job here, but I want to go and learn to work, so that I can get a job."'

(20) tāt-akē   mīr-ē   là'!ˈ 'ànàˈ   brāt-ī   ta-xa-nāš
     father-DEF say.PST-OBL.3SG.M no   I   daughter-1SG to-one-person
     là   k-əw-n-af   kē   ḥašta līt-ē=ū   'ēxa.ˈ
     NEG IND-give.PRS-1SG.M-3SG.F REL   work   NEG.EXIST-OBL.3SG.M=and this
     'The father said, "No! I shall not give my daughter to a man who has no job" and so forth.'

   bē-čāràˈ   na-rāḥàt xīr=ūˈ   hīyē-o
   without-help   upset   become.PST.3SG.M=and come.PST.3SG.M-TELIC
   bēlà.ˈ   hīyē-o   bēlà,ˈ   ta-dāak-ēf   mìr-ēˈ
   house come.PST.3SG.M-TELIC house   to-mother-3SG.M say.PST-OBL.3SG.M
   'The unfortunate boy became upset and went back home. He went back home and said to his mother,'

   dàykaˈ   'āt   zīl-at   m-dənyēxāē   ḥqè̇-laxˈ   la
   mother   you go.PST-2SG.F with-OBL.these   speak.PST-OBL.2SG.F NEG
   mīr-ax   'āna   ḥašt-ī   mà=ya.ˈ
   say.PST-OBL.2SG.F I   work-1SG what=COP.3SG.F
   '"Mother, you went and talked to these people and did not say what my job is."'

   wàlēˈ   tāta   brāt-akē   bəqr-ē   mə̀n-īˈ   mīr-ē
   but   father girl-DEF   ask.PST-OBL.3SG.M from-1SG say.PST-OBL.3SG.M
   'āt   ḥašt-ox   mà=ya?ˈ   mīr-ī   'āna   ḥašta
   you   work-2SG.M what=COP.3SG.F say.PST-OBL.1SG I   work
   līt-ī   tā-'atàˈ   g-bē-na   ḥašta taḥè̇-na.ˈ
   EXIST-OBL.1SG   to-now   IND-want.PRS-1SG.M   work   find.PRS-1SG.M
   '"But the father of the girl asked me saying, "What is your job?" I said, "Until now I have no job. I want to find work."""'

(21) mīr-aˈ   ròḷa   gyān,ˈ   'ata   g-ay   səna   dīdòxˈ   kē
     say.PST-OBL.3SG.F child   dear   now   in-this   age   OBL.2SG.M SBRD
     xīr-ètˈ   'əsrī   šə̀nèˈ   'əsrī=ū   xamša šə̀nè̇,ˈ   dàx
     become.PST-2SG.M twenty years   twenty=and   five   years   how
     k-ē-lox   ḥašta yalp-ēt?ˈ   har-jor
     IND-come.PRS.3SG.M-OBL.2SG.M work   learn.PRS-2SG.M   any-way
     xīra=y   yaləp-na.ˈ
     become.PTCP.SG.M=COP.3SG.M learn.PRS-1SG.M
     'She said, "My dear boy, now at the age that you are, twenty years old, twenty-five years old, how can you learn a job?" "Whatever happens, I shall learn."'

(22) zīl   ga-xa   tʷka   kḕ| kārxānà=yē-la,| pārčē
     go.PST.3SG.M   in-one   place   REL   factory=COP.PST-OBL.3SG.F   materials
     'ēxa tarṣ-ī-wa.| zīl   ga-dòka,| xāìš
     this make.PRS-3PL-PSTC   go.PST.3SG.M   in-there   request
     wīl-ē   mīr-ē|
     make.PST-OBL.3SG.M   say.PST-OBL.3SG.M
     'He went to a place that was a factory, where they made material, and so forth. He went there and pleaded saying,'

     'āna   ḥaštà   g-bē-na   čun| g-bḕ-na|
     I   work   IND-want.PRS-1SG.M   because   IND-want.PRS-1SG.M
     zəndəgī̀   taraṣ-na=ū̀| baxta   gòr-na=ū   'ēxa.|
     life   build.PRS-1SG.M=AND   wife   marry.PRS-1SG.M=and   this
     '"I want a job, since I want to build a life and get married" and so forth.'

     ga-doka   'lī-lū-ò-'əl-ēf=ū| ḥašta   hīw-lū
     in-there   know.PST-OBL.3PL-TELIC-on-3SG.M=and   work   give.PST-OBL.3PL
     bāq-ḕf=ū| hīyē-ò| rāba   pṣìx=ū|
     to-3SG.M=and   come.PST.3SG.M-TELIC   very   become_happy.PST.3SG.M=and
     'They got to know him there and gave him a job. He came back and was very happy.'

(23) mīr-ē   ta-dāak-ḕf| dàyka| 'ānà   xēt|
     say.PST-OBL.3SG.M   to-mother-3SG.M   mother   I   other
     mən-qomē=ū   xarē   g-bē   hēz-na   ḥaštà|
     from-tomorrow=and   after   IND-need.PRS.3SG.M   go.PRS-1SG.M   work
     wa-zəndəgī̀   nòš-ī̀| 'ədāra   hò-n-ēf| wa-ba-xa
     and-life   self-1SG management   do.PRS-1SG.M-3SG.M   and-in-one
     zəndəgī̀   maṭē-na.|
     life   arrive.PRS-1SG.M
     'He said to his mother, "Mother, from tomorrow onwards, I have to go to work and manage my own life, so I can make a livelihood for myself."'

     mīr-a   ᴴṭòvᴴ| sḕ!| 'ānà| rāba   paṣx-ana
     say.PST-OBL.3SG.F   good   go.IMP.SG   I   very   rejoice.PRS-1SG.F
     'āt   hēz-ēt   ḥaštà=ū| baška   hē-lox=əč
     you   go.PRS-2SG.M   work=and   perhaps   come.PRS.3SG.M-OBL.2SG.M=ADD

xa   baxta=č   gor-ət   b-ày   jora.|
one   woman=ADD   marry.PRS-2SG.M in-this way

'She said, "Fine. Go! I am very happy if you go to work. Perhaps you will be able to marry a woman in this way."'

(24) xolàṣa| zīl   ḥastà| bāqa xa-yarxa=ū   trē-yarxē
     in_short   go.PST.3SG.M   work   for   one-month=and   two-months
     ḥašta wìl-ē=ū| dubāra xa-brāta   xēt
     work   do.PST-OBL.3SG.M=and   again   one-girl   other
     'əly-ā-lē-ò.|
     know.PST-3SG.F-OBL.3SG.M-TELIC

'In short, he went to work and worked for one month, two months, then he became acquainted with another girl.'

'əly-ā-lē-ò,| dāak-ēf   šər-ā-lē
know.PST-3SG.F-OBL.3SG.M-TELIC   mother-3SG.M   send.PST-3SG.F-OBL.3SG.M
həjbì,| həjbī   brāt-akè̱| məntak=ē   tāta=ū
intermediary   intermediary   girl-DEF   with   father=and
dāak-af=ū   'ēxà.|
mother-3SG.F=and this

'He became acquainted with her and he sent his mother to ask for her hand in marriage, to request the hand of the girl from her father and mother, and so forth.'

(25) mīr-ū   mà   k-ol?| mīr-a   ga-xa   tʷka
     say.PST-OBL.3PL what   IND-do.PRS.3SG.M say.PST-OBL.3SG.F in-one   place
     xa-ḥastà   k-ol=ū| rāba bron-ī   'ayzà=y|
     one-work   IND-do.PRS.3SG.M=and   very   son-1SG   good=COP.3SG.M

'They said, "What does he do?" She said, "He works in a certain place. My son is very good."'

rāba   ta'rīf-èf   hīw-la=ū| mīr-ū
very   making_known-3SG.M give.PST-OBL.3SG.F=and   say.PST-OBL.3PL
g-bē   hamy-at-ē   xaē-xi̱-lē.|
IND-need.PRS.3SG.M   bring.PRS-2SG.F-OBL.3SG.M see.PRS-1PL-OBL.3SG.M
lə̀bl-a=ū| mē-la   bron-akè̱.|
take.PST-OBL.3SG.F=and   bring.PST-OBL.3SG.F   boy-DEF

'She described him in glowing terms. They said, "You must bring him for us to see." She took him. She brought the boy.'

(26) ləbl-a   lā   tāta=ū   dāak-akè̱=ū[|]   xa   'āṣər
     take.PST-OBL.3SG.F side   father=and   mother-DEF=and   one   evening
     zīl-ī   dokà=ū[|]
     go.PST-3PL   there=and
     'She took him to the father and mother. One evening they went there.'

   mēwa=ū   šīrnī=ū   'ēxa   kulē   mtū-lū   rēša   mèz=ū[|]
   fruit=and   sweeets=and   this   all   put.PST-OBL.3PL on   table=and
   ḥqè̱-lūn=ū[|]   brāta=ū   bron-akē   mən-ləxlē
   speak.PST-OBL.3PL=and   girl=and   boy-DEF   with-each_other
   ḥqè̱-lūn=ū[|]   mīr-a   ^Htòv^{H|}   tən-an   ləxlē
   talk.PST-OBL.3PL   say.PST-OBL.3SG.F   good   both-1PL each_other
   g-b-è̱xīn.[|]
   IND-love.PRS-1PL
   'They laid out on the table fruit, sweets and so forth. They talked. The girl and boy talked together. She (the girl) said, "Fine, we both love each other."'

(27) xolāṣa[|]   xìr-a[|]   barūxt-èf=ū[|]   taṣmīm
     in_short   become.PST-3SG.F   friend.F-3SG.M=and   decision
     dwəq-lū   xlūla   hol-ī   bāq-èf.[|]   xa   xlūla
     hold.PST-OBL.3PL wedding   do.PRS-3PL   for-3SG.M   one   wedding
     rāba   mojalàl   dəwq-ā-lē   bāq-af   tāt-akē.[|]
     very   grand   hold.PST-3SG.F-OBL.3SG.M   for-3SG.F   father-DEF
     'In short, she became his girl friend and they (the parents) decided to arrange a wedding for him. The father arranged a very grand wedding for her.'

   rāba   xoš-bàxt   xīr   'ay   brona-kačàl.[|]
   very   good-fortune   become.PST.3SG.M   this   boy-bald
   wa-ba-mra=ē   noš-ēf   màṭē[|]
   and-in-desire=EZ   self-3SG.M   reach.PST.3SG.M
   'The bald boy was very fortunate. He attained his heart's desire.'

(28) wa-xa   yāla=č   xè̱-lē[|]   har   mangol   noš-ēf   pərčē
     and-one   boy=ADD   see.PST-OBL.3SG.M   just   like   self-3SG.M   hair
     lìt-wā-lē.[|]   mīr-ē   mà   ho-na?[|]   'ay=əč
     NEG.EXIST-PSTC-OBL.3SG.M   say.PST-3SG.M   what   do.PRS-1SG.M   this=ADD
     mangol   noš-ī   xīra=y=ū   'ēxà.[|]
     like   self-1SG   become.PTCP.SG.M=COP.3SG.M=and   this
     'He had a son who had no hair just like him. He said, "What shall I do? He has turned out to be like me" and so forth.'

bar-do	xaṛåē	mīr-ē		ʾəlha	ruwà=y
after-OBL.that	afterwards	say.PST-OBL.3SG.M		God	great=COP.3SG.M
har-dax-dax	ʾāna-noš-ī	ba-xà	tʷka		mṭē-na
just-like-like	I-self-1SG	in-one-place	arrive.PST-1SG.M		this-boy=ADD
ʾày-brona=č	maṭē		ba-tʷkà.		
arrive.PRS.3SG.M	arrive.PRS.3SG.M		in-place		

'Then he said, "God is great, just as I attained a place (in life), this boy also will attain a place."'

xolåṣa	g-ay	xèta	xoš-ḥàl		xīr=ū
in_short	in-this	other	happy-condition		become.PST.3SG.M=and
zəndəgî-ēf	šəṛù	wīl-ē.		rāza	ʾay	brona
life-3SG.M	beginning	do.PST-OBL.3SG.M		story	this	boy
ʾày=yē-la		tīm-a.			
this=COP.PST-OBL.3SG.F		finish.PST-3SG.F			

'In short, he was happy with the situation and he began to live his life. This is the story of this boy. It has ended.'

Gorani

The following glossed text is a sample of a conservative Gorani (Hawrami) dialect. The recording was made by Masoud Mohammadirad at the village of Hawraman Takht in March 2016. The narrator is male, aged 74. The speaker talks about the customs of marriage in his village. He then elaborates on wedding ceremonies.

(1) | awaḷē-na | duē | žanī | Ø-kīyān-à. |
|---|---|---|---|
| first.F-ADP | two | woman.DIR.PL | IND-send.PST-3PL |

'First, they (i.e. the family of the boy) send two women (to the family of the girl).'

īsa	mən	dəḷ=əm	īnā	kənāčakē	ī
now	1SG	heart=1SG	DEIC	daughter.OBL.F	DEM.PROX.3SG
pīyā-y=a.					
man-OBL.M=DEM					

'(Let's say) I'm fond of (lit. my heart is with) this man's daughter.'

yām	pay	wè=m	yām	pay	kuř-akày=m.
either	for	REFL=1SG	or	for	son-DEF.OBL.M=1SG

'(And that I want to ask her in marriage) for either myself or my son.'

duē žanī kīyān-ù| kənāčakē=ū aḍằ=ū
two woman.DIR.PL send.PRS-1SG girl.DEF.OBL.F=and mother=EZ
kənāčakē don-ā.|
girl.DEF.OBL.F talk.to.PRS-3PL
'I send two women [who] talk to the girl and her mother.'

(2) m-āč-ā, ēma garak=mā=n b-ē-ymē
IND-say.PRS-3PL 1PL be.necessary=1PL=COP.3SG.M SBJV-come.PRS-1PL
ī̀ kənāčē=t=a Ø-wāz-mē.|
DEM.PROX.3SG girl.OBL.F=2SG=DEM SBJV-ask.PRS-1PL
'The women say, "We would like to come and ask your daughter's hand in marriage."'

m-a-ydḕ=mā| yā mà-ḍa-ydē=mā?|
IND-give.PRS-2PL=1PL or NEG-give.PRS-2PL=1PL
'"Will you give (her) to us or not?"'

ēḍ=īč yā m-āč-o, dē=na=mā
3SG.PROX=ADD either IND-say.PRS-3SG give.PTCP.F=COP.3SG.F=1PL
šū ba yo tar-ī̀|
husband to one.M else-OBL.M
'He either says, "We have married her off to someone else"'

yām m-āč-o, day qay čīš-ī̀ Ø-kar-o|
or IND-say.PRS-3SG well limit what-OBL.M IND-do.PRS-3SG
bā pars Ø-kar-mḕ.|
HORT investigation SBJV-do.PRS-1PL
'or he (the father) says, "No problem, let us make an investigation."'

haftà=y tar| dà řoē tar| xabar=tā m-a-ymḕ pana.|
week=EZ other ten day.PL other news=2PL IND-give.PRS-1PL to
'"We will let you know (about our decision) in a week, or in ten days."'

(3) mašūrat Ø-kar-å̀ bayn=ū wē=šān-ē.|
consultation IND-do.PRS-3PL among=EZ REFL=3pl-NA
'They (i.e. the bride's family) take counsel among themselves.'

m-āč-ā,   xwā   məbāràk=əš   Ø-kar-o.|
IND-say.PRS-3PL god   blessing=3SG SBJV-do.PRS-3SG
'(and after taking counsel and having a positive answer, the bride's family) says, "May God give his blessing to it (to the marriage)."'

ītər   ā   waxt-ī   pīyà̀   Ø-kīyān-mē.|
DISC   DEM.DIST.SG time-OBL.M   man.DIR.SG   IND-send.PRS-1PL
'Afterwards, we send some [senior] men (to the family of the girl).'

yarē,   čwằr   pīyā   Ø-kīyān-mē.|
three   four   man   IND-send.PRS-1PL
'We send three, four [senior] men (to the family of the girl).'

har   dasūr=ū   wḕ=tā.|
again   order=EZ   REFL=2PL
'Again, with your (i.e. the bride's family's) permission,'

das   mằč   Ø-kar-mē=ū|
hand.DIR.SG kissing IND-do.PRS-1PL=and
'we will perform "hand-kissing."'

dəmā=w   ānà-y| maḷà̀   Ø-bar-mē| žanī
after=EZ   DEM.3SG-OBL.M   mulla.DIR.SG IND-take.PRS-1PL woman.DIR.SG
māra   Ø-bəř-mḕ=ū|
marriage   IND-cut.PRS-1PL=and
'Afterwards, we will take a mullah and marry the girl.'

(4) īsa   čāwal   čāšt=ū   čìw   bē| īsa   šīrīnì̀=n.|
    now   in.the.past   meal=and   thing be.PSTC.3SG   now   sweets=COP.3SG.M
'Now, in the past there used to be a meal [that was served], nowadays it is sweets.'

bā   qəsa=y   qayīm-ì̀=t   pay   Ø-kar-ū.|
HORT   saying=EZ   old-OBL.M=2SG   to   SBJV-do.PRS-1SG
'Let me tell you about the past.'

jārē   bàr-ēn-ē=mā| xəzmàt=mā   pana   kar-ēn-ē.|
at.the.beginning take.PRS-PSTC-3PL=1PL   service=1PL by   do.PRS-PSTC-3PL
'In the beginning, they (the brides' families) would take us (the family of the fiancé) and make us do them some services.'

dřè̀=mā   pana   pēč-ēn-ē.ǀ
prickle=1PL   by   twist.PRS-PSTC-3PL
'They would make us twist the pile of prickles.'

ā   mən   žànī=m   ārdē-bē.ǀ
PTCL   1SG   wife=1SG   bring.PST.PTCP.F-be.PSTC.3SG
'[It is ironic] that I took a wife [and had to do all that labour.]'

(5) màn| mən   žàn-ē=m   ārd-a.ǀ
     1SG   1SG   woman-INDF=1SG   bring.PST-3SG.F
     'I, I took a wife.'

^A'ašhad-u-bīlā^A   yarè̀   sāḷ-ē   xəzmat=šā   pana   kard-ā.ǀ
by.God   three   year-DIR.PL   service=3PL   by   do.PST-1SG
'By God, they (the bride's family) made me work for them for a period of three years.'

bàrd-ā=šāǀ   ka   ba   hayàt=əm   ālf=əm
take.PST-1SG=3PL   SBRD   in   life=1SG   grass=1SG
na-kana=nǀ   bard-ā=šā   āḷə̀f   kan-ay.ǀ
NEG-mow.PST.PTCP.M=COP.3SG.M   take.PST-1SG=3PL   fodder   mow.PST-INF
'They took me—I have never mowed grass in my life—they took me to grass-mowing.'

dřè̀=šā   pana   kan-ā,ǀ
prickle.DIR.SG=3PL   by   mow.PST-1SG
'They made me cut down prickles.'

āḷə̀f=šā   pana   pēt-ā.ǀ
fodder.DIR.SG=3PL   by   gather.PST-1SG
'They made me gather the fodder.'

dəmằ=w   ānayǀ   jà̀   žan-ēkī=šā
after=EZ   DEM.DIST.OBL.SG.M   then   woman-INDF.OBL=3PL
dā-(ā)nē=ū.ǀ   àrd-a=m.ǀ
give.PST-1SG=and   bring.PST-3SG.F=1SG
'Only then did they give me a woman (my wife), and I took her.'

(6) mən žàn-ē=m   māra   bəřyē=na| sar=ū
    1SG woman.DIR.F-INDF=1SG marriage.portion cut.PTCP.F=3SG.F on=EZ
    ṣa   tmanà.|
    100   toman
    'I married (a) woman for 100 tomans (currency unit) as a wedding portion.'

    yūa=m   måra   bəřyē=na   sar=ū   yaraṣa
    one.F=1SG marriage.portion cut.PTCP.F=3SG.F on=EZ   300
    təmana|,   īna   har   pay wḕ=m.|
    toman   DEM.PROX   EMPH for REFL=1SG
    'I married another woman for 300 tomans as a wedding portion, that was for me.'

    yūà=yč=əm   māra   bəřyē=na| har   pay wḕ=m|
    one.F=ADD=1SG   marriage cut.PTCP.F=3SG.F EMPH for REFL=1SG
    yarḕ,| ba yaraṣà   tman-ī.|
    three   by 300   toman-OBL.M
    'I married another, again for myself—this makes it three women—for 300 tomans as a wedding portion.'

    īna   mārày=mā   bē.|
    DEM.PROX.SG   wedding.portion=1PL be.PST.3SG
    'The wedding portion used to be this much for us.'

(7) sara   yām   bəzḕ| yām   bəza-ḷḕ|
    sacrifice   either goat   or   kid.goat-DIM
    'The [animal] sacrifice [for the wedding was] either a goat or a kid-goat.'

    dasàř-ē   čīw-ē   wəz-ēn-mē   məl-ī=š=ū|
    kerchief-INDF thing-INDF put-PSTC-1PL neck-OBL.M=3SG=and
    'We would put a kerchief or something [similar] around its (the goat's) neck'

    d-ēn-mē=š   das   zāřòl-ēwa=w|
    give-PSTC-1PL=3SG   hand   child-INDF=and
    'and would give it to a child [to carry].'

bar-ēn-mē   čā   sara=š   bəř-ēn-mḛ̀ˈ   pay   yāna=w
take.PRS-PSTC-1PL there   head=3SG   cut-PSTC-1PL   for   house=EZ
ẉayẉḛ̀ˈ   yāna=w   hasūrà-y.ˈ
bride.OBL.F   house=EZ father.in.law-OBL.M
'We would take [the goat], and behead it over there. [It was] for the family of the bride, [i.e.] for the family of the [groom's] father-in-law.'

a   čē=č   sā   sar-ḛ̀ˈ   duḛ̀   sarē
PRSNT   here=ADD   then   CLF-INDF   two   CLF-INDF
haywān   sara   bəř-ēn-ē=ūˈ
animal   head   cut.PRS-PSTC-3PL=and
'Here [at the bride's family] too, they would behead one or two animals.'

yarḛ̀   řoē=wˈ   duḛ̀   řoē=wˈ   panjà   řoē=wˈ
three   day-PL.DIR=and two   day-PL.DIR=and   five   day-PL.DIR=and
ēnna   zamāwənà   kar-ēn-mē=w   hurpř-ēn-mē.ˈ
this.much wedding.ceremony   do.PRS-PSTC-1PL=and   dance.PRS-PSTC-1PL
'[For a period of] three days, two days, [or] five days, we used to hold wedding ceremonies this long, [and] dance.'

pànj   řoē   zamāwəna   [b-ē?]ˈ
five   day-PL.DIR   wedding.ceremony   be-PSTC.3SG
'Would the wedding ceremony last for five days?'

arē   panj   řoē   hurpř-ēn-mḛ̀.ˈ
yes   five   day-PL.DIR   dance.PRS-PSTC-1PL
'Yes, we would dance for five days.'

(8) *gorānīwằč-ē   ār-ēn-mēˈ   hēḻày=šā   pay   kar-ēn-mēˈ*
     singer-PL.DIR   bring-PSTC-1PL   egg=3PL   to   do.PRS-PSTC-1PL
     pīna   dang=šā   nà-gīr-ī-ē.ˈ
     for.DEM.PROX   voice=3PL   NEG-grab.PRS-PASS-3PL
     'We would fetch singers. We would give them eggs lest their voice be interrupted.'

āwdằx=šā   d-ēn-mēˈ   pīna   dang=šā   wàr
hot.water=3PL give.PRS-PSTC-1PL   for.DEM.PROX   voice=3PL   out
b-o.ˈ
be.PRS-3SG
'We would give them hot water so that their voice be clear (lit. be free).'

Ø-zān-ì̀| īsa   pāsa   nà-mana=n.|
IND-know.PRS-2SG now   this.way   NEG-remain.PTCP.M=COP.3SG.M
'You see, nowadays things have not remained like this.'

ba hasarè̀=č| ba hasarē swār-ē   kàr-ēn-mē.|
by mule=ADD   by mule   rider-PL   do.PRS-PSTC-1PL
'By mule, we mounted them (the bride) on a mule.'

yām   bərà̀=w   waywē| swằr=ū   war=ū   dam=ū
either   brother=EZ   bride.F.OBL   rider=EZ front=EZ side=EZ
waywa-(a)kē   b-ē| kənāčakè̀=š| wāḷakè̀=š|
bride-DEF.F.OBL be-PSTC.3SG   daughter.DEF.F=3SG sister.DEF.F=3SG
'Either, the bride's brother sat in front of the bride (on the mule), his daughter, (or) his sister,'

yām   māmo-akà̀=š   swār=ū   war=ū   dam=ū| bərāzākè̀=š
or   uncle-DEF.M=3SG   rider=EZ front=EZ side=EZ nephew.DEF.OBL.F=3SG
b-ē.|
be-PSTC.3SG
'or her (the bride's) paternal uncle sat in front of his niece.'

bar-ēn-mē=š   yānà̀=w   hīn-ī.|
take.PRS-PSTC-1PL=3SG   house=EZ   thing-OBL.M
'We took her to the house of thingummy (i.e. the bridegroom).'

(9) mən   wè̀=m| žanī=m   ằrdē-bē| tājguzārì̀=ū
     1SG   REFL=1SG   woman=1SG   bring.PST-PTCP.F-BE.PSTC.3SG   coronation=EZ
     šā-y   b-ē.|
     king-OBL.M   be.PRS-PSTC.3SG
     '[When] I got married, it was [at the time of] the Shah's coronation.'

Ø-wāč-à   ē|
SBJV-say.PRS-2SG.IMP   yes
'Then (lit. say, 'yes')'

kāka   gīyān   dwāngzà   řo-ē| pànj   dagē   b-ēn-mē.|
brother   dear   twelve   day-DIR.PL   five   village.DIR.PL be.PRS-PSTC-1PL
'[For a period of] twelve days [we danced]. We were from five [different] villages.'

dwāngzà ŗo-ē| čī panj dagā-na
twelve day-DIR.PL in.DEM.PROX five village.PL.OBL-POST
hurpřā-ymḕ.|
dance.PST-1PL
'[During these] twelve days, we danced in these five villages.'

nà-lā-ym=a yāna.|
NEG-go.PST-1PL=DRCT home
'We did not go [back] home [during these twelve days].'

(10) sàr=ū dwāngza ŗoa-y| a č-ĩ Bana-na|
on=EZ twelve day-OBL.M PRSNT in-DEM.PROX PN-POST
zamāwənà bē.|
wedding COP.PST.3SG
'On the twelfth day, there was a wedding ceremony in this village of Bana.'

pīyā-ka zamā-(a)ka nām=əš 'Alī Guḷāḷà bē.|
man-DEF bridegroom-DEF.DIR name=3SG PN COP.PST.3SG
'The man, the bridegroom's name was 'Ali Gulala.'

vāt=šā, Alī Guḷāḷa zamàwəna kar-o,| da'wat=əš
say.PST=3PL PN PN wedding do.PRS-3SG invitation=3SG
kàrdē=ndē.|
do.PST.PTCP.PL=2PL
'They said, "Ali Gulala is having a marriage ceremony. He has invited you."'

ba hurpřāy=ū čapḷā taqnằy| luā-ymḕ|
by dance.INF=and hand.clap knock.INF go.PST-1PL
yarà ŗo-ē=š pā-wa bīē=nmē.|
three day-PL.DIR =3SG foot-POST be.PST.PTCP.PL=COP.1PL
'While dancing and clapping hands, we went there. We stayed with him for three days.'

īna havdà ŗo-ē| haždà ŗo-ē.|
DEM.PROX.M seventeen day-PL.DIR eighteen day-PL.DIR
'That makes it seventeen or eighteen days.'

hažda ŗo-ē jā lūā-ym=a yānà.|
eighteen day-PL.DIR then go.PST-1PL=DRCT home
'Eighteen days, then we went [back] home.'

Kurdish

The following narrative is a sample of the Kurdish dialect of Sanandaj, recorded in the village of Khiarah, located 14 kilometres south-east of Sanandaj. The text is an anecdote about a man who is disgraced by his two wives. The narrator is female, aged 70.

(1) pīyàw-ēk   a-w-ē| dù   žən=ī   a-w-ē.|
    man-INDF IND-be.PRS-3SG two wife=3SG IND-be.PRS-3SG
    'There was a man. He had two wives.'

   ē   aw   waxt=a   mənāl=ī   nà-w-ē.|
   INTJ DEM time=DEM   child=3SG NEG-be.PRS-3SG
   'Well, he had no children.'

   mənāl=ī   nà-w-ē.| bo   xwa=y   žən-akàn=ī   řāwēž
   child=3SG NEG-be.PRS-3SG for   REFL=3SG wife-DEF.PL=3SG consultation
   a-ka-n.|
   IND-do.PRS-3PL
   'He did not have children. Well, his wives took counsel with each other.'

   a-řo-n   žən-ē   hāwsā=yān   mərd-ề=ya|
   IND-go.PRS-3PL   woman-INDF   neighbour=3PL   die.PST-PSTC=PERF
   kùř-ēk=ī   a-w-ē.|
   son-INDF=3SG   IND-be.PRS-3SG
   'Then (lit. they went), a woman who was their neighbour died. She had given birth to a boy.'

(2) kùř-ēk=ī   a-w-ē.| a-řo-n   t-èr-n=ī.|
    son-INDF=3SG   IND-be.PRS-3SG IND-go.PRS-3PL IND-bring.PRS-3PL=3SG
    'She had a boy. They (i.e. the wives) went and brought him.'

   kuř-aka   t-ēr-ən   a=y-nə-n=a
   boy-DEF   IND-bring.PRS-3PL   IND=3SG-put.PRS-3PL=DRCT
   nāwpà=y   šū-aka=yān.|
   between.the.legs=3SG husband-DEF=3PL
   'They brought the boy and put him in between the legs of their husband.'

a=y-nə-n=a   *nāwpằ=y*   *šū-aka=yān=ū*|
IND=3SG-put.PRS-3PL=DRCT between.the.legs=3SG husband-DEF=3PL=and
'They put him in between the legs of their husband.'

mənāḷ-aka   *tāzà*   *bū-w=a=w*   *xön=ū*   *xönāw.*|
child-DEF fresh be.PST-PTCP=PERF=and blood=and blood_soaked
'The baby was just born, (covered) in blood.'

šū-akà| *a=y-nə-n=a*   *nāwpằ=y*
husband-DEF IND=3SG-put.PRS-3PL=DRCT between.LEGS=EZ
šū-aka=yān=ū|
husband-DEF=3PL=and
'The husband, they put the baby in between the legs of their husband.'

(3)   *t-ē-n=a*   *dar-aw*   *hāwằr*   *a-ka-n*|
     IND-come.PRS-3PL=DRCT out-POST shouting IND-do.PRS-3PL
     'They (i.e. the wives) went (lit. came) out (and) shouted'

     a-yž-ən,   *waḷằ*| *ā*   *məhamàw=ī*   *nāw*   *a-w-ē*
     IND-say.PRS-3PL by.God mr. PN=3SG name IND-be.PRS-3SG
     pīyā-(a)ka| *šu-akà=yān*|
     man-DEF husband-DEF=3PL
     '(and) said, "By God"—the man, their husband was called Mr. Muhammad,"'

     īmšaw   *ā*   *məhamaw*   *zằ-w=a*   *kuř=ī*
     tonight MR PN give.birth.PST-PTCP=PERF son=3SG
     bū-w=a.|
     be.PST-PTCP=PERF
     '"last night, Mr. Muhammad gave birth to a boy."'

(4)   *aw*   *waxt=a*   *mardəm*   *t-ề-t=ū*|
     dem time=DEM people IND-come.PRS-3SG=and
     'Then people came by.'

     gəšt=yān   *t-ề-n=ū*| *ča*   *ama*   *mənằḷ!*|
     all=3PL IND-come.PRS-3PL=and EXCM PRSNT child
     'They all came by. "Look there [is] a child!"'

řås   a-kā=w| kuř-ēk=ī   bů-w=a=w|
right   IND-do.PRS.3SG=and boy-INDF=3SG be.PST-PTCP=PERF=and
'They were right. He had (given birth to) a boy.'

pīyà   zuwān=ī   a-č-ēt=a   bas.|
man   tongue=3SG IND-go.PRS-3SG=DRCT   fastening
'The man was speechless.'

(5) pīyā zuwān=ī   a-č-ēt=a   bàs.|
    man   tongue=3SG IND-go.PRS-3SG=DRCT   fastening
    'The man was speechless.'

takàn   a-xwā| zuwān=ī   a-č-ēt=a   bàs=ū|
trembling   IND-eat.PRS   tongue   IND-go.PRS-3SG=DRCT   fastening=and
'The man shuddered (and) was speechless.'

aw   wàxt=a| žən-akān   har   dək=yān   kuřānà-yk   a-nə-n.|
DEM   time=DEM   wife-DEF.PL   each   two=3PL   PN-INDF   IND-put.PRS-3PL
'Then, the wives hold a celebration called kuřāna (lit. relating to the boys).'

(6) a-řo-n   lotī   t-èr-n=ū|
    IND-go.PRS-3PL   singer   IND-bring.PRS-3PL=and
    'They went (and) brought a singer.'

la   hàwš-ā| hawš-ē   gawrà=yān   a-w-ē   wak   am
at   yard-POST   yard-INDF   big=3PL   IND-be.PRS-3SG   like DEM.PROX
hawš   ēma=w|
yard   1PL=and
'In the yard—they had a big yard, like this yard of ours.'

hawš-ē   gawrà=yān   a-w-ēt=ū|
yard-INDF   big=3PL   IND-be.PRS-3SG=and
'They had a big house.'

a-řo-n   kuřānà   a-nə-n.|
IND-go.PRS-3PL   PN   IND-put.PRS-3PL
'They went (and) held kuřāna.'

	īmšaw	ā	məhamaw	zằ-w=a		kuř=ī
	tonight	MR	PN	give.birth.PST-PTCP=PERF		son=3SG

bū-w=a.|
be.PST-PTCP=PERF
'"Last night, Mr. Muhammad gave birth to a boy."'

(7) ā   məhama=yč   la   xajāḷatì̀   xo=y-ā|
    Mr. PN=ADD   from   shame   REFL=3SG-POST
    'Mr Mohammad, in a state of disgrace,'

soḥ-ā   haḷ-a-s-ē   jəft-ē   sarpāyì̀
morning-POST   PVB-IND-set.PRS-3SG pair-INDF   sandal
a-xā   sar   pā=y-awa=w|
IND-throw.PRS.3SG on   foot=3SG-POST=and
'woke up next morning, put on a pair of sandals,'

gočằn-ēk   a-wr-ēt=a   das-aw|
crook-INDF   IND-grab.PRS.3SG=DRCT   hand-POST
'grabbed the crook in his hand,'

sar   xwa=y   haḷ-a-wr-ē   la   āwāyī   dàr-a-č-ē.|
head REFL=3SG   PVB-IND-grab.PRS.3SG   from   village   PVB-IND-go.PRS.3SG
'(and) set off (and) left the village.'

(8) la   āwāyī   dar-a-č-ē   la   xajāḷatì̀   xwa=y-ā.|
    from   village PVB-IND-go.PRS.3SG   from   shame   REFL=3SG-POST
    'As the result of the disgrace (inflicted on him), he left the village.'

ā   məhamàw| bā   pīyaw   kày   zā-w=a
mr.   PN   well   man   when   give.birth-PTCP=PERF
kuř=ī   bū-w=a?|
boy=3SG   be.PST-PTCP=PERF
'Mr Muhammad, well, since when does a man give birth to a boy?'

āxər   am   žən-gal=a   čə   kəḷằw-ēk=yān   nīā   sar
DISC   DEM.PROX   wife-PL=DEM   what   hat-INDF=3PL   put.PST head
am   šū=yān=a!|
DEM.PROX   husband=3PL=DEM
'What a trick the wives played on their husband!'

(9) aw   waxt=a   haḷ-a-s-ē   a-r-ȯ̀.|
    DEM   time=DEM   PVB-IND-set.PRS-3SG   IND-go.PRS-3SG
    'Well (lit. that time), he rose (and) went away.'

    ba   xwā   čàn   sāḷ   a-r-ö.|
    by   God   some   year   IND-go.PRS-3SG
    'Indeed, he left (the village) for some years.'

    sar   xwa=y   haḷ-a-wr-è̀.|
    head   REFL=3SG   PVB-IND-grab.PRS-3SG
    'He left home (for an unknown place).'

    žən=īč   mằḷ   bo   xwa=y| nāw   xo=yān-ā
    wife=ADD   house   for   REFL=3SG   between   REFL=3PL-POST
    māḷ   bàš   a-ka-n=ū|
    house   portion   IND-do.PRS-3PL=and
    'As for the wives, they divided the property between themselves.'

    a=y-ka-n=a   dukùt-aw   bo   xo=yān=ū|
    IND=3SG-do.PRS-3PL=DRCT   two.halves-POST   for   REFL=3PL=and
    'They cut (everything) in half (and kept it) for themselves.'

(10) aw=īč   a-ř-ȯ̀| ba   xwā   čan   sằḷ=ī   pē
     3SG=ADD   IND-go.PRS-3SG   by   God   some   year=3SG   to
     a-č-ēt=ū|
     IND-go.PRS-3SG=and
     'He left. Indeed, some years passed.'

     t-è̀-t=aw| la   nəzīk   àw   dēy-aw
     IND-come.PRS-3SG=TELIC   at   near   DEM.DIST   village-POST
     t-ē-t=aw.|
     IND-come.PRS-3SG=TELIC
     'He came back. He came back from somewhere close to the village.'

     a-yž-ē,   bāwa   mən   mằḷ-ēk=əm   bū.|
     IND-say.PRS-3SG   EXCM   1SG   house-INDF=1SG   be.PST.3SG
     'He said, "Oh, I had a house."'

jīya=ū   řè̂-k=əm   bū.|
place=and   road-INDF=1SG   be.PST.3SG
"'I had a place and a career.[5]'"

bā   bə-řo-m=aw   bə-zān-əm   čà=yān   pē
HORT   SBJV-go.PRS-1SG=TELIC   SBJV-know.PRS-1SG   what=3PL   to
hāt.|
come.PST.3SG
"'I shall go back to see what happened to it.'"

awa   mən   sar   xwa=m   haḷ-gərt-ē=a
PRSNT   1SG   head   REFL=1SG   PVB-grab.PST-PTCP=PERF
la   dāx   am   žən-àl=a.|
from   hatred   DEM.PROX   wife-PL=DEM
"'I have left home because of (my) hatred of these wives.'"

(11) t-ē-t   du   bərā   la   pə̀ř   āwāyī-aw| aw
     IND-come.PRS-3SG   two   brother   at   edge   village-POST   DEM.DIST
     āwāyì̂   xo=yān=a.|
     village   REFL=3PL=DEM
     'He came (towards his village). Two brothers (were) at the edge of the village, his (lit. their) own village.'

la   pəř   āwāyī-aw   dāwà̂=yān=a.|
at   edge   village-POST   fight=3PL=COP.3SG
'They were fighting at the edge of the village.'

dāwā=yān=a   aw=īž   a-řò̂-t,   a-yž-ēt|
fight=3PL=COP.3SG   3SG=ADD   IND-go.PRS-3SG   IND-say.PRS-3SG
'They were fighting. He went (and) said,'

a-řö-t=ū   nāwjī=yān   a-kà̂=w   a-yž-ē,|
IND-go.PRS-3SG=and   mediating=3PL   IND-do.PRS-3SG=and   IND-say.PRS-3SG
'he went (and) mediated between them (and) said,'

---

5 Literally: road.

bərā   bočà   a-wa-n   la   yak?
brother why   IND-give.PRS-2PL   at   one
"'Brother, why are you hitting each other?'"

ča=s   lasar   čà   bočà dāwā=tān=a?
what=COP.3SG because.of   what why   strife=2PL=COP.3SG
"'What is it? For what reason are you fighting?'"

(12) a-yž-ē,   bərā   tu   nà̇-zān-ī!
     IND-say.PRS-3SG   brother 2SG   NEG-know.PRS-2SG
     'He (one of the brothers) said, "Brother, you don't know [what the story is]!"'

àm   bərā=m=a   ēma   aw   sà̇ḷ=a   ā
DEM.PROX   brother=1SG=DEM 1PL   DEM.PROX   year=COP.3SG   mr.
məhamaw   zā-w=a   kuř-aka=y   bū-w=a
PN   give.birth.PST-PTCP=PERF boy-DEF=3SG   be.PST-PTCP=PERF
"'(Together) with my brother, the year in which Mr. Muhammad gave birth to a boy,'"

ēma   àm   zawī=mān=a   baš   kərd-ē=ya.
1PL   DEM.PROX   land=1PL=DEM   portion   do.PST-PTCP=PERF
"'we divided this land.'"

īsà   a-yž-ēt,   baš-aka=y   tu   xà̇s=a
now   IND-say.PRS-3SG portion-DEF=EZ   2SG   good=COP.3SG
"'Now, he says, "Your share is good,"'"

hēn-aka=y   mən   xərà̇w=a.
EZ.PRON-DEF=EZ   1SG   bad=COP.3SG
"'(however) mine is bad.'"

lasar   awà   xarīk=a   dāwā=ya   tak=mā.
because.of   DEM.DIST   busy=COP.3SG   strif=COP.3SG   with=1PL
"'That's why he is fighting with me.'"

(13) aw=īž   a-yž-ē,   ay   māḷ   wērān=əm   hay!
     DEM=ADD   IND-say.PRS-3SG   EXCM   house ruined=1SG EXCM
     'Mr. Muhammad (lit. he) said, "Oh, may my house be ruined!"'

nāw=əm   gum   nà-wū-w=a.|
name=1SG   lost   NEG-be.PST-PTCP=PERF
"'My name has not been forgotten!' (lit. it has not been lost).'"

yawāš-ē   hàḷ-a-s-ē| wa   šon-aka=y   xo=y=ā
slowly-INDF   PVB-IND-set.PRS-3SG   in   direction-DEF=EZ REFL=3SG=POST
a-wā   lē   a-ř-ò̩.|
IND-give.PRS.3SG   at   IND-go.PRS-3SG
'Then, he rose (and) went back in the direction he had come from.'

a-wà̩   lē   a-ř-ö| sar   xwa=y
IND-give.PRS.3SG   at   IND-go.PRS-3SG   head   REFL=3SG
hàḷ-a-wr-ē.|
PVB-IND-grab.PRS-3SG
'He set off. He left.'

(14) sar   xwa=y   hàḷ-a-wr-ē.|
      head   REFL=3SG   PVB-IND-grab.PRS-3SG
      'He left.'

a-wà̩   lē   a-ř-ö.|
IND-give.PRS.3SG   at   IND-go.PRS-3SG
'He set off.'

a-yž-ē,   bərā   bə-řò-n| xwā   har   xo=tān
IND-say.PRS.3SG   brother   SBJV-go.PRS-2PL   God   each   REFL=2PL
hàr   kār-ēk   a-ka-n   b=ī-ka-n.|
each   task-INDF   IND-do.PRS-2PL   SBJV=3SG-do.PRS-2PL
'He said, "Brothers, go (and settle it) yourselves. Do whatever you wish to do."'

a-ř-ö   ītər   nà̩-yē-t=aw   bo   aw   dē=ya.|
IND-go.PRS.3SG   no.more   NEG-come.PRS-3SG=TELIC   to   DEM.DIST   village=DEM
'He left. He did not go back to that village again.'

a-ř-ö   sar   xwa=y   hàḷ-a-wr-ē   a-ř-ö.|
IND-go.PRS.3SG   head   REFL=3SG   PVB-grab.PRS-3SG   IND-go.PRS-3SG
'He went away. He left (the village).'

bāqī	*wa*	*salåm*ꟾ	*nāma*	*wa*	*tamåm.*ꟾ
remaining	to	greeting	letter	to	finishing

'The rest (is) for (another) greeting. The letter (i.e. the tale) has come to end.

References

Abdul-Majeed Rashid, Ahmad. 1986. 'The Phonemic System of Modern Standard Kurdish.' Michigan: University of Michigan Ph.D. dissertation.
Ahmed, Zhwan, Othman. 2019. 'The Application of English Theories to Sorani Phonology'. Durham: Durham University Ph.D. dissertation.
Aikhenvald, Alexandra Y. 2003. *Language Contact in Amazonia*. Oxford: Oxford University Press.
Aikhenvald, Alexandra Y. 2004. *Evidentiality*. Oxford: Oxford University Press.
Aikhenvald, Alexandra Y., and Robert M. W. Dixon, eds. 2001. *Areal Diffusion and Genetic Inheritance*. Oxford: Oxford University Press.
Anonby, Erik, and Mortaza Taheri-Ardali. 2018. 'Bakhtiari'. In *The Languages and Linguistics of Western Asia: An Areal Perspective*, edited by Geoffrey Haig and Geoffrey Khan, 445–80. The World of Linguistics 6. Berlin: De Gruyter.
Ardalan, Sheerin. 2004. *Les Kurdes Ardalân. Entre La Perse et l'Empire Ottoman*. Paris: Guethner.
Avinery, Iddo. 1988. *Ha-Niv ha-ʾArami šel Yehude Zakho: Ṭeqsṭim be-Ṣeruf Targum ʾIvri, Mavo u-Milon* [*The Aramaic Dialect of the Jews of Zakho: Texts together with a Hebrew Translation, Introduction and Glossary*]. Jerusalem: The Israeli Academy of Sciences.
Bailey, Denise. 2018. 'A Grammar of Gawrajū Gūrānī'. Göttingen: Universität Göttingen Ph.D. dissertation.
Bar-Asher Siegal, Elitzur A. 2016. *Introduction to the Grammar of Jewish Babylonian Aramaic*. 2nd ed. Lehrbücher Orientalischer Sprachen III/3. Münster: Ugarit-Verlag.
Barry, Daniel. 2019. 'Pharyngeals in Kurmanji Kurdish: A Reanalysis of Their Source and Status'. In *Current Issues in Kurdish Linguistics*, edited by Songül Gündoğdu, Ergin Öpengin, Geoffrey Haig, and Erik Anonby, 39–71. Bamberg Studies in Kurdish Linguistics 1. Bamberg: University of Bamberg Press.
Becker, Laura. 2018. 'Articles in the World's Languages'. Leipzig: Universität Leipzig dissertation.
Benveniste, Émile. 1971. *Problems in General Linguistics*. Miami Linguistics Series 8. Coral Gables, Fla.: University of Miami Press.
Bickel, Balthasar, and Johanna Nichols. 2007. 'Inflectional Morphology'. In *Language Typology and Syntactic Description*, edited by Tim Shopen, 3:169–240. Cambridge: Cambridge University Press.
Blevins, Juliette. 2017. 'Areal Sound Patterns: From Perceptual Magnets to Stone Soup'. In *The Cambridge Handbook of Areal Linguistics*, edited by Raymond Hickey, 88–121. Cambridge: Cambridge University Press.
Bolonyai, Agnes. 1998. 'In-between Languages: Language Shift/Maintenance in Childhood Bilingualism'. *International Journal of Bilingualism* 2: 21–43.
Boneh, Nora, and Edit Doron. 2013. 'Hab and Gen in the Expression of Habituality'. In *Genericity*, edited by Alda Mari, Claire Beyssade, and Fabio Del Prete, 176–91. Oxford: Oxford University Press.
Boneh, Nora, and Łukasz Jędrzejowski. 2019. 'Reflections on Habituality across Other Grammatical Categories'. *Language Typology and Universals* 72 (1): 1–20.
Borghero, Roberta. 2015. 'The Present Continuous in the Neo-Aramaic Dialect of ʿAnkawa and Its Areal and Typological Parallels'. In *Neo-Aramaic and Its Linguistic Context*, edited by Geoffrey Khan and Lidia Napiorkowska, 187–206. Piscataway, NJ: Gorgias Press.
Botne, Robert, and Tiffany L. Kershner. 2008. 'Tense and Cognitive Space: On the Organization of Tense/Aspect Systems in Bantu Languages and Beyond'. *Cognitive Linguistics* 19: 145–218.
Brunner, Christopher J. 1977. *A Syntax of Western Middle Iranian*. Delmar, New York: Caravan Books.

Bulut, Christiane. 2018. 'The Turkic Varieties of Iran'. In *The Languages and Linguistics of Western Asia: An Areal Perspective*, edited by Geoffrey Haig and Geoffrey Khan, 398–444. Berlin, Boston: De Gruyter Mouton.

Butts, Aaron M. 2016. *Language Change in the Wake of Empire: Syriac in Its Greco-Roman Context*. Linguistic Studies in Ancient West Semitic 11. Winona Lake: Eisenbrauns.

Bybee, Joan L., Revere D. Perkins, and William Pagliuca. 1994. *The Evolution of Grammar: Tense, Aspect, and Modality in the Languages of the World*. Chicago: University of Chicago Press.

Carlson, Gregory. 2012. 'Habitual and Generic Aspect'. In *The Oxford Handbook of Tense and Aspect*, edited by Robert I. Binnick, 828–51. Oxford: Oxford University Press.

Carruthers, Janice. 2012. 'Discourse and Text'. In *The Oxford Handbook of Tense and Aspect*, edited by Robert I. Binnick, 306–34. Oxford: Oxford University Press.

Christensen, Arthur, and Åge Meyer Benedictsen. 1921. *Les dialectes d'Awroman et de Pawa*. Kobenhavn: B. Lunos.

Chyet, Michael L. 1995. 'Neo-Aramaic and Kurdish: An Interdisciplinary Consideration of Their Influence on Each Other'. *Israel Oriental Studies* 15: 219–49.

Chyet, Micheal L. 1997. 'A Preliminary List of Aramaic Loanwords in Kurdish'. In *Humanism, Culture, and Language in the Near East: Studies in Honor of Georg Krotkoff*, edited by Georg Krotkoff, Asma Afsaruddin, and A. H. Mathias Zahniser. Winona Lake, Ind: Eisenbrauns.

Ciancaglini, Claudia A. 2008. *Iranian Loanwords in Syriac*. Wiesbaden: Reichert.

Coghill, Eleanor. 2020. 'Northeastern Neo-Aramaic and Language Contact'. In *The Oxford Handbook of Language Contact*, edited by Anthony P. Grant, 494–518. Oxford: Oxford University Press. https://doi.org/10.1093/oxfordhb/9780199945092.013.19.

Cohen, Eran. 2012. *The Syntax of Neo-Aramaic: The Jewish Dialect of Zakho*. Neo-Aramaic Studies. Piscataway: Gorgias Press.

Croft, William. 2003. *Typology and Universals*. 2nd edition. Cambridge: Cambridge University Press.

Dawkins, Richard M. 1916. *Modern Greek in Asia Minor*. Cambridge: Cambridge University Press.

De Morgan, Jacques. 1904. *Mission scientifique en Perse. Études linguistiques. Dialectes kurdes Tome 5*. Paris: E. Leroux.

Dik, Simon. 1981. 'On the Typology of Focus Phenomena'. In *Perspectives on Functional Grammar*, edited by Teun Hoekstra, 41–74. Dordrecht: Foris.

Dixon, Robert M. W. 2000. 'A Typology of Causatives: Form, Syntax and Meaning'. In *Changing Valency: Case Studies in Transitivity*, edited by Robert M. W. Dixon and Alexandra Y. Aikhenvald, 30–83. Cambridge: Cambridge University Press.

Dorian, Nancy C. 1993. 'Internally and Externally Motivated Change in Contact Situations: Doubts about Dichotomy'. In *Historical Linguistics: Problems and Perspectives*, edited by Charles Jones, 131–55. London: Longman.

Durkin-Meisterernst, Desmond. 2014. *Grammatik des Westmitteliranischen (Parthisch und Mittelpersisch)*. Sitzungsberichte Der Phil.-Hist. Klasse 850, Veröffentlichungen zur Iranistik 73, Grammatica Iranica, Band 1. Wien: Verlag der Österreichischen Akademie der Wissenschaften.

Duval, Rubens. 1883. *Les Dialectes Néo-Araméens de Salamâs: Textes sur l'État Actuel de la Perse et Contes Populaires Publiés avec une Traduction Française*. Paris: F. Vieweg.

Ebrahimpour, Mohammad Taghi. undated. *Dastur-e Zaban-e Kurdi-e Sanandaji [A Grammar of Sanandaji Kurdish]*.

Emeneau, Murray. 1956. 'India as a Linguistic Area'. *Language* 32: 3–16.

Emeneau, Murray. 1980. *Language and Linguistic Areas*. Edited by Anwar S. Dil. Stanford: Stanford University Press.

Epps, Patience, and Kristine Stenzel. 2013. 'Introduction'. In *Upper Rio Negro: Cultural and Linguistic Interaction in Northwestern Amazonia*, edited by Patience Epps and Kristine Stenzel, 13–52. Rio de Janeiro: Museu Nacional Museu do Índio – Funai.

Fassberg, Steven. 2010. *The Jewish Neo-Aramaic Dialect of Challa*. Leiden-Boston: Brill.

Floyd, Simeon. 2013. 'Semantic Transparency and Cultural Calquing in the Northwest Amazon'. In *Upper Rio Negro: Cultural and Linguistic Interaction in Northwestern Amazonia*, edited by Patience Epps and Kristine Stenzel, 271–306. Rio de Janeiro: Museu Nacional Museu do Índio – Funai.

Fought, Carmen. 2010. 'Ethnic Identity and Linguistic Contact'. In *The Handbook of Language Contact*, edited by Raymond Hickey, 282–98. Chichester: Wiley-Blackwell.

Fox, Samuel E. 2009. *The Neo-Aramaic Dialect of Bohtan*. Piscataway: Gorgias.

Garbell, Irene. 1965. *The Jewish Neo-Aramaic Dialect of Persian Azerbaijan; Linguistic Analysis and Folkloristic Texts*. Janua Linguarum. Series Practica 3. London: Mouton.

Gardner-Chloros, Penelope. 2010. 'Contact and Code-Switching'. In *The Handbook of Language Contact*, edited by Raymond Hickey, 188–207. Chichester: Wiley-Blackwell.

Grant, Anthony P. 2020. 'Contact-Induced Linguistic Change: An Introduction'. In *The Oxford Handbook of Language Contact*, edited by Anthony P. Grant, 1–48. Oxford: Oxford University Press.

Greenblatt, Jared. 2011. *The Jewish Neo-Aramaic Dialect of Amadya*. Studies in Semitic Languages and Linguistics 61. Leiden: Brill.

Gutman, Ariel. 2018. *Attributive Constructions in North-Eastern Neo-Aramaic*. Studies in Diversity Linguistics 15. Berlin: Language Science Press.

Häberl, Charles. 2009. *The Neo-Mandaic Dialect of Khorramshahr*. Semitica Viva 45. Wiesbaden: Harrassowitz.

Haig, Geoffrey. 2008. *Alignment Change in Iranian Languages: A Construction Grammar Approach*. Empirical Approaches to Language Typology 37. Berlin New York: Mouton de Gruyter.

Haig, Geoffrey. 2015. 'Verb-Goal (Vg) Word Order in Kurdish and Neo-Aramaic: Typological and Areal Considerations'. In *Neo-Aramaic and Its Linguistic Context*, edited by Lidia Napiorkowska, 407–25. Gorgias Press. https://doi.org/10.31826/9781463236489-025.

Haig, Geoffrey. 2018. 'The Iranian Languages of Northern Iraq'. In *The Languages and Linguistics of Western Asia: An Areal Perspective*, edited by Geoffrey Haig and Geoffrey Khan, 267–304. The World of Linguistics 6. Berlin: De Gruyter Mouton.

Haig, Geoffrey, and Geoffrey Khan, eds. 2018. *The Languages and Linguistics of Western Asia: An Areal Perspective*. The World of Linguistics 6. Berlin: De Gruyter.

Haig, Geoffrey, and Ergin Öpengin. 2014. 'Introduction to Special Issue – Kurdish: A Critical Research Overview'. *Kurdish Studies* 2 (2): 99–122. https://doi.org/10.33182/ks.v2i2.397.

Hamid, Twana. 2014. 'Final Devoicing in Central Kurdish: An OT Analysis'. *Newcastle and Northumbria Working Papers in Linguistics* 20: 17–27.

Hamid, Twana. 2015. *The prosodic phonology of central Kurdish*. Newcastle: Newcastle University Ph.D. dissertation.

Haspelmath, Martin, and Uri Tadmor, eds. 2009. *Loanwords in the World's Languages: A Comparative Handbook*. Berlin, New York: De Gruyter Mouton. https://doi.org/10.1515/9783110218442.

Hazen, Kirk. 2000. *Identity and Ethnicity in the Rural South: A Sociolinguistic View through Past and Present Be*. Publications of the American Dialect Society 83. Durham, NC: Duke University Press.

Heine, Bernd, and Tania Kuteva. 2003. 'On Contact-Induced Grammaticalization'. *Studies in Language* 27: 529–72.

Heine, Bernd, and Tania Kuteva. 2005. *Language Contact and Grammatical Change*. Cambridge: Cambridge University Press.

Heine, Bernd, and Tania Kuteva. 2010. 'Contact and Grammaticalization'. In, edited by Raymond Hickey, 86–105. Chichester: Wiley-Blackwell.
Heinrichs, Wolfhart. 2002. 'Peculiarities of the Verbal System of Senaya within the Framework of North Eastern Neo-Aramaic (NENA)'. In *"Sprich Doch mit deinen Knechten Aramäisch, Wir Verstehen Es!" 60 Beiträge zur Semitistik. Festschrift für Otto Jastrow zum 60. Geburtsag*, edited by Werner Arnold and Hartmut Bobzin, 238–68. Wiesbaden: Harrassowitz.
Hickey, Raymond. 2010a. 'Contact and Language Shift'. In *The Handbook of Language Contact*, edited by Raymond Hickey, 151–69. Chichester: Wiley-Blackwell.
Hickey, Raymond. 2010b. 'Language Contact: Reconsideration and Reassessment'. In *Handbook of Language Contact*, edited by Raymond Hickey, 1–28. Chichester: Wiley-Blackwell.
Hoberman, Robert. 1988. 'The History of the Modern Aramaic Pronouns and Pronominal Suffixes'. *Journal of the American Oriental Society* 108: 557–75.
Holman, Eric W., Søren Wichmann, Cecil H. Brown, Viveka Velupillai, André Müller, and Dik Bakker. 2008. 'Explorations in Automated Language Classification' 42 (3–4): 331–54. https://doi.org/10.1515/FLIN.2008.331.
Hopkins, Simon. 1999. 'The Neo-Aramaic Dialects of Iran'. In *Irano-Judaica IV*, edited by Shaul Shaked and Amnon Netzer, 311–27. Jerusalem: Magnes.
Hopkins, Simon. 2002. 'Preterite and Perfect in the Jewish Neo-Aramaic of Kerend'. In *"Sprich Doch mit deinen Knechten Aramäisch, Wir Verstehen Es!" 60 Beiträge zur Semitistik. Festschrift für Otto Jastrow zum 60. Geburtsag*, edited by Werner Arnold and Hartmut Bobzin, 281–98. Wiesbaden: Harrassowitz.
Huddleston, Rodney D., and Geoffrey K. Pullum. 2002. *The Cambridge Grammar of the English Language*. Cambridge: Cambridge University Press.
Irvine, Judith T. 1979. 'Formality and Informality in Communicative Events'. *American Anthropologist* 81: 773–90.
Izady, Mehrdad. 1992. *The Kurds: A Concise Handbook*. 1st edition. Washington: Routledge.
Jaba, Alexandre. 1860. *Recueil de Notices et de Récits Kourdes*. Saint Petersburg.
Jakobson, Roman. 1971. *Selected Writings*. The Hague: Mouton.
Jastrow, Otto. 1979. 'Zur Arabischen Mundart von Mossul'. *Zeitschrift für Arabische Linguistik* 2: 36–75.
Jastrow, Otto. 1988. *Der Neuaramäische Dialekt von Hertevin (Provinz Siirt)*. Semitica Viva 3. Wiesbaden: O. Harrassowitz.
Jastrow, Otto. 1990. *Der Arabische Dialekt der Juden von 'Aqra und Arbīl*. Semitica Viva 5. Wiesbaden: Harrassowitz.
Johanson, Lars. 2000. 'Turkic Indirectives'. In *Evidentials: Turkic, Iranian and Neighboring Languages*, edited by Lars Johanson and Bo Utas, 61–87. Berlin: Mouton de Gruyter.
Joseph, Brian D. 1983. *The Balkan Infinitive*. Cambridge: Cambridge University Press.
Joseph, Brian D. 2010. 'Language Contact in the Balkans'. In *The Handbook of Language Contact*, edited by Raymond Hickey, 618–33. Chichester: Wiley-Blackwell.
Jügel, Thomas. 2014. 'On the Linguistic History of Kurdish'. *Kurdish Studies* 2 (2): 123–42.
Kahn, Margaret. 1976. 'Borrowing and Variation in a Phonological Description of Kurdish'. Michigan: University of Michigan Ph.D. dissertation.
Kalin, Laura M. 2014. 'Aspect and Argument Licensing in Neo-Aramaic'. Ph.D. thesis, University of California, Los Angeles.
Kaltenböck, Gunther, Bernd Heine, and Tania Kuteva. 2011. 'On Thetical Grammar'. *Studies in Language* 35 (4): 852–97.
Khan, Geoffrey. 1999. *A Grammar of Neo-Aramaic: The Dialect of the Jews of Arbel*. Boston, MA: Brill.
Khan, Geoffrey. 2002a. *The Neo-Aramaic Dialect of Qaraqosh*. Leiden: Brill.

Khan, Geoffrey. 2002b. 'The Neo-Aramaic Dialect of the Jews of Rustaqa'. In *"Sprich Doch mit deinen Knechten Aramäisch, Wir Verstehen Es!" 60 Beiträge zur Semitistik, Festschrift für Otto Jastrow Zum 60. Geburtstag*, edited by Werner Arnold and Hartmut Bobzin, 395–410. Wiesbaden: Harrassowitz.

Khan, Geoffrey. 2004. *The Jewish Neo-Aramaic Dialect of Sulemaniyya and Ḥalabja*. Studies in Semitic Languages and Linguistics 44. Leiden: Brill.

Khan, Geoffrey. 2007a. 'Grammatical Borrowing in North-Eastern Neo-Aramaic'. In *Grammatical Borrowing in Cross-Linguistic Perspective*, edited by Yaron Matras and Jeanette Sakel, 197–214. Berlin, New York: De Gruyter Mouton. https://doi.org/10.1515/9783110199192.197.

Khan, Geoffrey. 2007b. 'Indicative Markers in North Eastern Neo-Aramaic'. In *XII Incontro Italiano di Linguistica Camito-Semitica (Afroasiatica). Atti*, edited by Marco Moriggi, 85–97. Soveria Mannelli: Rubbettino.

Khan, Geoffrey. 2008a. *The Jewish Neo-Aramaic Dialect of Urmi*. Gorgias Neo-Aramaic Studies. Piscataway: Gorgias.

Khan, Geoffrey. 2008b. *The Neo-Aramaic Dialect of Barwar*. 3 vols. Leiden: Brill.

Khan, Geoffrey. 2009. *The Jewish Neo-Aramaic Dialect of Sanandaj*. Piscataway, NJ: Gorgias Press.

Khan, Geoffrey. 2012. 'The Evidential Function of the Perfect in North-Eastern Neo-Aramaic Dialects'. In *Language and Nature. Papers Presented to John Huehnergard on the Occasion of His 60th Birthday*, edited by Rebecca Hasselbach and Naʻama Pat-El, 219–28. Studies in Ancient Oriental Civilization 67. Chicago: University of Chicago.

Khan, Geoffrey. 2013. 'Phonological Emphasis in North-Eastern Neo-Aramaic'. In *Base Articulatoire Arrière. Backing and Backness*, edited by Jean Léo Léonard and Samia Naïm, 111–32. Munich: Lincon Europa.

Khan, Geoffrey. 2016. *The Neo-Aramaic Dialect of the Assyrian Christians of Urmi*. 4 vols. Studies in Semitic Languages and Linguistics 86. Leiden-Boston: Brill.

Khan, Geoffrey. 2017. 'Ergativity in Neo-Aramaic'. In *Oxford Handbook of Ergativity*, edited by Jessica Coon, Diane Massam, and Lisa Travis, 873–99. Oxford: Oxford University Press.

Khan, Geoffrey. 2018a. 'Eastern Anatolia and Northwestern Iran: Overview'. In *The Languages and Linguistics of Western Asia: An Areal Perspective*, edited by Geoffrey Haig and Geoffrey Khan, 31–45. The World of Linguistics 6. Berlin: De Gruyter.

Khan, Geoffrey. 2018b. 'Remarks on the Syntax and Historical Development of the Copula In North-Eastern Neo-Aramaic Dialects'. *Aramaic Studies* 16: 234–69.

Khan, Geoffrey. 2018c. 'The Neo-Aramaic Dialects and Their Historical Background'. In *The Syriac World*, edited by Daniel King, 266–89. London: Routledge.

Khan, Geoffrey. 2018d. 'The Neo-Aramaic Dialects of Eastern Anatolia and Northwestern Iran'. In *The Languages and Linguistics of Western Asia: An Areal Perspective*, edited by Geoffrey Haig and Geoffrey Khan, 190–236. The World of Linguistics 6. Berlin: De Gruyter.

Khan, Geoffrey. 2018e. 'The Neo-Aramaic Dialects of Northern Iraq'. In *The Languages and Linguistics of Western Asia: An Areal Perspective*, edited by Geoffrey Haig and Geoffrey Khan, 305–53. The World of Linguistics 6. Berlin: De Gruyter.

Khan, Geoffrey. 2018f. 'Western Iran: Overview'. In *The Languages and Linguistics of Western Asia: An Areal Perspective*, edited by Geoffrey Haig and Geoffrey Khan, 385–97. The World of Linguistics 6. Berlin: De Gruyter.

Khan, Geoffrey. 2019. 'Copulas, Cleft Sentences and Focus Markers in Biblical Hebrew'. In *Ancient Texts and Modern Readers: Studies in Ancient Hebrew Linguistics and Bible Translation*, edited by Gideon R. Kotzé, Christian S. Locatell, and John A. Messarra, 14–62. Leiden-Boston: Brill.

Khan, Geoffrey. 2020a. 'Contact and Change in Neo-Aramaic Dialects'. In *Historical Linguistics 2017*, edited by Bridget Drinka, 391–411. Amsterdam: Benjamins.

Khan, Geoffrey. 2020b. 'The Neo-Aramaic Dialects of Iran'. *Iranian Studies* 53: 1–19.
Khan, Geoffrey. 2020c. 'The Perfect in North-Eastern Neo-Aramaic'. In *Perfects in Indo-European Languages and Beyond*, edited by Robert Crellin and Thomas Jügel, 311–50. Amsterdam: John Benjamins.
Khan, Geoffrey. 2022a. 'Remarks on the Christian Neo-Aramaic Dialect of Shaqlawa'. *Israel Oriental Studies* 21: 192–231.
Khan, Geoffrey. 2022b. 'The Change in the Grammatical Category of the Copula In North-Eastern Neo-Aramaic'. *Journal of Historical Linguistics* 12: 446–475.
Khan, Geoffrey, and Christo H.J. van der Merwe. 2020. 'Towards a Comprehensive Model for Interpreting Word Order In Classical Biblical Hebrew'. *Journal of Semitic Studies* 65: 347–90.
Koch, Harold. 1995. 'The Creation of Morphological Zeroes'. In *Yearbook of Morphology 1994*, edited by Geert Booij and Jaap van Marle, 31–71. Dordrecht: Kluwer.
Korn, Agnes. 2009. 'Western Iranian Pronominal Clitics'. *Orientalia Suecana* 58: 159–71.
Korn, Agnes. 2011. Pronouns as Verbs, Verbs as Pronouns: Demonstratives and the Copula in Iranian. In Agnes Korn, Geoffrey Haig, Simin Karimi & Pollet Samvelian (eds), *Topics in Iranian Linguistics* (34), 53–70. Wiesbaden: Reichert Verlag.
Korn, Agnes. 2016. 'A Partial Tree of Central Iranian'. *Indogermanische Forschungen* 121 (1): 401–34. https://doi.org/10.1515/if-2016-0021.
Korn, Agnes. 2019. 'Isoglosses and Subdivisions of Iranian'. *Journal of Historical Linguistics* 9 (2): 239–81.
Krifka, Manfred. 2008. 'Basic Notions of Information Structure'. *Acta Linguistica Hungarica* 55: 243–78.
Kurdistānī, Saʿīd Khān. 1930. *Mizgānī (Nazānī)* [Good News (ignorance)]. Tehran.
Labov, William. 1972. *Sociolinguistic Patterns*. Philadelphia: University of Pennsylvania Press.
Ladefoged, Peter, and Ian Maddieson. 1996. *The Sounds of the World's Languages*. Oxford: Blackwell.
Lambrecht, Knud. 1994. *Information Structure and Sentence Form*. Cambridge: Cambridge University Press.
Lazard, Gilbert. 2000. 'Le Médiatif: Considérations Théoriques et Application à l'Iranien'. In *Evidentials: Turkic, Iranian and Neighbouring Languages*, edited by Lars Johanson and Bo Utas, 209–28. Berlin: Mouton de Gruyter.
Leezenberg, Michiel. 1992. 'Gorani Influence on Central Kurdish: Substratum or Prestige Borrowing?' ILLC – Department of Philosophy, University of Amsterdam.
Leezenberg, Michiel. 2020. 'Vernacularization as Governmentalization: The Development of Kurdish in Mandate Iraq'. In *Arabic and Its Alternatives: Religious Minorities and Their Languages in the Emerging Nation States of the Middle East (1920–1950)*, edited by Heleen Murre-van den Berg, Karène Sanchez Summerer, and Tijmen Baarda, 50–76. Leiden: Brill. https://doi.org/10.1163/9789004423220.
Lenneberg, Eric. 1967. *Biological Foundations of Language*. New York: Wiley.
Lyons, John. 1977. *Semantics*. 2 vols. Cambridge: Cambridge University Press.
MacKenzie, David Neil. 1961a. *Kurdish Dialect Studies*. Vol. 1. London: Oxford University Press.
MacKenzie, David Neil. 1961b. 'The Origins of Kurdish'. *Transactions of the Philological Society*, 68–86.
MacKenzie, David Neil. 1956. 'Bājalānī'. *Bulletin of the School of Oriental and African Studies* 18: 418–35.
MacKenzie, David Neil. 1962. *Kurdish Dialect Studies*. Vol. 2. London: Oxford University Press.
MacKenzie, David Neil. 1966. *The Dialect of Awroman (Hawrāmān-ī Luhōn): Grammatical Sketch, Texts, and Vocabulary*. Bind 4, Nr 3. København: Det Kongelige Danske Videnskabernes Selskab.
MacKenzie, David Neil. 2002. 'Gurānī'. In *Encyclopaedia Iranica*, vol. XI.4, 401–403. New York: Columbia University.

Macuch, Rudolf, and Estiphan Panoussi. 1974. *Neusyrische Chrestomathie*. Porta Linguarum Orientalium. Neue Serie 13. Wiesbaden: Harrassowitz.

Magnarella, Paul J. 1969. 'A Note on Aspects of Social Life among the Jewish Kurds of Sanandaj, Iran'. *The Jewish Journal of Sociology* 11: 51–58.

Mahmoudveysi, Parvin. 2016. 'The Meter and the Literary Language of Gūrānī Poetry.' Hamburg: Universität Hamburg Ph.D. dissertation.

Mahmoudveysi, Parvin, and Denise Bailey. 2013. *The Gorani Language of Zarda, a Village of West Iran: Texts, Grammar, and Lexicon*. Wiesbaden: Reichert.

Mahmoudveysi, Parvin, and Denise Bailey. 2018. 'Hawrāmī of Western Iran'. In *The Languages and Linguistics of Western Asia: An Areal Perspective*, edited by Geoffrey Haig and Geoffrey Khan, 533–68. Berlin, Boston: De Gruyter Mouton.

Mahmoudveysi, Parvin, Denise Bailey, Ludwig Paul, and Geoffrey Haig. 2012. *The Gorani Language of Gawrajū, a Village of West Iran: Texts, Grammar, and Lexicon*. Beiträge zur Iranistik, Band 35. Wiesbaden: Reichert.

Mann, Oskar, and Karl Hadank. 1930. *Mundarten der Gûrân, Besonders das Kändûlâî, Auramânî und Bâdschälânî, Bearbeitet von Karl Hadank*. Berlin: Verlag der Preussischen Akademie der Wissenschaften in Kommission bei Walter de Gruyter & Co.

Matras, Yaron. 2002. 'Kurmanji Complementation: Semantic-Typological Aspects in an Areal Perspective'. *STUF – Language Typology and Universals* 55 (1): 49–63. https://doi.org/10.1524/stuf.2002.55.1.49.

Matras, Yaron. 2003. 'Mixed Languages: Re-Examining the Structural Prototype'. In *The Mixed Language Debate: Theoretical and Empirical Advances*, edited by Yaron Matras and Peter Bakker, 151–76. Berlin-New York: Mouton de Gruyter.

Matras, Yaron. 2007. 'The Borrowability of Structural Categories'. In *Empirical Approaches to Language Typology [EALT]*, edited by Yaron Matras and Jeanette Sakel, 31–74. Berlin, New York: Mouton de Gruyter. https://doi.org/10.1515/9783110199192.31.

Matras, Yaron. 2009. *Language Contact*. Cambridge: Cambridge University Press.

Matras, Yaron. 2010. 'Contact, Convergence, and Typology'. In *The Handbook of Language Contact*, edited by Raymond Hickey, 66–85. Chichester: John Wiley & Sons.

Matras, Yaron. 2012. Review of *Review of Loanwords in the World's Languages: A Comparative Handbook*, by Martin Haspelmath and Uri Tadmor. *Language* 88 (3): 647–52.

Matras, Yaron. 2019. 'Revisiting Kurdish Dialect Geography: Findings from the Manchester Database'. In *Current Issues in Kurdish Linguistics*, edited by Songül Gündoğdu, Ergin Öpengin, Geoffrey Haig, and Erik Anonby, 225–41. Bamberg: University of Bamberg Press.

Matras, Yaron, and Jeanette Sakel. 2007. 'Investigating the Mechanisms of Pattern Replication in Language Convergence'. *Studies in Language* 31 (4): 829–65.

McCarus, Ernest N. 1958. *A Kurdish Grammar: Descriptive Analysis of Kurdish of Suleimaniya, Iraq*. New York: American Council of Learned Societies.

McCarus, Ernest N. 1997. 'Kurdish Phonology'. In *Phonologies of Asia and Africa: Including the Caucasus*, edited by Alan S. Kaye, 1:691–706. Indiana: Eisenbrauns.

Milroy, Leslie. 1987. *Language and Social Networks*. Oxford: Blackwell.

Minorsky, Vladimir. 1943. 'The Gūrān'. *Bulletin of the School of Oriental and African Studies* 11 (1): 75–103.

Mithun, Marianne. 2011. 'The Substratum in Grammar and Discourse'. In *The Substratum in Grammar and Discourse*, edited by Ernst Håkon Jahr, 103–16. Berlin: De Gruyter Mouton. https://doi.org/10.1515/9783110851847.103.

Mohammadirad, Masoud. 2020a. 'Pronominal Clitics in Western Iranian Languages: Description, Mapping, and Typological Implications'. Paris: Ph.D. dissertation. Sorbonne Nouvelle – Paris 3. https://tel.archives-ouvertes.fr/tel-02988008.

Mohammadirad, Masoud. 2020b. Predicative possession across Western Iranian languages, *Folia Linguistica*, 54(3), 497–526. doi: https://doi.org/10.1515/flin-2020-2038

Mohammadirad, Masoud. in prep. *The Takht dialect of Hawrami: Grammar, texts, Lexicon (working title)*.

Mohammadirad, Masoud. In review. 'Bound Argument Ordering across Central Kurdish and the Gorani Substrate.' In *Oxford Hanbook of Kurdish Linguistics*, edited by Jaffer Sheyholislami, Geoffrey Haig, Haidar Khezri, Salih Akin, and Ergin Öpengin. Oxford: Oxford University Press.

Mohammadirad, Masoud. 2022a. 'Gorani (Gawrajū)'. In *WOWA — Word Order in Western Asia: A Spoken-Language-Based Corpus for Investigating Areal Effects in Word Order Variation. 24 August 2022.*, edited by Geoffrey Haig, Donald Stilo, Mahîr C. Doğan, and Nils N. Schiborr. Bamberg: Bamberg University Press. multicast.aspra.uni-bamberg.de/resources/wowa/.

Mohammadirad, Masoud. 2022b. 'Kurdish (Central, Sanandaj)'. In *WOWA — Word Order in Western Asia: A Spoken-Language-Based Corpus for Investigating Areal Effects in Word Order Variation. 24 August 2022.*, edited by Geoffrey Haig, Donald Stilo, Mahîr C. Doğan, and Nils N. Schiborr. Bamberg: University of Bamberg. multicast.aspra.uni-bamberg.de/resources/wowa/.

Mole. 2015. 'The Three /r/s of Baṛtǝḷḷa'. In *Neo-Aramaic and Its Linguistic Context*, edited by Geoffrey Khan and Lidia Napiorkowska, 110–29. Piscataway, NJ: Gorgias Press.

Mufwene, Salikoko S. 2001. *The Ecology of Language Evolution*. Cambridge: Cambridge University Press.

Mufwene, Salikoko S. 2007. 'Population Movements and Contacts: Competition, Selection, and Language Evolution'. *Journal of Language Contact* 1: 63–91.

Mutzafi, Hezy. 2004a. *The Jewish Neo-Aramaic Dialect of Koy Sanjaq (Iraqi Kurdistan)*. Semitica Viva 32. Wiesbaden: Harrassowitz Verlag.

Mutzafi, Hezy. 2004b. 'Features of the Verbal System in the Christian Neo-Aramaic Dialect of Koy Sanjaq and Their Areal Parallels'. *Journal of the American Oriental Society* 124 (2): 249–64.

Mutzafi, Hezy. 2008a. *The Jewish Neo-Aramaic Dialect of Betanure (Province of Dihok)*. Semitica Viva 43. Wiesbaden: Harrassowitz.

Mutzafi, Hezy. 2008b. 'Trans-Zab Jewish Neo-Aramaic'. *Bulletin of SOAS* 71 (3): 409–31.

Mutzafi, Hezy. 2014. 'The Three Rhotic Phonemes in Ṭyare Neo-Aramaic'. *Aramaic Studies* 12: 168–84.

Mutzafi, Hezy. 2015. 'Christian Salamas and Jewish Salmas: Two Separate Types of Neo-Aramaic'. In *Neo-Aramaic and Its Linguistic Context*, edited by Geoffrey Khan and Lidia Napiorkowska, 289–304. Piscataway, NJ: Gorgias Press.

Myers-Scotton, Carol. 1993. *Duelling Languages: Grammatical Structure in Codeswitching*. Oxford: Clarendon.

Myers-Scotton, Carol. 2002. *Contact Linguistics: Bilingual Encounters and Grammatical Outcomes*. Oxford: Oxford University Press.

Myers-Scotton, Carol. 2006. *Multiple Voices: An Introduction to Bilingualism*. Oxford: Blackwell.

Nakano, Aki'o. 1969. 'Preliminary Reports on the Zaxo Dialect of Neo- Aramaic'. *Journal of Asian and African Studies* 2: 126–42.

Nakano, Aki'o. 1973. *Conversational Texts in Eastern Neo-Aramaic (Gzira Dialect)*. Study of Languages and Cultures of Asia and Africa 4. Tokyo: Institute for the Study of Languages and Cultures of Asia and Africa.

Nöldeke, Theodor. 1904. *Compendious Syriac Grammar*. London: Williams & Norgate.

Noorlander, Paul M. 2021. *Ergativity and Other Alignment Types in Neo-Aramaic*. Leiden-Boston: Brill.

Noorlander, Paul M. 2022. 'Neo-Aramaic (Jewish Sanandaj)'. In *WOWA — Word Order in Western Asia: A Spoken-Language-Based Corpus for Investigating Areal Effects in Word Order Variation.*, edited by Geoffrey Haig, Donald Stilo, Mahîr C. Doğan, and Nils N. Schiborr. Bamberg: University of Bamberg. (multicast.aspra.uni-bamberg.de/resources/wowa/).

Noorlander, Paul M., and Donald Stilo. 2015. 'On the Convergence of Verbal Systems of Aramaic and Its Neighbours. Part I: Present-Based Paradigms'. In *Neo-Aramaic and Its Linguistic Context*, edited by Geoffrey Khan and Lidia Napiorkowska, 426–52. Piscataway, N.J: Gorgias.

Öpengin, Ergin. 2016. *The Mukri Variety of Central Kurdish: Grammar, Texts and Lexicon*. Wiesbaden: Reichert.

Öpengin, Ergin. 2019. 'Accounting for Clitic and Affix Combinations in Central Kurdish'. In *Current Issues in Kurdish Linguistics*, edited by Songül Gündoğdu, Ergin Öpengin, Geoffrey Haig, and Erik Anonby. Bamberg: Bamberg University Press.

Öpengin, Ergin. 2020. 'Kurdish'. In *Arabic and Contact-Induced Change*, edited by Christopher Lucas and Stefano Manfredi, 459–87. Berlin: Language Science Press.

Öpengin, Ergin. 2021. 'The History of Kurdish and the Development of Literary Kurmanji'. In *Cambridge History of the Kurds*, edited by Hamit Bozarslan, Cengiz Gunes, and Veli Yadirgi, 603–32. Cambridge: Cambridge University Press.

Öpengin, Ergin, and Masoud Mohammadirad. 2022. 'Pronominal Clitics Across Kurdish: Areal Distribution, Structural Variation, and Diachrony'. In *Structural and Typological Variation in the Dialects of Kurdish*, edited by Yaron Matras, Geoffrey Haig, and Ergin Öpengin, 181–237. Cham: Springer International Publishing. https://doi.org/10.1007/978-3-030-78837-7_5.

Panoussi, Estiphan. 1990. 'On the Senaya Dialect'. In *Studies in Neo-Aramaic*, edited by Wolfhart Heinrichs, 107–29. Atlanta: Scholars Press.

Panoussi, Estiphan. 1991. 'Ein Vorläufiges Verbglossar zum aussterbenden Neuaramäischen Senaya-Dialekt'. *Rivista Degli Studi Orientali* 65 (3/4): 165–83.

Pattillo, Kelsie. 2021. 'On the Borrowability of Body Parts'. *Journal of Language Contact* 14 (2): 369–402. https://doi.org/10.1163/19552629-14020005.

Paul, Ludwig. 1998. 'The Position of Zazaki among West Iranian Languages'. In *Proceedings of the Third European Conference of Iranian Studies. Part 1: Old and Middle Iranian Studies*, edited by Nicholas Sims-Williams, 163–77. Wiesbaden: Reichert.

Paul, Ludwig. 2022. *An Analytical Bibliography of New Iranian Languages and Dialects Based on Persian Publications since ca. 1980*. Wiesbaden: Reichert Verlag.

Procházka, Stephan. 2018. 'The Arabic Dialects of Northern Iraq'. In *The Languages and Linguistics of Western Asia: An Areal Perspective*, edited by Geoffrey Haig and Geoffrey Khan, 243–66. The World of Linguistics 6. Berlin: De Gruyter.

Razi, Muhsin. 2009. *Wişe Gołînekanî Awyer [A Selected Lexicon of Abidar]*. Hewlêr: Aras.

Rees, Margo. 2008. *Lishan Didan, Targum Didan: Translation Language in a Neo-Aramaic Targum Tradition*. Piscataway, NJ: Gorgias Press.

Romaine, Suzanne. 2010. 'Contact and Language Death'. In *The Handbook of Language Contact*, edited by Raymond Hickey, 320–39. Chichester: Wiley-Blackwell.

Ross, Malcolm D. 1996. 'Contact-Induced Change and the Comparative Method: Cases from Papua New Guinea.' In *The Comparative Method Reviewed: Regularity and Irregularity in Language Change*, edited by Mark Durie and Malcolm D. Ross, 180–217. New York-Oxford: Oxford University Press.

Ross, Malcolm D. 2001. 'Contact-Induced Change in Oceanic Languages in North- West Melanesia'. In *Areal Diffusion and Genetic Inheritance*, edited by Alexandra Y. Aikhenvald and Robert M. W. Dixon, 134–66. Oxford: Oxford University Press.

Ross, Malcolm D. 2003. 'Diagnosing Prehistoric Language Contact'. In *Motives for Language Change*, edited by Raymond Hickey, 174–98. Cambridge: Cambridge University Press.

Ross, Malcolm D. 2019. 'Syntax and Contact-Induced Language Change'. In *The Oxford Handbook of Language Contact*, edited by Anthony P. Grant, 123–54. Oxford: Oxford University Press. https://doi.org/10.1093/oxfordhb/9780199945092.013.5.

Sabar, Yona. 2002. *Jewish Neo-Aramaic Dictionary*. Semitica Viva 28. Wiesbaden: Harrassowitz.

Sadjadi, Mahdi. 2015. *Jens-e Dasturī Dar Zabān-e Hawrāmī [Grammatical Gender in Hawrami Language]*. Marivan: Avin.

Sadjadi, Mahdi. 2019. 'Grammatical Gender in Arabic and Hawrami'. *International Journal of Language & Linguistics* 6 (2): 85–91.

Salmons, Joseph C. 1992. *Accentual Change and Language Contact: Comparative Survey and a Case Study of Early Northern Europe*. London: Routledge.

Sasse, Hans-Jürgen. 1987. 'The Thetic/Categorical Distinction Revisited'. *Linguistics* 25: 511–80.

Schiffrin, Deborah. 1981. 'Tense Variation in Narrative'. *Language* 57: 45–62.

Shirtz, Shahar. 2016. 'Indirect Participants as Core Arguments in Middle Persian'. In *Further Topics in Iranian Linguistics: Proceedings of the 5th International Conference on Iranian Linguistics, Held in Bamberg on 24–26 August 2013*, edited by Jila Ghomeshi, Carina Jahani, and Agnès Lenepveu-Hotz, 175–94. Cahiers de Studia Iranica 58. Paris: Association pour l'avancement des études iraniennes.

Shokri, Nawzad. 2002. 'Syllable Structure and Stress in Bahdinani Kurdish'. *Sprachtypologie und Universalienforschung* 55: 80–97.

Skjærvø, Prods O. 2009. 'Middle West Iranian'. In *Iranian Languages*, edited by Gernot Windfuhr, 195–278. London & New York: Routledge.

Smits, Caroline. 1998. 'Two Models for the Study of Language Contact'. In *Historical Linguistics 1997: Selected Papers from the 13th International Conference on Historical Linguistics, Düsseldorf, 10–17 August 1997*, edited by Monika S. Schmid, Jennifer R. Austin, and Dieter Stein, 377–90. Current Issues in Linguistic Theory 164. Amsterdam: John Benjamins.

Soane, Ely B. 1912. *To Mesopotamia and Kurdistan in Disguise; with Historical Notices of the Kurdish Tribes and the Chaldeans of Kurdistan*. London: J. Murray.

Stilo, Donald, and Paul M. Noorlander. 2015. 'On the Convergence of Verbal Systems of Aramaic and Its Neighbours. Part II: Past Paradigms Derived from Present Equivalents'. In *Neo-Aramaic and Its Linguistic Context*, edited by Geoffrey Khan and Lidia Napiorkowska, 453–84. Piscataway, N.J: Gorgias.

Tadmor, Uri. 2009. 'Loanwords in the World's Languages: Findings and Results'. In *Loanwords in the World's Languages: A Comparative Handbook*, edited by Martin Haspelmath and Uri Tadmor, 55–75. Berlin, Germany: De Gruyter Mouton.

Thomason, Sarah. 2001. *Language Contact: An Introduction*. Edinburgh and Washington, DC: Edinburgh University Press and Georgetown University Press.

Thomason, Sarah. 2010. 'Contact Explanations in Linguistics'. In *The Handbook of Language Contact*, edited by Raymond Hickey, 31–47. Chichester: Wiley-Blackwell.

Thomason, Sarah, and Terence Kaufman. 1988. *Language Contact, Creolization, and Genetic Linguistics*. Berkeley: University of California Press.

Treffers-Daller, Jeanine. 1994. *Mixing Two Languages: French-Dutch Contact in a Comparative Perspective*. Berlin: Mouton de Gruyter.

Treffers-Daller, Jeanine. 1999. 'Borrowing and Shift-Induced Interference: Contrasting Patterns in French–Germanic Contact in Brussels and Strasbourg.' *Bilingualism, Language and Cognition* 2: 77–80.

Trudgill, Peter. 2010. 'Contact and Sociolinguistic Typology'. In *The Handbook of Language Contact*, edited by Raymond Hickey, 299–319. Chichester: Wiley-Blackwell.
Trudgill, Peter. 2011. *Sociolinguistic Typology: Social Determinants of Linguistic Complexity*. Oxford: Oxford University Press.
Van Coetsem, Frans. 1988. *Loan Phonology and the Two Transfer Types in Language Contact*. Dordrecht: Foris.
Van Coetsem, Frans. 1995. 'Outlining a Model of the Transmission Phenomenon in Language Contact'. *Leuvense Bijdragen* 84: 63–85.
Van Coetsem, Frans. 2000. *A General and Unified Theory of the Transmission Process in Language Contact*. Heidelberg: Winter.
Weinreich, Uriel. 1953. *Languages in Contact: Findings and Problems*. The Hague: Mouton.
Wichmann, Søren, and Eric W. Holman. 2009. *Temporal Stability of Linguistic Typological Features*. München: LINCOM Europa.
Windfuhr, Gernot. 2009. 'Dialectology and Topics'. In *The Iranian Languages*, edited by Gernot Windfuhr, 5–42. London: Routledge.
Winford, Donald. 2003. *An Introduction to Contact Linguistics*. 1st edition. Malden, Mass: Wiley-Blackwell.
Winford, Donald. 2005. 'Contact-Induced Changes: Classification and Processes'. *Diachronica* 22: 373–427.
Winford, Donald. 2010. 'Contact and Borrowing'. In *The Handbook of Language Contact*, edited by Raymond Hickey, 170–87. Chichester: Wiley-Blackwell.
Wolfson, Nessa. 1979. 'The Conversational Historical Present Alternation'. *Language* 55: 168–82.
Yisraeli, Yafa. 1998. *Ha-'Aramit ha-Ḥadasha še-be-fi Yehude Saqqiz (Derom Kurdisṭan)* [*The Neo-Aramaic Spoken by the Jews of Saqqiz (Southern Kurdistan)*]. Jerusalem: Hebrew University Ph.D. dissertation.

Index

agency 529, 531
agentivity 137, 142, 143, 336, 529, 531, 532, 533, 534
agentivity of recipient language 531, 532, 533
agentivity of source language 531, 532

bilingual 10, 11, 17, 516, 517, 520, 527, 529, 530, 531, 532, 533, 537
bilingualism 13, 484, 516, 530, 537
borrower language 484
borrowing XX, 15, 17, 30, 104, 107, 130, 131, 222, 225, 314, 370, 452, 469, 481, 483, 484, 485, 486, 488, 490, 498, 499, 507, 508, 516, 517, 518, 520, 521, 525, 526, 527, 528, 529, 531, 532, 533, 534, 537, 539
borrowing language 520
borrowing, direct 166, 225
borrowing, lexical 483, 508, 532
borrowing, matter 15, 515, 516, 520
borrowing, morphological structural 520

calque 128, 350, 366, 475, 482, 486, 487, 489, 497, 498, 526
contact-induced change 14, 15, 17, 510, 513, 515, 531, 532, 536
convergence XIX, XX, XXI, 15, 16, 18, 25, 54, 59, 63, 64, 69, 73, 82, 83, 84, 88, 91, 112, 113, 122, 133, 137, 138, 140, 153, 156, 157, 161, 164, 183, 196, 225, 280, 281, 283, 339, 345, 357, 370, 371, 372, 373, 374, 390, 428, 429, 449, 450, 489, 512, 522, 525, 526, 527, 581, 583, 584
convergence, analogical 148
convergence, incipient 153
convergence, mutual 283
convergence, partial 79, 179, 196, 521, 524
convergence, structural 357, 406
convergence, total XXI, 427

dominance 529, 531, 532, 533, 534, 536, 537, 539
dominance, linguistic 531, 532, 536, 537, 539
dominance, shift in 532
dominant language 8, 13, 529, 531, 533, 538

formality 485, 508, 516, 532
formality, cultural 488
formality, linguistic 488
formality, social 488

hybrid 92, 110, 125, 128, 130, 475, 519
hybrid blend 519
hybrid constructions 130
hybrid form 475

imitation 15, 18, 138, 261, 372, 481, 514, 518, 526, 537
imperfect learning 529, 533, 538
imposition 17, 136, 528, 529, 530, 531, 532, 533, 534, 535, 536, 537, 538, 539
interference 528

language contact XIX, XX, XXI, 7, 9, 14, 15, 16, 17, 24, 25, 28, 30, 34, 35, 41, 44, 62, 63, 68, 69, 82, 89, 90, 97, 114, 117, 122, 124, 128, 130, 131, 132, 140, 153, 164, 171, 179, 194, 222, 223, 224, 225, 281, 283, 343, 373, 374, 427, 428, 450, 451, 483, 484, 485, 486, 488, 505, 508, 510, 511, 512, 513, 514, 515, 519, 521, 522, 524, 526, 527, 528, 529, 530, 531, 532, 535, 536, 537, 538
language shift 9, 11, 12, 13, 68, 483, 508, 510, 511, 513, 528, 529, 530, 532, 533, 537, 538, 539
levelling 134, 152, 172, 193, 223, 539
loan 19, 21, 92, 97, 99, 101, 115, 118, 121, 122, 126, 127, 128, 267, 347, 464, 476, 483, 486, 487, 497, 501, 504, 505, 506, 509, 514, 515, 526, 531
loan, phonological XIX, 62
loanblend 486, 488, 490, 499, 509, 518, 519
loanword 18, 19, 20, 21, 29, 30, 33, 34, 35, 37, 38, 44, 46, 50, 62, 91, 92, 96, 97, 98, 99, 102, 103, 104, 112, 123, 129, 131, 132, 267, 271, 483, 484, 485, 486, 487, 488, 490, 491, 492, 493, 495, 501, 502, 505, 508, 509, 511, 512, 513, 514, 515, 516, 518, 520, 527, 528, 531, 532, 533, 534, 536, 537, 538, 539
loanword, hybrid 519
loanword, unadapted 109, 264

maintained language 130, 529, 531, 533
matching XIX, XX, 12, 14, 16, 17, 18, 24, 25, 28,
   30, 35, 37, 40, 41, 42, 43, 46, 47, 51, 54, 60,
   64, 68, 72, 75, 79, 83, 84, 88, 89, 91, 92, 96,
   99, 100, 102, 108, 110, 113, 114, 124, 128,
   133, 134, 138, 142, 143, 152, 160, 166, 169,
   171, 172, 177, 179, 180, 182, 183, 184, 187,
   188, 189, 194, 201, 208, 209, 214, 218, 221,
   223, 225, 231, 236, 247, 268, 274, 276, 283,
   291, 292, 293, 297, 302, 322, 339, 357, 361,
   367, 368, 374, 383, 387, 391, 394, 406, 410,
   411, 415, 427, 429, 455, 460, 493, 511, 512,
   513, 514, 520, 521, 522, 523, 524, 525, 526,
   535, 537
matching, imperfect 522, 524
matching, morphosyntactic pattern 522
matching, paradigm pattern 69
matching, perceptual 25, 43
matching, phonetic 520, 521
matching, pivot 16, 171
matching, prosody 521
metatypy 527, 529
multilingual 1
multilingualism 13, 484

perceptual magnet effect 25, 40, 524
pivot 16, 171, 442

recipient language 17, 131, 132, 528, 529, 531,
   532, 533
replication 15, 16, 54, 82, 84, 88, 110, 128, 131,
   133, 134, 140, 208, 212, 226, 236, 265,
   268, 294, 343, 370, 469, 514, 515, 519,
   521, 522, 523, 524, 525, 526, 527, 529,
   534, 581
replication, grammatical 530
replication, partial 524
replication, pattern XIX, XX, 16, 89, 131, 222,
   521, 526

second language 529
source language 9, 15, 17, 91, 104, 209, 210, 483,
   485, 488, 489, 500, 509, 515, 517, 521, 528,
   529, 530, 531, 532, 533
substrate 11, 12, 13, 163, 171, 193, 438, 449, 511,
   512, 529, 538
superstrate 529

taboo 277, 488, 506, 508
transfer 15, 137, 515, 518, 528, 529, 531, 533, 537

www.ingramcontent.com/pod-product-compliance
Lightning Source LLC
Chambersburg PA
CBHW051531230426
43669CB00015B/2566